SQUARES
OF LONDON

SQUARES
OF LONDON

JOHN COULTER

First published 2016

Phillimore & Co. Ltd, an imprint of The History Press
The Mill, Brimscombe Port
Stroud, Gloucestershire, GL5 2QG
www.thehistorypress.co.uk

British Library Cataloguing in Publication Data.
A catalogue record for this book is available from the British Library.

ISBN 978 0 7509 6068 7

Typesetting and origination by The History Press
Printed in Great Britain

CONTENTS

PREFACE

This is an alphabetical guide to 578 London squares, large, small, famous, obscure, existing, long vanished, or merely projected. In each entry there is a brief history, a description of the architecture and atmosphere, if known, some account of notable former residents, and in many cases a photograph or other picture. For major squares there are several. Alternative names are included in the alphabetical sequence, with a cross reference to the main entry. Use of the apostrophe in place names has always been so whimsical that for any square where one could be included the reader should search with and without, especially in such cases as 'Queen' and 'Queen's'. These have not been cross-referenced.

I have assigned each square to a district and added the modern borough, where different, in square brackets. There is an index, a select bibliography, and lists of squares by district and modern borough. Most of the manuscript and printed authorities are indicated in the text, or will be obvious from the bibliography. I have made extensive use of ratebooks, but the lazy conservatism of the parish clerks reduces their value as a record of the development of names.

Because twentieth and twenty-first-century squares, in all but a handful of cases, were planned without any aspiration towards the classic forms, I have not dealt with squares built after 1900, except in cases of the complete rebuilding of an old example, as at Paternoster Square. I have tried to include all those built before 1900 that are or have been called 'square', even though many are nothing of the sort by even the loosest definition, plus two that are certainly squares although they have hardly ever borne that name.

Covent Garden and Lincoln's Inn Fields are the pioneer squares of London, without which no study of the subject would be complete.

That many tiny, occasional or short-lived squares have evaded capture is certain. Anyone who has studied the records of a London district intensively is likely to have discovered small squares that have appeared in no general list. Mary Cosh has unearthed several in Islington and I have found some in Deptford. There are undoubtedly many others. If authors waited for completeness few books would ever be published.

The large and famous squares are no doubt the ones that will be looked up most often in these pages. They have been the easiest to write about, especially where they have been covered by modern volumes of the *Survey of London*, or in Todd Longstaffe-Gowan's *The London Square*. In those cases there has been little left for the gleaner to pick up; but for that reason the obscure squares have been the most interesting to research and describe. I hope the reader will spare some time to explore these quaint and alluring byways. If the centre has the best squares, the suburbs certainly had the best names: Thessaly, Mortgramit, Mount Nod, Unicorn, Sweet Apple …

The colour photographs dated between 2006 and 2015 are copyright of the author. Unless otherwise credited, the remaining images are from postcards, prints, and photographs in the author's collection.

The book was finished in 2013 and only limited revision has been possible, so words like 'now' and 'still' should sometimes be understood with that limitation.

INTRODUCTION

It is easy to concoct an ideal definition of a London square: an enclosure of four sides of equal length set at right angles to each other, with a garden for the residents in the centre, a house or houses on each side, and a public road with outlets for access running all the way round between the garden and the houses. The difficulty is that such a definition would exclude nearly every square in London. If a complete stranger to the subject and the language were to define the London square not theoretically or etymologically, but on an average of all the places to which the name has been applied, he would perhaps conclude that a square is a widened section of road.

The history of the London square begins in 1631 with the great name of Inigo Jones, whose houses and church in Covent Garden were both started in that year. Lincoln's Inn Fields followed from 1638. Southampton (now Bloomsbury) Square was the first to bear that name formally, although it had been applied to Covent Garden as early as 1641 in a licence for Lincoln's Inn Fields. Building in front of Southampton House was begun in 1661 and the development was referred to as 'the square' from 1663.

After that they came with a rush: St James's Square from 1667, Leicester Square from 1670, Golden Square from 1675, Soho Square from 1677, Devonshire Square from 1678, Wellclose Square from 1682, Red Lion Square and Hoxton Square from 1684, Charles Square and Kensington Square from 1685, Bridgewater Square from 1688. There were other minor late seventeenth-century squares in the City, but after 1688 revolution and war discouraged new building projects, and it was not until the establishment of the Hanoverian peace that the second great wave of square building began.

In 1725 a Swiss visitor, César de Saussure, gave this account of the London Squares:

Covent Garden from the south in 1751.

London has many fine open spaces called squares, because they are of that shape. The centres of these squares are shut in by railings of painted wood, and contain gardens with flowers, trees, and paths. Those of Soho, of Leicester Fields, of the Red lion, and the Golden Square are in this style. Those of Hanover and Cavendish are not yet finished, and belong to a newly-built quarter. That of St James is fine; it is surrounded with handsome houses belonging to wealthy noblemen. In the centre of this square is a fine fountain, surrounded by iron balustrades, with lanterns at equal distances. Going towards the City you see another big place, named by the French 'Commun-Jardin', and by the English Covent Garden. Every sort of flower, fruit, and garden produce is sold here. It is surrounded on two sides by fine arcades, which are most convenient for shelter in bad weather. From this place you can continue to Lincoln's Inn Fields, where there is nothing in particular to be seen except some fine mansions, those belonging to the Duke of Ancaster and to the Duke of Newcastle being particularly magnificent.

Carl Philipp Moritz was equally complimentary in 1782:

It must, I think, be owned, that upon the whole, London is neither so handsomely nor so well built as Berlin is, but then it certainly has far more fine squares. Of these there are many that in real magnificence, and beautiful symmetry, far surpass our Gens d'Armes Markt, our Denhoschen, and Williams Place. These squares, or quadrangular places, contain the best and most beautiful buildings of London: a spacious street, next to the houses, goes all round them, and within that there is generally a round grass-plot, railed in with iron rails, in the centre of which, in many of them, there is a statue, which statues most commonly are equestrian and gilt. In Grosvenor-square, instead of this green plot, or area, there is a little circular wood, intended, no doubt, to give one the idea of *rus in urbe*.

Foreign visitors continued to be impressed, but the self-satisfaction of the natives did not last so long. As early as 1734 James Ralph's *Critical Review of the Publick Buildings* was contemptuous of almost everything, including the squares. In 1771 the anonymous *Critical Observations on the Buildings and Improvements of London*, now attributed to the wine merchant and politician John Stewart, referred to 'our so-much-vaunted squares' only as a prelude to cutting them to pieces; but the author did admit that if they were reformed along his lines 'London could boast of fifteen elegant squares (besides market-places and inns of court), while Paris, her proud rival, cannot show half so many that deserve the name'. This is how he stated his own ideal, which he found approached in London by St James's Square alone:

The notion I form to myself of a perfect square, or public place in a city, is a large opening, free and un-incumbered, where not only carriages have room to turn and pass, but even where the people are able to assemble occasionally without confusion. It should appear to open naturally out of the street, for which reason all the avenues should form radii to the centre of the place. The sides or circumference should be built in a style above the common; and churches and other public edifices ought to be properly introduced. In the middle there ought to be some fountain, groupe, or statue, railed in within a small compass, or perhaps only a bason of water, which, if not so ornamental, still, by its utility in cases of fire, etc. makes ample amends.

Stewart had evidently formed his taste abroad. This is very much the continental ideal of a 'place', and one increasingly out of step with the English love of privacy, domesticity and exclusiveness. What gentleman after 1780 would have wished to live in a square 'where the people are able to assemble'?

St James's Square did not long retain most of the features that Stewart admired, and today Trafalgar Square is the only one in London that comes close to meeting his specifications. Even that nearly took a different direction, as there were plans in the 1830s to make it into a garden square with the specific object of excluding the dangerous mob.

Stewart's views on the proper use of the open spaces in the centre of squares could not have been more at variance with the solution that London was well on the way to adopting in 1771. He was pained to find that:

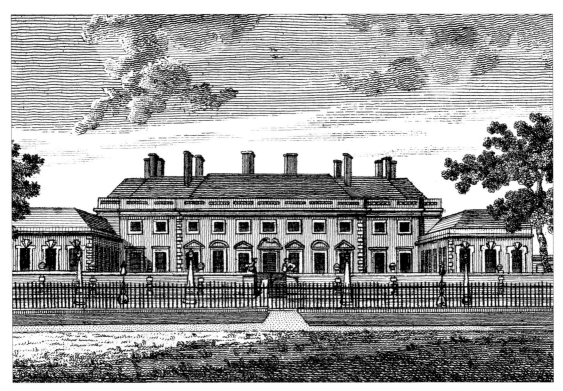

Bedford House, the former Southampton House, Bloomsbury Square, in 1784.

An early 1720s engraving of St James's Square from the south, altered to show the changes made to the garden after 1727.

… they are gardens, they are parks, they are sheep-walks, in short they are everything but what they should be. The *rus in urbe* is a preposterous idea at best; a garden in a street is not less absurd than a street in a garden; and he that wishes to have a row of trees before his door in town, betrays almost as false a taste as he that would build a row of houses for an avenue to his seat in the country.

He also made merry with the taste displayed in the statues of kings and princes erected in most of the squares. That of the Duke of Cumberland in Cavendish Square had been paid for by General Strode in gratitude for the duke's 'private kindness':

> If this fashion should prevail among great men and rich, of erecting publick statues to those who have been kind to them in private, it is not warriors in complete uniform, bestriding gilded steeds, who would be most frequently seen in our streets and squares, but beauty simple, unadorned, like the Venus of Medicis, and (could art do justice to nature in this country) finer forms than ever Grecian chizzle graved.

How sad that this suggestion was not acted upon!

The movement to convert the gravelled or muddy wastes in the centre of the early squares into the flourishing gardens of today began early in the eighteenth century, and was promoted vigorously by various nurserymen and gardeners who had spotted a commercial opportunity. The first was perhaps John James in his *Theory and Practice of Gardening* of 1712, but the great prophet of this movement was Thomas Fairchild, whose *City Gardener* was published in 1722. In this tract he argued the merits of 'Wilderness-Work', the 'prettyish kind of a little wilderness' that many residents of squares were familiar with at their country seats, and all the perfect trees and shrubs for which could be readily obtained from the author's nursery near Hoxton Square. Fairchild's ideas were widely adopted and contributed to the transformation of the gardens over the next fifty years. By 1770 this rural movement had sometimes degenerated into the bucolic masquerades satirised by John Stewart in his account of Cavendish Square (see p.109).

The squares over the proper planning of which Stewart and his contemporaries wrangled were the great ones of the West End, but they were not the only examples in London. Some of the early squares in the City (what William Weir described in 1844 as 'obsolete, or purely City squares') were built late in the seventeenth century in what had been the gardens of great houses, until the nobility migrated west. When the leading merchants later began to follow their example, the City authorities built or inspired a number of imitation West End squares from the 1760s with the hope of preventing this flight of wealth. Finsbury Square was the largest and best. The smaller City squares that sprang up in great numbers during the late eighteenth century had usually been known as 'Court' or 'Yard' or 'Alley' until fashion and ambition promoted them to 'Square'.

The rapidity with which the taste for squares swept westwards in the early eighteenth century was commented on by Henry Fielding in the *Covent Garden Journal* of 9 May 1752, while trying to fathom the phrase 'People of Fashion':

> It is moreover extremely pleasant to observe what wonderful Care these People take to preserve their Circle safe and inviolate, and with how jealous an Eye they guard against any Intrusion of those whom they are pleased to call the Vulgar; who are on the other Hand as vigilant to watch, and as active to improve every Opportunity of invading this Circle, and breaking into it.
>
> Within the Memory of many now living, the Circle of the People of Fascination included the whole Parish of Covent-Garden, and great part of St Giles's in the Fields; but here the Enemy broke in, and the Circle was presently contracted to Leicester-Fields, and Golden-Square. Hence the People of Fashion again retreated before the Foe to Hanover-Square; whence they were once more driven to Grosvenor-Square, and even beyond it, and that with such Precipitation, that had they not been stopped by the Walls of Hyde-Park, it is more than probable they would by this Time have arrived at Kensington.

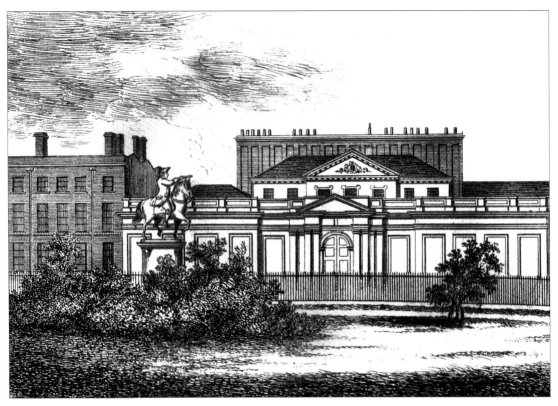

The Cumberland statue and Harcourt House, Cavendish Square, in 1808.

Finsbury Square from the north in 1796.

William Maitland found exactly fifty squares in London when he made a careful survey of all the streets in 1732, and John Lockie included 150 in the 1813 edition of his *Topography of London*. Samuel Leigh calculated that there were nearly 200 in 1834, but of these he found only twenty-five of any historic or aesthetic importance and most of the others undeserving of the name of square. He was unduly severe, as by that time excellent examples existed all over the capital, some in the most unpromising locations.

That London is adorned with so many fine squares is a signal triumph of hope over experience, for few of the projectors made a fortune from them and many were bankrupted. Even the landowners, usually so secure, sometimes ran themselves into the financial quicksand when they handled anything as ponderous as a square.

By the middle of the nineteenth century, squares with some pretensions to smartness had sprung up all over expanding London, north, south, west and even east. The way in which the tyranny of fashion shaped their destiny is illustrated in Trollope's *The Small House at Allington*, which was serialised between 1862 and 1864. An engaged couple are choosing a London house:

Crosbie himself had wished to go to one of the new Pimlico squares down near Vauxhall Bridge and the river … but to this Lady Alexandrina had objected strongly. If, indeed, they could have achieved Eaton Square, or a road leading out of Eaton Square – if they could have crept onto the hem of the skirt of Belgravia – the bride would have been delighted. And at first she was very nearly being taken in with the idea that such was the proposal made to her. Her geographical knowledge of Pimlico had not been perfect, and she had nearly fallen into a fatal error. But a friend had kindly intervened. 'For heaven's sake, my dear, don't let him take you anywhere beyond Eccleston Square!' had been exclaimed to her in dismay by a faithful married friend.

The triumph of the neo-Gothic style was the death sentence of the square, although its execution was lingered out through many appeals and reprieves. Formal groupings of buildings, whether in squares, crescents, or circuses, are a natural way of presenting classical architecture, but attempts to confine other styles within such geometry were never a great success. Tudor worked fairly well at De Beauvoir Square, but only as an imitation village green. It was overpowering

An Eaton Square scene in 1850.

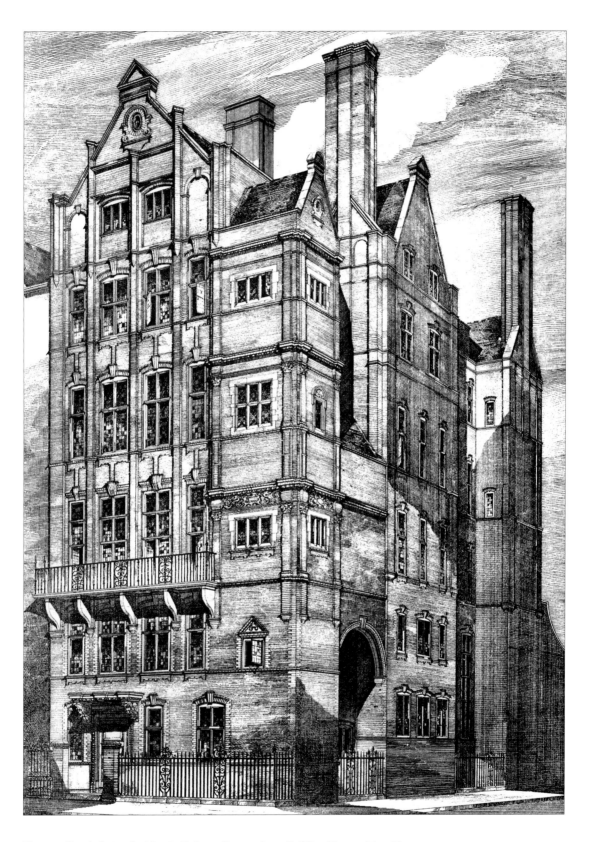

Norman Shaw's design for No. 62 Cadogan Square, from *Building News*, 11 May 1883.

in the more confined and regular Lonsdale Square. In Cadogan Square, magnificent individual houses in the Dutch manner do not achieve a coherent overall effect and gain little from their setting. If the square had been a canal, perhaps?

Fortunately, nobody ever thought of building a baroque square, which would have been the stuff of nightmares. Milner Square, the nearest approach, did disturb the sleep of Sir John Summerson. Gothic ones have been attempted, but the only way of grouping Gothic houses successfully would be around the most irregular possible shape: 'Balmoral Blob' might be a good name for the Gothic equivalent of a square.

A survey carried out by the London County Council in 1903 found 310 squares, which represented something of a decline from the peak, numerous small ones in the City having been swept away to make space for railway lines and offices. Very few new squares were created in London in the last thirty years of the nineteenth century. Percy Fitzgerald, writing in 1893, had an explanation for this:

> The formal rebuilding of London may be said to have set in seriously some forty years ago, at the close of the Exhibition of 1851, when the great tract about Cromwell Road was laid out and covered with terraces and houses. At this time, also, were introduced what were called 'gardens' as being more modest and less pretentious than the regular 'square'.

The abandonment of the word 'square' for quality building developments was to a much greater extent a response to adverse publicity from the east. The little courtyard squares of Whitechapel, Bethnal Green and other poor areas of London, were often much as described by *The Illustrated London News* in 1863, 'a number of black and crumbling hovels forming three sides of a miserable little square, like a fetid tank with a bottom of mud and slime'.

This hardly mattered so long as the wealthy never saw or heard of such places, but from the 1840s outbreaks of cholera and a growing taste for sociological research made the West End uncomfortably familiar with the horrors of the East. In the despatches from the front the word 'square' began to

crop up with unpleasant frequency. Thorold Square was usually featured in these reports because it was directly off the main road and easier for journalists to find than the more remote and even worse slums further into Bethnal Green. This publicity continued to have a damaging effect on the cachet of 'square' from the 1840s until the plague spot was demolished in 1872. It was a further blow to the prestige of the name when the Peabody Trust took to calling its groups of working-class tenements, to be found in the most squalid areas of the city, Peabody Square, Blackfriars Road; Peabody Square, Shadwell etc.

Bad publicity of this kind, combined with new architectural tastes and changes in social habits, meant that after two and a half centuries of triumph the square was finally losing its hold on the affections of the richer classes. The serviced mansion flat was becoming the London home of choice for many of the middle class who had formerly yearned for a house in a square. Criticism of the over-production of squares became

Peabody Square, Shadwell, in 1867.

common from the 1850s. The ones built in Bayswater in that and the next decade were failures, the houses quickly degenerating into cheap hotels and lodgings.

The squares attempted in Earls Court in the 1870s and 1880s were such a disaster that flats were resorted to before all the building plots could be let. After that hardly any squares of a traditional kind were promoted – Nightingale Square at Balham being a freakish exception – until a small revival late in the twentieth century. From 1890 to 1990 'square' was a name almost entirely abandoned to the providers of working and lower middle-class housing, in tenements, garden suburbs and council estates.

From quite early in the nineteenth century lone voices had been calling for the gardens of the London squares to be opened for the benefit of the general public, and more especially for the healthy exercise of poor children, but it was not until the 1860s that the call became a chorus. Flower shows held in one or two of the gardens in the 1850s and 1860s were the thin end

Wetherby Mansions (now Herbert Court Mansions), Earls Court Square, c. 1905.

of the wedge. Then permission began to be given for parties of poor children to visit underused gardens like Lincoln's Inn Fields. More important was the decision of the Marquess of Westminster to open the garden of Ebury Square, which had become neglected as the social standing of the area declined. He put the idea forward in 1872, but opposition from residents delayed its full implementation until 1884. By then permissive legislation had made it easier for landlords to dedicate gardens to the public, and the Metropolitan Public Gardens Association had been formed to encourage and assist such benevolent acts.

The harsher politics of the late nineteenth century shifted the emphasis from aristocratic benevolence to municipal coercion. One of the conclusions of the Charles Booth survey in 1898 was, 'With reference to the condition of the squares [their gardens, that is], it is a question whether Vestries should not have compulsory powers to take over such squares when the inhabitants fail to keep them in decent condition.'

The London County Council was usually ready to embrace any radical proposal, and its attention was repeatedly called to the subject by the efforts of the poorer parishes to secure their square gardens as children's playgrounds, and by the threat to the survival of many others when less scrupulous owners began to eye the gardens as valuable building sites.

Crisis point was reached in 1903, when the LCC had to buy the Ford and Sidney Square gardens in the East End at full market prices to save them from destruction, and a new threat arose of building on the huge Edwardes Square garden in Kensington. The council had been considering the possibility of legislative protection for the gardens since 1901, and now it began a tortuous process of promoting bills and negotiating with landlords and the House of Lords that led in 1906 to the London Squares & Enclosures (Preservation) Act. It was a very limited measure, covering gardens only where the owners were willing to have them included in the schedule, but its symbolic importance was considerable. It staved off some of the current threats and created the precedent that eased the passage of the comprehensive London Squares Preservation Act of 1931, the shield that still protects all our garden enclosures. That resulted from several acts of vandalism, both threatened and achieved, in the 1920s, including the building of the Friends' Meeting House on the southern garden of Euston Square.

The first half of the twentieth century was the bohemian phase in the long history of the London square. After the big houses began to be divided into flats, and before a flat in a good square became as great a status symbol as a house had been in more spacious days, there was an interlude when struggling writers and artists could afford to live amid this faded grandeur. To a mind focused more on historical associations than current realities a shabby flat in Russell or Brunswick Square was more attractive than a convenient house in Orpington or Hampstead Garden Suburb. Successful artists had favoured squares since the seventeenth century – for a fashionable portrait painter it was a professional necessity – and leading Victorian authors also began to affect them. Dickens, Thackeray, George Eliot, Trollope and Arnold were all square dwellers. In the twentieth century it was briefly possible for their less wealthy successors to imitate them.

That the society of the gardens became less select early in the twentieth century as more houses were divided into flats and residential hotels is suggested by this exchange between Lady Kellynch and her son in Ada Leverson's *Bird of Paradise* (1914). She suggests that he invite his school friend for a visit:

Brunswick Park, formerly the garden of Brunswick Square, Camberwell, *c.* 1905.

'I should think a beautiful house in Onslow Square, with a garden like this, was just the thing for a boy to like.'

He shook his head with a humorous expression of contempt.

'Pickering wouldn't go into a Square garden, mother!'

She waited a moment, wondering what shaped garden was suited to him, what form of pleasaunce was worthy of the presence of this exceptional boy …

The bohemian infiltration of the declining squares began, in a curious prefiguring of Bloomsbury, with the Pre-Raphaelites in Red Lion Square in the 1850s. Shabby Chelsea was the next area annexed by bohemia, but it was the arrival of the Stephen sisters in Gordon Square in 1904, and the growing influence of their set in nearly all the arts, that made Bloomsbury the classic ground for this new phase in the history of the square. The original Bloomsburyites began with houses, but under the pressure of war and social change most of them soon descended to flats and rooms. Countless writers, artists and musicians, some not at all allied to the Bloomsbury Group, found shelter in these mouldering squares until the relentless expansion of the University of London squeezed them out.

After the war there was a brief, dispersed revival in other areas. The residence of Ted Hughes and Sylvia Plath in Chalcot Square in the early 1960s comes at the end of this phase. Since then gentrification, or regentrification, has put all but the most squalid squares beyond the reach of struggling writers.

Artists were not the only disreputable group to colonise the squares at that time. In *The Military Philosophers* Anthony Powell contrasted Bayswater during and after the war:

… the area was not yet so squalid as it was in due course to become in the period immediately following the end of the war, when squares and crescents over which an aroma of oppressive respectability had gloomily hung, became infested at all hours of day and night by prostitutes of the lowest category.

The south side of Onslow Square, *c.* 1905.

The modern renaissance of the square began late in the nineteenth century with concerns about the survival of the gardens. It was only very gradually that more than an eccentric minority extended their interest to the fate of the surrounding houses. It took the widespread destruction of the Second World War and the even more widespread destruction by the local authorities afterwards to alert a wider public to what was being lost. The publication of John Summerson's *Georgian London* in 1945 was an important step towards the conservation of what was left of the older squares. It was only after such abrasive struggles as the battles of Union Square and Tolmers Square that a similar consideration was extended to the Victorians.

Today the rehabilitation of the square is complete. The reinstatement of the west side of Union Square, reversing as far as anybody could one of the worst examples of 1960s vandalism, is the proof of it. Many squares are better cared for now than in their early Victorian heyday. Fabulous prices are paid for houses, or even flats, in the good ones. The demand is such that for the first time in more than a century new squares with pretentions to the classic style are being built. Once again, developers are making the most inappropriate use of the name 'square', a practice that brought it into disrepute in the nineteenth century. This is a good time to look back at the long history of the square to see what lessons it has to teach.

WANTED—AN OPEN-AIR MINISTER.

Speculative Builder (*to London*). "IT'S YOUR LUNGS I WANT!"

Bernard Partridge's comment in *Punch* on the proposal in 1926 to demolish Brunswick Square, the Foundling Hospital, and Mecklenburgh Square as the site for a new Covent Garden market. It was a cliché to describe the squares as the lungs of the city.

SQUARES
OF LONDON

Acre Square

The first of the London squares in an alphabetical sequence is one of the least interesting. Acre Square was an insignificant court built in the 1830s off the west side of Acre Lane, now Clapham Park Road, between St Alphonsus Road and Holmwood Place. The entrance alley ran west from Acre Lane then turned ninety degrees to the south before being halted by the garden wall of a large detached house.

The cottages were all in the north–south section. There were originally four of them, one at the north end of the west side and a terrace of three on the east side, but with their detached gardens opposite. This two-storey terrace was soon subdivided into six cottages. In 1841 the occupants included a tailor, a whitesmith and several gardeners.

The large detached house to the south was replaced by Carfax Square in the 1870s. Parts of Carfax Square were badly damaged in the Second World War, and all the houses were demolished in the 1970s. Acre Square, although it escaped from the war with only blast damage, shared the fate of its larger neighbour, and the sites of both are now covered by the Carfax Estate.

Addington Square

Henry Addington, 1st Viscount Sidmouth, had only one brief period of acclaim during his long political career. It came in 1802, when he was able to wave the scrap of paper known to history as the Treaty of Amiens. For a few months of dearly-bought peace the weary nation hailed the prime minister as a hero. But 'The Doctor' gave his name to Addington Square only indirectly. The stretch of Camberwell Road from which the square is approached was christened Addington Place during the prime minister's moment of glory, and it was from there that the name spread to the new square when it was created a few years later.

The development of the square was closely connected with the Grand Surrey Canal, the section of which from the Old Kent Road to Camberwell Road was built between 1807 and 1810. The canal ran just to the north of the site of the square, with its basin extending almost to touch it. The south London canals were always in financial difficulties and on the lookout for any source of revenue. Here the company was glad to allow the establishment of a bath house in the angle of the canal and basin. It was probably the first building in the square, occupying the whole of the north side.

The filling in of the square was slow and halting, as the wide variety of styles indicates. The earliest houses are the two pairs on the west side flanking the entrance, and the widely contrasting terraces, three-storey and two-storey, on the south side. Six houses were occupied in 1820, twenty-five in 1826, and thirty-eight by 1830, but that total included small houses in the access roads. The grand east side was very slow-moving. The two tall houses with attics are much the oldest, but the north end of the terrace, and with it the square, was only completed in the 1840s.

The most celebrated early resident was the Reverend Dr William Bengo Collyer, preacher and hymn writer. He leased the present No. 48 in 1816 and left under a cloud in 1823. Despite being a doctor of divinity (minister of the Hanover Congregational Chapel in Peckham) his hobbies were medicine and anatomy. He liked to advise young men about hernias, for which purpose he would examine them naked, often in the private bath house on the north side of the square. The *Lancet* published several damaging articles on the subject and the resulting scandal aged the doctor (he said) ten years in a month; but he managed to live it down and continue his career to an honoured old age.

The other notable residents are very suitable for commemoration in a book about the London squares. Sir Robert Hunter, who was born at the old No. 3 in 1844 but soon moved to the old No. 7, was a founder of the National Trust and the great legal defender of open spaces of all kinds, including the gardens of the squares. G.R. Sims, editor of the valuable *Living London* and author of the immortal *Christmas Day in the Workhouse*, plus any number of successful plays, lived at the old No. 24 in the mid-1870s.

The garden was leased to the Camberwell local authorities from 1897 and bought with help from the LCC in 1914. It is now exceptionally public, as on

The east side of Addington Square in 2007.

the north side (where the canal and bath house once stood) it opens directly into Burgess Park. To extend the gardens of squares in this way, losing their identity and character in the process, was one of the many planning blunders of the LCC, pursued with vigour in south and east London after the Second World War. It is seen at its least destructive here. Not too far away, at the late Melbourne Square, it led to total extinction. A worse municipal blight is caused at Addington Square by Southwark's green wheelie bins, which have a most unfortunate effect parked on the pavement outside these undemonstrative Georgian houses.

Adelaide Square

ISLINGTON

Adelaide Square was built in the 1830s, close to the older and better Tibberton Square, and just to the east of Popham Road. The 1831 Dent/Rhodes map of Islington showed development south of Shepperton Street only just beginning. By 1840 there was a Nonconformist chapel in a former schoolroom in Adelaide Square, and later maps showed the St Bartholomew's National School there, presumably in the same building.

It was only a narrow alley, but for such a small place – a dozen cottages – it was lavishly provided with entrances, there being two from Shepperton Street in the north and one from South Street. This is perhaps why the square was much frequented by pickpockets in its early days. Later in the century costermongers lived there and stored their barrows in the yard.

In 1897 Charles Booth's assistant found that:

Adelaide Square, marked in map black [semi-criminal] is not so bad. [Inspector] Mason says not more than rather poor … All people in the square he says were of the same condition, most have been there for some years. No trouble to the police … 'Would not do for any in a place like this to have opposite views.'

The LCC marked Adelaide Square down for slum clearance in the 1930s, when it was renumbered as part of Basire Street, the former South Street. The houses were demolished in 1936, but redevelopment had to wait until the 1950s, when Parker Court was built on the site.

Albermarle Square

MAYFAIR [WESTMINSTER]

On 18 September 1683 John Evelyn went to view the demolition of Clarendon House in Piccadilly and the work being carried on there by a 'little armie of Labourers, & Artificers in levelling ground, laying foundations, & contriving great buildings'. The house had been bought by 'certaine inferior people, rich bankers & Mechanics … who designing a new Towne as it were, & the most magnificent Piazza in Europ, 'tis said have already materials towards it'. This magnificent piazza or square, to be named after the Duke of Albermarle, the last owner of Clarendon House, was intended to be built at what are now the north ends of Dover Street and Albermarle Street, the north side of the square being the present Grafton Street, the east Old Bond Street and the south more or less a continuation eastwards of Hay Hill.

The development scheme did not prosper. John Hinde, the chief of the 'inferior people', was bankrupted, Richard Frith of Soho Square and the Bonds of Bond Street got into difficulties, and the proposed square was never carried out, although still intended early in the eighteenth century. Its end was signalled by the *British Journal* in 1723: 'All the waste Ground at the upper End of Albermarle and Dover Streets, is purchas'd by the Duke of Grafton and the Earl of Grantham for Gardening, and the Road there leading to May-Fair is order'd to be turned.'

The purchasers were a syndicate who wished to preserve the open outlook of their houses in Old Bond Street, Albermarle Street and Dover Street by preventing building on the garden of the failed square. The road they grubbed up was its south side. Rocque's map of the 1740s showed only gardens south of Evans Row, now Grafton Street, and few buildings at the north end of Albermarle Street. Even then it would have been possible to resurrect the square by extending Hay Hill to Old Bond Street, and easy to make a smaller one with Albermarle Street as its east side.

Albert Square

BARNSBURY [ISLINGTON]

Much of the land around Highbury and Islington Station was occupied by Laycock's cattle lairs, where animals were freshened overnight before the final stage of their journey to Smithfield. The farmer is commemorated by Laycock Street, once Laycock's Yard. He was dead before the station was built in the early 1850s, but the business continued and was somewhat disrupted by the railway. It was as part of the resulting changes to the street pattern that Albert Square was built. Mary Cosh gives 1854 as its date.

Squashed against the cattle sheds on the south and west, the station on the north, and Swan Yard on the east, it can never have been anything but poor. It originally had four sides, with the entrance in the north-east corner, but in the late 1860s the railway was widened, requiring the demolition of the north side and part of the west.

The fragment survived for another fifteen years or so, only in the news when one of the residents made a court appearance, until it was demolished in the 1880s to make way for Highbury Station Road School. That survives, now as the Laycock Centre.

Albert Square

KENNINGTON [LAMBETH]

I first visited Albert Square and Bonnington Square on the same day. Such sketchy research as I had done suggested that Albert Square should be the more interesting and attractive in every respect. It was larger, more ambitious, and built at a much better date, the late 1840s. The style is certainly lavish and Kensingtonian, but has a curiously stilted air, perhaps because the detached corner houses are disproportionately tall. As their roofs make clear, each is merely one half of a semi-detached pair. The builder economised by not obtaining a separate design for his corner houses.

Even in the results of their war losses Bonnington Square comes out on top. The one original house entirely destroyed in Albert Square has been replaced by a hideous block of flats with the unfortunate name of Regency Court. The seven bombed houses in Bonnington Square have provided the site for the Paradise Garden.

Albert Square was built by John Glenn of Islington, who obtained a lease in September 1846. The square was fully occupied by 1851, with highly respectable private residents in all the houses except No. 19, which was a ladies' school. The tenants of No. 36 from 1854 to 1862 were the parents of Sir Ernest George, the architect. His father was a successful ironmonger. The young Ernest lived at home throughout that period while studying his profession at the Royal Academy Schools and elsewhere, but his flamboyant style was not in the least influenced (except perhaps in reaction) by what he saw around him in Albert Square.

At No. 27 there is a plaque to Arthur Rackham, the great book illustrator, who lived there from 1882 to 1885, except for the first half of 1884 when he was visiting Australia.

The east side of Albert Square, Kennington, in 1907 or a little earlier.

Albert Square escaped lightly in the Second World War, with only two houses, Nos 36 and 37 on the south-west side, being seriously damaged. As No. 36 formed an imposing group with 34 and 35, it was carefully restored or rebuilt; No. 37 was demolished and replaced by the egregious Regency Court in 1963–64.

The large garden of Albert Square is not public, being locked, but it gives little sign of private use either. There are no paths and no bushes and, but for a single seat, merely a featureless expanse of grass surrounded by tall trees. The garden was originally planted and laid out in the conventional manner, but perhaps has never recovered from the disruption caused by the sinking of a shaft for the Victoria Line extension in the 1960s. There is an Albert Square and St Stephen's Association that holds occasional events there, for the Diamond Jubilee for example, but as a traditional square garden it seems strangely underused. I may just have been unlucky in the days of my visits, but then the peace of the square was constantly broken by the passage of fast and noisy cars.

Albert Square

KENSINGTON [KENSINGTON AND CHELSEA]

Frederick Pratt Barlow, a lawyer who owned much of the south side of Kensington Square and lived at No. 24, bought 4 acres of land behind his houses, adjoining South End, in 1841. Here in the mid-1840s he built two small speculative developments that he called, almost inevitably, Albert Villas and Albert Square. The square consisted of eight cottages ranged around a small open space. They were never smart, but at first they were quiet and secluded.

That ended in the late 1860s, when the Metropolitan Railway track and tunnel between High Street Kensington and Gloucester Road cut across the corner of the little square. What survived of it did not last long, for by the 1880s the cottages had been replaced by a builder's works and the Kensington Studios, both entered from Kelso Place. They stretched back across the railway tunnel towards South End Row.

Albert Square

RATCLIFFE [TOWER HAMLETS]

(now Albert Gardens)

Albert Square was named after the Prince Consort, who married Queen Victoria in 1840. The name must have been an afterthought, as a square was being planned here by the mid-1830s, even before the accession of Victoria. The first idea may have been for a smaller square, not open to the Commercial Road on the north side.

The year of the queen's marriage was also that in which the London & Blackwall Railway was opened, its lines passing close to the south side of the intended square. The route had been known since the line was authorised in 1836 and must have been a factor in the planning from the beginning. The viaduct can never have been a welcome neighbour and it has moved uncomfortably close over the decades as the lines have multiplied.

The east side of Albert Gardens, Ratcliffe, (formerly Albert Square) in 2007.

Albert Square did not appear in the census of 1841. We know that David McIntosh was building houses there in the summer of 1842, because in June he had a barge load of bricks delivered to the nearby Stone Stairs Wharf and one of his enterprising carters diverted 1,000 of them to a house being repaired in York Square. McIntosh was perhaps the contractor who lived at No. 39 Bloomsbury Square, although he was mainly engaged in railway work.

In this area the early residents were not surprisingly, pilots, master mariners, boat builders and shipowners, but there were also lodging houses for less wealthy or more transient seafarers. Albert Square declined gradually during the nineteenth century, as the Booth surveyor found in 1898: 'Not so good as it used to be. 3½ storied houses, lodgers usual. Square fairly kept. Superintendent Mulvaney lives in it and says the place has seen better days. No Jews.'

In 1899 the owner of the square, Morris Cohen, advertised the garden for sale as a building site, and the alarmed residents petitioned the LCC to acquire it. The council entered into negotiations with Cohen, who

valued the garden at £20,000 for building purposes, but was willing to accept £12,000 for it as an open space. The council offered £6,500 and when that was refused obtained compulsory purchase powers. The garden was opened to the public in 1902.

The square escaped almost unscathed during the Second World War. Number 1, in the north-west corner, was the only house to be seriously damaged, and that has been carefully restored. The houses and garden are now attractive and in excellent preservation, but are surrounded on three sides by the tall blocks of a council estate and on the fourth by the busy Commercial Road. The residents must be glad that the LCC changed the name from Albert Square to Albert Gardens in 1938. Even so, they are apt to look wearily at sightseers and photographers as though they have encountered far too many of them.

Albert Square

STRATFORD [NEWHAM]

The residents of Albert Square, like those of Albert Gardens, have to put up with a surfeit of monotonous jokes, not helped by the fact that their local, now demolished, was called the Queen Vic in its declining years. The present form of the place makes the name seem like another pleasantry, as it has hardly any of the attributes of a real square. The explanation is the same here as at St George's Square at Upton, an even more extreme example of the current unfitness of the name. Here at Stratford it was evidently the intention to create a genuine square, rather like Edwardes Square at Kensington in form, but at an even humbler level.

The square was planned in the 1840s, as 'Albert' proclaims, but in 1851 the only resident, at No. 1, was Samuel Rookes, 'house proprieter'. (The census enumerator was a schoolmaster.) The large garden was to have been between the two arms of the present Albert Square on the west and north, Ash Road, formerly Albert Road, on the east, and the mews behind the Forest Lane houses in the south. The houses in Forest Lane between Albert Square and Ash Road, some of which existed in 1851, were intended to have the same relation to the square that Earls Terrace at Kensington bears to Edwardes Square.

The take up of plots on this new development was evidently very poor and in 1861 only Nos 1 and 2 were occupied; these early numbers have no relation to the present ones. Of houses built while the idea of a garden was persevered with, only Nos 43–45 Forest Lane can be confidently identified. There were certainly some on the east side of the present Ash Road, all demolished, and Nos 100–104 Albert Square, a terrace of three on the north side, and a few of the surviving houses on the west side of the western arm, may also be of that period.

Ambitions for a real square were soon given up, for by 1867 houses had been built over more than a quarter of the intended garden, a long terrace on the west side of what was then Albert Road (now Ash Road) and a few scattered houses on the east side of the western arm of Albert Square. By that time the west side was nearly complete, but the north side, and the east side of Albert Road, were still largely vacant.

Albert Square is now very dull, with two-storey terraces of various dates from the 1860s to the 1880s the main feature, plus a little modern infill on the site of the pub and elsewhere. The researcher is hampered by the peripatetic nature of the place. In the 1870s directories Albert Square appeared under West Ham, in the 1880s under Forest Gate and in the 1890s under Stratford. It is now in the borough of Newham.

Albion Square

DALSTON [HACKNEY]

It is a surprise to find one of the best squares in London concealed in deepest Dalston. That its presence there is more a case of carelessness than accident is suggested by the close proximity of the equally fine De Beauvoir Square; the landowners clearly had great confidence in the prosperous future of the district.

The field on which Albion Square was built belonged to Sir George Middleton, whose surveyor George Pownall was planning the development of the estate from the late 1830s. In 1840 Middleton entered into an agreement with Islip Odell, an Upper Clapton brickmaker and builder, for houses in Middleton Road that were completed in 1842. Odell then turned his attention to the new square, just

Numbers 13 and 14 Albion Square in 2007.

south of Middleton Road, where building was well advanced by 1844 and complete by 1849.

Numbers 5–8, held on a ninety-four-year lease from Lady Day 1844, were first occupied in 1845. If George Pownall did not design the houses, he must have approved the plans of others, that being a standard part of an estate surveyor's duties.

In the early days the typical residents were clerks, postal officials, merchants and stockbrokers. The unusual feature of the square was the Dalston & De Beauvoir Scientific & Literary Institute, a building that occupied the whole of the short west side. It was later the Albion Club, but in 1899 was acquired by the London School Board as a bath house.

The baths, which were at the rear, were destroyed during the Second World War, and the long-derelict hall at the front has now been replaced by very attractive flats (Nos 14–17) in the form of two pairs of bow-fronted houses in an 1840s style. Numbers 15–21 on the north side were also seriously damaged during the war, but have been beautifully restored. The garden has

been open to the public since 1899, when it was laid out by the Metropolitan Public Gardens Association.

The only thing Albion Square lacks is a glamorous list of former residents, but given its current status and attractions a writer on the squares 100 years from now should have a fine crop of celebrities to harvest.

Aldborough Square

MARYLEBONE [WESTMINSTER]

(now part of Stratford Place)

Stratford Place, off the north side of Oxford Street, was built for Edward Stratford in the 1770s to the designs of Richard Edwin, who was also the architect of the Hanover Square Rooms. The site had been a banqueting house for the use of the Lord Mayor. Like Panton Square, Stratford Place was built with a long approach road lined with houses, opening out into a small square. This was of the proprietor type, like Bloomsbury Square, with the owner's house taking the whole of the north side.

Derby House, Stratford Place (formerly Aldborough Square), *c.* 1907.

Stratford's father was created Viscount Aldborough in 1776 and Earl of Aldborough shortly before his death in 1777. It was probably then, on inheriting the titles, that Edward Stratford gave the name of Aldborough Square to the widened section of Stratford Place outside his own house. That was the name by which Lockie described it in 1813: 'Aldborough-Sq. – N. end of Stratford-place from 160 Oxford-st'. It was already in use in 1804, when, as the *Morning Post* recorded on 27 July, 'the Duchess of St Alban's masquerade in Aldborough Square, Stratford Place … was attended by all the fashionables remaining in town'.

As at Panton Square, the fact that the approach road and the square were numbered consecutively tended to make the separate name fade out of use quite soon. It was little heard of after 1813. The houses in the square were Nos 8–10 on the east side and 12–15 on the west. Most of them survive, but 12 and 13 are a 1954 rebuilding. Number 11 was Stratford House, later Derby House, on the north side. It was originally of five bays, with lower service wings. The present tall wings were added for the Earl of Derby in 1908–09.

Alexander Square

This is not a true square, but two terraces of fine late Georgian houses defended from the traffic of the Brompton Road by a plantation of trees. It is named after the nineteenth-century owners and developers of the estate, which also included Thurloe Square and its offshoots and part of the site of South Kensington Station.

John Alexander, a lawyer, inherited this land in 1799. It was then, like much of Brompton, being used as a market garden, but the area was changing rapidly. When John Alexander extended the lease of the market garden in 1821, he did so with the proviso that he could reclaim part of the land should he require it for building. This he did almost immediately, for in 1826 he took back the 4 acres closest to Brompton Road and agreed with a builder named James Bonnin for the construction there of Alexander Square (so named from 1827) and the associated roads. Bonnin or his subcontractors were to be granted eighty-year leases of the houses as they were

The south side of Alexander Square in 2006.

completed. James Bonnin was an active and successful figure in the development of Brompton, although his career ended, like those of so many nineteenth-century builders, in the bankruptcy courts.

Alexander Square consists mainly of two terraces, Nos 5–12 and 13–20, facing Brompton Road and separated by Alexander Place. There were also four houses on the short north side (Nos 1–4, now demolished) and the surviving 21–24 on the south side, and these eight were the first to be started, in 1827. There is no evidence that Bonnin built these first houses himself, but he was responsible for the two main terraces. The southern one (Nos 13–20, dated 1827) was built between 1827 and 1830, the northern (Nos 5–12, dated 1830) between 1830 and 1833.

The documents do not give the name of the architect, but Alexander Square has been attributed to George Godwin the elder. He did jobs for Bonnin and was the tenant of No. 24, the prominent corner house, which was the first to be occupied. Godwin was an obscure figure, but the father of a whole family of better-known architects, two of whom, George junior and Henry, lived here after him. The fine hand of Disraeli's cousin George Basevi has also been seen in the detail of the northern terrace, which was built after he became surveyor to the Alexander estate, probably in 1829.

The three associated roads, North Terrace, South Terrace and Alexander Place, were left as sawn-off stubs, pointing threateningly at the remaining part of the market garden, where Thurloe Square was to be built in the 1840s. Because Brompton Road, the highway to Fulham and Kingston-upon-Thames, was busy even in the eighteenth century, the houses built beside it from the 1760s were generally provided with long front gardens to protect them from the noise and dust. The plantation in front of Alexander Square gave a fashionable twist to this local custom.

Apart from the Godwins, there have not been many celebrated residents. William Nugent Glascock, RN, who lived at No. 21 from 1832 to 1834, was only intermittently employed by the Admiralty and spent his long years on half-pay writing useful naval manuals and novels a long way after Captain Marryat. Several other naval officers lived in the square in its early years. Dion Boucicault, the author of *London Assurance* and *The Colleen Bawn*, is thought to have been lodging at No. 23 in 1851, when 'Dion Page', 'gentleman, a dramatic author', appears in the census. 'Page' may have been an alias – he lived with his second wife for some years before marrying her and

was usually in debt – or the census taker's desperate stab at an unfamiliar name. He cannot have stayed there long, as the couple went to New York in 1853.

The short north terrace was demolished early in the twentieth century when the Rembrandt Hotel and Empire House were built in Thurloe Place. All the remaining houses received minor blast damage during the war and George Godwin's house was rather more seriously shaken, but the square is now in the most perfect condition.

Alma Square

ST JOHN'S WOOD [WESTMINSTER]

Although Alma Square was not built until the late 1850s, the planning must go back to 1854, when the Battle of the Alma was fought in the Crimea, or to a time not much later. In August 1859 the *Daily News* reported that ninety-six-year leases of Nos 1–7, the first houses built, had been auctioned at prices ranging from £290 to £450. If the building leases were originally of ninety-nine years, that would place the beginning of the development in 1856.

The west side of Alma Square seen from Hamilton Gardens, *c.* 1905.

Charles Maidlow, a builder who lived at No. 8 and was bankrupted in 1860, may have been responsible for these houses. He and other Maidlows had been engaged in the building of Pembridge Crescent on the Ladbroke estate earlier in the 1850s. The 1860 ratebook listed Nos 1–30 as 'building'. In 1861 only Nos 1 and 5 Alma Square had been disposed of, No. 1 to Samuel Joseph Mackie, the editor of *The Geologist* and a popular writer on geology. Ten more houses were to let and in the charge of policemen and other caretakers.

It should certainly have been called Alma Gardens, not Alma Square. Only on one of the very short sides do houses face the garden across a road. On the two long sides the backs of the houses open directly into the garden and on the north-eastern side it is confronted by a high brick wall. When Charles Booth's surveyor described it in 1898 as 'below the general level of St John's Wood' he was thinking socially, not geographically, for Alma Square forms a pleasantly secluded enclave, a cut above its neighbours to the south and west. The raucous world of the Abbey Road and its studio might be miles away.

The architecture has less to recommend it, being a mixture of starved Tudor and end-of-line Italianate. Number 11, now a house, was formerly the Heroes of Alma, a pub frequented by the Beatles when recording in Abbey Road.

Henry Vaughan Lanchester, one of the leading English architects of the early twentieth century, was born at No. 18 Alma Square in 1863. With his various partners, most notably Edwin Rickards, he was responsible for countless exuberant Edwardian town halls and other public buildings all over Britain and the Indian Empire. Elsa Lanchester, the Bride of Frankenstein, was his niece.

Alpha Square

Alpha Square, which was built in the early 1860s, was not a typical set of 'model buildings' of that decade, when ventures into the housing of the working classes were becoming popular. Despite their resemblance to that type, the fifty-eight flats of Alpha Square were aimed at a better class of tenant, and in the early days were occupied by clerks, commercial travellers and a surprising number of printers' compositors.

The exotic touch of a fountain in the centre of the courtyard was the only outward sign of this higher ambition. Otherwise, it was a dark and forbidding place, the tall buildings excluding the sunlight for most of the day. The narrow courtyard, with its entrance at the west end in Alpha Road, was surrounded by four-storey tenements with open stairwells on the long north and south sides and a five-storey block at the east end, backing onto older shops in the Walworth Road. The flats had very little depth, being hemmed in by houses in Olney Street on the north side and by other flats in Empress Street to the south. They had declined by 1899, 'some poor and others above the waterline'.

The flats survived the Second World War with only minor blast damage, but Alpha Square and all its neighbours were swept away in the early 1960s and the new street pattern is quite different. The square stood behind the shops directly opposite Merrow Street.

Alwyne Square

Alwyne Square (known as Canonbury Park Square until 1879) was built by Charles Hamor Hill, who signed an agreement with the Marquess of Northampton, the landowner, in 1857. Hill had already built much of Canonbury Park North and South, from which the style was carried over into the square. Four houses were occupied in 1861 and the development was complete by 1862. The first tenants were a wine merchant, a surveyor, an upholsterer and a builder. There were twenty-one houses, one detached, fourteen semi-detached and two terraces of three.

This was the last section of the Canonbury Park estate to be built. For the rest of the century the square settled down to quiet and prim respectability. In 1905 the marquess would only allow it to be included in the schedule of the *London Squares and Enclosures (Preservation) Bill* 'if there is a ban on bands playing in Alwyne-square'. Brass bands were the vulgar abomination that the aristocracy particularly associated with the LCC.

The north side of Alwyne Square, c. 1910.

With the new century the outlook for such large houses deteriorated, and between the wars the marquess began considering plans for redevelopment, perhaps doing away with the garden when the leases expired in 1936. Nothing had been done when the Second World War put a stop to all building. Five of the houses were damaged by bombing, but not beyond repair had there been the will to save such dinosaurs in the 1950s. Instead all twenty-one were demolished and replaced in 1954 by flats of no architectural interest. Now the shady private garden is the only attraction.

America Square

CITY OF LONDON

America Square was a product of the same wave of nervous City patriotism that produced Finsbury Square a few years later. The plutocrats of the City were being tempted away by the fine new squares in the West End and squandering their wealth among the wastrels there. To stem the tide, George Dance the younger, son and assistant to the City Surveyor and later his successor, designed this miniature homage to Bath on the extreme eastern edge of the City.

It was in three parts, diminishing in size from north to south: a square, a crescent and a tiny circus. The sixteen houses in the square were built between 1768 and 1774. The site chosen for this stylish exercise in town planning was the foetid and lethal ditch on the outer flank of the City wall. As Hughson reported in 1805, 'on this dangerous and filthy site are now constructed the convenient and elegant districts of Aldgate parish, denominated George Street, America Square, the Circus, and the Crescent'. George Street is now India Street.

The leading builder engaged in the work was Benjamin Hammett, an associate of Wilkes, and later alderman, MP and knight. A contemporary biographer remarked of him that 'rudeness, ignorance, and impudence, are frequently more valuable in the bustle of life than the most amiable qualities'. Because of his close involvement in City politics and his alignment with the Wilkes faction, Hammett has been regarded as the inspiration for this anti-court and West End scheme. Hammett Street was certainly the name given to the short approach to the Crescent from the Minories.

There was little chance that such developments would halt the drift to the west, or even slow it significantly. Sir James Shaw, Bt, who had been Lord

Mayor in 1805–06 and MP for the City from 1806 to 1818, died at No. 11 America Square in 1843, but he was almost the last survivor of the wealthy men Dance had in mind.

As early as 1840 only five of the sixteen houses in the square were occupied by private residents. The rest were in commercial use and No. 10 was, significantly, the office of the Blackwall Railway Company. It was the building of the approach to Fenchurch Street Station in 1841 that finally destroyed America Square's fading hope of success as a residential quarter. The railway viaduct cut across immediately behind the southern end of the square, bringing noise and dirt, and reducing light. Soon all the houses were being used as offices or low-grade commercial hotels. Widening of the viaduct chopped off the south side of the square and part of the west, and Victorian and Edwardian redevelopment and wartime bombing removed the other original houses one by one. The obelisk that was the main feature in the centre somehow survived the bombing, only to be removed by the Corporation after 1957.

Now America Square is a small paved area with two trees and a flowerbed and large modern offices all around. The only old building in sight is the pub at the corner of Crosswall and Vine Street. But in the Crescent (a few yards to the south, beyond the railway bridge) the style of Dance's development – now a startling one to encounter in the City – can still be admired in a few surviving houses and a number of careful replicas.

Ampthill Square

The common characteristic of the three squares on the Bedford New Town estate was that they were not even approximately square. Harrington was triangular, with houses on only two sides. The extinguished Ampthill and the partly surviving Oakley Square were in the shape of the longbow. Ampthill Square was named after Ampthill Park in Bedfordshire, one of the seats of the Dukes of Bedford.

America Square, looking north-east towards Crosswall in 2008.

The east side of Ampthill Square, looking north from Barnby Street, *c.* 1905.

The square was planned as early as 1834, but was not proceeded with for ten years. It began to be destroyed before a house was built, when the approaches to Euston Station were cut through it, dividing the garden into two sections, and the enlargement of the station in the mid-1840s replaced its southern half with carriage sheds. The railway company built a wall 200 yards long and over 20ft high to divide its property from the square, but as it was partially disguised by a plantation of trees, the *Morning Chronicle* comfortingly predicted in 1846 that 'the building property, of whatever character it may be, proposed as a continuation of Ampthill-square (the ground about which is fast being covered with good houses of the detached villa form), will not suffer, as far as appearance is concerned, from its proximity'. Building began seriously in 1845 and was completed by 1851.

Most of the early tenants were solidly prosperous merchants, manufacturers and clergymen of no distinction, but in 1851 they did include Richard Potter, professor of natural philosophy and astronomy at University College, at No. 11, and John Brandard, the lithographer, at No. 41. The square was never fashionable, so it is not surprising that its most celebrated resident was a man whose moment of fame lay seventy years in the past. William Henry Betty, the 'Young Roscius', was so much the fashion in 1805 that Pitt adjourned the House of Commons so that members should not miss his performance as Hamlet. He died at No. 37 Ampthill Square in the upmost obscurity, in 1874, fifty years after his second and final farewell to the stage.

In 1898 Charles Booth's researcher noted that 'the whole of this district is on the decline. Lodgers are coming in more and more', and in 1907 Beresford Chancellor found it 'composed of apartment-letting houses'.

All that had remained after the railway demolitions fell victim to bomb damage and 1960s redevelopment by St Pancras Council, the planners as usual accounting for more houses than the Luftwaffe. The name is insultingly perpetuated by the Ampthill Square Estate.

Angel Square

Angel Square was an occasional name, in use late in the eighteenth century and early in the nineteenth, for a court off the west side of Bishopsgate Without, leading to the long Angel Alley. The only justification for the name was the fact that four houses on the south side of the alley were set back from the building line, not unlike Audley Square, *mutatis mutandis*.

In the 1740s Rocque had shown Angel Alley extending to Bishopsgate, with no indication of a widening at its east end. The square had a little appendage to the south known as Smith's Buildings, insurance policies for which were taken out in 1819 and 1822. There had been one for Angel Square in 1793.

When most of Angel Alley was wiped out by the construction of the approaches to Broad Street and Liverpool Street stations in the 1860s and 1870s, the fragment that remained at the east end had long abandoned any pretensions, probably because the building of larger shops and offices in Bishopsgate had involved the demolition of the Angel Square houses, thus narrowing the alley to its original width. The last stub of Angel Alley was extinguished in 1891, when Liverpool Street Station was enlarged.

Arbour Square

In 1813 the site of Arbour Square was an open field in an area largely given over to rope walks. The square was laid out by the Mercers' Company in 1819 and named after Arbour Field, part of their St Paul's School estate here. The houses were built quickly, the inferior east side a little later than the others. A master mariner of 'Arbour-square, Commercial-road' was a bankrupt in April 1821.

By 1839 the square boasted two pubs, the Safe Harbour and the Star & Garter. The Safe Harbour was known to the locals, or pronounced by them, as the Safe Arbour, but by any name it was anything but safe, to judge from the experience of one Joseph Jones, who was robbed and nearly beaten to death there on an August night in 1833.

The south side of Arbour Square in 2007.

Nevertheless, it was a respectable square with mainly private residents, plus the odd solicitor and school, and of course pilots and master mariners.

In 1898 the garden was described as:

> … indifferently kept. Belongs to Mercers' Company, was done up two years ago but has since been allowed to go to waste. None allowed to use it, is now being tidied up. Houses round occupied by mixed class, Jews coming in. North side, southern and western sides better than the eastern. Houses 3½ storied, with fair gardens; most take in lodgers.

The garden was opened to the public in 1904, when the Mercers' Company leased it to the LCC, but this was only after the company had offered to sell the Arbour and York Square gardens for £3,000. (See York Square for details.) By that time the typical residents were clerks and commercial travellers, but there was also the odd stevedore or lighterman. In 1891 the landlord of the Star & Garter was also an architect, an unusual combination.

Arbour Square was never a smart address and no famous names are associated with it. One interesting man was born at No. 33 in 1892: Edward Merewether, the factory inspector who first demonstrated the medical dangers of asbestos.

Today the listed Raine's Foundation School of 1913, used as the Tower Hamlets College, fills the east side, and a 1937 block of flats the north, but the original terraces to south and west and the attractive garden still give it the atmosphere of a genuine square. The history could have been very different, as the Mercers' Company considered moving St Paul's School to the square before wisely deciding to go west, and Stepney Council had serious plans to build a new town hall on the north side in the 1920s.

Argyle Square

ST PANCRAS [CAMDEN]

The site of Argyle Square was part of the large Battle Bridge Field, which was cut in two when the New Road (Marylebone Road, Euston Road and City Road) was laid out in 1756. Part of the southern division of the field was used as the New Road Nursery – a hopeful speculation in an area where many houses and gardens were being created – until the land was sold in 1823 to developers named Thomas Dunston, William Robinson and William Flanders. In the next year they obtained an Act of Parliament empowering them to form, pave and light streets on Battle Bridge Fields. They immediately set out and named all the roads leading into the interior – including Argyle Street – and made some progress in getting houses built in a couple of them, but the site of the square remained a vacant space for a little longer.

Instead of houses, what first began to arise there was an ambitious private arts centre named the Panharmonic Gardens, which was intended to include a theatre, a dramatic school, concert and ballrooms, a picture gallery and a library, plus the more usual features of a London pleasure garden. It was the dream of Gesualdo Lanza, a music teacher who opened his gardens in 1830 and closed them (or had them closed by his creditors) in 1832.

Few of the planned buildings had got off the drawing board, so it took Dunstan, Robinson and Flanders no time to clear the ground and in the same year to offer building plots for sale 'in a new square called Argyle Square'. Their speed of response suggests that the square had always been a part of the grand design for the estate and that the Panharmonic Gardens was just an experiment, worth a brief trial.

Plots were offered, but builders were slow to take them up in an area already gaining a poor reputation. An 1834 parish map showed the roads laid out in their present form and had the word 'square' printed where the garden was to be, but there was no sign of any house. It was only in the late 1830s that building agreements were made, and the first houses in the square were not completed until 1840. Among the half dozen occupied in 1841 was No. 4, shared by Henry Ford, architect, and his father James Ford, architect and surveyor, men who may have been engaged in designing the houses. Progress was then a little quicker. Most of the square had been built by 1844, but the last few houses had to wait until 1849. At the southeast corner the Swedenborgians built their New Jerusalem Church in 1844.

The developers' hopes were not realised. The square was the star of the neighbourhood, but the neighbourhood was not a good one. It had been dragged down, even before building began on Battle Bridge Fields, by the poor streets established to the south and west in the first decade of the nineteenth century. Here poverty, drunkenness and overcrowding were entrenched. The situation was not improved by the building of King's Cross Station in 1851–52 and St Pancras in 1868–74, bringing waves of navvies, railwaymen and travellers into the area. In 1898 the local policeman reported that this was a centre of prostitution, for the convenience of provincials arriving at the stations. 'Number of streets in the neighbourhood of Argyle Square containing disorderly houses,' he said. There were good tenants, especially in the early days – Francis Oliver Finch, the artist, a follower of Blake, lived at No. 2 in the 1850s, and No. 47 was the vicarage of St Jude's, Gray's Inn Road – but by the early twentieth century the vicarage was one of only three or four private residences among the many small hotels and boarding houses. In the 1970s the square was thick with streetwalkers every night.

The New Jerusalem Church, Argyle Square, in 1844.

The north side of Argyle Square in 1908, or a little earlier.

The short north side was demolished in the 1930s. The square suffered a good deal of damage in the Second World War, especially in the south-east corner, where the Swedenborgian church was destroyed, but nearly all of the houses were carefully restored. Anything so close to King's Cross can hardly avoid being a little seedy even today, and Argyle Square is still dominated by small hotels, but it now seems thoroughly respectable, day and night. At lunchtime, office workers picnic on the grass of the public garden, just as they do at Finsbury or Russell Square. The attractive 1840s houses survive on three sides, but on the north the red brick wall of a singularly ugly warehouse breaks the spell.

Arlington Square

The Finsbury Fields, on which Arlington Square was built, were used as an archery ground from the sixteenth to the eighteenth century by the Archers' Company, one of the constituent parts of the Honourable Artillery Company.

Arlington Square was the work of Henry Rydon, a major developer in Islington, who signed an agreement with the landowners, the Church Commissioners, in 1847. He had also agreed terms with the Clothworkers' Company for the land surrounding the small plot belonging to the Church Commissioners, so the whole area was built at the same time, in a uniform style, characterised by unusually wide streets. Rydon did not build the houses himself, but sublet small plots to various contractors. The ones chiefly involved with Arlington Square were W.T. Catling on the west side and John Hill on the east.

The square was nearly complete by 1851, although only Nos 1–10 and 30–46 were occupied at the time of the census. The early residents were mainly clerks and craftsmen. The north end of the east side had been reserved by the Church Commissioners, and here St Philip's was built in 1855, with the vicarage beside it and the school behind. The church was designed by Alexander Dick Gough, the less extravagant of the two architects of Milner Square.

The south side suffered some blast damage during the war, but its restoration has not detracted from the unity of the design. This is a trim, respectable, well-maintained square of stucco and brick houses, the line of which is broken only by the block of flats on the site of St Philip's which was demolished in 1954, and by the surviving vicarage next door. The very mildly Gothic vicarage, now that of St James's, Prebend Street, looks brash beside the simple late 1840s terraces. The garden, which was taken over by the council after the war, is well maintained and popular. One curious feature of this pleasant district is that, unlike Regent's Canal

The north side of Arlington Square, Islington, in 2007.

suburbs to the west, it resolutely turns its back on the towing path, so that the casual visitor might easily have no inkling of the close proximity of water.

Arlington Square

MAYFAIR [WESTMINSTER]

Arlington Square was a project only, intended to be built on the site of Lord Arlington's estate in Piccadilly. *The Loyal Protestant and True Domestick Intelligencer* reported in March 1682 that:

> His Majesty has been pleased to give my Lord Arlington the ground at the farther end of the Park, where the Deer-harbour is, which is walled in as you go towards Hyde Park; in lieu of which His Majesty takes his house and garden into the Park for his use. The Lord Arlington has already sold the ground for £20,000, whereon will be built a stately square.

This was the site of Arlington and Bennett Streets, granted to Lord Arlington in 1681 and promptly sold to William Pym, who speculated in building development here and in Soho with unusual success. Gregorio Leti, writing in 1682, also confidently predicted that a square of the greatest splendour would be built on Lord Arlington's estate, but when this land was developed in the late 1680s only the two streets familiar to us today were laid out.

Artillery Square

WESTMINSTER

Artillery Square, which existed for only sixty years, was a court in Strutton Ground, now a popular pedestrianised shopping street, but then a slum. The name came ultimately from the Westminster archery ground – 'a pretty large Enclosure, made Use of by those that delight in Military Exercises', as Strype called it in 1720 – part of which was taken for the Artillery Brewery and afterwards for Artillery Mansions in Victoria Street.

Artillery Square was off the east side of Strutton Ground and lay rather closer to Duck Lane, now St Matthew Street. The 1813 revision of the Horwood map showed nothing there. It made its first appearance in the 1830 ratebook, when Joseph Wardell was the only man assessed. In 1833 a ground rent was auctioned, arising out of:

> … ten substantial Dwelling-houses in Artillery-square, Strutton's Ground, Westminster; also stables for six horses, and yard enclosed with folding gates. The whole let on lease for sixty-one years, at 75l. per annum, to a highly respectable tenant, who has expended a considerable sum in rebuilding the houses.

From the first it was occupied by labourers, bricklayers, shoemakers and charwomen. In 1891 the eleven houses were closed by the magistrates, and as nothing had been done to make them fit for human habitation they were pulled down by the St Margaret and St John's Vestry in 1892; 'thus,' as the Medical Officer of Health wrote, 'putting an end to a court which had, for many years, been a source of trouble to the sanitary authorities'. It was replaced by the much needed St Matthew's Mission. Award House is now on the site.

Arundel Square

BARNSBURY [ISLINGTON]

Arundel Square was built in the 1850s on land belonging to Samuel Pocock. The east side led the way, between 1850 and 1852, the north and west sides following, after a delay, between 1855 and 1860. The section of the North London Railway that bounded the garden on the south side was opened (after several years spent digging the cutting) in 1850, the year in which the first house was begun, so it was not a question of the railway disrupting or curtailing the development, but rather of a 'square' being resorted to so that the garden could protect the large houses intended from the noise of the trains. Before the railway was thought of there had been houses on both sides of what are now Westbourne Road and the west side of the square, some on the site of the later garden and railway cutting. These had to be demolished when the railway came through, and it was only then that the idea of a square was substituted.

The north side of Arundel Square, *c.* 1905.

The building dates make it easy to guess that the sixteen houses on the east side are much the best, achieving a satisfying, balanced composition despite the handicap of a sloping site. The style is still basically late Georgian. The north side is dull, jaded Italianate, more like Earls Court than Kensington. The west side is hideous.

The Charles Booth survey described Arundel Square in 1897, '4½ storied, with a fairly well kept private square [garden]. Most houses owned by one family. Lawn tennis court (grass) in square. Railway cutting running through south side of it.'

The houses escaped lightly during the war, with damage confined to a few on the west side, really part of Westbourne Road. The garden was not so lucky and dug for victory during the war, it fell into such dereliction afterwards that the residents were glad to be rid of the responsibility. It was acquired for the public in 1957, under the terms of the King George's Fields scheme, a memorial to George V, becoming largely a children's playground. The garden was enlarged and landscaped when luxury flats were built on the vacant south side (over the railway) in 2009.

Audley Square

Audley Square, sometimes called South Audley Square, is nothing more than a widening of South Audley Street on its eastern side, south of Hill Street. Only the recessed houses and those flanking them (eight in all) were ever considered part of the square, which is not even separately numbered. The original houses were Nos 2–8 South Audley Street.

Chesterfield House was No. 1, but the owners made little use of the number. Number 8, at the corner of Hill Street, which has been known as Cambridge House, Curzon House and Alington House, still occupies a large frontage, but it was a mansion almost as big as Chesterfield House when built before 1744, with a south wing that formed the north side of Audley Square. Before 1868 the wing was given up to an enlarged No. 7 and the house was separated from the square. It is now the Nehru Centre. Chesterfield House and No. 8 were shown on Rocque's 1740s map, with a vacant space between them that was filled by the other Audley Square houses in 1751–52.

Audley Square in 1926.

Most of the original tenants were prominent politicians or soldiers. The location, between Berkeley Square and Park Lane, makes it unsurprising that many men of rank and fashion have lived in Audley Square, most of them at No. 8. The Duke of York, George IV's brother, spent his last few years there and insured the house with the Sun in 1825. Mrs Arbuthnot recorded a visit in her diary for June of that year:

> I dined at the Duke of York's on the 16th to meet the Duke and Duchess of Cambridge and the Duchess of Gloucester. Nothing can be more magnificent than the Duke's dinner; all the ornaments of the table were gold plate, and the sideboards all round the room were also covered. The Duke is now living in the house in Audley Square where the Duke of Cambridge formerly lived, while his own in the Stableyard is rebuilding.

The Duke of Cambridge was the Duke of York's younger brother. The house in the stableyard is the present Lancaster House, which the 'grand old duke' did not live to occupy. Biographers say that

the unfortunate Prime Minister Spencer Perceval was born in Audley Square in 1762, but his father does not appear there in the ratebooks.

Audley Square did not have much architectural distinction as a group. The houses were of different heights and widths, and in various styles, and some were rebuilt in the nineteenth century. The square suffered severely during the war, with all the houses except No. 2 being damaged. Only Nos 2, 3 and 4 now survive in the square. The three to the north have been replaced by the Audley Square multistorey car park, a monstrous intrusion built between 1959 and 1962, and No. 8 is hidden behind it. Number 3 is the sole example of the original style of 1751–52. Number 2, on the south side, was rebuilt about 1880, in glaring red brick, for Lord Arthur Russell, whose terracotta arms are prominently displayed. It was one of the last works of Thomas Henry Wyatt.

Augusta Square

See Augustus Square

Augustine Square

See Augustus Square

Augustus Square

The tiny Augustus Square, which was originally called Augusta Square and sometimes appeared as Augustine Square on maps, was built in 1826–27, as part of John Nash's Park Villages scheme. Nash had taken the land to help the Regent's Canal Company, of which he was a major shareholder, through a financial crisis.

The detailed design was the work either of Nash or his assistant, James Pennethorne. The leases proved hard to sell and Nash had to take most of them himself. Although it was a toy, the square was perfectly formed, with its own miniature garden and a narrow road running round it. It had only ten houses, terraces of three on the north, south and east sides, and on the west a detached villarette with a garden on the brink of the canal. The east-side houses were a little removed from the others, on the far side of a road that was Park Village East to the north and the commercial Augustus Street, with its wharves alongside the Regent's Park Basin, to the south. The Regalia Tavern, which was No. 11 Augustus Square, was really part of Augustus Street, and was listed in Augusta Terrace when built in 1826.

One of the first residents was the dramatist and *Punch* humourist Douglas Jerrold, who lived at No. 4, the little villa, in the late 1820s. The square was a moderately good address until the 1850s, when Edward Rimbault, the historian of music, lived at No. 3. The appearance of lodging houses in that decade marked the beginning of a rapid decline.

In 1898 Charles Booth's assistant gave this description:

> 2 storey. Must once have been a pretty little square, tiny little houses probably given over to artists and Bohemians; now exclusively lodgers, 'all let out' said [Inspector] Wait. Here again the small square [garden] is in a disgraceful condition.

This pretty square was destroyed in stages between 1899 and 1901, together with the northern end of Augustus Street and most of Park Village East, to make room for the widening of the lines into Euston. Richmond House, a 1961 block of flats and the rerouted south end of Park Village East are now on the site.

Austin Friars Square

Despite the historic resonance of its name, Austin Friars Square has had a dull history. The seventeenth and eighteenth-century maps showed a small open space or yard north-east of the Dutch church, but treated it as part of the complex of passages known as Austin Friars. A large building protruded into the open space on the west side, preventing it from having a square shape. This building was apparently demolished in the nineteenth century, producing a larger and more regular space that maps from the early 1860s onwards described as 'Austin Friar Square'. The London directories, however, did not recognise it at all until well into the twentieth century.

The area was badly damaged by the bomb that destroyed the Dutch church in 1940. Austin Friars Square still exists as a name, but it serves mainly as a backyard to large 1990s office blocks in Old Broad Street. A few City workers take their lunch here on a bench beneath four gallant trees.

Avenue Square

Avenue Road was the uninspired name for the first suburban speculative development in central Lewisham, a cul-de-sac run off the west side of the High Street about 1840. It was later known as Romer Avenue and is now represented by the main entrance to the Riverdale shopping centre.

Avenue Road was entirely respectable, but a number of small courts and alleys that branched from it and its immediate offshoots in the 1840s were very different. Avenue Square was one of these, lying at the far south-western corner of the estate, close to the Riverdale Mill. It consisted of twelve two-storey, five-roomed cottages in two terraces, eight on the north

Numbers 5–12 Avenue Square, *c.* 1936. (Photograph courtesy of the Lewisham Local History and Archives Centre)

side and four on the east, each with a small garden. The west and south sides were occupied by the backs of granary and bakery buildings associated with the mill. In the centre there was a scrubby open space, more clothes-drying ground than garden.

Avenue Square was always isolated, obscure, almost forgotten. In 1900 it was classified as 'poor', a status from which it never altered in nearly a century of existence. When Lewisham Council was searching desperately in the mid-1930s for contributions to a London slum clearance programme, somebody remembered Avenue Square and it was put forward with other cottages that would have been considered quite comfortable in more deprived areas of the capital. It was demolished in 1937 or soon after. Molesworth Street, the Lewisham High Street bypass, now runs through the site.

Avondale Square

OLD KENT ROAD [SOUTHWARK]

Avondale Square was laid out on market garden ground in the 1870s. The lease of No. 15 ran from Christmas Day 1874, which means it was probably built in 1875. That was the date of the original St Philip's Church. An 1878 map showed houses only at the south end, close to the entrance from Old Kent Road, and on the east side, but none in the two large loops towards the west.

In the early 1880s some twenty houses were still standing empty. It was perhaps this slow take up that persuaded the owners to allow the Mawbey Road Board School to be built in the north-west corner of the square, a solution that cannot have been ideal for them or their tenants. There was no garden or communal open space (until bombing created one), so to introduce a little greenery into the waste of brick there were only the modest grounds of the church, which was built too late to need a burial ground, and the less modest garden of the vicarage. The style of the terraced houses – two storeys, with a deep semi-basement and a single dormer window – was harmless in itself, but became tiresome when endlessly repeated.

The attic room was for the single servant employed in most of the houses. In 1899 Charles Booth's researcher, who found the square quiet, described the typical household: 'City workers, a single man lodger usual, and a general drudge. Black coated and top hats, start for work by tram between 8 and 10 in the morning.' Avondale Square's most famous resident was Frederick Gard Fleay, 'the industrious flea' to his many enemies, who lived at No. 33 from the 1870s to the 1890s. His painstaking research into the life and works of Shakespeare and the other Elizabethan dramatists has introduced his name into a million footnotes ('Fleay says …') but his far-fetched theories have made 'Fleay absurdly says …' almost as common.

Avondale Square was nearly obliterated during the war, with three-quarters of the houses destroyed and

Avondale Square, *c.* 1910. St Philip's Vicarage is on the left.

the other thirty-five damaged. They survived, sur-rounded by prefabs, until the square was redeveloped in the 1960s. St Philip's Church was also so badly shaken that it had to be demolished, leaving the hall and the vicarage as the only original buildings in the square today. St Philip's was rebuilt in 1963, a date which makes it easy to guess that the job was not done well. The architect was N.F. Cachemaille-Day.

Azenby Square

PECKHAM [SOUTHWARK]

(later Azenby Road)

This was a large square, or triangle rather, built in the late 1860s. Separate names – Azenby Road, Aylmer Road and Aspenlow Terrace – were proposed for the three sides in 1868 at the request of Richard Gover, a Croydon architect and surveyor, but all were quickly dropped in favour of Azenby Square.

A ninety-one-year remainder lease of Nos 29 and 31, evidently running from 1868, was sold in 1876. A good many of the houses were still seeking tenants in 1871; those occupied harboured clerks, commercial travellers and taxmen. Gover began with high hopes, to judge

from the size of the garden and the ninety or so houses, but by the end of the century the square was already in serious decline. Charles Booth's assistant described it in 1899: 'Two storey, and two storey with basements houses. A great mixture, "mechanics and labouring classes", gone down, two and three families in most houses, the east end the poorer.' The words in inverted commas were the escorting policeman's comment. The summary for the district was, 'Deterioration is, perhaps, most marked in Azenby Square … a feature perhaps partly explained by its nearness to the railway, by the size of many of the houses (which are too large for single families) and by the fact that it leads nowhere.'

The complaint of its leading nowhere was dealt with soon afterwards, when a north-western entrance was made from Lyndhurst Grove, but for the size of the houses and the closeness of the railway no such easy remedy was available.

Azenby Square was renamed Azenby Road in 1903, for no obvious reason unless the LCC planners had been consulting the archives. On 6 January 1945 a third of the houses were destroyed by a V2 rocket and the square, under any name, was doomed. Today only a tiny fragment of Azenby Road survives at the west end, with one double-fronted house and a gaunt terrace of four. The rest of the houses were replaced in the 1950s by a park known as Warwick Gardens, which slopes gently downwards beside the railway line from Lyndhurst Grove to Lyndhurst Way.

Baldwin's Square

HOLBORN [CAMDEN]

(later Baldwin's Place)

Baldwin's Square was probably built early in the eighteenth century. The Strype map, published in 1720, but created earlier, indicated a large building with a courtyard, perhaps an inn, on the site. The list of streets given by William Stow in 1722 included Baldwyn's Square in Baldwyn's Gardens. John Rocque showed 'Baldwin's Sq.' in his 1740s map, but in the 1790s Horwood gave it the more appropriate name of Baldwyns Place. It was merely a court of nine or ten houses parallel with the north side of Baldwin's Gardens. There were two alleys leading from Baldwin's Gardens to this offshoot and a small opening at the north end of the western alley may have given rise to the name of 'square'.

Baldwin's Place can never have been a salubrious or quiet spot, being at the heart of some of the worst of the Holborn slums. In 1841 it contained a plaster works and the premises of a bone boiler. In the middle of the nineteenth century it was dominated by St Bridget's Roman Catholic Church, the schools occupying nearly the whole of the south side while the church was in the adjoining Leopard's Court. But the church was abandoned in 1876 and large business premises in Baldwin's Gardens to the south began to extend into Baldwin's Place. Alexander William Bain's bookbindery, for example, was rebuilt in such a way as to extinguish the opening that may once have suggested the name of 'square'. By the early twentieth century all the houses had been replaced by factories and workshops.

The whole area was badly damaged during the Second World War and now the St Alban's Church of England Schools, long established in Baldwin's Gardens, have been extended over the site of Baldwin's Place, which has been entirely extinguished. Baldwin's Gardens still links Leather Lane to Gray's Inn Road.

Banner Square

OLD STREET [ISLINGTON]

Banner Square was a substantially widened section of Banner Street halfway between Bunhill Row and Whitecross Street. Banner Street was created (largely along the line of the extinguished Goat Alley) soon after 1774. It was a humble companion to contemporary City improvement schemes like America Square and Finsbury Square, also located on the City boundary or just beyond. George Dance the younger, the architect of those schemes, set the ball rolling in Banner Street too with a plan submitted in 1774 that made a crescent the principal feature. In the event a square was substituted, but whether designed by Dance or an inferior hand is not known. Peter Banner is a possible candidate. The change was no doubt made because a crescent would have wasted too much valuable building land in a development aimed at 'middling sort of people'.

The name came from the builders who contracted for most of the plots – Henry, John and Peter Banner. Henry was City Carpenter at the time and thus a junior colleague of Dance, the City Surveyor. In the *Court and City Register* for 1776 Henry appears as a joiner and John as a plumber in the ward of Cripplegate Without, the nearest part of the City to Banner Square. Henry died in 1784.

Peter Banner of Old Street, builder, was one of the men who contracted to execute Dance's designs for houses in Finsbury Square in 1789, but he was bankrupted in the same year and fled to America. There he became a successful architect, designing several buildings for Yale College.

Maps of the 1790s and the early nineteenth century showed ten recessed houses on the north side and ten on the south of Banner Square, but all numbered as part of Banner Street. The houses at the two southern corners, Nos 52 and 63 Banner Street, became pubs as the Prince of Wales and the Hope. By 1841 nearly every house was in commercial use: watchmakers, fringe manufactures, a widows' cap maker and many other trades.

It was still shown as a square on maps up to the 1860s, but thereafter Banner Street was widened and rebuilt as workshops and warehouses, so that the square lost its distinctive existence. It was officially made a part of Banner Street, and the square name abolished, in 1895. The original houses of the square, at least on the north side, may have been destroyed when a refuge of the Houseless Poor Asylum was established there in the 1870s.

After serious bomb damage in the Second World War this part of Banner Street was left almost a blank sheet. It is now entirely modern, with offices on the north side and flats on the south.

Barnsbury Square

BARNSBURY [ISLINGTON]

It used to be believed, on the shaky basis of eighteenth-century archaeology, that Barnsbury Square was built on the site of a Roman camp, which led to the present No. 13 being called Suetonius House for a time. A more sober modern assessment of the evidence has concluded that it was the moated Barnsbury manor house that stood there. The house had become ruinous by the late fourteenth century, but remains of the moat survived at what is now the west end of the square until the 1830s and were not entirely effaced when the

square was laid out in that decade, as a small section was still shown in the back garden of Mountfort House on early twentieth-century maps. The last traces were destroyed when Mica House, a large factory, was built over the garden in the 1930s. The piece of land that included the moat, and on which the square was built, was usually known as Pond Field.

The first element of Barnsbury Square was Minerva Terrace, the attractive group of houses on the east side of Thornhill Road between Brooksby Street and Bewdley Street. This forms the east side of the square, but it has never been numbered as part of it and it is not certain that a square was in contemplation when it was begun in 1827. The first building in the square itself was Mountfort House, which still dominates the west end rather in the fashion of Hertford House in Manchester Square. But if Mountfort House was intended for the main developer, Thomas Whowell, as the style suggests, there was a rapid change of mind. It was first occupied by him in 1836, but promptly divided into the two dwellings it has ever since remained.

The original houses on the south side were built in 1835–36, those on the north in 1837. There two of the four were destroyed during the Second World War.

The south side of Barnsbury Square in 1908, or a little earlier.

Little more than half of these two sides were available because the long back gardens of Thornhill Road had preoccupied much of the land.

The elements that set Barnsbury Square apart from all others in London are the extensions to north and south of Mountfort House, known as Mountfort Crescent and Mountfort Terrace, which were built between 1841 and 1845. They were probably not the result of inspired design by developer or architect, but a utilitarian solution to the problems of an awkward plot of ground. These delightfully secluded retreats, miraculously surviving, give Barnsbury Square a unique charm. There can be few more desirable houses in any London square than the five in Mountfort Crescent.

The quality of Barnsbury Square persists despite a dull garden and unsympathetic architectural intrusions on the long sides. These were partly the result of bomb damage, but the process had begun much earlier when a factory and the red brick No. 5 (formerly 1a) were built in the garden of No. 35 Thornhill Road in the late 1890s. From the first, this was as individualistic a square as any in Mayfair, with each developer or owner choosing his own favourite style with no regard to uniformity. The garden was the subject of long disputes about ownership and upkeep, but since the 1930s it has been maintained by the council in uninspired municipal style.

Barnsbury Square was the home of Maria Louisa Charlesworth, the author of pious, best-selling stories for children. Most of them were written at West Lodge (the present No. 13) where she led a valetudinarian life in the home of her father, a clergyman. Her *Ministering Children* sold 170,000 copies in England between 1854 and 1881. The great Shakespearean actor Sir Johnston Forbes-Robertson was brought up at Mountfort House, where his family lived from 1859 to 1874. Ernest Henry Starling, the discoverer of hormones, was born at No. 2 in 1866. Number 27 was the last home of Douglas Cleverdon, the bookseller, printer, publisher and radio producer, in which last capacity he was responsible for *The Brains Trust* and *Under Milk Wood*. He died in 1987.

Mountfort Crescent, Barnsbury Square, in 2007.

Bartholomew Square

This is one of the oldest squares in or near the City of London, probably built late in the seventeenth century, when this area was developed. Hatton had two entries for it in 1708, as Old Street Square and St Bartholomew Square. It was shown fully formed, as St Bartholomew's Square, on the 1720 Strype map, which is a good deal earlier than its published date. The name came from the ownership of the land by St Bartholomew's Hospital.

In its early days the square stood on the edge of London, with only fields to the north. Its initial success must have been compromised by the proximity of the pest house, but by the 1740s it had the more encouraging French Hospital for a neighbour, although the road was still Pest House Row. (It is now Bath Street.) By then St Bartholomew's Square had become generally known as Old Street Square, and so it remained until about 1815.

The woolly-headed historians of framework knitting have complicated things by asserting that William Lee, the supposed inventor of the stocking frame, and his brother James, lived and worked in Old Street Square. As William is thought to have died in France about 1614, and James to have moved to Nottingham by 1620, that is evidently impossible.

The first reference to 'Old Street Square' in the Old Bailey records is found in 1732. There are several others in the 1730s and 1740s. The Bowl & Pin pub in Old Street Square is mentioned in 1743, and the Cock in 1758.

The houses were rebuilt early in the nineteenth century, as was evident from the style of the ones that survived until the 1970s. The name was changed at the same time to the present Bartholomew Square, although Old Street Square continued to appear as a variant until the 1830s. These changes were recorded as 'recent' in David Hughson's *Walks through London* (1817): 'Old Street Square is mostly taken down, and a new one, now called Bartholomew-Square, with an enclosed area in the centre, is nearly erected in its place'.

The first reference to Bartholomew Square, Old Street, in the Old Bailey records is in 1817. There had been about twenty-five houses in the eighteenth century but the rebuilding introduced a few more, the majority on the longer north and south sides. The new houses were of three storeys and a basement, lit by a shallow area. The doors and ground floor windows were round-headed. By the 1840s the houses were mostly in commercial use, and there was a pub, the White Bear, at the south-east corner.

The garden became public in 1894, four years before Charles Booth's investigator visited the square, with PC Machell as his guide, and made this report: '3 storey, asphalt playground in centre; on one bench Machell pointed out a respectably dressed middle aged lady eating her dinner out of a newspaper, who had been in prison "nearly as often as Jane Cakebread". Houses being done up, used to be a rough spot.'

Remarkably, in this area, the square came through the Second World War without any serious damage. Because this was just outside the City and its financial pressures, the square continued to be lined by houses until the 1970s. There were a few commercial buildings on the north side and the White Bear at the south-east corner, numbered in Leage Street. Nearly the whole area was then cleared for the second stage of the Greater London Council's St Luke's Estate, with the garden of the square retained at its centre. It is now just an irregular plot of grass with one or two old trees, bordered by flats on the south side and offices on the north, where alone the original street line remains.

Basing Square

The site of Basing Square was part of an estate purchased in 1704 as an endowment for the William Berman Trust, a charity intended to benefit poor ministers. The square was a tiny enclosure of five almshouses, built at the west end of the not much larger Basing Place in 1845. The name came from the Castle public house in Kingsland Road, one of the trust properties, which was 'formerly called the Basing House', as a lease of 1781 recorded. It later resumed the Basing House name, and still exists just south of Basing Place.

The Berman almshouses (replacing the original ones near Hoxton Square) were in Basing Square until they were destroyed by a flying bomb on 6 August 1944. The main block was a pleasing, modest composition of three two-storey houses, the central one dignified by stucco and a parapet. Basing Square was not reinstated after the Second World War and the Shoreditch Campus of the Hackney Community College now covers the site of that and most of the rest of the Berman estate. The almshouses were rebuilt at Brentwood in 1953.

Bath Square

OLD STREET [HACKNEY]

The piece of vacant land east of Tabernacle Square was filled about 1815 by John Street, this part of which was soon renamed Bath Street, and by a network of lanes and alleys leading north to Old Street. These came to be called Bath Place, Bath Court and Bath Square, the last of which appeared in the 1851 census, but not in 1841 or 1861. The central alley was Bath Place, which led from Bath Street to Old Street. Bath Court was a long cul-de-sac off its east side.

Bath Square must have rivalled Prince's Square, Holborn, as the smallest in London. In 1851 only No. 1 Bath Square appeared, listed between No. 35 Bath Street and No. 1 Bath Court. It was occupied by John Calvert, a type founder. Bath Street is now part of Rivington Street and of its northern offshoots only Bath Place retains its old name. The street pattern was greatly simplified during the second half of the nineteenth century, as larger shops and warehouses in Old Street, and larger workshops in Bath Street, were built back over the sites of the original cottages in the lanes.

Bathurst Square

See Sussex Square

Battersea Square

BATTERSEA [WANDSWORTH]

This is not to be thought of as a London square of the formal style that began with Covent Garden and Lincoln's Inn Fields in the seventeenth century. It is much older than that: a village square of a type that can be found all over the world. The four main streets

Battersea Square in 1908, or a little earlier, showing the view north from the High Street into Church Street.

meet in a broad, irregular crossroads and a market and meeting place is established. The idlers of Battersea no doubt spent their time here in the seventeenth century, and it is the same today; but then the idlers were poor and now they are the idle rich, dining outside the numerous restaurants and pubs.

Although Battersea Square has resumed some of its old appearance and functions, this is a recent change stemming from the rise of café culture and the pedestrianisation of most of the open space. For much of the twentieth century things were very different, with the motor car dominating and blighting a busy junction. Like any village centre it has been subject to piecemeal rebuilding: a few eighteenth-century houses survive behind shopfronts, but most of the square is Victorian.

Bear Garden Square

BANKSIDE [SOUTHWARK]

The Bear Garden and Hope Theatre was built between 1613 and 1615, on the site of an existing bear garden, and a little to the east of the Globe, by Philip Henslowe, the great Elizabethan impresario. The building, which could be easily adapted for plays or bull and bear baiting by the installation or removal of the stage, was demolished together with its associated kennels, stables and bear houses, by order of Cromwell, falling victim to a second Pride's Purge. A manuscript continuation of Stow's *Annals* records the event:

> The Hope on the Banke side in Southwarke, commonly called the Beare Garden ... pulled downe to make tennementes, by Thomas Walker a Peticoate Maker in Cannon Streete, on Tuesday the 25 day of March 1656. Seven of Mr Godfries Beares, by the command of Thomas Pride then his Shriefe of Surry were then shot to death, on Saturday the 9 day of February 1655 [1656 in modern terms] by a Company of Soldiers.

The development planned by Thomas Walker the petticoat maker must have been prevented or curtailed by political events, as the Bear Garden was restored with the monarchy in 1660 and was patronised by Pepys in 1666 and subsequent years, and by John Evelyn in 1670. Both thought it 'a very rude and nasty pleasure'.

In the reign of William III the Bear Garden was removed to Hockley-in-the-Hole, Clerkenwell, where it was established by 1701. Strype's 1720 revision of Stow, the text of which was written before 1720, had this to say:

> Bear Alley runs into Maiden Lane. Here is a Glass House, and about the middle is a new built Court well Inhabited called Bear Garden Square: so called as Built in the Place where the Bear Garden formerly stood, until removed to the other side of the Water: Which is more convenient for the Butchers and such like, who are taken with such rustick Sports as the baiting of Bears and Bulls.

Todd Longstaffe-Gowan quotes the last two lines as referring to the square, but they are surely intended for the new site across the river? The little unnamed square of six or seven houses shown near the south end of the street called Bear Garden on Strype's and Horwood's maps of 1720 and the 1790s was too small for bull or bear baiting. Rocque's map, published twenty-five years after Strype's, oddly still showed 'Old Bear Garden' here.

The little square – the 'wretched little square', as Arthur Dasent called it in 1895 – was almost surrounded by large warehouses in the nineteenth century. The White Bear pub at the north-west corner, which remained open until the 1920s, was the main feature, its address in the directories 'Bear Gardens'. One of the component parts of Philip Henslowe's Bear Garden was described in 1620 as 'another house there called the house for the white beares'.

The square passed through the Second World War with little or no damage and is still an anonymous feature of the south end of Bear Gardens, with a new block of flats and studios called the Bear Pit on the west side. The east side is being rebuilt as a hotel. Southwark's long report on the building application did not mention the square.

Bearbone Square

Bearbone Square was Rocque's name in the 1740s for the triangular opening now known as Newport Place, on the edge of Chinatown. The area was built by Nicholas Barbon in the 1680s on the site of Newport House. When he emerged as the leading builder of the Restoration, Barbon softened his name from the one gloried in by his notorious father, Praise God Barebones, but his many enemies liked to revive it.

Summerson referred to a Newport Square built by Barbon in Soho, but he was probably thinking of Newport Market, which was destroyed during the creation of Charing Cross Road. Barebone Square, a meeting place of nine streets and alleys, was not firmly named for most of its history, being usually regarded as part of Little Newport Street. It is a shame that the old name has not been revived, as this would be a suitably seedy memorial to the great rogue. Some battered examples of his houses survive around the corner in Newport Court.

Newport Place, formerly Bearbone Square, looking south towards Newport Court in 2013.

Beaufort Square

Beaufort Square was an unrealised scheme on the Ladbroke estate at Notting Hill. (See Ladbroke Square.)

Beaumont Square

Beaumont Square was the centrepiece of the Beaumont estate, built in the 1830s by the extraordinary John Thomas Barber Beaumont, artist, businessman, social reformer and philanthropist. Some houses were occupied by 1833 and the square was complete, or nearly so, by 1837. It was a large rectangle, running gently downhill from north to south. There were more than sixty small houses of three storeys, with round-headed doors and windows on the ground floor. Merchants with servants featured strongly among the early tenants, but a number of the houses were in commercial use by the 1850s. One notable resident in 1841, probably at No. 28, although the houses were not numbered in the census, was the artist John Robert Wildman, whose portrait of Sir James Clark Ross is at the National Maritime Museum.

Until 1894 the garden was available only to the residents of the surrounding houses. In that year it was offered to the LCC for public use by Captain William Beaumont, grandson of Barber Beaumont, and formerly a member of the council. His interest in the property was due to expire in 1928, so he could only offer the garden until then, should he live so long. It came also with the proviso that it must be closed to the public one day a year, to preserve the rights of the freeholder. The LCC accepted these terms and before opening the garden added such municipal touches as a drinking fountain and fences to protect the grass. The captain gave the seats, and the lawn mower, roller and tools that had been used to maintain the garden in its private days. The square was a centre of East End Conservatism at this period, the Beaumont Institute providing offices for the Tower Hamlets Conservative Club and the Stepney Conservative Association.

The southern half of the east side was destroyed during the Second World War and other houses were damaged. The square could have been restored, but instead the surviving houses were demolished in the late 1940s and early 1950s and replaced by council flats of varying degrees of ugliness. The garden is pleasant and some picturesque old cottages can be found in the neighbouring streets, but apart from that it is not an attractive place, a judgement in no way softened by the London Independent Hospital in the north-west corner. It stands on the site of what must have been an interesting building, the Philosophical Institution founded by Barber Beaumont in 1840. It was the ancestor of the People's Palace and Queen Mary College.

Beckenham Square

See Buckenham Square

Beckford Square

Beckford Square was on the south side of Old Street, between Whitecross Street and Bunhill Row. Its southern boundary was the back gardens of the houses on the north side of Banner Square. The name came immediately from the Beckford Head at No. 38 (later No. 122) Old Street, but ultimately from Alderman William Beckford (father of the author of *Vathek*) who was at his most famous in the 1760s, when he was twice Lord Mayor. The pub was the Beckford Head by the early 1790s, and probably before that, but Horwood's maps of the late eighteenth and early nineteenth century did not name the square. They showed a mixture of houses and larger buildings that looked like stables, so probably this began as the inn yard. It was common for courts and yards to be promoted to squares in the early nineteenth century, and here, with Banner Square and Bartholomew Square so close, the motive from emulation was strong. Rocque's map of 1746 called it Farm Yard and the 1720 Strype map probably Rain dear yard, suggesting that the pub was the Reindeer before it became the Beckford Head.

The square can never have been anything but a slum. In 1851 the fourteen houses sheltered nearly fifty families, mostly of labourers and men engaged in branches of the furniture trade. One woman was a 'dolls wigg maker'. In 1898 it was described as '14 houses, very rough … old red tiled houses, none on the south side, steep wooden staircases, wash hanging across the court, windows broken, dirty'. The houses were swept away a few years later, as the offices and workshops in Old Street grew larger, but the name Beckford Square persisted for a while, even outliving the Beckford Head.

Bedford Square

Bedford Square was first thought of in 1766 by the 4th Duke of Bedford. As a martyr to the gout, he was a frequent visitor to Bath, where he greatly admired the circus, then building. He thought that a square of similar architectural style would be an attractive and profitable addition to his Bloomsbury estate, where little had been built since the seventeenth century. The duke died in 1771 before anything could be done, but his idea was carried into effect by his widow, as guardian of her infant grandson.

Beresford Chancellor wrote in 1907 that 'the Square covers a portion of the notorious "rookery" of St Giles; Rowland Dobie, indeed, speaks of its arising "from a cow-yard to its present magnificent form"'. But both were wrong, to judge from Rocque's 1740s map, which showed the site as an open field between the Montagu House garden and the backs of small houses in Tottenham Court Road. The remains of an old stream or drainage ditch snaked through the field and there was a pond to the west and a timber yard to the north-west.

The houses were built between 1775 and 1782, mostly by Robert Crews and William Scott. The architect is generally supposed to have been Thomas Leverton, who took a building lease of No. 13 in 1775, and later lived there, but others think he was only responsible for the interiors of some of the houses. At this point in his career Leverton was a follower of the Adam brothers and he employed as an assistant Joseph Bonomi, who had formerly worked for the Adams.

Bedford Square escaped the censure heaped on nearly all the others by the early architectural critics. It was welcomed in 1783 as 'a proof of the improvement of our taste … without exception the most perfect square in town'. In 1807 it was compared favourably with the irregular St James's Square, because 'the houses in Bedford-square correspond exactly, and have a grand appearance'.

The square was popular from the first with eminent judges and lawyers. Lords Loughborough and Eldon both lived at No. 6 as Lord Chancellor. When Eldon urged George III not to hang a man condemned for a robbery in the square, the king acquiesced in these words, 'Well, well, since the learned Judge, who lives in Bedford Square, does not think there is any great harm in robberies there, the poor fellow shall not be hanged'.

Bedford Square was roughly treated by the mob during the Corn Law riot in March 1815 and the house of Eldon, the most unpopular member of the government, was attacked with great violence. Luckily the back garden communicated with the British Museum, to which Eldon evacuated his family. He then returned with a corporal and four men from the museum guard and this small force put the rioters to flight at bayonet point.

Another Bedford Square lawyer was Basil Montagu, a leading authority on bankruptcy, but better remembered as the friend of the Romantic poets. At his house, No. 25, lived his son-in-law Bryan Waller Proctor, barrister and poet, who wrote as 'Barry Cornwall'. The poetical talent descended to his daughter Adelaide Anne Proctor, who also lived at No. 25. Lord Glenbervie, the diarist, had a house in Bedford Square until 1794, while practising as a barrister, but moved to the West End when he took to politics and place-hunting.

Henry Cavendish, the great scientist, lived at No. 11 at the corner of Gower Street and Montague Place from 1784 until his death in 1810. There is a commemorative plaque on the house. He was an eccentric recluse, who ordered his meals in writing and never set eyes on his female servants. Cavendish assembled a semi-public scientific library of more than 12,000 volumes. When he himself borrowed a book from it, he always carefully left a receipt.

The north side of Bedford Square from Gower Street, *c.* 1905.

It was valued at £7,000, double the sum the house realised when sold in 1814. That was despite the valuer declaring 'I have scarce ever met with a more substantial or better built House'.

Although the square was never fashionable, it remained almost entirely residential. Bedford College, founded at No. 47 in 1849 as the Ladies' College, was a rare exception. There is a plaque at No. 48, into which the college expanded. The Bedford estate took over the management and upkeep of the garden when the original leases of the houses expired in 1874, but fortunately the duke's advisors did not follow the unhappy policy employed in Russell Square, of trying to bring the houses up to date by encasing them in terracotta.

In 1898 the local policeman told Charles Booth's researcher that Bedford Square was 'less good than formerly, better class Jews going in, many houses to let, no boarders allowed "by order of the Duke of Bedford"'.

Number 1 Bedford Square, *c.* 1907.

Lady Ottoline Morrell lived at No. 44 from 1906 and held her weekly bohemian parties there. It cost her husband £1,800, plus £300 for redecoration. When they became poorer after the First World War, they sold the house to Asquith, who made it his London home until his death in 1928. He also was economising, having moved from Cavendish Square, the home of his great days, but he was a barrister, a breed for which this was a natural habitat.

Another barrister, Sir Anthony Hope Hawkins, lived at No. 41 after his marriage in 1903, but like Asquith he was better known for his second career – as the novelist Anthony Hope, author of *The Prisoner of Zenda*. Other literary celebrities are Robert Bridges, who lived at No. 52 from 1877 to 1881, and Weedon Grossmith, the less eminent of the two brothers responsible for *The Diary of a Nobody*. He lived at No. 1 from 1902 until 1917. Sir Johnston Forbes-Robertson, the actor, lived for many years at No. 22 and died there in 1937. The house is marked with a plaque.

Bedford Square was also the home of a number of architects after Leverton, a tribute to its quality. The most eminent was Lutyens, who lived at No. 31 during the First World War. He hated the house, comparing it unfavourably with No. 29 Bloomsbury Square, from which he had been forced to move. His wife thought the Bedford Square house was haunted and had it exorcised. A very different architect, the Gothic William Butterfield, lived at No. 42, where there is a plaque, from 1886 to 1900. Lewis Cubitt, the brother of Thomas, lived at No. 52. The Society of Architects had its premises at No. 28 early in the twentieth century and the Architectural Association is now at No. 36.

Bedford Square is a miracle. Its swift and untroubled construction, the uniformity of the design and the immediate popularity of the houses were unprecedented and must have lured many speculators into disastrous attempts at emulation. No less astonishing is its survival and seemingly perfect preservation through two and a half centuries of changing tastes and fashions, riots, fires and destructive wars. Although today it gives the impression of having been miraculously preserved – by its beauty perhaps – from aerial bombardment, there was some Second World War bomb damage to houses at the west end of the north side and to one house on the south side. All was soon almost invisibly mended.

The shrinking of the garden in the 1970s had in general a bad effect, but it does at least make it possible to see the whole of any side of the square at an angle not too oblique to appreciate the design. The only drawback is the dreadful Gower Street traffic. If that noise and pollution could be removed, Bedford Square would be a paradise.

Bedford Square

CLAPHAM [LAMBETH]

Bedford Square was a short-lived name for half a dozen large houses on the west side of Clapham Rise, now the southern end of Clapham Road. There was nothing about their layout or their relation to the houses opposite to give any point to the name. It was clearly marked on A. & R. Bland's Clapham parish map of 1849, but the tithe map of 1838 and the census returns of 1841 and 1851 called the houses Bedford Place.

The ludicrous inappropriateness of the name must have prevented 'square' from being widely adopted. The houses, a little south of St John's Church, survived the Second World War, but were replaced afterwards by Callingham House on the Clapham Road Estate.

Bedford Square East

See Ford Square

Belgrave Square

BELGRAVIA [WESTMINSTER]

Belgrave Square, with its corner villas, was the one constant feature in the planning of the Grosvenor Five Fields estate from the first sketch made by 'Mr Wyatt' (thought to be James Wyatt) before 1813. The detail of the square changed as the surrounding streets were treated differently in succeeding plans, but the essentials remained the same. The name, which comes from Belgrave in Leicestershire, one of the properties and titles of the Grosvenor family, was also fixed at an early stage. The land was included in the portions of the estate leased separately to Thomas Cubitt and Seth Smith in 1824, but in 1825 they both prudently sublet the building of the houses to a group of bankers, George and William Haldimand and

The north-east side of Belgrave Square by T.H. Shepherd, 1827.

The north-west side of Belgrave Square looking towards No. 49, c. 1904.

Alexander Prevost. These plutocrats introduced George Basevi as their architect for the four terraces, Cubitt remaining responsible for the roads, sewers and garden.

The square was laid out, the sewers made and the building of the terraces begun in 1826. The four terraces are not identical, probably because it was obvious from the first that the large garden would prevent them from being seen as a whole. The immediate popularity of the square may also have encouraged Basevi and his backers to make the south and west sides more elaborate than the north and east, which were built first. The south side is the grandest of the four, with eight columns in the portico. Here Basevi put his name as architect on No. 31, which was George Haldimand's house, adding the date 1827. The sale of houses was brisk during the late 1820s, but slackened in the difficult political and financial conditions of the 1830s. Nevertheless, almost all the houses in the terraces were disposed of before the end of the decade, and to a distinguished group of tenants.

Although the four terraces are among the best in London, it is the corner villas that give Belgrave Square real distinction. The symmetrical Wyatt plan had large gardens at the corners, with a villa of

Downshire House, No. 24 Belgrave Square, decorated for the coronation in 1911.

equal size in each. The late change that introduced a third wide road, Grosvenor Crescent, into the north-east corner slightly spoilt the effect by setting the big house, No. 49, further back and reducing its prominence. This is not in a villa style like the others, but a standard London corner house which could have been linked to terraces with no diminution of effect. Thomas Cubitt designed it in 1847 and built it for Sidney Herbert in the early 1850s. It is now the Argentine Ambassador's residence. There is only a tiny triangle of garden in front, but that is enough to contain a tree that almost conceals the house.

Number 12 Belgrave Square, *c.* 1904.

Seaford House, No. 37 Belgrave Square, *c.* 1905.

Number 12, at the north-west corner (now the Portuguese Embassy), was designed by Sir Robert Smirke and built for Earl Brownlow in the early 1830s. It is slightly smaller than the two at the southern corners, because of the intrusion of the narrow West Halkin Street. At the south-west corner is No. 24, the Spanish Embassy, the earliest and best of the villas. It was built in the late 1820s for Thomas Kemp and designed for him by Henry Kendall, who also did work at Kemp Town in Brighton. Lewis Cubitt studied architecture in his office. The completion of the house was delayed by Kemp's financial troubles and it was much altered in the next decade for Lord Ducie. It was later known as Downshire House. The largest of the villas is Seaford House, No. 37, in the south-east corner. It was designed by Philip Hardwick for the Earl of Sefton and built between 1842 and 1845.

Despite the subtle differences between the terraces and the individual design of the villas, William Weir found the square too regular in 1843: 'We prefer individual character in the houses: we do not like to see them merely parts of an architectural whole, like soldiers who are only parts of a rank. But this regimental fashion is now the order of the day.'

The early and overwhelming success of Belgrave Square was shown by the 1841 directory which listed the Duchess of Kent, the queen's mother, at No. 36, and two dukes, three marquesses, nine earls and countesses, and four viscounts and barons in only forty-eight houses. Indeed, the eminent residents have been noted more for rank than personal distinction, although two of Wellington's colleagues in the Peninsular War, Lord Hill and Sir George Murray, who lived at Nos 24 and 5, qualify under both headings.

The last really distinguished resident was Sir Henry Campbell-Bannerman. He had downsized from No. 6 Grosvenor Place to No. 29 Belgrave Square in 1904, but lived there for only eighteen months before events beyond his control obliged him to downsize even further: into No. 10 Downing Street. Chips Channon, the diarist, who lived at No. 5 from 1935, was one of the last generation of private residents. Since then a large number of the houses have become embassies.

Bomb damage was confined to Seaford House in the south-east corner and to two houses each on the north, south and west sides. All the exteriors have been perfectly restored, an easier task with stucco than with brick, and Belgrave Square would now be close to perfection were it not for the traffic and the statues. Beresford Chancellor remarked in 1907 on the absence of a central statue, 'which, considering the general want of success of such effigies, is perhaps a want not to be greatly deplored'. From the point of view of the public there would be no value in a central monument, unless it were as tall as Nelson's column, but its lack has been overwhelmingly supplied by the array of statues around the edge. They are mainly naturalistic, something normally to be welcomed, but this heap of rubbish serves only to give naturalism a bad name.

Belgrave Square

PECKHAM [SOUTHWARK]

Belgrave Square was the short-lived name given to some houses built off the north side of Peckham Park Road in the early 1840s. The 1842 Camberwell parish map showed the south side built or being built, but gave no name. The January 1845 ratebook listed fifteen houses in Belgrave Square, only four of them occupied; by July ten had found tenants. It still had fifteen houses and was still Belgrave Square in 1850, but by 1851 the name had been changed to Belgrave Terrace. Perhaps the splendid Maismore Square (afterwards Leyton Square) only a few yards to the north had filled the owners with shame. Belgrave Square had houses of good quality, but it was only a slightly widened cul-de-sac. Several similar Peckham developments of the 1840s persevered with the name of square, but they were not so embarrassingly close to a real one.

When Belgrave Terrace was extended in the 1870s the same constraints that determined the form of Leyton Square forced the road to bend northwards towards the canal, by which it was eventually halted. It was renamed Haymerle Road in the 1880s. The northern extension of Haymerle Road survives, but it was diverted to link with Bird in Bush Road when part of the Friary Estate was built on the site of the original Belgrave Square houses after the Second World War.

Bell Savage Square

Bell Savage Square was an alternative name for La Belle Sauvage Yard, favoured by its more respectable residents in the early nineteenth century. John Mawley, attorney, gave his address as 'Bell-Savage-square, Ludgate-hill', in 1804. It was the yard of the ancient Bell Savage Inn at the foot of Ludgate Hill, scene of plays, animal shows, bull baiting and every sort of noisy popular entertainment.

By the end of the eighteenth century the part of the large yard nearest to Ludgate Hill had been reduced to a regular court of nine houses, and it was this that was presumably referred to as the square to distinguish it from the stabling to the north.

Any tendency to gentrification was soon stopped, first by the decline of the City as a residential area and finally by the building of the Ludgate Hill railway viaduct immediately to the west in 1865. The inn was demolished in 1873 and printing works soon surrounded the yard. The whole area was destroyed during the Second World War and Limeburner Lane is now on the site.

Bell Square (Blomfield Street)

CITY OF LONDON

The Moorfields Bell Square, presumably developed from an inn yard, was off the east side of Broker Row, which became Blomfield Street in the 1820s. The square was not shown on Rocque's map of the 1740s but was fully formed, with eight houses, by the 1790s. It did not appear on various ward maps published between 1756 and 1784, but as they are very imperfectly revised copies of earlier maps, their evidence is of little value.

Broker Row faced the much frequented open space of Moorfields and was thus a popular spot for pubs – a barmaid seeking work gave the square as her address in 1810 – but the main business of the area changed from pleasure to commerce after Finsbury Circus was built over Moorfields from 1815. The pubs vanished from Blomfield Street, which was occupied mainly by solicitors and the offices of charities. Bell Square was demolished in the late 1880s when Broad Street Avenue was constructed, so it lasted for about a century.

Bell Square (St Martins-le-Grand)

CITY OF LONDON

Bell Square was a sinuous alley leading from St Martins-le-Grand to Foster Lane. A slight widening near the west end was all that could possibly justify the second part of its name. The first came from the Bell public house, which was in the square. It was Bell Alley in 1540 and Bell Court on maps of 1676, 1720 and 1746. In 1708 Hatton called it 'Bell Court, a Passage from St Martins le Grand to Forster Lane.' By 1784 it had become Bell Square, the fashion for the name having swept the City in the 1770s.

Many courts and alleys were demolished to make way for Smirke's General Post Office, which was built (according to Colvin) between 1824 and 1829. Such monumental works require much preparation, and from the evidence in a coining case of 1821 it seems that Bell Square was an early casualty of this clearance, 'I went with him to the ruins in Foster-lane, where the new post office is building, we found the gate locked; we went round to Bell-square, and found that gate locked also, so that nobody could have been in the ruins. We got over the hoard …' It was obviously no longer possible to go through Bell Square, presumably because part of it, at least, was already 'ruins'.

Bell Square

CITY ROAD [ISLINGTON]

Where the City Road Brewery stood until the early nineteenth century, jutting rather unappetisingly into the Bunhill Fields burial ground, an open space named Bell Yard had emerged by the 1830s, although the conservative ratebooks continued to call it 'Up a Gateway'. As the industrial buildings were replaced by houses in a haphazard fashion, it may have been a continuation of the brewery yard, perhaps named after the tap. In the 1841 census the four houses were listed in Bell Yard, but the Finsbury Mechanics' Hall of Science in Bell Square. It may have been an alternative name, a mistake, or an attempt by the Hall of Science (a working men's institute established here in 1834) to give itself a more dignified address. If so it failed, as the 1850s directories listed it in Bell Yard.

The yard also contained a Bethel Chapel, which in 1849 was converted into the Birkbeck Finsbury School, but these outposts of civilisation did not last long; for most of its history Bell Yard was given over entirely to industry and commerce. The whole block was heavily bombed during the Second World War. The replacement buildings have now gone, and the site of Bell Yard will form part of a larger open space called Old Street Yard.

Bell Square

SPITALFIELDS [TOWER HAMLETS]

The Morning Post of 29 May 1805 reported a fire in 'Bell-square, Bell-lane, Spitalfields', that destroyed a sugar refiner's premises and two adjoining houses. The only candidate shown on Horwood's 1790s map was a small unnamed court off the west side of Bell Lane, just north of Cox's Square. It was open to Bell Lane and had a single house on the south side and larger industrial buildings on the west and north sides. Perhaps as a result of the fire, the court had gone by 1813, when the whole of the west side of Bell Lane north of Cox's Square was occupied by the Constitution Brewery. The Nido building is now on the site.

Belmont Square

SHOREDITCH [HACKNEY]

Greenwood's map of 1830 showed 'Belmont Square' forming a group with Reliance Square just to the south and New Inn Square to the west. It was drawn larger and more open than its neighbours, which were indicated but not named. In his 1827 edition Greenwood had shown all three openings but without naming any of them. Horwood's map of 1813 had a vacant space where Greenwood placed Belmont Square. I have found no other reference to it. It was perhaps an unrealised project.

Belsize Square

BELSIZE PARK [CAMDEN]

This had some slight resemblance to a true square while the garden of St Peter's Vicarage gave an open outlook to half the houses. That the green space was private was of little importance here, where nearly all the houses had back gardens of a reasonable size. But now this is only an 'H' shaped collection of streets with a bizarre numbering system, unconvincingly linked together by the name of 'square'.

St Peter's Church in Belsize Park was built in 1858–59, when Belsize Square was laid out behind it. At that time, before any houses were built, it had all the appearance of a genuine square (of the narrow, rectangular kind) with two distinct gardens. The larger of these, at the west end of the square, was linked to the rear of the church and was destined to provide a site for the vicarage built in 1862, the rest becoming its private garden. That would still have left the smaller enclosure at the east end of the square as a perfectly adequate communal garden, but it was sacrificed to squeeze in the twelve houses, in three terraces of four, that are now Nos 23–30 Belsize Square and 1–7 (odd) Lancaster Drive. When they were built together with the other houses in the square in the early 1860s, a small substitute garden or green was projected beyond them, but it was soon given up to make way for what is now the east side of Lancaster Drive. The houses in the square are large white three-storey pairs with bay windows and porches.

The north side of Belsize Square in the 1920s.

The original vicarage at the east end of the garden was demolished and a new one built in the centre in 1915. That was used until 1947, when the present vicarage was built adjoining St Peter's. Since then the Belsize Square Synagogue has occupied the garden and gradually filled it with buildings. At first the New Liberal Jewish Congregation worshipped in the former vicarage, but in 1957–58 they added the present synagogue to the 1915 house, and in 1975 built a hall on the site of the first vicarage, reducing the garden to almost nothing.

As Belsize Park is an outrider of Hampstead, it is not surprising that the square's celebrities have been associated with the fine arts. Ralph Wornum, the artist and art critic who was Keeper of the National Gallery for more than twenty years, died at No. 20 in 1877. George Clarkson Stanfield, son of the great Clarkson Stanfield and a landscape artist in a similar style, lived at No. 42 but died at No. 46, his sister's house, in 1878. Clarkson Stanfield had died at No. 6 Belsize Park Road in 1867. Patrick Caulfield, one of the leading post-war British

painters, died at No. 19 in 2005. He was often classified as a pop artist, which did not please him at all as he defined pop art as 'social realism without the realism'.

Belvedere Square

WIMBLEDON [MERTON]

Belvedere Square was so called after Belvedere House, the name from the 1830s of the second manor house of Wimbledon. These thirty-one Tudor cottages, including those in Church Road flanking the entrance, were built in the grounds of the house, for estate workers, in the 1860s. (Kelsey Square at Beckenham is a similar scheme of the same date, on a smaller scale.) The original and more suitable name was Belvedere Cottages, for this is a very pretty T-shaped cul-de-sac with little extensions in the north-east and south-east corners, like appropriately Gothic embellishments to the 'T'. The longer north-east extension used to give access to the greenhouses.

The east side of Belvedere Square in 2013.

Belvedere Square has no garden, but the pedestrian cross stroke of the 'T' forms a small open space like that at the end of Wellington Square, and decorated with a bench and flowers in tubs in the manner of Bonnington Square. The cottages have pointed gables of various sizes, all with decorative bargeboards, patterned brickwork, bay windows, and porches with wooden arches. From an early date they were not inhabited exclusively by estate workers, and now they are very expensive.

Ben Jonson Square

MILE END [TOWER HAMLETS]

Ben Jonson (or Johnson) Square was more often called Swatton or Swatton's Place. It was a spacious court of some twenty-four houses north of Rhodeswell Road (this part of which is now Ben Jonson Road) but entered via an alley in Johnson Street, now Harford Street. Even when the court was referred to as Ben Jonson Square, the alley was still apt to be called Swatton's Place. An appraiser named George Swatton (who died in 1853) lived in York Place, the terrace in Harford Street from which Swatton's Place was entered, and was described in the 1851 census as a house proprietor. In the 1840s and 1850s his son, William Swatton, lived next door as landlord of the Ben Jonson pub at the corner of Ben Jonson Road and Harford Street.

Swatton Place emerged gradually in the 1820s and 1830s and was fully developed by the 1840s. In 1851 the tenants were upper working class, but in 1881 the twenty-four houses were occupied mainly by labourers. Ben Jonson Square was an alternative name from the 1860s to the 1880s but in its last days the place was known as Johnson's Buildings. It was demolished in the early 1890s and Monteagle Street built on the site, but that has now been swept away in its turn. It was between Dongola Street and Ben Jonson Road.

Bentinck Square

See Manchester Square and Queen Ann's Square

Beresford Square

WOOLWICH [GREENWICH]

The square was created by the Board of Ordnance soon after 1811, by the demolition of twenty-seven small houses and shops that made a restricted and undignified entrance to the Royal Arsenal. The periphery of the cleared space incorporated older buildings, like the Salutation pub in the centre of the west side.

At first anonymous, the square was named after Lord Beresford, the Master General of the Ordnance, when the Beresford Gate of the Royal Arsenal was built by his order in 1829. It is now the only point of architectural interest in the square.

Holy Trinity Church was once another: a fine building in the style of the Waterloo churches, designed by John Douglas Hopkins, with a portico that dominated the west side of the square. It was built as a proprietary chapel between 1833 and 1835, on a narrow site between Beresford Street and Rope Yard Rail, but was closed in 1960 and demolished in 1962. The rerouted Beresford Street now crosses the site.

There had been a long contest in Woolwich over the location of the market which, being subject to tolls, was a valuable piece of property. Traders began to desert the old Woolwich market for the new Beresford Square in the 1830s, speeding the conversion of the houses to shops. In 1849 the permanent businesses included a bookseller (and registrar of births, deaths and marriages), a coachbuilder, a coal merchant, a surgeon and three pubs with military names, the Ordnance Arms, the Royal Mortar and the Salutation. Among the private residents was the Sluicemaster at the Royal Arsenal.

An improvement scheme of 1868 introduced better lighting and enclosed plantations in front of the shops on the west side. The authorities eventually admitted defeat and the market was formally moved to Beresford Square in 1888. As well as the market it became the great meeting place of Woolwich, the scene of demonstrations and political rallies. Gladstone made a rousing speech here before the 1874 general election, when he was returned for Greenwich but failed to carry the country.

Beresford Square during the First World War, with the Beresford Gate on the right, Holy Trinity in the centre and the Century Cinema (opened 1913, demolished 1968) on the left.

The Booth survey gave a good description in 1900:

> Beresford Square Market Place: broad, booths for market place, and crowded on Fridays and Saturdays. One of the main entrances to Woolwich Dockyard on the north side. Great crowd of men coming out at 1 p.m. dinner hour, majority gang men, bowler hats or caps, young men more often caps, middle aged and old men bowlers, majority wearing collars; some labourers making for home in S.E. or S.W. directions. Only one man that I saw had his dinner brought to him, but [PC] Clyne says a great number bring it with them and cook and eat it in the Arsenal. There is a large coffee house at the corner of Cross Street, which is much patronized, cut from joint and two veg 6d, roast beef or pork 4d and 6d, large rasher and two eggs 4d. Shouting among the crowd were six boys selling the 'News' and 'Sun', ½p papers, not many buyers. Clyne says they buy their papers, discuss it at their dinners, and then return and place their bets upon the horses they fancy with the bookies when they come back to work. The bookies are agents of bigger men, and wait in the square.

The spectacle of workmen streaming out of the Arsenal was a favourite subject of the postcard publishers.

A century has removed the gun makers, if not the bookies, and the great Beresford gate (its occupation gone, like Marble Arch) now vainly tries to screen the square from a horribly busy and noisy road. The buildings of the square have not changed much. The shops on the west side are mostly modern, but the Victorian ones survive on the east and older houses converted into shops on the south, none of any beauty. The open space, best seen when the stalls are removed, is impressively broad and deserves a better frame.

Berkeley Square

MAYFAIR [WESTMINSTER]

Berkeley Square is eccentric, aristocratic, inconsistent, dramatic, accidental. Its origin can be traced fifty years before a house was built there. On 10 June 1684 John Evelyn went to Berkeley House in Piccadilly to advise the widowed Lady Berkeley of Stratton 'about the building of two streetes in Berkeley Gardens, reserving the house, & as much of the Garden as the breadth of the house'. Stratton Street and Berkeley Street were built soon afterwards.

Stratton Street remained a cul-de-sac for 250 years, but the extension northwards of Berkeley Street in the 1730s was the beginning of the square. In the early leases it was 'a new intended street designed to be called New Berkeley Street', and in Horace Walpole's will, drawn up in 1793, his house on the east side of the square is described as 'situate in Berkeley Street otherwise Berkeley Square'. Equally important in the history of the square was the undertaking made by the 3rd Lord Berkeley of Stratton in 1696, when he sold Berkeley House to the Duke of Devonshire, that he would permit no buildings on his land within the width of the garden that 'might annoy' the purchaser's enjoyment of the house.

A development on Brick Close, the land later occupied by Berkeley Square, was planned in the 1680s but was not carried out because of the failure of the ambitious scheme for the estate to the east, which involved the abandonment of the intended Albermarle Square (q.v.). The fiasco ended in complicated lawsuits and nothing more was done until the 1730s. The immediate impetus was then no doubt given by the developments on the Grosvenor estate from 1720, with Grosvenor Square as the centrepiece.

Bourdon Street and Grosvenor Mews immediately to the north of Lord Berkeley's land were built in a haphazard way in the 1720s and soon became one of Mayfair's slums. In response, building agreements were made between Lord Berkeley and two carpenters and builders, Edward Cock and Francis Hillyard, for the east side of the new square in 1736 and for the west probably in 1740. They began making bricks on the site in 1736, began building on the east side in 1737, and quickly laid out a road along the north side to communicate with the Grosvenor estate via Davies Street.

Lord Berkeley may have expected that the north side would remain open, as at Queen Square, but the land belonged to Sir Robert Grosvenor, and inferior houses appeared there as quickly as fine ones on Lord Berkeley's east and west sides. Leases for the west side were granted between 1741 and 1745,

as the houses approached completion. They refer to 'a new intended square designed to be called Berkeley Square'. The south side, which was held on lease jointly by Lord Berkeley and the Duke of Devonshire, remained open.

Some attempt at overall design and architectural effect was made in Grosvenor Square, but none at all in Berkeley Square, where plots large and small were granted to all comers, who were left to build houses according to their own taste just as in St James's Square sixty years earlier. The only pattern was the grouping of most of the large plots and the best houses on the west side. The square was practically complete by 1747, when the garden, enclosed by 'Dwarf Walls and Wooden Rails and Pallisadoes set thereon', was leased to Cock and Hilliard.

In 1817 William Beloe reported Horace Walpole as saying that:

> ... in the time of Sir Robert Walpole it was the established etiquette that the Prime Minister returned no visits, but on his leaving office [in 1742] Sir Robert took the earliest opportunity of visiting his friends, and one morning he happened to pass, for this purpose, through Berkeley Square, the whole of which had been actually built whilst he was Minister, and he had never before seen it.

With houses of such various sizes the square was by no means exclusive, or exclusively residential. All but one of the houses on the north side were shops in the early days and they included a tavern from 1742. (In 1753 the proprietor, Morgan Gwynn, moved to a tavern or coffee house at No. 23 on the east side, which perhaps suggested to Horace Walpole his description of his own house on the same side as 'a little coffee-house in the morning when the town is full'.) In 1783 it was observed of the north side that 'an open fishmonger's stall and a lottery-office, contribute their mutual deformities to disgrace this finely elevated spot'. There were also at least two hotels in the square, Negri's (later Gunter's) at No. 7 from the 1750s, and Thomas's at No. 25 from 1798. The Gunters invested their profits in land at Brompton, including the site of Redcliffe Square.

The 1760s was an eventful decade for the square. In 1766, as 'the late Inclosure' was 'gone to Ruin', the residents obtained a private act empowering them to restore the garden. The newspapers reported that it was to be 'laid out and planted after the manner of Grosvenor-square'. As a centrepiece the king's aunt, the Princess Amelia, gave a lead statue of him, erected in 1772. In 1807 it was described as 'an equestrian statue of his present majesty in the character of Marcus Aurelius', an improbable masquerade dress for George III. It was removed before 1816 because the weight of the lead was causing the legs to crumple: a statue with the staggers.

Between 1762 and 1768 Lord Bute built a palace off the south-west corner (out of the way of the Duke of Devonshire's view) with its garden stretching across the whole of the south side. Lord Bute's daughter, Lady Louisa Stuart:

> … used to relate in her old age how she remembered when a child going with her father to see the first stone laid of Lansdowne House. The day was very wet, and the little girl's shoe got stuck in the mud where the present garden now is laid out, which was then 'like a ploughed field'.

Lord Bute never occupied the magnificent house, designed by Robert Adam, but sold it unfinished to Lord Shelburne, later Marquis of Lansdowne. Its mutilated remains survive in Fitzmaurice Place as the Lansdowne Club.

Berkeley Square was the scene of a riot in 1810, after the household cavalry assisted the sergeant-at-arms to arrest Sir Francis Burdett at his house in Piccadilly. The young Lord Keppel later recounted that when the cavalry advanced the mob of Burdett supporters fled:

> For my own part I did not stop running till I found myself safe and sound at my grandmother's house [No. 10] in Berkeley Square. That same evening a large and noisy multitude assembled in our square, and smashed every pane of glass in the windows of No. 12, the house next but one to Lady Albermarle's. The object of popular resentment was the Earl of Dartmouth, who rented that house of my father.

Lord Grosvenor's veteran surveyor, William Porden, came up with an ambitious scheme for the rebuilding of the unsatisfactory north side when the leases expired in 1818, but he overestimated the value of the land and found nobody willing to undertake the project. This failure led to his replacement as surveyor by the elder Thomas Cundy, who may have designed the houses that were contracted for by various firms, at a lower price, in 1821. Thomas Cubitt built two of them, his first works in the West End. Number 30 has been demolished, but No. 28 shows the style. That and No. 27 (by a different firm) are the only surviving houses from this rebuilding.

The west side of Berkeley Square, looking south, in 1813.

Berkeley Square comes behind only St James's Square, Grosvenor Square and Belgrave Square in the high rank of its former residents, but here the aristocrats were mainly to be found crowded together on the west side. Every house from No. 38 to No. 51 was occupied by a duke or duchess, an earl or countess at some time between 1745 and 1800, and this side continued to be very fashionable well into the twentieth century.

Most of the famous residents have been from the overlapping worlds of fashion and politics. Leading the way is Robert Clive, who died at No. 45 in 1774. It has always been supposed that he committed suicide by cutting his throat with a penknife or razor, but this (like almost everything else) has been questioned by recent writers. The unfortunate Admiral Byng lived at No. 41 until shortly before his execution. Horace Walpole lived at No. 11 (No. 40 in his day) from 1779 until his death in 1797, dividing his time between the square and Strawberry Hill. George Canning was at No. 50 in 1806–07 and Lord Grey, of the Reform Act, at No. 48 except when slumming at No. 10 Downing Street. Then he let the house to his uncouth Lord Chancellor, Henry Brougham, who left it in a dreadful condition, 'the bedrooms were simply unendurable'. Brougham afterwards lived

Lansdowne House, Berkeley Square, in 1808.

at No. 21. The political hostess Lady Jersey had her salon at No. 38, which was later rebuilt for another prime minister, Lord Rosebery.

The arts have been less well represented. The actor, playwright and Poet Laureate, Colley Cibber lived at No. 19 from 1745 or earlier, until his death in 1757. The architects Sir Robert Smirke and his younger brother Sydney succeeded one another at No. 24 during the 1840s and 1850s, and Sidney later lived at No. 28. Sir Squire and Lady Bancroft, the formidable theatrical couple, managers of the Prince of Wales and Haymarket theatres, lived at No. 18 after their retirement in 1885, and entertained lavishly.

The north side of Berkeley Square in 1906, with the present Nos 25–26 being built in the background on the site of Thomas's Hotel.

The destruction of Berkeley Square began in the 1920s, when the Mayfair Hotel was built at the northern end of the Devonshire House garden, towering over Lansdowne House. In the 1930s Lansdowne House was partially destroyed on conversion to a club, and cut off from the square. Over its garden, along the south side, a monumental block of flats insultingly called Lansdowne House was built at the same time, only to be hit by a VI rocket during the Second World War. It was rebuilt afterwards, but replaced by the present Lansdowne House in 1987–88. Most of the east side was demolished in the 1930s to make way for Nos 20–22 of 1938 and Berkeley Square House of 1937–38. Apart from the VI, serious bomb damage was limited to the north-west corner, where much of the Grosvenor rebuilding of 1821–23 was destroyed.

With very few exceptions, these demolitions have restricted the modern interest of the square to the west side, where much survives, although all the 1740s houses have become clubs or offices. The best are Nos 45 and 46, probably by Henry Flitcroft, and William Kent's magnificent No. 44 with its amazing staircase. The garden of the square is now open to the public. It falls gently from north to south, where Alexander Munro's *The Woman of Samaria* gazes out at the traffic. Herbert Spencer thought it superior to the *Venus de Milo* and was willing to prove it on the spot. The statue was given by the 3rd Marquess of Lansdowne, who could admire it from the upper windows of his house.

Bermondsey Square

BERMONDSEY [SOUTHWARK]

Bermondsey Square, which lies just to the south of the parish church of St Mary Magdalene, preserves the outline of the courtyard of Bermondsey Abbey and of the great house of Sir Thomas Pope that was built amid the remains of the abbey after the Dissolution. By 1679 Bermondsey House had been demolished and various small houses had been built or were being planned on parts of the abbey site. These included some on the west side of what was later Bermondsey Square. To the north of the courtyard the abbey gatehouse still stood and to the east the gallery of Pope's mansion, while the south side had a wide funnel-shaped opening that led to Grange Road. Rocque's map of 1746 gave the open space the fanciful name of King John's Court, but did not show dramatic changes to the buildings since 1679.

By 1780 there were forty houses in 'The Courtyard', most of them small, but over the next few years many were demolished and replaced by the larger terraced houses of which a few survive. By 1785 there were twenty-eight, a number that remained constant for many years, and it was probably then that the owners began to call the place Bermondsey Square. In the ratebooks the new name first appeared in 1788. The account of the abbey ruins published in 1804 in the first volume of Manning and Bray's *History of Surrey* made no mention of the square, but it was based on a survey made long before 1800.

The south-west corner of Bermondsey Square in 2010.

Hughson wrote in 1817 that all vestiges of the priory had been obliterated 'since the new buildings rose, called Bermondsey-Square'. Its social standing is suggested by the fact that a police constable was a resident in 1800, but the houses varied widely in size and quality. Other early tenants (like Jonas Blewitt, the organist and composer, who was there by 1794) were performers at the nearby Bermondsey Spa pleasure gardens.

The square was still largely residential in the 1830s, although there were three pubs (one the King John's Head), a school and a few surgeons and brokers. It declined over the next few decades, but remained above the level of the surrounding streets.

Big events have transformed Bermondsey Square at the turn of each century. In 1902 the building of Tower Bridge Road required the demolition of the east side and half of the south, turning the quiet backwater into a raucous public space where buses turned and waited. The north side and the northern half of the west side were destroyed during the Second World War. They have been redeveloped twice since then, most recently in the last decade, with the Bermondsey Square Hotel, plus shops, flats and a cinema giving the latest centennial makeover.

Billiter Square

Stow offered an explanation of the name in his account of Billiter Lane, now Billiter Street: 'Belzettar's Lane, so called of the first builder and owner thereof, now corruptly called Billiter Lane'. A bellezeter was a bell-founder, so 'bell-founders' lane' is another possible derivation. The name spread naturally from the lane to the square when it was created late in the seventeenth century or early in the eighteenth.

In 1805 David Hughson made the cryptic remark that 'Billiter Square also formed part of a lane, which was obliged to be stopped up on account of the iniquity of its inhabitants'. This is also derived from a passage in Stow's *Survey*, which reads thus in the 1603 edition:

Fenchurch Street … is of Aldgate Ward till ye come to Culver Alley, on the west side of Ironmongers' Hall, where sometime was a lane which went out of Fenchurch Street to the middest of Lime Street, but this lane was stopped up for suspicion of thieves that lurked there by night.

It is not at all clear that this refers to any part of Billiter Square, past or present, though no doubt many iniquities, of a subtler kind, are practised there still.

The site of the square was a great house in Billiter Lane with a large garden behind. It belonged to Sir Edward Darcy (a Groom of the Privy Chamber to Queen Elizabeth) who died in 1612. Part of the garden was still shown on the 1676 map. Billiter Square was mentioned by Edward Hatton in 1708, as 'very small, but pleasant, and good Buildings', and Strype described the buildings as new in his account published in 1720, although the passage may have been written before 1708. His map suggested that the square had not attained its full size, which it had done by the time of Rocque's map of 1746, but the map published in 1720 may also have been completed before 1708.

It has been said that Voltaire lodged in Billiter Square in 1728, on the evidence of this passage in his letter to John Brinsden, Lord Bolingbroke's secretary: 'Direct yr. letter by the penny post at Mr Cavalier, Belitery Square by the R. exchange.' It is more likely that Voltaire simply picked up his correspondence from the house of his banker, Pierre Cavalier, in Billiter Square, his own address being very uncertain during his travels in England.

Including the two at the corner of Billiter Lane there were twelve houses in the square in the later eighteenth century, seven on the north side, four on the south and one at the west end. The square continued to be a good address for wealthy merchants until the beginning of the nineteenth century, but from that time the houses were given up one by one to office use, a process completed by 1840.

The old houses were all demolished in the 1870s and 1880s and replaced by large offices, every one of which was damaged beyond repair during the Second World War. In the 1950s bigger and duller offices were built on their sites. These included the 1958 Lloyd's of

London, but that has been replaced by the towering Willis Building, completed in 2008, which occupies the whole of the north side.

The larger east–west section of Billiter Square is now counted as part of Fenchurch Avenue, from which it does not differ in any way; but only the eastern half of the present Fenchurch Avenue, formerly a good deal wider, was the original square. The name 'Billiter Square' has now been confined to the stubby cul-de-sac surrounded by tall modern offices that branches off the south side of Fenchurch Avenue. This offshoot formed a minor part of the square from its original creation. An archway at the bottom gives access to an alley leading to Fenchurch Street. This was perhaps Stow's Culver Alley. It was known as Smith's Rents in 1720, as Fishmongers' Alley in 1739, and is now called Hogarth Court.

Black Horse Square

DEPTFORD [LEWISHAM]

Black Horse Square was built over several decades, beginning in the 1780s, on a field behind the Black Horse public house in Evelyn Street, and the pub's stabling always occupied the whole of the short west side. The square first came to the attention of the rate collectors in 1788 when Edward Swift, the landlord, was charged 'for 16 houses' in addition to the pub. In February of the same year there was a burial from the 'new buildings near the Black Horse', which suggests that some of the houses were built in 1787.

It is not certain that a square was the original idea. In 1799 Horwood's map showed the long north side as Black Horse Row and the short east side as Pleasant Row, but gave no hint of a garden or south side in contemplation. By 1807 the south side had been built and Black Horse Square was established as the name.

The full complement of houses was thirty-six. They all had narrow private back gardens, the ones on the south side quite long. The parish registers indicate that most of the early residents were labourers, and no doubt good customers of the pub. Standing between the Surrey Canal and the Royal Dockyard, it was never likely to attract prosperous tenants, and it soon degenerated into a slum. The centre of the

square had ample room for a garden, but the 1868 Ordnance Survey did not show any laid out. Such uncared for open spaces were a natural dumping ground for rubbish. In the early 1880s Black Horse Square was demolished and Hood Street built on the site.

Blandford Square

MARYLEBONE [WESTMINSTER]

Blandford Square was laid out in the mid-1820s but built very slowly. Number 1 led the way in 1827, three years before work began on the rest of the south side. It was completed only in 1837 and the east side not until 1843. The north side was built in stages between 1843 and 1849.

More houses had been planned for the west side, but in 1851 the St Edward's Convent was built there instead. In 1813 a white lead factory had occupied the site, and fear of contamination was no doubt why it was left until last. There was no road on the west side until the 1890s, the garden of the convent abutting directly on that of the square. Beresford Chancellor says that the sisters, whose community had been founded near Queen Square, Bloomsbury, in 1844, worked among unemployed servants.

Blandford Square has recently been described as a project only, a planned but abandoned companion for Dorset Square. That would have surprised Sir Henry Taylor, the poet and civil servant, who settled at No. 16 after his marriage in 1839 and remained until 1845, and George Eliot and George Henry Lewes, who lived at the same address from 1860 to 1863, having

The convent on the west side of Blandford Square, c. 1910.

made the easy move from No. 10 Harewood Square. She wrote in December 1860, 'though we were in the house on Monday last, our curtains are not up and our oil-cloth is not down. Such is life seen from the furnishing point of view!' George Grossmith lived at No. 31 from his marriage in 1873 until about 1885, when he moved to Dorset Square.

Despite the slow development, Blandford Square settled down from the early 1850s as a prosperous and highly respectable place. That ended abruptly in the mid-1890s when the building of Marylebone Station, which had entirely destroyed Harewood Square, required the demolition of the east side of Blandford Square. The Great Central Railway Company became the landlord of the houses on the north and south sides, but found them a poor speculation. 'There is indeed great difficulty in letting them at all and "anybody has come in"', as the Booth survey reported in 1898.

The big houses survived the Second World War but were demolished in 1968. Modern flats and offices now stand on their site and that of the garden, and the St Edward's Convent in Harewood Avenue is the only relic of the old Blandford Square.

Bloomfield Square

See Gloucester Square

Bloomsbury Square

BLOOMSBURY [CAMDEN]

Thomas Wriothesley, 4th Earl of Southampton, decided in the 1630s to abandon the family town house in Holborn and build a new mansion on his Bloomsbury estate, in the fields north of the old manor house. As there were severe restrictions on building schemes with a tendency to enlarge London, the earl obtained a licence from Charles I and the Privy Council authorising his plan. Before he could act upon it the civil war began, and the earl spent the next few years in attendance on the king.

With the ruin of the royal cause came fines and a self-imposed exile in the country, and it was not until the mid-1650s that returning prosperity enabled him

to dust off his plans and begin to build 'Southampton House in the Fields' (see p.9). It was safely finished in time for the Restoration in 1660, when Southampton became Lord Treasurer, so nobody could allege that public money had paid for it. Clarendon, his great colleague in the new government, having sat out the Commonwealth on the Continent, had to begin his mansion from scratch on his return and was eventually overwhelmed by the wave of jealousy and slander that its magnificence aroused.

Under Cromwell, the careful attention that the kings paid to building standards had been replaced by a planning free-for-all. A shanty town of cheap wooden houses had grown up around the intended site of Southampton House, restricting scope for the magnificence envisaged by the 1640 licence. In 1661, secure in the favour of the king, the earl obtained a new patent that required him to repair or remove the substandard houses and allowed him to build on other parts of the estate. The most important of the new sites was in front of Southampton House, 'the void space in front of my lord's mansion', as the first building leases described it. These were issued in 1661, as soon as the earl had his new patent. The leases began to describe the development as 'the square' in 1663.

The plots leased to prospective builders and residents varied greatly in size, with frontages from 20ft to 145ft, but they were nearly all for single houses. The largest plots were on the east and west sides, closest to the mansion, which filled the whole of the north side. The inferior south side featured a public house, the Buffalo's Head.

Building went on briskly throughout the 1660s. The east side was known in the early days as Seymour Row, the west as Allington Row, the south side was Vernon Street and later Hart Street. On 9 February 1665 Evelyn recorded in his diary:

> Dined at my L: Treasurers the Earle of Southampton in Bloomsbury, where he was building a noble Square or Piazza & little Towne: his owne house stands too low, some noble rooms, a pretty Cedar Chapell, a naked Garden to the north, but good aire: I had much discourse with his Lordship whom I found to be a person of extraordinary parts, but Valetudinarie.

The earl, despite three marriages, failed to produce a son and heir, and Bloomsbury passed to his daughter Rachel, who married the traitor, Lord Russell. Their grandson, the 3rd Duke of Bedford, gained possession on the death of Lady Russell, so the mansion passed quickly through three names: Southampton House, Russell House and Bedford House.

John Noorthouck wrote in 1773 that 'it is hardly possible to conceive a finer situation then Bedford-house'. It was nevertheless demolished in 1800 by the agricultural 6th Duke, whose statue stands dismally in Russell Square, gazing down Bedford Place at the site of his old home. The new houses on the north side were built in 1800, or soon afterwards. It was then that the houses on the south side were first numbered in the square.

Bloomsbury Square, which was described by Hatton in 1708 as 'pleasant, large, and Beautiful', was very fashionable in its early days and, as in other aristocratic squares, the houses were frequently rebuilt to suit the tastes of new tenants. As a result, only a few houses on the east side retain any seventeenth-century

fabric, heavily disguised by alterations. The south side was the worst, with some houses 'that may even be called mean', as a critic wrote in 1783.

The aristocrats who settled in Bloomsbury Square were mainly obscure. The most interesting was the 2nd Earl of Chesterfield, more successful as a lover than a politician, who died at No. 45 on the south side in 1713. His plaque also records the residence of his famous grandson, the 4th Earl. He was largely brought up by his grandmother and probably spent as much time as he could in the family's town house, as he hated the country.

The other early celebrities were literary, their houses not known for certain as the ratebooks for the period have not survived. The dramatist and poet Sir Charles Sedley moved to the square after his bigamous marriage with Ann Ayscough in 1672. The Presbyterian writer Richard Baxter lived there from 1673 until 1681 or later, and Sir Richard Steele added a large house, 'the fifth on the east side', to his formidable financial burdens between 1712 and 1714. His 'fifth' was probably the later No. 33, although

Bloomsbury Square from the south in 1731, showing Bedford House on the north side.

subdivisions and combinations made the numbering of the east side inconsistent. Mark Akenside is said to have lived in the square from 1749 to 1759, in his character of doctor rather than poet. It must have been on the south side, as he does not appear as a ratepayer in any of the houses then numbered in the square.

In the eighteenth century, as fashion moved west, Bloomsbury Square was taken over by lawyers. Lord Chief Justice Mansfield lived at the old No. 11, later 28–29, from 1751 until it was partially destroyed during the Gordon Riots in 1780. An eyewitness left this account:

> The mob knocked at the door, and the servant opening it told them, it was not Lord Mansfield's, on which they quietly departed: but being better informed, they returned, and again knocking at the door, it was opened to them, but, for a length of time, not a person dared to enter, fearing resistance. At last one man ventured in, and being not even reproved, the rest became more bold, and rushing in, a scene of Bedlam ensued. The insane demons of religious bigotry flew to the bed-rooms, and from the second-floor, the first thing they did was to throw a grand piano out of the window, without any notice to their friends below, one of whom received the corner of it on his arm, and which drove the pike of the railing through it, so that it required two men to disengage the limb.

The barrister and politician Charles Yorke lived at the old No. 9 (later No. 31) in the mid-1750s, then at the old No. 10 (later No. 30) from 1758 until his death in 1770, immediately after being appointed Lord Chancellor. For No. 10 he paid a rent of £210 per annum, the highest on the Bloomsbury estate, although it was far from being the largest plot in the square. Lord Ellenborough, another Lord Chief Justice, lived at No. 41 on the south side from 1789 to 1808, when he moved to St James's Square. Lady Ellenborough's 'beauty was so great that passers-by would linger to watch her watering the flowers on the balcony of their house in Bloomsbury Square'.

In the nineteenth century the square became 'a very unfashionable quarter, though very respectable', as Sir Anthony Panizzi of the British Museum said when living at No. 31 between 1865 and 1879. Other literary men who found they could afford to live in the declining square were Isaac and Benjamin Disraeli at No. 6 from 1817 to 1829, and Herbert Spencer, that great lover of squares, who took lodgings at No. 29 on several occasions when requiring solitude for writing.

Bloomsbury Square has a good deal of architectural interest, in terms both of houses designed and houses occupied. The fine Nos 5 and 6, built in 1744, were the work of Henry Flitcroft, who acted as the Duke of Bedford's surveyor. They were rebuilt for the estate rather than a tenant, perhaps in an attempt to revive the declining fortunes of the square. (There is no evidence for the tradition that No. 6 was designed for himself by Isaac Ware.) Number 17, at the north end of the west side, and the terrace around the corner in Great Russell Street (where he lived) was John Nash's first, unsuccessful attempt to storm London in 1777–78. The failure of the development bankrupted him in 1783.

The east side of Bloomsbury Square, c. 1905.

Probably the staff and pupils of the College of Preceptors, posed in the garden of Bloomsbury Square, behind the statue of Fox, in 1906.

Eminent architects have chosen to live in the square. Ewan Christian was at No. 6 in the 1850s and Norman Shaw at No. 29 from 1876. Sir Edwin Lutyens moved to No. 29 in 1897, attracted by the association with Shaw, whose studio remained unaltered. As the house was expensive and Lutyens was poor, it was very sparsely furnished, something not at all to the taste of his aristocratic wife. Lutyens loved the house and when he had to move in 1914, because it was scheduled for demolition, he wrote, 'Yes, I am very, *very* sad leaving Bloomsbury Square and so much else along with it, a sea of surf and sorrow'. They moved to Bedford Square, which they hated.

Bloomsbury Square enjoyed nearly a century of peace after the loss of Bedford House, but then the shocks became more frequent. The first was the College of Preceptors, built at Nos 2 and 3 on the south side between 1885 and 1887. It was designed by Frank Pinches in florid stone and red brick and is much taller than its neighbours. The college was previously at No. 28, part of Lord Mansfield's house at the north end of the east side. Immediately after the First World War the whole of the east side was demolished to make way for the Liverpool Victoria Friendly Society offices, built from 1921 to 1934 over the block between the square and Southampton Row. The architect of what would be a fine building in Oxford Street was Charles W. Long.

The third shock was the digging of a deep car park beneath the garden in 1972–73. Otherwise Bloomsbury Square has been lucky. It passed unscathed through the Second World War, the 1800 terraces on the north side are unblemished, and a few fine houses survive on the south and west sides. The large public garden is attractive. At the north end is Westmacott's statue of Fox, seated in perpetual contemplation of his friend the Duke of Bedford.

Bloomsbury Square

NEWINGTON [SOUTHWARK]

Lockie, who did not mention this little Bloomsbury Square in 1810, gave this account of it in 1813: 'Bloomsbury-Sq., Church-Place, Newington, – 2d on the L. from op. the church'. Church Place (or Passage) was directly opposite St Mary's and if a yard behind the pub on the corner counted as its first turning on the left, then the second was a tiny court that might have been called a square. Rocque's 1740s map showed a small opening, but not obviously of the same form as that indicated by the Horwood maps of the 1790s and 1819: four houses on three sides of the court, with the north-east side vacant.

In the 1841 census, where it was known as Bloomsbury Court, two houses were occupied by shoemakers, another was empty, and two were being built, presumably meaning rebuilt. It was Bloomsbury Square in the 1847 ratebook, but in the 1851 census the sequence of Church Passage was broken by the six houses of Ann's Place, which was probably a new name for the rebuilt Bloomsbury Square. By 1871 the houses were somewhat crushed by the sperm oil works behind them on the north-east side. Only two were listed in Ann's Place in the census of that year and three in 1881. They had been entirely squeezed out of existence before 1891. The site is now the green in front of the shops opposite St Mary's churchyard.

Bonnington Square

VAUXHALL [LAMBETH]

Out of the most unpromising materials this has been turned into one of the remarkable squares of London. The main roads of Kennington are graced (amid the blocks of flats) by many fine late Georgian houses, survivors from the original development of inner south London, but much of the space between the highways remained as market garden ground long enough for the vernacular in English architecture to sink from unconscious grace to instinctive ugliness.

Bonnington Square was built on the site of a nursery at the low point in Victorian architecture: the leases ran from 1879 and 1880. The houses were designed to accommodate three families and have something of the look of tenement blocks. The builder set them directly on the road with no front gardens or even areas, and he did not provide a communal garden. Where it should have been, he set two more terraces of identical houses. The status of the early residents is suggested by the fact that one of them was sued in 1882 for the restitution of furniture supplied on 'the hire system' (which the newspaper reporting the case had to explain) and for which he had failed to make a single payment.

The only thing that gave the square, which hardly deserved the name, the least interest or distinction, was the survival within it of Vine Lodge. This is a double-fronted detached house of the early nineteenth century which had been occupied by the proprietor of the nursery. Before the building of the square it stood just inside the nursery gates, at the end of Langley Lane.

Salvation for the square, or the materials for salvation, came from an unlikely quarter. Hitler's bombers managed to demolish seven of the houses in the interior, where the garden should have been, without destroying anything else, although Vine Lodge just across the road was shaken, as were many of the other houses. The bomb site became an informal playground and was eventually dignified by the council with some swings and seats, but in the 1980s it degenerated into an overgrown rubbish tip. It seemed likely to become a builder's yard until the residents became alarmed and formed the Bonnington

The south side of Bonnington Square in 2008.

Square Garden Association. That was the beginning of an amazing flowering, not only in the exotic new Paradise Garden, but in all the streets, which have been brought to life with trees, shrubs, flowers and creepers. It is almost as if the old nursery had revived. This must be one of the few places in London where a garden party could be given in the street.

Bowling Square

Bowling Alley was a turning off the west side of Whitecross Street, near the southern end. Maps from 1676 onwards showed it with two offshoots to the south, and by the 1740s these had become nearly square in shape. They had five or six houses each by the 1790s. Bowling Square or Bowling Alley Square, which appeared in the census returns from 1841 to 1861, was the larger and more westerly of these two openings.

Mrs Susan Harris, whitesmith, was listed at No. 2 Bowling Square, Whitecross Street, in the 1840s directories. In 1851 two of the eight houses were occupied by framework knitters, another by a ginger beer dealer. The whole area was cleared in the 1860s for the digging of the Metropolitan Railway cutting and the building of the Midland Railway goods station.

After extensive Second World War bombing, the Barbican Arts Centre was built on the site.

Bown Square

This was one of the shortest-lived of the London squares. It was created in the 1820s, a few years after St John's Church in Waterloo Road, which was nearly opposite, and destroyed when Waterloo Station was built just twenty years later. It was not on Greenwood's 1827 map, but his 1830 revision showed the rather ill-defined square on the south side of Vine Street, which turned off Waterloo Road opposite what is now Exton Street. Greenwood showed the name very clearly as Bowys Square, but in the 1841 census it appeared as Bown or Bowne Square. At that time the dozen or so houses were occupied by a gardener, smith, waterman, engineer, milkman, car man, labourer etc. The Victory Arch of Waterloo Station is not far from the site horizontally, although a good way above it.

Bowys Square

See Bown Square

Brassey Square

BATTERSEA [WANDSWORTH]

Like Clarendon Square, this is now just an historical curiosity. It is in an obscure part of Battersea – if such a concept can be grasped – which is no doubt how the Artisans, Labourers & General Dwellings Company was able to afford land here for Shaftesbury Park, a philanthropic housing estate. They began to build it in 1872.

The managers had taken the bold and unusual decision to provide most of their new tenants with cottage homes (designed by Robert Austin,

Numbers 11 and 13 Brassey Square in 2008.

the founder of the company) instead of the traditional tenements, and in the middle there was to be a square with a garden, just like the West End. It was named after Thomas Brassey, the great engineer, who died in 1870. But the economics of a cottage estate were unfamiliar to the housing philanthropists. Their object was to make a small profit. Here at Battersea they found themselves in danger of making a loss, and to balance the books the garden was quickly sacrificed. Morrison Street now cuts across its centre.

Without the softening influence of a garden to set them off, there is not much in Robert Austin's houses to catch the attention, except the doorways, paired beneath a steep gable or open pediment, some with ornamental tiling, others with the date and the company's monogram.

During the Second World War a V1 flying bomb destroyed a number of houses in the south-east corner of the square, where flats now stand, but apart from that the 1870s houses are well preserved.

Bridgewater Square

CITY OF LONDON

Garter House in the Barbican was built early in the sixteenth century for Thomas Wriothesley, Garter King at Arms. His real name was Writhe, but as a herald he became dissatisfied with something so lacking in gentility. The house was an unofficial headquarters for the Heralds' College until his death in 1534.

It served as the Spanish Embassy during much of the reign of James I and was thus home to one of the most famous of ambassadors, the imperious Gondomar, during his first embassy from 1613 to 1618. This was an exciting interlude, when the house was a secret nunnery and a refuge for Irish priests and other Catholic fugitives. The chapel, a privileged place of worship, was called by Gondomar 'the parish and cathedral church for London'. The embassy was besieged by an angry mob in 1618 after one of Gondomar's servants rode over a child in Chancery Lane. 'They beset the Spanish ambassador's house, whither the delinquent had betaken himself, demanded the offender, and upon refusal, proceeded to break down the windows and threaten a forcible entry,' as Thomas Lorkin reported

on 14 July. Only the personal intervention of the Lord Chief Justice pacified the mob.

Late in 1618, after Gondomar went home, the house was bought ('for £3000 or thereabout') by the 1st Earl of Bridgewater, the head of another rising family, and became Bridgewater House. On 12 April 1687 it was destroyed by a fire in which Charles and Thomas Egerton, the two eldest sons of the 3rd Earl, were killed together with their tutor. As a result of the fire the earl joined the aristocratic migration westwards sooner than he might otherwise have done. Celia Fiennes mentioned this trend in 1701: 'There was formerly in the Citty severall houses of the noblemens with large gardens and out houses and great attendances, but of late are pulled down and built into streets and squares and called by the names of the noblemen …' The Egerton family settled first in Red Lion Square and finally in Cleveland House (now rebuilt as Bridgewater House) in Cleveland Square, St James's.

On the ruins of their Barbican mansion one of the first small wave of City squares was built and named inevitably Bridgewater Square. The developer was none other than Sir Christopher Wren, who bought the ruined house for £4,400 in 1688, in partnership with a backer named George Jackson. This was not the beginning of Wren's interest in the site, as in 1673 he had made an abortive development plan for the Earl of Bridgewater. The old drawings were perhaps dusted off and revised, and Wren disposed of building plots to friends and associates, including Nicholas Hawksmoor. It is unlikely that Wren or Hawksmoor designed any of the houses. They would have been within the compass of the experienced carpenters and bricklayers who contracted for most of the plots.

Building work probably proceeded slowly, as it was described in 1708 as 'a New, pleasant, tho' very small Square'. The defection of the earl did not encourage the builders to aim their houses at the aristocracy and gentry. They were designed with the City merchant in mind and in the early days that was the class from which the residents were drawn. One was Thomas Cromwell, great-grandson of Oliver. He was a grocer in Snow Hill but retired to Bridgewater Square, where he died in 1748. In 1720 (or perhaps earlier, as the date of Strype's text is uncertain) it was described as 'a very handsome open Place, with very good Buildings, well inhabited. The Middle is neatly inclosed with Palisado Pales, and set round with Trees, which renders the Place very delightful.' In 1806 Hughson reported that 'Bridgewater Square is small but neat, surrounded with plain, but handsome and convenient houses; the centre of the square is a grass-plat, shaded with trees, and encompassed by iron rails.'

When the merchants, following the lead of the aristocracy, began to desert the City towards the end of the eighteenth century, Bridgewater Square became the haunt of watchmakers, jewellers, gold-smiths and silversmiths. In 1843 the raised grass plot in the centre reminded William Weir of a disused City churchyard. He found 'on the windows of every alternate house a bill, "To let, unfurnished"'. A few schools and the first boarding houses appeared in the 1840s and 1850s, when it was also popular with furriers. In 1891 Henry Wheatley recorded that the square had been 'partially cleared away in the course of recent improvements'. This was the introduction of the new Cripplegate Street into the south-east corner. It did not cause much immediate

Bridgewater Square in 1844.

damage but the east side of the square was rebuilt not long afterwards.

By the twentieth century the whole surviving portion of the square was in commercial use in a wide variety of trades, except for the Cripplegate Boys' School, carried on in an incongruously tall building at No. 16, and a large temperance hotel occupying the whole of the south side. The style of the houses used as the hotel was more Regency than Queen Anne, and the east end of the south side,

Tranter's Hotel on the south side of Bridgewater Square, *c.* 1910.

at least, was certainly rebuilt at that time. The late seventeenth or early eighteenth-century houses on the other sides (not unlike those in Golden Square) survived until the 1840s, many of them probably for a century after that.

Because this was far from the centre of the City there was little Victorian office building and most of the houses were merely adapted to commercial use. Their luck ended during the Second World War, when the Barbican was badly damaged and most of the square flattened. It survives as a name, but is now just a children's playground between tall flats and offices. That it is preserved at all is the result of a campaign in 1928 that saved the garden from a planned building development and entrusted it to the care of the Corporation.

Brompton Square

BROMPTON [KENSINGTON AND CHELSEA]

Brompton Square is a narrow rectangle running north from Brompton Road with, crucially, no access to the north. Instead, the square ends in a small crescent that has its own little circular garden.

The speculation was begun in 1821 or a little earlier by James Bonnin, a local builder also involved with Trevor Square and Alexander Square. At first he dealt with the Irish owner, Mary Tatham Browne, who may have introduced as surveyor Robert Darley, the only architect involved in the early development. From 1821 William Farlar, a West End ironmonger, became interested in the development, at first no doubt as mortgagee. In 1823 he bought the estate from Mary Browne and Darley continued to act for him. Bonnin only had a building lease for the southern half of the square, which he had finished by 1826. Farlar, having given up his ironmongery business, dealt with the northern half directly, made much slower progress in the harsher economic conditions after 1826, and ended as a bankrupt.

Most of the long straight sides were complete by 1830. That left the northern crescent to be dealt with. Farlar believed that a communication with the more fashionable Kensington Gardens suburb to the north would be the salvation of his struggling square, so in 1834–35 he had the crescent built in two sections, with a gap between for a road. These eight houses are more elaborate than the rest of the square, completely faced in stucco and with porches. John Blore may have been responsible for their design or embellishment.

In 1835 the land to the north was still fields. By the time the Ennismore Gardens development was begun in the late 1840s Farlar had failed and Brompton Square had passed into other hands. The new owners tried to negotiate access for their road, but John Elger, the builder of Ennismore Gardens, would not permit it, fearing that the vulgar Bromptonians would damage the prospects of his exclusive estate. An acrimonious controversy raged for several years until Elger settled the issue by purchasing the disputed land and building the unmatching 31a Brompton Square in the gap. An ownership inscription survives there as a trophy of his victory. What was regarded as a disaster at the time has proved of equal benefit to Ennismore Gardens and Brompton Square, by saving them from through traffic.

Brompton Square was strongly associated from the start with actors and playwrights. George Colman the younger lived at No. 22 from 1825 until his death in 1836. William Farren, one of the great English character actors, who played old men exquisitely from his early twenties, lived at No. 23 from 1823 until 1836 and from 1854 until his death in 1861, but was at No. 30 in the years between. The comedian John Liston lived at No. 40 from 1829 to 1833, and John Baldwin Buckstone, the comedian and playwright, who was manager of the Haymarket Theatre for twenty-five years, lived at No. 6 from 1840 to 1854. Shirley Brooks, the playwright and editor of *Punch*, lived at No. 22 in 1859–60, writing soon after he moved that '"The wind is roaring in turret and tree", and the row it makes down here, in our open back, is perfectly pestering. But I look on a church (of England, mind), an Oratory (Popish), and the row of Brompton Boilers, which is the best of all.' (The Brompton Boilers was the nickname for the original, temporary Victoria & Albert Museum.) Many other actors and actresses have lived in the square.

Non-dramatic writers also favoured it. The witty man about town, Henry Luttrell, author of *Advice to Julia* and the hero of a thousand anecdotes, lived at No. 31 from the early 1840s until his death in 1851, socially if not physically a long way from his spiritual home at Holland House. His marriage in 1850 probably undermined his position in the same way as Charles Swann's to Odette. Number 31 was next to the gap through which the longed-for access to the more fashionable north was promised.

John Payne Collier, the Shakespearean forger, was at No. 24 from 1839 to 1843. E.F. Benson had his London home at No. 25 from 1915 until his death in 1940 and made the square the base for his alter ego's attempt to conquer the capital in *Lucia in London* (1927). A.W. Pollard, the literary scholar and bibliographer, was born at No. 1 in 1859. His researches into the text of Shakespeare made the square's amends for the harm done by John Payne Collier. Stanley Lane-Poole, the oriental scholar, died at No. 10 in 1932. Francis

Place, the social reformer, who lived at No. 21 from 1833 to 1853, seems out of place amid all this frivolity, but his second wife was an actress already associated with the square. There is a plaque on Place's house, and also on No. 6, where Stéphane Mallarmé lodged in 1863.

There were many lodging houses in the square by the end of the nineteenth century and it was a place where kept women lived, but Beresford Chancellor wrote in 1907 that it 'seems to have recovered from the not very good reputation it once suffered under, and its houses, though small, are respectable'. They are also very well preserved, Second World War bomb damage to the north crescent having been made good. Number 6 was rebuilt in 1889–90 and No. 31a in the centre of the north crescent was enlarged in the early 1980s.

The main changes have been at the south end, where James Bonnin had provided very elegant gates and railings. Road widening, bomb damage, and changes in architectural taste have destroyed them, and led to the corner houses being rebuilt several times.

The east side of Brompton Square and part of the northern crescent, *c.* 1905.

The present arrangement was not completed until the early 1980s. The garden, for the management of which Farlar obtained a private act in 1824, is too narrow to be secluded or elaborate but the long, gently sloping central lawn is attractive and the absence of through traffic makes this one of the quietest and most intimate of the central squares.

Brook's Square

Brook's Square was an alternative name for Brook's Court, which was probably built between 1810 and 1813, as it appeared in the second edition of Lockie's *Topography of London* but not the first. He located it as 'Brook's-Court, Vine-Yard, – 3rd on the R. from 110, Tooley-street'. Vine Yard was later Vine Street and is now represented by Vine Lane. That is only a short cul-de-sac, but Vine Yard used to continue to the Thames. Brook's Court or Square, which was about two-thirds of the way down, led east towards Brook's Wharf.

In 1851, when only thirteen of the fifteen houses were occupied, thirty families lived in Brook's Square and there were numerous single lodgers. Many of the men were sailors, dockers, or labourers at the wharves. Brook's Square had gone by 1861. In the 1860s the whole district was cleared to make way for large bonded warehouses and part of those were replaced at the end of the century by industrial dwellings called Vine Street Buildings. The Scoop, the sunken amphitheatre next to City Hall, is now on the site.

Broomfield Square

Broomfield Square was a name used a few times in the parish registers of St Paul Deptford in the years around 1820, but not found elsewhere. One example was the burial of a labourer in 1820. Broomfields was the old name for the eastern end of Evelyn Street, so if the square had a separate existence it was probably in that area. It may just have been an alternative name for Black Horse Square, which was off Evelyn Street, or for Deptford's Brunswick Square, which was close to it.

Brunswick Square

Samuel Pepys Cockerell, the surveyor to the Foundling Hospital, produced his plan for the development of the estate at the end of 1790. Its main features were the mirror image three-sided squares east and west of the hospital garden. Brunswick Square on the west side, named after the king's sister, the Duchess of Brunswick, was built first; work on Mecklenburgh Square was delayed for fifteen years by the war.

The main builder of Brunswick Square was the young James Burton, later so heavily involved in the development of the Bedford estate in Bloomsbury and the Nash terraces in Regent's Park. He began on the south side in 1792 and on the west in 1795, subletting some plots to other builders. Burton began to lay out the garden in 1796, but the difficulty of selling the houses already built now that war had begun prevented him from taking the north side. That was built instead between 1800 and 1807 by Charles Mayor, one of Burton's subcontractors. Brunswick Square's first residents appeared, on the south side, in 1799.

The houses – all now destroyed – were plain and solid, to suit the tastes of the wealthy merchants and lawyers they were intended for. They had four storeys plus basement and were three bays wide. The only serious ornaments were first floor balconies. On the north and south sides the central house had a three-storey bow flanked by taller round-headed windows. It is hard to apportion credit for the design. Burton was later an architect as well as a builder, in Russell Square, for example; here he may have worked from an elevation provided by Cockerell but is more likely to have submitted one for Cockerell's approval. For the north side Charles Mayor submitted a plan in 1800 which Cockerell accepted as being a good match for the existing houses on the south side. Like Gower Street, Brunswick Square became one of the examples the Victorians used to justify their contempt for Georgian architecture. Edward Walford remarked in the 1870s that 'the house-fronts of Brunswick Square have been described as "brick walls with holes in them"'.

The west side of Brunswick Square, Bloomsbury, c. 1905.

Jane Austen, writing in 1814, chose Brunswick Square as the residence of Emma's brother-in-law, John Knightley, a lawyer. Mrs John had this to say about it:

No, indeed – *we* are not at all in a bad air. Our part of London is so very superior to most others! – You must not confound us with London in general, my dear sir. The neighbourhood of Brunswick Square is very different from almost all the rest. We are so very airy! I should be unwilling, I own, to live in any other part of the town; – there is hardly any other that I could be satisfied to have my children live in; – but we are so remarkably airy! – Mr Wingfield thinks the vicinity of Brunswick Square decidedly the most favourable as to air.

Brunswick Square was home to many real lawyers too, mostly solicitors, and to solid City men. Rowland Dobie wrote in 1829, 'The square is smaller than many others in the metropolis, but elegant and pleasant, and from its near approach to the city, it has always been most respectably inhabited by merchants and others.'

John Leech is the most famous of the many artists who lived in Brunswick Square. He was at No. 32 from 1854 to 1862. His taste for large houses and high living, and the overwork required to pay for them, are blamed for his early death. Virginia Woolf, that most square-minded of writers, lived at No. 38, on the north side, in 1911–12. E.M. Forster had a flat at No. 26 from 1929 to 1939. Anthony Powell, who lived in the top-floor flat from 1932 to 1935, but never saw Forster, wrote that it was 'part of the Foundling Hospital Bloomsbury Estate, landlords, Constant Lambert remarked, who always made one feel like a foundling'.

The north side was demolished in or before 1938, when the Royal Pharmaceutical Society began to build its college there. Work was interrupted by the war and the building, by then known as the School of Pharmacy, was not completed until 1960. This was perhaps fortunate for the Society, as the houses on the west and south sides of the square, which would have put their new building to shame, were badly damaged and all demolished after the war. On the south side is now the University of London's very dull International Hall, built in the early 1960s.

The huge Brunswick Centre on the west side was built between 1968 and 1972. The beautiful public garden is now the only relief from the architectural horrors of the square.

Brunswick Square

CAMBERWELL [SOUTHWARK]

Brunswick Square was one of the most ambitious in south London, considerably bigger than its Bloomsbury namesake and surviving today in much better shape, yet to Beresford Chancellor in 1907 it was just 'Brunswick Square in the wilds of Camberwell in the south'. It was laid out in the late 1840s, but progress was desperately slow and the square was never completed in the grand manner intended. From the start it was hampered by the presence of the Camberwell Union Workhouse in Havill Street, just to the east. The workhouse, which had been built in 1818, grew more rapidly than its unfortunate neighbour.

Brunswick Square had more in common with contemporary suburban developments like Lewisham

Park than with its formal Bloomsbury namesake. There was a large irregular garden around which it was hoped that individually designed detached and semi-detached houses would congregate. The square had one most unusual feature: outside the road that encircled the big garden there were two small greens, on the south and east sides. The first was absorbed into the big garden when it became a public park and the second was overwhelmed by the growth of the workhouse. Most of the early houses of the square fringed these two greens.

In 1851 a dozen houses were occupied, some under the name of Brunswick Road, and four were being built. The tenants were merchants, manufacturers, solicitors and accountants. The slow take up of the plots and the inevitable bankruptcy of the developer led to early compromises. In the 1860s a terrace (now on the south side of Elmington Road) was built over the north edge of the garden and a Presbyterian church in the south-western corner. In the 1870s a pair of houses was built south of the church and a long terrace (now the east side of Benhill Road) over the garden to its north. The west side of the square

Numbers 1–4 Brunswick Park, formerly part of the south side of Brunswick Square, Camberwell, in 2008.

was completed with much smaller houses than the ones that had begun it.

The most serious breach in the integrity of the square came at the end of the century when the workhouse was extended west from Havill Road, requiring the demolition of the eight early houses on that side and the loss of the small eastern green. But at least E.T. Hall's administration block of 1904 (now flats) was a more attractive replacement than anyone could have expected.

The garden was bought by Camberwell Council in 1901 and opened as a park in 1907 (see p.16). The LCC contributed to the disintegration of the square in 1937, when it renamed the various parts as Brunswick Park, Benhill Road and St Giles Road. Now the relics are so scattered that they are hard to recognise, but it is an attractive place to explore in search of them. The oldest is No. 116 Benhill Road, the only detached house built in the square. The church is represented by its former Sunday school in Benhill Road. The two houses built south of the church in the 1870s hide rather mysteriously, almost inside the park. The south side of the square survives intact and epitomises the halting development. It was begun at the east end about 1850 with two very grand semi-detached pairs, but the terrace adjoining was added slowly, in three quite different styles, and took thirty years to complete.

Brunswick Square

DEPTFORD [LEWISHAM]

The Deptford Brunswick Square was a late eighteenth-century development on the Evelyn estate, probably named after Caroline of Brunswick, who married the Prince of Wales in 1795. Like Factory Square at Streatham it was T-shaped, but here the shorter stroke ran south from the entrance in Prince Street, with the longer stroke, a cul-de-sac, extending west to fill the awkward triangular plot between the present Evelyn Street and Prince Street. The two sections were widest at their meeting point, giving something like the sense of a square, and here from the early nineteenth century stood the most prominent building, the Duchess of Brunswick pub. It was named after the Princess's mother, who lived in exile at Blackheath.

Brunswick Square was close to the royal dockyard, which must have made it prosperous in its early years, but like the rest of riverside Deptford it declined with the dockyard in the nineteenth century. It was a slum by the 1870s. The enumerator noted in the 1881 census that three sides of Brunswick Square had been demolished, leaving only the east side, which included the pub. That was destroyed a few years later when Czar Street was extended south. It is now lined with very depressing 1960s flats.

Brunswick Square

HAGGERSTON [HACKNEY]

(later Godwin Square)

This might be called an opportunistic square, created to make the most of St Mary, Haggerston, a John Nash church built in the fields in 1825–27 with only a gasworks for company. It was one of two that Nash designed for the New Church Commissioners, the other being All Souls', Langham Place.

The house builders took a decade or more to catch up with the church. When they did, one quickly saw that with the new Brunswick Street in front of it and Weymouth Terrace nearly parallel just to the west, two short streets would form a ready-made square with St Mary's as a grand feature on its east side. The two short terraces to the north and south, the only houses ever numbered in the square, were built in the 1840s. Clerks, warehousemen, shopkeepers and craftsmen were the tenants. The whole of the centre was a garden at first, not quite square because Weymouth Terrace curved to the west, making the north side longer than the south. In the late 1850s the Shoreditch almshouses in Hackney Road were demolished to make way for Columbia Square, and the replacement was built here, on the west side of the garden, facing St Mary's.

By 1898 it was reported that 'the churchyard has been taken over by the parish and turned into a recreation ground'. This was useful, with the garden of the square occupied by the almshouses, but the arrangement did not last for long. The almshouses, St Mary's Church, and the houses on the north and

Bryanston Square

St Mary's, Brunswick Square, Haggerston, in 1829.

Bryanston Square was named after the Portman family seat near Blandford in Dorset. The architect principally responsible for Montagu and Bryanston Squares was Joseph T. Parkinson, but he was assisted by his talented pupil, George Ledwell Taylor. Both squares were laid out in 1811 (when the plans were exhibited at the Royal Academy) but Montagu Square was built first. As a result, Bryanston Square became a common district name years before any houses stood there.

It is lucky, perhaps, that any of the houses in the square *are* still standing, as most were the work of the notoriously slipshod Henry Peto. Building began in 1820, and the first great event was Mrs Portman's 'magnificent Ball and sumptuous Supper, at her superb Mansion in Bryanston-square' on 17 May 1821. It was attended by 'between five and six hundred Fashionables', as *The Morning Post* reported.

The houses were larger than those in Montagu Square and the six grand mansions were suitable for the lavish entertainment of which the landowner's wife had set the example. Number 38, the big house in the centre of the west side (destroyed in the Second World War), was sometimes used by the Portmans and sometimes let to such notable tenants as the Duke of Brunswick. The corner mansions were the showpieces, with stucco throughout, pilasters and pediments. Number 1 was the Turkish Embassy.

William Weir, who regarded Montagu and Bryanston Squares as 'twin deformities', remarked in 1843 that 'a range of balconies runs along the front of the houses in Bryanston Square; but the inmates appear to entertain dismal apprehensions of the thievish propensities of their neighbours, for between every two balconies is introduced a terrible chevaux-de-frise'.

Bryanston Square was, from the first, more fashionable than its neighbour and was popular with aristocrats, politicians and military heroes. One of the first tenants was Admiral Sir Richard Strachan, who lived in Montagu Square for a time but died here in 1828. This gallant sailor is sadly remembered chiefly

south sides of the square were destroyed by bombing in 1941, and the ones in Weymouth Terrace, which formed the west side, were badly damaged. In the post-war rebuilding a new street pattern was adopted and the square was extinguished. For its unhappy last few years it had been known as Godwin Square, a name imposed by the LCC in 1939, because William Godwin was educated nearby at the Hoxton Academy. He proved as much of a jinx to his square after death as he had been to his family during his lifetime.

for his part in the Walcheren expedition, that classic combined operations disaster when:

> The Earl of Chatham, with his sword drawn,
> Stood waiting for Sir Richard Strachan.
> Sir Richard, longing to be at 'em,
> Stood waiting for the Earl of Chatham.

Notable among the many politicians was the pertinacious reformer Joseph Hume, who lived at No. 6 for many years. It was the childhood home of his equally eminent son, Allan Octavian Hume, one of the founders of the Indian Congress party. In the twentieth century it was patronised by best-selling writers. Somerset Maugham lived at No. 43 in the 1920s and Eric Ambler spent his last years at No. 14, dying there in 1998.

Bryanston Square suffered severely during the Second World War, with more than half of the houses on the west side and some at the north-east corner destroyed. The Swiss Embassy at No. 21 is a good facsimile of the blitzed original, with large modern offices behind. The gaps on the west side have been filled with flats that blend in fairly well. The replacements in Bryanston Place, as the north side is called, are not so tactful.

Buckenham Square

Buckenham Square was sometimes called New Buckenham Square, which caused confusion to compilers of directories and other lists, who were apt to give it duplicate entries, but the variant does usefully indicate that it was named after the village of New Buckenham in Norfolk.

The Booth survey of 1899 noted an '1828' datestone, confirmed by the 1827 and 1830 editions of Greenwood's map, the first of which showed a vacant site, the second two sides of 'Beckenham Square' approached via 'New Beckenham Street'. New Buckenham Street was formerly known as Rope Walk, and between 1813 and 1819 some houses were built at its west end. When the square was formed ten or fifteen years later they became its north side. New

The west side of Bryanston Square, *c.* 1904.

Buckenham Street was afterwards Buckenham Place and Buckenham Street.

The land belonged to the parish of St George the Martyr, Southwark. It was a small and awkward plot, squeezed between the St George's burial ground in Great Dover Street and Union Crescent in New Kent Road, the complement to Michael Searles's ambitious Paragon opposite. As a result only the east side of the square, with its back to the graveyard, was added at first to the pre-existing north side. When a west side was built it had to be crammed against the back of the elegant Union Place, hastening its decline. A south side was never attempted and in 1864 the Pilgrim Congregational Church was built there. The burial ground, long disused, became a recreation ground in 1886.

The area was found to be in decline by the Booth survey of 1899: 'Buckenham Street and Square, two storey houses, all flush with sidewalks. Poor class; some broken windows and neglected children.' A few years later Union Crescent and the west side of the square were demolished to make way for the St Saviour's and St Olave's Girls' School, which was built in 1903. The school, the church and the small houses that survived on the north and east sides of the square were all damaged during the Second World War, and afterwards the school expanded to fill the whole site, or what was left of it after the construction of the Bricklayer's Arms roundabout.

Buckingham Square

See Cambridge Square, Edward Square
and Oxford Square

Buller Square

See Trafalgar Square, Peckham

Bull's Head Square

CLERKENWELL [ISLINGTON]

Two of the main offshoots from the west side of Turnmill Street were Peter Street and Bowling Street. Peter Street was nearly opposite the surviving Benjamin Street, Bowling Street about 100 yards further north. In 1813 Horwood's map and Lockie's *Topography* placed Flower de Luce (or Flower de Lis) Court between these two, but the name was not heard of subsequently.

By 1816 Bull's Head Court occupied the space, and in 1818 the ratebook included for the first time an offshoot named Little Bull's Head Court. 'Little' was perhaps thought inappropriate, as it had more houses than Bull's Head Court itself, and by 1821 the Bull's Head Square name had been substituted. In 1818 six of the eight houses were owned by Diana Weston, the other two by Robert Waker. In 1851 the square was occupied by labourers, lodging-house keepers and costermongers, most of them Irish.

Everything on the west side of Turnmill Street was demolished about 1860 to make way for Farringdon Station and Farringdon Road. The northern end of the station, opened in 1863, is now on the site of the square.

Burnham Square

BETHNAL GREEN [TOWER HAMLETS]

Burnham Square was not built, as it had no design, but it began to emerge before 1820 as cottages were gradually grouped around something that might pass for a square. The Horwood map of 1813 showed the first one. The immediately adjoining names, Pitt Street and Thurlow Place, suggest the date of the development.

In 1848 Hector Gavin described it in his *Sanitary Rambles* as Bernham Square, 'This square consists of scattered buildings in gardens, and forms a remarkable exception to the foulness of the places last visited, in being tolerably clean'. It became compressed as a more formal road pattern tightened around it. It was tiny by 1870, when it consisted of eight or ten cottages: precision is difficult, as they faced in various directions and merged into other streets, and the 1871 census duplicated numbers. Labourers and shoemakers figured prominently among the tenants. In its final form there were narrow entrances from Globe Road in the north-east and Chester Street in the south-west.

The square was replaced by the huge Burnham Court, flats built by Bethnal Green Council between 1937 and 1939.

Bury Square

Bury Square was a name used in the early 1850s for the small, square, northern extension of Bury Court, at its eastern end. The men listed in Bury Square in directories of that period were shown at the same numbers in Bury Court in later years.

Bury Court and the earlier Bury Street take their name from the house of the abbots of Bury St Edmunds in Bevis Marks. The Ogilby & Morgan map of 1676 and the Strype map published in 1720 had the house still standing, with a large garden behind. Rocque's 1740s map showed Bury Court built over the garden, with the northward extension towards Bevis Marks at its east end.

It has led a charmed life, escaping destruction when the adjoining Jeffrey's Square was replaced by the Baltic Exchange, passing unscathed through the Second World War and not even falling a victim to the Gherkin. Bury Court, with the sometime square still intact, is now surrounded by modern offices that would be thought tall elsewhere.

Busby Square

This was a tiny square of eleven two-storey cottages branching off the almost equally diminutive Busby Street. The name came from Henry Busby of Hanover Square, who in 1770 had married into the illegitimate branch of the Sclater family of Shoreditch, immortalised in the nearby Sclater Street. The immortality attached to the Busby names was temporary. Henry Busby's marriage gave him an interest in the Red Cow estate, a former Sclater holding named from a seventeenth-century pub, and he began granting building leases there immediately.

Busby Street existed by the 1790s, but the square was an afterthought. It had been built by 1813, when the Horwood map miscalled it 'Busby Court'. Lockie, who listed Busby Square and Busby Court in the same year – but neither in 1810 – placed Busby Court correctly east of the square, where Horwood showed nothing.

The thirty-seven-year unexpired lease of Busby Square was sold in 1820, when the estate was described as 'Eleven brick-built Houses, forming a Square, and situate in New King-street (otherwise called Busby-square), Bethnal-green'. If the original term was sixty-one years, the late 1790s would be the likely date of building. The west end of Busby Street was known as New King Street at that time.

Bethnal Green soon became London's most notorious slum and Busby Square was not far from the Nichol, the worst part of that dreadful district. In 1848 Hector Gavin gave this description of it: 'This square is perfectly dirty; the houses are two feet below the level of the court-yard; there are two privies in it, which are full, and one dust and garbage-heap; there is likewise one tap for the supply of water.' During the next fifty years a vast amount of social work was done in Bethnal Green, with the object of abolishing such horrors, but in Busby Square the results were not startling. In 1898 it was 'vicious, children all clean and with good boots, windows broken'.

Busby Square had already been marked down by the LCC as a clearance area before the Second World War, and the site was vacant in 1948. Since then both Busby Street and Busby Square have ceased to exist, as St Matthias Primary School has expanded south from its original site.

Cadogan Square

(now part of Cadogan Place)

Cadogan Square was the original name, in occasional use until the middle of the nineteenth century, for the northern third of what is now Cadogan Place, above Pont Street. It was part of Hans Town, the suburb built by Henry Holland from the 1770s on land leased from Lord Cadogan and named after Cadogan's father-in-law, Sir Hans Sloane. Sloane Street was the centre of Hans Town, the first Cadogan Square its eastern outpost, beyond which lay the fields later covered by Belgravia. The square was outlined in the agreement made by Holland in 1777.

The north side of Cadogan Place, formerly the first Cadogan Square, *c*. 1905, with Chelsea House on the right.

The building of Cadogan Place began at the north end with the square, where most of the houses were completed between 1800 and 1804. When the ninety-six-year remainder lease of No. 11 Cadogan Square was sold in 1806 it was described as 'recently built' and the views 'exceedingly cheerful'. The builder of the houses was Henry Rowles, Holland's nephew.

The fine garden laid out by Humphry Repton was guarded by a railing 4½ft high. In a description of the garden published in 1806, Repton called the place Cadogan Square. Holland's pupil, Peter Frederick Robinson, designed the Hans Town Assembly Rooms for Cadogan Square in 1805. This building was perhaps behind the larger No. 13, the eastern house of the north side, which was the home of Henry Rowles. It became Chelsea House in 1850, when Lord Cadogan made it his London residence. He rebuilt it on a much larger scale in 1874 but it was demolished in the 1930s.

The eastern terrace above Pont Street was also known as Upper Cadogan Place, but was numbered continuously with the north side, these two forming the square, with twenty-seven houses. Below Pont Street began the separately numbered Lower Cadogan Place, which was not completed until about 1815. Here the enclosure did not become a private amenity for the residents, but instead the London Botanic Garden, which hovered uneasily between a scientific resource for horticultural students and a public pleasure garden for subscribers.

Usage was inconsistent between 'Square' and 'Place', the former being applied mostly to the garden, the latter to the houses. In 1826 a thief being pursued down Sloane Street climbed the railings and hid among the shrubberies in 'Cadogan Square'. On the other hand, Lady Sarah Napier, who took over No. 13, the large house on the north side, from Henry Rowles, wrote in 1807, 'I think I shall be much better when I leave this odious old lodging [in Sloane Street] & am settled in my clean, airy, small house in Cadogan Place'. Lady Sarah, a daughter of the Duke of Richmond, had been brought up at Goodwood and Holland House, so her judgement of size was not that of the average observer. In her comparatively impoverished old age she owed this 'small house' to family favour, her mother having been a Cadogan.

The old 'Square' portion of Cadogan Place had few other eminent residents. Thomas Broadwood, a partner in the great piano firm, lived at No. 17, and Torrens McCullagh, the MP and social reformer, at No. 23. The old name was still current in 1843 when William Weir wrote that 'Cadogan Square is first cousin to Russell Square' in being inhabited by 'the aristocracy of the law'. He considered the whole of Cadogan Place to be part of the square. This was a late appearance of the old name, which had been obsolete for thirty years when the present Cadogan Square was created.

Bomb damage in the north-east corner and post-war commercial pressures have led to the demolition of all the north side and the northern half of the east side of the original Cadogan Square, so now only a few of its houses survive, north of Pont Street. They are more modest than the grand setting might lead one to expect.

Cadogan Square

KNIGHTSBRIDGE (2) [KENSINGTON AND CHELSEA]

The second Cadogan Square was the last truly and permanently successful one in London. With the failure of the contemporary squares in Earls Court undermining confidence, and with little prospect of another sufficiently big site becoming available close to the West End, clients and architects alike turned to this as a last chance to experiment in the uniquely favourable setting of a square. The result was a practical Royal Academy exhibition, where new money could flaunt itself and the leading architectural stars of the 1870s and 1880s could show their designs in solid brick and terracotta. The professional press recognised the importance of the moment by publishing drawings and plans of almost every house.

The site had not been secured without aesthetic and social cost. The square was built in the beautiful grounds of Henry Holland's house, the Pavilion, where Holland had himself toyed with the idea of building a square in the 1770s. The house did not long survive the loss of its grounds. To commemorate it, Pavilion Square was the name first chosen but quickly altered. Adjoining the site to the west was the fashionable Prince's Club cricket ground where W.G. Grace hit 261 for the South of England in 1877. It was a last flourish. The determination of the Cadogan estate to push Pont Street west to Walton Street and build

The west side of the second Cadogan Square in 1905, or a little earlier.

Cadogan Square to its south, made it impossible for the club to persevere with the cricket ground. Lennox Gardens was soon built in its place.

The garden of the new square was laid out in the mid-1870s. The original idea was for it to be cut in two by a road, as at Cadogan Place, and the road was actually constructed, only to be abandoned in 1886. Lord Cadogan set the terracotta tone by employing his favourite architect, William Young, to design the terrace of three houses now numbered 54–58. They were built in 1877. These houses are on the west side, which has more interest than the others. It features favourable examples of the work of A.J. Adams, F.G. Knight, George Devey, E.T. Hall, Norman Shaw (see p.13) and Ernest George, in whose houses it mounts to a crescendo of extravagant Dutch detail.

Constance Duchess of Westminster's furniture being sold up to-day at Cadogan Square. I went to look at it yesterday morning. There is no reason why the furniture of a Duchess should not be showy, or ugly, or dull, yet it shocks one to find it so. I was surprised at the smallness of the house, too. A policeman in the hall.

Bennett is one of several successful writers who have lived in Cadogan Square. He was at No. 75 from 1922 to 1930. In 1928 he invited H.G. Wells and another Reform Club friend 'to play a tennis match on the hard court in Cadogan Square for a quid'. A *Daily Mail* man infiltrated the garden to report on the match. Denis Wheatley was another best-seller who spent his royalties here. He lived at the more fashionable No. 60 from 1960 until his death in 1977. Other celebrities were the wonderfully named General Sir Bindon Blood, at No. 59 until his death at a great age in 1940, and Lord Maugham, brother of Somerset, who was Lord Chancellor on the eve of the Second World War. He lived at No. 73 until his death in 1958. Sir Thomas Andros de la Rue, the playing card maker, used to claim that he had arranged for the renumbering of the square so that his house could be No. 52, but he was known to be a joker.

Bomb damage was restricted to one house on the south side and two near the south end of the east side, fate, unusually, dealing its blows in the least interesting parts. Those rents have been seamlessly repaired and today it appears a rare example of a square without any later intrusions.

Cambridge Square

BAYSWATER [WESTMINSTER]

The layout of the Bishop of London's Paddington estate, 'Tyburnia', was subject to constant tinkering,1 and this involved not only the arrangement of the streets and square but also their names. The twin Oxford and Cambridge Squares were not immune to this. In the 1799 plan for the development of Bayswater in tandem with the Grand Junction Canal, the Oxford and Cambridge Squares area was occupied

At the north-west corner George Edmund Street designed the very different No. 4, which was built with many alterations after his death. The rest of the north side, and most of the east and south, consist of terraces of less individual houses mostly designed by G.T. Robinson and J.J. Stevenson, and built between 1879 and 1886. In 1893 Percy Fitzgerald thought that the Cadogan Square architecture was 'certain to disintegrate', which was curiously like the mid-Victorian view of the impermanence of stucco, but the terracotta seems as solid today as it ever was.

Only a dozen houses were occupied by 1882, but the tenants included the Marquess of Blandford, a baronet and a couple of hons. Success was assured, and the square has never lacked residents of rank, wealth, or fame. Taste was not essential, as the ever-inquisitive Arnold Bennett discovered in 1924:

The south-west side of Cambridge Square, *c.* 1905.

by a large Buckingham Square with two reservoirs in place of a garden. At a later stage Cambridge Square was to have been Stanhope Square and there was also a thought of applying that name to a huge polygon that would have taken the place of the twin squares and crescents.

The plans were not finally settled until after 1838 and building began in Cambridge Square only about 1839. A single house was listed in the 1840 ratebook, a few were occupied in 1841, twenty by 1843 and the full complement of thirty-two by 1844. The general style was laid down by George Gutch, surveyor to the estate, but different architects planned the interiors for individual clients. We know that Henry Harrison designed No. 7 for Charles Harrison, a solicitor.

Like the rest of Tyburnia, Cambridge Square was wealthy and highly respectable but failed to scale the social heights. It had just one star: Robert Stephenson moved to No. 15 in 1844, soon after his wife died, to be closer to his clubs, and remained until 1847. He had only slept once or twice in his new home when it was badly damaged by fire, at a time when his equally eminent father George was staying with him:

The first in the house to sniff the smell of fire, he lost no time in taking care of himself. When Robert Stephenson and his servants were in the act of flying from the house in their night-clothes, the prudent father made his appearance in the hall, dressed even to his white neckcloth, and with his carpet-bag packed and swinging in his hand.

The house took ten months to repair. On his election to Parliament in 1847, Robert moved to a larger house in Gloucester Square. Apart from him, the odd dowager, baronet, MP or general – and the Peruvian consul – were the best the square could boast.

It passed through the Second World War unscathed but could not escape the heavy hand of the planner. The Ecclesiastical Commissioners continued their pre-war policy of rebuilding in Tyburnia and the whole of Cambridge Square was demolished in the 1960s.

The garden remains but it is now surrounded by very dull town houses interspersed with fourteen-storey tower blocks. One interesting resident of the new Cambridge Square was John Boon of Mills & Boon. He was general manager of this family business and a major figure in the publishing world. He died at No. 7 in 1996.

Camden Square

CAMDEN TOWN [CAMDEN]

The original Camden Town of the 1790s, around the present High Street, had become distinctly seedy by the 1840s when a new Lord Camden made a fresh start on the land to the north-east with an expensive church and a new name, Camden New Town. The centre-piece was the long, narrow Camden Square which climbed dramatically towards St Paul's Church, set at nearly its highest point. When approaching completion in 1848 St Paul's was praised by the *Illustrated London News*, with elegant variation, as 'certainly one of the most picturesque ecclesiastical structures that have lately been raised in the neighbourhood of the metropolis'. The architects were Frederick Ordish and John Johnson.

The leases of the earlier houses ran from 1845, which was presumably the date of the building agreement and the laying out of the garden. The work was done in the usual way by letting plots to various men. Thomas Bishop, one of the small speculative builders involved in 1846–47, did so badly that he was in Southampton Gaol in 1849 as an undischarged bankrupt. A few houses were completed in the 1840s, Nos 1–6 being the first occupied, but most were built between 1850 and 1855. There were a few detached houses, many pairs and a terrace, called imaginatively The Terrace, north of the church. An estate agent promoted the development in 1850 as 'that beautiful and healthy locality, Camden-square, Camden New Town, within a threepenny omnibus ride of the Bank'. Leases of about ninety-five years were selling for between £900 and £1,000 in 1851.

The north-west side of Camden Square, Camden Town, in 1906 or a little earlier.

In this railway-plagued district destruction began almost as soon as the square was completed, when the Midland Railway laid its lines into St Pancras Station, which was opened in 1868. They ran through a shallow tunnel cut diagonally across the southern half of the square. Four houses had to be demolished then, and four more when the tunnel was widened. In all, Nos 8–11 were lost on the west side and Nos 45–48 on the east. The sites remained vacant until after the Second World War.

The square was so popular with artists and engravers in its early years that one might almost speak of the 'Camden Square Group'. One of the first residents, at No. 4 from 1849, was the Camden-born Frederick Goodall, RA, noted for his historical paintings on Egyptian themes. When he made his second trip to Egypt in 1870 he passed on the house to the Dutch specialist in similar subject matter, Lawrence Alma-Tadema, then a refugee from the Franco-Prussian War. Their work was handled by the same dealer. It was the beginning of a triumphant English career for the Dutchman, leading to a knighthood. Goodall ended a bankrupt.

A third eminent painter at No. 4, in the late 1870s and early 1880s was Frank Holl, RA. He began with sombre genre pieces but signalled an exceedingly profitable change of direction with a portrait of his neighbour Samuel Cousins. Cousins, one of only two engravers to be elected a Royal Academician – he also received the Légion d'honneur from Napoleon III – was at No. 24 from 1857 until his death in 1887. At No. 57 lived yet another Royal Academician, Henry Hugh Armstead, one of the sculptors employed on the Albert Memorial.

Literature was not so well represented, but in the 1890s No. 52 was the home of Annie S. Swan, one of the kailyard school of Scottish novelists. Under her own (maiden) name, and under the pseudonym of David Lyall she wrote over 200 novels, many of them best-sellers.

Camden Square retained its quality well into the twentieth century – 'with its respectability still protected by a Square keeper', as the Booth survey noted in 1898 – and after the great men had gone it still attracted minor artists. At No. 4, with its fine north-lit studio in the garden, the part-time sculptors,

Numbers 27 and 28 Camden Square, Camden Town, on the south-east side, in 2007.

Walter Roche and his brother Mark, lived from the 1880s until the First World War. In the daytime they were postal officials. The square's commemorative plaques, however, are to none of these. Camden Council erected one for V.K. Krishna Menon, Indian High Commissioner, at No. 57, where he lived from 1924 to 1947, and the Magic Circle remembered the illusionist Robert Harbin at No. 1, his home in 1928.

Hard times came with the Second World War. St Paul's Church, with the houses to its west and south-west and some on the south-east side, were damaged by bombing, and more were demolished after the war than was necessary. Ugly council flats filled the artificially widened gap on the west side and, as modern techniques and materials made it possible to build above the tunnel, more flats appeared there. St Paul's was replaced in the 1950s, 'temporarily', by one of the most shoddy and hideous buildings even of that decade. Since 2008 there has been an acrimonious planning dispute about the modern Church's typically philistine proposals for a replacement.

The lower end of the garden has been sacrificed to a play school and games courts and the rest is public, but the remaining houses have risen to favour again with Camden Town.

Camden Square

PECKHAM [SOUTHWARK]

(later Rosemary Gardens)

The old Camden Square at Peckham had no connection with a more recent one, now also gone, except that their names both came from the Camden Chapel in Peckham Road. The original was built in the early 1840s just north of the Rosemary Branch Tavern, at the junction of what are now Southampton Way and Commercial Way. It was a cul-de-sac square with eight houses on the north side and five on the south, behind the pub. It had one unusual feature: the entrance from Southampton Street was quite wide, but a third of the way in it narrowed to an alley, making the rest of the square of the front garden type. The alley then continued beyond the square into what is now Chandler Way.

It was a reasonably respectable backwater. In 1851, when half the houses were still awaiting tenants, the residents included a doctor, a teacher, a barrister's clerk and a fund holder. William Bernard Cook, who produced the plates for some of the major topographical works of the early nineteenth century and engraved many of Turner's drawings, died at No. 9 in 1855. He was described as an annuitant in 1851.

The Booth survey was polite in 1899, '2½ storey houses, stucco faced, fronts done up, improved'. The LCC changed the name to Rosemary Gardens in 1938, perhaps changing its luck as well, for a few years later during the Blitz the south side was destroyed and the north side seriously damaged. It had been cleared by 1954 and Rosemary Gardens had become a playground, but housing now occupies the site, which lies between Branch Street and Lidgate Road.

Camera Square

CHELSEA [KENSINGTON AND CHELSEA]

In its later days Camera Square was confusing and unsatisfactory because the roads ran in various directions without any focal point to unify them. Beresford Chancellor described it in 1907: 'Camera Square is to-day anything you like to call it – except a square. Its houses of tiny proportions; its ground of unequal elevation; its shape which might defy the most exact logician to properly define …' It was not always so.

Building began in 1821 with the smaller houses, but the ratebooks counted them as part of Camera Street until 1825, when the completion of the larger houses prompted the change of name. The result was an orthodox square with a central garden and terraces on all four sides. The only eccentricities were that the terraces extended beyond the garden on the north and west sides, and that the houses on the north and east sides had long front gardens. In the size and date of its houses and the class of tenants at which they were aimed, it might be compared with Edwardes Square at Kensington, although the communal garden was much smaller.

The square's celebrity was the Shakespearean actor William Blanchard, a famous Polonius, who died at No. 1 in 1835. It was also the childhood home

The north side of Camera Square, *c.* 1910.

of his son, Edward Laman (or Leman) Blanchard, the writer and actor, who devised the Drury Lane pantomimes from 1852 to 1888.

Perhaps the long front gardens of the houses made the tenants careless about the management and upkeep of the central garden. Whatever the reason, things went wrong in the 1860s when four quite large semi-detached houses were built over the west end of the garden. They were soon joined by seventeen very small houses in three tightly packed terraces facing the other three sides. From that moment all coherence was lost, something recognised officially in 1879 when the east side was numbered as part of Beaufort Street. Socially the square was very mixed, with wealthy people occupying the houses east of Beaufort Street, respectable tenants on the north side, but much poverty on the south and in Little Camera Street, the southern offshoot.

At the beginning of the First World War the growing prosperity of Chelsea encouraged the owners to plan the total rebuilding of Camera Square. A new name, Chelsea Park Gardens, was approved in 1915 but the severe restrictions on building during the war meant that the new development was not forward enough to be numbered until 1920. Nothing of Camera Square survives. The nearest examples of houses of the size and style of the terraces formerly round the square can be seen in Park Walk, north of St John's Church.

Campden Hill Square

In 1823 Joshua Hanson bought the site of Campden Hill Square from the Lloyd family, formerly of Aubrey House, which stands immediately to the south-west. Hanson was a property speculator then busy with the development of the similar Regency Square in Brighton, built between 1818 and 1828, where the Channel makes a more exciting fourth side than Holland Park Avenue.

It has been said that Hanson Square was the name originally intended, but the first document, a sewer application made in 1826, calls it Notting Hill Square. So it remained until 1893, when the present name was substituted. Adam Wayne's raid on the water tower in *The Napoleon of Notting Hill* (1904) might therefore be considered as the natural expression of a policy of *anschluss*. The 1826 application and a few later ones were made on Hanson's behalf by Edward Valentine of Furnival's Inn, an obscure architect and surveyor. Given the similarity with Regency Square, with which Valentine is not known to have been involved, the overall layout was probably Hanson's. Valentine may have dealt with the technical details and designed the early houses.

The first was No. 2, which Hanson occupied from 1828 to 1830. Number 52 was probably intended for

Valentine, but he never lived there and Hanson let it in 1831. These are near the bottom of the hill on the east and west sides, but building was also underway on the south side, for which Hanson had sold most of the plots in 1826 and 1828. Stephen Garrard, a solicitor who acted for Hanson, lived at No. 18 from 1828.

In May 1830 an unfurnished five-bedroom house in 'Notting Hill Square near Bayswater … delightfully situated at the top', was advertised to be let. That was the year in which Hanson's active involvement with the development ended. It had evidently not been a great financial success, but he had done enough to determine its general form and style. He laid out the large central garden and arranged for its upkeep by a committee of residents, and he stipulated building standards in his leases and sales. The most important were that the houses should be in exposed brick not stucco above the ground floor and should have front gardens of a uniform length.

The evidence of the houses built between 1826 and 1830 suggests that Hanson intended the kind of architectural unity possessed by Regency Square, but the ownership was fragmented after his withdrawal and progress was very slow during the difficult 1830s. The owners carried out their separate schemes at various dates between 1830 and 1851, which meant that Hanson's covenants were the only disciplines imposed. In general terms the northern houses of the east and west sides and the central houses of the south side were the earliest, but the progress was halting and haphazard. This was a positive recommendation to the Victorians. In 1899 the Booth surveyor commented:

> Old fashioned houses, mostly three floors and basement. Some have been modernised, and one new red bricked house (five floors) has been sandwiched between two of the older houses. Houses are clean and well kept, and there is a delightful absence of the uniformity that characterises most West End roads.

The numbering was settled at an early stage and grossly overestimated the quantity that would be needed, but the surplus numbers proved useful when extra houses were built off the north-west corner before and after the Second World War.

The south side of Notting Hill Square, now Campden Hill Square, in 1893.

Campden Hill Square was very respectable in the nineteenth century, but did not become fashionable until the second half of the twentieth. It has long been popular with writers. Norman MacColl, editor of *The Athenaeum* for thirty years, died at No. 4 in 1904. Evelyn Underhill, the theologian, lived at No. 50 from 1907 to 1940, and Siegfried Sassoon at No. 23 from 1925 to 1932. Charles Morgan and his wife Hilda Campbell Vaughan, both novelists, lived at No. 16 from 1933. He died there in 1958. Morgan had the odd fate of being regarded as a great writer by the French, while English critics never took him seriously. When he was made a member of the Institut de France in 1949 he wrote, 'Yes, there are other English "Immortals", Winston for example, but no other novelist except Kipling. I think I am at any rate unique in having bought the uniform!' Did he light up the square with his 'embroidered *habit vert*'?

More recently, Lady Antonia Fraser, the biographer, has lived at No. 52 with her husbands, Hugh Fraser and Harold Pinter. She persuaded Fraser to buy the house in 1959, acquired it from him in a swap after the break-up of their marriage, and was joined there by Pinter in 1977. She got a good deal because 'Notting Hill was not yet fashionable, and our house had twice been badly damaged by bombs, in the war and 1975'. Pinter, another writer more appreciated abroad than at home, lived here until his death in 2008. In 1979 he bought a small house at the bottom of the garden, in Aubrey Road, as a study. The square is normally very peaceful, but No. 52 was the focus of an IRA car bomb attack in 1975, shortly after Antonia Fraser moved out. Caroline Kennedy, daughter of

John F., was coincidentally staying there at the time, but the bomb was intended for Hugh Fraser, a former cabinet minister. It killed a neighbour, Gordon Hamilton-Fairlie.

As mentioned by the Booth surveyor, No. 18 was rebuilt in an aggressively clashing style in 1887–88, breaking up what was evidently a formal three-house centrepiece to the south side. It matters less here than in most squares.

The only serious Second World War damage was in the south-west corner, where a flying bomb took out five or six houses and the blast damaged others. The tactful replacements step down gradually in height and recede modestly from the building line. The steep hill on which it is built makes this the most exciting of the squares. The garden tumbles down dramatically to Holland Park Avenue. The square is illuminated on Christmas Eve with candles in the windows, a traditional London form of celebration, frequently in the past of an unpleasantly compulsory nature. Here, nobody thinks of breaking the windows of any Scrooges or other nonconformists.

The east side of Campden Hill Square in 2007.

Canonbury Square

CANONBURY [ISLINGTON]

Canonbury Tower, which stands just off the north-east corner of Canonbury Square, is the surviving fragment of the manor house, occasional home of the earls of Northampton until they built a new house further south (see Northampton Square) in the 1660s. When the 9th Earl of Northampton began to develop his Canonbury estate at the turn of the eighteenth and nineteenth centuries he laboured under two disadvantages: the land was well in advance of the London building line and the country was engaged in a long and expensive war. It may have been the short-lived Peace of Amiens that emboldened him to make a start, but by the time a builder had been found and agreements made war had begun again.

The developer was Henry Jacob Leroux, son of Jacob of the Polygon, who took a large area of land from the earl in 1803 on a ninety-nine-year building lease. He began his operations in Upper Street with the Union Chapel and the central part of Compton Terrace, but by 1805 there was mention of 'an intended square designed to be called Canonbury Square'. Leroux built the terrace at the western end of the north side of the square (Nos 42–47, 47 now demolished) and probably the two detached houses, Nos 48

Number 48 Canonbury Square in 2007.

and 39. He may also have begun the rest of the north side, which was finished by others between 1809 and 1818. Number 39, Northampton Lodge, a villa with a large private garden, Leroux probably intended for himself. If so, such grandiose plans were ended when on Christmas Day 1809 the newspapers announced the bankruptcy of H.J. Leroux of Canonbury-square, Islington, builder.

By 1809 Leroux's operations had been disrupted and his financial problems exacerbated by the planning and building of the New North Road, now Canonbury Road, which was opened in 1812. It ran through the centre of the square, dividing it into two halves with separate gardens. The road was both a symptom and a cause of Canonbury's closer integration with London and ensured that the square was a different, more urban place when building resumed after the end of the war.

For many years Richard Laycock had leased much of Canonbury and Barnsbury for his dairy farms and cattle lairs (see Albert Square), and he had taken over Leroux's land after his failure. In 1821, during a great building boom, Laycock reached an agreement with Lord Northampton (now the 1st Marquess) for the building of the south and east sides of the square. Laycock was a farmer not a builder, so he must have employed others to do the work. They began at the west end of the south side, where the terrace up to Canonbury Road was built between 1823 and 1829. The rest of the south side and the east side were built in the late 1820s and early 1830s.

For the next few decades Canonbury was very well placed to be a popular residential district, linked to the City by a new and convenient road but with open fields immediately adjoining to the north and east. The houses were occupied by merchants and lawyers, with a few doctors and private schools. The best-known school was the Reverend Arthur Johnson's at No. 36, where Joseph Chamberlain was a pupil from 1846 to 1850. He described his master as 'one of the handsomest men I have ever seen'.

A few literary and theatrical celebrities leavened the mass of solid citizens. Ebenezer Jones, a poet whose work was not appreciated until long after his death, was born on the north side in 1820. The satirical poet George Daniel lived at No. 18 and assembled there

The garden of Canonbury Square, *c.* 1910, looking towards the south-east corner.

a collection of Shakespeare first editions that caused great excitement when auctioned after his death in 1864. The most colourful early resident was the actor Samuel Phelps, manager of Sadler's Wells, who lived at No. 8 from 1844 to 1867.

The square declined with the rest of Islington later in the nineteenth century, which is why the gardens were opened to the public by the 4th Marquess of Northampton in 1884. In 1897 the Booth survey reported 'only 2 or 3 houses now inhabited by one family. Going down.'

The decline continued in the first half of the twentieth century, but the flats into which the houses were by then divided still attracted notable residents. The paths of the upwardly-mobile Lancing boy Evelyn Waugh, and the downwardly-mobile old-Etonian George Orwell both passed through Canonbury Square. Waugh lived at No. 17a during his disastrous first marriage in 1928–29, and Orwell at No. 27b from 1944 to 1947. Part of the square was then bomb damaged and derelict. At the end of this bohemian period, Duncan Grant and Vanessa Bell occupied No. 26a in the mid-1950s. That was when the rebuilding of the bombed houses at the east end of the north side and the restoration of the gardens began the gentrification of the square that has gathered pace ever since. Now only the relentless traffic along Canonbury Road detracts from the charm of a beautiful square.

Canonbury Park Square

See Alwyne Square

Canterbury Square

SOUTHWARK

Canterbury Square was part of a late eighteenth-century attempt to improve the Tooley Street area, a movement that also produced the Magdalen Street circus. Canterbury Square and Dean Street were complete at the time of Horwood's 1790s map, and the name appeared in the Old Bailey records for 1795 and on Cary's map of the same year. Rocque's map of the 1740s showed Flower de Lis Court more or less on the site of the later square and Flower de Lis Yard on the line afterwards taken by Dean Street.

Canterbury Square was of three sides, being open to Dean Street on the west, and had only nine houses. It was not separately numbered but consisted of Nos 30–38 Dean Street, an oddity that sometimes led to confusion: Johnstone's 1817 directory claimed that there were thirty-six houses in the square. An archway in the centre of the east side gave access to the older Silver Street. The square was demolished in 1836 to make way for London Bridge Station, which was opened in that year. The London Dungeon is now more or less on, or under, the site.

Its unfashionable location and early extinction were not likely to associate any great names with Canterbury Square, but it was a good business address, popular with estate agents, surveyors and attorneys, and it did have one notable resident. In the 1790s the landlord of the Canterbury Arms was the Welsh poet and republican John Jones, who popularised the ideas of Thomas Paine in his native Denbighshire and among London's large Welsh community.

Car Square

CITY OF LONDON

Car Square and Moor Square were tiny twins off the west side of Moor Lane, Cripplegate, the sites of both now covered by Willoughby House, Barbican. Maps of 1676 and 1720 (the second perhaps largely based on the first) showed Car Yard off Moor Lane, but its position corresponded with the later Moor Square rather than with Car Square. It was either the Ramshead Court or the Seven Star Court of the 1676 and 1720 maps that developed into Car Square, or possibly a combination of the two during a comprehensive rebuilding. It was called Star Court in 1746, but had become Car Square by the 1760s. The name was sometimes written as 'Carr'.

This was an even smaller place than its neighbour Moor Square, with only seven or eight houses often harbouring several families. In 1851 a number of the residents were porters and shoemakers, and cheap lodging houses were always a feature. The place can never have had any social pretensions, this being the very poor Grub Street area. Car Square was demolished during the extension of the Metropolitan Railway in 1864–65.

Carey Square

WOOLWICH [GREENWICH]

Carey (or Carey's) Square was a small court off the east side of Star & Garter Yard, between Powis Street and Union Buildings. The pub's skittle alley was at its south-west corner. There were only three or four houses, with front gardens protruding into the open

space, plus a few stables. The tenants were labourers, gardeners, washerwomen.

Union Buildings and Union Street were an early nineteenth-century development on land belonging to the Powis brewing family, and named after the parliamentary union with Ireland. Union Buildings is now Creton Street, but the Star & Garter, its Yard and the skittle alley are long gone. The Carey Square houses were swept away in the 1890s, most of the land being added to the gardens of houses in Creton Street, but the name remained in use a little longer for the alley between Star & Garter Yard and Creton Street, which was all that remained. The site is now a car park.

Carfax Square

CLAPHAM [LAMBETH]

Carfax Square, which lay off the west side of Clapham Park Road opposite Triangle Place, was built in the mid-1870s as an instant slum. There were twenty-two houses on the three sides. In the centre, where a garden should have been, were three houses facing Clapham Park Road and a Plymouth Brethren hall behind. Except for the hall, it was similar to Gillray Square at Chelsea.

In 1899 Carfax Square was described as, '2½ storey, roadway dirty and many of the houses, dirty children playing. Houses more modern and worse built than most in this poor area.' The hall and a number of the houses were badly damaged during the war, and in the 1970s the opportunity was taken to extinguish the square (with its little neighbour Acre Square) and build the Carfax Estate on the site.

Carlisle Square

LAMBETH

Carlisle Square was built late in the eighteenth century. It lay between Carlisle Lane and Upper Marsh, close to their junction with Westminster Bridge Road. A glance at a map will show why it no longer exists: the railway viaduct running into Waterloo Station destroyed it. It was a cul-de-sac square of about eleven houses, three at the west end and four or five to north and south. The east was open to Carlisle Lane. The building of the original viaduct between 1845 and 1848 removed the south and east sides of the square. The north survived until the tracks were widened in the 1870s. The site had a curious fate, as between 1902 and 1941 it was part of the sidings for the second terminus of the London Necropolis Railway, which took coffins and mourners to Brookwood Cemetery. The station closed after bomb damage, but its entrance survives as Westminster Bridge House.

Carlton Square

The East End Carlton Square was built in the early 1850s as the centrepiece of the Globe Fields estate at Mile End. The layout has been attributed to the architects Henry Lawrence Hammack and Thomas John Lambert of Bishopsgate, as surveyors to the landowner, William Pemberton Barnes. Hammack and Lambert, who had connections with Stepney and

Bow, were best known for their ornate public houses. The simple two-storey terraces of Carlton Square, standard designs of the period, would scarcely have needed the individual attention of an architect.

Very oddly, although more than thirty houses and the Lion pub faced the little garden, only the nine on the north side had Carlton Square as their address, the other three sides being counted as parts of longer streets.

As Carlton Square was poor and in an area with few parks, it became one of the early projects of the Metropolitan Public Gardens Association, which redesigned and replanted the garden and opened it to the public in 1885. The association was unable to afford the upkeep, a responsibility that was taken over by the LCC in 1890.

The south-east corner of the square, with the Lion, was lost to bomb damage during the Second World War. Here the houses were not replaced and the original garden now opens into a larger park created by the LCC in the 1960s and known as Carlton Square Gardens. On the north side Nos 5–9 are original; Nos 1–4 have been rebuilt in a paraphrase rather than a facsimile of their neighbours.

The garden of Carlton Square, Mile End, in 1907 or a little earlier.

Carlton Square

(later Pomeroy Square)

Carlton Square at New Cross, which was built in 1845, was a surprisingly formal and classical composition for its time and place. At the short west end there was a palace front – a miniature Balkan palace – with the name and date of the square in the pediment, and there were pediments also to the two houses at the corner of Pomeroy Street, which were set forward from the building line of the north and south sides to give added privacy and quietness.

The layout was unusual: the five houses at the west end were advanced, making the garden nearly square, but the houses on the north and south sides were splayed, so as to extend beyond the west side. This meant that four of the ten houses on the north and five of the eleven on the south side did not face the garden. The square lay off the west side of Pomeroy Street, near the north end. The houses on the east side of Pomeroy Street were built at the same time as the square but were pointedly excluded from it by the narrowed entrance, perhaps because one of them was a beerhouse called the Carlton Arms. The square, with its carefully planted private garden, clearly had social pretensions that a beerhouse might have undermined.

While never attaining to gentility Carlton Square continued to be thoroughly respectable during the nineteenth century, being classified as pink for 'fairly comfortable, good average earnings' on the two editions of the Booth poverty map. It was built in the parish of St Paul Deptford but became part of the new Camberwell Borough when the boundaries were simplified in 1900.

Another change came in the 1930s, when the LCC decided to call it Pomeroy Square, while confirming the original name to the younger Carlton Square in the East End. It did not long survive the shock of this change of name. The bulldozers came in the 1970s, and when a new square was built nearly on the same site, as part of a large housing estate, it was not called Carlton or Pomeroy, but Montague Square.

Carlyle Square

Carlyle Square might do as well as Robert Bruce to illustrate a sermon on perseverance. It is now one of the most expensive and exclusive in London, but in its early days it was notable, even in Chelsea, for its conspicuous failure. The original name was Oakley Square, the landowner from 1835 being, among other good things, Baron Cadogan of Oakley. The change to Carlyle Square was made in 1872 in compliment to Chelsea's most famous resident. It also marked a fresh

Carlton Square, New Cross, *c.* 1845.

start, like the renaming of a failing school, as the square had only just been completed after more than thirty years.

Oakley Square had been laid out in 1836 and the first six houses were built in 1837–38. The builder was the prominent local man Samuel Archbutt, father of Thomas Archbutt of Ovington Square. Any schoolboy can identify these original houses. The short terraces at the King's Road end of the west and east sides (Nos 1–3 and 40–42) are grandiose, the ground floor rusticated, a balcony on the first, and the central house adorned with four pilasters. This was evidently the pattern that Lord Cadogan wished to see repeated throughout the square: No. 1 was his estate office.

If tenants and builders had co-operated, it might have been one of the finest in London. Instead, the development stalled. Nothing more was built in the 1830s or 1840s, and in the 1850s only two semi-detached pairs next to the original terrace on the east side and three individually named houses on the north. Those sides were nearly complete by 1865, but the east was not filled in until 1867. The various builders made no effort to conform to the original style and were careless in matching their houses with the other new ones, even in such a basic point as the building line.

The east side of Carlyle Square, *c.* 1905.

Numbers 42–40 Carlyle Square in 2007.

Carlyle Square, like much of Chelsea, had a raffish reputation in the nineteenth century. Things began to change when Osbert and his brother Sacheverell Sitwell moved to No. 2 in 1919 and formed a salon that was one of the centres of modernism in London. It also became a temporary refuge for various friends and hangers-on. The most famous was William Walton, who was given a pension and a room in the attic, where he spent his time, according to Osbert, 'eating bags of black cherries and throwing the stones out of the window on to unsuspecting passers-by'. That was a game requiring patience if the square was as unfrequented then as it is today.

The 1922 premiere of *Façade*, Walton's first successful work, was given in the drawing room of No. 2. Osbert Sitwell continued to live there until 1963, when infirmity and domestic complications obliged him to move to a flat. Other literary and artistic figures followed the Sitwells' lead in the 1920s.

Sybil Thorndike, Lewis Casson and John Casson, for example, lived at No. 6, where there is a Sybil Thorndike plaque, from 1921 to 1932.

Most of the houses in Carlyle Square suffered minor blast damage during the war, but nothing that could not be quickly and seamlessly repaired. Since then it has become less bohemian and increasingly exclusive. When Edna O'Brien lived at No. 10 in the 1970s and early 1980s – she bought the house with the £39,000 she got for a screenplay – she found her neighbours 'fastidious' and disapproving. One of them was the 9th (and last) Duke of Portland, who died at No. 21 in 1990. David Frost, who lived at No. 22, was a more popular celebrity.

The present nature of the square and its residents is well indicated by the fact that when I made a photographic survey a police car drew up beside me within five minutes of my taking out the camera and the officers observed me silently until I left, the survey complete.

Carmarthen Square

BLOOMSBURY [CAMDEN]

The University of London, that great destroyer of squares, began its career in appropriate style by snuffing out this projected square to the east of Gower Street. It was shown boldly enough on layout plans for the Bedford estate and in the 1813 and 1819 editions of Horwood's map of London, but with so many new squares to be dealt with in Bloomsbury the tide of building advanced slowly and almost nothing had been done when the land was acquired as the site for University College in 1825–26.

The undated *Plan of Carmarthen Square* in the Crace Collection, showing only a ragged open space east of Gower Street, was no doubt intended to interest builders in the scheme. It probably brought the land to the notice of the founders of the university instead. The Horwood maps indicated four houses at the south-west corner of the square, which may have survived for a time. Greenwood's maps of 1827 and 1830 showed them coexisting with the unfinished college, but an 1830 estate map does not. The name of the square came immediately from Carmarthen Street, which became University Street before 1830.

Caroline Square

BROMLEY-BY-BOW [TOWER HAMLETS]

The little Caroline Square, a few cottages around a yard of irregular shape, existed for only about forty years. It was built in the 1840s in Four Mills Street, nearly opposite the Four Mills Distillery, but Four Mills Street was soon afterwards renamed St Leonard's Street. That still survives further north, but the section that contained the square, south of the Limehouse Cut, was destroyed about 1960 when the Blackwall Tunnel northern approach was built. Caroline Square, which was north of the junction of St Leonard's Street and St Leonard's Road, had been demolished long before that, when the School Board for London built St Leonard's Road School in its place in the 1880s. The site of the square and school is roughly where the northern arm of Teviot Street meets the A12.

Carr Square

See Car Square

Cartwright Square

Cartwright Street was formerly a cul-de-sac named Churchyard Alley, and Cartwright Square was part of a complex of lanes and yards at its southern end known as Crown Court. That name continued in use for the remainder after the largest courtyard became Cartwright Square between 1746 and 1792. Cartwright Street existed as a name by 1768, and perhaps as early as the 1720s, as an occasional alternative to Churchyard Alley. The square had eighteen houses at the end of the century, but whether they were built before the change of name it is impossible to tell from the maps. As a fashion for squares swept the City in the 1770s, it is most likely that the court was rebuilt and renamed then, or in the 1780s.

Many of the residents kept lodging houses and others were seafarers, tailors and woolcombers. The square was demolished as a slum by the Metropolitan Board of Works, under powers granted by the Artisans' Dwellings Act of 1875. The board altered the street pattern, extending Cartwright Street across the site of the square to make a through road to East Smithfield. In 1883 the East End Dwellings Company bought much of the land to its west and built tenements on the site of the square, facing the new part of Cartwright Street. But while one square was being destroyed by this slum clearance drive, another (Royal Mint Square) was being created at the north end of Cartwright Street.

Castle Square

Castle Square was an alternative name for Castle Court, a turning off the south side of Old Castle Street in the notorious Nichol area of Shoreditch and Bethnal Green. Old Castle Street already existed (as Castle Street) in the 1790s, and there was a Castle Court off the south side, but it did not have the same form as the later court and square. As more streets were squeezed in to the south it was shortened and compressed, and probably rebuilt. In its final form the nine or ten cottages were reached via an archway and were hidden from sight round a corner.

Hector Gavin described the place in 1848 in his *Sanitary Ramblings*: 'This court is abominably filthy; it has never been cleaned in sixteen or seventeen months; the yards and gutters are full of foetid fluid … The inhabitants complained loudly, deeply, and bitterly of the state of their court, and would willingly contribute 4*d* per week for relief.' The LCC swept it away with the rest of the slum in the 1890s, when it was replaced by Arnold Circus and its spokes.

Castle Square

Castle Square was a typical piece of back development in everything except its late date, for it was not built until the 1880s. Earlier maps showed an alley leading north from Rosemary Lane (now Road) to a single building that might have been a house or a stable with a small piece of vacant land to the east. It was there that Castle Square was built, a terrace of five two-storey houses on the east side, with two more attached to the terrace at right angles forming the south. The original building was left in sole possession of the north side and as much of the west as was not required for access. The centre was a patch of worn grass.

It got a fairly good report from the Booth survey in 1899: 'Castle Square, north-east corner of Rosemary Road, five or six 3 and 4 roomed cottages, the former letting at 7/- and said by an occupier to be dear at half the price, but not a bad looking little corner'.

Castle Square survived until the late 1950s, but was replaced soon afterwards by flats called Shurland Gardens, the name of which was approved in 1962.

Catherine Square

Catherine Square was built behind the houses on the north side of Artillery Place in 1843. The immediate position must have seemed a good one with the garden of Rushgrove House to the north-west and Mulgrave Pond to the north-east, but the larger picture was not so favourable, the Royal Artillery and Royal Marine barracks both being nearby.

Three of the five houses were in a terrace on the north side, the other two forming short wings to east and west. South of the court were the gardens of the Artillery Place houses. Whatever promise the situation had was not fulfilled. In 1900 the Booth survey described it as 'one of the roughest in the district. Five 3 storey houses looking on to a broad asphalted court, tap in center, built 1843. Irish, fights, a drunken row most nights. Mess of paper, no bread, children dirty.'

The square and the Artillery Place shops and houses in front were demolished early in the twentieth century. The Queen Victoria Memorial Children's Home, opened in 1909, was built on the frontage, with a yard behind where the square had been. The home, which was damaged in the Second World War, has now been demolished and the site of Catherine Square is occupied by the car park behind Centurion Court.

Catherine Wheel Square

CITY OF LONDON

John Lockie included Catherine Wheel Square in the 1813 edition of his *Topography of London*, but not in 1810. He gave its position as first on the left from Bishopsgate in Catherine Wheel Alley. The first turning on the left shown on the 1813 Horwood map was the short stubby southern section of Sandys Street that John Wallis called Sandy Square (q.v.) in 1801. It is just possible that the two were identical, but the 1873 Ordnance Survey included a much more square-like court at the second bend of Catherine Wheel Alley, a few yards south-west of Sandys Street, running back towards Bishopsgate. Horwood showed little more than an open space there, but if it did exist in 1813 it would have been the first on the left in the alley.

In 1841 the residents of the four cottages in Catherine Wheel Square included two porters, a carman and a mangler. By 1851 the number of houses had been increased to seven, into which twenty families were squeezed. The square did not appear in the 1861 census, but in 1871 there were entries for 'Dwellings in Catherine Wheel Alley known as Barker's Model Dwellings'. The 1873 map showed the tenements on the north and west sides of the court, with four houses on the south side. The building of the tenements did not obliterate the square.

There was a fire at Barker's Buildings, Catherine Wheel Square, in 1876, and in 1878 a man was charged with whipping a boy in Catherine Wheel Square. The place was then described as a court. In 1881 the thirty flats of Barker's Industrial Dwellings were occupied by single people and small families. The number of flats had been reduced to twenty-two in 1891, and by 1894 Barker's Buildings and the square had been overwhelmed by the growth of the shops and offices in Bishopsgate. This period of great change, when Middlesex Street was widened and extended to Bishopsgate, also saw the extinction of Sandys Street.

Cavendish Square

MARYLEBONE [WESTMINSTER]

Cavendish Square was laid out in 1717 for Edward, Lord Harley, later 2nd Earl of Oxford, by his surveyor John Prince. It was at first sometimes known as Oxford Square, but the permanent name was a just compliment to Harley's wife, Lady Henrietta Cavendish Holles, who had brought the estate to him as her marriage portion.

Number 20 Cavendish Square as the Cowdray Club in 1928.

'Oxford Square, in Tyburn Road', was William Stow's listing in 1722. Daniel Defoe, wondering at the prodigious growth of London between 1688 and 1725, referred to 'that new City on the North Side of Tyburn Road, called Cavendish-square, and all the Streets about it'. Later it was occasionally called Old Cavendish Square by contagion from Old Cavendish Street. Defoe described it as a city because John Prince, the self-styled 'Prince of Surveyors', had surrounded the square with a network of service streets, and provided the Oxford Market and the Oxford Chapel, intending to make it self-sufficient.

It was promoted to potential purchasers, many of them expected to be politicians or officials, as being more convenient for Westminster than older rivals like Red Lion or Bloomsbury Square. Robert Harley, the 1st Earl, was still alive and leading the dispirited Tory party in 1717, and it was from his friends and supporters that the early residents of the square were mostly drawn. In fact, it was a Tory counterblast to the predominantly Whig Hanover Square of a few years earlier. But if their creators were in deadly enmity at Westminster, here in Mayfair and Marylebone they co-operated in one of the West End's few examples of large-scale town planning. The long vista through the squares to and from St George's Church, available until the fashion for planting gardens obscured it, was one that even the severest critics could not fail to admire.

Defoe may have judged Cavendish Square more from Prince's plan, published in 1719, than from progress on the ground, as only one or two of the houses were occupied in 1725. The economic troubles of the country in the wake of the South Sea Bubble had slowed progress and by the time trade revived the bigger and better Grosvenor Square had begun to distract the attention of house seekers.

Cavendish Square was modelled on Bloomsbury Square, with the whole of the north side reserved for a single house, open to the fields behind. The Duke of Chandos, who had made a fortune as Paymaster in Harley's government, took this large plot, intending to build a palace there. The first architect involved was John Price (not Prince) who sketched an elevation in 1720; he was succeeded by Edward Shepherd, now only remembered as the creator of Shepherd Market. Some preparations were made, but Chandos lost money in the Bubble and Shepherd built only a pair of houses at the two ends of the north side, the centre remaining empty for fifty years. Chandos occupied the house at the north-west corner.

The north side of Cavendish Square in 1813.

Most of the west side was taken by Lord Bingley, formerly Harley's Chancellor of the Exchequer, who employed John Wood of Bath to design a large house for him there around 1724. There was a private garden behind, extending to Wimpole Street. The house was never admired, coming within half a century to be regarded as the nadir of Palladian dullness, with 'the same gloomy exterior as Burlington house' and the interior no better. It was known as Harcourt House (see p.11) from 1773 and was later owned by the Dukes of Portland. The eccentric and reclusive 5th Duke lived behind its high walls until his death in 1879.

There was also a big house at the south end of the east side, designed by Thomas Archer for Lord Harcourt, Harley's Lord Chancellor. The builder, Edward Wilcox, altered Archer's design as he proceeded with the work. Lord Harcourt died there in 1727, but it remained in the family until the 1760s. They shortly afterwards acquired Bingley House on the opposite side of the square, to which they transferred the name of Harcourt House. Most of the square was completed during the 1730s, but a few houses were not occupied until the 1740s or 1750s and the two fine villas that fill the centre of the north side were built only in 1769.

In 1771 the square fell foul of John Stewart's distaste for the *rus in urbe*:

> … the apparent intention here was to excite pastoral ideas in the mind; and this is endeavoured to be effected by cooping up a few frightened sheep within a wooden pailing; which, were it not for their sooty fleeces and meagre carcases, would be more apt to give the idea of a butcher's pen. [Art was better than nature, so] I would therefore recommend it to the next designer of country-in-town, to let all his sheep be painted. And I think if a paste-board mill, and tin cascade were to be added it would compleat the rural scene.

He was no happier with the modern dress statue of the Duke of Cumberland that replaced the sheep, remarking that the uniform might as well have been painted scarlet and blue 'as a pattern suit for the regimental taylors'.

The residents did not have to go far to find the real country, as the land to the north remained open for fifty years after building began in the square. J.T. Smith remembered that after taking a country walk with his mother in 1772 they 'entered London immediately behind the elegant mansions on the north side of Cavendish Square'.

The square was fashionable in the eighteenth century, with a number of dukes and earls among the residents. Even royalty patronised it: the Princess Amelia, daughter of George II, lived at No. 16, formerly the house of the Duke of Chandos, from 1760 until her death in 1786. Literature and fashion were represented by Lady Mary Wortley Montagu, who was an occasional resident from 1731 until her departure for the Continent in 1739. She was a close friend of the Countess of Oxford. The family had the big house on the south side, No. 19 on Horwood's maps but later several times renumbered and subdivided. Edward Wortley Montagu later moved to a smaller house, Horwood's No. 17. The John Lewis extension now stands on the site of both.

As fashion moved further west and south, Cavendish Square became associated with the arts. George Romney, known to his rival Reynolds as 'the man in Cavendish Square', lived at one of the smaller houses on the south side (No. 32, formerly 24) from 1775 to 1798. He sold the lease to Martin Archer Shee, later president of the Royal Academy, who remained until his retirement to Brighton in 1845. As Romney had bought the house from Francis Cotes, RA, its association with art and the Academy was a very long one. The house was demolished in 1904. Philip Hardwick, the architect, lived at No. 21, on the north corner of Henrietta Street, in the 1850s and 1860s. It doubled as the office of the Portman estate, of which Hardwick was surveyor.

In the nineteenth century, with Harley Street as one of its satellites, it was most famous as the haunt of fashionable doctors. 'Cavendish Square, that citadel of medicine,' Stevenson called it in 1885, in *The Strange Case of Dr Jekyll and Mr Hyde*. In 1905 nearly all the houses were occupied by doctors and dentists, but the Earl of Crawford was still at No. 2 and Viscount Duncannon at No. 17, and No. 20 was occupied by Asquith, soon to be prime minister. He was there from his marriage in 1894 until 1919, when not in Downing Street.

The philanthropist Quintin Hogg, father and grandfather of Lord Chancellors, lived at No. 5 until his death in 1903. The house communicated with the Regent Street Polytechnic, now Westminster University, which he revived in 1882. The most eminent doctors were Sir Jonathan Hutchinson, the expert on syphilis, at No. 15, and Sir Ronald Ross, who won the Nobel Prize for his work on malaria, at No. 18. Both houses have blue plaques. The unlikely name of the East End novelist Arthur Morrison has been given by the *Dictionary of National Biography* as a Cavendish Square resident of the 1920s, but he lived in York Mansions, Princes Street, the present John Princes Street.

The disintegration of the square began in 1893, when No. 9 on the north side, one of the Chandos pair, was replaced by luxury flats. Ten years later, Harcourt House on the east side was demolished and soon replaced by more flats, which took the same name. 'The Square has suffered, so far as the uniformity of its houses is concerned, by much rebuilding,' wrote Beresford Chancellor in 1907. The western half of the south side was demolished in the late 1930s to make way for the John Lewis extension, which was the most seriously damaged building in the square during the Second World War. The houses at the east end of the south side were demolished in the 1950s and replaced by a hideous office block. The final indignity was the destructive digging of an underground car park in 1970–71, with the loss of many trees and the severe curtailment of the garden.

Since then the tide has turned and the latest developments are more positive. The north side has been in a state of steady improvement since the war. The eastern house (No. 11) of the famous Palladian pair of 1769 was badly damaged by bombing, but it is hard to see any signs now unless the cleaner stonework and the patched bricks of the flank wall tell the tale of restoration. The awkward gap between the two villas was neatly filled in 1953 by Louis Osman's bridge, and now the flats at the east end have been demolished and replaced by a mirror image facsimile of Nos 15 and 16 at the west end, producing a symmetrical north side. Henry Keene's Nos 17 and 18 of 1756–57 are the highlights of the west side, and there are four houses of the 1720s, altered to various degrees, on the east.

The diminished public garden is very popular. Lord George Bentinck's statue, erected in 1851, shows that Cavendish Square remained a Tory stronghold, whereas the Whig influence on Hanover Square was transient. Pitt has presided there since the 1820s.

Chadwell Square

See Myddelton Square

Chalcot Square

PRIMROSE HILL [CAMDEN]

Chalcot Square was known as St George's Square until 1937, when the LCC gave exclusive use of that name to its slightly older Pimlico namesake. The land to the east and north-east of Regent's Park was part of the Southampton estate, the property of the Fitzroy family. They opened it up for development from south to north, beginning with Fitzroy Square in the 1790s, Euston Square from 1810 and Mornington Crescent in the 1820s.

In 1840 the land north of Regent's Park was sold, leading to the building of Gloucester Crescent and much of Regents Park Road in the 1840s. That left the Chalcot Farm fields between Regents Park Road and Chalk Farm Road to be dealt with. (Chalk Farm is just a variant form of Chalcot Farm.) The suggested layout for this area in the 1840 sale plan did not include a square, but proposed a circular plantation in the space now enclosed by Regents Park Road, Berkeley Road and Sharpleshall Street, and a smaller circle at the Chalcot Road and Fitzroy Road junction.

The oldest houses in the square are Nos 8–11 on the south side, which were built in the late 1840s, but it is not certain that even then they were intended to be part of a square. Their builder perhaps thought of them merely as a continuation of Alma Terrace, later St George's Road and now Chalcot Road. An 1851 map showed a naked square at the junction of Alma Terrace and Fitzroy Road, south-east of the present square, and that may possibly have been the first adjustment to the 1840 plan.

St George's Square, now Chalcot Square, in 1907 or a little earlier.

Alma Terrace existed for a decade before there was any development on the other three sides of St George's Square. Houses were built on the east and west sides only in the late 1850s, and on the north side in the late 1850s and early 1860s. Despite this halting progress, the houses facing directly onto the garden show a reasonable uniformity of style. The same cannot be said for the tall and gaunt Nos 34–39, set back from the garden in the south-west corner of the square. They were not built until the early 1870s, on part of the former pleasure gardens of the Chalk Farm Tavern in Regents Park Road.

The attempt to extend the world of fashion east and north of Regent's Park was never a great success and was running out of steam by the time it reached Chalcot Square, where the amenities of Primrose Hill were counteracted by the huge Chalk Farm marshalling yard to the north. The houses in the new square proved hard to let, attracted few eminent or wealthy residents and quickly fell into the hands of lodging-house keepers, vultures whose appearance marked the decay of a London square. In 1898 the Booth survey noted that it had 'gone down'.

Among the few celebrities was the scholar Frederick Furnivall, founder of the Early English Text Society and one of the creators of the *Oxford English Dictionary*. He lived at No. 3, but treated it as little more than lodgings, spending nearly all his waking hours in and around the British Museum. The square also appealed to artists: Harry Furniss lived at No. 10 in the 1880s and William Strang at No. 17 in the 1890s.

There was not much bombing in the area during the Second World War. The only houses seriously damaged were Nos 12–14 at the south-east corner, and they have been well restored.

The decline suffered by Chalcot Square during its first century has been more than recompensed by its rise since then. This began gradually after the war, for in the 1950s and 1960s it was still a place where young writers like Ted Hughes and Sylvia Plath could afford a flat. Her residence at No. 3 in 1960–61 is recorded by a blue plaque, and his name will presumably be added in due course. In 1960 he described it as 'a small flat in one of the most interesting corners of London – Victorian genteel houses overtaken by an Irish, Greek, Cypriot & Italian creeping damp'. Since the 1960s Chalcot Square has ceased to be a possible home for bohemians. Properties rarely come on the market, and when they do the prices are high.

If the rise in the fortunes of Chalcot Square had come sooner, the attractive and popular garden would probably have remained private, but the parents and children who use it seem responsible and well behaved and likely to cause the residents little annoyance. Gary Powell describes it as private, but if it is I must have been trespassing when I walked in and took photographs at will. The style of the houses and the gaily painted stucco of many of them – yellow, blue, salmon – gives the square something of a seaside atmosphere, an illusion aided by the cries of the seagulls that frequent the Regent's Canal. These might be boarding houses just off the front at Brighton.

Chamber Square

WAPPING [TOWER HAMLETS]

This little square of about fourteen houses had at least three names. It was Cooper's Rents on Strype's 1720 map and Watts Court during most of the eighteenth century. Early in the nineteenth it was in transition, and Lockie in 1810 gave a cross reference from Watt's Court (or Square) to Chamber Square. He defined its position as at No. 95 Upper East Smithfield, nearly opposite the London Docks. It was between Dock Street and the present John Fisher Street. The new name presumably had some reference to Chamber Street, although that was some way to the north.

The square led a charmed life during the nineteenth century, dodging railways, goods yards and slum clearance schemes, but fell a victim to commercial progress at the beginning of the twentieth century, when the Westminster Tobacco Company built a large warehouse on the site. Admiral House is there now.

Channelsea Square

STRATFORD [NEWHAM]

Channelsea Square was a name that emerged in the middle of the nineteenth century for the open space at the centre of an older network of working-class streets, formed between 1800 and 1820. It was named on the 1867 Ordnance Survey map, but because the houses surrounding it were numbered in Prospect Row and Channelsea Street it made no appearance in the census returns.

The name came from the Channelsea River, one of the natural and artificial tributaries of the Lea known collectively as the Bow Back Rivers. The Channelsea, which ran close to the east side of the square, was not the best neighbour: it was heavily polluted by industrial waste and suspected of being a carrier of cholera.

Many of the residents of the square and the surrounding streets were employed by the West Ham Gas Company, founded in 1846, which had its works immediately to the south.

The square had the potential to be large and airy, but two-thirds of the space was occupied by the long detached front gardens or allotments belonging to the cottages on the north side. These had existed before the square was formed and were known separately as Prospect Row. The gardens were divided from the cottages by a path. On the west side was the long terrace of Channelsea Street, which extended well to the south. On the east side were the back gardens of the houses in Channelsea Road, which faced the river.

South of the Prospect Row gardens was the open space that formed the real Channelsea Square, but even that was slightly reduced by a small infant school in its north-east corner. This was the cuckoo in the nest that was to destroy the square, for under the management of the School Board for London from the 1870s it swallowed up not only the open space but the Prospect Row front gardens. The Channelsea Square name continued in use for the school and sometimes for the Prospect Row cottages, but it no longer had any meaning.

Everything south of the school was demolished early in the twentieth century when the gasworks expanded, and the roads to north and west were cleared as slums shortly before the First World War. Prospect Row (renamed Channel Sea Street) lasted only a little longer, before being replaced by a rebuilt New Street. The whole area has been redeveloped again since the Second World War. The river has been hidden in a culvert and Kerrison Road is now on the site of the school and square.

Chant Square

Chant Square was created in the 1840s, its houses being among the first of the many thousands built for working people in the parish of West Ham during the reign of Queen Victoria. The Chant family owned the land. In 1851 the square was mainly occupied by bricklayers, carpenters and others engaged in the building trades.

The extraordinary thing about it was the disproportion between the large central garden and the diminutive houses, almost as great as at Edwardes Square in Kensington. Here there were quite long back gardens as well, though necessarily narrow. There were thirty or more tiny houses on the north and east sides of the square, and as many again in Chant Street on the west side and its continuation north to the High Street. Chant Street was sometimes counted as part of the square.

The south side remained open to the fields until the 1880s, when Pitchford Street was built as a continuation of Chant Street, and Bryant Street and Widdin Street filled the remaining space. From the 1870s a school, a hospital and a church hall had been built close to the square, and the growth of the first two increasingly hemmed it in. Chant Square survived the Second World War, but was swept away afterwards. The name has been revived for a modern upmarket successor, but it occupies only the northern half of the original and has a small paved oval in the centre, more like a traffic island than a garden.

Charles Square

In the 1680s enterprising builders experimented with squares in what were then the outer suburbs, far beyond the originals in Bloomsbury, Holborn and St James's. In the north the chief products were Hoxton Square and its neighbour Charles Square, loyally named in honour of the king. As it took nearly a century to complete the experiment was evidently not a great success.

The site of the north side, originally called Charles Street, and the northern halves of the east and west sides were included in a 900-year lease of 1684 from Isaac Honeywood to Anthony Ball and John Brown. They sublet the property to Charles Hills, who was the developer of the square, issuing building leases, for terms of about sixty years, between 1685 and 1690. A 1687 lease of one of the plots on the north side referred to the 'intended street called Charles Street'.

Some of the houses that survived into the twentieth century were of the 1680s, but others had apparently been rebuilt in the 1740s, when the leases expired. The Strype map published in 1720, but probably older, showed only the north and half of the east and west sides. The southern end of the west side was built in the 1720s and shown on Rocque's 1740s map. The south side was built over an orchard in the early 1770s and was known as Crocker's Row after William Crocker, the builder. Number 6 had a '1771' date stone, which was misread as '1776' by the Booth surveyor in 1898. These houses and those at the southern end of the east side, which were probably built at about the same time, were much smaller than the rest.

Hatton described it in 1708 as 'Charles Square, a pleasant tho' small one'. While Hoxton remained on the edge of London, which it did until the beginning of the nineteenth century, it was a popular residential square, especially with clergymen. The Reverend John Newton, the hymn writer and friend of William Cowper, lived on the north side from 1780 to 1786, enjoying views of the handsome trees in the central garden from his front windows and of open meadows from the back. The square's other celebrity was Frederick Catherwood, whose drawings of Mayan ruins did more than anything to bring that lost civilisation to the notice of the world. He was born in Charles Square in 1799 and continued to live there in the rare intervals when he was not travelling the world.

It became increasingly commercial in the nineteenth century, with cabinet makers and upholsterers predominating, but as from the 1840s the Shoreditch Crown Court was at No. 16, the largest of the 1720s houses at the south end of the west side, a number of solicitors continued to live in the square, preserving many of the houses in good condition into the twentieth century.

The garden was opened to the public in 1898, and is now a paved open space with trees and flower beds. There was serious bomb damage on the north side in the Second World War and afterwards everything except the Crown Court was replaced by council flats. Now the dignified No. 16, with its legal embellishments removed, stands forlornly among its plebeian neighbours, like better company at Tyburn tree.

Number 23 Charles Square, Hoxton, in 1922.

Charles Square

Charles Square was the name under which the late eighteenth-century Charles Court masqueraded during its last decades. It was a turning off the north side of Charles Street, now Raine Street, which is itself a minor offshoot from the east side of Old Gravel Lane, now Wapping Lane. Charles Court was still the name in 1813, but by 1840 Charles Square had taken over.

There were twenty houses, with many sailors, watermen and dockers among the tenants. It was lucky to survive the building of the London Dock in the first decade of the nineteenth century and the Eastern Dock in the 1820s. The square was finally destroyed when the No. 10 warehouse removed the north side of Charles Street in the 1850s. Part of the wall of the warehouse is incorporated into the flats that stand there now. The position of the square can still be easily found, as its entrance was opposite the beautiful Raine's charity school of 1719, which survives miraculously on the south side of Raine Street.

Charlotte Square

Charlotte Square grew slowly, and the builder probably had no original thought of its final form. The two houses of the short west side appeared on the Horwood map of the 1790s, but the north and south sides were not added until about 1820, when the area between Snowsfields and Long Lane was being developed rapidly. The east side was formed by West Street, later Lockyer Street, which is now only represented by a short stub at its southern end.

In the census returns the square generally appeared as Charlotte Place, but it was marked as Charlotte Square on the 1872 map. It began to disintegrate soon afterwards, the agent of destruction being Laxon Street School, now Beormund School. From its foundation in the 1870s the school grew relentlessly, removing first the greater part of Laxon Street, then one side of West Street and the north and west sides of Charlotte Square. Shortly after the Second World War the whole

of Laxon Street and the south side of the square were overwhelmed. The surviving fragment of Lockyer Street was originally called Little Charlotte Row.

Charterhouse Square

Charterhouse Square was usually known as Charterhouse Yard until the beginning of the eighteenth century. Despite its unpromising origin as the monastery's graveyard, and perhaps before that as a site for Black Death burial pits, it developed into a fashionable, aristocratic place of residence during the reigns of the Tudors and Stuarts, an almost suburban retreat from the bad air of the City and the Court. But as it was an unplanned cluster of houses gathered around an existing open space it cannot challenge the claim of Covent Garden to be the first genuine London square.

The Carthusian monastery founded in 1370 was suppressed in 1537. It was the home of various leading courtiers until 1611, when Thomas Sutton bought it for conversion into a school and almshouses. The open space outside the gate, known variously as Charterhouse Yard, Churchyard, Precinct and Close, became fashionable even before the Dissolution and more so afterwards, when such grandees as the Duke of Norfolk lived in the old monastery buildings. The Venetian ambassadors had a house in the Yard, and in the north-east corner, where Rutland Place is now, there was a mansion belonging to the earls of Rutland.

Literary celebrities included John Leland the antiquary from 1538 to 1546, Sir Kenelm Digby in the 1630s, Richard Baxter from 1686 until his death in 1691, and Sir William Davenant. In May 1656 Davenant obtained Cromwell's permission to stage musical entertainments in the hall at the rear of Rutland House. His productions are generally regarded as the first professional opera performances in England, although Dr Burney was of opinion that opera was more talked about than sung at Rutland House. The experiment continued until 1658, when Davenant moved his company to the Cockpit in Drury Lane.

The garden had first been laid out in walks soon after the chapel of the Virgin Mary & All Saints, which stood outside the Charterhouse gate, was demolished in 1615–16. James Howell reported in 1657 that Charterhouse Yard had 'lately been conveniently railed, and made more neat and comely'. This improvement was perhaps inspired by the success of Covent Garden and Lincoln's Inn Fields as luxury residential developments. But the aristocracy was deserting the City and its environs at the close of the seventeenth century, leaving the large mansions of Charterhouse Yard empty. As a result, nearly all the old houses were rebuilt in a much more nearly uniform style between 1688 and 1705, and at a scale to appeal to City merchants. A few of these houses survive on the east side. In 1708 Hatton described it as 'Charter House Yard, a pleasant place, of good, (and many New) Buildings'.

A wall with palisades on top 'as in Leicester Square' was built around the garden in 1715, and it was at this time that the name Charterhouse Square began to be used. In 1742 a private act created trustees to maintain the garden, three being officers of the Charterhouse, the other ten elected from among the residents. The oldest of the three gates, the one on the west side, was originally built in 1791.

The square remained popular with merchants and clergymen during the eighteenth century but the tenants became increasingly mixed in the nineteenth, with many doctors, the first hospitals and by the 1840s a number of printers, jewellers and watchmakers. The greatest change came in 1864–65, when the Metropolitan Railway Company bought the south side (in the City) and demolished most of it to build Aldersgate Street Station. Before long all the houses there were replaced by narrow commercial buildings fitted into the sliver of land that was left over.

Although the south side remained nominally part of the square, it became effectively a continuation of the busy Charterhouse Street after the Corporation of London extended it across the railway in 1873–74. In compensation, the corporation paid for the two southern gates to protect the garden from this new highway. The imminence of these changes was the signal for the Charterhouse School to move to the country in 1872. Its buildings were taken over by the Merchants Taylors' day school.

Charterhouses Square from the north side in 1731.

The north end of the east side of Charterhouse Square in 1906; all these buildings were demolished in the 1930s and 1950s.

Patterson's Hotel, Nos 2 and 3 Charterhouse Square, *c.* 1905.

After this upheaval the square became increasingly commercial and a number of the old houses that remained became hotels. Percy Fitzgerald referred in 1893 to 'one of the curious hostelries in Charterhouse Square, where he seemed to be in an ancient country town, or in one of those inns of fiction where say Mr Squeers might have alighted'. The extension of Charterhouse Street had shortened the west side of the square and there the houses were rebuilt as factories and offices. Sebastian Ferranti's company had its first premises at No. 27 from 1890. Sharing the building was another electrical engineer with the happy name of Charles Sparks.

The square was battered during the Second World War, with the north-east and south-west corners and the Charterhouse itself badly damaged. The ugly south side was untouched, but it has recently been smartened up and given a veneer of Victorian dignity, spurious but welcome all the same. The short west side was rebuilt in the 1950s and 1960s.

Now the only points of interest are to be found on the other two sides. The east is dominated by Florin Court, a block of service flats for businessmen built between 1935 and 1937, which would not be unattractive, somewhere else. Next door to the south, and dwarfed, are the oldest surviving houses, of the 1690s. There are good Georgian houses on the north side, flanking the early fifteenth-century archway of the Charterhouse. The garden remains private and the square remarkably quiet and peaceful.

Chatham Square

CITY OF LONDON

Robert Mylne's classical Blackfriars Bridge was built between 1760 and 1769 and, as it neared completion, equally elegant approaches were laid out at the City and Southwark ends. Chatham Square was a variant name for Chatham Place, the opening at the north end of the bridge, used on Cary's 1783 map among others. It was part of an extended but futile scheme for the glorification of the 'Great Commoner', as Hughson's description in 1806 makes clear: 'The east side of New Bridge Street is a pile of stately buildings, with a crescent, which extend to Chatham Square, and Pitt's Bridge, vulgarly Blackfriars Bridge.' The vulgar herd had its way as usual in the naming of the bridge, and the square, however called, was destroyed by the Victoria Embankment in the 1860s.

Chatham Place (or Square) had fourteen houses, seven on each side. They were of four storeys originally, but some were later raised higher. The doors and ground floor windows were round-headed. Lady Hamilton's first London job was here, probably in 1780, as nursemaid to the children of Dr Richard Budd, who was physician to St Bartholomew's Hospital from 1780 until 1801. At the same time his housemaid Jane was the young woman later celebrated as the tragic actress, Mrs Powell, whose roles included Hamlet. Brass Crosby (son of Hercules), the Lord Mayor and friend of Wilkes, was another early resident. He died at his house in Chatham Place in 1793. It was Crosby who gave the obelisk that stands in the centre of St George's Circus at Southwark.

From an early date the houses were more commercial than residential, but they had some literary and journalistic associations. Thomas Curson Hansard and his son of the same name, second and third in the dynasty that printed the parliamentary debates, lived

at No. 1, abutting the river on the east side, and John Delane, editor of *The Times*, lived at No. 4. Rossetti, who lodged for ten years on the second floor of No. 14, next to the river on the west side, sometimes gave his address as 'Blackfriars Bridge'. After his marriage he also rented the second floor of No. 13, knocking the two together. He wrote in January 1862 that 'there is something so delightfully quaint and characteristic about our quarters here that nothing but the conviction that they cannot be the best for her health would ever induce me to move'. A month later Elizabeth committed suicide and Rossetti fled to Chelsea. The Chatham Place rooms were taken over by another Pre-Raphaelite, George Price Boyce.

The corresponding open space at the south end of Blackfriars Bridge seems never to have been called anything but Albion Place.

Chatteris Square

NEWINGTON [SOUTHWARK]

Chatteris Square was built in the late 1880s on the site of Ash Street, a turning off the south side of the New Kent Road just east of Elephant & Castle Station. It was a good set of model dwellings, the tenements being on the east and south sides only, with an old terrace in New Kent Road to the north and the Crossway Central Mission Hall to the east. It was described by the Booth survey in 1899 as 'Sutton and Dudleys Buildings. All windows unbroken, a few flowers, respectable poor people. Curtains clean, white tiles to staircase. Police and City workers.' All the blocks in this square (which was closer to a triangle) were damaged during the Second World War, but most of them were patched up and survived until about 1970. They were replaced by the Deacon Way flats, tenements more monumental than anything the Victorians imagined, themselves now swept away.

Chelsea Square

CHELSEA [KENSINGTON AND CHELSEA]

All the Chelsea squares have suffered setbacks before achieving their present popularity, but none has followed such a rocky road as Chelsea Square. It began with South Row, which eventually became the north side of the square. This was a piece of back development off the Fulham Road, built in 1795–97, and was known as South Row until 1802, then as South Parade.

Serious exploitation of the land between the common and Church Lane, now Old Church Street, began in 1809 when a lease was granted to a builder named John Fielder. A square was beginning to take shape on Fielder's new estate by 1813, and at that date it was named, almost inevitably, Wellington Square. The district was a celebration of the great general, with a Salamanca Row, a Barrosa Place and an Arthur Street in close attendance. The square was on a suitably heroic scale, being much the largest in Chelsea, but the war that had provided the hero had severely hampered the building trades with heavy taxation of materials and shortages of labour, timber and capital. Economic recovery was delayed until 1818 and progress at Wellington Square was painfully slow.

Maps from the 1820s onwards copied each other in showing terraces all along the north and east sides and on the whole of the west side north of Bath Lodge. This was pure fantasy, based presumably on Fielder's intentions. Until 1830 the only house beyond South Parade and its continuation Barrosa Place was the detached Bath Lodge, later Catherine Lodge, which had begun in the eighteenth century as a villa lying back from the east side of Church Lane. Curiously, it was probably at Bath Lodge that the dashing cavalry general Lord Paget (later Marquess of Anglesey) lived in 1811 after being invalided home from the Peninsula, and while conducting a scandalous affair with Wellington's sister-in-law.

By 1830 Wellington had evolved from a national hero into an unpopular prime minister. In that year, perhaps for political reasons or merely to improve the luck of the place, it was given the new name of Trafalgar Square, which was first applied to the terrace on the east side. That was begun at the north end in 1830, but had only extended to four houses by 1834, to ten in 1838 and to eleven in 1840, when No. 1 was built. There it stopped, with less than half of the east side filled.

The houses were similar to those in squares on the New River estate at Clerkenwell. They were of two bays, with three storeys plus attic and semi-basement.

The north side of Trafalgar Square, now Chelsea Square, *c.* 1910.

The stucco ground floor was rusticated, with round-headed doors and windows. The corner house, No. 1 at the north end, was of three bays to the square, fully rendered and with a large porch. This incomplete terrace was probably intended to set the tone for the rest of the square, but the only other addition was the detached villa called Nelson Lodge, which the Fielders occupied through three generations. It was built on the short south side in 1841.

The square was therefore of the proprietorial kind, though not one in which the creator could take much pride. In 1843 William Weir remarked that, 'Chelsea has its Trafalgar Square, or at least two sides and a half of it'. The east terrace did have good tenants: merchants, barristers, surgeons, army officers. In the late 1860s the development was finally continued with a terrace on the northern half of the west side. It was the last attempt to complete the square. Over the next fifty years the work done by the Fielders unravelled.

The first of the many non-residential intrusions was a small fire station built in South Parade, at the north-west corner of the square, in 1868. When the north terrace was demolished in preparation for the extension of Brompton Hospital south of the Fulham Road, the fire station was rebuilt on an enlarged site in 1892. The building is now part of the hospital. The rest of the north side was filled by the nurses' home, a fine work by the hospital specialist E.T. Hall, built in 1898.

On the east side of the square the 1830s terrace was never extended. Instead a motley collection of buildings gradually assembled to its south: a joinery works, the Manresa Hall, a stone mason's yard and three sets of artists' studios, Elgin, Wentworth and Trafalgar. With the stone yard so handy, they were popular with sculptors, but Holman Hunt had No. 7 in the Trafalgar Studios for a time.

On the south side, the Fielders' own house, Nelson Lodge, was demolished in the early 1890s to make way for the huge South-West London Polytechnic. With so few residents left in the square the 2½-acre garden was little used, and in the early twentieth century it was leased to the Chelsea Lawn Tennis Club. In 1904 the LCC described it as 'Enclosure comprising garden, tennis courts, cricket ground and pavilion'.

When the leases expired in 1928 the Cadogan estate decided on comprehensive redevelopment. All the old houses, including the fine Catherine Lodge, were demolished in the early 1930s together with the miscellaneous buildings on the east side, and most were replaced by three-storey terraces in red brick designed by Darcy Braddell. Houses were also built on the north and south ends of the garden, substantially reducing its size, so that when the name was changed to Chelsea Square in 1937 Chelsea Gardens might have been a better choice.

The only distinguished buildings in the modern square (apart from the nurses' home) are Nos 40 and 41, which were designed by Oliver Hill and built on the site of Catherine Lodge in 1930 and 1934. Work at Chelsea Square was completed by 1938, just in time for the Second World War, in which a good deal of damage was done, much of the north-west corner being destroyed and the rest suffering more or less from blast. All was seamlessly repaired after the war.

An early resident of the new Chelsea Square was the painter Ethel Sands, who had not long acquired No. 52 when it was bombed in 1941. She later moved back to No. 18, where she died in 1962. It was a sign of the times that the modest No. 8 was the home of the 6th Earl of Clarendon, a former Governor General of South Africa and Lord Chamberlain, who died there in 1955. John Osborne, who was fond of squares, bought a fifty-one-year lease of No. 30 in 1968 and settled there for a while with his fourth wife, Jill Bennett. He had lost his previous house in Chester Square as part of his divorce settlement with Penelope Gilliatt. The Chelsea Square house was sold after his divorce from Jill Bennett in 1977.

Chequer Square

Chequer Square was an alternative name for Chequer Yard, a turning off the south side of Aldgate High Street, close to the Minories, which was named on the Ogilby & Morgan map of 1676. It was still Chequer Yard in the first edition of Lockie's *Topography of London* in 1810, but had become Chequer Square by the time of his 1813 revision. It was a substantial court, with as many as twenty small houses, mostly on the east side. If 'Square' was intended to replace 'Yard' it evidently failed to stick, as the old name continued to appear on maps until the completion of what is now the Circle Line in 1884 involved its total demolition. The Aldgate Bus Station is now on the site.

Chequer Square

OLD STREET [ISLINGTON]

John Lockie described this place in 1810 as 'Chequer-Square, Chequer-Alley, Bunhill-row, – a small open space on the N. side, the second on the R. from Bunhill-row', but in his second edition of 1813 he corrected this to '3rd on the R.' Horwood's 1790s map showed the open space with no houses. By 1813 there were six, three on the north and three on the south side. The square was at the south-eastern corner of the Friends' Burial Ground. It survived without change until this whole slum district was replaced by the huge Peabody estate in the 1880s. Chequer Street, the service road between the tenement blocks, preserves the name.

Cheriton Square

BALHAM [WANDSWORTH]

This is called a square because it branches off Elmfield Road, makes two right-angled turns and rejoins Elmfield Road, but there is nothing to suggest that the central portion was ever intended to be a garden. The houses on the inside of the bends appear to be of the same date as those on the outside. The name was approved in 1880.

Cherry Tree Square

OLD STREET [ISLINGTON]

Cherry Tree Square, off Whitecross Street, began as a rectangular opening on the north side of the long Cherry Tree Alley which extended to Bunhill Row. The site of the future square was shown as a garden on the Ogilby & Morgan map of 1676 and on Strype's of 1720. Rocque showed the space surrounded by houses

in the 1740s and Horwood by six or seven of them in the 1790s and in 1813. All of these treated the open space as part of Cherry Tree Alley.

The name was not used in the 1871 census but was given on the 1873 Ordnance Survey map, which showed the houses hardly altered from the 1790s. In 1881 it was 'Cherry Tree Alley, also called Court and Square, 1 to 6 only, no 7 and 8'. Nineteen families lived in the six houses. The change from alley to square was a deathbed conversion that cannot have corresponded to any moral reformation, for this was and remained a slum. In the 1880s, like Haberdasher's Square, it was destroyed by the relentless growth of Whitbread's Chiswell Street brewery.

Chester Square

BELGRAVIA [WESTMINSTER]

When the part of the Grosvenor estate that became Belgravia was let to builders in 1824 the largest portion was taken by Thomas Cubitt, but there was plenty left over for others to enjoy a share. The land between Eaton Square and Ebury Street was acquired in separate lots by Seth Smith of Mayfair and Joseph Cundy, brother of the Grosvenor surveyor, Thomas Cundy. The master plan for the development had envisaged simple roads here – Minerva Street and Pulford Street – but in 1828 Smith and Joseph Cundy proposed a more prestigious square instead and Thomas Cundy gave his gracious consent.

The *Dictionary of National Biography* says that Sir George Harman was born in Chester Square on 30 January 1830, but that is not correct: *The Morning Post* recorded the event at Croydon. The family later lived at No. 63.

E.T. Ward's 1830 map of improvements in the West End shows the square laid out, but without name or houses. Building began about 1832, in which year Joseph Cundy was living in Lower Belgrave Street and Thomas in Ranelagh Street, now Beeston Place. The north side of Chester Square was built by Seth Smith, the south and the short east side by Joseph Cundy, which has led to the assumption that Thomas Cundy designed only the higher numbered houses. But Thomas chose to live at No. 13, one of

The north side of Chester Square, *c.* 1904.

the Smith houses, at the corner of Eccleston Street, which was the first completed and occupied, late in 1833. It would certainly have made sense for Smith to employ him, to simplify his negotiations with the estate.

Work proceeded from the east end, with the highest and lowest numbers. Forty houses were built in the 1830s, but only twenty-seven were occupied in 1840. Number 77 in the corner is the only house with a good private garden, and like Clare House in Lowndes Square, it has its more important face to the side. The western end was added in 1843–45 and the square was almost fully occupied by 1847. The style remained consistent on the south side, but on the north it grew heavier and more Italianate between Nos 23 and 24.

Thomas Cundy designed St Michael's Church, which was built on an island site at the west end in 1844–46. It was enlarged by Cundy's son in the 1870s. Because the church is wider than the garden, Nos 42–47 on the south side are set back and form an individually designed terrace with pairs of pilasters (the only ones in the square) between the houses.

Even in the difficult 1830s Chester Square was an immediate success, despite the houses being only second-rate as compared with the grand Eaton Square. It soon had a sprinkling of aristocrats, especially dowagers, and being so close to Westminster it was popular with Members of Parliament and administrators, like Sir Arthur Helps. When a renumbering of the square in 1848 removed some houses into Chester Terrace, the dispossessed residents complained bitterly, as they had paid a premium for the kudos of having an address in the square, even though they had no view of the garden.

Chester Square has unexpected poetical associations. It was the last home of Winthrop Mackworth Praed, poet and politician, who died there in 1839 at the age of 36. Only a year before that he had become '… the first owner of 64 Chester Square, a large house in a newly-developed area of south-west London. Situated on a draughty corner and difficult to keep warm, with its high-ceilinged rooms, it was not the ideal home for a young man with lung trouble.' Praed's biographer, Derek Hudson, adds that by 1939 the house had become No. 39 Eccleston Street, but that is not the case now even if it was then.

Mary Wollstonecraft Shelley moved to No. 24 (where there is a plaque) in 1846 and remained until her death in 1851. She would not have agreed with Hudson's strictures on the square. This was her report to a house-hunter, probably in 1848:

> The houses are well built on 20 feet of gravel, well drained and the whole vicinity very airy. It is not a bracing air, but I never heard of fevers prevailing. I have had nothing of the kind in my house hold, which has been very healthy ever since I came here. I think it quite as healthy a spot as any part of London. Tiburnia is said to be more bracing, but it is cold, being on clay. The only part of town I should prefer as more bracing is Kensington Gore, but that is scarcely London.

This is curiously like Isabella Knightley's praise of Brunswick Square, Bloomsbury, in *Emma*.

Matthew Arnold lived at No. 2, where there is another plaque, from 1858 until 1868. In 1858 he wrote, 'We have taken a house in Chester Square. It is a very small one, but it will be something to unpack one's portmanteau for the first time since I was married'; and in 1867, 'We are fairly driven out of Chester Square, partly by the number of the children, partly by the necessity of a better school for the two boys who live at home.'

Harold Macmillan bought No. 14 on his marriage in 1920 and remained until 1937:

> It was the frontier between Belgravia and Pimlico. In those days we obtained the lease of a house on very modest terms, and lived there for the next sixteen years. Now with the steady migration westwards that has for centuries characterised the development of London, Chester Square has become both smart and expensive. In our day it was neither; it suited us very well.

Number 14 is a large corner house, corresponding to Praed's No. 64 on the other side.

Second World War bombing was largely confined to the south-west corner where St Michael's was damaged and several houses were destroyed. This is a rare instance of the least attractive houses in a square being hit. They have been replaced by slightly taller flats with exposed brickwork everywhere above the ground floor, where a gesture at uniformity is made with pillared porches and rustication.

The post-war residents of note have been an odd miscellany. John Osborne and his third wife Penelope Gilliatt lived at No. 31 in the 1960s during their brief marriage, after employing Sir Hugh Casson to make extensive changes. She attempted suicide there after Osborne left her for Jill Bennett in 1966, but did have the consolation of obtaining possession of the house in the divorce settlement. Osborne and his new wife went to Chelsea Square. Tony Curtis bought No. 49 while in London to film the television series *The Persuaders* in 1971–72, Yehudi Menuhin lived at No. 65 in his old age from 1983 until his death in 1999, and No. 73 was the last home of Margaret Thatcher. Chester Square continues, deservedly, to be one of the most fashionable in London.

Chester Square

KENNINGTON [LAMBETH]

Chester Square was the name given by the Charles Booth police notebooks in 1899 to the kink at the west end of Reedworth Street, where it changes course to pass round the Archbishop Sumner School. It had a squarer shape before the lane leading to Kennington Road on the south side of the school was widened. The name used in census returns for the square and the lane was Chester Gardens.

Booth's assistant described the two-storey houses of the square as being poorer than the rest of Reedworth Street, but none survive in either to be compared. Reedworth Street was built in the late 1860s, but Chester Gardens was older: two or three of the houses existed in 1841. The number soon rose to seven, occupied in 1861 by a dealer in chicory, a comedian, a hotel waiter etc. and in 1891 by a glass embosser, an electrical engineer, a bricklayer etc.

Chester Gardens became part of Reedworth Street in 1903, but a memory of the name is preserved by Chester Way, the next road to the south. The houses of the 'square' have been replaced by three-storey flats called Jubilee House.

China Square

LAMBETH

In the ambitious laying out of inner south London after the building of Blackfriars Bridge in 1769, a fine row of houses called China Terrace filled most of the south-west angle between Lambeth Road and Kennington Road. Behind them, perhaps originally as mews, there were two little courts surrounded with buildings and linked by a narrow passage. In the late eighteenth and early nineteenth centuries they were both known as China Court, but from the 1840s the northern half was China Court or Place, the southern becoming China Square. It had about a dozen cottages, with a narrow alley at the south end leading to St Alban's Street, just off Kennington Road. Several policemen lived there in 1881.

China Square was rebuilt with more regular terraces between 1881 and 1893 and enlarged by the annexation of China Court. The 1891 census called the whole complex China Place, but in 1899 Charles Booth's surveyor described China Square as, 'Poor, houses newish, three rooms for 8/- and 8/6 … This China area is rough, inhabitants chiefly costers and Irish labourers; no prostitutes, a few thieves, many drunks, both men and women.' The area was cleared by the LCC in the late 1920s and Wedgwood House, part of the China Walk Estate, was built on the site.

Chiswick Square

CHISWICK [HOUNSLOW]

Chiswick Square was built about 1680, at much the same time as Kensington Square, but is not to be compared with it as an ambitious or foolhardy attempt to transplant the new urban square into the country. It is more like the old Cleveland Square at St James's, a thrifty exploitation of the forecourt of a large house. Chiswick was a popular retreat for wealthy Londoners

Chiswick Square in 2013.

in the seventeenth century, so there would have been a ready market for the houses built as a prelude to what is now Boston House.

There were three of them, a two-storey pair on the west side and a three-storey detached house on the east. The framing of the court between was completed by the gates of Boston House on the south side and by Church Street on the north. While that was a narrow lane the houses on its north side might almost have been counted part of the square, but its widening as the Great Chertsey Road in 1933 began the isolation – the alienation – that was completed by the Hogarth Roundabout after the Second World War.

Boston House has had a chequered history. It was re-fronted in the middle of the eighteenth century

Choumert Square

North side, four room cottages, rents 6/- and 6/6, going up for new comers. Queer entrances behind out of a covered passage way, little garden fronts on each side, and 'all fronts', as an occupant said, proud, however, of her square. The south side very much the same, save that the entrances are in front, more after the way of the world. No tenants are taken with children, and the whole place appears to be very quiet, select, old-fashioned, and quaint. All pink [fairly comfortable] as map. No traffic for vehicles, private.

Sark in Peckham, in fact. Choumert Square appears to have changed hardly at all since this description was written by one of Charles Booth's research assistants in 1899. He was right about the 'adults only' rule, although in 1891 there was a two-week-old baby at No. 13, presumably just an unlucky accident. I cannot say whether the ban on children is still enforced. None were in evidence when I paid my visit, but that was during school hours. The residents were very shy, all vanishing from sight at my approach, but the cats were friendly.

The name comes from George Choumert (1746–1831), a French tanner who settled in England, became a British subject, and began to develop his estate west of Rye Lane in 1815. Building had begun in Choumert Place, now Choumert Road, before his death. Choumert Square was a much later development, its peculiar form dictated by an awkward and almost inaccessible site. It was built in the late 1880s over the long narrow gardens of two Rye Lane houses that had been converted into shops.

It has not the slightest right to be called a square, being merely a long, straight, narrow footpath or lane, but like a number of unsquare squares it does have a great deal of charm. It is protected from Choumert Grove by an elaborate double gate, unlocked. There is no communal garden, except for a picnic arbour with a table at the blind end, but in compensation all the tiny front gardens have been treated as a single composition, with a wonderfully profuse display of bushes, shrubs and country garden flowers.

and extended to east and west, then and later. It was described as being in 'the Square, Chiswick' when the contents were sold in 1837. It served as a boarding school for girls in the middle of the nineteenth century and as a home for inebriate women from 1889 to 1921, before becoming a social club for the employees of the Cherry Blossom boot polish company. It is now divided into flats, with a 1980s development called Boston Gardens built across its lawn.

The houses of its Chiswick Square forecourt are little altered and appear very prosperous. If the visitor looks determinedly southwards and wears earplugs, this might still be a fragment of civilised eighteenth-century Chiswick, but when he turns to the north and opens his ears it is upon all the horrors of twentieth-century traffic mismanagement.

Choumert Square, looking east, in 2010.

Choumert Square is divided into sections by trellis arches over the path, to which a mazy effect is given by the bushes encroaching upon it to different degrees. By communal effort, the residents have created something as delightful as the contemporary Bonnington Square, although here the original materials were far more promising.

Exploring Choumert Square is like strolling down the quietest of village side streets. Yet, on one side it backs on to a car park, on most of the other to the shops of Choumert Road, which is a turning off Rye Lane and almost as noisy and noisome. At its south-west corner the square has a much more pleasant neighbour in the Girdlers' Almshouses in Choumert Road, built in the Tudor style in 1852. They have their back entrances in the square and are sometimes counted as part of it.

Christopher Square

SHOREDITCH [HACKNEY]

Christopher Square, formerly Long Alley Square, was one of the many unsavoury courts in the crowded area between Bishopsgate and Finsbury Square. In modern terms it ran from Appold Street to the south side of Earl Street. The name came from Christopher Alley, which linked the square with Wilson Street, and the alley probably took its name from an inn. Rocque's map of 1746 showed a much wider open space called Three Bowl Alley in the position occupied by Long Alley Square in the 1790s. The eighteen houses shown there on Horwood's map had presumably been built within the open space of Three Bowl Alley, reducing its size.

Christopher Square became the usual name early in the nineteenth century. Its residents were frequently to be found in the criminal courts. The western third of Christopher Square, with seven houses, survived the building of the approaches to Broad Street Station in the 1860s, when the rerouted southern end of Long Alley was given the name of Finsbury Avenue. The remaining houses of the square were destroyed during the widening and smartening up of Finsbury Avenue when it became part of Appold Street in 1879.

Church Square

See St Mary's Square, Ealing

Clapton Square

HACKNEY

Clapton Square was built in the second decade of the nineteenth century. The man responsible for the layout is thought to have been the architect William Ashpitel, who owned land at Hackney, had collaborated in the design of the Well Street chapel, and lived in the square from 1812 until his death in 1852. It was the childhood home of his better-known son Arthur Ashpitel, architect, writer and connoisseur. According to Papworth's *Dictionary of Architecture*, William Ashpitel retired early and 'gave his attention chiefly to improvements upon his own property'.

The houses had good private gardens with mews behind, in addition to the large and well-planted central garden. Until Hackney declined late in the nineteenth century it was one of the best addresses in a good suburb, although there was already a school, Mrs Sargant's academy, in 1818. By 1896 several houses had become institutions, including the Salvation Army Rescue Home at No. 28, with Mrs Bramwell Booth as principal. In 1897 the Charles Booth survey found that there were 'a good many houses to let in Clapton Square, and they look rather past their prime'.

It is a narrow, three-sided square, with the Lower Clapton Road cutting diagonally across as the southern boundary. Like Campden Hill Square, although not so dramatically, it rises from the main road, of which the rush and noise is soon left behind. On the south side of Lower Clapton Road is the large churchyard of St John's, which more than doubles the green space provided by the square garden, the two forming a valuable park for the centre of Hackney.

The early nineteenth-century houses survive along most of the west and north sides of the square. The terrace on the north side, known as Clarence Place, was apparently intended to be more formal and decorative than the rest, but it was never completed. On the west side there are tall pairs linked by

The east side of Clapton Square, *c.* 1905.

single-storey entrance bays. Victorian mansion blocks occupy the north-east corner and bland Georgian pastiche has replaced the original houses on the east side. Bomb damage was restricted to the south-west corner, where the houses were replaced by ugly flats, tarted up with balconies like laundry baskets.

Claremont Square

CLERKENWELL [ISLINGTON]

The site of Claremont Square was the New River Company's Upper Pond, a reservoir dug in 1708 to supply the West End and enclosed by a high wall when the New Road – this part of which is now Pentonville Road – was built in the 1750s. The houses facing the reservoir in Pentonville Road did not belong to the company and have never been a part of the square. Indeed, when the brick wall of the reservoir was replaced by a less unsightly railing in 1826, it was reinstated on the north side to punish the Pentonville Road residents for refusing to contribute to the cost.

The plans of William Mylne, the company surveyor, were somewhat indefinite when he began to develop this part of the estate for building. The west side, Myddelton Terrace, was begun in 1815, perhaps before there was any firm decision to create a square. The other two sides were laid out between 1822 and 1825. At that time the intended name was River Square. The new name that soon replaced it came from the Claremont Chapel in Pentonville Road, which was opened in 1819. It recalled Claremont House in Surrey, home of the popular Princess Charlotte who had died in 1817. The east side of the square was built in 1823–25, the south in 1826–28.

Myddelton Terrace was delightfully quiet and secluded during its first decade and thus attracted one or two celebrities. George Cruikshank lived at No. 11 from 1821 to 1824. Thomas Carlyle saw the square's infancy when he lodged with Edward Irving at No. 4 on his visit to London in 1824. Writing his account forty years afterwards, Carlyle got the name of the square wrong, misled no doubt by Myddelton Terrace, and misleading many others since:

Irving lived in Myddelton Terrace, *hodie* Myddelton Square, Islington, No4. It was a new place; houses bright and smart, but inwardly bad, as usual. Only one side of the new square was built – the western side – which had its back towards Battle Bridge region. Irving's house was fourth from the northern end of that, which, of course, had its left hand on the New Road. The place was airy, not uncheerful. Our chief prospect from the front was a good space of green ground, and in it, on the hither edge of it, the big open reservoir of Myddelton's 'New River,' now above two centuries old for that matter, but recently made new again, and all cased in tight masonry; on the spacious expanse of smooth flags surrounding which it was pleasant on fine mornings to take an early promenade, with the free sky overhead and the New Road with its lively traffic and vehiculation seven or eight good yards below our level.

Irving's house, which he only occupied for a few years, is still No. 4 Claremont Square. Carlyle's is not the only gloomy ghost hovering here. The even more curmudgeonly writer B.S. Johnson (1933–73) had flats in Claremont and Myddelton Squares during his mercifully brief career.

After its early flourish Claremont Square was not fashionable, especially after the reservoir was covered over in 1854–56. The Booth survey described it in 1898 as 'a noted residence of medical students'. The New River Company formalised the trend towards multi-occupation by converting some of the houses into flats in the 1930s. There was bomb damage on all three sides of the square during the Second World War, as can be seen from the patched brickwork of many of the houses, but everything has been carefully restored. Islington Council carried the conversion to flats much further in the 1970s and 1980s and considerably altered some of the houses. Number 31, at the corner of Mylne Street, was rebuilt.

The houses, four-storey on the south side, three on the east and west, are attractive in the standard 1820s style and their outlook onto the green bank and trees of the reservoir is pleasant enough, but as it cuts off all view of the other sides there is very little sense of being in a square. The south side is the best, being the quietest and the least troubled with traffic.

The covering of the reservoir at Claremont Square, Clerkenwell, in 1856.

Claremont Square

The original name of Claremont Square was Union Court. It was a turning off the west side of New Gravel Lane, now Garnet Street, at its south end, nearly opposite Wapping Wall. It emerged during the second half of the eighteenth century. The various editions of Horwood's map showed it with only a single terrace of houses on the south side of the alley.

The change of name, which came in the 1840s, perhaps marked the building of the northern terrace. In 1851 nearly all the male residents were coal whippers. Claremont Square was snuffed out when the Ratcliff Gas Works, which had long existed to the west, expanded to New Gravel Lane in the 1860s. St Peter's Primary School is now on the site.

Clarendon Square

(enclosing the Polygon)

Clarendon Square was of little interest except as a frame for the Polygon, one of the boldest of the geometrical experiments indulged in by the eighteenth-century architects. It was really a circus, with an unbroken ring of houses on the inside looking out. Each of the sixteen pairs of houses formed one side of the polygon, but with the road and pavement following an unbroken curve this was scarcely noticed.

The Polygon and St Aloysius, Clarendon Square, in 1850.

Because of its early decline, the Polygon is remembered, if at all, as something squalid, but it was in fact similar to the contemporary and much admired Paragon at Blackheath. Here in Somers Town the curve was convex rather than concave and the outlook restricted once the square was built around it, but the design and proportions of the paired houses were much the same.

On the early maps, before the framing streets were built, it had a strange, even sinister, appearance, standing alone in the fields like a model prison. Oddly enough, the architect did also design the Middlesex House of Correction in Coldbath Fields. He was Jacob Leroux, who had built something very similar to the Polygon at Southampton twenty years earlier. Leroux was a speculative developer with a shady reputation, which may account for the slow progress of the Polygon and its early failure. It was the central feature of Somers Town, which Leroux had been building since the 1780s. The Polygon was begun in 1793 and largely completed within the decade, but the framing houses of Clarendon Square took much longer. The east side and the south, where Leroux himself lived, were only beginning to take shape in the 1790s, and the north side was barely begun in 1813.

William Godwin and Mary Wollstonecraft lived at No. 29 the Polygon during their brief marriage in 1797, and Godwin remained there until 1807, bringing up their daughter Mary (later Mary Shelley) and various other children and stepchildren. The curious form of the Polygon may perhaps be blamed for giving a disastrous new direction to his life, as it enabled his second wife, Mary Jane Clairmont, to introduce herself to him from a neighbouring balcony with the irresistible words, 'Is it possible that I behold the immortal Godwin?'

Number 17 the Polygon was one of the many London addresses of the young Charles Dickens. The family lodged there in 1827–28 during Dickens' spell as a solicitor's clerk and his earliest days as a reporter. He later made it one of the shabby homes of Harold Skimpole in *Bleak House*.

It was popular with painters and engravers: Henry Bone, James Neagle and Edward Scriven lived in Clarendon Square in the early nineteenth century, James Tibbitts Willmore at No. 23 the Polygon, Thomas Colman Dibdin at No. 25 and John Thomas (*Rainy Day*) Smith at No. 4. Others were to be found in the neighbouring streets. In the 1850s the Polygon was also home to a surprising number of pianoforte makers.

The purity of the Polygon was breached in the 1840s when the northernmost four houses, Nos 19–22, were demolished to build the Polygon Infants' School. In 1891 Henry Wheatley wrote of the Polygon as 'now enclosed by the dirty neighbourhood of Clarendon Square'. The rest of it was swept away in that year and quickly replaced by Polygon Buildings, four large ranges of industrial dwellings running north and south, which completely filled the centre of the square.

The LCC abolished the Clarendon Square name in 1938, renumbering the houses in what are now Polygon Road (the north side), Chalton Street (east), Phoenix Road (south) and Werrington Street (west).

Polygon Buildings were replaced by Oakshott Court in the 1970s, with an open green at the south-west corner, the first garden the interior of the square has known. The streets that used to form the frame are some of the ugliest in London. All the original houses have gone and the only point of interest (not beauty) is the Maria Fidelis Convent School in Phoenix Road. This is the successor to the Roman Catholic chapel of St Aloysius, founded here as early as 1808.

Cleaver Square

KENNINGTON [LAMBETH]

Cleaver Square was known as Prince's Square until 1937 and the old name can still be read in faded paint on the wall of No. 1. The prince in question was the future George IV.

'Cleaver' was not intended to be descriptive: if that had been the idea Bottle Square would have been the new name, the neck being at the Kennington Park Road end. Mary Cleaver was the landowner who initiated the development and gave her name to Cleaver Street, from which it has migrated to the square. Its building began about 1790, was three-quarters completed by 1813 and ended in the middle of the century. The houses built on fresh sites after 1813 are the partly stuccoed Nos 21–33 around the neck of the bottle (about 1850) and the smaller Nos 42–46 on the north side (about 1820). In addition Nos 49–61, by the pub, which had been part of the original development, were rebuilt about 1850.

The square was not always as prosperous as it is today. As early as the 1830s there was a fair scattering of tradesmen among the private residents:

The north side of Cleaver Square in 2008.

bricklayer, plumber, carpenter, engraver, house agent, shopkeeper, in addition to the surgeons and proprietors of schools found in many squares. By 1891 most of the houses were in multiple occupation, some with numerous lodgers. In 1899 Charles Booth's research assistant described it as being occupied by 'mechanics working over the water. The square in the centre is taken up by a florist and nursery garden. There may be a servant in three houses in the east corner.' He classified the square as pink, which meant 'fairly comfortable, good ordinary earnings'.

In 1928 the garden was said to be surrounded by 'working-class houses and flats'. The florist and market gardener had been ousted by then and the garden had been opened to the public. Lambeth Council bought it for £2,000 in 1927, as the only means of preventing the owners from building garages there. In the 1930s it was described as a playground. The square escaped the Second World War with only light damage on the south side.

This is now one of the best of the London squares, with attractive modest houses of various styles, all in excellent preservation, and a pub handily placed in the corner. The Prince of Wales was rebuilt in 1901, but still has 'Prinny' on the sign. The delightfully shaded public garden is gravelled not grassed, and enclosed by a low post and chain fence which gives it, in conjunction with the pub, something of the atmosphere of a village green. The square is very quiet, except when the London Pétanque Club has its meetings, and the seats in the garden are popular with readers.

Cleveland Square

BAYSWATER [WESTMINSTER]

Cleveland Square and Cleveland Gardens were built between 1852 and 1859 by Henry de Bruno Austin, who lived at No. 40 in the square. He was later responsible for Kensington Gardens Square and many other developments, but was bankrupted in 1872. The work on Cleveland Square was eventful: one of Austin's carpenters committed suicide in 1852 by cutting his throat with a razor, and one of his labourers killed another with a shovel in 1853. Despite these interruptions, two of the big houses were occupied in that year, and ten in 1854, but most were slow to let, contributing to Austin's mounting financial problems. Austin built the adjoining Cleveland Gardens at the same time.

The west side of Cleveland Square, Bayswater, *c.* 1904.

Some eminent men did settle in Cleveland Square. The great judge Sir George Jessel, the first Jew to fill any of the major legal offices, lived at No. 8 from 1856 to 1873. The first Lord Hailsham, Lord Chancellor 1928–29 and 1935–38, lived at No. 5 in his early days as a barrister, and his son, Quintin Hogg, the second Lord Hailsham (also Lord Chancellor 1970–74 and 1979–87) was born there in 1907.

Austin's houses are of no great interest, being the standard grandiloquent Bayswater stucco, five storeys and three bays, with large balustraded porches. The interesting feature is the double garden, for Cleveland Square and Cleveland Gardens are a single composition and if two names were needed they should have been reversed. In Cleveland Gardens a road runs all the way round the central enclosure, but in the Square the houses have direct access to the garden on the north side, with no intervening road. Austin made use of the same unusual plan at Kensington Gardens Square, combining the two names into one.

Three houses on the east side were totally destroyed during the Second World War and others seriously damaged. The gap was filled with tall brick-built flats that attempt some perfunctory stucco assimilation only on the ground floor. Most of the original houses are now flats or hotels. The two gardens are still private.

Cleveland Square

(now part of Cleveland Row)

Cleveland Square, St James's, was the unwitting creation of Charles II's mistress Barbara Villiers, Duchess of Cleveland. The king gave her Berkshire House, a mansion nearly opposite St James's Palace. She renamed it Cleveland House and about 1670 had advanced east and west wings added, forming a large forecourt. These wings were separated from the main building after the duchess parted with Cleveland House, the west wing in 1691, the east early in the eighteenth century, and were converted into several houses. The three on the west side were

the best, having gardens running back to Green Park, and proved popular and long-lasting. The east wing was rebuilt at least once and its new houses faced south into Cleveland Row. The open space between the wings was known as Cleveland Court for much of the eighteenth century, but Cleveland Square had become established as the name before 1800.

The houses on the west side, Nos 1–3 Cleveland Square, had many fashionable tenants. The most distinguished were Lord Godolphin, Marlborough's ally, who was at No. 1 from 1692 to 1694; George Selwyn, the connoisseur of public executions, also at No. 1 from 1781 to 1791; and Lord Castlereagh, who lived at No. 2 from 1795 to 1804. But these desirable houses were always at the mercy of the plutocrats who lived in the great mansion on the north side. Since 1696 Cleveland House had been owned by the Earl of Bridgewater (see Bridgewater Square) and by his heirs. In the 1790s the 3rd Duke of Bridgewater bought No. 3 and added it to Cleveland House, which he was altering extensively at that time.

The great house was inherited by the Marquess of Stafford, who in 1805 built stables on the site of the houses in the east wing, which had been burnt down in the 1780s. In 1833 Cleveland House passed to Lord Francis Egerton, later Earl of Ellesmere, who demolished it in 1840–41, together with No. 2 (which he had bought) and built Bridgewater House on the enlarged site between 1846 and 1854. That left No. 1 (now the much-altered Selwyn House) marooned on an island site between Cleveland Row and Bridgewater House.

Cleveland House, Cleveland Square, St James's, in 1795.

Beresford Chancellor wrote in 1907, 'These residences, various in size and interest, constitute Cleveland Square, but anything less like a square, even among the varied enclosures in London so called, it would be difficult to find.' It is not at all difficult, in fact, to find 100, but the name of Cleveland Square did become less appropriate after the building of Bridgewater House. This fact was formally recognised in 1938, when the houses were renumbered as part of Cleveland Row.

Nevertheless, it is still a distinct and distinguished square, with the north side formed by Sir Charles Barry's Bridgewater House – Marchmain House in television's *Brideshead Revisited* – the west by Selwyn House and the decorative flank of a late seventeenth-century house in Cleveland Row, the east by the early twentieth-century No. 7 Cleveland Row, and the south by the mellow brickwork of St James's Palace.

Clifton Square

PECKHAM [SOUTHWARK]

This was a cul-de-sac, with all the houses on the north and south sides, but it was more square-like than the nearby Buller Square in that it was shorter and had a narrow entrance from Albert Road before widening out when the houses were reached. There were six on each side, of two storeys, with good back gardens. Albert Road is now Consort Road and retains some pleasant 1840s houses looking lost among the post-war flats, but Clifton Square was an addition of the early 1860s. The name came immediately from the adjoining Clifton Lodge and Clifton Place in Albert Road.

This was not one of the common slum cul-de-sac squares, but a respectable offshoot from a prosperous road, occupied by clerks, shopkeepers, commercial travellers and the like. There was no bomb damage in Clifton Square during the Second World War, but the whole area was cleared in the mid-1960s for a large council estate. Martock Court now occupies the site.

Clifton Square, New Cross

See Carlton Square

Cloudesley Square

BARNSBURY [ISLINGTON]

Cloudesley Square is named after Richard Young, alias Cloudesley, who in 1518 left to the parish of Islington the charity estate called Stonefields on which the square was built. The trustees of the charity obtained an Act of Parliament in 1811 empowering them to grant building leases, but it was only in 1824 that agreements were made for the square. John Emmett of Pentonville, who later lived at No. 1, was the developer.

Holy Trinity, Cloudesley Square, in 1842. The houses are Nos 29 and 30, on the north side.

The houses were built between 1824 and 1826; their typical early residents were merchants and lawyers. The church in the centre, Holy Trinity, completed the square between 1826 and 1829. Its architect was the young Charles Barry, getting his first chance to show his talents in London. A fanciful portrait of Richard Cloudesley is a feature of the east window.

Cloudesley Square itself is complete, unspoilt and very attractive. It is like a miniature version of Myddelton Square, with similar houses and a Gothic church in the centre. The square being so much smaller, Holy Trinity occupies the whole enclosure, which is never a satisfactory arrangement,

but at least the sides of the church are well planted with trees.

The individual features of Cloudesley Square are the two detached houses that flank the eastern entrance and take the rest of that side, and the pairs of houses (with large gardens) set at an angle across the two western corners. There was originally another detached house, Cloudesley Villa, on the south side of the western approach road, but that was replaced by a photographic factory late in the nineteenth century. Holy Trinity is now the Celestial Church of Christ.

Cobden Square

ISLINGTON

Cobden Square was known until the 1860s – probably until 1865, when Richard Cobden died – as Water's or Walter's Court. It was built, at least in part, early in the nineteenth century, before 1827, but the name did not appear in the ratebooks until 1838. Before that the fifteen houses were listed in 'Lower Side'. This was one of the unsavoury slums off the east side of Islington High Street, its narrow entrance through an archway under a schoolroom nearly opposite Liverpool Road.

When the infant daughter of a labourer died of cholera at No. 9 Water's Court in 1853, the registrar commented, 'If asked to point out where cholera would be most likely to commence, this is one of the places I should have mentioned; there are but three privies for all the houses in this court, and other things in proportion.' It must surely have been a Protectionist who changed the name.

As Cobden Square it had two interesting inhabitants: in 1868 'Professor' Kelvin, patentee of the dedicon ('fits pleasantly the mouth') as used by 'Negro Performers, Ventriloquists, Swiss Warblers, Magicians, etc.'; and in 1880 the 13-year-old Michael Clancy, who conspired with other boys to set fire to the Shoreditch Workhouse. That was perhaps the final straw, for Cobden Square was cleared as a slum soon afterwards and industrial dwellings built on the site, immediately north of the Islington Empire. The Royal Bank of Scotland building is there now.

Coldbath Square

There was a craze for medicinal springs, wells and baths in the late seventeenth century, amply catered for by landowners who were lucky enough to find, or inventive enough to claim, the right properties in their waters. In 1697 Walter Baynes of the Middle Temple, who had bought some land at Clerkenwell in the previous year, hired Edward Baynard of Bath as the essential quack doctor and announced a great new medical discovery in a blaze of puffing advertisements. The new spring, 'strongly impregnated with Steel and Sea Salt', was claimed as a certain cure for practically every disease known to man. Baynes built an elegant three-gabled bath house over the marble pool, with a rectangular garden surrounded by a high brick wall. He became the resident manager, though prudently retaining his day job in the Custos Brevium Office.

From 1719, Baynes was the main mover in the development of the surrounding fields for housing. On the north, east and south sides of the bath and its garden terraces of houses were built, mostly in the 1730s, that could be described in 1743 as 'handsome regular Buildings which may very well pass for a fine Square, tho' it was a very little while ago nothing but Dunghills'. The west side remained open to the fields. It was between 1733 and 1736, during this brief period of fashion, that the square could boast of its only celebrity. Eustace Budgell, a cousin of Addison and one of the contributors to his *Spectator*, was then busy writing his own series of periodical essays, *The Bee*.

The square's prosperity began to decline in the 1750s when the Sir John Oldcastle public house and pleasure garden in the fields to the west was converted into a smallpox hospital. Worse quickly followed, when the hospital was rebuilt on a much larger scale immediately opposite the square, becoming in effect a most unwelcome west side. It was completed in 1762. With squalid streets crowding around it to

The Cold Bath, Coldbath Square, in 1811.

north, south and east, and the smallpox hospital on the west side, the square was in rapid decline and it might have seemed that things could not possibly get worse. They could, of course, and when the hospital moved away in 1793 it was replaced by the even larger and uglier Middlesex House of Correction, commonly known as the Coldbath Fields Prison.

The trustees of the London Fever Hospital bought the cold bath in 1811 and partly demolished it, intending to build a typhus hospital on the site. When local opposition proved too strong the garden was sold to a developer, who built some thirty houses around the edge. The remains of the bath house continued in business, approached through an archway under the new houses on the north side of the former garden. In its later days, up to 1886, it was known as Nell Gwynne's Baths, after a nude porcelain figure that became one of the attractions.

Coldbath Fields Prison was closed in 1886, not 1877 as often stated. The Clerkenwell Vestry wanted to build industrial dwellings – a new type of prison – on the site, or to make it a much-needed open space. Instead it was put up for sale in 1887 ('it would do for a misanthrope or a pessimistic philosopher,' said the *Daily News*) and was bought by the Post Office for a parcel depot, later the Mount Pleasant Mail Centre.

But before the residents of Coldbath Square could celebrate the removal of their unwelcome neighbour, the construction of Rosebery Avenue between 1889 and 1892 proved the worst of all their many misfortunes. The new road sliced diagonally across the square, removing half of the south side and a third of the north. The interior houses and the cold bath were demolished and the industrial dwellings intended for the prison site were built there instead. Just a few of the 1730s houses survived as slums on the north and south sides.

Arnold Bennett provides a last glimpse of the old Coldbath Square in *Riceyman Steps* (1928): 'Coldbath Square easily surpassed even Riceyman [Granville] Square in squalor and foulness; and it was far more picturesque and deeper sunk in antiquity, save for the huge, awful block of tenements in the middle.'

There was serious bomb damage at the south-east corner in the Second World War and the houses that were not destroyed had already been scheduled as a clearance area by the LCC. The tenements, known as Coldbath Buildings, survived until 1982. Coldbath Square still exists as a name, but it is now one of the most depressing spots in London. The short arm, the old south side, has withered away altogether. The north side is a featureless stretch of road between the sides of intensely dull modern buildings, and much of the site of the tenements is occupied by one of those thoroughly un-English developments, a gated estate.

Colebrook Square

HOXTON [HACKNEY]

This was an extremely short-lived little square. Horwood's 1790s map showed it as a nameless alley without any houses, off the west side of Hoxton Street, south of Turner Square. Lockie named and located it in 1810, and a few houses were shown north and south of the short cul-de-sac on the 1813 revision of Horwood's map. James Elmes included Colebrook Square in his 1831 list of streets, but he was probably out of date, as usual: the 1820s maps indicated that the square had been replaced by the first part of Upper John Street. It must have been a rebuilding rather than a mere renaming, of the south side at least, as the street was much wider than the square.

By 1841 Upper John Street had been extended west almost to St John's Road (now part of Pitfield Street) where its progress was stopped by Westby's almshouses. The street pattern has been disrupted by council estates but the short Homefield Street is the modern successor to Colebrook Square and Upper John Street.

College Square

CITY OF LONDON

College Square was the great quadrangle of Doctors' Commons near St Paul's Cathedral, haunt of the ecclesiastical and Admiralty lawyers of the College of Advocates. The square was immediately south of the main entrance in Knightrider Street. The smaller rectangular quadrangle to the east was Little College Square.

Dickens described College Square in 1836 as 'a quiet and shady courtyard, paved with stone, and frowned upon by old red brick houses'. The houses were of three storeys with attics, opening directly onto the square. The college, a miniature temple but with courts of law as well as chambers, was rebuilt after the Fire of London and remained little altered until the society was dissolved in 1867. Many of the buildings, including the ones around the square, were then demolished and the new Queen Victoria Street soon passed over the garden to the south. Walford quotes from a description of the deserted college in 1867:

> … cross Knightrider Street and enter the Commons. The square itself is a memorial of the mutability of human affairs. Its big sombre houses are closed. The well-known names of the learned doctors who formerly practised in the adjacent courts are still on the doors, but have, in each instance, 'All letters and parcels to be addressed …'

The eastern half of the Faraday Building is now on the site.

Collins Square

The very small and insignificant Collins Square at Blackheath is now of importance as a unique example of what was once to be found all over London: the slum court dignified with the name of square. Others persist as empty shells, but here some of the humble cottages are still standing to give an idea of what the hundreds of lost courtyard squares were like.

The name came from John Collins of Greenwich, a small-scale developer who obtained the freehold of most of the west side of what is now Blackheath Village in 1783, or a little earlier. The square was probably built soon afterwards, and certainly by 1798. It was originally more like a square, having a wider opening to Tranquil Vale, and cottages, nine in all, on the west and south sides. It then included the older cottages now numbered 45 and 47 Tranquil Vale.

The rebuilding of the Tranquil Vale shops to the east in the 1850s and the creation of Collins Street to the south in 1867 reduced the square to a terrace

The demolition of College Square, Doctors' Commons, in 1867.

Collins Square from the south in 2013.

of four weather-boarded cottages on the west side, and one of those was demolished early in the twentieth century. In 1961 Lewisham Council proposed to clear the survivors as a slum, but the invaluable Blackheath Society mounted a campaign that saved them. The prosperous residents have now emulated Choumert Square's gate and greenery, but as the tiny space is on a slope with steps, it resembles a rockery more than a garden.

Columbia Square

BETHNAL GREEN [TOWER HAMLETS]

Columbia Square was an expensive and elaborate estate of industrial dwellings built for Angela Burdett-Coutts between 1859 and 1862, with amateur advice from Charles Dickens and professional from Henry Astley Darbishire, later architect to the Peabody trustees.

Columbia Square in 1862.

The site was a huge rubbish tip south of the Hackney Road, not far from the notorious Nichol rookery. There were four blocks of bleak, mildly Gothic five-storey tenements. The ones on the north and south sides were set forward, which made the central space narrow and rectangular, but it was dignified with a clock tower. There was a slightly earlier church (St Thomas's) and a church school to the north, and the huge Columbia Market, bigger than the square, to the west. This elaborate Gothic folly was where the expense came in. It was meant to attract the costermongers from the streets, but failed entirely.

The square suffered badly in the Second World War, with all four blocks damaged, one of them severely. The other three were cleared about 1960 and replaced by the twin tower blocks called Sivill House. The undamaged market had been demolished in 1958.

Colville Square

NOTTING HILL [KENSINGTON AND CHELSEA]

George Frederick John Tippett was the creator of some of the ugliest squares in London, monstrosities that helped to bring the whole concept of the square into disrepute and very nearly banished it from the developer's vocabulary for more than a century. As he took complete responsibility as owner, chief builder and probably architect, Tippett thoroughly deserved to end his career in the bankruptcy courts in 1885.

He was already building in Prince's Square and Leinster Square in Bayswater when he purchased 17 acres in Notting Hill in 1860. They were the scene of a failed 1850s development by Samuel Walker that had produced only some sewers and the unfinished All Saints' Church. Over the next fifteen years Tippett and the men to whom he let many of the plots built a compact estate with Powis Square, Colville Square and Colville Gardens at its heart. Some of the houses in Colville Square were occupied by 1863, but the north side had not been begun in 1865.

In all his squares Tippett attempted a cheap imitation of the 'Gardens' architecture of South Kensington and Bayswater. His nearest and most recent model was the work of Henry de Bruno Austin in Cleveland Square and Kensington Gardens Square. The difficulty was the treatment of the double-sided houses, giving dignity to the garden front without relegating all the utilitarian detail to the street front. It is instructive to compare the relatively elegant solution achieved by Austin in Kensington Gardens Square with the appalling clutter with which Tippett surrounded the front doors of his back-to-front houses. To make matters worse, the communal gardens of Colville and Powis Square, for the sake of which these compromises were made, are meanly narrow strips.

With so many better squares to choose from much closer to the West End, few of the carriage folk Tippett

The west side of Colville Square in 1910, or a little earlier.

hoped to attract were willing to face the long trek to the north end of Notting Hill. Such little success as the square achieved was over by the 1880s, when more and more of the houses were divided into flats or let as cheap lodgings. Others were schools or institutions. By 1900 very few were in single occupation and the square was declining into a slum.

The council began to acquire houses in the area soon after the First World War and became the main landlord after the Second, gradually reducing the piecemeal conversions of the houses to some regularity. The south end of the west side of Colville Square, facing the garden,

was destroyed in the Second World War. The houses there have been replaced by very dull flats. Dullness and quiet are now the main characteristics of the whole square, except during the Notting Hill Carnival.

Colville Square North

(now Colville Houses)

Colville Square North was the original name for what is now Colville Houses. It was not a square, but a cul-de-sac with two terraces of seven houses running north from Colville Square, opposite the garden. It was part of George Tippett's development and just as ugly as the square, but was built a little later, in the early 1870s. Only the eastern terrace survives, plus an interesting coach house conversion (No. 9) on the west.

Compton Square

Compton Square, which probably came into existence in the 1830s, was called after the family name of its owner, the Marquess of Northampton. It cannot be said to have been built, as it was the more or less accidental open space left between six houses in Canonbury Road and four little terraces to the east. No more than five scattered cottages had Compton Square as their address. It was a mews more than a residential square and the name did not appear in the census before 1861. The 1848–51 skeleton map and the 1851 census called it Carters Yard.

Mary Cosh quotes from the Vestry minutes of 1878 a complaint of 'a nuisance caused by cabs being washed and goats running about unrestrained in the square'. In 1905 the marquess objected to its inclusion in the schedule of the *London Squares and Enclosures (Preservation) Bill*, because it was 'only a small paved court at the rear of premises in Canonbury Road'. Compton Square was badly damaged during the Second World War and the area was redeveloped. No. 124 Canonbury Road is the solitary survivor of the six houses behind which the square was hidden.

Connaught Square

Connaught Square was the first of the many in Bayswater, unless one counts the evanescent Cressey Square. The original name when building started in 1821 was Frederick Square, which is why the mews to the south is still Frederick Close. Portsea Place and Stanhope Place used to be Upper and Lower Frederick Street. 'Connaught', which had become the name by 1825, was taken from Connaught Place, the first of the Tyburnia developments, begun in 1807. It was the second title of the Duke of Gloucester.

Samuel Pepys Cockerell was surveyor to the Bishop of London's estate until his death in 1827, so he must have approved the designs for Connaught Square, if he did not provide them. The houses are not unlike his in Brunswick Square and far more conservative in style than those in the parts of Tyburnia begun after 1827. It may be significant that Thomas Allason, best known for his work on the Ladbroke estate at Notting Hill but active in Bayswater in the 1820s, lived at No. 1 Connaught Square. An architect might receive a house as payment in kind.

Cockerell died before the square was complete. The builder and architect James Ponsford took a lease of some remaining plots in 1829 and dislodged a factory that existed in the south-west corner until 1830. The square is in fact a rectangle, sloping gently from north to south, remarkably regular and well preserved, with only the ugly flats of Connaught Street in the north-east corner to distract from the late Georgian mood.

'It was typical of Lionel to live on the wrong side of the Park,' was the aristocratic Louis's comment in *Kind Hearts and Coronets* and its source, *Israel Rank*, when Lionel Holland committed suicide at a house with a fictitiously high number in Connaught Square. Nevertheless it was, and is, a better address than the other Bayswater squares and has had its celebrities, despite being at the back of beyond. The Earl of Thanet, at No. 15 in the mid-1830s, was a rare peer, but most of the distinguished residents represented the arts. 'I found my way to Fonblanque's, beyond Tyburn Turnpike,' wrote Crabb Robinson in 1831. He was visiting Albany Fonblanque, one of the leading journalists and editors of the early nineteenth century, who lived at No. 48 until his death in 1872. Marie Taglione, one of the most highly paid of ballet dancers, spent her old age running a school of deportment successively at No. 14

The west side of Connaught Square, *c.* 1904.

and No. 6 in the late 1870s. There is a plaque at No. 14. Mrs Humphrey Ward, Matthew Arnold's niece, after an extravagant career launched by her best-seller *Robert Elsmere*, died almost penniless in 1920 at No. 4.

Cook Square

CITY OF LONDON

This tiny square was so insignificant that Harben failed to include it in his *Dictionary of London*. It was approached via an archway on the west side of Staining Lane, between Lily Pot Lane (alas no more) and Oat Lane. In 1842 it was referred to as Cook Square, Noble Street, so there may perhaps have been some access from the west. Early nineteenth-century maps showed no development in the interior of that block and the name was not recorded by Lockie in 1813 or Elmes in 1831. The square certainly existed in 1837, when a whalebone cutter insured Nos 3 and 4.

It was included in the 1841 census as Cook Square, and as Cooks Court in 1851 when the five houses were occupied by a charing woman, a mangling woman, a labourer, a tailor and a dealer in fruit. The pages of the 1861 census covering the square have not survived and it was passed over in 1871 and later returns because there were no residents in what had become an entirely commercial court.

It was shown without name on the 1873 Ordnance Survey map, by which time the five large buildings surrounding it had their main entrances in Staining Lane, Oat Lane or Lily Pot Lane, reducing the square to a mere backyard. Later maps indicated that its size had been reduced still further, but it survived in some form as late as 1940. The whole area was flattened during the Second World War and the Lloyds Bank head office now occupies the block.

Cook's Square

CITY OF LONDON

The area west of Bishopsgate and Norton Folgate was a wilderness of alleys, the most prominent being Long Alley, which ran all the way from the north side of Moorfields, now Eldon Street, to Hog Alley, now part of Worship Street. Its northern half is represented today by Appold Street.

The alley that somehow came to be called Cook's Square was a minor part of this network. It ran from Long Alley to Primrose Street, with a right-angled turn three-quarters of the way along. Strype's map of 1720 (probably surveyed long before that date) did not show it, but it appeared without a name on Rocque's survey of 1746. By the 1790s it was Cook's Court.

John Lockie made a rare mistake in the 1813 edition of his invaluable *Topography of London* by describing it twice, as Cook's Court when approached from Primrose Street and as Cook's Place when approached from Long Alley. Only the former was in his 1810 edition.

By 1829 when George Pitt, a New Broad Street auctioneer, insured twelve houses, it had blossomed into Cook Square – but pride comes before a fall. Most of it was demolished in the 1860s, when the land (or more exactly, something far below it) was required for the lines running into the new Broad Street Station. The eight houses that survived at the west end were briefly more like a square, of the cul-de-sac type, than the place had ever been before, but they were destroyed and the square extinguished when the goods depot was created at the corner of Appold Street and Worship Street in the 1870s.

Now, with Broad Street Station a fading memory, ground level has been re-established and huge offices stand on the site of Cook's Square.

Coopers Square

RATCLIFFE [TOWER HAMLETS]

Lockie gave the position of Coopers Square in 1810: 'School-House-Lane, Ratcliffe, – is a few doors on the R. from Cockhill towards Brooke-st.' This describes the Coopers' Almshouses on the east side of Schoolhouse Lane, towards the south end. They did form a three-sided square, with the chapel in the centre of the east side flanked by the two-storey houses of the pensioners, which also extended along the whole of the north and south sides; but many almshouses had this form without the courtyard being called a square. Lockie was supported in giving the name here only by his usual follower, James Elmes.

The almshouses had been rebuilt in this form in 1796 after being destroyed in the great Ratcliffe fire of 1794. They were demolished in 1894 after becoming surrounded by foundries. Cock Hill is now the Highway and Brook Street is Cable Street. School House Lane is still Schoolhouse Lane, but has become one of the most dull and dreary streets in all of London – no mean feat. The whole of the east side is now occupied by the red brick wall of the Highway Business Park.

Copperas Square

DEPTFORD [LEWISHAM]

Copperas Square was an early nineteenth-century court with entrances through archways from Copperas Lane, now Bronze Street, in the north and from John Street, later Alvar Street, in the south. Six houses were listed there in the 1824 ratebook.

In the 1860s, when there were houses only on the west side, the court was quite large, extending east between the backs of the houses in the two streets to a large building. It was probably a factory or workshop, for this was a poor industrial area, with paint, tar, soap and manure works all within easy reach, and smell. By the 1890s the large building had gone and the court had been reduced to an alley by the addition of houses on the east side.

The LCC was already redeveloping the area with flats when the Second World War interrupted work. A V1 flying bomb obliterated the last of the old houses in Alvar Street, Bronze Street and Copperas Square, and Congers House was built on the site.

Cornwall Square

BETHNAL GREEN [TOWER HAMLETS]

Cornwall Place was opposite the entrance to the Bethnal House lunatic asylum, off the south side of Cornwall Road, now Cornwall Avenue. It was a short alley of about five houses and Cornwall Square was an offshoot to the west with three or four more.

Cornwall Road was created in the 1820s. The name of Cornwall Square did not appear before the 1860s; until then Cornwall Place and Cornwall Square were known collectively as Fountain Place, perhaps after the fountain in the garden of Bethnal House. In 1871 the three houses listed in the square were occupied by cabinet makers, a cork cutter, a butcher and a pegged boot maker.

Charles Booth's assistant recorded a police inspector's estimate in 1898:

'Mark it as bad as you like,' said Pearn, 'for it is vicious, and as bad as any place in Bethnal Green, a great source of trouble to the police. Haddock curers its inhabitants, many juvenile thieves. Though so bad it is a small place. Belongs to the Commissioner of Police, who made us smile one day by sending down to say that his tenants complained of constant row, & absence of any police from the neighbourhood.'

Despite its bad reputation it survived unaltered until the Second World War, when bomb damage was taken advantage of to demolish the remaining houses and add the ground to Bethnal Green Gardens. The site had been cleared by 1948.

Cory Square

BANKSIDE [LAMBETH]

Prince's Square on the South Bank, which was later known as Cory Square, was built soon after 1815, and like Cleaver Square it was named originally in honour of the Prince Regent. This part of Lambeth was a piece of Duchy of Cornwall land known as 'Prince's Meadows', for the development of which as 'Prince's Town' an Act of Parliament had been obtained in 1810. This authorised the regent to grant building leases from 1815.

The immediate site of Prince's Square was a group of tiny cottages in a complex of alleys called Back Walk, alleys even narrower than Narrow Wall from which they branched. The cottages probably dated from the Commonwealth, when there was no Prince of Wales on hand to prevent encroachments.

The developers of the Prince's Town estate were John and Thomas Lett, timber merchants of Narrow Wall. They widened and straightened Narrow Wall to create Commercial Road, now part of Upper Ground, as the main feature of the new town. Prince's Square was built off the south side of Commercial Road, just east of Duke (now Duchy) Street, before 1820. A narrow entrance led to a slightly wider court, with eleven small houses on each side and two at the south end. Had the Prince ever visited his new square the compliment of the name would not have pleased him, as this dismal court can never have been anything but a slum.

Prince's Square did not often come to the attention of the great world on the other side of the river, and then its moments of fame were of a most unwelcome kind. The land had been reclaimed from the Thames in a haphazard way, probably early in the seventeenth century, and remained subject to flooding. In November 1875 and again in January 1877 during an exceptionally wet winter, this man-made inlet was completely filled with Thames water. A flood was a rare occasion – a moonlight flit was another – whcn a paucity of possessions was a positive advantage.

Prince's Square, Bankside, later Cory Square, flooded in 1875.

The name was changed to Cory Square in 1897, to avoid confusion with Prince's Square at Kennington, which was itself later renamed Cleaver Square in deference to the much later Prince's Square in Bayswater. Why Cory? If it was in honour of William Cory, who died in 1892, it was no more flattering to the poet than to the prince. It is not impossible, given that the LCC chose to rename the adjoining Thomas Street as Aquinas Street. There was, unexpectedly, somebody in County Hall with a sense of humour.

Charles Booth's assistant gave this description in 1899:

> Cory Square (late Princes Square), three storied houses, court in course of being well laid with cement. Children very dirty but well fed. Poor and very poor, and a few fairly comfortable. All doors open, some bread about, a few Irish. West side poorer than the east. Five roomed houses let at 10/-, all the east side at this price. Small glass bottle factory out of the east side. Old tenants: one has been 26 years in the court, another boy of about 16 had lived at various times with his family at every one of the various houses in the court.

Cory Square must have been demolished in 1913 or not long before, as the Ordnance Survey map of 1913–14 showed the buildings entirely cleared. The southern half of Bernie Spain Gardens now occupies the site.

Cottage Square

NEWINGTON [SOUTHWARK]

Cottage Square was built in the 1840s behind the Cottage of Content public house. In 1851 it consisted of only four or five houses occupied mostly by shoe-makers. The pub stood opposite Elsted Street, at the complicated junction where Rodney Road now meets Flint Street, Elsted Street and Catesby Street, which is the modern successor to Cottage Row. The description of the enumeration district in 1871 included both Cottage Square and Gotobed Cottages, but had the note, 'Gotobed Cottages now known as Cottage Square'. (A John Gotobed lived nearby in 1851.)

As the number of families in Cottage Square was greater in 1871 than in earlier censuses, it had perhaps annexed the terrace a little to the north-west that was described as Oaksbury Cottages on the 1871 map. That name did not appear in the census and was probably an alias of Gotobed Cottages. Cottage Square was demolished in the 1880s, when Hillery Road was built across the site. Since the Second World War the whole area has been redeveloped as council housing and Locksfield House has replaced Hillery Road and the Cottage of Content.

Cottage Square

STEPNEY [TOWER HAMLETS]

Cottage Square was part of Dawson's Gardens, the land enclosed by Commercial Road on the south, Sidney Street on the west, Clark Street on the north and Jubilee Street on the east. Doran's Row, which formed the southern boundary of Dawson's Gardens, predated Commercial Road and was made an awkward part of it when the new highway was created in the first decade of the nineteenth century.

In the 1790s there were scarcely any buildings in Dawson's Gardens north of Doran's Row, but when Commercial Road made the land more accessible Jubilee Place, the present Jubilee Street, was built on the east side and named after George III's golden jubilee of 1810. Cottage Lane was added just east of Sidney Street and Cottage Square soon branched east from the north end of Cottage Lane. Numbers 1–6 Cottage Square were insured with the Sun in 1822.

The haphazard rural development was regularised in the 1860s, when Cottage Lane became Bromehead Street and three short roads were built off its east side. The northern one, Gardom Street, later Mayland Street, replaced Cottage Square, although a few old houses survived in a narrow offshoot from Bromehead Street, just south of Clark Street. The area was rebuilt as council housing after extensive Second World War bomb damage and the site is now occupied by Jubilee Gardens, a real square, though without the name.

Covent Garden

Covent Garden, London's first square, was built in the 1630s before that term had been invented, although it was sometimes applied to it in later descriptions. In 1756, for example, William Maitland called it 'Covent Garden Square' in his *History of London*.

It was the product of a change in taste that began under James I and intensified under his son. Sir Henry Wotton had published *The Elements of Architecture* in 1624 and the Banqueting House at Whitehall was the new boast of London. From being the passion of a coterie, the classical principles of the art were becoming a commonplace of small talk, and no aspect of the subject was so much discussed as Covent Garden. Two plays set in the unfinished square were produced in or around 1632–33. Richard Brome's farcical comedy *The Weeding of the Covent-Garden* opens with a foolish Justice of the Peace standing in the square and holding forth on taste to one of the builders, who has 'pil'd up a Leash of thousand pounds in walls and windows there', not to mention the 'Bellconeys' before some of the houses, a novel attraction featured in both plays:

'I Marry Sir! This is something like! These appear like Buildings! Here's Architecture exprest indeed! It is a most sightly situation, and fit for Gentry and Nobility.'

'When it is finished, doubtlesse it will be handsome.'

'It will be glorious: and yond magnificent Peece, the Piazzo, will excel that at Venice, by hearsay, (I ne're travell'd). A hearty blessing on their braines, honours, and wealths, that are Projectors, Furtherers, and Performers of such great works … You cannot think how I am taken with that Rowe! How even and straight they are! And so are all indeed. The Surveyor (what e'er he was) has manifested himself the Master of his great Art. How he has wedded strength to beauty; state to uniformity; commodiousness with perspicuity! All, all as't should be!'

'If all were as well tenanted and inhabited by worthy persons.'

There was the rub, for already bawds and whores had made a lodgement in the new buildings, discouraging the gentry and nobility from settling there. In *Covent Garden*, the rival play by Thomas Nabbes, the machinations of lodging-house keepers are a further drawback.

Covent Garden from the east in 1741.

The Projector whose wealth and enterprise gave rise to Covent Garden was the 4th Earl of Bedford. The site was the land behind the garden of Bedford House in the Strand, the name recalling that it was the kitchen garden of Westminster Abbey until the Dissolution. The inevitable surveyor was Inigo Jones. In 1631 the earl paid Charles I £2,000 for a licence to build the square and the employment of the king's architect was almost certainly a condition of the grant.

The earl's plans for the layout of the land were viewed by the king and his commissioners for new buildings (of whom Jones was the chief) and altered in ways that made them considerably more expensive. Jones provided the designs for St Paul's Church, which was paid for by the earl, and for the arcaded houses on the north and east sides. The church was begun in 1631 and consecrated in 1638; the houses were built between 1632 and 1637. Jones's models were various ceremonial public spaces seen on his travels in Italy and France. The earl had the first three houses built on his own account to set the standard that others

The Covent Garden arcades in 1768, looking from the north to the east side.

The Covent Garden Market House in 1829.

north side, the Great Piazza. The most celebrated was the poet and dramatist, Sir William Alexander, Earl of Stirling, from 1638 to 1640. Other society figures who dabbled in literature were Thomas Killigrew from 1636 to 1640 and again in 1661–62, Sir Kenelm Digby from 1662 to 1665 and Roger North from 1686 until about 1694. Almost the last was Lady Mary Wortley Montagu in 1730–31. As a member of the landlord's family, Admiral Edward Russell, Earl of Orford, was a special case. He lived at No. 43 King Street from about 1690 until 1727.

Like several later squares, Covent Garden passed from the aristocracy to the artists. The first of importance was Sir Peter Lely from 1650 until his death in 1680. Sir Godfrey Kneller, his successor as the fashionable portrait painter, lived in the square from 1682 to 1703. Sir James Thornhill was there from 1722 to 1734 and his pupil and son-in-law William Hogarth until his move to Leicester Square in 1733. The last artist of real eminence was the landscape painter Richard Wilson, who had his studio in the Great Piazza from the late 1750s to the early 1770s.

Competition from the rush of new squares in the 1670s and 1680s, all based upon the model of Covent Garden, contributed to the social decline of the prototype. Edward Hatton described it in 1708, just before it was substantially altered:

> Covent Garden, a pleasant Square, on the NW and NE sides whereof, are very stately Buildings, partly elevated on large pillars, which makes very fine Piazzas: On the SW side is the Church, and on the SE the Market for Earthenware, Fruit and Herbs; the Area is 3 acres, and the Column in the Center, is from Charing Cross, northwesterly, 670 yds.

Bedford House had been demolished in 1705, soon after the Russells moved to Bloomsbury Square. The market was moved into the central enclosure where it quickly expanded (see p.7), and between 1706 and 1714 a south side was added to the square. At first it was thought of as a continuation of Henrietta Street, but it was later known separately as Tavistock Row.

Strype's account, although not published until 1720, was also written before the building of Tavistock Row:

were required to follow. A number of Jones's friends and associates took building leases, as did the courtier William Newton, who was later the main developer of Lincoln's Inn Fields.

The problems common to new districts – the pot-holed roads, the footpads, the defective sewers, the noise and dirt of building work – and the local difficulties with brothels and rowdy taverns were largely overcome by the late 1630s when Covent Garden began a brief period of fashionable success. From 1657 the tenants contributed to the maintenance of the railing around the central space. It was known as the Mount, the ground rising gently to the centre to aid drainage. A tree was its only ornament until a sundial column replaced it in 1668–69. The market was at first hardly a problem, being only a cluster of stalls (replaced by shops in the 1670s) sheltering under the wall of the Bedford House garden on the south side. The earl did not even procure a charter for it until 1670.

Covent Garden had many aristocratic residents during its early years, most of them favouring the

On the North and East Sides are erected stately Buildings for the dwelling of Persons of Repute and Quality, their Fronts standing on Pillars and Arches of Brick and Stone Rustick Work, with Piazzas, or Walks, like those in the Royal Exchange in London, and imitating the Rialto in Venice … Covent Garden, particularly so called, is a curious, large, and airy Square, enclosed by Rails, between which Rails and the Houses runs a fair Street. The Square is always kept well gravelled for the Accommodation of the People to walk there, and so raised with an easy Ascent to the Middle, that the rain soon draineth off, and the gravelly Bottom becomes dry, fit to walk on. In the Midst of this Garden, within the Rails, is a Stone Pillar or Column raised on a Pedestal, ascended by Steps, on which is placed a curious Sun-dial four Square; having above it a Mound gilt with Gold, all neatly wrought in Freestone. On the North and East Sides are Rows of very good and large Houses, called the Piazzo's, sustained by Stone Pillars, to support the Buildings, Under which are Walks, broad and convenient, paved with Freestone. The South Side lieth open to Bedford Garden, where there is a small Grotto of Trees, most pleasant in the summer Season; and in this Side there is kept a Market for Fruits, Herbs, Roots, and Flowers, every Tuesday, Thursday, and Saturday; which is grown to a considerable Account, and well served with choice Goods, which makes it much resorted unto. And on the West Side is the Church of St Paul's Covent Garden.

From this time the fashionable inhabitants drifted away to the west, more of the houses were turned to commercial use and the profitable market became the main concern of the dukes of Bedford and their agents. Later comments on the square were focused on the market, in praise or blame. César de Saussure gave this account in 1725:

Going towards the City you see another big place, named by the French '*Commun-Jardin*,' and by the English Covent Garden. Every sort of flower, fruit, and garden produce is sold here. It is surrounded on two sides by fine arcades, which are most convenient for shelter in bad weather.

James Ralph was sour as usual in 1734:

The piazza is grand and noble, and the superstructure it supports light and elegant. The market in the middle may be a matter of much profit to the ground-landlord, but I am sure it is a great nuisance, with respect to the beauty and regularity of the square, and, in a great measure, defeats the very intent it was first calculated to serve.

Noorthouck agreed in 1773:

… a fine square, the area of which is the greatest market for greens, fruit, and flowers in the metropolis; a circumstance which it must be owned has more of utility than elegance in it … Had Inigo Jones's plan been compleated, this would have been the most finished square any where to be found.

Contagion from the local theatres was another cause of the square's social decline. The Theatre Royal in Drury Lane was built in 1663 by the Covent Garden resident, Thomas Killigrew. It brought actors and playwrights into the district and encouraged the growth of taverns, coffee houses and brothels. These were brought even closer when Covent Garden Theatre was opened in 1732, with its principal entrance through the portico buildings in the north-east corner. Thereafter, coffee houses proliferated in the square itself, plus bagnios and hotels, some of them of suspicious reputation.

By the early nineteenth century, with the growth of London and the conversion of so much land in the suburbs into market gardens, the centre of the square could not contain the stalls of all the tradesmen. The 6th Duke's income from the market rents and tolls exceeded that from the houses, and the traders' convenience naturally took precedence. In 1827 he decided to build a market house to replace the clutter of shops and stalls and to take the management of the market into his own hands instead of leasing it to the highest bidder. The architect of the new building was the market expert Charles Fowler, who also did work for the Bedford estate at Bloomsbury. The contract for building it went to William Cubitt, his first

Covent Garden in the 1920s.

major job after separating from his brother Thomas. The work lasted from 1828 to 1832.

The arcaded houses of Inigo Jones had been eroded by faulty workmanship, fire and changes of use and taste even in the seventeenth century, and the destruction increased in the eighteenth. Family influence enabled Admiral Russell to rebuild No. 43 King Street in an entirely discordant style in 1716–17. The east side south of Russell Street was destroyed by fire in 1769 and rebuilt without the arcades. Other sections were altered or rebuilt as shops and hotels.

By 1876 the sections flanking James Street were all that remained of the original arcaded houses, and that to the west was crumbling. After much debate about the claims of tradition and profit, the 9th Duke decided to rebuild this section with the arcades replaced. Henry Clutton's Bedford Chambers of 1877–78 are a Victorian interpretation of Jones, on a larger scale but remarkably successful. Several other blocks around the square were rebuilt by Clutton, or under his influence, in the 1870s and

1880s, in a similar style but without the arcades. East of James Street the arcades survived in front of the Tavistock Hotel (largely rebuilt in the 1860s) until 1928.

The great expansion of the market buildings in the late nineteenth and early twentieth century was a desperate attempt to keep up with the growing demand for space and to fend off mounting criticism of the duke's monopoly. The first addition outside the original enclosure was the flower market in the south-east corner, which began in a small way in 1860 but had grown by 1905 into the huge complex now occupied by the London Transport Museum. Tavistock Row, the south side of the square, was demolished after the leases expired in 1883 and at first left entirely open as parking space for the traders' carts, but in 1904 the eastern half was covered by a foreign flower market, the original half of the present Jubilee Market Hall.

E.M. Barry's Floral Hall of 1858–59 was part of the rebuilding of Covent Garden Theatre and intended as a rival flower market, but it failed and was bought by the duke in 1887 as a foreign fruit market. At the same time he demolished most of the houses between Russell Street and the Floral Hall to provide more space for the traders, but all this exertion and outlay failed to satisfy the public and divert criticism. The duke despaired, and the whole of the Covent Garden estate was sold in 1918 to Sir Thomas Beecham, the conductor, and his family company, for £2 million. In 1962 the company sold most of it (but not the Royal Opera House) to the Covent Garden Market Authority for £4 million.

That proved the end of the 330-year history of the market in Covent Garden, for the Authority immediately resolved on finding a larger site and completed the move to Nine Elms in 1974. In anticipation, the GLC and the local councils put forward extraordinarily far-reaching proposals for the rebuilding of the area. Public opposition to them and their gradual modification and virtual abandonment proved a turning point in the history of London and began the great age of improvement through conservation and adaptation.

Fowler's central market buildings were restored as shops and restaurants between 1977 and 1980 and became an immediate and overwhelming success. At the same time the flower market was converted as the London Transport Museum and the Jubilee Hall on the south side became a sports centre and flea market. Since then the magical name of Inigo Jones has led to the gradual reappearance and extension of the arcades, restricted between 1928 and 1984 to Clutton's short stretch west of James Street.

The tentative first step was on the south side, where arcades had not been seen before. The 1984–87 extension to the Jubilee Hall features a crude and heavy arcade intended to shelter market stalls. A much more sophisticated tribute to Jones followed between 1997 and 1999, when the long-debated extension to the Royal Opera House was built, with a light and elegant arcade from James Street to Russell Street that restores something of the spirit, though not the form, of the Great Piazza. Elsewhere canopies and sun shades have appeared. If one could return in 100 years it would be no surprise to find neo-Jones on every side.

Cowper's Square

WHITECHAPEL [TOWER HAMLETS]

'Cowper's Square, Goodman's fields' was one of the fifty listed by Maitland in 1756 in his *History of London*, and from there has found its way into several books on London squares as an unlocated puzzle, but it is evidently only a mistake for Hooper's Square (q.v.) which was at the south-east corner of Goodman's Fields. Maitland does not include Hooper's Square, although it certainly existed in his time, being named on Rocque's map.

Cox's Square

SPITALFIELDS [TOWER HAMLETS]

The land between Petticoat Lane and Bell Lane belonged to the Montague family. By the early eighteenth century the houses built there before 1600 had become ruinous and Elizabeth Montague was trying to improve the estate by granting repairing and building leases. One of these, taken about 1708 by John Cox and Henry Philip of Stepney, probably resulted in the formation of Cox's Square.

The site was shown as a garden on the 1676 and 1720 maps, but was fully formed and named Coxes Square by Rocque in 1746. It had a dozen houses, distinctly bigger than those in the surrounding streets. John Strype, who was born a few yards to the north and took a natural interest in the area, made no mention of the new square in his 1720 revision of Stow's *Survey*. That may suggest it was built later, but much of Strype's text, like his map, was completed long before 1720.

In the eighteenth century the square must have seemed quite eligibly situated with open garden ground close by in most directions, but by 1810 the gardens to the north had been covered by the huge Constitution Brewery, to which a newly widened opening on the north side of Cox's Square gave all too ready access. This southern portion of Spitalfields, originally a garden suburb, had grown ever more crowded during the eighteenth century.

The creation of the square was no doubt an attempt to halt this decline, but by 1800 the downward spiral was unstoppable. The old houses were broken up into ever smaller tenements and the population grew dramatically. Petticoat Lane developed into one of the chief Jewish quarters of London and the surrounding streets and squares became mere offshoots of its teeming market. Cox's Square was destroyed in the last year of the nineteenth century, as part of a comprehensive slum clearance programme agreed between the freeholder and the LCC. Strype Street was one of the new roads that replaced it.

Cressey Square

BAYSWATER [WESTMINSTER]

Cressey (or Cressy) Square is a fascinating oddity. It was part of a short-lived shanty town that rose and fell in Bayswater between 1800 and 1820, when it was swept away in preparation for the splendours of Tyburnia. It wrapped round the north and west sides of the St George's burial ground in Bayswater Road. The usual name for this haphazard collection of huts was Tomlin's New Town and its main thoroughfare was Harpur's Fields, which ran west from Edgware Road opposite King Street, now Nutford Place.

John Lockie listed Cressey Square in his 1813 edition, but not in 1810. He described Cressey Place as being in Harpur's Fields, an eighth of a mile west from No. 37 Edgware Road, and Cressey Square he located on the west side of Cressey Place. Number 37 Edgware Road was between Upper Berkeley Street and George Street. It was chosen as the landmark because there were no permanent houses on the west side.

The 1813 edition of Horwood's map showed a lane directly opposite No. 37 that ran west for 100 yards before turning north and ending abruptly after another 100 yards or so. Almost no buildings were shown west of it. Darton's 1817 map indicated that Tomlin's New Town had spread west very rapidly from the modest settlement shown by Horwood. If Lockie's eighth of a mile is accurate, Cressey Square was north of the burial ground, roughly where the west end of Kendal Street is today. Darton showed some terraces at odd angles there that might just be construed as a square.

Until 1817 the ratebooks did not include the names of Cressey Square or Cressey Place, the two being lumped together as Byers Cottages, named from the proprietor. From 1817 to 1820 they do appear, as Cressy Square and Place, the square having twelve cottages with a tiny £6 rateable value. At first an attempt was made to 'collect of Biers', but in 1820, when the square made its last appearance, the tenants were all described as poor and excused rates. The shanties had been built on very short leases, terminable at six months' notice, issued by the Bishop of London's lessees while they waited until the time was ripe for their great Tyburnia development. In 1820 the leases were called in and Tomlin's New Town was demolished. The dislodged pig keepers, who were then its main occupants, decamped to Pottery Lane, Notting Hill, where they caused havoc for fifty years. (See Tobin Square and St James's Square, Notting Hill for more about them.)

Crosby Square

CITY OF LONDON

Crosby Square was built over the garden and on the site of the rear offices of Crosby Place, the great Bishopsgate mansion famous for its association with Richard III. Various writers follow one another in saying that Crosby Place was largely destroyed in the Great Fire and that Crosby Square was built about 1671, but the Ogilby & Morgan map of 1676 shows the house and garden unaltered, although their peace was then disturbed by the clatter of the General Post Office's wagons in the forecourt. Strype says of Bishopsgate that 'this Ward within the Wall suffered not much by the Fire of London, 1666, and the Parts without nothing at all'.

Crosby Hall, Crosby Square, City of London, in 1829.

Edward Hatton in 1708 was the first to mention 'Crosby Court, or square, on the easterly side of Bishopsgate street within, near the middle, a Passage to St Mary Ax'. That he said nothing about the houses may be significant. It does not inspire confidence that Hatton had a second entry for 'Crosby court', mentioning Crosby Hall, the surviving relic of Crosby Place, but placing the court on the wrong side of Bishopsgate, as 'a Passage into Broad street'. Strype's map of Bishopsgate ward, following as usual Ogilby & Morgan, does not show the square, but includes the name in the key, the reference being to the forecourt of Crosby Place. In his text, Strype mentions Crosby Square twice and the second description certainly refers to the true one:

> This large and convenient House is now built into a Square of good Houses, and called Crosby Square … This large Building hath been of late Years converted into a curious open Square, with fair Brick Buildings, well inhabited by Gentry and Merchants, the Houses having Palisado Pales before, and Gardens behind them. Out of this Square is a passage through a Back-gateway, passing by a large Warehouse belonging to the East India Company, and so into Great St Helen's.

David Hughson gave further details in 1806: 'On the other side of the square, eastward, are the Baggage Warehouses of the East India Company, which occupies a large space of ground. The building is for the reception of contraband goods before sale.'

Crosby Square was small, with only eight substantial three-storey houses. Crosby Hall was in the north-west corner by the narrow entrance from Bishopsgate. The square was always a good address. From 1782 No. 3 was the London home of Sir Robert Wigram, Bt, the shipbuilder, who died in 1830.

Two of the eight houses were still private in 1843 and Nathan Adler, the Chief Rabbi, lived at No. 4 in the 1850s, a synagogue having replaced part of the old East India warehouses. The other houses were occupied by substantial merchants.

All were rebuilt as tall offices during the twentieth century. The east end was severely damaged in the Second World War and not rebuilt, leaving more a courtyard than a square, with steps down from the east side to the new street, Undershaft. The steps, the nameplate and one office on the north side still exist, but since 2007 all the other buildings have gone and a huge redevelopment has been in progress around the site of Crosby Square.

Crosby Square

SHOREDITCH [HACKNEY]

Crosby Buildings was not shown on Horwood's 1790s map and was not included in Lockie's 1810 *Topography of London*, but it was noticed in the 1813 revisions of both. Lockie gave its position as 'French-Alley, 1st on the L. from 150 Shoreditch'. It was a court of eight houses, four on each side, turning south from French Alley, which ran from Shoreditch High Street to Curtain Road. It had been promoted to a square by 1841 but the old name still cropped up afterwards.

Like the similar New Inn Square to the south, it was at least partially destroyed in the early 1860s by the building of the North London Railway viaduct into Broad Street. The west side may have survived as part of Norfolk Place, which was later incorporated with French Place but has now been demolished. The site is between Dereham Place and Bateman's Row, under the viaduct and immediately to its west.

Crosley's Square

CITY OF LONDON

This was an occasional name for a yard off the north side of Hart Street, opposite St Olave's. It was called Crossley's Court on the 1676 Ogilby & Morgan map and Crosleys Square on the Strype map of 1720 (probably surveyed earlier), but was Three Tuns Court on Rocque's map of 1746. In 1667 Pepys recorded a visit to 'the new tavern come by us, the Three Tuns, where D. Gawden did feast us with a chine of beef and good other things, and an infinite dish of fowl; but all spoiled in the dressing'. It was only a few yards from his home at the Navy Office.

Hatton mentioned 'Crossleys court' in 1708, but said nothing about the buildings. In 1720 Strype described it as 'Crossleys, or Angel Court, which is a pretty open Place with good Buildings well inhabited'. In the 1790s London Street, formerly a cul-de-sac running south from Fenchurch Street, was clumsily extended to Hart Street under the name of New London Street, and Crosley's Square was one of several small places either incorporated in it or obliterated during its construction. The very irregular shape of New London Street at its southern end in those early years suggests that a number of the Crosley's Square houses survived there. New London Street still exists, but it is now occupied entirely by huge modern offices.

Cross Key Square

CITY OF LONDON

Cross Key Square is nearly always called Cross Keys Square in popular speech. It still exists off the north side of Little Britain but has passed through four transformations on the way to its present state.

The 1676 Ogilby & Morgan map showed a small Cross Keys Court, presumably an inn yard. The Cross Key was perhaps the forerunner of the White Horse in Little Britain, which still exists as a building but is no longer a pub. An entrance to the square survives as a passage through the former pub, but the gate is always locked.

In 1720, Strype described it as 'Cross Keys Court, a pretty handsome Place, with good Buildings, and Gardens behind some of them'. In 1746 Rocque showed a fairly long and narrow Cross Keys Court leading to a large, formal, rectangular garden with a pond or fountain in the centre. The garden beyond had gone by the 1790s, but the court, still narrow, had become Cross Keys Square with fourteen houses, seven on each side.

In 1820 Washington Irving wrote a gently satirical account of the society of the district, in which he recorded that 'bitter rivalry has also broken out as to the most fashionable part of Little Britain; the Lambs standing up for the dignity of Cross-Keys square, and the Trotters for the vicinity of St Bartholomew's'.

The Little Britain entrance to Cross Key Square in 2007.

(The Lambs were the social-climbing children of a butcher). There were still a few 'esquires' living in the square in the 1840s, but the area was becoming more and more commercial.

The houses were intact in 1875 but by the 1880s the whole of Cross Key Square had been rebuilt as towering warehouses and factories connected with various branches of the clothing trade. Most of them surprisingly survived the Second World War but they were empty and derelict in the 1980s, the area having been blighted by the demolitions for the London Wall/Aldersgate roundabout, which was built in the previous decade. In 1991–92 the huge '200 Aldersgate' building arose, bridging over and wrapping round the new Montague Street, for the sake of which numerous small courts and alleys had been destroyed. In the process a larger Cross Key Square emerged as practically a private garden for No. 200 Aldersgate, which mountainously defines its western, northern and eastern sides, while its obsessive security blocks public access from all directions.

Crossland Square

Crossland Square was built about 1820 during the rapid development of the land south of Bethnal Green Road. Grosvenor Square was the original name. The angle imposed on Mape Street by a stream left more than the usual amount of space north of Sale Street. This was used to build the two terraces, set far apart, that constituted Crossland Square. There would have been room for a central green, had one been desired, but instead the land was divided into ten front gardens, all accessed via a narrow alley running north from Sale Street.

It was already a slum when Hector Gavin visited the area in 1848 as part of his *Sanitary Rambles*: 'Crossland or Grosvenor-Square, ten houses in a kind of court planted on the damp undrained soil, presenting a rheumatic aspect.'

The houses on the west side (Nos 1–5) were rebuilt in conventional bay-windowed style around 1890, when the terrace to the south in Sale Street was demolished and left as an open space. This had been a semi-criminal 'black spot' on the original Booth poverty map of the late 1880s. On the east side of Crossland Square the original terrace of tiny late Georgian cottages survived until the whole area was cleared in the late 1950s and early 1960s. The peculiarity of this terrace was the very large window with a slightly curving top that filled almost the whole first floor of each cottage.

The site of the square is now the part of Weavers Fields between Kelsey Street and Derbyshire Street.

Crown Square

Crown Square is one of London's oddest survivals. It was probably built late in the eighteenth century, and certainly by the 1820s, on the east side of what was then part of Windmill Lane, now Crown Street. The 1815 ratebook listed under Windmill Lane four cottages called Carpenters Place and four called Mr Savages Rents. The 1848–50 skeleton map called the south side Crown Square and the north Carpenters Place.

The square was of the front garden type, the terraces on the north and south sides having long front gardens separated by an alley that gave access to the houses on the east side. The west was open to Crown Street. When the London, Chatham & Dover Railway viaduct was built between Crown Street and Camberwell Road in the early 1860s nearly all the houses on the east side of Crown Street were demolished, and with them went the north and south sides of Crown Square. That left half a dozen houses of the east side, stranded on the wrong side of the viaduct, tight up against it and only to be reached through one of the arches. Their name was soon forgotten. They seemed doomed, but somehow other uses were found for them and there they still are after a century and a half, although recent rebuilding to south and west has reduced the inaccessibility that has protected them for so long. The open railway arch just south of Sultan Street leads to this secret place.

Crown Square

Deacon Street was a turning off the north end of Walworth Road, opposite Hampton Street. The first turning on the north side of Deacon Street was Williams Place and off the west side of that was Crown Square. It was given the name because the terrace of shops in Walworth Road that bounded it on the west was known as Crown Row. Williams Place was built in the 1830s, but Crown Square was not heard of until the 1840s and had a very short life. It did not appear in the 1871 census and the 1872 map showed the cottages demolished. The cleared space was rebuilt as a mews, with stables for the enlarged shops in Crown Row.

Early in the twentieth century Williams Place, by then known as Winch Place, was also cleared to form a larger yard which was soon covered by a garage. All this was demolished after the Second World War and two generations of tower blocks have since covered the site.

Crown Square

See Three Crown Square

Cumberland Square

Cumberland Square was a project only, one of the many anticipations of John Nash's developments included in the 1813 revision of Horwood's map but never realised. It appeared as a large rectangle with a fancifully planted garden at the north-east corner of Regent's Park.

In the event, the various terraces around the park were given different names and positions, the canal took its great loop south of Lords instead of running straight and the land adjoining it was developed as avenues of villas rather than old-fashioned squares. The Duke of Cumberland was honoured instead by the Cumberland Hay Market on the east side of the park.

Cummings Square

Just outside the charmed circle of the Crown's Regent's Park estate there was an awkward triangle of land north of Euston Road, much of which is now occupied by Triton Square. In the 1790s, perhaps inspired by the creation of Fitzroy Square directly to the south, an attempt was made to plant a rival here on the north side of the New Road.

As the plot available was a quarter of the size of Fitzroy Square, itself quite small, the prospects for success were never good. They disappeared altogether when the building of Fitzroy Square was suspended after only two sides had been completed.

Lockie did not include Cummings Square in his 1810 edition but gave its position in 1813: 'Fitzroy-Row, New Road,– N. end on the R.' The name came from James Cummings, who appeared in the 1813 ratebook as the owner of two houses listed in Fitzroy Row. The ill-defined open space remained until at least the 1830s, but was increasingly hemmed in by the backs of cottages in the lanes and alleys that sprang up all around it. The name had passed out of use by 1841 and as Euston Road grew in commercial importance the shops there extended their showrooms and warehouses across the site of the abortive square.

Dacre Square

When Lee Place, the moated mansion of the Boone family, was demolished in 1824–25 for a road improvement, a working-class enclave called Lee New Town was built over its garden, at the heart of a very wealthy parish. The little terraced houses were mostly in a regular grid of streets, but in the 1840s an even meaner piece of back development called Dacre Square was squeezed into the last remaining space. It had two terraces of six cottages facing each other across a paved court. The only entrance was through an archway on the south side of Dacre Street, later Fludyer Street. The whole district was poor, but this was a slum and demolished as such in 1935–36. The surrounding streets followed in the 1950s and 1960s and now hardly any of the Lee New Town houses survive. The very dull block of council flats numbered 25–35 Boone Street is on the site of Dacre Square.

Dacre Square, c. 1935. (Photograph courtesy of the Lewisham Local History and Archives Centre)

Dalston Square

Dalston Square was not in Dalston. It was a court of no more than eight houses built in the 1830s off the south side of Storer Street, now Nelson Street, at the Sidney Street end. In 1841 it was occupied by coopers, tailors, shoemakers and bricklayers, in 1861 largely by dockers. By 1871 the south side had been demolished for the extension of a Commercial Road warehouse and only five houses remained.

Bacon's 1888 map showed the Seamen's Christian Friend Society office in Commercial Road, south of the square, with the Bethel Oak Chapel behind, either on its south side or in the centre. Among the objects of the society were 'the establishment and maintenance of bethels, free reading-rooms, libraries, and schools'. By the 1890s the office, the bethel and the square had been overwhelmed by the relentless expansion of the Commercial Road linen drapers, William Longuehaye & Co., whose showrooms and warehouses stretched back almost to Nelson Street. Some of the cottages on the north side survived for a time incorporated in the Longuehaye premises.

The tall block of flats called Siege House is now on the site.

Davey Square

Davey (or Davy's) Square consisted of ten or eleven houses tucked behind the north side of Albert Road, east of Fernhill Street. There was a terrace of seven on the north side and three or four more on the west. The square was begun in the 1860s when this area was created to house the workers in the docks and the heavy industry along the Thames. The eastern four houses of the northern terrace had been built by 1869. Nearly all the tenants were dockers or labourers in the gas or electric cable works.

The LCC designated the square a clearance area in the 1930s and the site (now just south of the London City Airport) was used for a library after the Second World War. Its current successor is the Royal Docks Learning & Activity Centre.

Davis's Square

Davis's Square at Deptford stood next to Russell Square in the largely criminal and entirely poor Gravel Pits area, and shared its character and fate. These slums were built late in the eighteenth century and early in the nineteenth on the John Addey charity estate. In 1824 the square had twelve houses, none of them paying rates. They were destroyed in 1835–36 by the London & Greenwich Railway viaduct.

De Beauvoir Square

This is one of London's rare Jacobethan squares and, with its more spacious setting and better designed houses, it is superior to Lonsdale Square, the other notable example, despite having lost its east side to an unsympathetic range of modern flats. It was the surviving element of a much more ambitious plan for the development of De Beauvoir Town that involved four squares and an octagon.

The scheme was devised in the early 1820s by a developer named William Rhodes, but he could not afford anything so grand in the difficult financial conditions of the second half of that decade and little had been done when Richard Benyon de Beauvoir regained control of his estate in 1834. Building then proceeded more rapidly, but with only the one square.

The east side, now demolished, had been built in the early 1820s under the Rhodes regime. It featured a terrace of sixteen houses that were known as Park Place. They were inferior to the later houses, smaller and with meagre gardens. Completion of the square began on the north side in 1838–39, with the west and south sides following in the early 1840s.

Thomas Smith was the chief builder employed and the architect was probably William Conrad Lochner. He designed St Peter's Church, built in 1840–41 at the south-eastern corner of the square. Lochner held building leases for Nos 1 and 2, the first to be built in this second wave of development. They established the style followed on the rest of the north side

The north side of De Beauvoir Square in 2007.

and on the west and south sides. That style features shaped gables in various designs on the north and south sides, sharply pointed ones on the west, oriel windows and castellated bays. (Pevsner attributed the pairs, on the basis of style, to the notorious partnership of Roumieu and Gough, which was responsible for Milner Square.)

The square did not (until our own day) attract the class of residents that its creators had hoped for. Charles Booth's researcher remarked on this in 1897:

> De Beauvoir Square (pronounced locally de Bover square) is surrounded by old fashioned looking stone built houses with odd shaped window-panes … They looked good enough but Inspector Flanagan had been surprised at the poorness of the inhabitants and the insides … The west side has good large gardens and should be the better side. The east has practically none.

The houses in the north-west corner were destroyed during the Second World War and have been replaced by flats that imitate the style of the square in a greatly simplified form. The inferior east side was replaced by Hackney Council's Lockner Estate in the 1960s.

The original round garden, laid out in the 1820s, was formally arranged, with paths in a series of concentric circles. It has been public since the 1890s and is now less complicated, with all the trees crowded together on the east side. The De Beauvoir Square residents enjoy the best of both worlds, with the large public garden plus back and front gardens for each house. The front gardens add much to the beauty of the square, giving it a unique spaciousness. There are fine mature trees in many of them, producing the effect of cottages facing a village green, or ranges of luxurious almshouses.

Devonshire Square

Devonshire Square was built from 1678 by the notorious Nicholas Barbon, his first but by no means his last essay in the form. The site was a large mansion in Bishopsgate known originally as Fisher's Folly. It was built for Jasper Fisher, Queen Mary's goldsmith, who overreached himself and was ruined. His house then passed through the hands of more suitably aristocratic owners, including the Earl of Oxford in the 1580s, followed by Sir William Cornwallis, his son-in-law the Earl of Argyll, who offered it to the East India Company in 1615, the Marquis of Hamilton until his death in 1625, and then by the earls of Devonshire until 1675, when it was sold to Nicholas Barbon.

Devonshire House stood at what is now the eastern end of Devonshire Row. The square was built over the garden. Two Dissenting chapels were established in the purlieus of Devonshire House before Barbon's purchase and were not ejected by the son of Praise-God Barebones. One was William Kiffin's Baptist chapel, referred to by Samuel Butler in *Hudibras* as 'Fisher's Folly Congregation'. According to Walter Wilson's *History and Antiquities of the Dissenting Churches* (1808) it was built about 1653: 'The meeting-house … stands in a paved yard, behind Devonshire-square, called Meeting-house Yard'.

Meeting House Yard was off the east side of the square, where the Metropolitan Free Hospital later stood. The modern extension leading towards Cutler Street now occupies the site. But the Ogilby & Morgan map did not show any buildings there, in what was then the Devonshire House garden.

The meeting house of 1653 was probably in the stable yard, off what is now the south-west corner of the square, with an entrance in Houndsditch. In the 1740s Rocque showed it in the position indicated by Wilson. This was presumably the chapel opened by William Kiffin in 1687, on a new site provided by Barbon.

The other chapel in existence before the square was the Quaker meeting house established in 1666. A new meeting house was built in 1678 or soon after, probably on or near the same site, as part of Barbon's development. This was in Cavendish Court, formerly the Devonshire House stable yard.

Barbon had not yet perfected his style of diagonal alleys at the four corners of a square, but he did include them as entrances to mews at the two eastern corners, approached through archways under the houses. The one in the south-east survived until the 1870s. The seventeen three-storey houses were closer to the collegiate style Barbon was soon to employ at Gray's Inn and Lincoln's Inn than to Red Lion Square. There was no garden, but trees were planted around the yard and the statue of Mercury in the centre added a modish West End touch.

Devonshire Square from the west side in the 1720s.

Devonshire Square from the south-east corner in 2011.

In 1708 Hatton called the square 'a pretty (tho' very small) one, inhabited by Gentry and Eminent Merchants'. Strype's account in 1720 was:

> Devonshire Square, made out of an House called Fisher's Folly, an airy and creditable Place, and where the Countess of Devonshire in my Memory dwelt in great repute for her Hospitality; It consisteth of good Buildings, and they well inhabited by Merchants and Persons of Wealth. In this Square on the North West Corner, is a very large House which is severed from the rest by a pair of great Gates, being the Seat of Sir Samuel Dashwood, Knt. and Alderman, now deceased. In the midst of the Square, upon a Pedestal carved with Figures on each side, and ascended by three Steps, and enclosed with Iron Bars, stands a naked Figure guilt. Hence is a Passage called Cavendish Court, which hath good Buildings, with a Free Stone Pavement, leading to Houndsditch.

The mansion of Sir Samuel Dashwood, who was Lord Mayor in 1703, may have been part of Devonshire House. It did not long survive him and was replaced by smaller houses matching Barbon's originals. A fragment of old Devonshire House wall still exists off Devonshire Row.

The 'merchants and persons of wealth' included Sir Francis Baring, the founder of the great bank, who had his London home in Devonshire Square, above the firm's offices, until 1802, when he moved to Hill Street in Mayfair. Chandos Pole, a governor of the Bank of England, continued to live in the square until about the same period.

From 1769 the square began to be encircled and overshadowed by the great ranges of the East India Company's warehouses, beginning in New Street to the north, swinging round behind the east side, and breaking into the north-east corner of the square itself, where there had always been an entrance, around 1820. This virtually ended its days as a residential square but the houses continued to be occupied as the offices of merchants, bankers, solicitors and architects.

A decline began around 1850 when the Metropolitan Free Hospital was established at No. 8. It expanded to fill the southern half of the east side, but was demolished in 1876 when a tunnel was dug across the centre of the square. This was for the Metropolitan Railway's extension from Moorgate to Aldgate, which opened in that year. Thereafter most of the houses were rebuilt as larger offices shared between many businesses.

The south side was entirely destroyed by bombing during the Second World War, but through all the changes Nos 12 and 13 on the north side have remained intact. They may well be Barbon's original houses, altered in the middle of the eighteenth century. Number 13 is now Coopers' Hall.

Serious revival began in 1978 with the conversion of the East India Company warehouses into the offices, flats and shops known as Cutlers' Gardens, which now dominate the east side. On the south side there is a telephone exchange valiantly disguised as a chapel and in the centre, in place of Mercury, a pleasant circle of dwarf trees and seats. It is an attractive, retired spot with a choice of sun or shade on the brightest day, no through traffic and an interesting miscellany of buildings.

Devonshire Square

See Gloucester Square and
Queen Square, Bloomsbury

Dickens Square

SOUTHWARK

The little Union Square was built in 1844 on land belonging to the Dean and Chapter of Canterbury. The 'D.C.C.' initials of the landlords, with the date and the initials of the builders responsible for the different terraces, appeared on tablets set in the walls of several houses. Also included were the remaining terms of the builders' leases so that there should be no quibbling when the Dean and Chapter resumed possession in 1942. By then the tenants had other things to worry about.

Union Square was described as quiet and working class in 1899 and in 1907 as 'a little back square of small houses'. Most of the houses were quite small,

two storeys with attic and semi-basement, but there was a taller pair in the north-west corner. The centre of the square seems never to have been planted as a garden, but was merely a featureless paved space.

The exciting event in its history was the decision of the LCC to rename it Dickens Square in 1937, south London as usual losing out to its north London rival in one of these beauty contests. The new Dickens Square passed through the war fairly well, with only two houses on the north-west side of the square itself badly damaged. With that exception, the modest terraces were in good condition in the 1950s. The houses in the approach from Harper Road (formerly Union Street) were destroyed by the V1 that hit Bath Terrace on 13 July 1944.

A curiosity of this last phase was the establishment of the Dickens Square Temporary Court in prefabricated buildings on the bomb site at the entrance, where a mosque has now been built. It was an annex to the Crown Court in Newington Causeway which was enlarged in the 1970s. Southwark Council had been plotting the destruction of Dickens Square since the 1950s, so it was allowed to fall into dereliction and the houses were demolished in the 1970s. Since then nothing has been done and the road and the paved space in the centre survive as the ghost of a square.

Dorset Square

MARYLEBONE [WESTMINSTER]

The site of Dorset Square was a 7-acre field on the Portman estate where Thomas Lord, a professional underarm bowler, encouraged and underwritten by various aristocratic enthusiasts, established the original Lord's cricket ground in 1787. The Marylebone Cricket Club was founded there in that year and immediately took upon itself the unofficial government of the game. When the lease expired in 1810 Portman required a much higher rent for land that was now ripe for building development, so Thomas Lord moved to a new site north of Regent's Park, though not immediately to the present Lord's. The square that was built on the site of the original ground is supposed to have been named in honour of the 3rd Duke of Dorset, one of the

The north side of Dorset Square, Marylebone, *c.* 1905.

founders of the MCC and the best known aristo-cratic cricketer of the eighteenth century.

Much of the square was built by David Porter, the extraordinary sweep's climbing boy who made good in spectacular fashion. He was also the principal builder of Montagu Square, but here the houses are more conventional, without the bow windows of the earlier scheme. The architect is not certainly known. Howard Colvin records that an obscure surveyor named Charles Day was involved in the work; H. Gilbert Bradley suggested Joseph T. Parkinson, the architect of Montagu Square and Bryanston Square.

A private act for the management of the Dorset Square garden was obtained in 1813. The Horwood map of that year showed only the houses at the east end of the south side, with their gardens not set out. Some were occupied by 1815 and the east side was quickly added, but the rest of the square was not built until after 1824.

Fashionable society proved difficult to entice north of Marylebone Road and the square attracted few tenants more exalted than knights, generals and the odd MP. Boarding houses were appearing by the 1850s. The square's celebrities are mostly connected with the arts. George Grossmith lived at No. 28 from about 1885, when he left Blandford Square, until 1909, so it was from this address that he set out for many of his Gilbert & Sullivan triumphs, and it was here that he wrote *The Diary of a Nobody* in collaboration with his brother Weedon. Another theatrical star was the Edwardian matinée idol Lewis Waller, who lived at No. 18. The playwright and novelist Dodie Smith lived in a top-floor flat at No. 19, as Miss Dorothy Gladys Smith, from 1932 to 1934.

An odd man out was Sir Laurence Gomme, clerk to the LCC and a major force in local government. He lived at No. 24 from 1895 until 1909. Gomme is particularly deserving of his blue plaque as he was one of the founders of the *Victoria County History*, a strong supporter of the *Survey of London* and the man who persuaded the LCC to finance the commemorative plaque scheme.

A number of eminent men died at the Cambridge House Nursing Home at No. 4 Dorset Square, including, in 1922, the great cartoonist Sir Leslie Ward, 'Spy' of *Vanity Fair* (who had been born nearby in Harewood Square) and in 1923 Sir Charles Hawtrey, the actor-manager.

Dorset Square suffered widespread bomb damage in the Second World War, the most serious being to the oldest houses at the east end of the south side. Much patching and repair was required and a number of houses on the south and east sides were rebuilt in pastiche, not always accurate. It is a great shame that the verandas were not reproduced on the east side.

Dorset Square

Dorset Square was the last name for Dorset Court, which was built in the 1680s and is noted as the place where John Locke lodged while completing his *Essay concerning Human Understanding*. In 1720 Strype described it as:

> Dorset Court, built on the Place where Dorset House stood: It is a very handsome open Place, containing but six Houses, which are large and well built, fit for Gentry to dwell in; of which those towards the Thames have Gardens towards the Water Side very pleasant: In one of these Houses dwells Mr Emmet, the son of Mr Maurice Emmet, the Builder of them, where he dyed.

In 1810 Lockie gave this direction for 'Dorset-Square (or Court), Cannon-Row, Westminster, – the first on the L. under the arch, three doors from Derby-st. entering from 46 Parliament-st. in which is the Transport Office'. In his 1813 revision, Lockie dropped the 'or Court'.

The archway on the east side of Cannon Row led to what was by then a small rectangular square, which had the Transport Office on the east side in place of the best riverside houses. There were still two houses on the west side, flanking the entrance. These were not public offices: occupants included 'T. Stewart of Dorset-square, Canon-row, broker', who was a bankrupt in 1801, and Edward Medley, a house agent.

Dorset Square ceased to exist in 1816 when a much larger and grander Transport Office, designed by William Pilkington, covered the whole area between the Thames and Cannon Row, where it had a small carriage sweep. This building was later the Indian Board of Control and the Civil Service Commission. It survived the construction of the Victoria Embankment and Westminster Bridge Station, but was demolished in the 1890s to provide the site for the southern building of New Scotland Yard.

Duncan Square

Like its neighbour Warburton Square, Duncan Square, which was begun in the late 1850s, was of the false type that had houses in the centre instead of a garden. In fact, it had more houses in the centre than on the edge in the early days, as the surrounding streets were in a state of flux. The 1872 map showed no houses on the south side, which was Duncan Road, and few on the east or west.

It was a very poor area – the Booth survey in 1897 found chronic want, 'street littered with rubbish' – and was demolished in 1935 as part of a slum clearance drive. The displaced families were settled in Duncan House, later known as Alden House.

Dunstan's Square

'Dunstan's Square, in Whitechapel' appeared in William Stow's 1722 list of London streets, but not in any other. It could have been his name for Montague Square, Spitalfields, which was close to Whitechapel Road, or just possibly for Stepney Square, which was near St Dunstan's Church, but far from Whitechapel.

Eagle Square

Eagle Square was an alternative name for Eagle Place, an enclosed yard with half a dozen houses to the north of Eagle Court. It was Eagle Place in the 1820s ratebooks but Eagle Square in the 1830s. In the 1841 and 1851 census returns Eagle Square was inhabited mainly by charwomen and laundresses.

Eagle Court was Vinegar Yard in the seventeenth century, when the north side was largely occupied by the garden of Berkeley House. Vinegar Yard was rebuilt with houses instead of stables around 1680 and the name was soon changed to Eagle Court. It became a slum, and for that reason was chosen by the School Board for London as the location for one of its early schools, designed by E.R. Robson and built in 1873–74. *The Survey of London* reports that 'Eagle Court was so notoriously lawless that a police guard had to be mounted to protect the workmen and site during construction'. Eagle Square and the north side of Eagle Court were demolished to make way for the school. It is still standing, now converted into the Goldsmiths' Centre: the chief attraction of the narrow Eagle Court, which runs from Britton Street to St John's Lane.

Earls Court Square

Earls Court Square was among the last luxury examples of the form. Its failure (with that of its neighbour Nevern Square) discouraged any further attempt. The land was part of Lord Kensington's estate, the developer Edward Francis, who began to build in Earls Court Road in 1872, probably employing Frederick Nesbitt Kemp as architect.

His original idea for the land to the west was a comparatively modest and safe Farnell Road, running north and south. The fateful decision to build a square instead, which led Francis directly to bankruptcy, was a last-minute change of plan in 1874. Farnell Square was briefly the name of the new development and Farnell Mews, which was built before the change of mind, is the permanent memorial to this first thought. Because the square took so long to build and was not finished by its originator, the houses and flats are in a wide variety of styles.

The first and best house, No. 1 at the corner of Earls Court Road, was built before the change to a square was decided on. It was first occupied by Sir William Palliser, a soldier of inventive genius who patented various improvements to cannon and shells. He was a financial backer of Francis and lived at various houses in the square, dying at No. 21 in 1882.

Francis also built the north-eastern approach road and Farnell Mews behind its south side before the plans were changed. In 1875 he continued the road as the north side of the square, switching to the fatally

The east side of Earls Court Square in 1907 or a little earlier.

grandiloquent style that was to be his ruin. He also changed, though not immediately, from brick to stucco and added to the disjointed appearance of the north side by placing his widest and tallest houses off-centre. Francis had built the north and west sides and most of the east before he was forced to the bankruptcy courts early in 1879.

After a delay of nearly a decade the square was continued by the more prudent John Douglas of South Kensington, who built a terrace of smaller red brick houses – miniature imitations of Cadogan Square – on the south side, and blocks of mansion flats on the other vacant plots. Wetherby Mansions, now Herbert Court Mansions, on the east side (see p.15) is the most attractive.

The square was finally complete in 1896. The huge houses built by Francis had proved very hard to let, quickly becoming schools, institutions, or lodging houses, but Douglas's more modest creations were popular. Val Gielgud was born at No. 36 on the south side in 1900, but the family moved away shortly before his brother, Sir John, was born in 1904.

There was bomb damage on the north side, quite serious to two or three houses, but all has been made good. The objection made to stucco by Victorian critics, that it was a mere theatrical sham, works

to its advantage when major repairs are needed. The double porch of Nos 25 and 27, the most seriously damaged houses, is still supported by the two emergency props that replaced the original three pillars after the bombing.

The square is now more prosperous than at any stage in its career. The private garden is well planned and maintained, and protected by an unusually dense hedge.

Eaton Square

BELGRAVIA [WESTMINSTER]

In 1824 Thomas Cubitt, then quite a young and inexperienced builder, entered into an agreement with Earl Grosvenor for the development of the most important part of the Five Fields, on which Belgrave Square, Eaton Square and all the associated roads were to be built. The names came from Eaton Hall in Cheshire, the seat of the earl, and Belgrave in Leicestershire which provided his second title. Eaton Square was called Eaton Place in the early plans, after the fashion of the neighbouring Cadogan Place, but the example of the very similar Euston Square, on which Cubitt was engaged at this time, may have emboldened the

Eaton Square, looking north-east from Eccleston Street, *c.* 1904.

estate to make the change. The long square was still novel and regarded as an anomaly by conservative critics. At a ⅓ mile, this is the longest of them all.

The square began with the church, always considered a good way of attracting the best tenants. St Peter's was a Commissioners' or Waterloo church intended to relieve pressure on St George's, Hanover Square. It was designed by Henry Hakewill in a Grecian style (after his original Gothic plans were rejected) and built in 1824–27; begun before any of the houses in the square and consecrated when few, if any, were occupied. It was burnt down in 1836 but rebuilt by Hakewill's son according to the original plans. Blomfield rescued it from Victorian contempt in the 1870s by adding the chancel and remodelling the interior.

The north side of the square was built by Cubitt in three terraces, separated by what are now Belgrave Place and Lyall Street. The first, east of Belgrave Place, was built between 1825 and 1830 and presumably designed by Lewis Cubitt, who was then in partnership with his brother. It has four-storey houses similar to their contemporary work in Bloomsbury, with stucco only on the ground floor except in the centrepiece. The long terrace between Belgrave Place and Lyall Street is the grandest in the square, or indeed in Belgravia, with four Corinthian porticoes (one in Belgrave Place) and a continuous colonnade on the ground floor. The design, published in 1829, was again probably by Lewis but the building was not completed until the late 1830s. The less ambitious and more Italianate third terrace, west of Lyall Street, was built in the 1840s and early 1850s, long after Lewis had gone his own way, so Thomas was probably the architect. He built the part of the short west end north of the main road in 1851.

Most of the south side of Eaton Square was built by Seth Smith, who was also responsible for the north side of Chester Square which lay behind on the same plot of land. His architect is not known. The houses he left unfinished were completed by Sir Charles Freake, who also built the west side, south of the main road. Unlike Cubitt, with his regular progression from east to west, Smith worked on all three terraces together, with the result that in 1840 parts of each were occupied but other houses

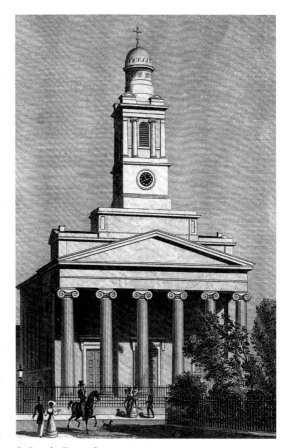

St Peter's, Eaton Square, in 1829.

were not even begun. Work lasted from the 1820s to the 1840s.

Symmetry of a sort is achieved within the square, as on the south side it is the western terrace that has stucco only on the ground floor. The Smith and Freake houses have porches instead of colonnades and are, in general, not as well built as Cubitt's.

The square has six gardens, created by the old (rerouted) King's Road and the two roads that cross from north to south. Because the market gardeners and nurserymen who held the land before building began had time remaining in their leases, the northern gardens were granted to them in compensation until the 1840s. They had their cottages and shops and sold their produce direct to the new residents of the square, a mutually advantageous arrangement. In 1841 the two nurserymen were John Rogers and James Tuck. The tenants of the northern houses were given keys to the southern gardens in the meantime.

Although the Duke of Bedford lived at No. 81 in the 1880s, Eatons Square's lists of residents have never, like those of Belgrave Square, read like an abridgement of *Debrett*, but in the early days they were an epitome of Dod's *Parliamentary Companion*. The Speaker of the House of Commons had his official residence at No. 71 in the 1830s and 1840s during the rebuilding of the Palace of Westminster after the fire, and in 1841 eleven other members of parliament were among his neighbours. In 1856 there were twenty-two.

Two lord chancellors lived in the square: Lord Truro died at No. 13 in 1855 and Lord Chelmsford at No. 7 in 1878. His grandson, the 1st Viscount Chelmsford, who was Viceroy of India from 1916 to 1921, was born at No. 7 in 1868. Stanley Baldwin lived at No. 93 from 1908 until he moved to No. 10 Downing Street in 1924, and his successor Neville Chamberlain lived from 1923 to 1935 at No. 37, where he was followed by Ribbentrop, as German ambassador. Leo Amery, whose motion brought Chamberlain down in 1940, lived at No. 112 from 1924 until his death in 1955 and it was the home of his son, Julian, for most of his life.

Like many others in London, Eaton Square gave up part of its garden for a military club during the First World War, but here, naturally, Queen Mary's Club was for officers only. It closed in 1920.

During the Second World War the gardens were needed for air-raid shelters. The Mayor of Westminster, L. Eaton Smith, was killed on an official visit to one opposite Nos 40–48, when it received a direct hit on 11 May 1941. In the previous month St Peter's had been bombed and the vicar killed, but in spite of these and other incidents the church and the houses survived the war with remarkably little damage. The most serious was to Nos 74 and 75, at the west end of the south side, a fact that may account for their mismatching attic windows.

Between 1945 and 1956 the Grosvenor estate converted most of the Eaton Square houses into flats, employing to oversee the work Raglan Squire, who had come to prominence as one of the designers of the Arcon prefab. He was amused to find that the most expensive flats, the penthouses, were the former servants' quarters. These changes introduced more glamorous residents after the war. Terence Rattigan lived in one of the penthouses, at No. 29, in the 1950s and 1960s, Vivien Leigh died at No. 54 (where there is a plaque) in 1967, and Julie Andrews lived at No. 70 in the 1960s.

Queen Mary's Club for officers, in the Eaton Square garden, *c.* 1919.

Ebenezer Square

Slum squares proliferated in the Houndsditch and Petticoat Lane area on the eastern edge of the City. Ebenezer Square was built in the middle of the eighteenth century and had its double form from the first. The main section, entered via an archway in Stoney Lane, was square in shape and had a dozen houses. A second archway opposite led to a narrow, rectangular court with eight more. This offshoot was later rebuilt or subdivided as sixteen houses.

Ebenezer Square was not shown on Rocque's map of the 1740s. The earliest two residents we hear of were Samuel Whale, who described himself as 'a Jew schoolmaster', in 1767, and Israel Abrahams, a pedlar – 'I travel with a box' – in 1778, when Simon Moses and Samuel Isaacs were tried for burgling his house.

Ebenezer Square had one famous son, the novelist and Zionist, Israel Zangwill, author of *The Children of the Ghetto* (1892), who was born there in 1864. He was the son of a pedlar and glazier who had fled from Russia at the age of 12.

Ebenezer Square narrowly escaped destruction in 1876 when the Metropolitan Railway's Aldgate extension shaved past it, but that only put off the end for a few years, the whole area being cleared as a slum by 1879. In 1884 the City began to build artisans' industrial dwellings on its Petticoat Square estate, and Artizan's Street (now Artizan Street) was built over what remained of the site of Ebenezer Square to provide access to the new tenements.

Ebury Square

Ebury Square is much the oldest on the Grosvenor Estate in Pimlico and Belgravia. It was begun about 1790, more than thirty years before Thomas Cubitt appeared on the scene. It was in 1790 that William Porden's Ebury Chapel was built nearby, as the Grosvenors began a tentative development. The lease of No. 1 Ebury Square was for ninety-nine years from 1791, probably the year in which the building agreement was made.

Hopes for a fashionable suburb were damped by developments just to the south. In 1843 William Weir supposed that 'Ranelagh, seeing the tide of fashionable houses rising up towards it, bewails the precipitancy of its owners, in allowing it to be covered by inferior houses, water-works, and factories'. Ebury Square was on the edge of this original working-class Pimlico which Cubitt arrived too late to gentrify.

The site of the square was the yard of the ancient Avery Farm. In 1614 and 1723 the Eybury Manor map and the Grosvenor estate plan showed the farmhouse surrounded by an impressive collection of outbuildings. By the 1740s there was a little ribbon development in what are now Buckingham Palace Road and Pimlico Road, and by the 1790s the square was taking firm shape. The farmhouse had been demolished, or possibly converted into the pub called the Flask, after which the north side came to be called Flask Row. The east side was Avery Farm Row. They were complete, but the centre was still a rough field rather than a garden.

It had a more defined shape by 1813, with paths crossing it from corner to corner just as they do today. The Ebury Square name was slow to emerge. In his 1810 and 1813 editions Lockie had a cross reference from Ebury Place to Avery Place, which he defined in 1813 as the north end of Avery Farm Row. The name was firmly established as Ebury Square by 1820, when Mr C.F. Warden lived at No. 1.

The original cottages were small and humble – in 1801 'a maker of hogs puddings, commonly called black puddings' lived in Avery Place, Avery Farm Row – and dragged down the better houses built around 1820 on the south and east sides.

The difficulties in the way of establishing a fashionable square in this district are illustrated by a lawsuit of 1824. Mr Wilson, a surveyor, 'had taken one of the new houses in Ebury-square, Pimlico, for his residence'. A whitesmith had then built a forge in the next garden, 14ft from Mr Wilson's house. He sued for damages caused by the noise, smoke and dirt, but the judge said that 'if a person comes to a place where an unpleasant trade has been long carried on he can not complain of nuisance because he comes to the nuisance', and the jury found for the defendant. There could be only one long-term winner where such contests were necessary. The wealthy residents departed and the square became almost wholly commercial and working class.

Avery Farm Row was demolished in 1868, when Buckingham Palace Road was extended south and widened, destroying a network of alleys and yards east of the square and also the second Pimlico Literary Institution. (The first survives as No. 22 Ebury Street, the third was in Winchester Street.) New schools for St Michael's, Chester Square, were built on the cleared space, replacing cramped ones in Spring Garden Place to the north. The new east side was completed by the St Michael's Vicarage, which enjoyed the whole of the busy corner site (now occupied by Fountain Court) where Buckingham Palace Road, Ebury Bridge, Ebury Bridge Road, Ranelagh Grove, Pimlico Road and Avery Farm Row all meet.

The north side of the square was disturbed at the same time by the construction of what is now the District and Circle underground line, this section of which opened in 1868. Ebury Buildings, tenements belonging to the Improved Industrial Dwellings Company, replaced nearly all the remaining houses there between 1869 and 1873, only the Flask and one or two others surviving. The Grosvenors were closely involved in the planning and financing of Ebury

Buildings and may have had a hand in selecting the architect, William Ward Lee.

The Marquess of Westminster first suggested the opening of the garden to the public in 1872. The local authorities had less confidence than the noble philanthropist in the public's ability to treat a public space with respect, and his idea was not fully carried out until 1884, despite experimental openings in the 1870s.

Ebury Square was not a place where the eminent chose to live, but they cannot choose their place of origin. Edith Evans was born at No. 12 in 1888 and was educated at St Michael's School in the square. She was associated with this area for much of her life. Her first job was at Martin Blackaller's drapery shop at Nos 81 and 83 Buckingham Palace Road. She became the protégé of George Moore of Ebury Street, and later lived in Ebury Street herself.

A parachute mine in Semley Place shattered many houses in May 1941. The flying bomb that fell in the garden of Ebury Square late in the war destroyed the last of the original houses, which had survived on the west and part of the south side, and seriously damaged the St Michael's Schools and various ranges of tenements. Here something approaching a blank slate was presented to the post-war planners, whose

The garden of Ebury Square, *c.* 1905.

Ebury Buildings, Semley Place, Ebury Square, *c.* 1905. (Photograph courtesy of Maurice Friedman)

unsurprising solution was blocks of flats. They or their successors still occupy the north and south sides, but there are new luxury flats to the west and the back of the Belgravia Police Station to the east. The quiet garden is a pleasant relief from them all.

Eccleston Square

PIMLICO [WESTMINSTER]

Thomas Cubitt was no more reticent about his plans than John Nash had been twenty years earlier, with the result that map makers were apt to anticipate his developments. Eccleston Square appears on maps as early as 1827 under the name of 'New Square', and is even given unbroken terraces on the long sides. In fact, although the ground was marked out, nothing was built until 1836 when Cubitt primed the pump with Nos 1–3, the smallest houses and perhaps the best. They were let immediately, but the tenants must have been lonely. Nothing else was built until 1842, and the square was not completed until the late 1850s, after Cubitt's death.

Elsewhere, many of Cubitt's houses were designed by himself or his brother Lewis, but Lewis was pursuing a career of his own by the late 1830s. Thomas may therefore have looked elsewhere for advice at Eccleston Square. Colvin mentions a plan for a terrace on the north-west side, thought to be Nos 8–10, by Robert Garland and Henry Christopher of No. 11 John Street, Adelphi. The name of the square came from the earlier Eccleston Street. Eccleston in Cheshire, close to Eaton Hall, was one of the manors belonging to the Grosvenor family.

This was the final outpost of fashion in the early 1860s, according to Trollope. In *The Small House at Allington* a bride is warned, 'For heaven's sake, my dear, don't let him take you anywhere beyond Eccleston Square!' Beresford Chancellor agreed in 1907 that 'Eccleston Square forms a twin square with that of Warwick, but there is not much comparison between them as fashionable centres'.

The list of famous residents confirms this judgement. Sir Michael Costa, the leading London conductor of the mid-nineteenth century, lived at No. 7 in the early 1850s and at No. 59 from 1857 to 1883.

William Edward Forster, MP for Bradford and the man behind the 1870 Education Act, was the first of the eminent politicians. His biographer Wemyss Reid wrote: 'In this year, 1863, Mr Forster took the house, No. 80, Eccleston Square for the season. He liked it so much, that he finally took a lease of it; and it was for the remainder of his life his London residence.' Forster died in 1886.

F.E. Smith, Lord Birkenhead, lived at No. 70 from 1907 to 1913 and his friend Winston Churchill took No. 33 when he was married in 1908, passing it on to Sir Edward Grey, the foreign secretary, in 1913. One modern celebrity was Ian Nairn, the explosive, hard-drinking and short-lived scourge of modern British architects and planners. He had a flat at No. 3 until his death in 1983, but his real home was the St George's Tavern in Belgrave Road.

Its proximity to Victoria Station is perhaps a reason for the louche reputation the square acquired after the First World War, when some houses became private hotels and others were divided into flats. Rooms in Eccleston Square were a favourite place of convenience for H.G. Wells when conducting his many love affairs, and the civil servant and poet Humbert Wolfe set up home with his mistress Pamela Frankau in a flat at No. 75 when he left his wife in 1936. To preserve the proprieties she discreetly effaced herself when he died there in 1940 and left the estranged wife to deal with the formalities.

Being so close to the station was certainly a disadvantage during the Second World War, from which the square emerged far more battered than the others in Pimlico. More than three-quarters of its houses suffered blast damage, some of it quite severe, but crucially few were destroyed or so badly shaken that demolition was necessary. The square is now in excellent condition. The large garden remains private, despite an attempt to have it opened to the public as early as 1885.

Edward Square

ISLINGTON

Edward Square was built gradually throughout the 1850s off the east side of Caledonian Road, just north of the Regent's Canal. The name came from Edward Terrace, older houses in the Caledonian Road immediately to the west of the square. This was a

The Belgrave Road side of Eccleston Square, *c.* 1905.

poor part of Islington, so the houses were of two storeys and semi-basement only, though dignified with round-headed windows and rustication to the ground floor. The tenants were always working class.

Edward Square had a curious form: it was roughly rectangular, but widened slightly from south to north, like a tall vase. The garden was divided into two sections by a path that cut across the centre from east to west. This was a broadened continuation of the passage that still leads from the Caledonian Road to the site of the square. Access from the north was only via an archway through the shops in William Street, now part of Copenhagen Street, and the canal lay to the south, so the residents enjoyed a good deal of seclusion. The terraces on the north, south and west sides extended beyond the garden. Only the two on the east side, divided by the entrance passage, faced it for their whole length.

The garden was open to the public from 1888. In 1897 the Booth survey found 'Edward Square, poor … at the north but distinctly worse at the south end. Northern half of square kept up by vestry, the southern half has been destroyed and is now an untidy waste.' A later note to this passage gave a brighter picture, 'Improvement here. The waste at south end is now bounded with stone, and tidy. Houses look better. The southern half of the east side is still markedly poor, but the whole might be purple [some comfortable, others poor]. Square well tended and open to public.'

The jazz trumpeter and band leader Nat Gonella was born in Edward Square in 1908, the son of a taxi driver of Italian descent. The cabbie died when his son was 7 and the children were all placed in the Islington poor law school. From this unpromising start he rose via the school band and Billy Cotton to found and lead the Georgians, one of the most successful British jazz bands of the thirties.

Part of the square was already being considered for slum clearance before the Second World War. There was not much bomb damage but the houses were left to decay and were all demolished in the mid-1960s. The site was intended for a new school, but it was never built and the area of the garden and the demolished houses gradually became a park, now well planted. The cobbled access passage retains the name of Edward Square.

Edwardes Square

KENSINGTON [KENSINGTON AND CHELSEA]

This delicious square, thus stowed away in a corner, must have been designed by one who wished to carry the finest amenities of Patrician life into the domestic habits of the narrowest incomed families of the middle class. We regret to add that so delightful a plan did not originate with an Englishman: Edward Square was a Frenchman's speculation.

William Weir got the name wrong when giving this account of Edwardes Square in 1843, but he was right about the charm of the place, and the developer.

He was Louis Léon Changeur, a French émigré who in 1811 made an agreement with Lord Kensington for 11 acres on the south side of what is now Kensington High Street. The landowner's family name was Edwardes. Changeur sometimes described himself as an architect, but he seems to have employed David Bunning to plan the layout of his 11 acres and perhaps to design the houses. Most of them were built, or started at least, in 1812–13, but they sold slowly, leading to the bankruptcy of poor Changeur. His disaster was not the result of xenophobia: builders of all nationalities were more likely than not to be ruined when they fell among thieves and moneylenders. Few squares produced any profit for their original projectors. Changeur fled to France, whither he was soon followed by his main backer, an Englishman. It took some time to unravel the tangle in which their affairs had been left and to complete the unfinished houses, but by 1821 the square was almost fully occupied.

Edwardes Square is one of the strangest in London, as well as one of the best. The plan is eccentric in the extreme. The houses are small – disgracefully small, Carlyle thought – but the garden is huge. It is not quite so large as Grosvenor Square, but bigger than any of the others in the West End. Yet it makes as little use as possible of one of the chief advantages of a large garden, an open outlook for the houses, as they were originally built only on the short east and west sides of the rectangle. The long north side is confronted by the back garden wall of Earl's Terrace, a fine group of twenty-five houses built by Changeur at the same time as the square, but facing north onto the High Street.

The long south side was intended for mews, but they were never built in any systematic way, as few of the tenants kept carriages – something that might have been anticipated from the size of the houses. Redeveloped from the late nineteenth century, the south side is now a pleasant miscellany of small houses, studios and flats, with the separate name of South Edwardes Square. As a glorious crowning oddity, the gardener's cottage facing the middle of the south side is a Greek temple.

Such a square was sure to attract artists and bohemians. The most famous of them was Leigh Hunt, who lived at No. 32 from 1840 to 1851. During that period he was collecting material for *The Old Court Suburb* (serialised 1853–54, collected 1855), a book that propagated a number of Kensington myths, including two about Edwardes Square: that Changeur built the houses with the idea of letting them to Napoleon's officers after an invasion, and that Coleridge was a resident. Hunt's autobiography, which was written

during the 1840s, suggests that Edwardes Square was not always as idyllic as it seems today, for he says of his move to Kensington that 'we unfortunately got into a part which had been denounced in the books of the Sanitary Commissioners'.

Other eccentric inhabitants were G.K. Chesterton, who lived briefly at No. 1 around 1901, Goldsworthy Lowes Dickinson at No. 11 from 1912 to 1919, and Frankie Howerd at No. 27 from 1966 to 1992. The larger houses of Earl's Terrace were popular with more prosperous writers, including Elizabeth Inchbald at No. 4 in 1816–17, and three at No. 12: George Macdonald from 1865 to 1867, followed by George du Maurier until 1870, and Walter Pater from 1886 to 1893. The novelist May Sinclair lived at No. 4 the Studios, on the south side, from 1907 to 1914. The square and Earl's Terrace bristle with blue plaques, but there is none on Leigh Hunt's house.

Edwardes Square has an important place in the history of squares. It was the threat to the garden, which was advertised as building land in 1903, that galvanised the LCC into action to protect the gardens of all the London squares. This led directly to the London Squares & Enclosures (Preservation) Act of

The east side of Edwardes Square, *c.* 1905.

1906, a largely symbolic measure that did not protect Edwardes Square.

In 1907 Beresford Chancellor thought that it might 'pass before long from its present retirement to a metamorphosis of flats or a palingenesis of so-called Queen Anne houses'. The square was not safe until 1912, when the residents' garden committee defeated the dastardly developers in the House of Lords.

A couple of the houses in Earls Terrace were destroyed in the Second World War, but they have been rebuilt in facsimile. There was no damage in the square itself. Since the war it has gone from strength to strength as the present owners are far better able to maintain and improve the houses than such notoriously impecunious tenants as Leigh Hunt. The charm is one of contrast between a wide, busy and (on the north side) ugly stretch of Kensington High Street and the narrow lanes of the square. The one on the north side might be running along the wall of a country house.

Elder Square

ISLINGTON

Elder Square was a tiny court of five houses off the north side of Elder Walk. It was named on the 1871 Ordnance Survey map where there was scarcely room to fit the two short words into the space. A fragment of Elder Walk is still to be found looping between Essex Road and Popham Street, the last survivor of an old tangle of lanes and courts.

Mary Cosh reports that Elder Square first appeared in the ratebooks in 1848, one Francis Weaver paying. It lasted less than forty years. In 1874 the Medical Officer of Health condemned twenty-five courts in this area, including Elder Square, and they were soon put forward as a clearance area under the Artisans' and Labourers' Dwellings Act of 1875. There were problems rehousing the displaced tenants, but the site was cleared in 1881/82, Popham Street was extended west to Essex Road across the site of Elder Square and other slums, and artisans' improved dwellings (grim courtyard tenements) were built on either side of the new street. They have now been replaced by Islington's less grim Popham Estate.

Elger Square

WHITECHAPEL [TOWER HAMLETS]

Elger Square was a court off the west side of Essex Street, formerly Catherine Wheel Alley. Rocque showed stables on the site in the 1740s. In 1810 and 1813 John Lockie gave the position of 'Elgers Square' and Essex Court in almost exactly the same terms, as the fourth turning on the left in Essex Street from No. 105 Whitechapel High Street. The Horwood maps of the 1790s and 1813 gave the fourth turning as Essex Court. Lockie also included Elgers Place, which he called 'the north end of Elgers-square' in 1810, but in 1813 'the last on the left in Essex Street'. The Horwood maps showed a nameless offshoot just north of Essex Court, and certainly 'the last on the left'. It may still have been essentially a stable yard at that time, its emergence as a square causing Lockie's confusion between the fourth and last turnings.

In the 1841 census Elger Square and Essex Court appeared as separate, adjacent places. There were then three houses in Elgers Place and sixteen in Elger Square, occupied by labourers, tailors, shoemakers, etc. Essex Street and all its courts were demolished when required as part of the route for the very much wider Commercial Street, this southern section of which was laid out between 1843 and 1845. The site of the square is just south of the junction of Commercial Street and Wentworth Street.

Elliott's Square

DEPTFORD [GREENWICH]

Elliott's Square was a court of ten or fifteen houses at the north end of French's Fields, in the old riverside quarter of Deptford. To the north-east it had an outlet in Butcher Row, now Borthwick Street, and to the west it communicated, via the even smaller and narrower Elliott Court, with New Street and Old King Street, now Watergate Street.

The name may have come from William Elliott, a victualler who held land at Deptford Green and Hughes Fields in the 1740s and 1750s. That was when the street pattern here began to take shape:

a 1753 map showed the entrance from Butcher Row but only a field where the main part of the square was built. It was a poor area, inhabited by sailors, fishermen, rope makers and the like. Its demolition in the 1880s and 1890s was an early example of LCC slum clearance. Trevithick Street replaced Elliott Square on a widened and simplified line, but has now been truncated, so that Twinkle Park covers the site.

Ellis Square

NEWINGTON [SOUTHWARK]

Ellis Square was built in the first decade of the nineteenth century on a piece of ground where Horwood had shown two ponds in the 1790s. Lockie gave explicit directions in 1810: 'Ellis-Square, Penton-Street, Walworth – the second on the L. along Amelia-st. from Walworth High-st. or road, or a few doors on the R. from Penton-place in the op. direction.'

It was more a curving lane than a square, with perhaps a dozen houses in 1813, but twenty-five in 1821 and thirty-five or more in the 1870s, branching off in all directions. This wild profusion must have alarmed the authorities, for in the late 1880s Ellis Square was swept away and the very dull and regular Thrush Street was built in its place, with a non-residential Clarence Yard to its south, close to Manor Place. These have vanished in their turn and Lockie's excellent advice now leads to a public garden with the uninspired name of Pullens Open Space, and to a private housing development called Clarence Yard (north of the old one) that is far more like a square than Ellis Square ever was.

Euston Square

BLOOMSBURY [CAMDEN]

As originally built, Euston Square was like Eaton Square, with a long rectangular garden bisected by a main road, great terraces of fine houses lining the two long sides, and St Pancras New Church having the same relation to one as St Peter's does to the other. Although the rectangle at Euston Square was not so

long, the sense of space was extended at both ends by sections of Euston Road where the houses had long private front gardens.

The name came from the Fitzroys, barons Southampton, a cadet branch of the family of the Duke of Grafton, whose second title is Earl of Euston. Lord Southampton was the landowner. The development scheme was inspired by that of the Duke of Bedford to the south, with which it was integrated.

The short west side was built in 1813–14 and the short east side in 1817–18. The important part of the square architecturally was the north side. Its two beautiful terraces, divided by Euston Grove, were built between 1811 and 1818. Number 1, the earliest house, was occupied by January 1812. Various architects have been suggested but none with any confidence.

The date of their demolition has caused confusion. Pevsner, through a misreading of the old editions of Summerson's *Georgian London*, said 1937, but both were intact until the Second World War. Although there was severe bomb damage to the east terrace, the west survived almost complete until the early 1960s, when the station was rebuilt.

The south side, known as Endsleigh Gardens after 1879, was built very slowly between 1824 and 1860 as part of Thomas Cubitt's north Bloomsbury development on Lord Southampton's land, and survives in part. The terrace between Endsleigh Street and Taviton Street, which can be glimpsed from Euston Road through the gap at the east end of Friends' House, was built in the late 1830s. Cubitt also laid out and planted the southern half of the garden. On the undated Carmarthen Square plan in the Crace Collection it is called 'Bedford Nursery or Euston Square', and the northern garden 'Euston Square'.

The extraordinary St Pancras New Church was built between 1819 and 1822, to designs by William and Henry Inwood. William lived at No. 68, south of the church, a house later known as Woburn Lodge.

Various authorities say that the satirist John Wolcot ('Peter Pindar') died in 1819 at Montgomery Cottage, on the site of the square, but as the square was then complete except for the south side and the garden had been laid out earlier, Montgomery Cottage is perhaps more likely to have been in Ossulston Street, another address given for Wolcot late in his life.

Charles Aders, a German merchant and art collector, settled at No. 11 Euston Square after his marriage in 1820 and entertained an extraordinary collection of poets and artists at his musical parties there, until his extravagance led to financial disaster. Wordsworth, Coleridge, Blake, Landor, Rogers, Campbell, Lamb, Flaxman and Lawrence were all his guests. Coleridge greatly enjoyed the music, but

The west terrace of the north side of Euston Square, *c.* 1905.

A square within a square: the YMCA soldiers' hostel in the southern garden of Euston Square, *c.* 1918.

Wordsworth covered his face with a handkerchief and was suspected of sleeping through the performances.

John Payne Collier, the Shakespearean scholar and forger, lived at No. 25 from 1834 to 1839, and Frederic Harrison, the leading English disciple of Comte, was born at No. 17 in 1831. His father was a stockbroker. Christina Rossetti lived with her mother and sister at No. 56 (later No. 5 Endsleigh Gardens) from 1867 to 1876, when they moved the short distance to Torrington Square.

In 1907 Beresford Chancellor gave this assessment:

Its quaint and dreary houses, many with the old wooden lattice-work verandahs to the first-floor front windows, are now chiefly occupied by small hotels and 'apartments,' presumably on account of their proximity to Euston Station; but in past days, thirty or forty years since, they were tenanted by people of some standing if not of any particular importance, and its gardens, connected by a passage beneath the roadway joining the Euston Road and terminus, was the favourite promenade of the younger generation and their attendants.

Chancellor was aware that Endsleigh Gardens had once been part of Euston Square, yet he said very oddly that it was 'rather an excrescence from the Euston Road than a proper square, and has an analogy in shape, though in nothing else, to such curious apologies for squares as Hereford and Alexander Squares'. In 1898 the report of the Booth inspector had been 'respectable hotels and boarding houses'. In the twentieth century the respectability was sometimes more dubious, as it often is in the vicinity of a railway terminus.

Apart from those in Endsleigh Gardens, the only surviving houses are Nos 70 and 71 Euston Square, a fine bow-windowed pair now unhappily marooned between Grafton Place and the fire station. The only other buildings of interest (besides the church) are Beresford Pite's London, Edinburgh & Glasgow Assurance offices of 1907 at the west end, now the Royal College of General Practitioners, and the Friends' House of 1925–27, which it is impossible to look at without anger as it stands on the southern half of the garden.

The garden had been under threat from various directions since 1890, and during the First World War the southern half was covered by a temporary soldiers' hostel, so its loss in the 1920s was long anticipated. The present horror of Euston Square is a price worth paying for the London Squares Preservation Act of 1931, the all-important measure that was passed in response to the Euston Square and Mornington Crescent scandals.

Factory Square

Factory Square existed by 1840 and was probably twenty years older. It was named after Stephen Wilson's Streatham silk mill, which was built about 1820 and later became a factory used for making crêpe.

The former silk mill at Factory Square in 2011.

Cow & Co., India rubber manufacturers, moved to it in 1857 and expanded the buildings considerably during more than a century in Streatham. (At the height of the Jack the Ripper panic, Douglas Cow, one of the partners, was arrested for grinning at a woman on Westminster Bridge, an incident straight out of *The Mikado*.)

The factory and square were built, like the neighbouring Greyhound and Histed's Squares, on the large Crooke, Ellison & Bates estate. The square was intended to accommodate the mill workers, an odd transposition of the Lancashire system to rural and wealthy Streatham. It had the shape of a capital 'T'. The narrower cross stroke ran east to west from Streatham High Road to the mill gate, and the down stroke, with most of the cottages, ran parallel with the east side of the larger and lower factory building.

There was originally an open space at the junction, with only a substantial semi-detached pair of houses on its north side. The open space was destroyed by the growth of the factory and the replacement of the semi-detached pair in 1861 by George Gilbert Scott's Emmanuel Church School.

The silk mill survives in part, incorporated into the supermarket that obliterated the square in the late 1980s. The cross stroke of the 'T' is now the entrance to the supermarket from the High Road, the down stroke part of the car park. Another relic of the factory is the former Beehive Assembly Rooms on the south side of the entrance, which was built in 1878–79 for the benefit of the workers. It was designed by Sir Ernest George, a friend of Douglas Cow.

Falcon Square

Like many in the City, this was not a true square but an open space where various streets converged, in this case Falcon, Castle, Monkwell, Silver and Noble Streets. There was no garden in the centre, merely a drinking fountain and public convenience. But Falcon Square was not without its leafy shade, as the north-eastern corner was occupied by the graveyard of St Olave, Silver Street, a church destroyed in the Great Fire and not rebuilt. Shakespeare lived at the corner of Silver Street and Monkwell Street during his most fertile years, but his house and all his haunts were burnt with the church in 1666. The square took shape late in the eighteenth century, with the creation of Castle Street.

Falcon Square's most famous resident was Sir Matthew Wood, who was Lord Mayor in 1815–16 and 1816–17 (a rare distinction) and MP for the City from 1817 until his death in 1843. He made himself famous, or notorious, in 1820 by his enthusiastic championing of Queen Caroline during the divorce proceedings. He went to France to escort her to London and she took up residence at his house in South Audley Street. Wood, who was a druggist and hop merchant by trade, had his City address at Falcon Square from 1801, and his son William Page Wood was born there in that year. He had

Falcon Square from the St Olave graveyard in 1926.

a highly successful career as barrister, politician and judge (he was described as 'a mere bundle of virtues without a redeeming vice') and rose to be Gladstone's Lord Chancellor from 1868 to 1872, as Lord Hatherley.

The most prominent building from the middle of the nineteenth century was the Falcon Square Congregational Chapel, which stood on the north side, next to the Falcon public house. Otherwise Falcon Square was given over to offices and workshops.

It was reduced to rubble in 1940, like so many other places in this part of the City. When the new section of London Wall (the road) was created in the 1950s, Falcon Square provided part of its route. Its site now lies under the section of the road between Ironmongers' Hall and Bastion House.

Falcon Square

SOUTHWARK

Falcon Square was an alternative name for Falcon Court, a turning from the north side of St Margaret's Court, Borough High Street. In the 1740s Rocque had shown a much larger '3 Faulcon C' with its entrance directly from Borough High Street, and the Horwood maps of the 1790s and 1813 showed the much reduced open space as '3 Falcon'. John Lockie made an uncharacteristic error by including it twice, as Three Falcon Court and Falcon Court.

As the borough had several other places called Falcon Court it is not surprising that this one made spasmodic attempts to differentiate itself as Falcon Square, the name used by the skeleton Ordnance Survey map of 1848–49, or as Three Falcon Square, which appeared in the 1871 census. The novelties failed to stick and it was Falcon Court in 1861 and 1872. The place was contracting throughout this period; the six houses of 1861 had been reduced to four by 1871, when they were occupied by labourers and charwomen, and soon afterwards it was extinguished altogether.

Farnell Square

See Earls Court Square

Fassett Square

DALSTON [HACKNEY]

Fassett Square was planned with the rest of the Massie estate at Dalston in 1853, but progress was slow and the square was not built until the 1860s. The 1862 Stanford map showed two plain roads on the site, the north–south one nameless and the present Fassett Road called Prior Road. One or two houses were marked at the junction, but no indication was given of a square. It appeared fully formed as Fawcett Square on the 1864 revision, but that name was presumably just a blunder.

William Hodson, a local man, was the chief builder involved. His houses are not of the kind one would look at twice in an ordinary street but they are attractive enough when seen across a garden. Charles Booth's investigator reported in 1897 that 'Fassett Square is very well kept and tidy, with beds of geraniums and some trees about fifty years old'.

In 1871 the typical tenants were clerks, accountants, commercial travellers and commission agents. The only celebrated resident was the novelist Mrs G. Linnaeus Banks (Isabella Varley), who died at No. 34 in 1897, only kept from poverty by help from the Royal Literary Fund and a civil list pension. She is best known (or least badly known) for *The Manchester Men*, published in 1876.

Almost from the time of its creation the square was under threat from its neighbour the German Hospital, hospitals being always apt to expand until they burst. The threat took shape in 1935 when much of the west side of the square was replaced by a new wing of the hospital, designed by Thomas Tait: five storeys of bright yellow brick to confront the mellow two-storeyed houses. The hospital was closed in 1987 and the wing converted into flats in the 1990s. It is the only listed building in the square and looks as bad as one would expect.

The attractive and well-maintained garden is private – a rarity in north London – but so narrow that it can hardly be called secluded.

Fassett Square escaped ruinous notoriety in the early 1980s, when the creators of the BBC soap opera *EastEnders* used it as a model for Albert Square and even thought of filming the series there. Fortunately

The north side of Fassett Square, *c.* 1905.

for the residents' peace and quiet, the German Hospital, so damaging to the square in other respects, came to the rescue. It was then still open and the producers of *EastEnders* thought it would prove indigestible in terms of plot.

Fawcett Square

See Fassett Square

Fells Square

BERMONDSEY [SOUTHWARK]

Fells Square was known for most of its existence as Union Court. On Horwood's 1790s map it was shown without a name as a turning off the north side of the tiny lane known as Alexander Buildings which was destined to grow into a part of Tooley Street. Cary's 1795 map showed only a field there, so possibly a new development received its name or had it topically changed in 1800 or 1801 when the union with Ireland was in agitation. The 1813 revision of Horwood gives the Union Court name. It was a cul-de-sac with four cottages on each side.

The change to Fells Square was made in 1891, perhaps because the proximity of the St Olave's Union offices was causing confusion. Like so much of Tooley Street it was destroyed during the Second World War. The huge block of flats numbered 255 Tooley Street, east of Three Oak Lane, is now on the site.

Ferry Square

BRENTFORD [HOUNSLOW]

Ferry Square is now just a short cul-de-sac off Ferry Lane, wrapping around the Old Fire Station. Ferry Lane was one of the many narrow passages from the High Street to the river that were a feature of Brentford from the sixteenth century. It led to the ancient ferry to Kew, which survived until 1939. Ferry Square, although not under that name, may have been as old as the lane. It certainly had the same form in the 1740s that it retained for another 150 years: that of a genuine square, though a small one.

In the nineteenth century it had seven houses on the south side and two on the west. The east side was formed by Ferry Lane, the north by the widest part

Ferry Square, Brentford, from the High Street in 2013, with the old fire station on the left.

of the High Street. In the central open space there was a small building on the line of the south side of the High Street, which did not materially reduce the sense of a square, as there were still wide openings on either side. In 1839 this intruder was called the 'Lock up House', in 1897 'The Cage'. It must have been rebuilt at least once, as the cage demolished in 1897 was only about fifty years old. When these short-term cells for minor offenders were made redundant by police stations, the building was adapted for use as a shop, No. 52 High Street.

The opening was known as the Square, Old Brentford, from the 1850s to the 1870s when the present name was adopted. It did not mark any physical change; that came when the much larger fire station, designed by the leading Brentford architect, Nowell Parr, replaced the former cage in 1897–98. Although there were still nine houses in the square and it retained a narrow second entrance from the High Street, it was reduced to a minor back street. It cannot have been salubrious, with the Thames Soap Works immediately behind.

In the mid-1930s the cottages (which appear from the scanty photographic evidence to have been of the eighteenth century or earlier) were demolished in stages. Now there is only a plain 1937 terrace on

the south side of Ferry Square; the section of road west of the Old Fire Station has become a mere parking area, decorated by a few struggling shrubs and separated from the High Street by a fence. On a smaller scale it is like Bromley's Market Square, eaten by a public building.

Finsbury Square

DEPTFORD [LEWISHAM]

Like Russell Square and Davis's Square, the little Finsbury Square was part of the Gravel Pits estate at Deptford, between Church Street and the Creek, which belonged to John Addey's charity. It was a slum district built late in the eighteenth and early in the nineteenth century, with very little control from the landlord or the parish. The worst part of the Gravel Pits, the notorious City, was swept away in the 1830s by the London & Greenwich Railway.

Finsbury Square was well to the south of the railway viaduct and survived rather longer. The name was perhaps a cruel allusion to the great Finsbury Square on the edge of the City of London. Deptford's version was a typical square of the front garden type, found in poor areas all over London. There were ten cottages, arranged in terraces on the north and south sides facing each other across long front gardens. Access was from an alley off the east side of Hosier Street, or Finsbury Street as it was sometimes called. The square was replaced in the 1880s by a terrace opening directly into Hosier Street. That survived until shortly after the Second World War, when the LCC built Wilshaw House on the site.

Finsbury Square

OLD STREET [ISLINGTON]

In 1806 Hughson gave an account of the recently completed Finsbury Square in his *History of London*:

> This handsome pile of buildings is situated on the waste, formerly denominated Moorfields … The west side of the square, except two houses at the north end, was built in 1777, and from that time it lay dormant many years … in 1789, the north side was let, in 1790, the east side; in the following year, the south side … The original design was to make the centre of the square a piece of water … and that it might be a reservoir, in case of fire, or accident to the New River; but from the apprehension that it would be a deposit for filth, and unwholesome, it was changed to a garden, by far the more agreeable accommodation to the inhabitants … The object was, to accommodate the merchants with dwellings, and create a respectable neighbourhood near the city … At present Finsbury Square does not give place in beauty, and not much in size, to the most boasted at the west end of the metropolis.

The City might still boast of the size of Finsbury Square if it chose, but not of its beauty. The writer of a London guidebook published in 1825 found that 'Finsbury Square forms a collection of very handsome houses, with stone basements. The garden in the interior is extremely well laid out, and tastefully planted.'

The square was a continuation of the City's rearguard action against the fatal attraction of the West End that had inspired America Square and its

An unrealised scheme for the laying out of a public Finsbury Square garden in 1910. It shows some of the original houses on the north side.

pendants in the 1760s. Although the site was just outside the City boundary, the corporation held it on a long lease. Finsbury Square was planned by George Dance the younger, the City Surveyor, and there seems little doubt that he designed the fine terrace on the west side, despite attempts to shift the credit to his assistant, James Peacock. It was not built as quickly as Hughson thought. The plans were approved in 1777, but the building took from 1778 to 1790. The other three sides were built to a simpler design in the early 1790s. (See p.11) The south took the longest, as the four central houses collapsed in 1792 during construction.

In 1783 Dr Johnson drew a characteristic moral from the houses on the west side, the only ones he lived to see:

> Mrs Burney wondered that some very beautiful new buildings should be erected in Moorfields, in so shocking a situation as between Bedlam and St Luke's Hospital; and said she could not live there. JOHNSON. 'Nay, Madam, you see nothing there to hurt you. You no more think of madness by having windows that look to Bedlam, than you think of death by having windows that look to a church-yard.' Mrs BURNEY. 'We may look to a church-yard, Sir; for it is right that we should be kept in mind of death.' JOHNSON. 'Nay, Madam, if you go to that, it is right that we should be kept in mind of madness, which is occasioned by too much indulgence of imagination. I think a very moral use may be made of these new buildings: I would have those who have heated imaginations live there, and take warning.'

The slow construction makes it plain that building speculators had little faith in the square's chances of halting the flight to the west, and from the first it was occupied more by ordinary merchants, solicitors and doctors than by the great City magnates it was designed to retain. When No. 26 was advertised in 1794 it already included a counting house among its attractions. Numerous successful physicians and surgeons have lived in Finsbury Square, which was the Harley Street of the City. Hotels and boarding houses began to appear in the 1840s.

Beresford Chancellor gave this portrait of the place in 1907:

The life of Finsbury Square is a particularly complex one. Here we find to-day solicitors and doctors, architects and engineers and surveyors largely predominating, while other businesses are interspersed among these; here is a hospital – that for Diseases of the Skin – at No. 12A; a Consulate – the Italian – at No. 44; the German Branch of the Y.M.C.A. at No. 23; while a number of Building Societies, as well as hotels, are scattered about within it, and, most interesting to most of us, at Finsbury House, the Income Tax Recovery Agency.

There was a long campaign to make the garden public. In 1898 Charles Booth's researcher commented on the 'large, well kept square in centre, used only by the residents! Should be converted into open space, much needed here.' In 1910 *The Graphic* reported:

It has been proposed that the owners and occupiers of houses round Finsbury Square should hand over that garden to the London County Council under the Open Spaces Act of 1906, but at a meeting of the residents to decide the point only six votes were given in favour of the proposal and eighteen against it. Fears were expressed that if the gardens were handed over to the County Council residents and business men in the Square might have to put up with bands and noisy games.

The bands and noisy games came in due course, but by then the private residents were long gone.

Most of Finsbury Square was rebuilt as large offices and hotels early in the twentieth century. It suffered less damage in the Second World War than might have been expected in this area, but the most attractive feature, the fine original terrace on the west side, was all but destroyed. The loss of the big German hotel in the north-east corner was more easily borne.

The present design of the garden dates from the early 1960s, when the car park was dug underneath it after a long and heated debate over the principle of desecrating squares in this way. Business won the argument and more gardens were damaged after the precedent was created.

Fish Street Square

See Monument Square

The west side of Finsbury Square, Islington, *c.* 1905.

Fitzroy Square

Fitzroy Square is one of those places that seem always to be just off the edge of the map, but which nobody can ever find without the help of a map. Yet it is among the finest squares in London, one of the very few that conforms to the ideal definition in every particular, and ought to be well known to every native and on the itinerary of every discerning tourist. It was the last London work of Robert Adam, undertaken when the fashion for his style had retreated to his native Scotland, and was part of the effort by the Adam brothers to recover from the financial disaster of the Adelphi.

The name of the new square came from the Fitzroys, barons Southampton, who owned a large estate wrapping round the east and north sides of what was soon to be the Regent's Park. The Adam brothers presumably approached Lord Southampton with a proposal for a square, as they were the developers as well as the architects of the east and south sides. They seem also to have been confident of completing the other sides, as the numbers assigned ran anticlockwise, with Nos 1–9 on the east side and 27–34 on the south. When more houses than anticipated were eventually squeezed into the north and west sides the southern houses had to be renumbered.

The Adams built the east side first, in 1792–93, and the south side in 1793–94. Robert Adam, the genius of the family, died in 1792 and with his death the energy went out of the firm. The completed houses let reasonably well but no move was made to build more in the unfavourable conditions of wartime.

For thirty years the square stood as a classic torso. As late as 1825 an architectural critic wrote, 'Were it but completed, in accordance with the designs upon which it was some years since commenced, [it] would probably form the most splendid ornament of its kind in the metropolis'. Just in time, his plea was answered. In the 1820s it was still possible to find builders who could work with instinctive grace within the Adam style, and the north side of 1827–28 and the west of 1832–35, although simpler and more conventional, are a dignified complement to the work of the master. Thirty years had been enough to show that the tide of fashion would not flow in this direction, so the new houses were smaller and less expensive. Old and new were alike in having no back gardens.

The Marquess of Salisbury, in his comparatively impoverished youth before inheriting the title, and long before becoming prime minister, lived at the small No. 21 from 1859 to 1862, but he was a rare bird in these parts. Only a year or two after he left Trollope wrote in *The Small House at Allington*, 'We know how vile is the sound of Baker Street, and how absolutely foul to the polite ear is the name of Fitzroy Square'. But what society scorned, many artists found very much to their taste. William Weir gave a reason for this in 1843: 'Its vicinity is much affected by artists, who find it convenient to live between their aristocratic patrons and employers in the West End squares, and their possibly more lucrative employers in the houses of commons which surround the Bedford Square group.'

Only the most notable artists can be mentioned. Sir Charles Eastlake, PRA and Director of the National Gallery, lived at No. 7 from 1842 until his death in 1867; Lady Eastlake retained the house until her death in 1893. William Dyce, RA, was at No. 2 in 1850–51. Edward Orme, the engraver and publisher, and the creator of Orme Square, died at No. 6 in 1848. Sir William Ross, RA, the painter of portrait miniatures, lived for many years at No. 38, where he died in 1860. Ford Madox Brown lived at No. 37 during his most prosperous years, from 1866 to 1881, although towards the end of that period he was spending more time in Manchester. His departure was protracted, 'the Fitzroy Square house being held on a long lease, and proving almost unlettable'. William De Morgan had his studio at No. 40 until a fire in his kiln destroyed the roof of the house and he was asked to leave. Sir Frank Dicksee, PRA, lived at No. 2 in the 1890s. Poorer artists and their clubs and societies swarmed in the surrounding streets.

Writers also favoured the square. George Bernard Shaw lived at No. 29 from 1887 to 1898, and figures in directories after that because his mother remained until 1907. It was perhaps Shaw who recommended the square to his friend William Archer, the dramatist and critic, who occupied ground-floor rooms at No. 27 from 1909 until his death in 1924. But Archer was already well acquainted with this style of life, having lived earlier in Gordon Square and Queen Square. Virginia Woolf was at No. 29 from 1907 to 1911, between spells at Gordon Square and Brunswick Square.

There were still a few artists and architects at the beginning of the twentieth century, but by then most of the houses had been turned into hospitals or other institutions. In 1898 the Booth survey recorded that the houses were occupied by a 'private hospital, schools, clubs, hotels at south-west corner of questionable repute, not so good as it used to be'. Beresford Chancellor wrote that by 1907, 'Fitzroy Square has become largely the home of hospitals and institutions of various kinds … In fact as a residential centre Fitzroy Square has, in common with so many others in this quarter, become almost a thing of the past.' As it was full of hospitals and nursing homes a great many minor celebrities died there.

The east side of Fitzroy Square in 1807.

The south side of Fitzroy Square in the 1920s.

Two houses on the north side, Nos 13 and 14, were rebuilt in the 1920s in an unhappy imitation of Adam. During the Second World War the German bombers, with impeccable taste, picked out the two Adam sides for attack, but did no damage to the inferior north and west sides. The south terrace was very nearly destroyed and had to wait thirty-five years before it was partly restored and partly rebuilt in facsimile.

The square is now pedestrianised on three sides and wonderfully quiet. The garden neatly combines public and private, with seats on the paved perimeter and the circular inner garden given over to the traditional lawn and trees.

Ford Square

Ford Square was built in the early 1820s, a few years before its close neighbour Sidney Square. It was originally known as Bedford Square, a name changed first to Bedford Square East and then to Ford Square in deference to its great Bloomsbury namesake. It was superior in status to most of Whitechapel and had at least one moderately eminent resident. Francis Louis Barrallier, a French-born officer in the British Army, died at No. 24 in 1853, by which time he had the honorary rank of lieutenant colonel. He did important surveying work in Australia from 1801 to 1803 and in the West Indies from 1805 to 1817. The square was popular with shipowners and the proprietors of ladies' schools, and there were two pubs, the Hermit and the North Briton.

In the mid-1870s the square was seriously disrupted when the East London Railway dug its cut-and-cover tunnel down the west side of the garden and demolished the last two or three houses at the west end of the north and south sides. That was presumably when the remaining houses of the north and south terraces were renovated and given their stucco finish.

In 1898 Charles Booth's researcher found 'Ford Square (late Bedford Square) a rough field uncared for, shut and entirely neglected. All Jews living round it, 3 storey houses and four families in each house.' The central enclosures of Ford and Sidney Square were bought by the LCC for £10,000 in 1903 and laid out in 1904, Ford Square as a playground ('its present use' at that time), the smaller Sidney Square as a garden. They were opened to the public 'without ceremony' on 20 June 1904.

The whole square was badly knocked about during the Second World War, the damage on the east side being particularly severe. There the late Victorian No. 27, a fine double-fronted house, is now the only

The garden of Ford Square, from the south side, in 2007.

pre-war building. A restored 1820s terrace survives at the north end of the west side, now part of Cavell Street, and parts of the stucco terraces at the east ends of the north and south sides. The three houses at the west end of the south side are a modern pastiche over the railway tunnel.

Frederick Square

See Connaught Square

Frith Square

See Soho Square

Fulmer's Square

WESTMINSTER

Fulmer's Row and Fulmer's Square were in Palmer's Village, a shanty town off the east side of the present Artillery Row, named after the nearby Palmer's Almshouses. Fulmer's Row grew rapidly in the late 1780s. The ratebooks list four houses in 1789, sixteen in 1790.

John Lockie did not include Fulmer's Row in the 1810 edition of his *Topography of London*, but gave this direction in 1813: 'Fulmer's Row, Palmer's Village, Westminster – 1st on the R. in Providence-row from Paradise-row'. The name came from Samuel Fulmer, a lamplighter, who gave his address variously as Providence Row and Fulmer's Row, Palmer's Village, and was a voter in Westminster.

Fulmer's Row was named in the 1813 edition of Horwood's map. Fulmer's Square first appeared in the 1851 census, but it was merely an alternative name for part of the Row, where two of the 1851 residents of the square were living ten years earlier. Fulmer's Row was far from salubrious: in 1846 it contained two brothels and was the residence of six prostitutes, according to a survey by a local clergyman. Evidence in a trial for theft in 1829 gave reason to believe that Mrs Fulmer let rooms to the prostitutes.

Palmer's Village was an area where regularity of building or consistency of naming was hardly to be expected. *The Mirror of Literature* described the place in 1839:

You are not to suppose that there exists only one avenue through Palmer's Village, or only one street of the straggling tenements above mentioned. There are as many avenues, lanes, holes and bores, as there used to be in the catacombs – houses huddled upon houses, without regard to discipline or good order; in short, were I a magistrate, I should feel inclined to read the riot act, Palmer's Village being strictly within the spirit and meaning of that enactment – a neighbourhood tumultuously assembled!

Most of Palmer's Village was demolished between 1845 and 1851, during the construction of Victoria Street. Fulmer's Row and Square were off the direct route of the new road and survived long enough to appear in the 1851 census, when the fourteen houses of the square were occupied by dustmen, scavengers and coal porters. The remaining fragments of Palmer's Village were acquired by the Westminster Improvement Commissioners in 1853 to await redevelopment. Howick Place is now roughly on the site of Fulmer's Row.

Gainsborough Square

HACKNEY

Gainsborough Square was of the cul-de-sac variety, running south from a narrow entrance in Wick Road to the viaduct below the Stratford line platform of Victoria Park Station. There were thirteen houses on the east side, only seven on the west, where the viaduct cut across diagonally. Although the road widened a little where the houses began, there was no room for any communal garden or even yard and thus no real sense of a square. The site had been occupied by the Wick Hall Academy until the land was required for the station (the second of the name, replacing one on the north side of Wick Road), which was opened in 1866. The square was built at the same time as the station and was known at first by the more appropriate name of Gainsborough Street. The three-storey houses had bay windows on the ground floor and small front gardens.

Gainsborough Square passed through the Second World War with little damage, but its fate was nevertheless sealed then, because the station was closed in 1943. This had no immediate effect, but in the

1960s it became part of the route of what is now the A12 and the square was demolished with the redundant station in 1970, during the building of the new road.

George Square

George Square was built in the first decade of the nineteenth century immediately to the north of Hoxton Square. John Lockie did not include it in the first edition of his *Topography of London*, published in 1810, but in 1813 described it as 'by the Coffee-house, N.E. corner of Hoxton-square'. Hoxton Square was very solid and respectable, its new neighbour anything but. It had some twenty tiny cottages ranged around three sides of a small open space with no garden, and there was later a pub called the Prince Albert in the square.

The west side had a southward extension that was halted by the back gardens of the north side of Hoxton Square. The east side was occupied by a large building that was Claxton & Sons' cotton mill until it was nearly destroyed by a fire in 1856. Robert Claxton, who regularly appeared in game certificate lists in the 1840s and 1850s, was the square's respectable resident; many of his neighbours were burglars. The restored large building had become a corn mill by the 1870s, when half of the north side of the square had been demolished to extend it. By that time the name St George's Square was sometimes being used.

In 1883 the George Square cottages were demolished and replaced by four-storey tenement blocks usually called George's Square. They were financed on the 5 per cent philanthropy system by the publisher George Murray Smith, founder of the *Dictionary of National Biography*. The flats were a failure, socially and financially, and Smith sold them in 1891.

The Charles Booth survey gave 'St George's Square' a bad report in 1898: 'Nearly opposite the Hoxton lunatic asylum. A messy square, surrounded on north, west and south sides by four-storied Buildings; poor, rowdy, much trouble to police, haunt of Sunday gamblers who escape up the open staircases … Is becoming worse, much bread lying about.'

Despite their obvious shortcomings the tenements survived until the 1970s, when St Monica's School expanded north from Hoxton Square to cover the site.

Gibson Square

In 1823, with new developments, and especially new squares, being built or planned all around them, the trustees of the Milner-Gibson estate (for the owner was a child) decided it was time to join in. After much hesitation and various changes of mind, the plan resolved itself into some minor service roads supporting what eventually became the narrow, rectangular Gibson Square and Milner Square. The first thought was to call Gibson Square Milner Square, and other rejected ideas were Theberton Square and Upton Square. *The Morning Post* announced it as forthcoming, under its final name, in October 1829.

The trustees were fortunate in their choice of architect, for they lighted on the talented and highly efficient Francis Edwards, then just starting his own practice. He later designed Wellington Square at Chelsea. Edwards made the grand plan for the estate and designed the houses in Gibson Square and the minor roads, but the later Milner Square was entrusted to other and less practical hands.

The south side of Gibson Square was built first, in 1831, and some of the houses were occupied by 1832. It has now long been counted as part of Theberton Street (named after a Milner-Gibson estate in Suffolk) which continues to east and west, but it was separately and distinctly designed to set the tone for the square, in which it was originally

The west side of Gibson Square in 2007.

numbered 1–13. The three central houses are of four storeys plus basement, instead of the three of the rest of the terrace; the penultimate house at each end was given two pairs of pilasters and a pediment, though the one at the east end has been removed.

The long east and west sides of the square were built between 1834 and 1836. They have the three end houses at north and south decorated with pilasters and a pediment, and the four in the centre set forward and given an attic storey and round-headed windows on the first as well as the ground floor. The very short north side and its westward continuation are now part of the square, but were built in a simpler style as Charles Street. As at Wellington Square, Edwards's fine design has survived in almost perfect condition.

An incident in the early history deserves recording. In December 1832 a gentleman walking through Gibson Square saw a man:

… without his coat, waistcoat, and shoes, running round a pool of water, in the middle of the square. After a few minutes he stripped himself stark naked, and ran up to his knees in the water. Thinking this rather strange, the passer-by told a policeman, who took the paddler into custody.

He turned out to be an escaped pauper lunatic from St Pancras. The 1828 plan of the estate showed a circular feature in the centre of the garden, evidently the pond, but it was gone by the time of the 1871 map.

Gibson Square was solidly middle class in its early years, with insurance agents and music teachers the least respectable inhabitants, but like others in Islington it declined late in the century. The Booth surveyor noted in 1897, 'Houses built for a better class than now inhabits them … Square ill kept, inhabitants can't afford to pay a square keeper.'

For the first half of the twentieth century Gibson Square was mostly given over to lodging houses, with the occasional bootmaker, surgeon or dressmaker. The garden was handed over to Islington Council in the 1930s. The square passed through the Second World War safely with only two houses on each of the long sides damaged, none of them fatally.

The gentrification of Islington has introduced a different class of residents since the war.

The rehabilitation of Gibson Square was started by Angus McBean, the photographer, who bought No. 34 in 1945 and later added No. 35 to it. The sociologist Michael Young, Lord Young of Dartington, who died at No. 67 in 2002, is the most eminent former resident. He was the author of many books, including *Family and Kinship in East London* (1957) and *The Rise of the Meritocracy* (1958), which added a word to the English language. He founded the Consumers' Association and *Which*.

The wealth and pugnacity of the new inhabitants enabled them to beat London Transport in the 1960s, when a monstrous ventilation shaft for the Victoria Line was planned for the garden. In a landmark victory for the London square, the residents forced the substitution of an elegant mock temple, designed by Raymond Erith and Quinlan Terry.

Gillray Square

CHELSEA [KENSINGTON AND CHELSEA]

Strewan Square was the original name for this unhappy eyesore. It came from the short section of the King's Road to the west of Milman's Street, which was known as Strewan Place from early in the nineteenth century. This terrace was immediately to the north of the future square.

Greenwood's map of 1830 showed only a single house in a garden behind Strewan Place; by the 1860s it was known as Strawen House. It was acquired by a developer named George Stephenson, who built Strewan Terrace on the Milman's Street frontage in 1875 and Strewan Square behind it soon afterwards. There were twenty-two houses in total on the north, west and south sides, and ten more in the centre, where a garden should have been. Five of those ten (forming part of Strewan Terrace) had their entrances in Milman's Street.

When Nos 23 and 24 Strewan Square were vainly offered for sale in 1879 they were described as having 'eight rooms, small garden in rear, forecourt enclosed with iron railings, rental £42 each'. The lease was for ninety-nine years from 1873.

In 1888 the square was renamed in honour of James Gillray, the caricaturist, who was born in Chelsea in 1756. His father, a one-armed Chelsea Pensioner, served for forty years as sexton to the Moravian Burial Ground in Milman's Street, opposite the square, presumably executing the digging part of the job by proxy. Beresford Chancellor said the change of name was suggested by Sir Charles Dilke. It followed the precedent set with Carlyle, of commemorating famous residents of Chelsea in the names of its squares. The compliment was less flattering in this case, for No. 10 Strewan Square was a brothel as early as 1879, and in 1887 Chelsea Vestry received a complaint that the square was used for gambling purposes, particularly on Sundays. When the vestry referred this to the police, the answer was, 'Strewan-square is a very rough neighbourhood and there is much overcrowding. The police have done, and will continue to do, all they legally can to check the nuisance complained of.'

In 1899 Charles Booth's assistant described Gillray Square as '3½ storey, asphalte paved, nearly all one room dwellers. Street clean, but broken windows, open doors, filthy plaster, etc. Very rough, drunken, and troublesome: almost the worst place in the [police] division.'

All the houses suffered blast damage during the war, but they were not seriously injured. Nevertheless, the whole area was cleared by Chelsea Council in the late 1940s to build the Cremorne Estate, one of the blocks on which is called Gillray House.

Gloucester Square

Gloucester Square, the largest in Tyburnia, had a long prehistory like the rest, with changes of plan and name. Bloomfield Square and Devonshire Square were considered, before the final choice was made in 1838. Building began in the early 1840s in standard Bayswater stucco. The west and south sides were the first, in progress by 1842, but the circuit of houses was not completed until the end of the decade.

Gloucester Square is unlike its orthodox neighbours; in Kensington it would have been called Gloucester Gardens, for only on the north and south sides do the houses face the garden across a road. The most important elements of the square were the large back-to-front houses on the two short sides, which communicated directly with the garden.

George Ledwell Taylor designed those houses, all now demolished, and also the ones on the south side, which have survived better than the rest in a sadly butchered square. His nearly complete terrace west of Hyde Park Square is very grand, with six engaged Corinthian columns in the centre, but the houses at the sharp-angled corners, with their profusion of

The houses on the west side of Gloucester Square, Bayswater, opening into Sussex Place, *c.* 1904.

seaside bow windows, are the most attractive features. Of the long north side, the last built, only four original houses are standing.

Being 'on the wrong side of the park', Gloucester Square, like the others in Bayswater, was inhabited more by wealth and talent than by fashion. Robert Stephenson, formerly of Cambridge Square, lived at the larger No. 34 Gloucester Square from his election to parliament in 1847 until his death in 1859. In the directories the great engineer is listed as MP for Whitby. Joseph Samuda, the engineer and Liberal politician, died at No. 7 in 1885. Number 11 was the home of the Irish swindler and MP Michael Sadleir, who killed himself on Hampstead Heath in 1856 by drinking prussic acid when his embezzlements could no longer be concealed. He was the inspiration for shady financiers in a number of Victorian novels, including Merdle in *Little Dorrit*. A more respectable businessman was George Murray Smith, publisher and founder of the *Cornhill Magazine*, the *Pall Mall Gazette* and the *Dictionary of National Biography*. He also lived at No. 11, from 1859.

The destruction of Gloucester Square began before the Second World War as part of the estate policy of replacing the 1840s houses with small, dull, brick terraces as opportunity offered. What little bomb damage the square suffered was nearly all concentrated on the south side at the link with Hyde Park Square. Since the war larger-scale replacement of houses with flats has nearly completed its ruin.

Gloucester Square

CITY ROAD [ISLINGTON]

Gloucester Square, which was off the east side of Whitecross Street, south of Banner Street, was known until the 1860s as Gloucester Court. It was a purely cosmetic change, as the place looked much the same on the Ordnance Survey of 1873 and the Ogilby & Morgan map of 1676. The narrow alley leading from Whitecross Street continued to be called Gloucester Court after the opening to its north was promoted to a square.

It must once have been a place of some pretensions, as the early Georgian Gloucester House, which filled most of the west side, was of five bays and three storeys plus attics. The other houses, a dozen or more, were much smaller.

The whole area was cleared in the early 1880s to build the huge Peabody tenement estate that still dominates Whitecross Street and looks as though even an earthquake would not disturb it.

Godwin Square

See Brunswick Square, Haggerston

Gold Square

See Gould's Square

Golden Square

BRENTFORD [HOUNSLOW]

Golden Square was a group of cottages set around a yard off the north side of Back Lane, very close to its junction with Half Acre. It grew quite slowly and for most of its existence was counted as part of Back Lane. There were a couple of cottages in 1839, half a dozen in 1865 and ten in 1881, when the Golden Square name made its only appearance in the census returns. It was then occupied mainly by Irish agricultural labourers.

In 1887 the Brentford inspector of nuisances brought the state of Golden Square to the notice of the local board, and its committee of inspection shortly afterwards made a damning assessment:

> In making their report on those [cottages] in Golden Square, the Committee are unanimously of opinion that every one of them are utterly unfit for human habitation, being bereft of every qualification necessary for that purpose, and being dirty, damp, crumbling to pieces, insufficient in air space, with no proper means of ventilation, bad in their original construction both in material and design, and in a state of decay that renders futile any attempt at repair, altogether representing a most deplorable state of insalubrity. Under these circumstances the Committee recommend the Board to close the whole of them as being to the individuals inhabiting them very dangerous.

Notices were issued for seven cottages, and that they were effective was shown by the 1891 census, which did not include Golden Square, and the 1893 Ordnance Survey, which showed the site cleared and vacant. It is now occupied by the police station, which has cut off the west end of Back Lane.

Golden Square

RICHMOND [RICHMOND UPON THAMES]

The lanes and alleys that link Richmond Green with George Street and King Street were built late in the seventeenth century. One of them, Golden Court, between George Street and the southern corner of the Green, preserves some memory of the vanished Golden Square.

Until well into the twentieth century Golden Court was called Pensioners Alley and had offshoots to the south-west known as Golden Square, with three houses, and Gosling's Court, with four. Golden Square existed by 1823, when the name appeared in the baptism entry of a bricklayer's son. There were no examples between 1813 and 1823, and before 1813 the Richmond parish registers did not give addresses.

The growth of the George Street shops in the early twentieth century overwhelmed the square and the court. Gosling's department store was the main

agent of destruction and now, as the House of Fraser, covers the site. The square used to be very obscure and secluded because the entrances to Pensioners Alley from George Street and the Green were under archways through shops, now removed. Golden Square and Pensioners Alley were entirely working class, housing labourers, laundresses, gas fitters, bootmakers and the like. Golden Court is filled with restaurants and expensive shops.

Golden Square

SOHO [WESTMINSTER]

Although it lies so close to Regent Street and Piccadilly Circus, Golden Square is the least known and the hardest to find of all the original squares of the West End, being the smallest and 'not exactly in anybody's way to or from anywhere', as Dickens said in *Nicholas Nickleby*.

It was the idea of John Emlyn, a brickmaker, and James Axtell, a bricklayer or carpenter, who adjusted their rival claims to the land and proceeded jointly. As there was strict royal control over new building in London, their scheme had to be referred to Sir Christopher Wren, the Surveyor General. The first application in 1671 was unsuccessful, but in

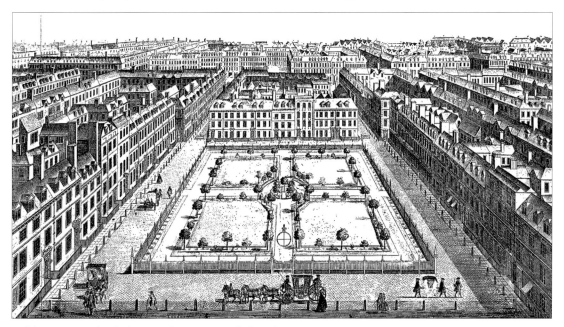

Golden Square, Soho, looking north, in 1731 or a little earlier.

1673, after some judicious bribery, they obtained permission to build the square in accordance with a plan attached to their petition. This is signed by Wren, but whether it was drawn in his office or submitted by Emlyn and Axtell is not known.

The land was Gelding Close or Field, so the development was originally called Gelding Square, 'but the inhabitants, indignant at the vulgarity of the name, changed it to the present'. This was recorded by Thomas Pennant on the authority of William Pulteney, who was born in 1684. The new name was established by 1688 although Golding Square was a variant form used in the early eighteenth century.

Emlyn's half-share soon passed (by somewhat dubious means) to Isaac Symball, 'an eminent builder', who took a leading part in the development until he was murdered in 1695. Symball and Axtell divided the land equally, but Axtell's death in 1679 delayed any building on his half. Symball managed to dispose of his plots at the south end of the west side quite quickly. Number 24 was begun in 1675 and Nos 19a–24 were occupied by 1686. Most of the north side was also built during Symball's lifetime.

Numbers 2 and 3 Golden Square in the north-east corner, in 1905 or a little earlier.

The Axtell share was taken in hand by James's sister-in-law, Martha, who seems to have been a capable businesswoman, and all the houses there were built and let in the 1680s and 1690s. The square was completed in the first years of the eighteenth century with Nos 1–4 at the north end of the east side, part of the late Symball's share. From the 1680s the various builders involved aimed fairly successfully at uniformity of style. The garden was laid out in the 1680s in professed imitation of Leicester Square. Its design was changed at least once in the first sixty years to keep abreast of the latest style. In 1773 Noorthouck reported that the wooden pales had lately been replaced by 'handsome iron rails'.

The 'very new and pleasant Square', as Hatton called it in 1708, was fashionable during its first half-century, with many peers among the residents. In one of her gossiping letters to her son in 1705, Lady Wentworth described her niece Mrs Hanbury's house, No. 25 in the middle of the west side:

> They have a lees for five years of it: thear is a little garden, a gravel walk in the midle, and a gras walk of each syde, at the end an arber the hole breadth of the garden, and a doar in to the stables. The rent for the hous, stables, and coachous is threescore pd a year, very good water both to drinck and wash with; the landlord pays the Queen's taxis, they have of all sorts of provetion just by them; it is in Golden Square.

Henry St John, Viscount Bolinbroke, Secretary of State from 1710, lived at No. 22 near the south end of the west side from 1702 until 1714, when he fled the country. In February 1712 Swift noted that 'Prince Eugene dines with the Secretary to-day, with about 7 or 8 General Officers or forein Ministers. They will be all drunk, I am sure.' In August 1714 Peter Wentworth wrote to his brother that for the proclamation of George I, 'Lord Bullingbrook Sunday made a Bonfire and the finest illuminations in town at his house in Golden Square, but that might be out of Policy, fearing the mob'.

Two other celebrated statesmen are thought to have been born in the square: Pitt the elder at No. 28 in 1708, and William Windham at No. 6 in 1750. Sir Edward Knatchbull, a prominent MP for Kent, lived at No. 5 until his death in 1730. The odd baronet or Irish peer was still to be found there throughout the eighteenth century and the square was popular with minor ambassadors, but high fashion had migrated further west.

It was in a poor state by 1783, the garden 'more neglected than is usual in these places of ornament' and 'the coach pavement, near the railing' exhibiting 'very offensive symptoms of neglect'.

After its brief spell of glory, Golden Square was much occupied by artists, doctors and merchants. Angelica Kauffman and Sir Martin Archer Shee are the most important of the artists. The Kauffmans moved to No. 16 soon after their arrival in England in 1766. J.T. Smith records that 'when I was a boy my father frequently took me to Golden Square to see her pictures, where she and her father had for many years resided in the centre house on the south side'. Shee lived at No. 13 in the south-east corner from 1796 to 1799, when he moved to Cavendish Square.

The most famous of the medical men was John Hunter, who set up his London surgical practice at No. 31 in 1763 and remained until 1768. The famous Lady Holland grew up in Golden Square where her father, Richard Vassall, a sugar planter, occupied No. 11 on the east side from 1782 to 1786, when she was married. He later lived at No. 6 until his death in 1795.

It has frequently been stated that the Bavarian Embassy Chapel in Golden Square was looted by the mob during the Gordon Riots of 1780. In fact the chapel was in Warwick Street, where its successor, built ten years after the riots, is now known as Our Lady of the Assumption. It was the house of the Bavarian envoy, Josef von Haszlang, which stood, and still stands, at Nos 23 and 24 on the west side of the square, immediately behind the chapel. Horace Walpole says:

Old Haslang's chapel was broken open and plundered; and as he is a prince of smugglers, as well as Bavarian minister, great quantities of run tea and contraband goods were found in his house. This one cannot lament, and still less, as the old wretch has for these forty years usurped a hired house, and though the proprietor for many years has offered to remit his arrears of rent, he will neither quit the house nor pay for it.

The chapel in Warwick Street and the house in Golden Square had belonged to the Portuguese minister until the Bavarians took it over.

It was no doubt this long association that led to No. 35 on the north side becoming the official residence of the Roman Catholic Vicar Apostolic of the London District. Nicholas Wiseman was one holder of that office and lived here from 1847 until he went to Rome in 1850 to be made a cardinal. The Roman Catholic connection also helped to make Golden Square popular with foreign visitors, for whose convenience Italian, French, German and other hotels were opened.

In 1898 the Booth survey found that 'the square is well kept but shut. Great pity, none ever uses it!' This was because there were few private residents left. In 1907 Beresford Chancellor noted that 'nearly the whole of Golden Square is occupied by woollen manufacturers' offices'. They had moved into the square from the late 1860s, making use of the old houses at first, but in the early twentieth century rebuilding many of them as offices, warehouses and showrooms.

The statue in the centre, which was erected in 1753, is said to be of George II and to have been bought at the sale of the Duke of Chandos's collections at Cannons in 1747–48, but the authors of the *Survey of London* suspect that it was merely one of the many decorative figures from the roof of Cannons, successfully passed off as the king even during his lifetime.

The square escaped surprisingly lightly in the Second World War with only some blast damage to the south side, but the garden emerged as a wreck. It was restored by Westminster Council and opened to the public in 1952. It has trees and grass around the edge and a raised area of seating surrounding the 'king'. Only four houses survive: No. 11, a rebuilding of 1778, re-fronted in 1954, and the late seventeenth-century Nos 21, 23 and 24, all altered to various degrees. The rest of the buildings are a miscellaneous collection of twentieth-century offices and shops. Numbers 34–36, on the north side, is a block of offices designed by Leonard Stokes, the Catholic architect, and built in 1914 partly on the site of the Wiseman house. The massive No. 25, which occupies much of the west side, was built in 1924 for the woollen firm, Dormeuil Frères.

Golden Square

SEE THE MOUNT SQUARE

Goldrings Square

WALHAM GREEN [HAMMERSMITH AND FULHAM]

The pub at No. 541 Kings Road, just west of Stanley Bridge, began seriously as the Earl Grey, turned to frivolity as the Nell Gwynne, and has now, like so many others, become merely silly as the Jam Tree. Goldrings Square was one of a series of names for a terrace of seven or eight houses that lurked behind the pub, by Gas Factory Yard, the entrance to the Imperial Gasworks. Many of the residents worked there.

In 1841 the terrace was called Goldrings Rents and Buildings, in 1851 Goldrings Square, in 1861 Goldrings Place, and from 1871 to 1891 Goldrings Buildings again. The name may possibly have come from Robert Goldring, a tobacconist who lived in neighbouring Chelsea in 1841. Shopkeepers often invested their savings in small building developments.

In the 1890s the terrace was replaced by lodging houses, but they had gone in their turn by 1914. Now the smart flats of Astor Court and Maynard Close are on the site.

Goldsmith Square

STOKE NEWINGTON [HACKNEY]

(later St Matthias Square)

Goldsmith Square had three names in its brief history, but they were not enough to save it from destruction. William Butterfield's remarkable St Matthias Church was completed in 1853 and the square was built in the early 1850s as its forecourt. It was nearly square in shape, with six houses each on the north and south sides and St Matthias on the east. Howard Road continued it to the west, but the houses of the square – of two or three storeys, with semi-basements – were set further apart than those in the road to give an unrestricted view of the church. Some early maps called it Gloucester Square, but as most of the other roads on the National Freehold

St Matthias and the site of Goldsmith Square (now a school playground) in 2011.

Land Society's Albert Town estate were named after poets – Cowper, Spenser, Shakespeare and Milton – that was probably just a mistake for Goldsmith. It was Goldsmith Square in the 1861 census.

This was one of the better addresses in a far from wealthy area, but the square did not remain entirely residential: a builder and a bricklayer had two of the houses by the 1890s. The celebrity was the eminent

Goldsmiths' Square

The name came from the long vanished Goldsmiths' almshouses of 1703 that stood further down what is now Goldsmith's Row, on the west side. The square was built in the 1830s. It had a very odd form, determined in part by the fact that the garden – which stood to one side rather than in the centre – had been a pond and was presumably not suitable for building. There was an irregular terrace of houses to the north of the garden, but these were known separately as Goldsmiths' Grove.

The square was a right-angled alley that wrapped around the east and south of the big garden, with houses on both sides separated by small front gardens. None of these houses faced the big garden, although seven of them backed onto it. The alley, which was sometimes known confusingly as Grove Square, quickly became a slum which Shoreditch Vestry was keen to demolish by the late 1880s. In 1891 they were able to persuade the LCC that only a third of the cleared space should be used for new housing, the rest becoming a much needed recreation ground. It was laid out between 1892 and 1894.

George Duckworth, the Charles Booth surveyor who visited Goldsmiths' Square in 1898, found:

> … great changes here, new LCC playground on the south side in place of the dark blue [very poor] of the map. On the north side eleven new two-storied houses, inhabitants now fairly respectable … The playground is divided into two, the eastern half gravelled with swings, bars, giant stride, etc., for children. The western half more of a garden with grass, flowerbeds, and asphalt paths. On the west side of it, fronting on Goldsmiths Row, is a row of dwellings put up by LCC when the old places were demolished, 'but quite a different class came into them: the old ones had a job to find homes, they most of them settled into the neighbouring streets.' [The words in single inverted commas were the accompanying policeman's comment.]

church architect James Brooks, a churchwarden of St Matthias, who lived at No. 6 in the late 1850s and early 1860s.

In 1937 the LCC changed the name to St Matthias Square, probably to avoid confusion with Goldsmiths' Square at Haggerston. The houses and the nearby vicarage were wrecked in the Second World War and St Matthias and its school were damaged. The church has been restored, but the ruined houses were cleared away to provide part of the site for a new and enlarged school.

The 'row of dwellings put up by LCC' between 1894 and 1898 are in fact two rows and now much the most attractive feature of the former square. The rest of the 1890s changes failed to last. All the houses were replaced by large blocks of flats in the 1930s and 1940s and the recreation ground is now a very dismal hard court with not a flowerbed or giant stride in sight. The cheerful Albion, the modern successor to an old beerhouse, is a welcome relief.

Goodman's Square

See Goodwin Square

Goodwin Square

In 1813 Lockie, who had not mentioned it in 1810, described 'Goodman's Square' as being opposite the east end of Church Street, Blackfriar's Road. Church Street is now Burrell Street.

Horwood's 1790s map showed an unnamed alley opposite Church Street leading to a garden or open space with a building in the south-west corner. The 1813 revision of the map indicated two terraces on the north and east sides of the space, forming a rough square, with the original building standing in for the south and west sides. By 1821 Gardner's map of the parish of Christ Church was calling it Goodwin Square, and that usage was followed in all later references.

Under either name it did not last long, for it was one of the many places cleared in 1861 for the new Southwark Street. The census of that year recorded that the houses in Goodwin Square were unoccupied. Their epitaph was this advertisement in the *Daily News* of 26 April:

Metropolitan Improvements, Southwark and Westminster Communication, Seventh Sale, Building Materials of 18 Houses. Pullen, Horne, and Eversfield are instructed by the Metropolitan Board of Works to sell by auction, on the premises, on Monday, May 6, at 12, in lots, all the valuable building material of eighteen houses in Bear-lane, Price's-street, and Goodwin-square, Gravel-lane, Southwark …

The Holiday Inn Express, Southwark Street, is now on the site.

Gordon Square

Thomas Cubitt made an agreement to build a large part of the Duke of Bedford's Bloomsbury estate, including Gordon Square, in 1824. The name came from the second wife of the 6th Duke, Georgiana, who was daughter of the 4th Duke of Gordon.

Work began in 1829 with the south side. This was a rare example of Cubitt accepting a design by an outside architect. The plans for the terraces on either side of Woburn Square were provided by Charles Fowler, architect of Covent Garden market (built by William Cubitt) and thus well known to the Duke of Bedford. Fowler lived at No. 1 on the west corner of Woburn Square with the benefit of gardens outside

The east side of Gordon Square, *c.* 1905, showing the Bloomsbury Group houses.

The Catholic Apostolic Church, Gordon Square, c. 1905.

his windows in all directions. His house was demolished with the rest of that terrace in the 1950s but the similar Nos 55–58 survive at the east end of Gordon Square's south side.

After that promising start the development stalled in the depression of the 1830s, and never recovered momentum because of Cubitt's other commitments and the desertion of Bloomsbury by the fashionable world. The only other houses built before 1840 were the eight at the north end of the east side. One of them, No. 36, was occupied in 1838. A single house, No. 7, was built at the south-west corner in the 1840s, but it was fatally undermined when the foundations of the Irvingite church were dug, and had to be demolished. The north side was started in the late 1840s and completed before Cubitt's death in 1855, but most of the houses on the east and west sides were built by his executors between 1855 and 1860. They were a poor match for the existing terraces, in finish on the west side and in size at the south end of the east side.

Gordon Square suffered more than the others in Bloomsbury from the declining popularity of the area. The small houses in Torrington and Woburn Squares sold readily enough, but the great merchants and lawyers who were the intended tenants of the larger squares were being nagged away to Belgravia by their socially ambitious wives and daughters. This persuaded the Bedford estate to permit two unusual features at the south end of the west side, to fill an embarrassing gap.

The first was University Hall, which was built in 1848 through the initiative of Crabb Robinson and other friends of University College, as a non-denominational hall of residence. It soon came to be dominated by Unitarians, which was an embarrassment to Arthur Hugh Clough, the first principal, who had just escaped from Oxford dogmatism. It did not survive for long, and since 1890 the building has been the home of Dr Williams's Library. University Hall was designed by Thomas Leverton Donaldson, the Professor of Architecture, in a Tudor style equally at odds with Cubitt's houses and the church that was about to be built to the south.

The Catholic Apostolic Church was designed by Raphael Brandon, one of the theorists of the Gothic revival, and built in 1852–53 as a church – almost a cathedral – for the followers of Edward Irving (see Claremont Square). The church is now known as Christ the King. The historian Samuel Rawson Gardiner was (like his father) a deacon of the church and he married Edward Irving's daughter. It has been said that Gardiner lived in Gordon Square, but it was at the family home at No. 22 Gordon Street, just off it, that the first volumes of Gardiner's history of the early seventeenth century were written.

Gordon Square is famous mainly for its writers. Before the Bloomsbury Group there were several of a very different kind: Clough at University Hall, the philosopher James Martineau at No. 35 and Brandon Thomas, the author of *Charley's Aunt*, at No. 47.

Number 46 was the original home of the Bloomsbury Group: Vanessa and Virginia Stephen lived there from 1904, and it was later occupied by John Maynard Keynes. Other 'Bloomsbury' houses in the square were No. 50 (Clive & Vanessa Bell and Arthur Waley), No. 41 (James & Alix Strachey, the translators of Freud, and David Garnett), No. 51 (Lytton Strachey) and No. 57 (Bertrand Russell). Charles Laughton and

Elsa Lanchester had a flat at No. 34 from 1934 to 1939. The south-east corner of the square is alive with blue and brown plaques.

Gordon Square suffered a good deal in the war, with several houses ruined in the north-west corner and general blast damage along the rest of the north and west sides. The west side was saved, but the north was demolished. It was replaced by a building in a manner for which 'style' would be the wrong word. It looks like a telephone exchange of the worst period but is in fact the Institutes of Archaeology and Classical Studies, much praised by the architectural press in the 1950s.

Gough Square

The Ogilby & Morgan map of 1676 showed the gardens of one large and two smaller houses on this site. Strype did not mention Gough Square in 1720, but its southern arm he described under the name of Hind Court, 'large, and broad at the upper end, where the Houses are much better built and inhabited; and to the whole is a very good Freestone Pavement, cleanly kept'. Gough Square was not in William Stow's 1722 list of streets, but Rocque showed and named both parts in the 1740s. William Maitland described Gough Square in his 1756 history as 'a place lately built with very handsome houses and well inhabited by persons of fashion', but his survey of the London streets was made in 1732, so 'lately' should probably be understood as meaning recently built then rather than in 1756.

It is likely that the southern section was a late seventeenth or early eighteenth-century improvement of the upper end of Hind Court, and that when the main western section was built out of it in the 1720s the new name of Gough Square was applied to both. The name came from Sir Richard Gough, the owner of the land.

Gough Square is now almost entirely associated with Dr Johnson, whose great name has preserved it and its only original houses, No. 17 where he lived from 1749 to 1759 and the adjoining No. 1. That he could afford to settle here suggests that the 'persons of fashion' had not lingered for long. Number 17, in a prominent position at the west end, was not a typical Gough Square house: the five in the southern arm and the three on the south side of the main section were bigger and the seven on the north side smaller. Properly understood, No. 17 is the end house of a terrace in Pemberton Row that happens to have its door at the side. Johnson wrote his dictionary during the decade at No. 17, while his humble assistants prepared the materials in the 'dictionary attic'.

Gough Square has had its other minor celebrities. Hugh Kelly, the Irish dramatist and barrister, died at No. 17 in 1777. Johnson assisted the widow and children by writing the prologue for a benefit performance of his play *A Word to the Wise* at Covent Garden. George Chinnery, an artist who spent most of his life in India and China painting portraits of the ex-patriots and a few of the natives, was born at No. 4 in 1774. His father was a writing master.

Gough Square from the east in 1891.

Gough Square became increasingly commercial in the nineteenth century, although there was still the odd private resident even in the 1850s, when No. 17 was a boarding house. Most of the square was occupied by firms engaged in printing and publishing, the best known being Henry Vizetelly, who had Nos 15 and 16. Virginia Woolf described it in 1917 as 'a little square, folded in behind Chancery Lane, & given over to printing presses'.

Number 17 became a printing works too, but was rescued by Cecil Harmsworth and opened as a Johnson museum in 1914. Heroic efforts by its devoted custodians saved most of the house from destruction during the Second World War, but the rest of the square was less well tended and the north and east sides were ruined.

The restored square is now a delightfully quiet spot with red brick offices to the south and east and pastiche eighteenth century on the north side. One quaint addition is the statue of Dr Johnson's Hodge, 'a very fine cat'. His saucer is often filled with milk or meat.

Dr Johnson's house, No. 17 Gough Square, in the early nineteenth century.

Gould Square

Gould Square was built about 1720, as a speculation, by James Gould, a surveyor much employed by the South Sea Company and its officers. Dorothy Stroud has suggested that he was assisted in the development by his son-in-law, the architect George Dance the elder, who married Elizabeth Gould in 1719. The names of James Gould and his square were very frequently spelt 'Gold', which may indicate the pronunciation. It was quite a good address until the early 1840s, occupied by private residents and merchants, especially wine merchants.

The Fenchurch Street Station viaduct that blighted America Square in 1841 had an even worse effect on Gould Square, shearing off its south side and blocking most of its entrance from Cooper's Row. By the 1870s it was reduced to a backyard for shops in John Street and hotels in America Square, and in the 1880s the widening of the viaduct destroyed it altogether.

Goulston Square

The name came from Sir William Goulston, MP for Bletchingley and New Romney in the 1680s, who inherited property in the parish of St Mary Whitechapel from his mother. The site of the square was shown on the Ogilby & Morgan map of 1676 as the formal garden of a large house on the north side of 'White Chapell Street'.

'Gulston Square' was listed in the key to the Strype map of 1720, but the map itself seemed to show only a vestigial Goulston Street with no square at the top. It may be that the map was prepared for the intended publication in 1708 and that the square was built between then and 1720.

Goulston Street, which developed into a route of some importance, served in the eighteenth century merely as an approach from Whitechapel High Street to Goulston Square. There was a wooden gate leading into the square, but whether at the top or bottom of Goulston Street is not clear.

In the early days the street and square had continuous numbering, the square being Nos 15–33 in a sequence of forty that began and ended at the High Street. This started to change very early in the nineteenth century, when two houses at the north-west corner of the square were demolished to open the way for a continuation of Goulston Street over an open space with the fascinating name of 'Blackguards Gambling Ground'. New Goulston Street was the original name for this northern extension – a name later transferred to a side turning – but soon both parts were known as Goulston Street and the square, once the main feature, had become a mere incident on its eastern side.

From that time the square began to wither away, shrinking in size, and from the 1840s no longer receiving a separate entry in the London directories, although it continued to be named on maps.

In 1839 there was a fair range of trades in the square – cap maker, cap peak maker, umbrella maker, picture frame maker, pencil manufacturer, cooper – but ten years later the Whitechapel public baths and wash-houses were the only Goulston Square buildings listed, and they were placed in Goulston Street. These were the first public baths in England. They were built over the north and east sides and most of the centre of the square in 1847, displacing nearly all the residents and effectively ending its independent existence. The surviving trace is a slight indentation on the east side of Goulston Street, at the entrance to Calcutta House, one of the buildings of the London Metropolitan University. This was the south side of the square.

The only resident of any celebrity was the bibliographer, publisher and book collector William Herbert, who had a house and shop at No. 27 from 1765 to 1776.

Grafton Square

Grafton Square was the creation of Captain (later Major) Thomas Ross, an Irish property developer who made great play with his military rank, although it was based on very limited active service with the militia. He did have considerable experience in building fine houses, especially at Blackheath Park, before he bought an estate at Clapham Old Town in 1846.

Numbers 1–3 Grafton Square in 2008.

Two detached houses and a terrace of three had been built on the land a little earlier, almost certainly with no thought of a square, and Ross decided thriftily to incorporate them in his own scheme. That determined the position and the rectangular shape of the square. The existing terrace easily became Nos 1–3, perhaps the most attractive feature of the square, but the detached houses required a good deal of alteration before becoming Nos 7 and 8, also on the west side, and Nos 16 and 17, on the east.

Thomas Ross was probably living in one of these earlier houses when he addressed a letter from 'New Square, Clapham' in November 1850, and that name also appeared in the 1851 census. By the spring of 1851 it was known as Grafton Square, a name honouring the Duke of Grafton, Ross's commanding officer in the West Suffolk Militia.

Ross quickly built Nos 4–6, to fill the gap between the existing houses on the west side. He then added the east side south of Nos 16 and 17 and the whole of

the south side, where he lived at No. 39 from 1852 to 1861. There he stuck. The northern half of the west side was the back garden of Clapham Hall in Old Town, and that Ross did not expect it to become available is shown by his numbering scheme. He did leave sufficient numbers for the north side but built nothing there.

The reason was the common one of unrealistic ambitions. If he had taken the modest Nos 1–3 as his model all might have been well, but there were not enough customers for the much larger houses he chose to build. He struggled for a decade to improve the prospects for Grafton Square by promoting railway development in Clapham, but in 1861 he left to pursue adventures in the tea trade. The north side was built in a very different style, abandoning Ross's stucco, in the 1860s.

The square had two Nonconformist churches. There are references to eighteenth-century ministers of the Grafton Square Congregational Chapel, but this was a mere carrying back of the name, after it was rebuilt in the square in 1851–52, to the original chapel in Old Town. The 1851–52 building, a much-admired design by John Tarring, was demolished after Second World War bomb damage. It was in the southern of the two arms that link the real square with Old Town, as is the modern replacement, now an evangelical church. In the square itself, but with its entrance in the northern arm, was the Grafton Square Baptist Church, which was built at the end of the garden of Clapham Hall. The foundation stone was laid in 1882. It is now converted into flats and the Grafton Square Surgery.

Grafton Square declined late in the nineteenth century, as the Booth survey found in 1899, 'Here is a great change. The northern end and the east up to Belmont Road are still middle class … but the 4½ storey houses at south are all let in tenements.'

The garden was a private one for the use of the residents until the 1920s, when the breaking up of so many houses into flats and lodgings persuaded the owners to let it to a tennis club. It did not become available for public use until 1953, when Wandsworth Council was able to buy it for £1. The two access roads have been largely rebuilt, but the main part of the square is well preserved and the houses beautifully

maintained by their prosperous new owners. Two of the less attractive houses on the north side, which were damaged during the Second World War, have been replaced by flats that make the survivors look a good deal more distinguished.

Granville Square

CLERKENWELL [ISLINGTON]

Granville Square should have been the showpiece of the Lloyd Baker estate but it was unlucky from the first. The land had been used by tile makers for sixty years and much clay had been removed before there was any serious thought of development in the 1820s. The pits were gradually filled from that time, but so slowly and carelessly that the land became a general rubbish tip and its solidity for building purposes was doubtful.

The commissioners for the 'Waterloo' churches asked William Lloyd Baker for a site in 1828 and were given the centre of the intended square, which meant there would be no space left over for a garden. The architect assigned was the dull Edward Buckton Lamb, who produced a dull church, built in 1831–32, that was soon nicknamed 'St Philip's-in-the-Dustheaps'.

The Grafton Square Baptist Church in 1908, or a little earlier.

St Philip's, Granville Square, and the Granville Place steps, *c.* 1860.

John Booth, the Lloyd Baker surveyor, was approached by prospective builders in 1833, but he thought the infilled ground needed more time to settle and delayed the start of development until 1839. At that time the intended name was Sharp Square, after the philanthropist Granville Sharp, a relation of Lloyd Baker's wife. The name was printed in anticipation on the 1827 Storer map of Clerkenwell. The builders, naturally sensitive to wounding puns, disliked that idea and Granville Square was substituted.

The houses were built in two stages by different men. The half furthest from what is now Kings Cross Road came first in 1839–41, the rest following in 1840–43. Five houses were occupied in 1843. The design of the fine houses in Lloyd Square at the top of the hill has been attributed to John Booth's talented son and assistant, William Joseph Booth, but the much more orthodox terraces of Granville Square would have been well within the range of the father, or indeed of the builders.

Because the square is on higher ground than King's Cross Road, its most unusual feature is still the flight of steps leading up from Gwynne Place. This was originally much more dramatic. Gwynne Place (known at first as Lightfoot Street after another Lloyd Baker family connection, then as Granville Place) was carefully designed to frame the west front of St Philip's, the church's only good feature. Here again, the bad luck that dogged the square ruined a fine effect. The route of the Metropolitan Railway, dug between 1860 and 1863, was directly along the west side of the square, on which all the houses had to be demolished, together with the corner houses on the north and south sides. Also destroyed were the steps and all the delicate houses and shops that framed them. When the railway company rebuilt Granville Place and the west side of the square in 1873–74 they greedily squeezed in an extra house, narrowing the steps and ruining the vista. The new houses in the square were similar to those they replaced, but cruder in detail and with meretricious decoration around the windows and doors.

In the 1860s, while it was rudely exposed to public view by the vacancy of the west side, St Philip's became a stronghold of Puseyism and the scene of

The north-east corner of Granville Square, *c.* 1910.

anti-ritualistic riots. The vicar took advantage of the railway excavations to call in William Butterfield to look at the foundations, and incidentally reorder the church more in accordance with High Church principles. This was the first parish where pew rents were abolished, according to Beresford Chancellor.

With all these disruptions, Granville Square had little chance of attracting good tenants. Its only celebrity was Joseph Grego, the art historian, who was the great nineteenth-century expert on the English caricaturists, especially Gillray, Rowlandson and Cruikshank, and a major collector of their works. He was born at No. 23 in 1843, the son of a looking-glass maker, lived there throughout his life and died in the house in 1908, so even in its dingy days one part of the square glittered, secretly, with all the wit and malice of the Regency.

Gray's Inn Square

Until the 1680s the chambers of the lawyers at Gray's Inn were arranged around three main courts or quadrangles: Holborn Court, the ancestor of the present South Square; Chapel Court, of similar size, to the north of the chapel and hall; and the rather larger Coney Court to the north of that. Spurred perhaps by the fashion for squares, brought forcibly to its notice by New Square at Lincoln's Inn and Red Lion Square, and more immediately by a serious fire in Coney Court in 1678, the Society demolished the chambers between the two northern courts in 1685.

In 1688 a surveyor was appointed to superintend, among other works, the building of a new gateway from Grays Inn Road. This was a 'Mr Rider', tentatively identified by Howard Colvin as Richard, son of the builder-architect Richard Ryder, who was active in the development of Soho. Between 1685 and 1693 the new, enlarged court was entirely rebuilt as fourteen sets of four-storey chambers in a uniform style. It was not immediately named Gray's Inn Square. Hatton described it as 'Coney court, a fair new Square, a great improvement' in 1708 and Rocque still showed it as Coney Court in the 1740s, but the permanent name was established before the end of the eighteenth century.

It was mostly occupied by lawyers, of course, but a number of eminent architects also lived there. George Frederick Bodley, Lutyens – his first office, in the 1890s – and Sir Giles Gilbert Scott all had chambers at Nos 6 or 7 on the north side. Bodley previously had an office in South Square. There were also one or two disreputable *fin de siècle* literary tenants: it was the last home of the poet Lionel Johnson, who drank himself to death in 1902 on two pints of whisky a day, and the bibliographer of pornography Henry Spencer Ashbee ('Pisanus Fraxi') kept his huge collection in his chambers at No. 4, well away from the family home.

The centre was an entirely open, paved space until some trees were planted around the edge late in the nineteenth century. The garden was not introduced

The state of the square after the First World War, when it sank almost to the level of a slum, is graphically described, as Riceyman Square, in Arnold Bennett's *Riceyman Steps* (1923). The demolition of the church in 1938 made no immediate difference to the fortunes of the square, which suffered serious bomb damage in the Second World War, when the shops and houses in 'Riceyman Steps' were destroyed.

Islington Council bought the houses in the square in the 1970s for conversion to flats. They had been so weakened by the original poor foundations, the railway works, and war damage that many of them had to be nearly rebuilt. Since then the approach from Kings Cross Road has been ruined by the building of a hotel over Gwynne Place, but the square itself probably looks better now than it ever has, with the houses tidy and the garden freed from the frightful church.

until after the First World War. Most of the west side and the north-east corner were destroyed by bombing during the Second World War and the hall and chapel on the south side and most of the other houses were badly damaged.

Today, only No. 1 survives more or less intact. Elsewhere shreds and patches of original brickwork are to be seen among Sir Edward Maufe's post-war restoration and rebuilding, but there is enough to preserve a sense of antiquity quite missing from South Square.

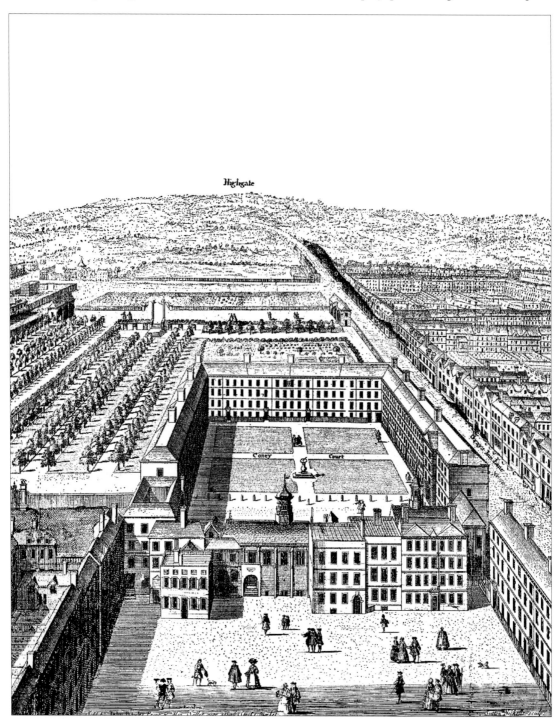

Gray's Inn Square (and South Square in the foreground) in 1731, or a little earlier.

Great Eastern Square

Great Eastern Square was an intermediate stage in the sanitising of an old name out of rural Essex. It was originally a long, narrow green called Ducking Pond Row, north of and parallel with the Whitechapel Road. In the 1740s Rocque showed the pond near the east end, which was the widest point.

The building of the London Hospital immediately to the south in the 1750s began the serious urbanisation of the village of Whitechapel. Ducking Pond Row was still the name for the open space, but the pond had been drained before the end of the century and by 1813 houses were being built on its site and across all of the wider east end of the green. That left a smaller, triangular open space at the west end. In the 1830s its name was softened to Buck's Row.

Railways transformed the area from the 1860s when the Great Eastern Company acquired Smith's distillery on the north side of Buck's Row and established the southern entrance of its great Spitalfields coal depot there. As a result the open space began to be called Great Eastern Square, although Buck's Row continued to dispute the name. Whitechapel Station on the East London Railway was opened in 1876, the cutting passing just east of the square. In 1884 the Metropolitan District Railway demolished all the buildings on the south side of the square and opened its Whitechapel (Mile End) Station there. This left the old church school at the east end (rebuilt by the London School Board in 1876) as the only substantial building in the square.

Early in the morning of 31 August 1888 the body of one of Jack the Ripper's victims, Polly Nichols, was found in the square. As a result Buck's Row, mentioned repeatedly in the police reports, was dismissed in disgrace and replaced in 1892 by the romantic name of Durward Street.

Great Eastern Square continued to be used occasionally for the western end until the middle of the twentieth century. After decades of dereliction and redevelopment, some sense of a square has now been regained, with the Whitechapel Sports Centre on the north side and the new Crossrail station on the south, although the wide section of Durward Street between them is little more than a car park. Only the former school at the east end, now converted into flats as Trinity Hall, adds some dignity and a reminder of the past.

Green Arbour Square

This was an alternative name for Green Arbour Court, the last turning off the west side of Old Bailey at its northern end. It existed before the Fire of London and had the same form in 1676 that it retained until the 1870s. In the best Cockney tradition it was sometimes written Green Harbour Court.

Its only celebrity was Oliver Goldsmith, who in 1759 was living at 'Mrs Martin's in Green Arbour Court, Little Old Bailey'.

In December 1818 a man was killed in 'the conflagration of the house of Mr Neale, of Green Arbour-square, Fleet Market', that destroyed Nos 12, 13 and 14.

It was more like a square than many courts that assumed the name, being quite large, with more than twenty houses and a nearly square open space in the middle. Break Neck Steps led from the north-west corner towards Fleet Market. In the 1840s there was a pub, the Green Parrot, at No. 1 Green Arbour Square and a number of the houses were occupied by printers and publishers spilling over from Paternoster Row. The square was demolished to provide part of the site for Holborn Viaduct Station, which opened in 1874, but Green Arbour Court survives as the name for the mews behind the Victorian offices in Holborn Viaduct.

Greyhound Square

Greyhound Square lay immediately behind the Greyhound public house, opposite Streatham Common. The square was of the front garden type, where the ground that might have made a communal garden was divided up between the cottages. That was common enough in back development, but here the alley that gave access to all the front gardens opened directly from Greyhound Lane, leaving the three-sided square anatomised. There were twenty cottages, eight each on the east and west sides and four tiny ones without front gardens on the north. The variations in size and shape suggested piecemeal development, probably from the late eighteenth century. The land on which this and the neighbouring Factory Square and Histed's Square were built was part of the Crooke, Ellison and Bates estate. The plan of the estate made by John Willcock in 1780 shows only a few scattered buildings here, probably part of the Greyhound yard.

The inhabitants of the square were always working class, agricultural labourers in the early days, but changing to more urban occupations as Streatham became a commuter suburb.

Wandsworth Council cleared Greyhound Square and the neighbouring houses in a late 1930s slum clearance drive, and the flats known as Sanders House were built on the site.

Grosvenor Square

CAMBERWELL [SOUTHWARK]

(now Grosvenor Park and part of Grosvenor Terrace)

Grosvenor Square was intended to be the centrepiece of an ambitious development stretching from Camberwell Road almost to the Camberwell New Road. The name first appeared in Grosvenor Place, the terrace of fine late eighteenth-century houses still surviving in Camberwell Road to the south of Urlwin Street.

By the 1820s the first section of Grosvenor Street (now Urlwin Street) had been built, pushing westwards into a large triangular area of open fields. It still features an almost unbroken succession of original houses, with terraces dominating the north side and detached tea-caddy houses the south. Grosvenor Street was completed in the 1840s.

Before 1850 Grosvenor Square had been laid out at its western end with a private garden in the centre, and the east and north sides had been built. The shape of the field meant that the 'square' had to be an elongated triangle. The original square is now represented by the houses on the east and south sides of Grosvenor Park and on the north side of Grosvenor Terrace west of Grosvenor Park.

Grosvenor Park, formerly the south side of Grosvenor Square, Camberwell, *c.* 1910.

The north side was originally continued west by another Grosvenor Street.

The earliest and best houses are in the perfectly balanced and perfectly preserved North Terrace and South Terrace on either side of Grosvenor Street. They were planned in conjunction with it and have two taller houses to mark its entrance. The other 1840s houses, on the north side of what is now Grosvenor Terrace, are less satisfactory: they were not so good originally and have been disfigured by Second World War bomb damage. Two stretches of the long terrace were destroyed and have been replaced by flats that have only the virtue of being no higher than their neighbours.

The houses on the south side of the square, now the south side of Grosvenor Park, were mostly built in the 1850s. At the west end there is a plain three-storey curving terrace, with stucco ground floors and semi-basements, but the east end of the south side is far more interesting. First there are twenty-two houses in quasi semi-detached pairs with shared gables, linked by lower entrance bays. The last two pairs break

All Souls', Grosvenor Park
(formerly Grosvenor Square, Camberwell), *c.* 1871.

away to the south, forming a small open space that survived when the big communal garden was sacrificed. Obliquely opposite them are four matching houses that continued the 1840s terrace on the east side of the square. That left a little space to be filled in the sharp angle of the south-east corner, where a miscellaneous collection of houses was built in the early 1860s. The pair at the end of the west side are called 'South Villas 1861' and in a quaint annex the detached 'Albert House 1862' is almost hidden from sight.

In the 1860s the houses looked out onto the ornately laid out triangular private garden, which was about the size of Camberwell Green. The square had by that time been renamed Grosvenor Park. The spoiling of this fine piece of town planning began in 1871, when All Soul's Church was built at the east end of the garden, opposite Grosvenor Street. The architect was Henry Jarvis, who designed St Paul's in Lorrimore Square, another church that has failed to survive. If the church had been the only intrusion on the garden the damage would not have been too great. There would have been enough open space left, as at Myddelton Square. Sadly, it was decided to build two short

terraces of four houses on either side of the church and a terrace of twenty-five all along the north side of the garden. These 1870s houses are at least of good quality and built with such a tactful desire to blend with their neighbours that it is hard to believe they were built twenty or thirty years later than the terraces opposite. The same cannot be said for the ugly bay-windowed houses that were squeezed into the remaining land on the south side of the garden. The absurd conceit of four taller houses with gables in the centre only draws attention to the meanness of this terrace.

The road leading west from the square, originally another Grosvenor Street, became Grosvenor Terrace in the 1870s and the north side of the square was later renumbered as part of it.

The Second World War bombs that disfigured the north side also damaged All Souls'. It was restored and renamed St Michael's, in combination with another parish, but declared redundant and demolished in 1973. In its place a large and entirely unsympathetic block of flats was built. A happier result of the bombing was the restoration of part of the garden. As at Bonnington Square, a few of the 1870s houses of the interior were destroyed. They were replaced only by prefabs and the area is now a small community garden and playground close to the point of the triangle. Maimed as it is, Camberwell's Grosvenor Square is a great deal more attractive than its illustrious namesake in Mayfair.

Grosvenor Square

MAYFAIR [WESTMINSTER]

Sir Richard Grosvenor began the development of his 100-acre Mayfair estate in 1720. One of his first acts was to appoint the experienced builder-architect Thomas Barlow, the man probably responsible for the form of Hanover Square, as his surveyor. Barlow planned the layout of the estate, with the huge Grosvenor Square at its centre. Although much larger, it is similar to Hanover Square, with which it is aligned, and the two are directly linked by Brook Street. Barlow built some houses on the estate himself and negotiated with other speculators over leases and building lines, but he is unlikely to have designed any of the houses in the square or even to have vetted the plans of others. The craftsmen and investors who took plots employed their own architects and very little attempt was made to enforce uniformity, or even quality.

Building agreements for the square were made in 1724 and 1725 and all the houses were completed by 1731. Noorthouck disliked the miscellany of houses, complaining in 1773 of 'some being of stone, others of brick, some ornamental, and some plain'.

The most eminent architect involved was Colen Campbell, but his design for the east side was not carried out, although it seems to have influenced the plan followed by the builder, John Simmons. Edward Shepherd (of Shepherd Market) designed Nos 18–20 on the north side as a unified group, but was apparently unable to secure the co-operation of other builders in a more extensive plan. Several other notable architects, like Thomas Ripley and Roger Morris, had an interest in the early development of the square, but it is not known which houses, if any, they designed.

The centre was carefully planned from the first. Grosvenor paid the considerable sum required for enclosing it and making the garden, which was laid out by John Alston, and reimbursed himself, or attempted to, from the additional ground rent charged for the plots around the square. In return for these continuing contributions the tenants received keys and the right to 'walk' in the garden. Grosvenor also paid for John Nost's statue of George I which

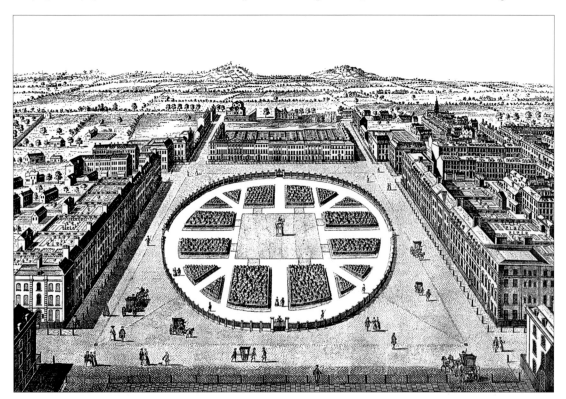

Grosvenor Square, Mayfair, from the south, in 1731 or a little earlier.

The north side of Grosvenor Square, Mayfair, seen from the south-east corner, *c.* 1905.

stood in the centre, but six months after it was set up in 1726 'some villains dismembered it in the most shameful manner and affixed a traitorous paper to the pedestal', which meant an extra expense for repairs.

In 1771 John Stewart was scathing about:

> Grosvenor square, which is generally held out as a pattern of perfection in its kind. It is doubtless spacious, regular, and well-built; but how is this spaciousness occupied? A clumsy rail, with lumps of brick for piers, to support it, at the distance of every two or three yards, incloses nearly the whole area, intercepting almost entirely the view of the sides, and leaving the passage round it as narrow as most streets, with the additional disadvantage at night of being totally dark on one hand. The middle is filled up with bushes and dwarf trees, through which a statue peeps, like a piece of gilt gingerbread in a green-grocer's stall.

The residents responded in 1774 by obtaining a private act for the better management of the garden, which was soon re-planned with a neat fence and shrubberies instead of Alston's formal paths.

Carl Philipp Moritz, a German tourist, remarked in 1782 on the different arrangement of the garden from the usual 'round grass-plot': 'In Grosvenor-square, instead of this green plot, or area, there is a little circular wood, intended, no doubt, to give one the idea of *rus in urbe*'. This wood was favourable to other country pursuits. In 1779 a satirical writer in the *Morning Post* claimed that:

> Grosvenor Square is, without doubt, the happiest spot … in this metropolis, the air being perfectly favourable to the votaries of Venus; a subscription, we are informed, is set on foot, to ornament the centre, by building a temple dedicated to that goddess, in which, to give preference to the inhabitants of the Square, those who are best initiated in the mysteries of love, will be appointed priestesses of the temple.

He went on to name, under transparent initials, some of the aristocratic votaries of Venus that he had in mind, including Lady Grosvenor.

The take up of the houses was slow at first, in the aftermath of the South Sea Bubble, with the result that many of the builders were bankrupted, but there was a rapid improvement in the 1730s and 1740s. A Grosvenor Square resident reported in 1746 that the newly engaged Lord Petersham and Lady Caroline Fitzroy 'are looking out for a house in this square, where there is scarce any to be let, and if any, at a prodigious rent'. By that time the list of tenants was very aristocratic and so it remained for nearly 200 years. In 1807 it was described as 'undoubtedly the finest square in London'.

Lord Chesterfield and his mother-in-law the Duchess of Kendal (George I's mistress) lived only two doors apart, the duchess at No. 38 (later 43) from 1728 to 1743 and Chesterfield at No. 40 (later 45) from 1733 to 1748. Lord Hardwicke leased Powis House in Great Ormond Street during his long tenure of the office of Lord Chancellor, but on his retirement in 1758 he moved to No. 26 (later 29) Grosvenor Square, which was his London home until his death in 1764.

In the later eighteenth century it was a common place of residence for prime ministers past, present and to come. The Duke of Grafton lived at No. 32 (later 37) from 1765 to 1768; Lord Rockingham at No. 4 from 1742 to 1782; and Henry Addington at No. 17 (later 18) from 1792 to 1795. Lord North had three spells at No. 46 (later 50) in 1753–54, 1755–56 and from 1782 until his death in 1792, by which time he had succeeded as 2nd Earl of Guilford. During this period many of the houses were extensively altered or even rebuilt, most of the eminent architects of the time being engaged on one or more.

John Wilkes was a less respectable political resident. According to John Almon:

> Mr Wilkes changed his winter-residence in London, in the year 1790 … to a house in Grosvenor-square, the corner of South-Audley-street, – a salubrious situation, and better suited to the preservation of his health. Here he resided with his daughter during the winter months for several years; constantly walking to Guildhall every day …

The house was No. 30 (later 35). He died there in 1797, and his daughter in 1802.

The most famous event connected with the square was the Cato Street Conspiracy of 1820, when revolutionaries plotted to assassinate the whole cabinet during a dinner at the 1st Earl of Harrowby's house at No. 39 (later 44), his home from 1804 to 1847. According to a report sent to Lord Fitzharris:

> They must have watched Lord Harrowby's house narrowly, where to put persons at the areas and mews' doors so as to prevent the egress of servants when the alarm was once given. When the conspirators had ascertained the Ministers were seated at table, one was to knock at the door as with a message or letter, the rest rush in and murder the porter, meanwhile a grenade or stone was to be thrown into the eating-room window to divert the attention from the noise in the hall, then they were to rush in and murder Ministers and servants.

In the event, the conspirators were surprised at their meeting place and no action took place in the square.

The nineteenth-century politicians were not quite so eminent. Earl Canning, the last Governor-General and 1st Viceroy of India (during the Mutiny) lived at one of the two old houses on the site later occupied by No. 10 from 1834 until 1862, except for the years in India. He died in the house only a few weeks after returning to England. The philanthropic Earl of Shaftesbury was born in 1801 at No. 24 (later 27), the family's London home since 1731. What with school and college and a quarrel with his father, he saw little of the house for the first fifty years of his saintly life, but he lived there again from his succession in 1851 until his death in 1885.

The arts were less well represented, except where supported by trade. The Thrales moved to No. 1 in 1781, to further her social ambitions according to Boswell, and for the convenience of his doctors by her own account. That Henry Thrale died there after a few months supports her defence. Dr Johnson was as usual encouraged to treat their home as his. Hannah More wrote to her sister, 'Think of Johnson's having apartments in Grosvenor Square! But he says it is not half so convenient as Bolt Court.'

William Beckford lived at No. 2 from about 1796 to 1801 and lent the house to Sir William and Lady Hamilton when they came to England in 1800.

The west side of Grosvenor Square, Mayfair, *c.* 1904. Most of these houses survived the Second World War, but were demolished in 1957 to make way for the American Embassy.

The artist and patron of the arts, Sir George Beaumont, lived at No. 34 from 1785 until his death in 1827, and the last London home of Lord Lytton, the novelist, was at No. 12 from 1868 until his death in 1873. Lord Clark (of *Civilisation*) was born at No. 32 in 1903.

The first slight crack in the aristocratic exclusiveness of the square was the introduction of embassies from the 1850s. At least ten nations have had their embassies there at one time or another. The longest running have been the Americans and the Italians, who were at No. 20 (formerly 19) from 1887 to 1932 and then at No. 4. The intermittent American presence began with John Adams at No. 9 in 1785–86 and has ended by completing the destruction of the square.

That destruction was begun by the Grosvenor estate. In 1844 Thomas Cundy, the surveyor, persuaded the Marquess of Westminster to introduce a policy of modernising the houses, as the leases came up for renewal, with 'Stucco Work to the fronts with Porticos, Window Dressings, Cornices and Balustrades to such of the Houses as may be thought to require it'. The 2nd Marquess, who succeeded in 1845, made this compulsory for any tenants wishing to renew their leases. Number 38 on the south side is a result of this policy: a house of the 1720s re-fronted by Cundy in 1854–55.

By the end of the nineteenth century the exterior of the square had come to resemble Bayswater or South Kensington, but with less regularity. The changes failed to halt, or perhaps accelerated, a sharp decline in the value of the houses in the early twentieth century. The estate was ready to consider desperate measures, which began with the rebuilding of the south-east corner as flats in the late 1920s, during the last days of Edmund Wimperis as surveyor. From 1928 his successor Detmar Blow devised a grand plan for the complete rebuilding of the square in a similar style. The American Embassy of 1936–38, now the Canadian High Commission, was a part of this scheme, as was the whole of the north side (finished only in the 1960s) and most of the south. Only existing long leases of the 1860s saved two houses from destruction: No. 4 on the east side, the Italian Embassy, and No. 38 on the south side, now the Indonesian Embassy. Number 9, the John Adams

The Italian Embassy at No. 20 Grosvenor Square, Mayfair (the west end of the north side), *c.* 1904.

house, the other survivor, escaped through being only partly in the square.

The takeover by the American armed forces during the Second World War changed the destiny of the square again. Afterwards the garden was re-planned as a Roosevelt memorial surrounding his statue, which was unveiled in 1948.

The previously untouched but bomb-damaged west side was demolished in 1957 to provide the site for the present American Embassy, which was built between 1957 and 1960. Since the Vietnam War demonstrations of 1967–68 the ever-intensifying security around the building, reducing the square to three sides, has made it seem more and more like a grim robber baron's castle with a frightened village cowering in its shadow. Speed the day of its removal!

Grosvenor Square

See Crossland Square

Grove Square

See Goldsmiths' Square

Gun Square

CITY OF LONDON

The Gun Yard of Ogilby & Morgan's 1676 map, just north of St Botolph Aldgate, looked in shape and buildings almost the same as Horwood's Gun Square of the 1790s. In 1720, Strype described it as 'Gun Yard, a very handsome square Court, with good large Houses, very well inhabited, with an Entrance wide enough for Coach or Cart'. The change of name occurred during the 1790s, when both forms were used.

The fine entrance from Houndsditch declined into a narrow archway during the first half of the nineteenth century and the fourteen good large houses were increasingly turned to commercial use, low-grade manufacturing more than retail. In 1806 most of the tenants had Jewish names.

All the buildings in the square were destroyed during the Second World War and their replacements did not last long. The area was cleared early in the twenty-first century and the huge St Botolph Building now squats on the site of Gun Square.

Gun Square

Gun Square, Limehouse, was a court off the south side of Gun Lane, now Grenade Street, and behind St Peter's Church in Spread Eagle Street, which is now part of Gill Street. It was a group of about ten houses built in the 1840s round a small open yard. Very early in the twentieth century it was demolished and rebuilt in a larger and more regular form, with an extra entrance in Three Colt Street but no yard, under the name of Padstow Place. That has been replaced in its turn by large council tenements, called collectively Padstow House.

Haberdashers' Square

Haberdashers' Square was built a little before 1720 on an estate in the famous Grub Street bought by the Haberdashers' Company in 1622/23. In the seventeenth century the site of the future square was occupied by two alleys named Robin Hood Court and Paviours Court, but on Strype's 1720 map Robin Hood Court was shown as Sun Alley and Paviours Court as Haberdashers Square, though neither had apparently changed in size or shape. Strype's map was earlier than his text, which reads:

> Haberdashers Square, very genteel, with new well built Houses. The Court is square, and inclosed in with Palisade Pales, except a handsome passage to the Houses round about; and in the midst is a Dial. This Court was made out of two old ones, viz. Paviers Court, and Robin Hood Court. Sun Alley, but small.

The map may show the first stage in the creation of a formal square, but it is more likely that it was hastily revised in deference to the updated text. On Rocque's 1740s map Sun Alley had vanished and Haberdashers' Square covered the whole site. It had eighteen houses arranged on the north, south and west sides, the east side being occupied by the entrance and the backs of houses on the west side of Grub Street. The regular shape of the garden and the uniform size of the houses suggest that the square was entirely rebuilt in the years before 1720 and did not incorporate any of the houses in the old courts it had displaced.

The gentility remarked on in 1720 did not last long. Grub Street soon became a byword for literary poverty and bohemianism, and in 1750 the square acquired an unwelcome neighbour to the north, when Samuel Whitbread established his great Chiswell Street brewery. As the decades passed, the brewery crept closer and its buildings grew taller, overshadowing Haberdashers' Square. The elegant garden with its sundial sank into a sordid courtyard criss-crossed by washing lines, but the attractive Queen Anne houses survived on the west and south sides until the bitter end. That came in the late 1880s, when Whitbread's brewery was extended southwards across the site of the square.

Hamilton Square

Nelson Square was a set of tenement blocks built in 1855 off the west side of Nelson Street (later Kipling Street) by the Metropolitan Association for Improving the Dwellings of the Industrious Classes, and designed by its architect, Charles Lee. At first they were sometimes known as Metropolitan Chambers.

Kipling Street is just south of London Bridge Station and Guy's Hospital, so now within the shadow of the Shard. St Paul's Church and its school occupied the whole of the south side (but divided by a wall from the courtyard of the square) with the flats on the other three. The eastern block extended further up Nelson Street and faced towards it, so only the back of its southern half faced the courtyard.

As there were several Nelson Squares in London, the most important as near as the Blackfriars Road, the name was whimsically changed to Hamilton Square in 1874. In 1899 the square had 'Good class of tenants, always let, so said the caretaker, a very quiet and capable Scotchman, "I can pick and choose"'.

The buildings suffered only minor blast damage during the Second World War, but they were demolished about 1970. The name lives on, having been attached without much justification from its form to the new housing on the site.

Hammond Square

HOXTON [HACKNEY]

North Hoxton was in a state of rapid development at the end of the eighteenth century. Dirty Lane was about to become King's Road and tiny squares were springing up like mushrooms. Hammond Square was part of this crop. It existed, at least in part, by the 1820s, being named on the 1830 Greenwood map but not the 1827.

In its most developed form it was a right-angled alley, branching off the west side of Hoxton Street, turning sharply south and ending in Ivy Street. The square element came from the long front gardens of the houses on the south side, which also gave an open outlook to half of the western terrace. The social status of the place was indicated by the presence of a large dye works hard behind the west side and a ragged school at the north-western corner. The Booth survey describes this as 'the Chapel where Lord Shaftesbury first started work among the costers'.

Hammond Square lost its south and east sides and, more damagingly, its long front gardens when the London School Board took over the Hoxton Ragged School in 1871, and over the next two years bought land to enlarge it as the Hammond Square School. It is now Burbage Primary. After that there were houses only on the west side, with an interesting view of the school wall. The Booth survey called these survivors Ebenezer Place, probably from a name plate displayed on them.

It also said that Hammond Square, that is the east–west section, had 'no living houses', meaning none that were residential. Ebenezer Place was destroyed in the Second World War and its site was added to the school playground. Hammond Square still exists as a name, but since the 1950s it has been a blind alley off Hoxton Street leading to the back of the school. To mark its diminished state it has dropped an 'm' and is now called Hamond Square.

Hampstead Square

HAMPSTEAD [CAMDEN]

The three squares at Hampstead were unplanned and accidental. In this sprawling hillside village, built gradually in haphazard fashion, much of it on

Hampstead Square, Hampstead, in 1911. Vine House on the right and Nos 7–9 on the left.

manorial waste, there were numerous other open spaces and greens at the junctions of roads that could equally well have been given that name.

Hampstead Square, a space occupied by 'a high hill and a sand pit' in the middle of the seventeenth century, evolved between 1700 and 1730 and was known at first as 'the Square'. Demand for good houses in the village was growing rapidly at that time, following the building of the Great Room and the Pump Room and the systematic promotion of Hampstead as a health resort to rival Tunbridge Wells.

The two big houses of the square, No. 6 (Vine House) and No. 12 (Lawn House) were built at the beginning of the eighteenth century, Nos 1 and 2 about 1720 and the terrace numbered 7–9 about 1730.

The open space in the centre of the square was bigger in the early days: Rocque showed it as a well-planted rectangle in 1746. It was sometimes used by strolling players for a temporary theatre 'near the Square, Hampstead', as a playbill of 1807 called it, and was later the Victoria Tea Garden. The open space was greatly reduced when Christ Church was built on part of the green in 1851–52. It was designed by Samuel Daukes, with additions by George Gilbert Scott (senior and junior) and Ewan Christian. The late Victorian Nos 10 and 11, which were built partly in front of the church, are the square's only ugly intruders.

Thomas Barratt described the place in 1912: 'Then, there is the Square, now called Hampstead Square, another term that calls up ideas of space and distinction: but here too the reality tells a different story, for the Square is not large, and some of the houses are certainly not palatial.'

Since the building of Christ Church the square has had a strange and confusing form, with two arms thrusting south and west from the garden, which is a small, steeply sloping shrubbery. The western arm, on the higher level, contains Vine House and Nos 7–9. Number 7 has a plaque in honour of Christopher Newman Hall, the Congregational minister, who died at Vine House in 1902. The lower and wider south arm has Lawn House and Nos 10 and 11 on its east side, Nos 1 and 2 on its west.

Hampstead Square has some literary associations, though not perhaps of the expected kind. Evelyn Underhill, the religious writer, died at Lawn House in 1941. Her fellow scribe Jeffrey Bernard had been born at No. 11 in 1932, far from his spiritual home in Soho, and Norman St John Stevas, journalist and politician, lived at No. 1 more recently.

Hampstead Square

SOUTH HAMPSTEAD [CAMDEN]

The other Hampstead Square was part of an ambitious, and therefore unrealised, plan for the development of the Eyre estate between St John's Wood and Hampstead, published in 1794. The plan, which may have influenced Nash's Regent's Park, also included a crescent and a circus. The square was large with each side of 366 yards, but it was dwarfed by the circus, 'one mile round'.

This being the outer suburbs, the houses proposed for the square were not in terraces, but semi-detached pairs with long private gardens in addition to a round communal garden in the centre. No architect's name was attached to the plan. It can hardly have been by John Shaw, who was only 18 at the time, but in 1802–03 he published proposals for a similarly lavish British Circus on the Eyre estate. The land was eventually developed with many semi-detached villas but with no circus, unless College Crescent is a pathetic fragment of an abandoned attempt, and certainly with no square.

Hanover Square

CITY OF LONDON

Hanover Square was an occasional name for a place of no importance that was usually called Hanover Court and sometimes Hanover Yard. It left the east side of Grub Street opposite Silk Street, turned ninety degrees to the south and ended in Butler's Alley, later Butler Street. The north–south section was wider than the east–west. Its only claim to notice was a large house popularly known as General Monck's, though with no justification. This house had a '1653' date on a rainwater head. It stood on the west corner of Butler's Alley and the Ogilby & Morgan map of 1676 showed that Hanover Court was built over its garden, presumably after 1714, if that was the original name.

Strype noted in 1720 that Grub Street was 'sufficiently pestered with Courts and Alleys', but he did not mention Hanover Court.

It survived the building of Moorgate Street Station in the 1860s but not the Second World War bombing of this whole district. Part of Grub Street still exists as Milton Street, but the north-eastern corner of the Barbican Estate is now on the site of Hanover Court.

Hanover Square

KENNINGTON [LAMBETH]

(now Hanover Gardens)

Hanover Gardens is one of the most attractive squares in London, and one of the least known. I would not wish to alter that, so perhaps I should print this entry in very small type or invisible ink. The builders contributed to this precious obscurity by the cunning kink they introduced into the approach from Kennington Park Road, and the change of name from Hanover Square to Hanover Gardens in the 1870s has also helped. After 170 years of quiet prosperity it still hides successfully a few yards from the Oval tube station and within a lusty blow of the cricket ground.

The land had belonged to the Cleavers of Cleaver Square, but by 1843 was divided between Joseph and Josiah Williamson. A private act of that year paved the way for joint development of their shares, and Hanover Square and Albert Square were among the results.

Hanover Square was built in the late 1840s and early 1850s. An 1850 map showed it without a name and rather more square and regular than it eventually turned out. In the 1851 census eleven of the thirty-four houses were awaiting tenants. Among the predictable clerks and commercial travellers, some of the early residents had less common occupations: a fishmonger and builder, a parliamentary reporter, a parliamentary agent's managing clerk and a man who worked in the chamberlain's department at Buckingham Palace.

After the curving approach, originally called Hanover Place, the square opens into a shape for which there is no name, but closer to a triangle than a square. Because the west terrace was continuous with

The garden and the south-east side of Hanover Gardens (formerly Hanover Square), Kennington, in 2010.

Hanover Place it consisted at first of twenty houses. The north side has ten, the east side nine and the south only two or three. In the centre there was in the early days a small circular garden. The houses are three-storey with semi-basement or two-storey with semi-basement and attic. The main architectural effect is the gradual stepping back of the last few houses of the terraces, something suggested by the irregular shape of the land. The obscure and retiring houses in the north corners have the largest gardens.

Hanover Square

Richard Lumley, 1st Earl of Scarborough, was brought up a Catholic and served under James II, but converted to Protestantism in 1687, played an important part in establishing William III on the throne, and fought with him at the Boyne. He was liberally rewarded with titles and offices, becoming a pillar of the Whig party. After a spell in the wilderness in the later days of Queen Anne, when he turned his thoughts to the development of his Mayfair estate, he returned to favour at the accession of George I and celebrated the new dynasty by naming the first of the second wave of London squares in its honour.

The layout of Hanover Square was probably the work of Thomas Barlow, who acted for Lord Scarborough in negotiations concerning St George's Church and is known to have built some of the houses in the square and St George Street. Barlow had previously done a good deal of work in Covent Garden and on the Berkeley estate in Mayfair and was later employed in the design of Grosvenor Square. The other architect largely involved was the Frenchman Nicholas Dubois, probably a Huguenot refugee, who designed Nos 8, 9, 19, 20 and 21 in the square (of which only No. 20 survives in anything like the original form) and No. 15 in St George Street. It used to be said that as a further compliment to the new king the houses in St George Street and some in the square were designed in a German style, but the exotic impression created may have been French.

Hanover Square is quite small and most of the plots were large, so there were only twenty-five houses. According to James Ralph in 1734 'the west side of Hanover-square is uniform, argues a very tolerable taste in the architect, and deserves a good deal of approbation; but all the rest are intolerable, and deserve no attention at all'. It filled John Stewart with sorrow more than anger. In 1771 he wrote:

As to Hanover square, I do not know what to make of it. It is neither open nor enclosed. Every convenience is railed out and every nuisance railed in. Carriages have a narrow ill-paved street

This delightful backwater would probably have remained quite unaltered had Second World War bombing not introduced unwelcome changes. There was serious damage to the west side of the approach, reducing the long terrace to its eight northern houses. In the gap some very unsympathetic blocks of flats were introduced in the 1950s, and a new road called Elias Place reduced the privacy of the square. Blast damage elsewhere has been tactfully repaired. The central garden being now an open lawn with a few trees, the atmosphere is more like a village green than a formal London square.

to pass round in, and the middle has the air of a cow-yard, where blackguards assemble in the winter, to play at hussle-cap, up to the ancles in mud. This is the more to be regretted, as the square in question is susceptible of improvement at a small expense. The buildings are neat and uniform. The street from Oxford road falls with a gentle descent into the middle of the upper side, while, right opposite, George street retires, converging to a point, which has a very picturesque effect; and the portico of St George's church, seen in profile, enriches and beautifies the whole.

The criticism evidently stung, as only two years later Noorthouck was able to report that the garden:

> … was till lately railed round from carriages, but left open for cross paths to foot passengers; this however has been remarked as an ill-judged plan, as the area was thus rendered a dirty place of resort for the idle and vulgar. It is now just enclosed with neat iron rails, so that this evil is remedied.

The first leases were granted in 1717, the first house was occupied in 1719 and the square was nearly complete by 1728. Many of the early tenants were Whigs and generals like Lord Scarborough, who died in 1721, too early to take up residence himself, if that was ever his intention.

The square was a glittering success in its early years. Sir Francis Dashwood was the first resident. He lived at No. 16 (later 18) from 1719 until his death in 1724. Sir Theodore Janssen, of the South Sea Bubble, was the first tenant of No. 20 (later 22), followed by the Duke of Bolton and his mistress Lavinia Fenton ('Polly Peachum'). The Earl of Coventry was the first at No. 15 (now 16); the Earl of Pomfret (and his more interesting countess) succeeded him there from 1721 to 1737. The Duke of Montrose was the first at No. 18 (later 20) and the Dukes of Roxburgh were at No. 12 (later 13), from 1721 to 1795. The great Roxburgh library, afterwards moved to No. 13 St James's Square, was founded in this mansion, which became Harewood House in 1795.

The aristocratic names did not come without the aristocratic vices. In 1724 Lady Mary Wortley Montagu described a hell-fire club just established at No. 19 (now 21):

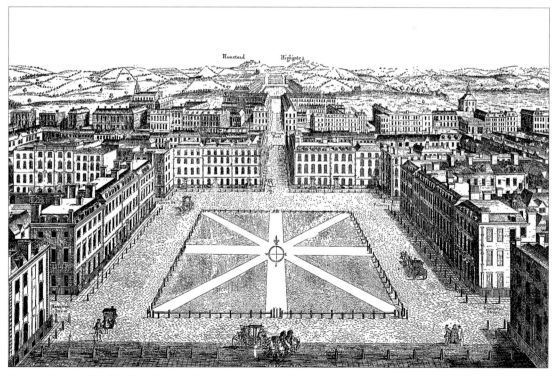

Hanover Square, Mayfair, from the south in 1731, or a little earlier.

Hanover Square, Mayfair, from the north in 1787.

They call themselves Schemers, and meet regularly 3 times a week to consult on Gallant Schemes for the advancement of that branch of Happyness which the vulgar call Whoring. Viscount Hillsborough … has turn'd his house, one of the handsomest in Hannover Square, into an Edifice appropriated to this use.

The square continued to have notable residents until the middle of the nineteenth century. The house at the south-west corner (No. 20, later 22), long the home of the Duke of Bolton, was let in 1748 to the poet Ambrose Philips, of 'Namby-Pamby' fame, who died there in 1749. By that time he was an Irish MP and legal functionary. Lord Rodney died in 1792 at No. 10, at the south corner of Princes Street, which was at least nominally the home of his son and successor. This was probably made necessary by the admiral's chronic debts.

The 2nd Viscount Palmerston lived at No. 23 (formerly 21), which he bought in 1790, as he recorded in his accounts: 'Paid Lord Cadogan for his house in Hanover Square, fixtures and some furniture, £10,878 7s 6d'. But he then employed the notoriously slow and expensive Henry Holland to make alterations, and the house was not ready for the family to occupy until 1796. Even then the chimneys smoked, threatening to spoil the new furniture. (In 1790 Holland was the inevitable architect for a Whig, but by 1796 Palmerston had gone over to Pitt.)

This was the childhood home of the 3rd Viscount, the prime minister, but he was glad to get rid of it soon after succeeding, as it was large and costly to maintain. It included a sizeable private garden behind the houses in George Street. In 1808 he wrote from the Albany, 'I am happy to say I *have* got a house & have let my own in Hanover Square to Lord Cawdor, who takes it on.'

Later it was the home of the Duchess of Brunswick, sister of George III. In November 1810 Lord Glenbervie noted in his diary, 'I went in the evening last night to meet her Royal Highness [the Princess of Wales] and Lady Glenbervie at the Duchess of Brunswick's, who has taken Lord Palmerston's house in Hanover Square for the season.' The duchess died there in 1813. The house was demolished in the 1920s.

The old No. 15, now 16, was the home of the unfortunate Sir Godfrey Webster, who committed suicide there on 3 June 1800. The house may then have included all or part of the adjoining No. 1 Tenterden Street, if the account in the diary of his former wife, the famous Lady Holland, is accurate. (Egg's shop was in the Haymarket, at the corner of Coventry Street):

> On Tuesday he went out at nine o'clock, and purchased at Egg's a brace of pistols, and after various devices and stratagems to get his servants out of the way, he but too fatally succeeded, and at half past four shot himself in his front drawing-room in Tenterden Street.

Prince Talleyrand lived at No. 21 from 1830 to 1834, as French ambassador, carrying on at least in spirit the great tradition established there by Lord Hillsborough in 1724. When Wellington told William IV that he would have to receive the Duchesse de Dino, Talleyrand's niece, companion and reputed mistress, as ambassadress, the king replied, 'Oh, very well; I will tell the Queen; and you had better tell her too'. The 3rd Earl of Lucan, the Crimean general and one of the central figures in the controversy over the charge of the Light Brigade, lived at No. 20.

But no mere resident could equal the fame and glamour of the Hanover Square Rooms, later the Queen's Concert Rooms, on the north corner of Hanover Street. They were built in 1774–75 for the fashionable Bach-Abel concert series, directed alternately by Johann Christian Bach and Karl Friedrich Abel. The architect was Richard Edwin, who also

The Hanover Square Rooms, Hanover Square, Mayfair, in 1844.

designed Stratford Place (see Aldborough Square). The Rooms remained open for 100 years and for most of that time this was London's leading concert venue. It was here that Haydn directed his London symphonies for the Salomon concerts between 1791 and 1794, and Berlioz conducted his own music in 1848 and 1852.

But the glorious progress of the hall was nearly ended in the first year, as Mrs Harris reported to her son, our man in Berlin, in February 1775:

> 'Tis a great stroke of Bach's to entertain the town so very elegantly. Nevertheless Lord Hillsborough, Sir James Porter, and some others, have entered into a subscription to prosecute Bach for a nuisance, and I was told the jury had found a bill against him. One would scarce imagine his house could molest either of these men, for Bach's is at the corner of Hanover Street. Poor Sam Clarke may complain, but the others can have no reason.

The square had another important musical institution in its immediate vicinity. Between 1823 and 1912 the north-western corner was haunted in summer by a discordant medley of sounds from the pupils of the Royal Academy of Music in Tenterden Street, practising their various voices and instruments with the windows wide open. These were early indications of the change coming over the square. Others were the building of the Oriental Club at No. 16 in 1827–28 and the establishment of two hotels, the Hanover at No. 3 and the Brunswick at No. 10, both on the east side. By 1843 there were only nine private residents, but they included Lords Harewood, Portman, Downshire and Lucan.

In 1899:

> … 'becoming less and less residential every month, I think,' was [PC] Gunn's remark. Except in two blocks of chambers there are hardly any private houses now; any number of Societies, which run to agriculture, bibliography, or medicine, for the most part. The Zoological is also here, the St George's Club, the Oriental Club; and the New County Club for Ladies is now being fitted up … Harewood House now the home of the Royal Agricultural Society.

Beresford Chancellor noted in 1907 that:

> … no Square in London has undergone such a transformation … where used to dwell notable sailors, soldiers, statesmen, and people generally of light and leading, is now given over to the dressmaking art; to learned societies with portentous names; or to business establishments with the most uncompromising exteriors.

There are now only four old houses remaining in the square, or five if the one at the corner of Princes Street is counted. The rest is a medley of Victorian, Edwardian and late twentieth-century vulgarity. The novelty is a Crossrail entrance to Bond Street Station at the corner of Tenterden Street, where the Oriental Club stood until the early 1960s.

But in spite of all changes, Hanover Square, with its small, shady public garden, retains a certain dignity. Chantrey's 1820s statue of Pitt still admires the famous view down St George Street to the church, and on the north side a rare 1897 cabmen's shelter in green camouflage nestles against the railings.

Hare Square

HOXTON [HACKNEY]

Thomas De Quincey, unaware of the pronunciation, thought that John Donne's name had doomed him to write unmusical verses. On the same argument, a poet could not be expected to emerge from Hare Square, and in fact nobody of any fame seems ever to have been born, or to have lived there.

There was only ribbon development in Hoxton Street and the Kingsland Road until late in the eighteenth century, the land between remaining agricultural. Hare Square was shown on Cary's 1795 map between the tiny Hare Street, later Tyssen Street, and the rather longer Hare Walk, part of which survives. Cary exaggerated the size of Hare Square, which was so small as not to be named on most subsequent maps. Even Lockie overlooked it in the first edition of his *Topography of London*, published in 1810, but had located it by 1813: 'Hare-Sq. Hoxton – 1st on the R in Hare-st., from Hoxton'.

The Booth survey also missed it in 1898 but found Tyssen Street inhabited by costers, 'too busy on Saturday nights to make a noise, but apt to be troublesome on Sundays & Mondays when business is slack', and noted that Hare Walk was popular with burglars, '2 or 3 men now away from here doing time'.

The area survived with surprisingly little change until the Second World War, through which it passed almost unscathed, but since then all the houses have been demolished and much of the street pattern has been lost in the creation of a large council estate. The square had disappeared by 1953: the curve in the middle of the new Tyssen Street more or less marks its site.

Harewood Square

MARYLEBONE [WESTMINSTER]

This was the shortest-lived of all the great West End squares. It formed a group with Dorset Square and Blandford Square, but was built later, in the 1840s. The land was used until then as the Portman Nursery, which no doubt supplied plants for the gardens of the others. Number 10, at the east end of the north side, led the way in 1843, and Nos 30 and 33, in the south-west corner, completed the square in 1849. It was a little smaller than its neighbours to east and north, but still had forty-five substantial four-storey houses with iron balconies, ranged around a nearly square garden.

Harewood Square existed for only fifty years, but could boast of a few famous residents. George Eliot and George Henry Lewes lived at No. 10 for three months in 1860, before moving around the corner to Blandford Square. In September Lewes wrote of it as 'a furnished house we have taken for 6 months, all our efforts to find a suitable house having failed, and from there we shall be able to look about us and

Survey mankind from Pimlico to Kew'.

The other celebrities were artists: John Graham Lough (1798–1876), the sculptor, who lived for many years at No. 42, and the great cartoonist Sir Leslie Ward ('Spy' of *Vanity Fair*) who was born at No. 33 in 1851. He was the son of the painters Edward and Henrietta Ward.

Harewood Square was destroyed between 1895 and 1897, when all the houses were demolished to make way for Marylebone Station and the Great Central Hotel. The north side of the hotel (now the Landmark) in Melcombe Place follows the line of the south side of the square.

Hargreave Square

BERMONDSEY [SOUTHWARK]

Hargreave or Hargrave Square was a cul-de-sac built in the 1840s off the west side of Alice Street, Bermondsey. Its only faint approaches to anything square-like were a slight widening from east to west, and a single house across the end, which it would be a gross exaggeration to call the west side. It was a very poor street, with a rag and bone store immediately behind it and large tanneries to north and south. The Booth survey found it declining further in 1899: '2 storey houses with forecourts … Crowds of children here, many doors open, dirt abundant. The houses are formed with wash-houses and small yards, rents 9/-. Most were said to be sub-let by the occupier who gave me information.'

The north end of Alice Street and Hargreave Square were among the places demolished when the Meakin Estate was built in the late 1930s.

Harland Square

HOXTON [HACKNEY]

Harland Square formed a group with Whitmore Square and Louisa Square, west of Kingsland Road and south of the Regent's Canal, this part of which was dug between 1816 and 1820. That was when the square was formed, even though Mill Road (now Mill Row) existed before the canal. Harland Square was a court opening out at the western end of Mill Road, immediately south-west of Whitmore Square. Only the four houses on the north side and the five on the south were numbered in the square. Mill Road entered from the east.

The slightly later west side, which extended north and south of the open space, reaching almost to Canal Road (now Orsman Road) and Philip (now Phillipp) Street, was separately known as Berry Place. The name came from Daniel Berry, 'proprietor of houses', who lived at No. 7 Harland Square in 1851. He was a pastry cook in Great Turnstile, Holborn, until he retired to manage his little estate. Eleanor Place in Mill Road was named after his youngest daughter, who was born in 1839, and Harland was perhaps another family connection.

The square was sharply reduced in the 1870s, when a board school built in Canal Road required the demolition of the north side and half of Berry Place and also took the open space in the centre, which became part of the playground. In this truncated form Harland Square survived until the 1920s, when the whole area was replaced by an estate of LCC flats. Tiller House covers most of its site.

Harriet Square

SHOREDITCH [HACKNEY]

Harriet (or Harriett) Square was a very insignificant thing in itself, but it formed part of a large and symmetrical pattern on the east side of Kingsland Road. The Ironmongers' Almshouses (now the Geffrye Museum) was the centrepiece, flanked on the north and south by the much smaller Framework Knitters' and Drapers' Almshouses. Maria Street (now Geffrey Street) ran behind all three, and in the gaps between Maria Street and the two small sets of almshouses were fitted Elizabeth Place at the north end and Harriet Square at the south. Elizabeth Place is now represented by Sovereign Mews, but Harriet Square only by the south entrance to the museum.

The roads framing the three sets of almshouses were built in the 1820s and 1830s. The style of the development can be seen in a surviving terrace of houses in Pearson Street to the north. The names sound like the daughters of the developer, but Harriet Square was not built until the early 1860s. It was a mere cul-de-sac of nine houses on each side, with the north end closed by the southern range of the Ironmongers' Almshouses. The only possible excuse for calling it a square was a slight widening of the road after its narrow entrance from Thomas Street,

now Cremer Street. Perhaps the name was suggested by Harris Square just to the south, which was extinguished as Harriet Square was created.

The Drapers' (or Harwar's) Almshouses to the west were replaced by shops in 1879, but otherwise Harriet Square remained undisturbed until it was slightly damaged by bombing in the Second World War. The houses were demolished in the late 1950s, and after a spell as a playground the land was acquired to extend the museum. Its southern entrance and the 1990s horseshoe wing are now on the site.

Harrington Square

SOMERS TOWN [CAMDEN]

Harrington Square was part of the Bedford New Town development that also included the extinguished Ampthill Square and the partly surviving Oakley Square. The name recorded the fact that Anne, Duchess of Bedford, the wife of the 7th Duke, was a daughter of the 3rd Earl of Harrington.

Bedford New Town was planned in the 1830s, but there was a delay between conception and building; the square was begun in 1843 and completed in 1849. It was only ever two sides of a triangle, with the busy Hampstead Road on the third, but it was planned to form part of a huge irregular square with the slightly earlier Mornington Crescent, which had a much larger garden on the other side of the Hampstead Road. Together, Harrington Square and Mornington Crescent were a larger and less formal version of Euston Square, with a main road running through the middle.

One noteworthy resident was the novelist and journalist William Mudford, who was at No. 5 from 1844 until his death in 1848. At that time he was editor of the high Tory paper *John Bull*. His tales of terror, written for *Blackwood's Magazine* in 1829–30, influenced Edgar Allan Poe. Another minor celebrity was the private detective and former Bow Street Runner, Henry Goddard, who lived at No. 7. In 1861 he gave his occupation as 'Doorkeeper Ho[use of] Lords', but that was a largely ceremonial duty.

Harrington Square was already 'on the decline' in 1898. Beresford Chancellor described it in 1907 as

The south side of Harrington Square, *c.* 1905.

'chiefly composed of houses where apartments are let; and it is most conveniently situated for those who use the North-Western line'. Things began to go seriously wrong in 1926, when the Carreras tobacco factory was built over the Mornington Crescent garden.

It is now a particularly dismal remnant of a square. The only ten houses precariously standing, on the east side, are the sad remains of a terrace of twenty-four, the rest of which was destroyed during the Second World War. The south side was much less seriously damaged, but was demolished in the 1960s to form the ugly prelude to the council estate that replaced Ampthill Square. This is all the sadder because the south side was more elaborate than the east, with the two end houses sporting fine Venetian windows. The square is now part of a one-way system so that the triangular public garden, which was slightly enlarged when the south side was demolished, is difficult to reach, noisy and little used.

Harris Square

SHOREDITCH [HACKNEY]

Harris (or Harris's) Square was in the tapering gap between Hackney Road and Kingsland Road, just south of Thomas Street, now Cremer Street. Much of this land belonged to Christ's Hospital and was known as White Bear Gardens after the White Bear pub, which was at No. 96 Kingsland Road until quite recent times. The land began to be built over late in the eighteenth century.

Horwood's 1790s map showed the unnamed square, apparently new, with open fields to the north and east. It was of the front garden type, with terraces of seven cottages on the west side and nine on the east, facing each other across long gardens. The tenants were entirely working class. By 1851 the name was fading away, with only four houses numbered in the square, the rest having been annexed by the neighbouring Harris Place. The whole area was severely disrupted in the early 1860s by the building of the North London Railway's line into Broad Street. The viaduct – now part of the London Overground system – was built through the square, obliterating it.

Haydon Square

Haydon (or Heydon) Square was in the Little Minories, a former convent that was one of the detached portions of the Tower Liberties, as was Wellclose Square. This gave them something of the privileged status enjoyed by Pimlico in *A Passport to Pimlico*. The name came from Captain John Heydon, who had his official residence in the Minories as Master of the Ordnance from 1627 to 1642. His house was still marked on Ogilby & Morgan's 1676 map. Its garden became the site of the square.

Edward Hatton described it in 1708 as 'a way to Mansel street by Goodmans fields', with no mention of the houses. In 1720 Strype gave this account:

Heydon Yard, being broad enough for Coach or Cart; at the upper end is a good large Square, or open Place railed about, with a Row of Trees, very ornamental in the Summer Season, having on the East Side Coach Houses and Stables, on the West Side a very handsome Row of large Houses, with Court Yards before them, and are inhabited by Merchants, Persons of Repute: On the North a Square of good brick Houses; out of this Yard, on the West, is a Passage into the Little Minories, on the East another into Goodmans Fields.

Strype's 1720 map agreed with the text in showing the square fully formed, with a formal garden in the centre, railed and planted with trees, but named it Heydon Yard, while a small court off the north side, entered through an archway, was called Heydon Yard Square. In 1746 Rocque named the larger space Heydon Square and the small northern offshoot Heydon Court. It was later known as Little Haydon Square. Holy Trinity Church, the old convent chapel, stood to the west of it.

In 1805 David Hughson wrote that 'in Haydon Square are large warehouses belonging to the East India

The Haydon Square goods depot, *c.* 1905.

Company, one range being appointed for the housing of tea and drugs, the other for the reception of drugs only'. But these warehouses, larger than the square, were to the north of it, stretching almost to Aldgate High Street. During the nineteenth century, with the flight of private residents from the City, the square became entirely commercial. In the 1830s one of the tenants was an importer of leeches and cigars. God send he didn't import them in the same pot!

The London & North-Western Railway acquired the East India Company warehouses and converted them into the Haydon Square Goods Depot, opened in 1853. The tracks serving it branched from the main line into Fenchurch Street and ran through the middle of Haydon Square. In spite of these destructive changes, the old houses on the east side survived until the end of the nineteenth century, with a close-up view of the viaduct instead of the ornamental garden of happier days.

On the other side of the viaduct Holy Trinity Church survived even longer, with the goods depot built against its northern wall. Beresford Chancellor gave this description in 1907: 'Nowadays it is practically monopolised by the goods office of the North-Western Railway Company and the offices of the Excise Bonded Spirit Warehouse, and what few other houses are in it, for it is a small square, are mostly connected with these.'

Haydon Square Goods Depot survived until the Second World War, in which it suffered a good deal of bomb damage. It was closed in 1962. Holy Trinity, long relegated from church to church hall, was also destroyed. The area has now been shared out between offices, flats and the Aldgate Bus Station.

Heath Square

PENGE [BROMLEY]

Penge was a tiny hamlet until the 1850s, when the rebuilding of the Crystal Palace in its north-west corner set off a frenzy of building, of decreasing quality as it receded from the palatial precincts. Heath Square was a humble part of this rapid growth. It was built in the early 1860s off the north-east side of Laurel Grove, this part of which is now known as

Blean Grove. The entrance was behind the London Tavern, at the corner of Maple Grove.

It was a typical piece of back development, squeezed behind the larger houses in those two roads. There were only nine cottages, in terraces of four and three tucked away around two corners and a pair facing the entrance. Heath Grove and Clifford Grove, two culs-de-sac, were immediately adjoining, which might suggest a builder's name behind one or both. Edward Clifford, a carpenter, lived at No. 1 Heath Square in 1871, when labourers and gardeners occupied most of the cottages.

Heath Square survived until the Second World War, but afterwards everything but the London Tavern was cleared for blocks of council flats. The pub building still stands, converted into housing. The site of the square has been taken by Heath Grove, equally sinuous but winding in quite different directions.

Hereford Square

SOUTH KENSINGTON [KENSINGTON AND CHELSEA]

The name came from Hereford Cottage, the villa in Brompton Road that was for a time the home of the Day family, the owners of the estate. Hereford Square, which was built over its paddock, was designed by James Day's surveyor, John Blore, who is also thought to have been responsible for the northern crescent at Brompton Square. Work began in 1845 and continued until 1851. Completion of the project was delayed by the routine accident of the bankruptcy of the builder, Thomas Holmes, who had previously worked on Thurloe Square.

Hereford Square consisted of three terraces, a long one on the west side and short ones to north and south. It has been haughtily dismissed by some critics as no square at all, because it has only three sides, but there is a great difference between this and something like Alexander Square. Where the road forming the fourth side is not excessively wide and the buildings not ugly, the different name is of little consequence. In this case the 1820s and 1830s houses on the east side of Gloucester Road add to the attractions. The three terraces numbered in the square had palace fronts, the central houses set forward and taller, with pilasters. The handsome stucco houses,

The north side of Hereford Square, *c.* 1905. On the right is No.125 Gloucester Road.

all with balconies, can now be best appreciated on the undamaged north side.

The chief lion of Hereford Square – and he was more leonine than most celebrities – was George Borrow, who lived rather unhappily at No. 22 from 1860 to 1872, equally far from wild Wales and La Mancha. There is a blue plaque on his house. Number 16 was the home of Mrs Jane Brookfield, the friend of Thackeray and Tennyson, and the centre of one of those rare things in London, a literary salon. Her husband, William Henry Brookfield, who was considered by some to be an even wittier clergyman than Sydney Smith, died there in 1874. Fanny Kemble, the actress, lived at No. 26 from 1884 to 1890.

Hereford Square suffered severely in the Second World War: a flying bomb caused much damage in the south-east corner and five houses were shattered at the north end of the west side. Numbers 22 and 23 are a post-war rebuilding retaining the original facade; Nos 24–26 could not be salvaged. There the replacements are defiantly modern and unaccommodating flats, an early work of the brutalist Sir Colin Wilson, built in 1956–58, with balconies and concrete bands, but in the south-east corner the bland 1950s houses hide behind creepers with justified modesty.

Heydon Square

See Haydon Square

Histed's Square

STREATHAM [LAMBETH]

Histed's Square, Greyhound Square and Factory Square, the three at Streatham, were all built on a large estate that belonged in 1780 to John Crosse Crooke, Henry Bates and Thomas Ellison, and remained in the same extended family until all the fields had been covered by houses. The three squares, close together off the west side of Streatham High Road, were part of a tentative early nineteenth-century cottage development on the estate, when Streatham was still almost entirely rural.

Histed's Square was built behind a row of small shops in Streatham High Road, nearly opposite Streatham Common South. The nine cottages of the square were back-to-back in a single block, some facing east and some west. The man responsible may have been Daniel Histed, a Streatham builder who died in 1844. In 1840 William Histed, a job master, occupied two of the cottages and also had a field to the west where he no doubt kept his horses. One of the shops on the High Road, at the entrance to the square, was then occupied by Thomas Histed.

The square was demolished about 1870 and the shops, which were growing in importance with the village, extended their gardens and yards back across its site. The Histed shop became quite a large drapery business eventually numbered (after the Histeds had given it up) as 470 Streatham High Road. Now the shops and the site of Histed's Square have been overwhelmed by a supermarket that destroyed Factory Square.

Holborn Square

See South Square, Gray's Inn

Holford Square

CLERKENWELL [ISLINGTON]

Holford Square, Vernon Square and Percy Square were built in the 1840s on the last plot of land available on the New River Company's estate at Clerkenwell. Vernon was begun first, then Holford, with the tiny Percy filling the gap between them, but work on the three went on concurrently. All were named after figures associated with the government of the company.

William Chadwell Mylne, its surveyor, was responsible for the layout of the squares and the general style of the houses but may have delegated the job of preparing the elevations. The architect James Harrison, who lived at No. 1 Holford Square, the first house built, is a possible candidate. Numbers 1 and 2 appeared in 1841, but afterwards progress was slow and the square was not completed until 1848.

The architecture must have seemed crude and heavy to those accustomed to the grace and lightness of the early nineteenth century, but can be appreciated by those familiar with the excesses of later decades. It was a peculiarity of Holford Square that the east and west sides were extended northwards with the idea of linking with the Pentonville Road. When that aim was frustrated the opening on the west side became the forecourt to a single detached house and the one on the east was occupied by St Philip's Vicarage and Holford Mews. This meant that the classical symmetry of the terraces on those sides, complete with palace fronts, was not mirrored by the garden, which had been forced awkwardly to the south as though slipping down the hill.

The north side of Holford Square, *c.* 1905. (Photograph courtesy of Maurice Friedman)

The square was very respectable in the nineteenth century, which is why the vicar of St Philip's preferred it to Granville Square. Herbert Spencer was an early resident, at No. 42 in 1847. It declined after 1900, when lodging houses became common: Lenin had rooms at No. 30 in 1902–03. (A plaque was put on the ruined house in 1942, after it had been bombed, and the various Lenin memorials that succeeded it became the focus for a long political battle.)

The garden ceased to be private in 1932 and was opened by the council as a bowling green in 1934. More than half the houses were destroyed in the Second World War and only three escaped without any damage, so here there could not be much complaint about the decision to clear the site and start again. The first idea was to retain the form of the square. That was found to be too expensive and the Lubetkin flats built here in the early 1950s obliterated all trace of it.

Holsworthy Square

HOLBORN [CAMDEN]

Holsworthy Square, or Holsworthy Square Buildings as it was called at first, is a group of six-storey tenements of the late 1880s built on the site of a slum alley called Fleur de Lis Court. They were a side-blow

The entrance to Holsworthy Square in 2011.

of Rosebery Avenue, the creation of which disturbed a great many streets and courts not immediately in its path and provided an opportunity for speculators to build new working-class housing. The flats, which abut directly onto the south side of Elm Street, are called 'square' because there is a courtyard behind them with a few trees.

There was Second World War bomb damage to the eastern block, at the corner of Mount Pleasant, but that was made good. Holsworthy Square was modernised by the St Pancras Housing Association in the 1980s and now these industrial dwellings have become a gated community with pretensions.

Honesty Square

CITY OF LONDON

Honesty Square appeared without a name on the Ogilby & Morgan map of 1676 and was named on Rocque's map of 1746 as the first turning on the right in St John's Court, when walking south from Chick Lane (later West Street). It is unlikely to have been called Honesty Square in 1676. Honesty Court or Yard are possible, or it may have been regarded merely as a part of St John's Court.

Honesty Square was listed in Boyle's *View of London* (1799), but Horwood's 1790s map showed it removed and a gap in the Chick Lane houses immediately north of where it had been. By the time of the 1813 revision much larger houses had been built in Chick Lane, perhaps extending back over the site of the square. The whole area was cleared in the 1860s for the new Smithfield Market. West Poultry Avenue is roughly on the site of Honesty Square.

Honeysuckle Square

CITY OF LONDON

Honeysuckle Court was one of the many offshoots of Grub Street in which poor authors scribbled in garrets during the eighteenth century. It was on the east side, towards the south end. In 1676 it was a cul-de-sac, but by 1746 it had been linked with the former Horse Shoe Alley to form a new route to Moor Lane.

During the next century it only appeared in the news in connection with pickpockets, drunken fights and robberies. Model lodging houses, tenement blocks with a common staircase leading to the various flats, were built there in the middle of the nineteenth century, and in 1863 they were the occasion of a test case to decide whether their residents were entitled to vote as householders. They were not, although the denizens of that better-known model lodging house, the Albany, were.

When the Metropolitan Railway was being extended to Moorgate in the early 1860s, Honeysuckle Court was severely truncated, losing nearly all the houses on the north side to the cutting. This moment of diminution was chosen for promoting what remained from Honeysuckle Court to Honeysuckle Square, although as usual it took some time for the new name to stick. Only Nos 4, 5 and 6 were listed in the 1871 census, but the three houses were occupied by eighteen families.

Honeysuckle Square survived the Second World War as a name, but the Moorgate area was very heavily bombed and was comprehensively redeveloped in the 1960s. The site is now occupied by the escalator that leads from Moorfields towards the Barbican Estate.

Hooper's Square

WHITECHAPEL [TOWER HAMLETS]

Hooper Square was mentioned by Edward Hatton in 1708 as 'a small one, at the E. end of Prescot street, in Goodmans fields', and Hooper's Square was named on the Strype map of 1720, which may well be a dozen or more years older than its published date. It was small and irregular in shape, with only half a dozen houses pointing in all directions, as this was really just the enlarged meeting place of Lemon (or Leman) Street, Rupert Street and Lambeth Street.

Two of the houses were pubs, the Brunswick Arms and the White Hart. Hooper Street came much later, forcing its way eastwards from the square through a tangle of old courts and alleys – one of them called Bone Yard – from the 1870s onwards. In its

first tentative phase it was regarded merely as an extension of the square. It reached its objective of Back Church Lane only in the 1880s, whereupon it immediately swallowed its parent, Hooper's Square being abolished as a name and its houses numbered in the new Hooper Street. But Hooper Street was created just in time to be chopped in half by the many lines running into the London, Tilbury & Southend Railway's Commercial Road goods depot, which was opened in 1886. The old Hooper's Square thus became the detached western portion of Hooper Street, and might just as well have kept its old name.

With the closure of the goods depot in 1967 and the subsequent removal of the tracks, Hooper Street regained its integrity. The kink at the west end is the last relic of Hooper Square. Not many old buildings are to be found in the area, as a flying bomb fell at the south end of the depot during the Second World War, but on the south side of Hooper Street, just at the kink, the impressive hydraulic engine house that powered the depot's cranes has survived, now converted into offices. It was built in 1885–86. The ecclesiastical style of the engine house may echo the German Reformed Chapel, which formerly stood on the site.

Horsleydown Square

See New Square, Bermondsey

Hoxton Square

HOXTON [HACKNEY]

The site of Hoxton Square was land belonging to the Austen family known as Brick Close or Church Field. In 1683 Katherine Austen let it to Samuel Blewitt and Robert Hackshaw, and in 1684 it was described as 'intended to be built on'. Blewitt and Hackshaw laid out the square and sublet the plots on building leases between 1684 and 1700.

Most of the houses were of two storeys plus basement and attic. In the suburban style, many enjoyed private front and back gardens in addition to the use of the communal garden in the centre.

Number 48 Hoxton Square in 1921.

In 1708 Hatton called it 'a pleasant Square, being an oblong or Parallelogram', and said of Hoxton that, 'This seems (with the Square) a little Town of it self'.

The Strype map published in 1720, but of earlier date, showed Hoxton Square complete, with open fields close by in all directions. Like other early squares it was designed to be self-supporting, with its own market immediately to the west. In 1725 Daniel Defoe mentioned Hoxton Square as one among many examples of the amazing growth of London:

To come to the North Side of the Town, and beginning at Shoreditch, West, and Hoxton-Square, and Charles's-Square adjoining, and the Streets intended for a Market-Place, those were all open Fields, from Anniseed-clear to Hoxton Town, till the Year 1689, or thereabouts.

The Austens retained the freehold until 1730 when Sir John Austen sold his Hoxton estate, including the square, to Israel Wilkes, the father of John.

Hoxton Square was popular with Presbyterian ministers, some no doubt attracted by the various non-conformist schools there, like that of Joshua Oldfield, which had a fine reputation in the early years of the eighteenth century. Edmund Calamy, the historian and biographer, is the most celebrated of the Presbyterian residents. He says in his autobiography, 'I continued (1694) preaching with good Mr Sylvester at Blackfriars, and living in Hoxton-square; Mr Thomas Reynolds and I lodging together, under one roof. We chose to live there for greater retirement, and that we might have more leisure and conveniency for study.' Today, it is not the first square one would recommend to the scholar in search of peace and quiet.

Another notable resident was the surgeon, geologist and active radical, James Parkinson, after whom Parkinson's disease is named. He was born at No. 1 in 1755 and remained loyal to Hoxton all his life. The square was very respectable then and even procured its own private act for the management of the garden in 1776.

There were businesses in the square from an early date and it became increasingly commercial in the nineteenth century. Only a dozen of the fifty-seven houses were privately occupied by 1850 and none but the vicarages by 1900. Fourteen or fifteen of the seventeenth-century houses were still standing in the 1920s, nearly all adapted for use as workshops and warehouses. An Anglican church, St Peter's, was built at the north-west corner in 1874–75, but was closed in 1937 and demolished after the Second World War. The vicarage, by the same architect, R.W. Drew, survives as No. 10.

Hoxton Square was badly damaged during the Second World War, with houses destroyed at the south end of the west side and the north end of the east. There was also less serious damage to a number of buildings on the north side, to the Shoreditch Vicarage on the east and to the house at the east corner of Rufus Street on the south side.

Hoxton Square is now one of the most lively, inconsistent and bewildering in London, with only the popular garden to bring relief to the mind and senses. Smart restaurants rub shoulders with seedy tenements, churches with warehouses, Gothic vicarages with pretentious offices, art galleries with rundown shops. There is no architectural unity or even *détente*,

The garden of Hoxton Square from the south-east corner, in 2007.

the many styles clashing violently. The best building is Edward Welby Pugin's St Monica's of 1864–66, on the north side. The style least represented is that of the late seventeenth century, which only appears in the pretty pastiche of No. 32 on the east side, which was reconstructed after the war.

Hudson's Square

STRATFORD [NEWHAM]

Hudson's Square was a tiny court of four houses off the west side of Stratford Broadway, nearly opposite St John's Church. It was behind the Hudson's Head beerhouse, named in honour of George Hudson, the railway king. He established the great depot of the Eastern Counties Railway at Stratford in 1847 and began to build Hudson Town, now Stratford New Town.

Hudson's Square appeared in the 1851 and 1861 census returns, occupied in the latter entirely by road labourers. It thus survived the disgrace and ruin of its sponsor, but by 1871 had succumbed to the growth of the Broadway drapers' shops. This area was soon engulfed by Roberts' department store, now largely Wilkinson's.

Hudson's Square

See Webb's Square

Hyde Park Square

BAYSWATER [WESTMINSTER]

Because there was such a long delay between the drawing up of the first plan for the development of Bayswater and the completion of the building, most of the squares passed through various shapes and names on the journey from paper to brick. Hyde Park Square, the second (after Connaught Square) to be begun, was less protean than the others, but in 1828 George Gutch was planning only a single Stanhope Square instead of the Hyde Park Square and Gloucester Square eventually laid out.

Only when building began in the 1830s did Hyde Park Square achieve its final form: a rectangle with short east and west sides. The work went on slowly from the east end, with only a single house listed in the 1839 ratebook. Nine, with the highest and lowest numbers, were occupied by 1840, twenty by 1843,

The north side of Hyde Park Square, *c.* 1904.

thirty-seven by 1845. All were complete by 1850. George Ledwell Taylor designed some of them and lived first at No. 50, which later became 45. Others were the work of Sir Matthew Wyatt, who retired from his profession on the proceeds of these and other jobs in Pimlico and Bayswater to a life of leisure at No. 5. Neither house survives.

Writers of very different kinds have lived in the square. Mary Coleridge, who achieved her main success with poetry, as ancestry demanded, was born at No. 29 in 1861, and the novelist Ada Leverson, Oscar Wilde's 'Sphinx', lived at No. 21, now 20a, from her birth in 1862 until 1881. John Buchan's first home after his marriage in 1907 was at No. 40, but he soon drifted to more fashionable regions east of the Edgware Road.

The unlikely socialist leader H.M. Hyndman, who used to address mass meetings of the workers in a top hat and frock coat, and who would take sabbaticals from politics to make money promoting public companies, was born at No. 7 in 1842. At No. 11 lived another unconventional politician, Samuel Laing (1812–97), who had a second career as a railway pioneer and late in life developed a third as a popular writer on evolution.

There was serious bomb damage at both ends of the square during the Second World War and other houses were demolished from 1957 as part of the estate policy of modernisation. Now the original houses survive only on the north side and in the western half of the south side. The gaps have been filled with flats, low on the south side, taller at the two ends.

Imperial Square

WALHAM GREEN [HAMMERSMITH
AND FULHAM]

Visions of grandeur called up by the name could not be further from the truth. Imperial Square is as unassuming as any in London and none the worse for that. It was built to house the workers of the Imperial Gasworks Company, which was established at Walham Green in 1824.

The design has been attributed to Francis Edwards, the company's architect, but as he died in 1857 and the square was not built until about 1870, that seems unlikely. The present name has only recently become firmly established. Although the LCC called the open space Imperial Square in 1904, it described

Imperial Square in 2010.

the approach from Imperial Road as Emden Street and the houses as Imperial Cottages. The last two were the only names given by the 1913 map. In 1899 Charles Booth's researcher described it as, '2½ storey, asphalt in centre, not attractive looking. Belongs to gasworks and is tenanted by their employees; some poor. Many foreigners, employed on a special gas process, live here.'

After more than a century the cottages have come to look attractive, especially when compared with later attempts at working-class housing, but the square is still overshadowed in dramatic fashion by a huge rusty gas holder. Despite that, the value of these humble cottages must be rising as dramatically as a gas holder in a heat wave as the luxury developments of Chelsea Harbour and Chelsea Creek ooze ever closer.

Ion Square

BETHNAL GREEN [TOWER HAMLETS]

Ion Square was built in the 1840s on the Pritchard estate in Hackney Road, land then owned by Andrew Pritchard, the optician and writer on microscopy. Ion Pritchard was Andrew's son, born about 1844; his name presumably came from Thomas Noon Talfourd's tragedy *Ion*, which was the theatrical sensation of 1836 and was republished in a popular edition of Talfourd's plays in 1844.

Before the square was built part of the site had been Nag's Head Yard, the rest market garden ground. In 1848 Hector Gavin gave this report on its condition:

> Thirty-eight new houses, forming three sides of a square. Close by the southern end runs the filthy black ditch spoken of under the head of Willow-walk. [For 77 yards in this most filthy walk, does a stagnant foetid gutter extend.] Nearly all the houses in this square are remarkably damp, so much so as to be very injurious to health.

There were houses only on the long east and west sides and the short north side of the square. To the south there was a shrubbery and a brick wall that barred all access from the mean streets beyond, even though they had been built with the clear intention

of linking with the square. The situation did not change until 1895, when an entrance was made from Durrant Street. That was the year in which the garden was opened to the public after the Pritchards had leased it to Bethnal Green Vestry until 1934.

In 1898 Charles Booth's researcher, reporting his conversation with the local policeman, noted that it was a 'well kept square, should be pink [fairly comfortable, good ordinary earnings], but "a bad lot here", prostitutes, windows broken, 2 storey houses. "They tried to improve it by doing up the square, putting in benches, but nothing came of it."'

All but a few houses in the approach road from the north were destroyed during the Second World War and an estate of prefabs stood on the vacant plots until about 1960. In 1953 the LCC and Bethnal Green Council had agreed that there should be no permanent replacement of the houses so, after the prefabs and the surviving terrace had been removed and some neighbouring houses demolished, the wider area became a park known as Ion Square Gardens.

Jeffrey's Square

CITY OF LONDON

The Ogilby & Morgan map of 1676 showed a large house with an even larger formal garden dominating the east side of St Mary Axe. It belonged to the Jeffreys family, who owned huge tobacco plantations in Virginia. The founder of their fortunes is buried in St Andrew Undershaft, at the south end of St Mary Axe: 'John Jeffreys Esq; of an ancient Family in the County of Brecknock, and in the Parish of Llywel, Merchant of London, deceased Nov. 5, 1688'. He left the St Mary Axe mansion to his nephew Sir Jeffrey Jeffreys, and it was after his death in 1709 that it was demolished and the site made available for development.

In 1720 Strype, in his account of St Mary Axe, noted that 'here was lately the fair House of Sir Jeffrey Jeffryes, Knt. and Alderman, which is now taken down, with divers others, in the Places whereof are other good Houses now erecting by Mr John Blunt, the Gardens backwards having been spacious, and designed for a Square'. Was this the chairman of the South Sea Company, soon to be Sir John, who was busy moving his fortune from stock into land in this year of the Bubble?

The square was quiet, for the entrance was a passage beneath the houses in St Mary Axe that opened into a court of three times its width. The eight large houses remained popular with wealthy merchants throughout the eighteenth century, but some became business premises. The great firm of Coutts, for example, had their first London offices in Jeffrey's Square. Boswell was a frequent visitor in 1762–63, as his banker lived there. In March 1763 he wrote, 'I then went to Jeffrey Square beyond Cornhill and dined with Mr William Cochrane, merchant. He has got an excellent house and lives well.'

The medical profession was also fond of it. The great surgeon Sir Astley Cooper, who lived there between 1791 and 1806, was not the perfect neighbour. When he moved from his original house to a larger one he accidently left a live viper behind and he later dissected an elephant in his front garden. By 1840 there was an early fire station in the square – the firemen living at No. 3 – and all the other houses were offices. Few were occupied by single firms, most being shared by as many as seven.

In 1895 the square had become a business slum, home to more than forty firms, and the writing was soon literally on the wall in the form of bills announcing that the site had been acquired for redevelopment. Jeffrey's Square was demolished in 1899 to make way for the Baltic Exchange, which was built between 1900 and 1903, but the site is now covered by the Gherkin.

Jeffrey's Square

WHITECHAPEL [TOWER HAMLETS]

Jeffrey's Square was the same as Jeffrie's Yard, which Lockie included in the 1813 edition of his *Topography of London* (but not in 1810) as being the first turning to the right in Chamber Street, Goodman's Fields, coming from Mansel Street. That was close to the east side of Little Prescot Street, which was given as the location of Jeffrey's Square in the 1841 census. It was no doubt accessible from both sides. Mordecai Moses

of No. 2 Jeffreys Square, Chamber Street, Goodman's Fields, insured his brick and timber house with the Sun on 9 December 1834.

Much of Little Prescot Street was destroyed during the construction of the London & Blackwall Railway and its Minories Station, which opened in 1840. What was left of Jeffrey's Square was squeezed against the south side of the viaduct. In 1841 the five dwellings were occupied by shoemakers, a labourer, an excavator and a lighterman. Some of the 1841 residents were still there ten years later, by which time the maimed square had adopted the new name of Prescot Place. It was destroyed soon afterwards when sidings were built to serve the goods depots between the railway and Royal Mint Street.

Jeffrys Square

WALTHAMSTOW [WALTHAM FOREST]

Jeffrys (or Jeffreys, or Jeffries) Square was an occasional name for ten houses off the east side of Wood Street, immediately south of the Duke's Head. They had something like the form of a square, with cottages on two and a half sides and the pub on the fourth, but the central space was divided into front gardens.

In 1851 the occupants of Jeffrys Square were working people: carpenter, agricultural labourer, gardener, shoemaker, fishmonger, hair dresser. Some of them were living in the same houses ten years earlier and later, but then they were regarded merely as a part of Wood Street.

Jeffreys Square and Jeffries Square appeared as variant names in late nineteenth-century census returns and directories. In the 1901 census eight cottages were occupied, mostly by men engaged in the building trades, but Nos 9 and 10 were listed as 'old houses to pull down'.

Most of the west side was destroyed when Marlowe Road was extended to Wood Street early in the twentieth century. The south side lasted longer, but has now been replaced by a children's playground. The weather-boarded cottage on the south side of Marlowe Road, attached to the rear of No. 116 Wood Street, is a relic of the square, of which it formed the short east side.

Jerusalem Square

Jerusalem Square was in Mare Street, Hackney, opposite the town hall. The site is between Mare Street and Valette Street, the successor to Jerusalem Passage, which continued the east side of the square south to Paragon Road. The square featured small houses, built from about 1700 and inhabited by working people. A dairyman, a smith and a carpenter were the tradesmen listed in an 1856 directory.

It was demolished between 1902 and 1904 when the LCC rehoused many families from the square and other cleared streets in its new tenement block, Valette Buildings.

John's Square

John's Square, a small court of nine houses on the east side of Church Lane (now Back Church Lane), was part of the tentative early development of Whitechapel. It was shown on the 1790s and 1813 Horwood maps, but not by Rocque in the 1740s. It was swept away about 1820, when intensive building began on the east side of Church Lane. The site, between Boyd Street and Ellen Street, is now occupied by the Dog & Truck, a pub by no means so old as it tries to seem. The area has been rebuilt several times since John's Square was demolished.

Johnson's Square

See Wellington Square, Chelsea

Kelsey Square

Although on a much smaller scale, Kelsey Square is comparable with the contemporary Belvedere Square at Wimbledon. This opening from Beckenham High Street became one of the main entrances to the Burrell family's Kelsey Park estate and was dignified

Numbers 4–7 Kelsey Square in 2013.

with a lodge after the new northern mansion was built in the 1760s.

The Hoare family, of the bank, acquired Kelsey Park when the Burrell interests moved elsewhere. The lodge was rebuilt by Peter Hoare in the 1860s and the seven matching cottages that form the square were added to accommodate servants and estate workers, a purpose for which the Tudor style was then almost inevitable. It is handled with less delicacy here than at Wimbledon.

The cottages are in two short terraces facing one another, with the former gate of the mansion at the south end; there was little justification for calling the arrangement a square. To the western terrace was added the corner building now numbered 153 High Street. In the early 1880s it was the headquarters of the volunteer fire brigade and the offices of the Beckenham Local Board, so modest were the local government requirements of our ancestors.

Kensington Gardens Square

The name must often have caused confusion, as the square is a long way from Kensington and not very close to Kensington Gardens. The reason for the eccentric choice may be that the builder, Henry de Bruno Austin, had just finished work on Cleveland Gardens and Cleveland Square when he began this new development. Allowing for the different shape of the two sites, the design is much the same, but at the earlier job Austin had given the two parts individual names, calling the northern section Cleveland Gardens and the southern Cleveland Square, names that should really have been reversed. At his new site Austin decided to use a single name, but managed to find one that expressed the two elements of his scheme. As at the Clevelands, the design involved a small northern garden with a road and houses all round it and a larger southern garden with no road on the north side where the houses opened into it directly.

The Norfolk Hotel, Nos 80 and 82 on the east side of Kensington Gardens Square, in the 1920s.

Austin was building the square in 1857 when *Building News* described the houses as being in the French Renaissance style, 'vieing to a certain extent' with the Louvres and the Tuileries. Some of the houses were occupied by August 1860 and the Victoria College for Ladies was well established at No. 21 by January 1861, moving later to 20. It was the first of many schools.

One George Henry de Strabolgie Neville Plantagenet Harrison lived at No. 22 in 1861, when not in prison. If he is a fair sample of the early tenants it is not surprising that the square failed to prosper and attracted nobody of eminence. This chronic bankrupt used his schedule of debts to libel all his creditors.

The houses proved difficult to let and a number of boarding houses had appeared by the 1890s. The Booth survey noted in 1899 that other houses were being divided into flats. They are as large as the ones in the Clevelands but more attractive, with lighter porches, many of them doubled, and triple round-headed windows on the first and second floors. The grand houses opening directly into the southern garden have large, shallow bay windows.

As at Cleveland Square, the most serious Second World War damage was on the east side and the clumsy replacements are very similar. The stubby extension in the north-east corner, originally the mews, became part of Whiteley's department store quite early in the career of the square but has recently been rebuilt as inoffensive flats.

Many of the houses are now hotels, but the gardens remain private. The southern one is well looked after, but the little northern garden is perhaps the most untidy in London, a lawn and a few spindly trees surrounded by a wire mesh and concrete fence, with an outer circuit of dustbins and motorbikes.

Kensington Square

Kensington Square is so strongly associated with William and Mary and Queen Anne that it is odd to consider that it was begun three years before the Revolution of 1688 and was originally named King's Square in honour of James II. It was quixotic to expect to make a success with the newly fashionable urban square in so very remote a location as the Kensington of 1685, but as countless blunders have been made in estate development when following seemingly solid trends, the odd freakishly lucky anticipation is only to be expected.

Thomas Young, the wood carver and joiner after whom Young Street is named, bought a house and land south of Kensington High Street in 1682 and began to lay it out as a square three years later. Young had worked as a carver on some of the Wren churches and was employed under the pioneer square builders, Richard Frith and Nicholas Barbon, in Soho. It was to the tradesmen associated with him in these and other jobs that Young leased most of the plots on his own development at Kensington.

He and his lessees set to work quickly and the north, east and south sides were largely complete by 1690; complete but sparsely occupied, for like many other projectors of squares, Young and his friends found the houses easier to build than to let. Young's hopes of making the square popular rested on the pleasure garden, refreshment house and bowling green that he established just to the south.

The asthmatic William III bought Kensington House in 1689 as a winter retreat from the smoke and fog of Whitehall, and it was in 1690 that William and Mary began to occupy the repaired and enlarged Kensington Palace. This entirely unforeseen piece of good fortune transformed the prospects of the new square, and the existing houses were quickly disposed of to courtiers and followers of fashion, although the west side was built only gradually and not completed until the 1730s. But as happened so often with squares, the success did not benefit the original projector but the capitalists who had lent him money. Young had been deposed and imprisoned by his chief mortgagee in 1688, even before James II was deposed and driven into exile by William of Orange.

Young's name lived on in Young Street, but the man himself was soon forgotten. His misfortunes could not dent the prosperity of the square under the patronage of William and Queen Anne, and even in the early years of George I the palace was regularly occupied and the village full of fashionable residents. Things changed later in his reign, and Defoe had this to say in 1725:

It is no wonder if the Court being so much at Kensington, that Town has encreased in Buildings … On the South Side of the Street over against the Palace, is a fair New large Street, and a little way down a noble Square full of very good Houses, but since the Court has so much declin'd the Palace, the Buildings have not much encreased.

George II was there as little as his father, and after the death of Queen Caroline in 1737 (just as the square was completed) the palace was almost abandoned by the royal family.

As even in the great days the court was only at Kensington in the summer, the courtiers tended to take lodgings in the square rather than acquire their own houses. Some famous names stand out among the crowd of royal grooms, barbers and laundry women. The Duchesse Mazarin, one of Charles II's mistresses and the niece of Cardinal Mazarin, lodged in the square, probably from 1692 until 1694, when she moved to Paradise Row, Chelsea. Her lodgings were not at No. 11, where her name is inscribed above the door, as that house was not built until after her death, but perhaps at No. 15 ('Mrs Margaret's house') where one of her women died in 1692. The 3rd Duke of Schomberg lived at No. 13 in 1696–97 and another of William III's officers, Lord Cutts, at No. 23. Richard Steele lived with him there as his secretary in 1696–97.

With the departure of the court after 1737, Kensington resumed its interrupted progress as one of London's satellite villages, a place to which successful tradesmen could retire, where clergymen and ladies could establish moderately fashionable schools, and where the odd man of fashion could maintain a convenient suburban retreat. The square was a sleepy place for eighty years until the birth and upbringing of the Princess Victoria – the heiress on whom all eyes were fixed – brought the palace and the village back to prominence early in the nineteenth century. The square was still isolated among the fields during Victoria's childhood, but by the time of her accession expanding London was drawing near.

Being so out of the way of fashion, Kensington Square had avoided the wholesale rebuilding that transformed most of the other seventeenth-century squares. As a result, the most notable of those who rediscovered it in the nineteenth century were writers, artists and musicians charmed by its Queen Anne quaintness. Leigh Hunt, the inventor of much of its legendary history, lived in the less expensive Edwardes Square, but the house of Thackeray, its other romantic historian, was just around the corner in Young Street.

The square itself was the childhood home of Peter Mark Roget, the compiler of the *Thesaurus* which was first published in 1852, and John Stuart Mill lived at No. 18 from 1836 to 1851. William Nassau Senior, the economist, was at No. 32 from 1820 to 1827, and Henry Mayhew, author of *London Labour and the London Poor*, at No. 2 from 1858 to 1861. The Whig historian, John Richard Green, and his wife and fellow-worker Alice Stopford Green, lived at No. 14 from 1879, except when his precarious health drove them to Mentone. After his death in 1883, she lived there alone until 1903. The house was frequented by historians, writers and politicians.

The most notable artist was Sir Edward Burne-Jones, who lived at No. 41 from 1865 to 1867. Chief among the composers was Sir Hubert Parry at No. 17 (which he bought from Alfred Huth, the book collector) from 1886 until his death in 1918. Being a man of the widest culture, he made it a meeting place not only for musicians, but for artists and writers. Other celebrities were Sir John Simon, the pioneer of public health, who lived at No. 40 from 1871 to 1904, and the great actress Mrs Patrick Campbell, who was at No. 33 from 1899 until 1918, after which she moved to the cheaper Tedworth Square. Number 33, where Ernest Thesiger organised the placing of a memorial plaque in 1950, is now the property of the National Trust.

The Booth account of the square in 1899 was ominous:

> Old fashioned houses, mostly four floors, some double fronted. Many of them are passing into the hands of the great drapers, who are using them for sleeping apartments. One, fitted as tenements, was offered to Inspector King for police lodgings. A few good families still remain.

The great drapers were Barker and Derry & Toms, who began to infiltrate the square about 1890. After Barker & Co. took over Derry & Toms in 1920 and set about the rebuilding of the two department stores, the threat to the future of the square became acute, and it was not until the late 1940s that a compromise was reached that preserved the houses at the cost of nearly all the garden ground on the north side.

The south end of the west side of Kensington Square, *c.* 1904.

The north side of Kensington Square in 1926.

Kensington Square has now outlived its department store enemies and its residential future seems assured, but its original houses had already suffered a good deal before the happy days of listing and protection began. The east side, where the Greyhound has been a feature since the infancy of the square, was almost entirely rebuilt at various dates during the nineteenth century. The possible exception is No. 7, where some of the original fabric may have survived the rebuilding of 1808–09.

The south-west corner of the square was rebuilt in the 1870s and 1880s as the Convent of the Assumption with its chapel and schools. Elsewhere houses of the late seventeenth or early eighteenth century survive, but few in anything like the original state. Most have been raised a storey or two, others have been re-fronted, and where the exterior is little altered the interior has usually been gutted. There is no uniformity of size or style, but the medley is strangely attractive.

The best houses are Nos 11 and 12 on the south side. They were an afterthought, built about 1700 in a south-east offshoot known as Hell Corner. These are the only ones in the ornate style of Queen Square (Queen Anne's Gate) at Westminster. In the earlier houses Thomas Young and his colleagues had imitated Soho or Red Lion Square. The best preserved of these are Nos 17–19 on the south side, No. 29 on the west and Nos 43–45 on the north. The best of the early eighteenth-century houses on the west side are Nos 32, 33 and 35.

The shady garden remains private. The diary of the poet William Allingham gives a glimpse of its society in 1867, when he visited Burne-Jones ('Ned') at No. 41:

Ned and I in garden of square; to us enter Mr John Simon (from next door) and his niece. Mr S. is a kind, bright pleasant man and good talker, as well as eminent surgeon, boyishly merry at times. He and his niece run a race to the house, then he jumps on the low wall and lies flat on it as if exhausted.

Kilburn Square

The Kilburn Chapel, later rebuilt as St Paul's, was opened in 1829 to serve a scattered village that had grown up along the Edgware Road, far from any parish church. Serious development had to wait until the opening of Kilburn and Maida Vale (now Kilburn High Road) Station a little to the south of the chapel in 1852. In anticipation, a narrow square was begun about 1851 with a terrace on the south side of the chapel and four semi-detached houses on the north. The first houses were optimistically given the highest numbers.

The chapel occupied the whole of the east side of the square, with the garden behind it. The north and south sides made slow progress, jerking westwards over several decades, and the square was eventually completed with a semi-detached pair on the short west side.

The original builders were Bishop and Sirkett. On 20 May 1854 this advertisement appeared in *The Morning Chronicle*:

> To be let in this healthy neighbourhood, facing the square about to be finished as Kilburn-square, an elegant eight-roomed house, with every domestic convenience, and gardens back and front. The locality is highly respectable, and there are constant facilities for reaching London by omnibus and rail. To a respectable tenant very moderate terms will be offered. The house has a south aspect, and adjoins excellent church accommodation. Apply on the premises, to Mr Bishop, Kilburn-square.

The square achieved a fair measure of the respectability Mr Bishop so ardently desired, but the excellent church accommodation was lost when St Paul's was demolished in 1936. This was by then the heart of

St Paul's, Kilburn Square, *c.* 1905, with part of the north side on the right and the west side on the left.

the busy Kilburn shopping centre and no longer the place for a respectable Victorian square. Beginning in 1964, Willesden Council rebuilt the whole area as the depressing Kilburn Square Estate, with shops in front. The only thing in sight that can now raise the drooping spirits is the Cock Tavern, a lively 1900 gin palace in the High Road. It used to stand directly behind the houses on the north side of the square.

Kildare Square

BAYSWATER [WESTMINSTER]

In the schedule attached to its abortive *London Squares and Enclosures (Preservation) Bill* of 1905, the LCC gave this name to 'Garden enclosure bounded on the north by the roadway of Kildare-terrace, and on the east, west and south by the roadway of Kildare-gardens'. This, which survives as one of the most attractive of the small London garden enclosures, and one now open to the public, has generally been called Kildare Gardens. It was created between 1855 and 1858, when the surrounding houses were built.

King Square

CLERKENWELL [ISLINGTON]

King Square on the east side of Goswell Road, opposite Northampton Square, was built between 1822 and 1825 on land belonging to St Bartholomew's Hospital, under the supervision of Thomas Hardwick, the veteran surveyor to the estate. Hardwick designed St Barnabas, the 'Waterloo' or Commissioners' church that occupied the centre of the east side, but probably only supplied specimen elevations for the three-storey houses. They were small and modest, making the large garden seem even larger. At the same time as the square, Rahere Street, named after the founder of St Bartholomew's Hospital, was built to the north.

In this poor area the square was as much commercial as residential from the start. In 1840 watchmakers, jewellers and others engaged in the local metal-working trades already outnumbered the private residents. However, it was distinctly better than the surrounding streets, partly because the garden remained private. The Booth surveyor made an interesting comment on

The west side of Kildare Gardens (occasionally Kildare Square), *c.* 1904.

this in 1898: 'In the middle a good square [garden] belonging to inhabitants and not open to the public. Would be an advantage to the neighbourhood if it were, though not to the square.'

King Square grew poorer in the twentieth century and was little above the level of a slum in the 1930s. Radical Finsbury Council was already looking upon it as a redevelopment site when the Second World War put a stop to all such projects. There was a good deal of bomb damage, especially to St Barnabas and the east end of the square, but most of the houses survived and could have been restored as the church was, had the will existed. Instead, all the houses were demolished in the 1950s and 1960s and replaced by the tall blocks of prefabricated flats that now surround the enlarged garden. Rahere Street was extinguished and is now only commemorated by Rahere House. The roads around the north, south and west sides of the square were abolished, leaving only the east side to give access

to the church. Even that has lost its identity since the war: it was united with the demolished St Clement's in Lever Street and given that name. It is a sad story, and a sad place.

King Square

SHOREDITCH [TOWER HAMLETS]

King Square was a small court off the west side of Brick Lane, with twelve houses in three terraces of four on the north, south and west sides. It was built late in the eighteenth century and quickly gained a bad reputation. In 1795 an officer from the Worship Street Police Office testified to arresting a gang of thieves 'in a place called Queen's-square, or King's-square, in the neighbourhood of Brick-lane'. His uncertainty probably arose from the fact that Queen Street lay immediately south of the square and King Street to the north.

Fortunately, perhaps, the life of the square was short. It was one of many places in the East End – Webb's Square was another – destroyed in the late 1830s as the Eastern Counties Railway prepared the route and laid the tracks leading to its new terminus at Shoreditch Station. This was later known as Bishopsgate Station, then as the Bishopsgate Goods Depot. It was destroyed by fire in 1964. The London Overground viaduct now passes over the site of King Square.

King's Head Square

SHOREDITCH [HACKNEY]

By the 1790s King's Head Court, an alley entered via an archway on the west side of Shoreditch High Street, had replaced the Nag's Head Yard of Rocque's 1740s map, so the name was in a state of improvement even though the place was probably deteriorating throughout. It was just north of Hog Lane, soon to be given more dignity as part of Worship Street. Around 1820 King's Head Court was extended west to Curtain Road and to its north, between the Court and Cumberland Street, King's Head Square was formed.

It did not remain undisturbed for long, for by 1830 the Chartered Gas Light Company of Curtain Road had begun to expand east along the south

St Barnabas, King Square, Clerkenwell, in 1828.

side of King's Head Court, where it soon built six gas holders extending along the south side of the square. The twelve houses that survived on the other sides were destroyed when the whole block north of the old Hog Lane part of Worship Street was demolished in the 1860s and early 1870s, during the construction of the approaches to Broad Street and Liverpool Street stations. A coal depot was established on the surplus land to the west of the tracks. The site of King's Head Square is now a little southeast of Hearn Street.

King's Square

CITY OF LONDON

Was it prescience of its glorious future as Broadgate that led the builders of Shoreditch to create King's, Queen's and Prince's Squares in the far from palatial block east of Wilson Street?

Queen's Square was the oldest, Prince's Square the youngest of the three. King's Square was unnamed on the Horwood maps of the 1790s and 1813, and looked more like stabling than housing, but Lockie described it

as King Square in 1810 with the direction, 'Horseshoe-Alley, Moorefields, 1st on the L. from Wilson-st'. Horseshoe Alley was old, but had only gardens on the north side in the 1740s.

King's Square was little more than an alley, with a regular row of six cottages on the west side and three houses of different sizes on the east. In 1851 the tenants included sofa makers, French polishers, tailors and shoemakers. King's Square was destroyed when the Broad Street goods depot was extended on the west side of Finsbury Avenue in the 1890s. Number 1 Finsbury Avenue is now on the site of the square.

King's Square

See Kensington Square

Knight's Hill Square

WEST NORWOOD [LAMBETH]

For such an insignificant place, Knight's Hill Square has got through a great many names, most of them uncomplimentary. Rocque showed an enclosure on

Knight's Hill Square, probably in the 1920s.

the common at about this point in the 1740s, and the northern range of buildings was already in existence when the land was awarded to William Blanchard by the Lambeth enclosure commissioners in 1806.

The square was shown complete but for the south-eastern block on the tithe map of 1843. There were six short terraces scattered in a random pattern, but four of them did form a rough square. It was called Soot Street on the 1870 and 1894 maps, but the different parts were given as Powles Row or Powell's Road and Beaconsfield Terrace in directories and census returns. To the locals it was Soapsuds Square or Alley, or sometimes Washerwomen's Square. The LCC replaced all of these with Knight's Hill Square in 1896.

The old single-storey cottages were destroyed by a V1 on 13 August 1944 and prefabs were erected there after the war. The name survives, but now only to indicate a loose collection of workshops and warehouses.

Ladbroke Square

NOTTING HILL [KENSINGTON AND CHELSEA]

Thomas Allason, an expert on Greek architecture, acted as surveyor to James Weller Ladbroke, the owner of much of Notting Hill. A decision to build on the land was made around 1820, when Allason drew up a plan that fixed the main outlines of the estate with Ladbroke Grove as its axis. A start was promptly made, but the financial crisis of 1825–26 halted development and there was hardly any building on the estate during the 1830s. Instead, an experiment was made with the Hippodrome, a racecourse opened by an enterprising gambler named John Whyte in 1837. This extended over the site later occupied by Ladbroke Square, land which was, according to the leases, 'part and parcel of a piece of ground called heretofore Pond Field'. The racecourse quickly failed and its last proprietor, Jacob Connop, began to look instead to the development potential of the land.

Connop employed several surveyors to draw up schemes, all of whom had to negotiate with Thomas Allason, as the man with overall responsibility for the Ladbroke estate, and to co-ordinate their plans with those of James Thomson, who was laying out the land to the west of Ladbroke Grove. It was probably

Ladbroke Square, looking east from Ladbroke Terrace, c. 1904.

John Stevens (a pupil of William Wilkins of the National Gallery) who came up with the idea of three great squares to the east of Ladbroke Grove. The two northern ones, Beaufort Square and Lansdowne Square, were never built, but Ladbroke Square did survive from drawing board to bricks and mortar.

The building of the square began in 1842, with Nos 23–27 undertaken by William Gribble of St Marylebone and Nos 28–31 by W.J. Wells of Islington. By 1843 Nos 32–37 were also well enough advanced for ninety-nine-year leases to be granted by J.W. Ladbroke. John Stevens may have designed some or all of these houses.

But Jacob Connop had only been able to get the project started and pay for the roads and sewers by borrowing heavily, and slow progress in completing and letting the houses did not bring in enough to service the debt. He was bankrupted in 1845. This enabled Ladbroke to enter into fresh agreements

with Connop's creditors. One of them was his former surveyor Martin Stutley (the predecessor of John Stevens) and it was he who took a new lease of Ladbroke Square. Stutley failed to carry out his agreements and the square was not completed until 1856–60, when William Wheeler built Nos 4–17. An early occupant of No. 35 was the architect Benjamin Broadbridge, who played a part in the early development of Notting Hill and designed the Old Vestry Hall in Kensington High Street.

Although only the houses on the south are numbered in the square, it has four sides and the other three were once more integrated with it than they are today. The houses to the north, with their front doors in Kensington Park Gardens, are two-sided designs with the lives of the tenants focused as much towards the south, where their small sloping private gardens give them access to the large garden of the square, as to the north.

To the west the large formal terrace between St John's Church and Ladbroke Walk (sadly maimed in the Second World War) exactly faces the garden of the square, which it was clearly intended to enhance. These houses were less detached from the square before Ladbroke Grove became a major highway and

The section of Kensington Park Road that formed the east side of Ladbroke Square, *c.* 1910.

the lawn in front of the terrace was heavily planted in self-defence. In Kensington Park Road, which formed the east side, four individual and attractive detached villas originally faced the garden, but in the 1930s they were replaced by large mansion flats set further back from the road and having no relation to the square.

Ladbroke Square was quite fashionable in the 1850s, when the scientist and Liberal politician Lyon Playfair, later Lord Playfair, lived at No. 32, but it declined towards the end of the century with a number of lodging houses intruding, and even the Holy Cross Society of Trained Nurses at No. 2. Beresford Chancellor was dismissive in 1907, noting that 'its formation is too relatively recent for it yet to have any historical or antiquarian importance'.

Numbers 38–40 were badly damaged during the Second World War but they were rebuilt in facsimile, and since then Ladbroke Square has risen higher and higher in popularity. A second eminent liberal is the most famous resident since this renaissance. Roy Jenkins lived at No. 33 from 1954 until he became president of the European Commission in 1977.

Lamb Square

CLERKENWELL [ISLINGTON]

Lockie included 'Lamb's Court or Square' in the 1810 edition of his *Topography* as being entered next to No. 23 Clerkenwell Green, on the south side of the Sessions House, but in his 1813 revision he made 'Lamb Square' 'the S. end of Lamb-court'. The eighteenth and early nineteenth-century maps showed Lamb Alley (Rocque's name) or Lamb Court as a cul-de-sac, with no difference in form between the north and south ends. The 1873 map showed some widening at the south end and a way through to the alleys beyond.

The 1841 census listed twelve houses in Lamb Court and nine in Lamb Square, occupied by labourers, tinkers, fruiterers, a dustman and a drover. In 1851 only Nos 3–6 Lamb Square were occupied, in 1861 Nos 1–4, inhabited mainly by costermongers, and in 1871 Nos 2–6. Court and square were destroyed during the construction of Clerkenwell Road, which was completed in 1878.

Lambeth Square

LAMBETH

Lambeth Square was built in the early 1830s off the south-east side of Lower Marsh, near the Westminster Bridge Road end. A number of the houses were insured between 1835 and 1839. It came closer than most in London to the ideal definition of a square, being nearly square in shape, with houses on all four sides, a small garden in the middle and a road all round it. The houses were of a reasonable size, too, three storeys plus semi-basement, though narrow. They were provided at first with cesspits: a report published in 1854 noted that the death rate fell from fifty-five to thirteen per 1,000 when the houses were connected to good sewers.

Despite its unpromising location close to Waterloo Station, with the raucous market to the north and poor streets hemming it in on the other three sides, it remained largely residential and reasonably respectable throughout the nineteenth century. In 1899 Charles Booth's assistant classed it as fairly comfortable: 'a small neglected square, grass and trees, no flowers in the centre. One takes a house and lets off. Talleymen going the rounds.'

There was a decline in the twentieth century and the whole area had been set down for slum clearance even before Second World War bombing did considerable damage. Immediately afterwards what remained of the square was replaced by the Munro House council flats.

Few traces remain. In Lower Marsh the 'Lambeth Square' name used to be displayed on the old entrance between Nos 13 and 14, until those shops were rebuilt. This was the minor western entrance, originally called Colman's Place. The main entrance to the square no longer exists. The attractive garden courtyard of Munro House, in Murphy Street, is the modern successor to the Lambeth Square garden, but moved slightly to the south and with no access from Lower Marsh.

Lancaster Gate

See The Square, Upper Hyde Park Gardens

Lansdowne Square

Lansdowne Square was an unrealised scheme on the Ladbroke estate at Notting Hill. See Ladbroke Square.

Leavis Square

Leavis Square was part of the intense late eighteenth-century development of the Vauxhall riverfront, between Fore Street and Back Lane, when the gardens shown by Rocque in the 1740s were covered with courts, alleys and wharves. Before *Scrutiny*, Leavis was perhaps a less familiar name than now. It certainly gave trouble in Vauxhall. Lockie described this place in 1810 as 'Leaves-Court or Square, Fore-Street, Lambeth, – is between Free-court and Francis's Stone-yard, about ¼ of a mile on the L. from the church'. It was Leavis Square in 1841, but Leviss Square in 1851. The six houses were then occupied mainly by fishermen and labourers.

Fore Street was swept away with its many courts and alleys when the Albert Embankment was built between 1866 and 1870. The part of the road in front of the Riverbank Park Plaza passes directly over the site of the square.

Leicester Square

The history of Leicester Square has some similarity to that of Bloomsbury Square, but here the proprietor's house occupied the whole of the north side only briefly and he was certainly not without a son and heir, although at times he might have wished it. The development of the square was held up by a bitter dispute between the 2nd Earl of Leicester and his son Lord Lisle, later the 3rd Earl. The father bought the estate in two parts, in 1630 and 1648. The earlier purchase included most of the land on which Leicester Square was later developed, and at the northern edge of it the earl built Leicester House between 1631 and 1635. The open ground in front became known as Leicester Fields.

Leicester House, Leicester Square, in the middle of the eighteenth century.

The earl did not make much use of the house during the Civil War and Commonwealth, but soon after the Restoration, inspired no doubt by the development of Bloomsbury Square and St James's Square, he began to think of building on Leicester Fields. However, when he granted a lease in 1664, under which some houses were built on what became the western end of the south side, his son claimed that this was in breach of his marriage settlement and the dispute halted further action for six years.

In 1670 the earl obtained from Charles II a licence to lay out a square in Leicester Fields and a pardon for the houses already built without licence. The rest of the south side was then completed and the east and west sides built within a few years, according to very precise specifications laid down by the earl for the guidance of the various speculators. The plots were smaller and the houses less grand than most of those in Bloomsbury Square and St James's Square. The royal licence had called for a regular shape, but the pre-existing street pattern forced the nipping in of the east side. Leicester House and its garden occupied the whole of the north side until the 2nd Earl's death in 1677. Soon afterwards his son sacrificed most of the garden for further houses at the western end, built in the 1680s by Richard Frith, the developer of Soho Square. In the 1690s single-storey lock-up shops were built in front of the Leicester House courtyard, on either side of the gate, in Parisian fashion.

Leicester Square from the south in 1750.

The east side of Leicester Square from Leicester Place in 1813. The former Sans Souci Theatre on the left.

Because the parishioners had some residual rights over Leicester Fields, the centre remained open to all for a time and was enclosed only with rails and posts until the 1720s, when the 6th Earl began to charge his tenants for the upkeep of the garden and fence. When the fashion for planting gardens in a more elaborate manner arose, Leicester Square shared in the movement in 1737. A large pond was intended to be the main feature, but in 1748 an equestrian statue of George I was erected in the centre instead. This came from Cannons, the house of the Duke of Chandos, which was soon to be demolished.

When not being used by its owners Leicester House had a unique succession of royal tenants.

The Queen of Bohemia, Charles I's sister, died there in 1662, Prince Eugene was lodged in the house during his visit to London in 1712, and the unhappy family life of the Hanoverians made it the 'pouting place of princes' for much of the eighteenth century, as each heir to the throne quarrelled with the king.

George, Prince of Wales, lived here from 1718 until his accession in 1727. His son, Frederick, Prince of Wales, sulked and plotted here from 1742 until his death in 1751. The erection of the statue of George I was probably his calculated insult. Leicester House remained the home of Frederick's son, the future George III, until he succeeded in 1760, and then of his mother, the Princess of Wales, who held court there in as much state as the king at St James's.

Leicester Fields gradually became Leicester Square during the eighteenth century, the names competing over a long period. Leicester Square appeared as early as the Edward Hatton map of 1707 and in his text of 1708 he called it 'Leicester square (by some called Leicester fields)'. It had a number of aristocratic residents in its early days and retained a few through-out the eighteenth century, but the royal presence tended if anything to depress its status. Placemen and officials would not wish to be associated with the factious court, and many houses were required by the servants of the Princes of Wales, or by tradesmen and artists keen to offer their services.

The most eminent statesmen associated with the square lived there before and after the pouting period: Lord Chancellor Somers at No. 28 from 1701 until his death in 1716, and Henry Dundas, Pitt's right-hand man, at No. 25 from 1783 to 1785. Matthew Prior, who was a politician as well as a poet, lived at No. 21 in 1699–1700.

From its earliest days Leicester Square was popular with artists, great and small. The great included William Hogarth at No. 30 from 1733, Sir Joshua Reynolds at No. 47 from 1760, the architect James ('Athenian') Stuart at No. 35 on the south side from 1766 – all three until their deaths – and John Singleton Copley at No. 28 from 1776 until 1783. Sir Thomas Lawrence began his assault on London at No. 4 in 1787, when Reynolds was still living within sight of his windows. He settled for a year in 'a suite of handsome apartments, the house being occupied by a confectioner'. The rooms cost him 4 guineas a week. While there, 'he opened a public exhibition of his works, his father performing the office of exhibitor'. The small artists included the French portrait painter, Théodore Gardelle, who murdered his landlady at No. 37 in 1761 and tried to dispose of the body piecemeal.

Leicester Square was also occupied by many physicians and surgeons. The most eminent was John Hunter, who lived at No. 28 on the east side from 1783 until his death in 1793. He made many alterations and additions to the house to accommodate his collections, the museum he built in the garden stretching back to Castle Street, the forerunner of Charing Cross Road.

After 1800 the square was increasingly deserted by society and one by one the houses were converted to shops, hotels, or places of entertainment. The hotels, mostly on the east side, often had foreign proprietors and contributed to the distinctly cosmopolitan and dubious atmosphere of the square. Dickens described 'the tributary channels of Leicester Square' on a wintry morning in *Bleak House*: 'Behind dingy blinds and curtains, in upper storey and garret, skulking more or less under false names, false hair, false titles, false jewellery, and false histories, a colony of brigands lie in their first sleep.'

Ownership was fragmented after the Leicester title became extinct, and the garden began to be neglected. In 1817, when half the houses were in commercial use, David Ricardo nearly obtained permission to build a Benthamite school in the centre; he was eventually frustrated by opposition from the shopkeepers, already a more powerful lobby than the private residents.

With only narrow and intricate exits at three of the corners, Leicester Square was very quiet and free from traffic until the 1840s, when New Coventry Street was formed and Cranbourn Street widened, creating a major through road on the north side. By then, only seven or eight houses on the west side remained in private occupation.

More serious threats of building over the garden arose at that time, and from 1851 to 1862 almost the whole of the centre was occupied by James Wyld's Great Globe, which in form was a forerunner of the Albert Hall. It was used for exhibitions. After the Globe was removed and the battered statue of

Leicester Square from the south-east in 1921.

George I reinstated, the square fell into a disgraceful state. It was again under threat of building until rescued, redesigned and presented to the public in 1874 by the shady financier Baron Grant.

The transformation of Leicester Square into London's leading entertainment centre had begun in 1774, when Sir Ashton Lever took a lease of Leicester House for the display of his huge collection of natural curiosities, many of them associated with Captain Cook's voyages. The 'Holophusikon', as he called the show, remained there until 1788.

When Leicester House was demolished in 1791–92 the future of the square might have taken quite a different course if a plan to build a magnificent opera

The Empire, built on the site of Savile House, was opened in 1884. Daly's, in Cranbourne Street just off the north-east corner, was built in 1893.

Venues for entertainment and pleasure proliferated in the late nineteenth and early twentieth centuries. In addition to the theatres and hotels there were restaurants, oyster rooms, clubs and Turkish baths. The Leicester Galleries, the chief showcase for modern art in London, opened in 1902 at No. 20 Green Street, now Irving Street, just off the south-east corner. The Leicester Square Hall, part of the premises of Thurston & Co. the billiard table makers at Nos 45 and 46, was the main venue for professional snooker in the 1930s and the 1950s. Compton Mackenzie presented the world championship trophy there in 1939:

> I look back to that evening in Leicester Square with a sigh for what was, and is no more. Sir Joshua Reynolds's studio is gone; the Alhambra is gone; Thurston's Hall is gone. In memory I am sitting again with various Savilians on that tier of comfortable seats rising above the green cloth at which Joe Davis, the supreme snooker player of all time, is bewitching us with his artistry.

Cinemas replaced the theatres between the wars: the Empire on the north side was built in 1927, the Leicester Square Theatre on the south side (now demolished) in 1930 and the Odeon on the east side, on the site of the Alhambra, in 1937.

In addition to all these palaces of pleasure and the many shops and offices there were several hospitals and schools in the square. The biggest of the offices was Fanum House, the headquarters of the Automobile Association, which began fairly modestly in 1923 but extended in stages to occupy the whole of the west side by 1959. As a result of all these changes, only one building survives from the early domestic days of the square: No. 22 on the east side, sheltering bizarrely below the great black tower of the Odeon.

There has been much tinkering with the centre of the square since the Second World War. First there was a wish to exploit the serious bomb damage between Leicester Square and Trafalgar Square to create a visual link, but the National Gallery extension made much better use of the gap.

house along the whole of the north side had been carried out. Instead, the old and new buildings there became a miscellany of shops and entertainments, including the panorama set up at No. 16 in 1793 by the Barkers of West Square, Miss Linwood's gallery of needlework pictures at Savile House, which adjoined Leicester House, and Charles Dibdin's Sans Souci Theatre in Leicester Place, where he gave his entertainments from 1796 to 1804. It was the forerunner of the huge theatres – the Alhambra, the Empire and Daly's – that dominated the square until the 1920s. The Alhambra took over the building of the Royal Panopticon of Science and Art, an uneasy alliance of instruction and entertainment, rather like the Crystal Palace, that lasted only from 1854 to 1856.

The GLC first considered a pedestrianisation scheme for Leicester Square in 1976 and it was partially implemented when the layout of the garden was re-planned about 1990. In 2010–12 the garden was altered again to leave ample space for the chief modern function of the square, as a screaming place for teenage girls.

Leinster Square

BAYSWATER [WESTMINSTER]

This was one of the series of very similar back-to-front squares in Paddington and Notting Hill with which the builder and developer George Tippett helped to discredit the name and form. At Leinster Square some at least of the houses on the south and west sides were designed by George Wyatt, one of the last of an extraordinarily prolific architectural dynasty.

They were built between 1856 and 1859. *Building News* reported that some were complete and ready for occupation in September 1857, and praised Wyatt's design of the houses on the west side, where the front of each had a 'segmental curve across its entire elevation', by which plan 'the windows command a view obliquely on each side as well as in front'. This was just what William Weir had censured in Montagu Square in 1843.

Numbers 1–6 on the north side of Leinster Square were designed by William Willmer Pocock of Trevor Terrace, Knightsbridge (the architect of Ovington Square and the son of the architect of Trevor Square), and others by Tippett himself. He financed his many developments by borrowing heavily from insurance companies and inevitably ended as a bankrupt.

The fashionable world increasingly lost interest in Bayswater as the tide of development washed further and further from Hyde Park, with the result that the celebrities of Leinster Square are literary. When the eccentric philosopher Herbert Spencer lived in a boarding house near Lancaster Gate, he had a room in Leinster Square to which he came for three hours every morning to read and write. He was a friend of the controversial novelist and journalist – the first professional female journalist in England – Mrs E. Lynn Linton, who lived at No. 27 during the early years of her disastrous marriage. The Lintons settled there in a new house in 1858. She hoped to form a salon, in pursuit of her social and literary ambitions, and spent all her savings on

The north side of Leinster Square, *c.* 1904.

furnishings and hospitality. Her much older husband, the socialist engraver and poet William Linton, hated the life. 'Sitting with his friend Mr W.E. Adams in the smallest room in the big house, he had said, "All I want is this little room – the rest is a worry and an encumbrance".' He was delighted when the money ran out and they had to move to Hampstead Heath in 1862.

W.H. Hudson and his wife ran a struggling boarding house at No. 11 Leinster Square in the 1870s and 1880s, long before his books began to achieve success at the end of the century.

In 1899 the Booth survey found Leinster Square better than Powis Square, but had this general observation:

> The notable features are … the deterioration of the squares in the north, Leinster, Princes, and Kensington Gardens Square. The prevailing type of these is the heavy fronted four to five floored dwelling, which estate agents delight to term a 'mansion' or 'desirable residence'. Many are to let and they are gradually being converted into flats.

That trend continued and there are now many hotels. The best part of the square is Wyatt's west side where the two groups of bow-fronted houses flank a grand palace front. The weaknesses, as with all Tippett's developments, are the mean strip of garden and the ugly street fronts of the back-to-front houses.

Leonard Square

OLD STREET [HACKNEY]

Leonard Square was the old name for the opening at the junction of Leonard Street and Paul Street. Those roads run east–west and north–south, and the four short sides of the square were set obliquely between them, north–east, north–west, etc. When originally built in the 1790s, the northern half before the south, there were two or three houses on each side. The 1813 edition of Horwood's map mistakenly attached the Leonard Square name to Tabernacle Square, the next opening to the north, and left the real Leonard Square anonymous.

The former Leonard Square in Paul Street, seen from the west in 2013 with Victoria House in the background.

The houses were at first residential, at least in part, but had become entirely commercial by the middle of the nineteenth century, with a miscellany of shops, pubs and small factories. For a century from the 1860s the south-eastern side was dominated by institutions connected with the vigorous Anglo-Catholic church of St Michael in Mark Street: first its school, set back behind a playground, and later the convent, built directly on the square. As the old houses were replaced by larger factories and warehouses with entrances in Paul Street or Leonard Street, the Leonard Square name passed out of use in the 1880s.

During the Second World War there was serious bomb damage to the north-west and south-west sides, which are now occupied by large offices built with no relation to the square. The site of the convent and school is now an untidy car park, so only the old warehouse on the north-east side still indicates the original building line. It is called Victoria House. The centre now boasts a one-way roundabout and, if not a garden, at least a paved area with seats, a tree or two and a strange sculpture in the form of a huge typewriter ribbon.

Leonard Square

See also Tabernacle Square

Leyton Square

PECKHAM [SOUTHWARK]

The oblique angle at which the Surrey Canal struck westwards from the Old Kent Road created problems for the landowners when they came to lay out streets over the market gardens on either side. To the north of the canal the new streets had to break to the left soon after leaving the Old Kent Road, and to the south they had to break to the right soon after branching from Peckham Park Road.

It was this necessity that determined the curious form of Maismore Square (afterwards known as Leyton Square) when it was built between Peckham Park Road and the canal in the 1830s. It had two entrances from Peckham Park Road, the northern one very short, the other (now Maismore Street) necessarily longer and with houses on both sides. These two roads turned forty-five degrees to the right, and that was where the real square began, with a large private garden in the centre and a continuous terrace of substantial houses on the east, west and north sides. The fifteen on the west side were particularly good, with large private gardens and fields behind.

It was a remarkably ambitious plan for this area, as ambitious as the nearby Surrey Square and even more ill-judged. The extra experience of thirty years should have convinced the developer that a luxury square was not a good long-term investment in this part of south London. Things went smoothly until 1870, but after that mean streets crowded in from the south, east and west, and the canal attracted industry to the north side of the square, with a tannery and other factories, a timber yard and a wharf. Another

Maismore Street, formerly part of Leyton Square, in 2013.

timber yard took the place of the long gardens of the western terrace. A declining reputation perhaps explains the change of name to Leyton Square in 1881.

Charles Booth's researcher made an interesting report in 1899:

> Houses generally eight rooms and scullery. An occupier I spoke to was paying 15/-. Two families the rule, and some extra sub-letting. Improved, the great trouble now being the noise and disorder of larrikins who come and play in the square. This is soon to be laid out as an open space by the vestry.

In 1901 he added a note that the garden was 'now open'. It had been bought by Camberwell Council for £3,000, half contributed by the LCC.

The south-east corner was the worst part of the square: 'Opposite this bit a small row of houses has been built, very shoddy and rapidly deteriorating'. This was on the short approach road, where a small part of the garden had been stolen to build this terrace of five houses.

Every house in the square was seriously damaged during the Second World War, the *coup de grâce* being a V1 in the north-east corner. The wreckage was cleared and the Friary Estate – five-storey blocks of flats – was built around the garden in the 1950s. The short approach road survived until about 1960 as access to the factory that had grown out of the shoddy terrace. The garden remains a public park, enlarged by the removal of the factory and the houses at the Peckham Park Road end.

Lime Street Square

CITY OF LONDON

Lime Street Square was behind the east side of Lime Street, where its main entrance lay, but it could also be reached via Billiter Court, off the north-west corner of its neighbour, Billiter Square.

Lime Street Square is not heard of until 1732, but in this passage from Strype's 1720 revision of Stow, perhaps written well before 1720, the 'new court' mentioned may be its beginning:

And in this Part is Axe Yard, which is but indifferent, Lime Street Alley, by some called Billiter Alley, as leading into Billiter Square, and through that Square East into Billiter Lane. Betwixt this Alley and Axe Yard is a new Court built out of some Houses pulled down.

The most important houses in Lime Street Square were in a terrace of four or five on the east side, but there were at least four more in the entrance passage from Lime Street. Although it was scarcely wider than Billiter Square, it was half the length and largely enclosed at both ends, which gave it more the appearance and atmosphere of a square. That changed in the late 1870s, when two new streets broke into it, greatly reducing its seclusion. Fenchurch Avenue entered at the south end, replacing Billiter Court, and Billiter Avenue made an entirely new opening in the middle of the east side.

Lime Street Square had not been residential since the eighteenth century and the new streets made no difference to the type of business that was carried on there: merchants, ship brokers, solicitors and the odd architect were established in the square before and after the changes of the 1870s, but gradually the old houses gave way to larger offices. They were destroyed by bombing in 1941, and after the war an entirely new street pattern, involving the extinction of Lime Street Square, was imposed for the convenience of the 1950s Lloyds of London. That in its turn has now been replaced by the Willis Building, completed in 2008.

Lincoln's Inn Fields

HOLBORN [CAMDEN AND WESTMINSTER]

Lincoln's Inn Fields has only occasionally been given 'Square' as part of its name – Edward Hatton called it 'Lincolns inn square' in 1707 and William Maitland 'Lincoln's Inn fields Square' in 1756 – but it was 'the largest and most beautiful square in London, if not in Europe', as Hughson wrote in 1817. It cannot be ignored here, as London's second square, preceded only by Covent Garden, and the first to approach the classic form.

Being well aware of the eagerness of James I to grasp at any source of revenue, the lawyers became nervous about the future of Lincoln's Inn Fields, the royal pasture land that they had come to think of as their own. Besides its use as a place for exercise, it was an invaluable buffer against the growing and noisome suburb of St Giles. In 1617, in the hope of preventing building on the fields, the Inns of Court and the officers of the adjoining parishes presented a petition to the king urging him to follow the recent precedent of Moorfields and have Lincoln's Inn Fields laid out and planted as a public recreation ground. James was pleased with the idea, especially as a means of impressing ambassadors and other visiting foreigners, and in 1618 Inigo Jones was instructed to prepare a plan of the proposed walks. No action followed, probably because the subscription set on foot failed to raise enough money to pay for the works.

In 1636 a courtier named William Newton, who had acquired the leases of the two principal fields, petitioned Charles I – as short of money as his father – for leave to build fourteen large houses on the west side, and in 1638 he sought permission for thirty-two houses. The prospect of a greatly increased revenue was too tempting to refuse. The licences were promptly granted and Newton began to build immediately.

The gentlemen of Lincoln's Inn responded with petitions to the king and queen, negotiations with Newton, complaints to Parliament once it was sitting again, and even by direct action.

Lindsey House, Nos 59 and 60 Lincoln's Inn Fields, c. 1910.

More effective than any of these in saving the fields was Newton's own plan. He had evidently been inspired by the recent success of Covent Garden – where he had dabbled himself – and was anxious to preserve the greater part of the open space as a means of attracting builders and tenants to an estate of the highest quality. A 1641 licence for a plot on the south side had specified that the land in front should be left 'in an open square, much alike that in Covent Garden'. By the time of his death in 1643, Newton had built or arranged for the building of most of the west side and part of the south.

Whether a single architect was responsible for the plan of the square, or for the design of the early houses, has been much argued over since the early eighteenth century. Lindsey House, now the only surviving original building, was attributed to Inigo Jones on stylistic grounds, and knowledge of his involvement in the abortive commission of 1618 led many to regard Jones as the man chiefly responsible for the whole development. In fact, the commission is the only document linking Jones with Lincoln's Inn Fields and modern opinion inclines to the view that the builders of the various houses, or their clients, chose their own architects with very little supervision from Newton or the king, beyond a general desire that the houses should be large and of good quality. Even Lindsey House is not now firmly attributed to Inigo Jones. Howard Colvin was inclined to favour the claims of Nicholas Stone, Jones's friend and associate.

The Civil Wars put an end to work at Lincoln's Inn Fields for ten years, but in 1653 Newton's brother sold the west end of the north side to Arthur Newman, who built the houses known as Newman's Row. The south side was Portugal Row, from the residence there of the Portuguese ambassador, the west side Arch Row from an archway beneath two of the houses. The garden of Lincoln's Inn occupied the whole of the east side.

In 1657 an agreement was made to continue the north and south sides in a manner acceptable to Lincoln's Inn, and a year or two later the filling of the last gap on the west side completed the square. On 19 August 1661 the Dutch artist William Schellinks noted in his journal:

From [Smithfield] we went to Lincoln's Fields, a large square lying behind Lincoln College, where law students are taught. Round this square are many fine palace-like houses, all with forecourts behind high walls; one can count there seventy entrances with stone pillars and double doors and many of the nobility live there. The Protector Cromwell had a row of new houses built there and established a place of execution in the square.

His seventy entrances was barely an exaggeration: Horwood showed sixty-four houses in the 1790s, and there were sixty-eight in the London directory of 1843.

The agreement of 1657, which transferred the freehold of the eastern half of the open space (Cup Field) to Lincoln's Inn, arranged for its laying out as a pleasure ground with trees and gravel walks. The western end, Purse Field, which was controlled by the occupants of the houses, was left as a much less formal open space, available for the exercise of troops, for bonfires, puppet plays, rope dancing, public executions and various other entertainments. It also became a rubbish tip and a useful lurking place for footpads.

The builders of the eastern houses, who held a 900-year lease of Cup Field from Lincoln's Inn, had great trouble in maintaining the distinction between their more formal half of the open space and the disorderly west, which was one of the Londoners' favourite spots for a riot. In 1693, in his *Guide de Londres*, Colsoni described it as '*une belle grande place, où pour la plus part du tems les Bateleurs et Charlatans sont en action*'. No wonder the lawyers were unhappy, if the development of Lincoln's Inn Fields had brought jugglers, quacks and mountebanks to their gates: they had a monopoly to defend.

Two finishing touches remained. In 1657 Bulstrode Whitelocke noted in his diary that he had 'by the desire of the E. of Clare furthered a Bill for a Market in Lincolns Inne fields'. Clare Market, south-west of the square, declined into a slum in the nineteenth century but was a food market of a high standard in its early days. The Lincoln's Inn Fields Theatre was not in the square but in Portugal Street, behind Portugal Row on the south side. There was an entrance from the Fields via a passage through No. 37. It opened in 1661 and during a chequered career saw the first performances of *The Provok'd Wife*, *The Way of the World* and *The Beggar's Opera*. The rear of the Royal College of Surgeons now covers the site of the theatre, or theatres rather, as it was several times rebuilt.

As Schellinks reported in 1661, the early tenants of the houses, especially the bigger ones on the west and south sides, included many peers. The greatest was Lord Halifax, 'the Trimmer', who lived at Carlisle House (on the site of the present Newcastle House) from 1653 to 1659 and from 1662 to 1672.

The opening of the theatre added a new element. After becoming Charles II's mistress, the actress Nell Gwyn lived at the old house on the site of Nos 57 and 58 from 1669 to 1671; her son, later Duke of St Albans, was born there in 1670. From 1670 the 2nd Earl of Rochester lived at Arbor House on the south side, next to the theatre entrance, and devoted himself to plays, prologues and affairs with actresses. Another poetical peer, the 6th Earl of Dorset, a former lover of Nell Gwyn – her 'Charles the first' – lived at Lindsey House for the first few years of the eighteenth century.

Edward Hatton gave an unusually full and enthusiastic description in 1708:

> Lincolns inn square (or the great Field) is reckon'd one of the finest and largest Squares in the World. It has on the northerly side Holbourn Row, south Portugal Row east Lincolns inn Walks, i.e. the strong Wall that supports a fine Terrace Walk, and westward the Arch Row. It is a Trapezium (tho' near a Square) whose Area is upwards of 10 acres, mostly Inhabited by Eminent Gentry and some Nobility.

In 1725 César de Saussure noted 'some fine mansions, those belonging to the Duke of Ancaster and to the Duke of Newcastle being particularly magnificent'.

After an unsuccessful attempt to improve the amenities in 1707, the inhabitants obtained a private act in 1734 that enabled them to enclose and plant the garden and restrict access to the residents only. Soane's key can be seen at his museum. A huge basin of water was made the centrepiece of the garden.

The speed with which the houses of the 1630s and 1640s were rebuilt is a proof that the square remained fashionable. In 1734 Ralph's comment was, 'Several of the original houses still remain to be a reproach to the rest'.

One of the earliest rebuildings was enforced. Carlisle House in the north-west corner, where Lord Halifax had lived, was burnt down in 1684, the family of Lord Powis just escaping, and rebuilt in something like its present form soon afterwards. Powis House was bought by the Duke of Newcastle, later prime minister, in 1705, and was his town house until his death in 1768. By that time fashion had migrated west and Lincoln's Inn Fields was falling into the hands of the lawyers.

Powis House itself had served as an official residence for lord keepers and lord chancellors before the duke bought it, and between 1705 and 1732 the combined Nos 51 and 52 were used for the same purpose. Nearly all the lord chancellors of the eighteenth century lived in the square at some point in their careers.

Other celebrated lawyers were Lord Mansfield, who lived at No. 56 from 1739 to 1756 and at Nos 57–58 from 1786 until 1793, and Sir William Blackstone, who was at No. 55 from 1768 until his death in 1780. Spencer Perceval, the square's second prime minister, lived there as a lawyer rather than a politician. He was at No. 59 from 1790 to 1808, adding No. 60 to it in 1803.

Lincoln's Inn Fields had a long association with Roman Catholicism, and in London that also meant a long history of rioting and destruction. The principal location was the chapel behind Nos 53 and 54, on the west side. It was established in 1688, as part of a Franciscan monastery, and sacked by the mob in the same year after the overthrow of James II. It was subsequently attached first to the Portuguese and then to the Sardinian Embassy. It was burnt down, apparently by accident, in 1759 and its replacement was nearly destroyed during the Gordon Riots in 1780.

The events of that year may have contributed to the change that came over the square in the second half of the eighteenth century. The artist Johann Zoffany lived at No. 43 in the 1760s and left without paying his rent. Sir John Soane, the architect, moved to No. 12 on the

Newcastle House, Lincoln's Inn Fields, in 1754.

north side in 1792 and gradually expanded into Nos 13 and 14, altering, enlarging and rebuilding until he had created the great museum that he left to the nation in 1837. An earlier institution is the Royal College of Surgeons on the south side. It moved to No. 41 in 1797, acquired No. 42 to house the Hunter Collection in 1803, and had the two houses rebuilt by George Dance the younger between 1806 and 1813. When No. 40 was added the college was rebuilt by Sir Charles Barry between 1834 and 1836, retaining the old portico, repositioned. An extension back to Portugal Street in 1855 replaced the old theatre. Finally, wings were added in 1888–89 on the sites of Nos 39 and 43.

Other non-domestic infiltrators of the early nineteenth century were the Insolvent Debtors' Court at No. 33, a family hotel at No. 34, the Society for the

Suppression of Vice at No. 57, the Society for the Diffusion of Useful Knowledge at No. 59 and the Society for the Promotion of Christian Knowledge at No. 67. There was even a nefarious proposal to build new law courts over the whole of the garden.

The great lawyers of the eighteenth century lived in complete houses, sometimes in two combined, but their successors in the high legal offices tended to follow fashion further west, abandoning Lincoln's Inn Fields to lesser men. Most of the houses were divided into chambers, 'and in those shrunken fragments of its greatness', as Dickens put it, 'lawyers lie like maggots in nuts'. The square became 'those pleasant fields, where the sheep are all made into parchments, the goats into wigs, and the pasture into chaff'.

There were a few architects among the solicitors and barristers, and because there has long been a connection between literature and the law, there was also a sprinkling of writers: Robert Smith Surtees at No. 27, John Forster at No. 58 and James Spedding at No. 60, where Tennyson stayed with him in 1842 while correcting the proofs of his *Poems*, the work that made him famous. Thomas Campbell had chambers at No. 61 from 1838 to 1841, when he moved to Victoria Square.

As the number of family houses in the square declined, pressure grew on the trustees to permit the general public to enjoy the huge garden. Requests to give limited access to children and invalids grew during the 1870s and eventually Octavia Hill and others were permitted to organise strictly controlled visits by parties of poor children. The agitation for a wider opening rose to a crescendo in 1890, when the LCC was moved to seek compulsory purchase powers. They were refused by the House of Lords, but in 1894 the LCC was able to purchase the garden for £13,000. It was opened in 1895. Ramsay MacDonald, the square's third prime minister, who lived in a flat at No. 3 from 1896 to 1911, contributed the most striking feature to the garden: the memorial seat surmounted by a bronze group of his wife Margaret surrounded by children. She died in 1911 and the monument was erected in 1914.

The first decade of the twentieth century was the most destructive in the history of Lincoln's Inn Fields. The eastern end of the south side was demolished for the sake of the land registry, and the building of Kingsway sliced off the back premises (including the Sardinian Chapel) of all the houses on the west side. Half of them were demolished and those that

The College of Surgeons, Lincoln's Inn Fields, in 1829.

were saved by their architectural or historic associations were blighted by the huge offices built immediately behind them in Kingsway. The old houses that survived at the west end of the south side were sacrificed after the Second World War for the Cancer Research Fund building, eight storeys of glass.

The old parish boundary ran through the houses on the south side, but this was simplified in 1900, and now the south side is in Westminster, the rest in Camden.

Despite its twentieth-century disasters, Lincoln's Inn Fields is still the best square in London in which to spend a day filled with pleasure and instruction. There are architectural treasures on three sides: Lincoln's Inn on the east, ten or a dozen eighteenth-century houses on the north side, and on the west Lindsey House of 1639–41, the much-altered Newcastle House of the 1680s and later, and Nos 57 and 58 of 1730. On the north and south sides there are the two museums, Soane's and the Hunterian. But above all, there is the garden, the biggest and one of the best in the London squares.

Lincoln's Inn Square

See New Square, Lincoln's Inn

Little College Square

CITY OF LONDON

Little College Square, so called to distinguish it from its larger neighbour College Square (q.v.), was the eastern of the two quadrangles at Doctors' Commons. It immediately adjoined the Bennett's Hill entrance, just south of Knightrider Street. Little College Square shared the fate of its big brother, being demolished soon after the society was dissolved in 1867. The eastern block of the Faraday Building is now on the site.

Little Haydon Square

CITY OF LONDON

Little Haydon Square was one of the names for the northern offshoot of Haydon Square (q.v.).

Little Louisa Square

HOXTON [HACKNEY]

Little Louisa Square, containing only two houses, was off the west side of the not much bigger Louisa Square (q.v.). It was demolished with Louisa Square in the 1920s.

Lloyd Square

CLERKENWELL [ISLINGTON]

John Booth, who was appointed surveyor to the Lloyd Baker estate in 1817 to plan its development, had many problems to overcome. With Lloyd Square at the top of the hill, these were the reservoirs and conduits of the New River Company. The scheme he prepared in 1819 circumvented these as far as possible and building began in the early 1820s with Nos 9 and 10 on the south side.

Their design has been generally ascribed to Booth's talented son and assistant, William Joseph Booth, who travelled in Greece and came home fired with enthusiasm for its architecture. The style is certainly expressive of youthful freshness and naivety.

One of the New River Company's conduits ran beside No. 10 and the curiously-shaped house now numbered 12 was built to the east of it soon after 9 and 10. When the conduit was later removed the quaint No. 11 filled the gap. After the building of the first three houses the 1820s financial crisis brought the development to a halt and it did not resume until 1830. The men who then came forward wished to build more houses than the original plan had called for, so John Booth adapted the design for Nos 9 and 10 to serve for houses of two instead of three bays. This modified plan was used for the rest of the south side. The square was then completed in a rush between 1830 and 1832.

The man who contracted for the north and west sides was the architect James Blackburn, who was later transported to Tasmania for forgery, and had a successful career there. The houses he built in Lloyd Square were a faithful copy of the style established by the south side. It was Blackburn who laid out the garden.

The tapering of the square meant that there were only two houses, the original Nos 12 and 13, on the east side. They were demolished to make way for an Anglican convent, built in 1881–82 for the Sisters of the Order of Retreat, later known as the Sisters of Bethany. The architect was Ernest Newton. When the sisters moved to the seaside in 1962, the building was taken over by the YWCA, but it is now divided into flats.

Lloyd Square has only recently become fashionable, but it has been solidly respectable throughout its history, which is why the garden is one of the very few in North London that is still private. The celebrities of the square have been artists. Linley Sambourne, who was born at No. 15 in 1844, is best known for the thousands of drawings he contributed to *Punch* between 1867 and his death in 1910. He succeeded Tenniel as the chief cartoonist of the magazine. Sidney Paget, the classic illustrator of *Sherlock Holmes*, grew up at No. 19, and Henry Mee the portrait painter has lived more recently at No. 14.

Blocks of flats have been built just off the square on its two western approach roads in wildly contrasting styles, defiant modernity and respectful pastiche, but the square itself is delightful. The unusual houses are perfectly preserved, the garden is an excellent blend of mature trees, lawn, shrubbery and encircling hedge,

and the slope of the ground adds excitement, as it always does in a square. John Arlott would probably not have agreed that a finely framed view of the Post Office Tower is one of the attractions.

Lock Square

WALWORTH [SOUTHWARK]

Lock Square was built about 1790, during a period of rapid development in the part of Walworth known as Lock's Fields. It had only two numbered sides, terraces of eight houses on the south and west, with a triangular garden in front. The west side was originally called Lock's Row, the south Lock Place, but Lock Square was supplanting them by 1841. The north side was formed by York Street, now Browning Street, the west by the curving Queen Street, the curve dictating the triangular shape of the garden. Queen Street is now quite straight and dull at this northern end, but in compensation has acquired the ornate name of King and Queen Street.

In 1861 the fifteen houses of Lock Square were occupied largely by men engaged in the building trades. There was a beer-shop, the Green Man, between Nos 1 and 2. Charles Booth's assistant, visiting in 1899, found the square poor, with the slightly larger houses

The south side of Lloyd Square in 1906, or a little earlier, with the tower of St Mark's, Myddelton Square, in the distance.

of the west side a little better than those on the south: 'The square in front [the garden] is boarded round and used as a yard by a carman and contractor; used to be Locks Fields. The west side, made by the east side of King and Queen Street, is better.'

The area was cleared between the wars and replaced by an estate of the standard LCC flats of the period, but the garden remained an open space, now used as a playground and all-weather games court.

London Bridge Square

[CITY OF LONDON]

London Bridge Square was a feature of the old London Bridge for about seventy-five years until the houses were demolished and the bridge widened between 1760 and 1763, one of the first of London's many sacrifices to the idol 'Traffic'. The square was the open space slightly nearer to the north than the south bank, shown between the 'N' of London and the 'B' of Bridge on Rocque's map of the 1740s. This was immediately to the north of the former chapel of St Thomas, by that time converted into houses and shops.

There had been houses on the stone bridge from soon after its completion early in the thirteenth century. They were frequently destroyed by fire, and after the Great Fire of 1666 the section that became the square remained open until the 1680s. When it was rebuilt, the name of London Bridge Square may not have been applied to it immediately: the first reference noted by Harben was in 1732.

The narrow roadway ran across the centre of the square, with shops flanking it on the north and south sides. The east and west were open to the river. The shops had prominent signs hanging outside. A trade card survives for 'John Grant, Brush Maker, And late Partner with Mr John Thomas decea'd, Son of the late Mrs Ann Pitham, At the Four Brushes, the Corner of the Square, London Bridge'. When his shop, with the others in the square, was demolished in 1760, Grant moved his business to Leadenhall Street.

Long Alley Square

See Christopher Square

Lonsdale Square

BARNSBURY [ISLINGTON]

In line with the other Barnsbury landowners, the Drapers' Company made plans to develop their estate in the 1820s, but there was a slump, and the local builders and speculators willing to gamble were spoilt for choice. As a result, it was not until the late 1830s that progress was made. Two brothers, Richard and Thomas Carpenter, in partnership as cattlemen, leased the land for grazing during the 1830s. In 1839 Richard Carpenter, who had branched into property development, took a building lease. The Drapers' Company envisaged the typical late classical square of the time, but what they got was very different, indeed extraordinary and unique.

This is the best preserved of the Jacobethan squares – it has been called Tudor-Gothic – but the rigid uniformity of the design, though seemingly appropriate to a square, is at odds with the spirit of this architectural style when displayed in such formidable terraces. The detached houses and pairs of De Beauvoir Square and Lyndhurst Square carry the Tudor banner more effectively. Mary Cosh has suggested that the contemporary popularity of the style for the almshouses of City companies was the reason for its use here on the Drapers' estate. The architect, not surprisingly, was Richard Cromwell Carpenter, otherwise noted almost entirely for his scholarly Gothic churches. He was the son of the developer, here receiving his first major commission.

Lonsdale Square was built between 1840 and 1845. It appeared as 'New Square, Liverpool Road' in the 1841 census, when the first nine houses were being built. When the leases of five houses were auctioned in August 1843, four of them were already occupied and the permanent name was established. They were described as:

… Five elegant residences, designed in the Elizabethan style, and decorated in a very expensive manner; the situation of this property is the highest in a locality which has always maintained the first character for the salubrity of the air. Nos 13, 14, 19, and 21 are let to highly respectable tenants at rents amounting to £270, and No. 22 is in hand; each house is held for seventy years at a ground rent of £10. The house in hand may be viewed daily.

For once the tenants were as respectable as the auction-eers boasted. One of the first was the deputy cashier of the Bank of England, and others were clergymen, pub-lishers, barristers and architects. Richard Carpenter, the developer, lived at No. 24. One of the few celebri-ties was the writer G.R. Sims, formerly of Addington Square, who lived at No. 30 in 1878–79.

Among the many unusual features of Lonsdale Square is the fact that there are only two entrances, at the middle of the north and south sides. This left the architect to deal with four awkward corner plots. His solution for three of them was to build bigger houses with only deeply recessed front doors and two narrow windows onto the square. The life of these houses was all turned to the large gardens behind, from which their light was derived. Number 5, the big house at the south-east corner, was the first in the square to fall into commercial use when a factory was built over the garden in the 1860s. The large garden at the south-west corner was enjoyed by one of the orthodox houses flanking it until it was built over about 1970.

Lonsdale Square remained respectable longer than most in Islington, but declined in the early twentieth century as the houses were divided into flats. It has recovered in spectacular style in recent decades. There

was a good deal of blast damage during the Second World War but everything has now been beautifully restored. The garden remained private until the 1960s, longer than the others in the area, and even now the gates are so hard to open that a good imitation of privacy is achieved.

Lorrimore Square

WALWORTH [SOUTHWARK]

Lorrimore Square is a dispiriting place to visit even on a sunny day. In the rain it must be desolate. The builder was perhaps William Cook, who was listed in the square in the 1856 directory, which showed only seven other residents.

The original 1850s houses can never have been objects of much beauty. One terrace of them survives on the south side but it has been municipalised on conversion into flats and is disfigured by most unsympathetic street lamps. The modern flats on the east, north and west sides (part of the Brandon Estate) respect the scale of the original houses, but have no more positive virtue. The east side had no houses in the original layout, just Manor Road leading directly to the church.

The east side of Lonsdale Square, *c.* 1905.

The early residents were clerks and commercial travellers, with the odd merchant or solicitor. The celebrity was the journalist, historian and novelist, Justin McCarthy, who was the tenant of No. 28 from 1861 to 1864. He was not a prophet in his own parish, where he appears in the ratebooks as 'Justice'.

The Booth survey found the square declining in 1899: 'Parsonage with rather ill-kept garden and churchyard in the middle. 3½ storey, south side better than north or west. A few servants on south.' Beresford Chancellor wrote in 1907:

> Lorrimore Square was once a favourite residential quarter, but to-day it is a poor neighbourhood, and it is, perhaps, only by its superior size and the presence of a church in its central garden that it is enabled to take precedence of the neighbouring Sutherland Square and the little Alpha Square with its odd blocks of buildings.

The houses were in a state of progressive decay, and in June 1931 there was a dramatic incident when the parapets of several collapsed, carrying the front steps with them into the areas and coal cellars.

There was general blast damage to the square during the Second World War and two houses were lost on the north side. The only other building destroyed was Henry Jarvis's St Paul's Church of 1856, which occupied the eastern end of the garden with the vicarage taking the west. It was ritualistic in its early days and Chancellor claimed that the first modern harvest festival in London was celebrated there.

The church and vicarage were rebuilt between 1955 and 1960, uncompromisingly in the style of that period. The new St Paul's looks like Cape Canaveral, with several satellites about to be launched. The children's playground beside the church leaves only a small part of the garden as a public open space.

Louisa Square

HOXTON [HACKNEY]

The alliterative instinct would lead one to say 'little Louisa Square' as it could boast only six houses, were it not for the fact that it had an even smaller offshoot with two more that really *was* called Little Louisa

St Paul's, Lorrimore Square, and the vicarage, in 1909 or a little earlier.

Square. They formed a group with Whitmore Square and Harland Square, west of the Kingsland Road and south of the Regent's Canal. Louisa Square was a wedge-shaped court with four houses on the south side and two on the west. It was built in the 1840s, south of Phillipp Street, running back halfway to Hoxton Street.

An LCC slum clearance drive removed Louisa Square and many of its neighbours in the 1920s. They were replaced by the familiar balcony entrance flats of the period, of which Catherine House is a surviving example. Both the name and the form of the square are remembered in Phillipp Street. On its site there is a pleasant courtyard between Catherine House and the modern Bow House flats, with a shady tree and a flower bed at the entrance, and on the other side of the road there is a better than average modern block called Louisa House.

Love Lane Square

RATCLIFFE [TOWER HAMLETS]

Love Lane Square was a short cul-de-sac off the east side of Love Lane, now Brodlove Lane. Facing it on the west side was Elm Row (now Elf Row) where Peabody Square, Shadwell, still stands.

Love Lane Square was far less substantial, with only three houses in a terrace on the north side. It was cut off short by the back of an iron foundry in Glasshouse Fields. Love Lane Square was the name from the 1860s until the foundry was extended over it early in the twentieth century, but the houses had existed since about 1820. In 1861 the place had the more honest name of Love Lane Gap. Dull modern flats now cover the site of the square and the foundry.

Lower Square

ISLEWORTH [HOUNSLOW]

Lower Square is almost certainly identical with Isleworth Green, where a Church House was built about 1528 on waste land granted by the lord of the manor, thus reducing the open space to something like its present size. This building is thought to have developed into the Town House or Court House, where a charity school was established soon after 1630. It was the ancestor of the Blue School, the 1841–42

Lower Square, Isleworth, looking north-east from Swan Street, c. 1910.

building which still dominates the square, by quality if not by size, although it has not been used by the school since 1939.

The square was the centre of village life. On gala days the children were treated in the school room, or the 'piazza' under it, to roast beef, plum pudding and good ale, and the senior parishioners feasted at the Northumberland Arms on the duke's venison and champagne from Syon House. Until early in the twentieth century it was called just the Square. Apart from the Blue School it was mainly commercial, with several inns and beer-houses – the Northumberland Arms, the Bell, the Horse & Groom – and many of the village's best shops.

The centre of Isleworth suffered bomb damage during the Second World War and much of what remained was swept away afterwards in preparation for a 'comprehensive redevelopment' that was never thoroughly carried through. That left the way open for a 1980s scheme that was of much better quality than anything possible in the 1950s and 1960s, and more tactful in its handling of the architecture.

In Lower Square the principal buildings had survived the war and the clearances and were finely restored in the 1980s. It now consists essentially of four elements, one on each side: the old Blue School on the south, the former Northumberland Arms on the north, John Day House (long occupied by the principal doctors of the village) on the east and a modern shopping centre, small and pleasantly detailed, on the west. The cream-coloured school and the two white painted eighteenth-century buildings dominate the scene. The modern pastiche red brick buildings on either side of John Day House are set back behind it, so that they are hardly noticed.

The space is more like a true square, in shape and arrangement, than ever before. A major road used to cross it from Swan Street to Church Street, which meant that the west and north sides curved to merge with those roads. When the through road was abolished the west side was rebuilt at right angles to the school, so now only the north side is splayed. At the same time the centre was turned into a sunken paved area with trees and seats around the edge.

Lowndes Square

KNIGHTSBRIDGE [KENSINGTON AND CHELSEA, AND WESTMINSTER]

From the 1670s the site later occupied by Lowndes Square was one of the several pleasure resorts in London known as Spring Gardens. It was somewhat disreputable. Defoe had one of the lovers of Moll Flanders take her there for drinks, and in *Colonel Jack* some highwaymen rob a coach 'between the Park Gate and Knight's-bridge; there was in it, only a Gentleman and a Punk; a Whore that he had pick'd up, it seems at the Spring-Garden a little farther'.

Later in the eighteenth century it was known as Grove House, and it was there that Teresa Cornelys of Soho Square made her last stand in 1795 as a milk woman, before sinking into hopeless bankruptcy. Grove House then became a resort for the fashionable sport of archery, with the butts presumably at the south end of what is now the Lowndes Square garden. In its last years it became a builder's works.

The land had been in the possession of the Lowndes family since 1692, first as tenants of the Crown and later as freeholders. The owner from 1808, William Lowndes, was in such serious financial trouble that his trustees were anxious to turn the estate into money. They made their development plans in conjunction with the much larger Grosvenor estate, which was separated from the Lowndes land only by the Westbourne stream.

Lowndes Terrace was built on the Knightsbridge frontage (where the Sheraton Park Tower is now) in 1824–26. Thomas Cubitt took a lease of the remainder of the land in 1826, but his commitments in Belgravia and Pimlico meant that the building of Lowndes Square did not begin until 1836, on the east side, and was only completed late in the 1840s.

The north, east and west sides were much in the style of Eaton Square. The five houses on the south side were designed and built in 1837–39 by Lewis Cubitt, the architect brother of Thomas, 'with greater regard to architectural effect than anything which had up to then been attempted in London', according to Beresford Chancellor. A reporter for *The Surveyor* noted that 'at a very short distance, they appear as one magnificent palace', a deception despised by many later critics.

Number 1 was occupied in 1839, Nos 1–8 and 67–70 in 1840. Cubitt's name must have given confidence, for No. 1 was soon shared by two prominent members of parliament, John Leader of Westminster and Sir William Molesworth of Leeds. Success was assured, especially after Cubitt persuaded the government to authorise the making of Albert Gate for direct access to the park. Eighteen houses had been completed by 1843 and thirty-nine by 1846.

As the square filled up in the 1840s and 1850s it continued to be very popular with politicians (including Robert Lowe at No. 34) and also attracted many aristocrats. One was the Earl of Clare, for whom Cubitt built the great house of the square, No. 35, now the Pakistan High Commission, with its large garden in the south-west corner. The square was also popular with architects and engineers: Sir William Tite lived at No. 42, Sir John Rennie at No. 7 and Thomas Brassey (after whom Brassey Square is named) at No. 56.

Lowndes Square was very fine in the nineteenth century, but is now seriously diminished. Lewis Cubitt's 'palace' survives at the south end, but two-thirds of the houses on the long sides were replaced by luxury flats in the 1930s and the Sheraton Park Tower was built on the north side of the square, facing Knightsbridge, in 1970–73. The architects were Seifert & Partners. This Brobdingnagian municipal litter bin now dominates the square, but has not deterred some from spending huge fortunes on the few remaining houses.

Ludgate Square

This is not remotely like a square. At a pinch it might be called a crescent, but it is really just a curving lane. It is so narrow that I assumed it was

The south side of Lowndes Square, c. 1840.

The west side of Lowndes Square, c. 1904.

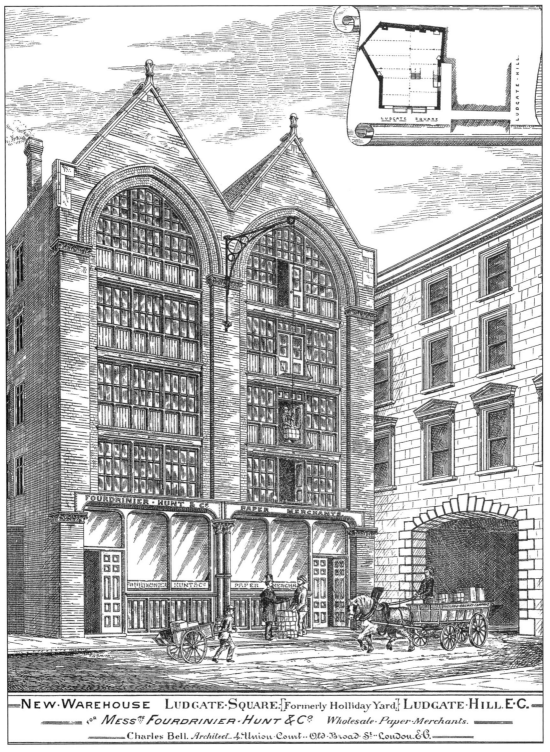

Charles Bell's design for No. 1 Ludgate Square, 1878.

a purely pedestrian one until a van turning out of Ludgate Hill nearly knocked me down when I was photographing there.

Maps from the seventeenth to the nineteenth century showed something much more like a square in this area, under the name of Holliday Court.

It was part of a complex of alleys and smaller yards that had two entrances from Creed Lane but none from Ludgate Hill.

At first the open space at the west end of the complex was the only large one, but during the eighteenth century another, closer to Carter Lane, outgrew it. That was still the situation in 1873, when the eastern court had about twelve houses, the western six. The name applied equally to both. Holliday Court or Yard was not much above the level of a slum and hardly ever figured in directories, but cutlers and tin men had premises there. We know from court records that in 1799 a thief kept 150 rabbits in a cellar at No. 22, which cannot have added to the amenities, and in 1873 the yard was the scene of a fatal brawl between two labourers.

In January 1878 *The Builder* published this paragraph about 'A New Square in the City':

A new business centre in the City is at present in course of formation in the immediate neighbourhood of Ludgate-hill. Ludgate-circus has recently been added to the last-named well-known thoroughfare, and now the locality is about to be still further distinguished by Ludgate-square. Some time ago the dilapidated blocks of buildings known as Holliday-yard, entered from Creed-lane, were demolished by the Ecclesiastical Commissioners as the owners, and the site so cleared has just been leased by the London and County Building Company, who are now laying it out for the erection of buildings of a mercantile character. The roadway through the square is being laid with blocks of wood pavement. Although nominally designated a square, the ground is angular in form, and the roadway curves in a south-easterly direction from the Ludgate-hill entrance towards Creed-lane, at the point which formed the old entrance to Holliday-yard. This approach will remain, there being two entrances to the square – the new one in Ludgate-hill, and the original approach from Creed-lane. The first block of buildings erected in the new square has just been completed. It has been built for Messrs. Fourdrinier, Hunt, & Co., the well-known paper manufacturers, at a cost of £5,500.

This first warehouse, designed by Charles Bell, was demolished around 1990, but its replacement is in a similar style. It stood next to the new entrance from Ludgate Hill, which was via an archway that did not align exactly with the road, introducing an awkward kink at this north end: the developers presumably had to take the best access they could get in this crowded and expensive district. Progress was slow, with Fourdrinier & Hunt the only firm listed in the new Ludgate Square in the 1882 directory. The other warehouses were built in that decade.

Later in the century, as might be expected in this area, the square was popular with printers, publishers and booksellers, but there were also mantle makers and other miscellaneous trades. The buildings have changed little to outward view in 130 years, but the north-east side is a 1980s rebuilding in a vaguely late Victorian idiom.

Lyndhurst Square

PECKHAM [SOUTHWARK]

The polite lady who told me the dates of all the houses in Lyndhurst Square hoped I had come to arrange for the replacement of the standard municipal street lighting with something more appropriate to the spirit of the place. The lamps and the deliberately ugly modern block of flats at the north-east corner (built at the expense of the one bombed house) are all that detract from the charm of this unexpected Peckham survival. It reminded me of Orme Square, although here the houses are in quite a different style, Lyndhurst being one of the small and distinguished band of London's Jacobethan squares. The lucky residents not only have the pleasure of the small communal garden, really just a decorative green, but private gardens too, most of them a good deal larger.

Dewhirst's Camberwell map of 1842 showed the square laid out and named, but with no houses. The original plan was for nine, two detached on both the north and west sides, with one detached and four semi-detached on the south. These houses were all the work of the same developer.

When the estate was auctioned in 1844 only three houses (described as Nos 1, 4 and 5) had been completed, the remaining lots being pieces of building

The west side of Lyndhurst Square in 2008, showing Nos 6 and 7 and one of the offending street lamps. Choumert Square (see p.126) would provide a better model.

land. Most of the other houses were added after-wards, but No. 6 (according to Tim Charlesworth in *The Architecture of Peckham*) not until ten years later. The style was remarkably well matched. The Tudor theme breaks down at Nos 8 and 9 in the north-west corner, an afterthought built in a commonplace 1860s style on what had been part of the garden of the present No. 10. They are not even a genuine semi-detached pair, but have the appearance of a shorn-off terrace that was designed to extend further west.

The Booth surveyor was fairly complimentary in 1899, although detecting a slight decline: 'A leafy corner, small detached and semi-detached villas, gabled. Linen out to dry in the gardens. Some servants.'

There was bomb damage on the north side, serious at the Lyndhurst Road end, which gave the council the ever-welcome pretext to damage a square, in this case with the egregious Falcon House. If Southwark would follow Islington's example at Union Square by reinstating the lost No. 11 in facsimile it would possess one nearly perfect square here in Peckham – or it would once it had replaced those dreadful street lamps.

Lyons Square

WOOLWICH [GREENWICH]

Lyon's Square was an occasional name for a court usually called Lyon's Yard and sometimes Lyon's Place. It was built in the 1840s behind the shop of J. Lyons, army and navy cap maker of No. 12 Artillery Place, just west of Rushgrove Street. He was listed in the 1849 directory.

The square was of the same vintage and general character as Catherine Square to the east of Rushgrove Street. There were twelve cottages, later reduced to ten. The Booth survey described it in 1900 as 'a court of small 1-storey houses called Lyons Place. One room in each, 2/3d. Old women, lean cats but clean yard.' A few years later almost the whole block was demolished to make way for married soldiers' quarters. The successor to that block, the 1937 Cambridge House, is now on the site.

Mackay Square

See Nightingale Square

Maismore Square

See Leyton Square

Manchester Square

MARYLEBONE [WESTMINSTER]

Manchester Square was first projected early in the eighteenth century when, according to the *Picture of London* for 1825, it 'was intended to have been called Queen Anne's Square, and to have had a handsome parochial church in its centre'. That scheme did not survive the death of the queen in 1714, but it was revived later in the century.

Henry William Portman succeeded to the estate in 1761 and immediately began to plan its laying out for building, with Portman Square as the main feature and a smaller square as a pendant. A church was always an asset to a new development, so when the St Marylebone parish sought a site for a new one in 1770, Portman offered the centre of his small square. It was accepted at first, but when the vestry changed its mind an orthodox garden was substituted. The new square is described on two maps of 1777 as Bentinck Square. The definitive name was settled only some time after the 4th Duke of Manchester became involved in 1776.

When Portman granted the first building leases in 1771 it was with no thought of a dominant house, but in most of the early squares built on the edge of London the north side, with its views of Hampstead and Highgate, was the most coveted. Samuel Adams, the man who took the lease of the north side, and who had already built much of Portman Square, took the risk of beginning a large house in the centre of his take, but did not go far with it until he had secured a client in the Duke of Manchester.

The duke was a poor man for one of his rank, which no doubt explains why he had to be content with a comparatively small and simple house that never attracted any praise from the critics. It had only five bays of three storeys. The basic design was presumably by Samuel Adams, and to complete the house the duke did not employ any of the great architects available but the extremely obscure Joshua Brown.

Hertford House, Manchester Square, in 1813, the 'old yellow chariot' emerging.

Manchester House was largely built between 1776 and 1780, but not finished until 1788, in which year the duke died at the age of 51. His house was taken for use as the Spanish Embassy, a brief association that has left a permanent legacy in the name of Spanish Place, the north-eastern entrance to the square.

The 2nd Marquess of Hertford bought the house in 1797 and gave it the name that it still bears. He is chiefly remembered on account of the Prince Regent's infatuation with the marchioness. Prinny's daily visits to Lady Hertford in his incognito coach (celebrated by Thomas Moore in *Extracts from the Diary of a Politician*) added to his unpopularity:

Through M-nch-s-r Square took a canter just now –
Met the *old yellow chariot*, and made a low bow,
This I did, of course, thinking 'twas loyal and civil,
But got such a look – oh! 'twas black as the devil!

It was the 2nd Marquess who added the wings and built out the portico to support a conservatory.

His notorious son, Disraeli's model for Lord Monmouth in *Coningsby* and Thackeray's for the Marquis of Steyne in *Vanity Fair*, did not use Hertford House very often, and his grandson spent most of his life in Paris, making the house available for letting to several French ambassadors in the 1830s and 1840s. The bachelor 4th Marquess was a great art collector and when he died in 1870 these treasures passed to his son Sir Richard Wallace, who greatly extended and altered Hertford House to receive them. He left everything to his wife, and on the death of Lady Wallace in 1897 the house and its contents were bequeathed to the nation.

The houses on the other three sides were mostly built between 1776 and 1780, but the last not until 1790. Samuel Adams was the most prominent of a number of speculative builders involved. There were twenty-nine houses in the square but only twenty-six numbers, as most of the corner houses were included in the side streets. They were originally of three bays and four storeys plus basement, but half of the surviving houses have had a fifth storey added at different times, one as late as 1912.

Hertford House, Manchester Square, *c.* 1904.

In 1783 the square was declared to be 'too small to promise any considerable addition to the magnificence of the capital. The buildings already erected have nothing but regularity to recommend them.' In 1813 they were described as 'neat, respectable dwellings, which have nothing worthy of particular notice'. The nearly circular garden was laid out in the late 1780s and placed under the care of trustees by a private act of 1789.

It took a long time for Manchester Square to become accepted as part of fashionable London. In 1808 Palmerston, having let his large house in Hanover Square, wrote to his sister, 'I do not know what we shall do for a house; how far upwards should you mind going? There is a nice house in Manchester Square, but it is, to be sure, sadly out of the way.' He chose Lower Grosvenor Street instead.

In the middle of the nineteenth century the square was mainly occupied by physicians and surgeons, but it had become more aristocratic by the 1890s. The square can boast a miscellaneous collection of celebrities. The most eminent of the doctors was John Hughlings Jackson, who made important discoveries about the workings of the brain and the nerves. He lived at No. 3 from 1871 until his death in 1911. The once fabulously wealthy William Beckford, the author of *Vathek*, had squandered most of his money by the 1820s, the decade throughout which he had his town house at No. 12. He even thought it worthwhile to appeal against his rate assessment in 1825.

Samuel Warren, the novelist and commissioner in lunacy, died at No. 16 in 1877 and Stopford Augustus Brooke, the preacher and literary critic, lived at No. 1 from the late 1860s until 1914. The prolific Gothic architect Edward Blore lived at No. 4 from about 1839 until his death in 1879, and Sir Julius Benedict, the composer and conductor, at No. 2 from 1845 until his death in 1885. So far from Westminster, the only important political figure was Alfred, Viscount Milner, who lived at No. 14 from 1921 to 1925, after his retirement.

Of the eighteenth-century London squares this is second only to the immaculate Bedford Square in the survival of its houses. Three-quarters of them still exist in something like their original form and the square is unique in retaining its great house. There have been many changes, but none that spoils the pleasant atmosphere. Some houses have been given porches. Number 21 was practically rebuilt in 1873 at the time of the Hertford House alterations next door, and No. 6 was most inappropriately refaced in 1926.

Number 15 was destroyed during the Second World War and its neighbours to the north were damaged. It was replaced by an office in 1953 and EMI House was built on the site of Nos 16–19 in 1960. The whole block was rebuilt in 2000–01 as the ICI headquarters and was taken over by the Boston Consulting Group in 2008. The new building, while not a pastiche, fits sympathetically into the style of the square. It even has railings and an area.

Although there have been few residents since the First World War, after which most of the houses became offices, the garden remains private like all those on the Portman estate.

The south-west corner of Manchester Square, *c.* 1904.

Mansion House Square

(later Wesson Square)

Not many streets had struck west from the southern end of Camberwell Road before the London, Chatham & Dover Railway was built in the early 1860s, its viaduct restricting further access. As a result, several mean culs-de-sac were built between the road and the railway. One of them was called in derision Mansion Street, after the Mansion House Baptist Chapel that stood to the south, with Mansion House Place in front of it in Camberwell Road.

Around 1862 the five tiny cottages of Mansion House Square were built immediately south of

Mansion Street, tight against the viaduct. The only justification for the name would have been the open space between the new development and the backs of the shops in Camberwell Road, but half of that space, and the half nearest the Mansion House Square cottages, was filled by the Baptist chapel, 'blocking up the centre and blocking out the light', as the Booth survey said in 1899. The sole mitigation was an oblique glimpse of the Emmanuel Vicarage garden to the south.

In 1912 the LCC changed the name to Wesson Square, which was at least less ridiculous, but real relief had to wait until the Second World War, when the chapel was badly damaged. Unfortunately the houses suffered too, to a lesser extent, and the whole area had been cleared by 1951. Camberwell Council respected tradition by building equally mean flats on the site, between Wyndham Road and Blucher Road, in the 1960s.

Mansion House Square

Mansion House Square was an occasional name for the great open space in front of the Mansion House, the Royal Exchange and the Bank of England. It is usually Mansion House Street, which was what Horwood called it in the 1790s and Hughson in 1817.

An example of the less common usage is this advertisement in *The Standard* for 31 May 1842: 'Bankers in London … Messrs. Smith, Payne, and Smith, Mansion House-square.' The address of Smith, Payne & Smith was more often given as No. 1 Lombard Street, which was almost next door to the Mansion House, but the building of King William Street in the 1830s had separated it from the rest of Lombard Street and made 'Mansion House Square' less confusing.

The name was evidently not familiar to William Weir, when he wrote in 1843 about the new fashion for ceremonial squares, the French *places*, in London: 'At the Mansion House they are gradually excavating a place, which promises to be fine, though irregular. The Bank, the Exchange, and the Mansion House will make a goodly City place.'

Marian Square

Marian Square was built slowly between 1845 and 1855 on the estate of the Pritchard family, who were just completing Ion Square on the south side of Hackney Road when they turned their attention to this more ambitious project.

What they now had in mind was a serious and classical square, with houses of a good size and a private garden formally laid out with trees and a circular lawn. It was also nearly square in shape. But Marian Square laboured under serious disadvantages, which no doubt explains the slow development. The square was very close to the Regent's Canal and its wharves, with the associated industry, noise and smells; and it was only just completed when the Imperial Gas Company acquired a huge site immediately to the south-east, formerly occupied by fish ponds. There it built a gas holder into which the garden of the square could have been comfortably fitted. It was the first of four, and the third, built before 1872, almost touched the south-east side of the square.

In 1851, when only ten houses were occupied, with sixteen empty or being built, the tenants included the secretary of the Merchants' Protection Association and a backgammon board maker.

In 1898 the Booth survey reported:

> Marian Square, 2½ storied, square shews signs of being well-cared for spasmodically, beds and paths well laid out & planted, but covered with weeds. 'The inhabitants look after it themselves.' Some fairly well to do. The west side [furthest from the canal and gas holders] is the best.

By the early twentieth century it was evident that this was not the spot on which to imitate the amenities of the West End. Marian Square was demolished bit by bit and soon a stone yard with immediate access to the canal made far more appropriate use of the space. In 1914 just three houses survived on the south-west side, which was the only piece of road that remained. The three houses had gone by the 1930s, but the name lived on as a ghost and still appeared on some recent maps, even though the last trace has vanished on the ground.

Today, of course, a classical square beside the canal, if it could only be recalled, would be a valuable piece of real estate. The expensive development named Darwen Place, which has recently appeared on the site, does not take the form of a square but makes picturesque use both of the canal and the gas holder.

Marine Square

See Wellclose Square

Mark Lane Square

Mark Lane Square was the short-lived final name for a place that had been known for hundreds of years as Red Cross Court or Red Cross Square. It lay off the north side of Tower (or Great Tower) Street, between Mark Lane and Seething Lane. The Ogilby & Morgan map of 1676 showed Red Cross Court in exactly the form it still had in 1873: a narrow alley opening to the right at the north end into a small square court. As this was on the edge of the Great Fire area it may have existed in the same form long before 1676. The name presumably came from an inn.

The Horwood map of the 1790s was the first to call it Red Cross Square, a name that continued in use (although Court was sometimes revived) until the 1870s. It was an obscure place, but certainly not a slum: a respectable tailor lived there in 1805, in 1841 a customs officer, a corn meter, lightermen, porters, a letter carrier and a few labourers.

The change to Mark Lane Square in the 1870s was perhaps the result of a rise in status, for by that time it had become something of a centre for the tea trade: in 1882 seven tea companies or tea merchants had offices there. If there had been improvements they were labour in vain, for between 1882 and 1884 work began on the first stage of the new road now known as Byward Street, which struck north from Great Tower Street, obliterating Mark Lane Square.

Market Square

Market Square at Bromley only acquired that name after it ceased to resemble a square. The market established in 1205 by the Bishop of Rochester, which was the basis of the town's prosperity, was held in an open space east of the High Street known as the Market Place. There was a small timber market house in the centre.

Market Place was nearly square in shape, tapering slightly from north to south. On the west side it was separated from the High Street by a terrace of shops on an island site. In 1863 a large Gothic town hall was built on the northern half of the Market Place and it was then that the greatly reduced open space began to be called Market Square. The traders still crowded their stalls into it once a week.

With the growth of traffic and local government in the twentieth century, the stalls and the town hall were found inconvenient and in 1933 the market was moved elsewhere, the town hall and the island shops between the square and the High Street were demolished and the present block of mock-Tudor shops was built over nearly all the enlarged space. Market Square is now just the busy road to the north of this block and the pedestrianised street to its east. That section does have seats and trees and a few old shops on the east side that once overlooked the market.

Markham Square

CHELSEA [KENSINGTON AND CHELSEA]

Two houses on the north side of the King's Road – Box Farm, with a 1686 date stone, and Box Farm Cottage – belonged to the Markham family in the early nineteenth century. Between the two houses they created Markham Street in the 1820s, and in the mid-1830s they laid out Markham Square over the rough ground behind Box Farm Cottage.

The name appeared in the printed index to the 1836 ratebook, but with no page reference. The first resident, in 1838, was the surgeon Thomas Gaskell, whose house on the east corner was first No. 1, then 42, then 49, but eventually not numbered in the square at all and known as Markham House.

Market Square, Bromley, and the town hall, *c.* 1905.

As with most of the Chelsea squares, planning proved much easier than execution. Work on the square proper did not begin until 1841, with Nos 1–3 occupied in 1843 and 41–48 by 1846.

On 17 May 1844 *The Morning Post* reported:

Yesterday morning, shortly before seven o'clock, a fire, attended with considerable destruction of property, broke out in a large uninhabited house, situate No. 39 Markham-square, King's-road, Chelsea … The owners of the house are Messrs. Thirst and Humphries, the extensive builders of Chelsea; and although the premises were insured in the Guardian Fire Office, these gentlemen will be losers to a considerable extent, there being between 500l and 600l worth of prepared work in the place …

Thirst and Humphries were evidently using this house, in the middle of the east side, as a base for further building work. Edward Thirst was of No. 11 Halsey Terrace, Cadogan Street, in 1851.

Twenty-five houses were occupied in 1851, when Matthew Markham Evans and John Evans were at Box Farm, and Edward Dench, patent hothouse manufacturer, and William Piper, dairyman, shared Box Cottage. Demand for the houses was evidently very slack. Seventy-five-year leases of Nos 5, 7 and 8 (running from Christmas 1851) were auctioned in November 1852, but only No. 5 was sold; and when an eighty-year lease of an unidentified house (running from 1846) was offered in May 1854, it was bought in at £440.

The numbering of the houses, which was fixed at an early stage and was always meant to jump from No. 22 at the north end of the west side to No. 30 on the east, proves that there was not originally any thought of a church in the square. If one *had* been contemplated, it would not have been a Congregational church, which Victorian developers considered destructive to any social pretensions. It is a mark of the desperation of the owners, with only half of the intended houses built and tenanted after twenty years, that they were willing to let the whole of the north side for such a purpose. The Chelsea Congregational Church, designed by John Tarring, was built in 1858–59. It did nothing to spur on the development, for even in 1865, when the east side was complete, little more than half of the west side had been built.

Markham Square from the King's Road, *c.* 1900.

Markham Square did not recover from this poor start until the second half of the twentieth century. The Booth survey found it declining in the 1890s. In 1901–02 P.G. Wodehouse lived in Markham Square, in what he called 'horrible lodgings off the King's Road', while working in a bank by day and churning out journalism by night. It was certainly seedy enough at the time: at least nine of the houses were let out as apartments in 1902, and others were occupied by a plumber, a dressmaker and a midwife.

The Chelsea Congregational Church was damaged during the Second World War and demolished soon afterwards, an event that can be taken as the turning point in the square's fortunes. Then it was found fortunate that the planning had not included a church, as there were enough vacant numbers for the six new houses built in its place. They are small, modest and inoffensive, all that one requires – but so rarely finds – of infill in a square.

The subsequent social change in Markham Square was illustrated by the fatal police siege in 2008, when press comment concentrated on the incongruity of such sights in this quiet and exclusive place. In 1911 a siege of Markham Square would have been only a little more surprising than a siege of Sidney Street.

Marlborough Square

CHELSEA [KENSINGTON AND CHELSEA]

The site of Marlborough Square was part of Chelsea Common, which was gradually built over without any formal enclosure act from the late 1790s, with development gathering pace after 1808. Marlborough Square was built in stages between 1810 and 1818, but at first the ratebooks listed the new houses as Chelsea Common, then as Marlborough Place, and the Marlborough Square name did not appear until 1816.

The district continued to trade on its rural virtues after they were destroyed. In 1819 a laundress 'who lives in an airy situation, and who would take great pains to give satisfaction', gave her address in an advertisement as '1 Strathaven-place, Marlborough-square, Chelsea Common'.

The Greenwood map of 1827 showed the square fully built as a nearly triangular space enclosing a circular garden and surrounded by a mixture of detached houses and terraces. Being on the northern edge of Chelsea, it was sometimes called Marlborough Square, Brompton. The name presumably came from the Marlborough tavern and pleasure garden in Blacklands Lane, which existed by 1794. Blacklands Lane became Marlborough Road, but is now known as Draycott Avenue.

Number 18 was the birthplace in 1840 of the indefatigable literary scholar, Richard Herne Shepherd, who edited the works, or unearthed the juvenilia, of countless standard English authors, often in defiance of the copyright laws. He was a heavy drinker and ended his life in 1895 in that deceptively charming building, the Camberwell House lunatic asylum.

The Public Gardens Association managed to open the garden as a playground for children in 1884. In 1899 this was 'a quiet little square, with the centre not railed, and therefore all the grass gone'. Beresford Chancellor reported that there was once a statue in the centre of the garden, thought to be of the great Duke of Marlborough, but it had vanished before 1907.

Not long after that the square and its surrounding streets were bought by the recently founded Sutton Model Dwellings Trust, which cleared them all as slums about 1909 and built a large estate of fifteen tenement blocks, completed in 1913. The space formerly occupied by the garden was left open and remains a triangular green within the estate. The tenements are unaltered too, except for the crude removal of 'Model' from the name of the buildings on the central block in Cale Street.

Marlborough Square

WESTMINSTER

Marlborough Square was a tiny court of five houses, lying south of Great Peter Street, but entered from Whister's Ground (now Monck Street) to the east. The name suggests the early eighteenth century, but Rocque's 1740s map did not show it. At first the houses were treated as part of Whister's Ground for rating purposes, but they became Nos 1–5 Marlborough Square in 1790.

For such an insignificant place, Marlborough Square had a distinguished end. The world's first gasworks had been opened in Horseferry Road in 1813. It spread gradually northwards over the next three decades, replacing slums with retort houses as it did so. In the 1830s it crossed Whister's Ground to plant three small gas holders in the place of Marlborough Square. They were removed early in the twentieth century. The offices of the Society of Motor Manufacturers & Traders in Great Peter Street and Ashley House behind it in Monck Street are now on the site. The nearby Seacole Building has a plaque commemorating the Gas Light & Coke Company's works.

Marlborough Square

See Warwick Square

Maryland Square

STRATFORD [NEWHAM]

Maryland Square is one of the last, least and most remote of the nineteenth-century London squares. It was built in the early 1890s on the site of the Forest Lane Nursery and, unsurprisingly at that time and place, it was not a true square at all, having no communal garden and the original houses in the centre being of the same date as those of the periphery. They are of the very dullest standard of that dull period.

The only point of interest was the mews, a remarkably late example, occupying the centre of the centre, behind the interior houses. Some of the buildings there are now used by Whitechapel College. The St Paul's Vicarage, which stood behind the south side and had its address in the square, was really part of Forest Lane.

However shabby an imposter a square may be at first, it is surprising how often the magic of the name helps it move a little closer to the ideal. Like St Philip's Square and Bonnington Square, Maryland Square eventually received a garden courtesy of the Luftwaffe. There was serious bomb damage to various parts during the Second World War and the terrace on the west side facing Maryland Park was not rebuilt. It is now a lawn, with trees, but more private than public, being part of the grounds of the St Francis School.

The similar Torrens Square, just to the south, does not qualify for inclusion here as it was built after 1900.

May Square

CITY OF LONDON

May Square was a fancy nineteenth-century name for an old inn yard off the west side of Whitecross Street formerly known as Tiger Court. It was apparently an entirely cosmetic change, as the half-dozen small houses of the court and square looked no different on the maps. Some confusion has been introduced by what seems a mere mistake in the Horwood maps, where the place was described as Tyson Court. It was Tiger Court on Rocque's 1740s map and Tyger-Court in Lockie's 1813 list of streets. Maps before Rocque's showed only a garden.

May Square had taken over as the name by 1841, when the eight houses were occupied by twenty-six families. The 1895 Ordnance Survey showed the west side still standing, but the houses on the east side and those attached to them in Whitecross Street demolished, leaving the square momentarily doubled in size. But this was only an illusion: the new space was a building site, soon filled by a large office block in Whitecross Street that occupied the east side and the former courtyard of the square. The houses on the west side were necessarily demolished too and replaced by a building approached via an alley at the junction of Beech Street and Beech Lane. These new buildings were flattened during the Second World War and the site is now occupied by Cromwell Tower in the Barbican Estate.

Mecklenburgh Square

BLOOMSBURY [CAMDEN]

In Mecklenburgh Square, as befitted the girls' side of the Foundling Hospital, the houses were more delicate and decorative than in Brunswick Square. The reasons for the greater elaboration were the difficulty of attracting tenants to a remote and somewhat inaccessible spot and a change of architect.

In 1790 the square was planned in conjunction with Brunswick Square by Samuel Pepys Cockerell, the Foundling Hospital's surveyor, but little had been done on this eastern side when Cockerell quarrelled with the committee and resigned in 1808. He was succeeded by his pupil Joseph Kay, who immediately turned his attention to Mecklenburgh Square. Its name came from Mecklenburgh-Strelitz, the home of Queen Charlotte.

The first two houses on the south side were built in 1808, in accordance with an earlier agreement, even before the garden was laid out in 1809. The south side was completed in 1810, much in the style of Brunswick Square. Kay's ambitious plan for the long east side was approved in 1810 and the houses were built in stages between then and 1820. Thomas Cubitt twice applied for the north side, in 1819 and 1821, but both his offers were refused. It was eventually built in stages by several men between 1821 and 1825. The design was again similar to Brunswick Square but approved by Joseph Kay, who was still the surveyor.

The glory of the square was and is Kay's grand east side, which verges towards the new style of Nash. It is divided into five sections, with highly decorated stucco features in the centre and at the ends and plainer brick between. The stucco sections are each of five houses, but those in the centre are larger, having either an extra bay or wider windows. Thanks to the 'architectural embellishment' of the east side, Mecklenburg Square was spared the total

contempt with which Victorian critics regarded Brunswick Square.

Mecklenburgh Square has had many notable residents, mainly writers and artists. The earliest was Henry Thomas Buckle, the historian, who lived at No. 35 from 1825 (when he was 3 or 4 years old) until his father died in 1840. The sensational novelist Mary Elizabeth Braddon lived at No. 26 for a few years from 1861, while passing as the wife of John Maxwell; they were not married until 1874. The journalist George Augustus Sala, a great lover of squares, had his final home at No. 46 from 1878 to 1884.

In the early twentieth century the square became an outpost of 'Bloomsbury', with No. 44 having a remarkable list of writers. Richard Aldington and his wife 'H.D.' lived there in 1917–18, D.H. Lawrence briefly in 1917 and Dorothy L. Sayers around 1920. John Masefield lived at No. 18 from 1932 to 1935 and Virginia and Leonard Woolf had their last Bloomsbury home in a flat at No. 37 from 1939 until 1940, when they were bombed out. Leonard Woolf later moved to Victoria Square.

Professor R.H. Tawney, the economic historian, lived in four houses: No. 17, 1913–15; No. 44, 1922–40; No. 26, 1947–51; and No. 21 from 1951 until his death in 1962. One who visited this last address recalls that

The long east side (on the right) and the north side of Mecklenburgh Square, *c.* 1905.

'the house was a mess – books everywhere'. Other celebrities were the painter Sir William Nicholson at No. 38 from 1906 to 1911, and the actresses Fay Compton at No. 35a in 1933–35 and Flora Robson at No. 6 in 1936–37. William Cubitt, Thomas's brother and later twice Lord Mayor of London, was at No. 43 from 1832 to 1844. The family works were only a few steps away in Grays Inn Road. Number 21 has plaques to Tawney and Sir Syed Ahmed Khan, 'Muslim Reformer & Scholar'.

There was considerable Second World War bomb damage in the square, most serious at the north end of the east side and to varying degrees all along the north side. Mecklenburgh Place, the south-western approach to the square (formerly Caroline Place and briefly Sally Place) was destroyed.

The south side of the square was not so badly damaged, but it was already doomed. From the 1930s it was being encircled by London House, the students' hostel designed by Sir Herbert Baker and obviously intended to fill the whole block. The south and east wings were built in 1936–37, the west, on the site of the Mecklenburgh Place houses, in 1949–50, and the north wing, filling the south side of the square, in 1961–63.

On the north side, the eastern half was demolished and replaced by a student hostel (now William Goodenough House) in a style reasonably sympathetic to the surviving Nos 43–47 in the western half. The most important part of the square, the long east side, has been well restored. Here the advantage of stucco is seen, for the patchwork is noticeable in the centre and at the ends only in the attics, but is much more visible in the brickwork of the two plainer sections.

Theodore Hook described it in 1842 as the 'bleakest and most inhospitable-looking of squares, in whose road the grass grows all the year round, and where a carriage, or even a pedestrian, is seldom seen'. But Hook's life revolved around the bustle of St James's Street and the clubs, so he could not be expected to appreciate a quiet backwater. That is today the great charm of one of the best of the London squares. With the postgraduate Goodenough College now having premises on all three sides, and a beautifully tended private garden, it is becoming more and more like a displaced fragment of Oxford or Cambridge.

Melbourne Square

STOCKWELL [LAMBETH]

The site of Melbourne Square was part of the Archbishop of Canterbury's manor of Lambeth Wick. The manor was leased to the Fox family from the beginning of the eighteenth century and was developed as a building estate by the 3rd Lord Holland (Charles Fox's nephew) from 1820. Melbourne Square was built about 1831 and named after the future prime minister, who was Holland's friend and cabinet colleague. The building lease for the square was granted to Holland's agent, Benjamin Currey. He was the father of the well-known architect Henry Currey, but Henry was only 11 when Melbourne Square was built.

The square had an unusual form. There was a long approach from Brixton Road leading to a small garden of a nearly square shape. The approach was called Addison Place on the tithe map of 1843, but Melbourne Square on maps of 1862 and 1871. The garden could also be reached from a point further north in Brixton Road via a second long approach named Normandy Road in 1843, Cowley Road in 1862 and Addison Place in 1871.

There was a terrace on the south side of the long section of Melbourne Square which continued along the south side of the small garden. Its houses were of two storeys plus semi-basement, arranged in pairs linked by lower, recessed sections, what Summerson called quasi-semi-detached. On the east side of the garden there were three houses, one of them, Melbourne Lodge, large and detached. It should have been No. 13, but was known as 12a. There were no houses on the west side where the two approach roads entered, or on the north, but there was an offshoot from the north-east corner of the garden with two more houses.

The square was thoroughly respectable in its early years, when Brixton was still a good suburb, and even in 1899 was classified as 'comfortable', but the area declined rapidly in the twentieth century and houses of this size were broken up into flats and bedsits. There was some blast damage during the Second World War, but it was only serious in the little north-east offshoot, which was hardly a vital element.

Melbourne Square from Normandy Road in 1966, with the spire of the Mostyn Road Methodist Church (since rebuilt) in the background. (Photograph by M.D. Trace, courtesy of Lambeth Archives)

Most of the houses survived until the 1970s or later, but they were allowed to become derelict and have all been demolished. Both parts of Melbourne Square, the long approach road and the small garden, have now been extinguished. The former Cowley Road, which was built in the 1820s, survives under the name of Normandy Road. The garden, which was supposedly protected by the 1931 London Squares Act, was tossed back and forth by Lambeth Council and the LCC, being enlarged first as Melbourne Fields and then as Mostyn Gardens, by which time all semblance or memory of its name, form or purpose had been lost.

Merrick Square

SOUTHWARK

Merrick Square, like its elder brother Trinity Church Square, was built on land given to Trinity House in 1661 by Christopher Merrick. Trinity Church Square was completed in 1832, but demand for houses of that quality was not strong enough to encourage the corporation to build on the remainder of its estate until 1853. Plans were then drawn up and elevations made by Richard Suter, who had been a pupil of Daniel Asher Alexander when the estate was first laid out and succeeded him as the Trinity House surveyor in 1822.

The new square was named in 1854 and built by Cooper and Bottomley of the Old Kent Road, who had finished it by 1856. The east and south sides were built first and were occupied in that year. Given the lapse of more than two decades, the style is surprisingly similar to that of Trinity Church Square, evidence of a conservative institution and continuity of architectural advice. The houses are much smaller, however, in realistic recognition of the changing nature of the area: it was just at this time that many of the big houses in the older square began to be used as lodgings.

In Merrick Square the houses are of two storeys plus basement and attic, and mostly of two bays, although a few at the north ends of the east and west sides have three, in compensation for shorter gardens. On the east side this was made necessary by the pre-existing Catholic Apostolic Church, which stood until the 1950s where Shaftesbury House is now. (It is interesting to note that Richard Suter's son gave up architecture, went to Australia, and became a minister of the Catholic Apostolic Church.)

A gap was left in the centre of the south side, between Nos 16 and 17, probably for a road but possibly with the idea of building a rectory for Holy Trinity, a long-felt need. That was what eventually filled the gap, in 1872, or possibly just before as it was shown on the 1872 map. It is a tall, red brick house with Gothic trimmings, designed by Henry Jarvis & Son, but being hidden by the garden from most points of view it is less disruptive than it might have been anywhere else.

There were two lodging houses among the fourteen occupied in 1856 and that set the pattern for the standing of the square until its modern ascent. In 1899 it consisted of 'two storey houses with basements, something like Trinity Square, but rather better. Apartments the rule however.'

There have been few notable residents, but it was at No. 22, the home of his brother, that the great cricketer Alfred Mynn died in 1861. He was a farmer's son, but played as an amateur and was the mainstay of the Gentlemen in their matches against the Players. Despite his 18 or 19 stones, he was the first successful fast round-armed bowler and, not surprisingly, a powerful hitter.

The whole square suffered blast damage during the Second World War, quite severe at the north end of both long sides and fatal to part of Trinity Street, which forms the north side. There some ugly council blocks can be glimpsed in the north-east corner, and the houses that could be saved or reconstructed have been turned into flats, with most of their doors blocked. In the square itself everything has been beautifully restored and many of the houses have reverted to single occupation. The well-maintained private garden seems popular and is in regular use for parties and barbecues.

Midway Square

DEPTFORD [LEWISHAM]

Midway Place was a collection of cottages built on the marshy ground of the Deptford-Rotherhithe boundary. It began to form around the large house of the Reverend Thomas Beck and the chapel he built in its garden in 1790. The house was demolished soon after Beck's death in 1844 and more cottages were then built on its site. Midway Square was the name given to four

The garden of Merrick Square in 2007, with Trinity Street in the background.

of these cottages in the 1851 census. It was probably the same place as the Midway Yard of 1841, also with four cottages. Neither name appeared in the 1861 census.

The 1868 map showed what might have been the remains of a little court south of the chapel, but if that was Midway Square it had by then been nearly extinguished by Lee Terrace, now Trundley's Terrace, which was built along the south side of Midway Place in the 1850s. The large block of flats in Trundley's Terrace has covered the site of most of Midway Place since the 1960s.

Milner Square

The second square on the Milner-Gibson estate only acquired that name and form at a late stage in the planning. Francis Edwards, the estate surveyor and the architect of Gibson Square, had envisaged only a wide road here, and it was not until Gibson Square was completed in 1839 that firm proposals were put forward for continuing the development northwards in a more ambitious style. Even then, the application was for Milner Terrace, not Milner Square.

By 1839 Francis Edwards was perhaps too busy with his breweries and gasworks to have time for this minor suburban estate work, so the job was given to the young architects Robert Lewis Roumieu and Alexander Dick Gough. They had recently made their mark in Islington with two churches and the Literary & Scientific Institute in Wellington Street, now the Almeida Theatre in Almeida Street. The Milner-Gibson trustees could not complain of being taken unawares by the young partners' designs for the new square, as the Institute gave fair warning of Roumieu's extraordinary aspirations to altitude and elongation.

Milner Street, now Milner Place, the link between the two squares, was built in 1840, the style modulating between the well-mannered conventions of Edwards and the eccentricities of Roumieu. The east side of the square itself, by this time avowedly a square, was begun in 1841. The houses were considerably bigger than those in Gibson Square, three bays wide and with four storeys plus basement, and clearly aimed at much wealthier tenants. This, together with the bizarre design, must have made the houses difficult to dispose of, and it took until 1844 to complete the twenty-five houses of the east side. Seventeen of these faced the garden, with four at each end numbered in the square but fronting the approach roads. Seven houses were occupied by 1843.

After 1844 there was a long delay. This may have been caused by deliberations about a church proposed for the middle of the west side, or the church may have been intended, in traditional style, to revive a flagging development. The fact that the undated elevation of the church is signed by Roumieu alone may point to a date after the partnership with Gough was dissolved in 1848. The church would have been one of the most remarkable in London, though far from the most beautiful, as it was to be an extreme exaggeration of the traits already exhibited in the Institute and the square.

The church remained a dream, or nightmare, and eventually the west side became a mirror image of the east. The houses on the west sides of the two approach roads were built in the late 1840s, but the long west terrace was not completed and occupied until the late 1850s. It reflects great credit on the builder, William Spencer Dove, that he managed to achieve such unusual uniformity over so long a period. The only serious difference between the terraces is Almeida Passage, the arch on the east side leading to Almeida Street, which is disguised as a doorway.

The design of the houses, which has sharply divided critical opinion, has been universally attributed to Roumieu far more than to Gough. In his later career Roumieu was noted as one of the extreme Goths, but here the style is baroque. The motive behind every detail seems to be the joy and pride of the architect rather than the comfort and convenience of the tenant. To make a fair assessment of the original effect one should look at the reconstructed houses on the east side of the northern approach road, where the porches, balconies and balustrades have been replaced. They certainly soften the extreme bleakness of the houses, but even when every allowance is made, these still look like City warehouses of the very best kind. One is surprised not to see hinged cranes attached to the walls between the tall windows.

In the struggling early days, when the square was only one-sided, Nos 13–15 were occupied by the Church Missionaries' Children's Home, a clear admission of failure, but the orphans were removed as the square filled up, and from the mid-1850s the only exceptions to the solidly respectable private residents were a few doctors and ladies' schools. There have been no residents of real distinction.

In line with the others in Islington, Milner Square declined late in the nineteenth century. In 1897 the Booth survey found that it had been 'evidently built for a very good class, now all tenements. Clerks live here – furnished apartments. Whole house costs £60 a year. Square [the garden] has a keeper of its own.'

The decline grew steeper in the twentieth century and in the 1930s the porches, balconies and balustrades were removed, no doubt to avoid the expense of repair. The south end of the east side was damaged in the Second World War and the square was in a very decayed state when Islington restored it as council flats in the 1970s. Apart from the failure to replace the porches, the disappointment of the restoration is the dull municipal garden, part children's playground, part hard games area. It is significant that Gary Powell describes Milner Square as 'closely associated with its much smarter neighbour Gibson Square'. This is a fair enough comment today, but the reverse of the developers' intention and the early status of the two squares.

Mint Square

SOUTHWARK

Mint Square was the only one south of the river included by William Maitland in his list of London squares published in 1756, but probably compiled in 1732. The Strype map of 1720 (or earlier) and Rocque's map of the 1740s showed it as the central feature of the fully formed Mint district, so it had a good claim to be the oldest formal square in south London. It had little else to boast of, being merely an opening at the crossing of King Street and Queen Street, in which the eight houses surrounding the square were probably numbered; and the district was very bad, a debtors' sanctuary until 1722 and a slum ever afterwards. Being outside the jurisdiction of the City it was a haunt of thieves and prostitutes.

The square became less distinct during the first half of the nineteenth century as the St Saviour's Workhouse encroached from the south-west and the pubs and shops at the other corners nibbled away at the open space when they were rebuilt. As a result, the name gradually passed out of use. Mint Square was destroyed in the 1880s when the new Marshalsea Road was built directly across the site. Mint Street survives, together with fragments of Caleb, formerly King, and Quilp, formerly Queen Street.

The garden and west side of Milner Square, c. 1905.

Mitre Square

The names of Mitre Square and Mitre Street, from which the square is approached, are thought to be taken from the Mitre tavern, which occupied a surviving fragment of the Holy Trinity Priory buildings. The site of Mitre Square was shown as an open space on Greenwood's map of 1827, but marked and named in his 1830 revision, and a Mitre Square jeweller appeared in a list of bankrupts in 1830.

The square had a ready-made south-east side in St James's, one of the rare early seventeenth-century London churches, which was named in honour of James I in 1622. It was rebuilt in 1727 and demolished in 1874.

The new square that emerged to its north had a mixed population. The 1841 directory listed a merchant at No. 1 and a surgeon at No. 8, but lodging houses were then the general rule. In 1851 there was an accountant, a beadle, a dairy, a merchant, a builder, plus porters and carpenters.

Mitre Square declined later in the century and the low point was reached when it was the scene of one of the Jack the Ripper murders, that of Catherine Eddowes, early in the morning of 30 September 1888.

No old buildings survive in Mitre Square, which has been rebuilt as offices several times since the 1870s, but it is still a distinct open space, with seats and a small flower bed. The south-east side is now bounded by the playground of Sir John Cass's Foundation, the school buildings on that part of the site having been removed.

Molesworth Square

Molesworth Square was built between 1841 and 1845. Like Harrington Square at Somers Town it was a triangle with, in this case, houses on the west and south sides and Weston Street cutting across diagonally to form the third side on the north-east. There was a short terrace on the south side and a long one on the west.

Mitre Square and Sir John Cass's Foundation School in 2007. The square has been largely rebuilt since then.

All the houses were of three storeys and two bays, in a heavy early Victorian style. The name was displayed on a large and solid stone tablet above the second storey of the south terrace. Molesworth Square was presumably named after Sir William Molesworth, who was popular in radical circles from the 1830s and served as MP for Southwark from 1845 until his death ten years later. The square can hardly have been named in honour of his election, as the tablet was an integral part of the fabric, and only two months after the close of the poll the *Morning Post* published an account of the drowning of a baby in a washing tub at No. 6 Molesworth Square, Weston Street.

Clerks and commercial travellers were the typical tenants, plus the odd master mariner and wool-stapler, and medical students were often found as lodgers.

Three houses on the west side were destroyed during the Second World War; the rest of Molesworth Square stood until the early 1960s. The triangular green survives, nearly opposite Leathermarket Street, but it now has twenty-storey blocks of flats on the south and west sides.

Monmouth Square

See Soho Square

Montagu Square

MARYLEBONE [WESTMINSTER]

The lesser squares on the Portman estate, Montagu and Bryanston, were laid out behind Montagu House in Portman Square about 1800, when the long, narrow gardens were planted, but the problems of the building trade during the Napoleonic War delayed construction of the Montagu Square houses until 1811–13, and Bryanston Square had to wait even longer.

The architect was Joseph Parkinson, District Surveyor of Westminster, whose designs for the two squares were exhibited at the Royal Academy in 1811. The main builder was David Porter, the former chimney sweep's climbing boy who was also responsible for much of Dorset Square. The unusual features of the Montagu Square houses are the shallow bay windows, some carried through two or three storeys, 'after the most approved Brighton fashion, each with its little bulging protuberance to admit of a peep into the neighbours' parlours', as William Weir described them in 1843. The same device was later used in a more thoroughgoing and overpowering way in Gloucester Terrace.

The east side of Montagu Square, *c.* 1904.

Some idea of the arrangement of the houses in the early days can be got from *The Moonstone*, where Miss Clack takes the reader on a tour of Lady Verinder's house while secreting her tracts in all the rooms. They are a little smaller than those in Bryanston Square, and it does not have the great mansions at the ends and centres of the terraces. As a result it was less fashionable and had fewer distinguished residents. The great lion was Anthony Trollope, who lived at No. 39, where there is a plaque, from 1873 to 1880. Sir Arthur Blomfield, architect of innumerable dull churches and if not the last of the Goths, certainly one of the last, lived at No. 28 for many years. It is notable how many architects in other styles choose Georgian houses for their own occupation.

Number 28 had earlier been the home of another man of celebrity, or at least notoriety. Robert 'Romeo' Coates, who died there in 1848 after a road accident, had unwillingly convulsed audiences across the country between 1810 and 1816 by his attempts to perform his favourite roles, notably Romeo, in theatres hired for the purpose, and supported by professional actors. He was so bad that he was nearly always booed off the stage before he could reach his death scene, but he was allowed to perform it in Montagu Square. Various Beatles lived at No. 34, where there is a John Lennon plaque, between 1965 and 1969.

Eight or nine houses in various parts of the square were seriously damaged during the Second World War. The worst incident was at the north end of the east side, where two houses were destroyed. There a block of flats has been built, much taller than the houses it has replaced, but elsewhere the damage has been tactfully repaired. The railings, removed during the war, were replaced in 1999.

Montague Square

SPITALFIELDS [TOWER HAMLETS]

Edward Hatton described it in the past tense in 1708: 'Montague Square was a pretty pleasant Square, in the most easterly part of Spittlefields; its Area upwards of 1¾ acres, and from the Tower of London

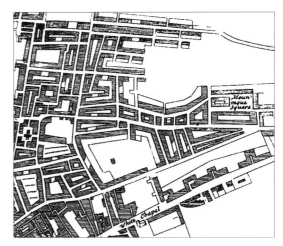

Montague Square from the Hatton map of 1707.

northeasterly, 1760 yards, or one mile.' Hatton also mentioned Church Street as being 'a little south from Montague Square'.

Henry Montague, Earl of Manchester, and members of his family, bought large estates in Spitalfields and Mile End New Town in 1640 and 1643, and the land was retained by the Montagues and their heirs for three centuries. They began to let this part of it for building around 1680. Hence there was a Montague Street, now Old Montague Street, north of Whitechapel Road, and another Montague Street that is now the central section of Hanbury Street, between Brick Lane and Spital Street. Hatton's Church Street, 'a little south from Montague Square', is now the section of Hanbury Street east of Greatorex Street.

Hatton's map dated 1707, and others of the 1720s and 1730s, show a Mountague or Montague Square occupying most of the area known as Coverley's Fields, now represented by Coverley Close. The editors of the *Survey of London* supposed that the map-makers were anticipating an unrealised development, but in view of Hatton's appreciative but valedictory account, perhaps they were only showing the remains of an abandoned attempt at a square. Rocque portrayed the space as largely open ground in the 1740s. The mysterious 'Whitechapel Square, at Whitechapel' mentioned by William Stow in 1722 may be another name for the same place. Montague Square, which was close to Whitechapel Road, is not in Stow's list under that name.

Montpelier Square

This is a rare example of a square with an estate agent's name, intended to suggest to potential buyers that the air of Brompton was as pure and invigorating as that of Montpelier in France. William Weir's comment in 1843 was 'so called probably because it is more shut in from a free current of air than any other'. The developer was Thomas Weatherley Marriott, a Knightsbridge ironmonger, who acquired the land in 1824 in conjunction with a partner who was soon bought out. The layout of the estate was planned and the name chosen in that year.

The square grew very slowly, the original impulse being broken by the banking crisis of 1825–26. The south side was built in the mid to late 1820s, the west in the 1830s and mid-1840s, and the entire east side in the early 1840s. The north was begun in the 1820s but not completed until the early 1850s. The south side, the only one with any striking unity of composition, and the only one with the houses fully stuccoed, may have been designed by the builder, William Darby, who some years after his bankruptcy in 1828 re-emerged as a surveyor. This style would no doubt have been continued round the square if the original plans had not been thwarted. It was lucky that the square was ever finished, as in 1845 a representative of the London & Exeter Direct Railway Company stated at a public meeting 'that it was the intention of the company to have their London terminus at Hyde Park-corner, close to Montpelier-square'.

In its early years the square came to share the unsavoury reputation of its smaller neighbour Trevor Square, although there is little to suggest the presence of brothels. There were certainly schools and boarding houses, and one of the first buildings occupied was the George IV public house, built about 1827, where inquests were held. Shops adjoined the pub, giving the north-east corner a commercial air until modern times.

There were persistent proposals to change the name to Beaufort Square, Knightsbridge Square and several other smart alternatives from the 1860s to the 1890s, to shake off the dubious associations of the old one; just what is done today with failing schools. These attempts at a fresh start were evidence of a gradual improvement in the square that became marked from the 1880s. Despite claims to the contrary, Galsworthy was not wrong to put the house of Soames Forsyte at 'No. 62', as the square would have been respectable enough in his day and the sharp Forsytes would have been able to spot at that early stage its potential as an investment.

The north side of Montpelier Square, *c.* 1904.

The actor Walter Lacy and his wife Harriett, an equally well-known actress, lived at No. 38 from 1852 until the 1870s as part of the Brompton theatrical community. Frederick William Fairholt, the engraver, artist and antiquary, author of *A History of Costume in England* among many other works, lodged successively at Nos 9 and 22, where he died in 1866. The great Mayan archaeologist Alfred Maudslay lived at No. 32 from the 1890s until the First World War.

Edmund Gurney, the psychologist, best known as the principal author of *Phantasms of the Living*, one of the pioneering works of psychical research, lived at No. 26 from about 1880 until his death, probably by his own hand, in 1888. It is curious that Arthur Koestler, the other eminent literary resident, ended his career with a series of books on similar subjects, notably *The Roots of Coincidence*. In 1983 Koestler and his wife Cynthia committed suicide at No. 8, his home since 1952. The novelist Robert Hichens had lived there in the 1890s when it was a lodging house.

Montpelier Square grew steadily more fashionable throughout the twentieth century, in tandem with the rise of Knightsbridge as a shopping centre, and alterations were made to the houses – bay windows, conservatories, etc. – by the wealthy new owners. The width of its appeal after the Second World War, through which it passed unscathed, is shown by the residence there in the 1960s of the actress Leslie Caron at No. 31 and the politician Anthony Barber at No. 15. Shops and boarding houses had long been banished and the closure of the George IV in 1995 severed the last link with trade. It was demolished in 1997 and new houses in a convincing pastiche were built on the site in 1998–99.

Monument Square

(now part of Monument Street)

This was London's first attempt at a public, ceremonial square. Various theorists had wished to take advantage of the Great Fire to create such open spaces but they had been frustrated by vested interests. The rebuilding acts, however, called for an assessment of the City

Monument Square from the west, *c.* 1905.

churches to decide which should be reinstated, and decreed that a monument to the fire should be erected close to the spot where it had broken out. Both tasks fell in part to Christopher Wren, who combined them creatively to achieve this single square. St Margaret, Fish Street Hill, close to the fatal bakery in Pudding Lane, was put in the list of churches not to be rebuilt, and on its site an open space was formed as a fit setting for Hooke and Wren's monumental column, which was built between 1671 and 1677.

In 1708 Hatton called it 'Monument Yard, a pretty small square on the east side of New fish-street hill'. Monument Yard it remained for its first two centuries, but if the name was less dignified the position was more important while Fish Street Hill was the approach to London Bridge, as it continued to be until 1831. In this busy spot, and so close to Billingsgate, the square could never be residential, except for the odd solicitor, but it was home to a wide range of businesses.

The change to Monument Square in the early 1890s was in response to the building of large office blocks – Monument House, Monument Square Chambers and Monument Buildings – on the three sides. They have all been rebuilt at least once since then, but they lasted longer than the new name. Since 1911 the open space has been counted a part of Monument Street, which was created in the 1880s to reduce traffic chaos at Billingsgate.

Moor Square

CITY OF LONDON

There has been some confusion between Moor Square and its close neighbour Car Square because the Car Yard marked on maps of 1676 and 1721 has been taken as the forerunner of Car Square, when it seems more likely that it developed into Moor Square.

Car Yard was described by Strype in 1720 as 'a pretty large place for Stabling'. On the Rocque map of 1746 it appeared as Star Yard, suggesting that it was then attached to an inn, but by the 1760s it was Moor Square with fourteen houses. The change of name probably accompanied a total or partial rebuilding, as (to judge from the maps) the square was smaller than the yard and had a more regular shape.

Moor Square, part of the poor Grub Street area of the City, was occupied mainly by bootmakers in 1851, with cigar and playing card makers adding exotic variety. It was demolished when the Metropolitan Railway was extended to Moorgate in 1864–65. Willoughby House on the Barbican Estate now covers its site.

Morgan Square

See Tredegar Square

Mortgramit Square

WOOLWICH [GREENWICH]

Mortgramit Square was a triangle between Powis Street and Dog Yard, approached through archways in each. It was built in 1807–08, on a lease from the Powis brothers of the Dog Yard Brewery, by George Graham,

with financial backing from two local tradesmen, John Mortis and Thomas Mitchell. The peculiar name of the square was concocted from their three surnames. It was originally called Mortgramit Buildings, but had been promoted to a square by 1841.

Twenty-one cottages faced the open space, but behind the terraces on the south and east sides, back-to-back, were twenty-two more opening into alleys. The back-to-back cottages, having no yards, shared fifteen privies tucked into the corners of the square.

These slums were cleared in the 1880s and Mortgramit Square began a second, commercial, life as the premises of a job master. That business developed naturally into Furlong's Garage, which now occupies the site of the cottages. The name remains in use for a sinister network of cobbled lanes between Hare Street and Powis Street, where an archway is still the entrance. The section entered next to the Prince Albert in Hare Street was formerly Dog Yard.

Mount Nod Square

GREENWICH

Mount Nod Square was built on former market garden ground around 1840. The 1841 census listed a dozen houses in Mount Nod Brickfields, although only one was occupied by a brickmaker, and a couple more in Mount Nod. Some of these were no doubt in the square, but that name did not appear.

It must then have been very secluded, the perfect sleepy retirement home, perhaps, for the small shopkeeper or clerk, except when a house was totally destroyed by fire, allegedly by an arsonist, in April 1843.

Like so many squares it suffered serious damage from the railways: in this case, the building of the ill-fated Greenwich Park Branch, which was opened in 1871. The line sank from a viaduct to a cutting as it swept across the corner of the square. All but one of the houses on the north side had to be demolished and several at the north end of the west side. The parts of the square that survived had the quiet promised by the name rudely shattered. The nuisance did not end even when the line closed in 1917, as the decaying viaduct and cutting quickly became rubbish dumps.

Eureka Cottage, Mount Nod Square, c. 1953. It was the only house on the north side after the building of the railway. (Photo courtesy of Godfrey Smith)

In 1899 the Booth survey had nevertheless found the square going up in the world:

Two storey houses, some with basements. Centre of square is garden belonging to the houses – vegetables, etc., growing. On the west side are two entries; one leads to two cottages and a double fronted house. Brethren hold services here, notice at entrance, 'To Arlington Room'. The other entry leads to four cottages, numbered in the Square. The Square has improved greatly during the past three years. People were very poor, better now.

In an area that suffered severely from bombing during the Second World War, Mount Nod Square escaped quite well. The school, for which houses in the south-east corner had already been demolished, was itself destroyed, but only one more house shared its fate, the rest receiving minor blast damage. It was a mere stay of execution: all the surviving houses were demolished in the early 1960s to make way for the Orchard Estate.

Mount Square

BETHNAL GREEN [TOWER HAMLETS]

Mount Square was a tiny court off the west side of Mount Street (now Swanfield Street) in Shoreditch. In 1813 John Lockie defined its position as 'Mount Street, Bethnal-Green, at 67, 1st on the left from Rose Street'. Rose Street was the southern continuation of Mount Street.

The 1813 Horwood map showed the building of the southern end of Mount Street in progress and an open space where Mount Square was to be fitted in, so it was evidently new when discovered by Lockie. Mount Street marked the eastern edge of the notorious criminal district known as the Nichol, which was demolished in the 1890s for the Boundary Street Estate, with Arnold Circus at its centre. Mount Square was one of the many courts and yards swept away during the clearance. See Reform Square for more details of conditions in these slums.

What we know about Mount Square comes mostly from the account Hector Gavin gave of his inspection of it in *Sanitary Ramblings* (1848):

The whole place is very dirty indeed; there are two privies in a beastly condition, and a refuse-heap in a recess in the back yard. The houses here are two-roomed, one above the other; the place is dark and dismal. One pipe without a cock supplies the place with water. A slaughter-house abuts on this square, the smell from which is complained of by the inhabitants as most dreadful and scarcely endurable; the blood of the slaughtered animals is stated to be retained in holes for a week or a fortnight together; the untrapped drain in the centre of the square likewise, occasionally, creates most offensive smells. At least a dozen cases of fever have been attended by the parochial medical officer in this court during the last twelve months, besides scarlet fever, &c. Nine years ago, a similar story was told by Dr Smith. He then stated, on the authority of the then parochial medical officer, that seven persons were attacked in succession in No. 2, six in No. 3; in the next house three, and in the next one. For nine years, then, at least, has this court continued to do its work in poisoning by fever the unfortunate poor who ignorantly take up their abode in this nest of fever. How long shall it be permitted thus to injure the health and destroy the lives of its occupants?

Fifty years was the answer.

The Mount Square

Until 1937 The Mount was known as Silver Street and The Mount Square as Golden Square. The awkwardness of the current name is a good indication of modernity: 'the' would not have survived a few centuries of use.

This was one of the slums of Hampstead: the streets and alleys here were already crowded with cottages, shops, pubs and stables by 1762, but the square did not achieve its present form until much later. The buildings that surround it now are eighteenth and early nineteenth-century houses on the south side, nineteenth-century cottages on the north and east and on the west the stable yards of Old Grove House and New Grove House (with its George Du Maurier plaque) in Hampstead Grove.

In 1851 Golden Square was occupied by labourers, laundresses, shoemakers, a gardener, a pipe maker. In 1898 Booth's survey found 'cottages and 3 storey tenement houses' occupied by a mixture of poor and

Golden Square, now The Mount Square, looking east, c. 1910.

The Mount Square, looking east, in 2007.

fairly comfortable inhabitants. In 1903, according to Caroline White's *Sweet Hampstead*, Silver Street and Golden Square had 'nothing in their present appearance, except irony, to suggest the etymology of their names', and in 1912 Thomas Barratt wrote that 'Money Cottages, Silver Street, and Golden Square arrest our attention; but suggestive as the names are of wealth, it has to be admitted that the houses are of the humblest'.

There is no garden, just a tree in front of one of the houses. The paved open space is now filled with expensive cars and the affluent modern residents of the square have forgotten the old names with the old poverty. The very polite gentleman of whom I enquired for Golden Square directed me to Golden Yard. Bridget Cherry was apparently given the same misleading information when revising *Pevsner*.

Munster Square

REGENT'S PARK [CAMDEN]

In the planning of the working-class service area to the east of the Regent's Park, John Nash provided three markets of ascending size, with Osnaburgh Street running through the centre of them to the Regent's Park Basin of the canal. They, like Osnaburgh Street, took their names from titles of the royal family. The smallest was York Market, the second Clarence Market and the northernmost Cumberland Market.

The conservatism of the London tradesman often frustrated such grand schemes. Cumberland Market was the only one used as intended, for hay and corn, the others becoming residential as soon as built, as Clarence Gardens and York Square. The northern end of Osnaburgh Street was soon renamed Munster Street, and in 1844 York Square became Munster Square, probably in an attempt to shake off the dubious reputation of the old name.

Although the three markets were part of the Regent's Park plan from an early stage, and were shown confidently in prediction on the 1813 Horwood map, the York Square houses were not built until 1823–24. Once the decision was taken to make the square residential Nash, or perhaps his assistant James Pennethorne, took great trouble with the design of the houses. Some accounts call them cottages. They were certainly small, but elegant, with a round-headed door and window on the ground floor, a single large window with balcony on

St Mary's, Munster Square, *c.* 1905.

the first and a square window on the second. The most prominent corner house, in the middle of the north side, had pilasters, a balustraded roof and just a single window on each floor, the entrance being at the side.

Pennethorne had designed a church, St George's in Albany Road, to serve the district, but in 1849 a wealthy curate there decided to build a daughter church more in accord with his high architectural and liturgical tastes. The south-eastern terrace of Munster Square was acquired and demolished and the church and its school built there between 1849 and 1852. Richard Carpenter, the architect of St Mary Magdalene (and earlier of Lonsdale Square), based the design upon the Dutch church in Austin Friars, which was destroyed in the Second World War. St Mary's was at first entered from Munster Street, with the school occupying the frontage to the square.

The Munster Square houses tended at first to be occupied by tradesmen and craftsmen – tailors, shoemakers, cabinet-makers, carvers and gilders, and the like – whose customers lived in the great terraces around the park. There was also a large pawn-broking establishment occupying two houses.

The square declined rapidly as the Albany Street district sank into something close to a slum. The houses, small as they were, became subdivided and many were occupied by prostitutes. In November 1843 the *Morning Post* reported that:

> … for a number of years past nearly all the houses in York-square … have been inhabited by females of the most loose and abandoned character. Their riotous and disgusting behaviour by day and night in the public streets have given an infinite deal of trouble to the police, and rarely a week has passed without fifteen or twenty of the occupants and their visitors being brought before the sitting magistrate.

The brothels were closed in 1843–44, and the name of the square changed.

Munster Square bore the brunt of the long Victorian reaction against Georgian architecture and town planning. In 1898 the Charles Booth surveyor reported, 'Narrow fronted 3½ storey houses, two or three families in each house. The square is wretchedly kept.' Beresford Chancellor was scathing in 1907:

Munster Square, which is intersected by Osnaburgh Street, consists of tiny two-storied houses, built probably at that terrible period of domestic and all other architecture in this country, the decade from 1830 to 1840. The two central gardens are of a bare and desolate appearance, but form a refuge for the inhabitants from their dwellings, and for the casual wanderer (for they are open to anyone) to contemplate the exiguous habitations by which they are surrounded.

The twin gardens, with the revived Osnaburgh Street running between, had been leased to the LCC by the Office of Woods & Forests for thirty-one years from 1905, the lease to be renewed if the gardens had been properly looked after. They were opened to the public in 1906. The eastern part was a cemented playground, the western had a lawn and flower beds.

Munster Square suffered only blast damage during the Second World War, but on the LCC bomb damage map 'condemned property' was scrawled across the houses, which had all been demolished by 1949. Only St Mary Magdalene was spared. In the 1950s St Pancras Council built the Regent's Park Estate around Nash's three markets, the centres of which were protected by the London Squares Preservation Act. A reaction in favour of Munster Square and its architecture came just too late. *The Survey of London* was already full of praise in 1949 and in 1980 Sir John Summerson recalled that 'it was lined with houses whose tiny dimensions and single-window fronts made the square seem magically large and serene'.

Myddelton Square

Myddelton Square is the centrepiece of the New River Company's estate at Clerkenwell, which was planned in 1818 by William Chadwell Mylne. He had succeeded his father as surveyor to the company in 1811 and held the post for fifty years. Chadwell Square was the name during the planning stage, but when building began the superior claims of Sir Hugh Myddelton, the founder of the company, proved irresistible. Mylne had to be satisfied with

St Mark's, Myddelton Square, *c*. 1840.

Chadwell Street, the eastern approach to the square, and the little Mylne Street in the north-west corner. It is as the engineer of canals and bridges that Mylne is best known, but the houses and church in Myddelton Square demonstrate his talent as an architect.

Building began in 1822 on the south side, which was completed, except for the two central houses, in 1826. The other three sides were all begun in the 1820s and finished in the 1830s. The two taller houses on either side of the alley leading to Myddelton Passage filled the gap on the south side in 1842–43. Although thirteen different builders took plots in the square, Mylne achieved an impressive overall unity, despite many small differences of design and size.

The square is large and nearly square in shape, with the south side slightly splayed to meet River Street at a comfortable angle. The garden is large enough to accommodate the substantial St Mark's Church without any sense of overcrowding. The church was set facing the approach from the west, Upper Chadwell Street (now Inglebert Street), leaving ample private pleasure grounds for the residents on

three sides. The Commissioners for New Churches naturally applied to Mylne to design St Mark's, which was built between 1825 and 1828, in the pleasantly mild Gothic of the period.

None of the Clerkenwell squares have been fashionable until our time, and Myddelton Square was no more than highly respectable in its early days, with merchants, clergymen, solicitors and surgeons among the tenants, but also the odd watchmaker. The least obscure residents have been Thomas Dibdin, the playwright who lived at No. 7 in 1826–27 while stage manager at Sadler's Wells, and Jabez Bunting, the Methodist leader, who died at No. 30 in 1858 after a residence of twenty-five years. Richard Cromwell Carpenter, the architect of Lonsdale Square, who lived at No. 61, was married at St Mark's in 1840, but probably disapproved of it, being a dedicated follower of Pugin. (Edward Irving, who is placed at No. 4 by many writers, lived at No. 4 Claremont Square.)

Myddelton Square looks pristine at first glance, but there have been changes. Numbers 3 and 4 on the south side were demolished just before the Second

World War to improve access to Myddelton Passage. During the war the north side was severely damaged and Nos 43–53 were rebuilt in facsimile (as flats) in 1947–48. At the same time the garden was re-planned and opened to the public. St Mark's was also bomb damaged and restored without a gallery in the early 1960s. Conversion of the houses to flats began in the 1930s and accelerated after the war, but with the increasing popularity of Islington the trend has been reversed in recent decades.

Nelson Square

(now part of Furley Road)

Peckham's Nelson Square was built in 1842. The neighbouring Trafalgar Square was part of the same development and featured very similar houses, all demolished. Nelson Square was formed of two terraces facing one another across what is now part of Furley Road. Until the 1870s there was access only through a narrow entrance at the north end. There was no communal garden in the centre, but the private front gardens of the houses gave a sense of space.

In 1861, when more than half the twenty-five houses were unoccupied, the few tenants included clerks, a commercial traveller, an accountant, an attorney and the sub-editor of a newspaper. The Booth survey found the square occupied by the 'mechanic class' in 1899. The only known resident of any distinction was the landscape artist Charles James Lewis, who was here in the mid-1850s, when first married.

The square was renumbered as part of Furley Road in 1937. The houses remained intact until the 1970s when the west side was sacrificed for the new estate that also destroyed Trafalgar Square, known by then as Buller Square. The original east side survives as Nos 80–98 Furley Road. The three houses to the south of this terrace (which almost turn it into a shallow crescent) were added around 1880. The 1842 houses are a surprising and attractive survival amid the wasteland of post-war Camberwell redevelopment.

The east side of Furley Road, formerly part of Nelson Square, Peckham, in 2011.

Nelson Square

This is one of the saddest squares in London because of the dismaying contrast between the four original houses in the south-east corner and the appalling council flats that now surround them on all sides. The wasted public garden, messily divided into small enclosures, does nothing to lighten the gloom.

The Horwood map of 1813 described it as 'Nelson Square, so to be called when built on', but the map showed the west side and part of the north side completed. In fact, the square was laid out in 1807, the north side was occupied by 1808 and the development was finished by 1814, with William Hansard as the main or sole builder. The design of the houses has been attributed to Samuel Pepys Cockerell, who planned important parts of Bloomsbury and Bayswater.

Three of the four houses that survive in Nelson Square are on a grand scale, three bays wide and with five full storeys plus basement, which makes them taller than those in almost all the great West End squares and rarely outdone anywhere in London. They may have seemed intimidatingly tall when first built, but they are now dwarfed by the eight and nine-storey flats that confront them. These survivors were not the standard type in the square but restricted to the south side and part of the north; most of the houses were of three or four storeys plus basement.

Nelson Square had some literary associations in its early days. Lodgings at No. 26 were one of the temporary homes of Shelley, Mary Godwin and Claire Clairmont in 1814–15, during the messy collapse of Shelley's first marriage. Thomas Barnes, editor of *The Times*, lived at Nos 48 and 49 successively from 1821 to 1836 with his mistress, Mrs Dinah Mondet. She accompanied him to Soho Square, where he died in 1841, and inherited all his money. Joseph Haydn, of the *Dictionary of Dates*, has also been associated with the square. He moved to London in 1839 and died in poverty in 1856.

The square did not remain residential for long. There were several factories by the 1840s – spring works, file manufacturer, wood engraver – and a pub, the Lord Nelson, at No. 64. By the mid-1850s only half the houses had private residents. In 1899

Numbers 44–47 Nelson Square, Southwark, in 2013.

the Booth survey found 'old fashioned balconied 4½ and 5½ storied houses. Good trees, but barely kept square [garden]. Women's University Settlement on the south side and one good private house on the north side, but many let in tenements, and servants only occasional.' The Women's University Settlement, a slum mission encouraged by Octavia Hill, opened at No. 45 in 1887 and expanded into the neighbouring houses, which is how they came to survive.

There was extensive bomb damage in the Second World War, worst on the east and west sides and at the east end of the south side beyond the Women's University Settlement houses. Most of the south side and the east end of the north might perhaps have been saved, as they only suffered blast damage, but Southwark Council began buying houses immediately after the war as the site for a housing estate, for which all but the sad survivors were sacrificed in the late 1940s and early 1950s.

Nelson Square

See Hamilton Square

Nevern Square

Nevern Square was the last desperate attempt to breathe life into a dying architectural and social model. After 250 years the fashionable London

The west side of Nevern Square, *c.* 1905.

square had run its course. Its popularity had been waning since the 1850s and by 1880 it was no longer possible to sell enough houses of this size to the people of rank and wealth the developers needed to attract. The trend towards smaller families and fewer servants meant that many of the rich were attracted to the serviced luxury flats springing up everywhere. Others preferred a detached house with a garden in the outer suburbs, and for those who still wished to live in a square there was plenty of choice in the old, aristocratic squares of the West End. Failure was confessed at Nevern Square by the flats known as Nevern Mansions that were built flanking its southern entrance in 1889–91.

Lord Kensington's surveyors had originally intended to build a network of simple streets on this part of his estate, but in 1877 they decided to include a square, and in 1880 they found a builder, Robert Whitaker, willing to take the risk. Undeterred by the recent and local failure of Earls Court Square, he agreed high terms for the land and borrowed heavily to finance the project. As architect he chose the young and inexperienced Walter Graves, who supplied a tame design that borrowed some of the less interesting features of the contemporary Cadogan Square.

Building began in 1880 and in August 1882 Whitaker was advertising his houses in these terms:

To be let or sold, first class family residences, situate within two minutes' walk of Earls-court Station, and 15 minutes of Kensington Gardens; they are fitted throughout with electric bells, speaking tubes, hot and cold water services, and all the modern arrangements … the square, which is in a very fine open locality, is planted with shrubs, and well turfed, suitable for lawn tennis and croquet; rents on lease 150l. per annum; price 2200l.; term 98 years.

Some were occupied in that year and most of the north, east and south sides had been completed when Whitaker died at No. 3 in January 1885. The west side, which he had barely begun, was built in 1885–86 by George Whitaker, an architect as well as a builder who, if he was a relation, was not a close one. His houses follow the main lines of the Graves design, but are simpler and more conventional.

At first, while a new square in a fairly new style was a novelty, Robert Whitaker had done quite well in selling and letting his houses and servicing his debt. After his death things fell apart and his widow was forced to surrender possession to the mortgagees early in the twentieth century. The Booth survey had noted many empty houses in 1899.

Boarding houses began to appear before the First World War and after it the division of houses into flats became commonplace. The only celebrities of the square were the actor Edward Compton and his wife and leading lady, Virginia, who lived at No. 1 from 1901 to 1918. It was a large family home, so their son Compton Mackenzie was an occasional member of the household until his marriage in 1905, and his sister Fay Compton, the actress, and her husband Harry Pélissier, the writer, producer and star of comic reviews, also lived there from time to time. The house was destroyed in the Second World War.

Every house in Nevern Square was seriously damaged by a flying bomb that fell in the north-west corner of the garden in July 1944. That makes its present neat and coherent appearance a miracle of careful restoration and tactful rebuilding, sometimes in a simplified style. The replacement for No. 1, the old Compton Mackenzie house, for example, lacks the ornamentation of the original, and the west side has suffered from the loss of the first floor verandas that used to enliven a number of houses. Only on the north side, west of Nevern Road, did the restorers admit defeat, and even there the flats that were built respect the proportions and materials of the surrounding houses. The private garden is large and well maintained and has unusually fine gates, designed by Walter Graves.

New Alley Square

LIMEHOUSE [TOWER HAMLETS]

New Alley at Limehouse ran east from the south end of the now extinct Church Row to Three Colt Street, where it emerged nearly opposite Gun Lane, now Grenade Street. New Alley Square consisted of three or four small cottages off the south side of the alley.

Horwood's 1790s map named New Alley and clearly showed the unnamed square with a terrace of three cottages on the east side and a single house on the west. Fifty years earlier Rocque had shown gardens at this point. The district was a rough one, many of the houses being brothels for foreign seamen or dangerous thieves' dens. The LCC had scheduled the alley and the square as part of a slum clearance area before the Second World War, and anything the council failed to remove was effectively cleared by German bombs. Brewster House was built on the site in the 1960s.

New Buckenham Square

See Buckenham Square

New End Square

HAMPSTEAD [CAMDEN]

New End was a seventeenth-century development of cottages on the manorial waste, gradually encroached from the heath by brickmakers and others. By the early eighteenth century, with the exploitation of the mineral well giving the village a new popularity as a health resort, it had grown into a substantial addition to Hampstead.

Burgh House, the biggest in New End Square, was built in 1703 and enlarged for the physician to the wells, perhaps in the 1720s. Numbers 16–20 on the west side of the square are also of early eighteenth-century origin, but heavily restored or rebuilt.

A single large house and its garden occupied the whole of the south side until a terrace of three houses was built over the garden late in the nineteenth

The south-west corner of New End Square in 1909.

century. The big house, at the west end, was destroyed in the Second World War and has been replaced by a blatant block of flats. The ancestor of No. 40, near the corner of Flask Walk, was a pub named the Hawk until late in the eighteenth century. The house was rebuilt in 1815.

The New End area declined during the nineteenth century, with many of the larger houses being divided into tenements. In 1898 the Booth survey found 'New End Square, at the north end of which are four houses rather poorer than their neighbours; at the south end it becomes middle class'. In 1905 the residents included a carpenter, a farrier, a boot maker, an upholsterer and a firm of plumbers. There was severe bomb damage during the Second World War, with the north-west corner destroyed, the west side badly damaged and the south side shaken by blast.

As a result the square, always a very miscellaneous triangle, now features original houses of various dates (some heavily restored), new houses, and two blocks of flats, one trying to blend in, the other defiantly out of keeping with its surroundings. Nevertheless, the gentrification that transformed Hampstead after the war extended eventually to include New End Square when the supply of houses in the better preserved streets ran short. Burgh House, surrounded by blocks of council flats, is now the Hampstead Museum.

New Inn Square

SHOREDITCH [HACKNEY]

New Inn Square was created in the second half of the eighteenth century, before 1783. It was fully formed by the 1790s, when this area was in the process of rapid development. There were ten houses, four on each side and two at the south end, separated by a narrow passage leading to Socrates Place.

If this was ever a spot for philosophic retirement, the peace was shattered in the early 1860s when the North London Railway viaduct into Broad Street brushed past the east side of the square. Widening of the line in 1874 took out the east side altogether, leaving five houses confronting a high wall. In 1898 it was described as 'poor, noisy, Irish, windows broken, used to be quiet but not so now'.

New Inn Square from the north in 2009.

Today New Inn Square is a yard alongside the Overground viaduct, looking rather like Reliance Square, its near neighbour to the south; but it is given a little more atmosphere by its cobbles and the warehouses that occupy the west side. The narrow entrance to Socrates Place still exists, but enquiry into it has to be abandoned in face of a dead end.

New Square

BERMONDSEY [SOUTHWARK]

New Square, which was known at first as Horsleydown Square, took its names from Horsleydown New Stairs on the Thames, and from New Street which led directly to the stairs from Gainsford Street. Hatton mentioned New Street in 1708 and Strype's map published in 1720 showed it as a lane of uniform width. In the 1740s Rocque indicated a distinctly widened northern half, which he called Horsleydown Square, a name that persisted during the eighteenth century. By 1810 it had been superseded by New Square.

This close to the river, it was soon dominated by granaries and warehouses, but some slums survived in an offshoot on the west side called Morris's Court. Charles Booth's research assistant wrote the last word on New Square in 1899:

> Women, loud voiced and foul tongued. ('A little bit of Bermondsey,' said [Constable] Watts, as they flung threatening words at some children that were playing near.) Dirt, squalid children, with the continuous and miserable wailing of one inside. One woman, sitting outside her house, handsome, strong, and stupid with drink. All the signs to make one suspect that this out of the world corner of London is also one of its most drunken and low-lived spots. While we were there a crowd of urchins who had been bathing in the Thames rushed up, naked, to dress: a little public, perhaps, but the best thing we saw.

The square ceased to exist in 1906, when the LCC demolished most of it and widened New Street, giving the name of Maguire Street to both. The changes were made to accommodate the LCC's storm water pumping station which (in its cunning disguise as a nonconformist chapel) still dominates the centre of Maguire Street, where Morris's Court used to be. One building does survive from New Square: Wheat Wharf, the large granary that occupied half of the west side from early in the nineteenth century. The granary is now confronted on the other side of what was the square by the staring white wall of the Design Museum.

New Square

(now part of Vine Street)

The Ogilby & Morgan map of 1676 and the Strype map of 1720, which relies heavily on its predecessor, showed a small, elongated open space between Vine Street and Minories called Pope's Yard by the first and Goodwin's Yard by the second. A Pope's Yard was mentioned there in 1708 and 1732. In 1746 Rocque showed New Square on this same site as a small, distinct entity, square in shape, approached from Vine Street and Minories by narrow passages. It had seventeen houses in 1752.

The building of America Square and John Street (now Crosswall) in the 1760s disrupted the street pattern and Vine Street, moved eastwards, had to take a most awkward detour around New Square, as Horwood's 1790s map indicated. By 1813 the inconvenience of this had evidently been felt and gaps had been made in the north and south sides of the square to allow the Vine Street traffic to pass through it. As a result, the detour section ceased to be used but remained to the west of the square like an oxbow lake.

As a name, 'New Square' was probably meant to be merely descriptive and temporary, although it lasted so long. A possible alternative name is suggested by the fact that Maitland included a Union Square, Minories, in his 1756 list, which was probably compiled in 1732. This may have been Maitland's name for New Square, as that and Haydon Square were the only two shown off Minories on Rocque's map of the 1740s, and Haydon Square appears in the list, as 'Hydon'. At that date the name 'Union' usually referred to the parliamentary union of England and Scotland in 1706.

Vine Street in 2008, showing the former New Square, City of London.

New Square, its name less and less appropriate, continued to enjoy an independent existence until about 1913, when the confusion of having two distinct parts of Vine Street to the north and south led to its abolition. But although its name could be taken away at a stroke its shape could not, and it remains an unmistakeable square to this day. There was bomb damage during the Second World War to all the buildings except those in the north-east corner. It was most severe on the west side, where the buildings had long been part of a huge range of bonded warehouses and there the old building line has been lost.

St Paul's Church. The building also housed the church school, which took it over completely when the 'permanent' St Paul's was built in Pear Tree Street in 1875. (That church was bombed in 1940 and not rebuilt.) The school became redundant in 1881 when the Compton Street School was built behind. In 1889–90 the old school was converted into industrial dwellings called St Paul's Buildings, and later the Cavendish Dwellings. They survived until 1959, but an office block has been built over the site since then.

New Square

New Square, otherwise known as New Place Square, was built in the 1830s off the north side of New Street, from which it was approached through an archway. New Street, a development of the 1820s, was off the east side of Limekiln Hill, now the southern end of Three Colt Street. New Street was later part of Phoebe Street, but that no longer exists. The square, which had eight houses on three sides, was demolished about 1890 for the sake of the Gill Street School. Its successor, the much larger Cyril Jackson Primary School, still occupies the site.

New Square

New Square was begun about 1680 on a piece of ground known as Little or Lower Lincoln's Inn Fields, by Henry Searle (or Serle) one of the benchers of Lincoln's Inn. His brethren objected to this intrusion on their privacy and from 1682 the project was a joint venture by Searle and the inn, with chambers instead of houses. After Searle's death the work was carried on by Nicholas Barbon, formerly the bitter enemy of the lawyers. The finishing touch was the gateway to Carey Street on the south side, built in 1697. The north side was left open.

For more than a century the name remained unsettled, with Searle's Court or Square appearing as often as New Square. In 1708 Hatton called it 'Searls court, a fine new Square, being a great improvement,

New Square

New Square was formerly one of the 101 places named New Court. It was a cul-de-sac of ten cottages off the north side of Allen Street, now Dallington Street, occupied by such craftsmen as gold beaters and bookbinders. The land, which belonged to the Charterhouse, was built over in the seventeenth century, but almost entirely rebuilt between 1760 and the 1790s, and it was then that New Court appeared.

The change to New Square in the 1840s was short-lived, as all the cottages were demolished around 1860 to make way for the first, temporary, very pleasant Chambers; in the Center of which, is a Fountain, also a fine Fluted Column and Clock, etc.' In 1722 William Stow called it 'Lincolns Inn Square, in Lincolns Inn. Otherwise call'd Serle's Court.' The address of Samuel Illidge, the publisher, appears in 1725 on the title page of *The Amorous History of the Gauls* as 'under Serle's Gate Lincolns-Inn New-Square'. The originator is now commemorated by Serle Street, which runs behind the west side of the square.

Even James Ralph liked New Square. In 1734 he wrote:

Lincoln's Inn may reasonably boast of one of the neatest squares in town; and though it is imperfect on one side, yet that very defect produces a beauty, by giving a prospect to the gardens, which fills the space to abundantly more advantage. I may safely add, that no area is anywhere kept in better order, either for cleanliness and beauty by day, or for illumination and decorum by night.

In 1804 William Herbert described Searle's Court as 'surrounded on three sides by large handsome brick buildings, the chambers of which are spacious and convenient, but for the most part want rebuilding'.

The 'Inigo Jones' fountain in the centre was, he thought, 'in itself a handsome decoration; but if it were still kept playing, would preserve its name with more propriety, and give far greater pleasure than the basin of stagnant water which at present scandalizes the place'. The garden was planted and enclosed with railings in 1845, but sadly disturbed in 1867, mercifully only for a season, when a miniature version of the Brompton Boilers was built there to display the rival designs for the new law courts. (See Victoria Park Square for the Brompton Boilers.)

The tenants of the chambers in New Square were more exclusively legal than most of the others in the Inns of Court, but there have been a couple of literary associations. The Irish actor, playwright and journalist Arthur Murphy also pursued a busy and successful legal career and was a bencher of Lincoln's Inn. He had chambers at No. 1 New Square from 1757 to 1788. At No. 8 Charles Dickens worked in 1828–29 as a clerk to Charles Molloy. He thought well enough of his boss to employ him later as his own solicitor. A few architects crept into No. 2 at the beginning of the twentieth century.

Fortunately, William Herbert's advice was ignored, except in the case of emergencies. Numbers 10 and 11,

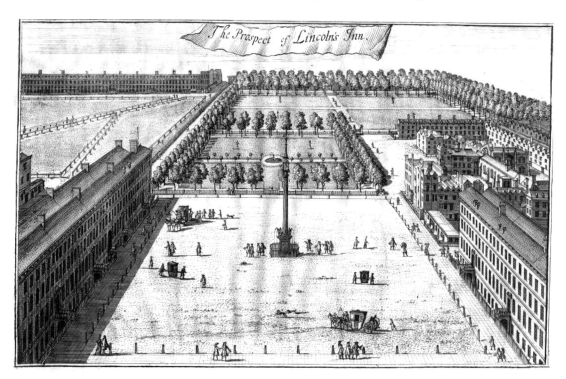

New Square, Lincoln's Inn, from the south in 1720 or a little earlier.

The building used in 1867 to display the law courts designs in the garden of New Square, Lincoln's Inn.

for example, had already been largely rebuilt after a fire in 1752 and No. 11 was rebuilt again after Second World War bomb damage. With such minor exceptions, this is the only example in London of an intact seventeenth-century square. It even incorporates something a good deal older, as Nos 12 and 13 at the north end of the east side are part of the Tudor Old Buildings.

The only qualification to the enjoyment of this lovely square is the ugly modern fountain, with a mound that obstructs views across the garden.

New Square

WESTMINSTER

Westminster's New Square was a small court off the south side of Orchard Street, just west of St Ann's Street. It was built in 1790 and first appeared in the 1791 ratebook, with only four of its twelve little houses occupied. The name came from New Street, which ran north from Orchard Street, nearly opposite the entrance to the square, until it was removed to make way for Victoria Street.

The square was much frequented by prostitutes, who could pick up plenty of tipsy clients around the Palace of Westminster and the abbey. The square just survived the large clearances required for the construction of Victoria Street, but was demolished in the early 1880s when the Peabody Abbey Orchard Estate was built on the site of this and a number of other small streets and alleys. The Peabody tenements are a little less dismal than the courts they replaced.

New Square

WHITECHAPEL [TOWER HAMLETS]

This was a short cul-de-sac, no wider than an alley, off the east side of Upper North Street (now Brady Street) opposite the Jews' Burial Ground. It contained eighteen cottages, eight on the north and south sides and two at the east end. The use of the name 'square' was a brief affectation of the middle to late nineteenth century. The only excuse for it was the sense of space created by the long front gardens of the cottages on the north and south sides. The alley was called Howe Place in 1830 and Holme's Avenue in 1913. It was demolished soon after the First World War to provide part of the site for the LCC's large Collingwood Estate. Rutherford House replaced the square in the 1920s.

New Square

See Grafton Square and Quaker Square

New Street Square

CITY OF LONDON (1)

New Street Square was a new name, probably adopted very early in the eighteenth century, for a place that had already existed for fifty years or more as West and East Harding Street. Those names came from Agnes Hardinge, who gave the land to the Goldsmiths' Company in 1513. The 1676 map showed the square as West and East Harding Street in exactly the form it retained until recent years. 'Westharding Street alias New Street' was mentioned in 1664.

All the maps from 1676 showed buildings in the centre of the square. In 1666 and 1676 there were sixteen and in the 1790s twelve of them, facing outwards to the street with small private yards in the middle, accessible only through the houses. The change to New Street Square was most likely made (for reasons of fashion) before 1708, when the Harding names migrated south. 'New Street Square, near Fetter lane' was William Stow's name in 1722. New Street became a general name for the district.

There were at least two pubs in the square. The White Swan, which existed by 1730, was at No. 1 and the Gentleman & Porter at No. 30. Many of the other houses were occupied by brass founders, printers and engravers. The most important building on the outer ring was the works of Spottiswoode & Co., the Queen's printers. Andrew Spottiswoode was the son-in-law and eventual successor of William Strahan, who had been printing in this district since the 1740s. The Spottiswoode premises eventually occupied the whole of the east side and stretched south to Little New Street and east to Shoe Lane. There was even a Spottiswoode Institute in the square, for the recreation of the workers.

The houses around the edge were rebuilt from time to time as the leases fell in. Numbers 19, 20 and 21 on the south side were described in 1806 as 'small well-built brick dwelling houses, held on a 43 year lease from the Goldsmiths' Company by John Lowington, carpenter'.

In 1852 or soon after the centre was transformed into McLean's Buildings, a large set of chambers entered via a glazed passage opposite Dean Street, later Dean Lane. The 1930s map showed the centre occupied by 'McCleans', with the northern two-thirds a solid building and the southern third glass, so there must have been some rebuilding between 1914 and 1937. The journalist William Titterton described it in 1926:

> I know a square which is no square at all – it is just a dreary street running (or rather crawling) round a maze of streets and houses: they call it New Street Square. It is given over to printing and publishing, and devoted to the befogging of strayed revellers. If you have had old ale at the Cheese, and turned right instead of left when the little fat waiter has wafted you to the door, beyond a peradventure you will at last find yourself in New Street Square. It is even money that you will not find your way out again. 'Last seen heading for New Street Square' might be the epitaph of any of us.

There was serious bomb damage on the west and south sides of the square, which was rebuilt in the 1950s and 1960s with tall, ugly office blocks, mostly by Richard Seifert, and a multistorey car park.

New Street Square (1), City of London, from the south in 2011.

Now at last there is an open space at New Street Square after 350 years without one. The power of the name ensured that when it was entirely rebuilt in 2007–08 a large, handsomely paved courtyard was included as a fashionable centrepiece to ranges of huge office blocks. The recipe is some shops and restaurants, a wine bar, a few seats, a few trees, and a security guard to say 'You can't take photos here, Sir, this is private property'. The new New Street Square is Paternoster Square, in fact, without the location, the flair or the Wren.

New Street Square

CITY OF LONDON (2 AND 3)

In 1831 James Elmes created two imaginary places called New Street Square in his *Topographical Dictionary of London*, through an error in cutting and pasting from the first edition of Lockie's *Topography of London* of 1810. Both were simply New Street. His New Street Square, Aldersgate Street, is the present Newbury Street, Cloth Fair. His New Street Square, Blackfriars, is the present Burgon Street.

New Street Square

OLD STREET [ISLINGTON]

This was probably another error of James Elmes, who listed it in 1831 with his two false City of London New Street Squares. Here also the direction was merely to a New Street, this one now extinguished. It turned off the north side of Old Street just east of Ironmonger Row, the present St Luke's Close.

Newport Square

See Bearbone Square

Nicholl Square

CITY OF LONDON

Like its close neighbour Falcon Square, Nicholl Square was merely a widened converging point of several streets, in this case Castle Street, Red Cross Square (later Hamsell Street), Well Street and Maidenhead Court.

Henry Harben was mistaken in saying in his *Dictionary of London* that it was formerly called Red Cross Square. It emerged in the second half of the eighteenth century from the tangle of alleys shown at this point on Rocque's map of 1746. Horwood named it Nicols Square in the 1790s and indicated about eight houses around the open space, but all numbered in one or another of the converging streets. That must have changed almost immediately, as the address of the coal merchants J.&E. Barnard was given as Nicholl's Square, Aldersgate, in a 1794 directory, No. 13 was insured by a toyman in the same year, and there were eventually at least twenty-three numbered properties.

Number 16 was a pub named the Gentleman & Porter, which existed by 1803. An 1817 directory noted eighteen houses, but in 1841 there were only nine inhabited, including the pub, with a mixture of middle-class and working-class tenants. The square became entirely commercial soon afterwards and in its later years was popular with the clothing trades. It was destroyed by bombing in 1940, and the southern end of Mountjoy House on the Barbican Estate now covers the site.

Nichols Square

Nichols Square was quite large and must have been pretty when first built, but its location between Hackney Road and Kingsland Road gave it no chance of retaining these attractions. Walford said the square was named after the talented Nichols family, printers, publishers, editors and antiquaries through three generations, who owned the land on which it was built in 1841. Peter Chassereau's 1745 map of Shoreditch showed 'Nichols Esqr.' as the owner of a good deal of the land to the east, but the field on which the square was later built as belonging to 'Pippit'. This explains the mysterious 'Papiet Square, or Allports' that appeared in the correct position in the 1841 census, but with only two houses occupied: it was clearly a tentative name for Nichols Square. John Allport was the nurseryman who occupied the land until it was ripe for building.

The terraces on the perimeter of the square were in a late classical style, with porches to add dignity.

By the late 1840s twenty-eight semi-detached houses had been built in the centre, perhaps replacing a transient garden. These were in the Tudor style, something along the lines of the nearby De Beauvoir Square. There was also a charming little Tudor lodge, complete with heraldic beast presiding over the gable. Beside it was a tiny triangular green where the entrance from Hackney Road divided to approach the south and east sides of the square.

There were some moderately prosperous residents in the early days. The actor and theatre manager Robert Honner, one of the first exponents of the role of Ebenezer Scrooge, died in Nichols Square in 1852.

The west side was destroyed as early as the 1860s when the viaduct of the North London Railway, running into Broad Street, cut a swath through Shoreditch. More of the west end was lost when sidings were added late in the century, and at that point the twenty-eight houses in the centre became twenty-six, the last two now detached. Several houses were also demolished in the north-east corner of the square to make way for St Chad's. The church of 1867–69 and the vicarage of 1873–74 were designed by

The Queen Victoria Jubilee Institute for Nurses occupied Numbers 76, 78 and 80 Nichols Square, at the north-west corner of the inner section. The recessed part of the building was infill, quite new when the photograph was taken *c.* 1910.

James Brooks, the favourite architect of the London Anglo-Catholics.

Any social pretensions the square started with were long gone when the Booth surveyor visited in 1898: '2½ storied houses, only one entrance, almost monopolised by policemen … plasterfronts, 2 families to most of the houses, rents 17/-'.

Nichols Square got through the Second World War with hardly any bomb damage, which was remarkable next to a railway line and near a major road junction, but all the 1840s houses were demolished in the early 1960s to make way for a council estate. Now the only surviving buildings, St Chad's and its vicarage, have addresses in Dunloe Street. They are surrounded by blocks of flats in various styles, all bad.

Nightingale Square

BALHAM [WANDSWORTH]

Nightingale Square is traditional in its planning and organisation, but extraordinary in being so late an example of the traditional style. It was laid out in the late 1880s on the site of a house called Woodlands. The original idea was to call it Mackay Square: that name was approved in 1888, but changed to Nightingale Square in the following year. (Woodlands had had its entrance in Nightingale Lane, to the north.)

The oldest houses are the few at the east end, but they are numbered in and belong to Endlesham Road, which existed before the square was thought of. The long north and south sides were built gradually during the 1890s; the drainage applications were made in batches between 1889 and 1896.

There is nothing memorable about the houses, which are typical late Victorian pairs and terraces. They are well built and well maintained, but the slope of the land from north to south and from west to east is all that gives them any interest. The shady private garden is the attractive feature. It is a long oval, higher than the surrounding road, and enclosed by a stepped brick wall and sturdy railings.

The only buildings of note are at the east end of the square in a Roman Catholic enclave consisting of the Church of the Holy Ghost, the former Convent of Perpetual Adoration and two schools. The convent was built in the late 1880s, the Church of the Holy Ghost (designed by Leonard Stokes) in 1897. The church school and Oak Lodge School for the Deaf, with buildings of no interest whatever, are fitted discreetly into the two corners, almost out of sight.

The south side of Nightingale Square, *c.* 1910, showing the church and convent at the east end.

Nixon's Square

Nixon's Square appeared as quite a well-formed feature on Rocque's map of the 1740s and was included in Maitland's list of 1756, which probably meant that it existed by 1732. The Ogilby & Morgan map of 1676 showed Goldsmith's Alley, which later led from Jewin Street to Nixon's Square but in 1676 merely turned to the east and ended in Bull's Head Court.

The Strype map of 1720 or earlier showed an intermediate stage, with an open space emerging between Goldsmith's Alley and Bull's Head Court. Strype called Bulls Head Court 'a handsome Place, with good Buildings, and well inhabited'. Two adjoining sentences may be of equal significance:

> Lauderdale Court, a good large Place, well built and inhabited; being built out of the Garden belonging to Lauderdale House, seated in Aldersgate street; but some of the ground lieth yet unbuilt. And on the East side of the Entrance into this Court, going up Steps, is Goldsmiths Court, which is but ordinary.

Lauderdale Court, which was named by Hatton in 1708, did not appear in later sources, so may perhaps have been one of the constituent parts of Nixon's Square. On Strype's map Goldsmith's Alley was called Lauderdale Court. Nixon's Square, then, was a widening of the east–west section of Goldsmith's Alley, undertaken early in the eighteenth century, perhaps by a developer or landowner named Nixon. Dodsley called it 'a very mean little square' in 1761.

Nixon's Square was still shown on Cary's 1795 map. It was cleared, or largely cleared, when the Jewin Crescent scheme was put forward in the 1790s, but Jewin Crescent took so long to complete that the western end, where the square had been, remained a vacant space for many years. Jewin Crescent was as unsuccessful as the square, being consumed by fire in 1897 and bombed to extinction during the Second World War. The City of London School for Girls in the Barbican Estate is now more or less on the site.

Norfolk Square

In the development of Bayswater the Grand Junction Road (now Sussex Gardens) was a social barrier. To the south lay the squares and crescents of middle-class Tyburnia, to the north the shops and houses of the tradesmen who catered to the needs of the middle classes.

The three physical features that reduced the value of these northern acres were the Paddington Basin of the Grand Junction Canal with its associated wharves and industry, Paddington Station, and the reservoirs of the Grand Junction Waterworks Company. The third of these drawbacks was removed in the 1840s when the Waterworks Company closed its Bayswater reservoirs, which were quickly drained and made available for building. The estate surveyor decided to lay out squares in the two southern reservoirs, in an attempt to push the boundary of fashionable Bayswater from Grand Junction Road to Praed Street. Norfolk Square, on the site of the South Reservoir, was the first of the two new developments. Talbot Square followed a few years later.

Faced with a difficult property to market, Victorian developers would often begin with a church as a solid and unmissable symbol of the quality and respectability of the houses that were to follow. Here the church, which occupied the whole of the short east side of the square, was ready long before the first house was begun. The original All Saints', designed by Henry Clutton, was consecrated in November 1847.

The square has only two sides of houses, the west end being formed by the older London Street. Building began at the west end, as being closer to civilisation. Numbers 1–10 were first occupied in 1854, fifteen houses (of an eventual fifty-five) had found tenants by 1856 and the square was completed in 1859.

The original plan was to give variety to the terraces by arranging them in alternating blocks of five and four storeys, and an anticipatory lithograph was published showing this arrangement. In the event, when the builders returned to five storeys after the first dip they could not bear to drop again and continued at the same height to the east end. They also added

The north-east front of All Saints', Norfolk Square, seen *c.* 1905 from Cambridge Place, now Norfolk Place.

porches to a number of houses. Most of them were owned by the Bloomsbury solicitors, Harrison & Beal.

The square succeeded fairly well in its first half-century, with many barristers, doctors and senior army officers among the residents. With its tall trees and houses and narrow garden this is one of the darkest and gloomiest of London squares. Is that why it has been the home of some serious thinkers? The most notable residents were the historian John Addington Symonds, who lived at No. 47 from 1865 to 1868, J.M.E. McTaggart, the philosopher, who was born at No. 28 in 1866, and the classical scholar Walter Headlam, who was born at No. 24 in the same year. Two distinguished scientists lived at No. 41, Professor William Edward Ayrton from 1903 until his death in 1908, and his wife Hertha Ayrton from 1903 until 1923. The house has a high and easily missed plaque to her. The fine arts are represented by the sculptor Richard Westmacott the younger, who was one of the first residents, at No. 18 from 1855 to 1857.

All Saints' Church was destroyed by fire in 1894 and rebuilt in 1895. The architect was Ralph Nevill, a pupil of Sir George Gilbert Scott. The composer Sir Edward Bairstow was organist and choirmaster in the 1890s. The church was closed in 1919 when the parish was united with St Michael & All Angels, Star Street, and the building was used as the headquarters of the Royal Association in Aid of the Deaf and Dumb. It was called back into service as a parish church when St Michael & All Angels was bombed in 1941, but was closed again and demolished in 1961. Flats providing sheltered accommodation for the elderly were built on the site. The block is called Edna House, and deserves the name.

In the twentieth century the influence of Paddington Station made itself felt, with a few hotels, clubs, hostels and nursing homes intruding among the private houses by 1914. This is a trend that nearly always accelerates once it begins. There was quite serious Second World War bomb damage to the east end of the north side and blast damage all along the south side. On the north the disruption is still obvious from the denuded appearance of the houses. Since the war the square has been almost entirely given over to hotels, most of them small. At the shabby east end there is also a student hostel. The atmosphere is rather that of Kemp Town, some way from the front.

Norfolk Square

In the 1820s, before the nearby Tibberton and Adelaide Squares were built, the land behind the houses and intended houses in Rotherfield Street, Queen Street, New Norfolk Street and Morton Road began to be filled with a dense network of alleys and courts. Such back development was characteristic of this poor area south of the Essex Road and the result was usually a slum. The three main elements of this warren were known as Norfolk Court, Norfolk Gardens and Norfolk Square, names that did not become established until the 1840s. The only entrance was along a narrow alley entered beneath an archway in New Norfolk Street. Norfolk Square was the part closest to the entrance; the name was suggested by a slightly wider and squarer opening between the cottages.

The Islington Vestry demolished the fifty-two slum houses in the late 1890s, using powers granted in the Housing of the Working Classes Act. The vestry wanted the cleared ground to be a park, but the Local Government Board thought there was an obligation to use it for housing, and that was the decision of the

inspector who reported in 1901. But in 1904 Islington Council was able to overturn this decision and create the desired park or playground with the assistance of £4,000 from the LCC. It was small, being bounded on three sides by the backs of houses and open only to Morton Road.

As a result of the subsequent clearance of the houses backing onto the playground in Ecclesbourne Road (formerly New Norfolk Street) and Queensbury Street (the old Queen Street), and the treatment of most of the open space as a lawn, something like a real square has now been created. The fact has been recognised in the design of the flats facing the garden in Queensbury Street and Morton Road, which pay homage to the architecture of the humbler Georgian square.

Norland Square

The square was built on the site of Norland House, formerly a school, which belonged from 1792 to Benjamin Vulliamy, a Pall Mall watchmaker and the father of the architect Lewis Vulliamy. It was let

The west side of Norland Square, showing the Notting Hill and Bayswater High School, *c.* 1920.

to Henry Drummond, the Charing Cross banker. In February 1825, when sublet to 'a respectable family from India', the house was destroyed by fire, the tenants escaping with only the clothes they could 'hurry on'. Two years later Vulliamy offered the ruins and 25 acres to the Middlesex justices as a site for a county asylum. Luckily for the future prosperity of Holland Park, the price asked was too high and a new institution for the lunatics was built at Hanwell instead.

It is odd that Benjamin Vulliamy, with free domestic architectural advice so readily available, did not think of developing the estate himself. Perhaps he was too wise to get involved in the perils of Victorian building speculation. Instead, in 1839 he sold the estate to Charles Richardson, a Golden Square solicitor, who sank huge sums in the development and was eventually bankrupted in 1855. The southern part of the estate, which included Royal Circus as well as Norland Square, was laid out by Richardson's surveyor, Robert Cantwell. He was the architect of the circus and probably of at least some of the houses in the square.

The building work did not run smoothly. Holland Park was still considered too far west for fashion or convenience and although Richardson managed, by hook or by crook, to lease all the plots in the square by 1844, bricks and mortar lagged far behind paper commitments. Only No. 1 was occupied in 1843. The development proceeded haltingly through the 1840s and it was not until 1853 that all the houses were completed and tenanted.

Considering the number of builders involved and the protracted development, a surprising uniformity was achieved. The terrace on the north side features plain pilasters between the houses, but in other respects the three sides are almost identical. The houses have ground floor bows like Montagu Square, but with windows only at the front allowing no glimpse into the neighbours' parlours.

Despite the shortcomings of the windows the square attracted many ladies of private means and a number of solicitors and doctors. The celebrity was Robert Fitzroy, captain of the *Beagle* during Darwin's momentous voyage and the father of weather forecasting. He lived at No. 4 in the early 1850s, before settling in Onslow Square.

There were several private schools for boys and girls, and in 1873 the first two houses in Holland Park Avenue, at the south-west corner, were replaced by a large new building for the Notting Hill and Bayswater High School. It became No. 53 Norland Square. This was the second venture of the very successful Girls' Public Day School Company, now known as the Girls' Day School Trust. When the school moved to Ealing in 1930 the building was replaced by Norland Square Mansions, the only blot on the classic unity of the design.

Norland Square was overwhelmed with boarding houses in the early twentieth century, but after passing through the Second World War unscathed it recovered strongly and has now achieved a status far higher than that of its earliest and most optimistic days. The large and attractive garden is private.

North Square

BETHNAL GREEN [TOWER HAMLETS]

North Square was built about 1820. It was of the front garden type, two terraces of seven cottages facing each other across long gardens. The square branched south from the east end of Portman Place, a road formerly known as North Street. It has now been reduced to little more than a drive to Morpeth School.

There were originally two entrances to the square, from North Street and from Prospect Place to the south. When the Eastern Counties Railway built its line into Shoreditch in the late 1830s, Prospect Place had to be rebuilt further north and its prospect was changed from fields to a close-range view of the viaduct. The building of the railway also destroyed the passage south from the square, which had a terrace of cottages on the east side. Thereafter the only access was from the north.

The square was doomed from the moment the School Board for London opened its Portman Place School in 1878. It was steadily enlarged, in 1884 and again in 1896, taking over more and more of the south side of Portman Place. North Square was gobbled up before the First World War, and since the Second the renamed Morpeth School has swallowed most of Portman Place as well.

North Square

North Place was a turning off the east side of Love Lane, now Putney Bridge Road; North Passage is its present representative. It was an old lane that gave access to market gardens and water meadows. In 1787 it had a garden on the south side owned by John Wilmot, Esq.

The element that led to its sometimes being called North Square was the pair of terraces, twelve cottages in each, built over Wilmot's garden early in the nineteenth century. They formed a square of the front garden type, the terraces facing each other across long gardens, with an access path down the centre. In 1838 the cottages belonged to various members of the Cumbers family, who gave their name to the nearby Cumbers Yard.

Such amenities as the square originally possessed – quiet and a view of the river – were lost when the London & South-Western Railway viaduct was built a few yards to the north in the late 1830s. It did not sound a pleasant spot as described by the Booth survey in 1899: 'North Place and large court south out of it, 2 and a few 3 storey; large front gardens in court; poor and rough. Corner of North Place a great gathering place for gangs of rough lads and loafing men.' It was marked down as a slum clearance area in the 1930s. The smart new Adelaide Road is now on the site.

Northampton Square

The earls of Northampton owned an estate at Clerkenwell from 1610 and in the 1660s the 3rd Earl built a great house in St John Street. The timing was bad, as the aristocratic migration to the West End had already begun. The Comptons soon followed the fashion and Northampton House spent most of the eighteenth century as a lunatic asylum and two-thirds of the nineteenth as a school. It was demolished in 1869. Much of its land had been shorn off in the 1790s as the family set about developing the estate for building.

They appointed Samuel Pepys Cockerell as surveyor in 1791. He had occupied the same position with the Foundling Hospital since 1788 and was an expert in estate development, especially in this part of London. Cockerell drew up a plan, but problems with the New River Company, whose pipes ran across

The unveiling of the George Baxter plaque at No. 11 Northampton Square in 1928.

The south-west side of Northampton Square in 2007.

the land, delayed building operations for a decade. The company's entrenched rights determined the unique diagonal layout of the estate's centrepiece, Northampton Square.

Cockerell provided elevations that were followed faithfully by the various builders engaged on the square, so that a charming external uniformity masked considerable internal differences between the houses. The roads were laid out in 1803–04 and the houses built between 1805 and 1814. The way in which the six service roads entered the square produced the unusual pattern of two long terraces and four short ones.

The square, which had always been surrounded by mean streets, suffered an early social decline. By 1840 only half the houses were occupied by private residents, the rest by businesses. All were in business use by 1880 and many had been converted into factories, with additional workshops built over the gardens. Watchmaking and metalworking were the main trades. Number 18, at the corner of Ashby Street, was the Ashby Castle pub in the 1860s and 1870s.

The most famous residents were connected with printing. One was George Virtue, the publisher of illustrated books and art journals, who lived at No. 2 in the 1840s. His printing works were in the City Road, nearby. The other was George Baxter, the pioneer of colour printing, who had his home and works at Nos 11 and 12 from 1844 to 1860. In 1928 Finsbury Council erected a commemorative plaque at No. 11. When the house was demolished a simpler replacement was put on one of the City University buildings.

It was the future 5th Marquess of Northampton (managing the estate on behalf of his father) who sowed the seeds of the square's destruction. He had opened the garden to the public in 1885 and in 1894–98 he sponsored the building of the Northampton Institute. This had its main front in St John's Street, but the triangular site tapered back to the square, involving the demolition of the shortest of the six terraces, with three houses. It is an attractive building, but it did great harm by bringing the institute into connection with the square and setting the example of demolition.

The institute grew into a polytechnic, a college, and finally into the City University in 1966. This, it was decided, required a new campus, and what could be cheaper and more convenient than to build it straight across the north side of the square? These monstrous eight storeys of concrete and glass were built between 1971 and 1979. Seventeen houses were demolished, leaving less than half of the original thirty-six standing and ruining the shape and coherence of the square.

The destruction of most squares can be blamed on bad luck, bad management, carelessness, or cupidity in various combinations, but Northampton Square was destroyed by sheer vandalism, sheer brutalism and sheer academic philistinism. Today the darkness of the brickwork of most of the surviving houses – merely the result of its never having been cleaned – together with the black railings and balconies, gives the square a pleasant sombreness little in tune with the gambols of the students in the garden. It is as though the houses were in mourning for their lost companions.

Oakley Square

SOMERS TOWN [CAMDEN]

The name comes from Oakley House near Bedford, a property of the landowner, the Duke of Bedford. The square has roughly the shape of a longbow, with a curving east side and a straight, shorter west side. There is also a terrace of six houses on the south or south-west side, which might just as well have been numbered in Eversholt Street.

Like the two other oddly shaped squares in Bedford New Town, Ampthill and Harrington, it was planned in the early 1830s. That was a difficult decade for building speculations, even in more promising locations than this, and no progress was made until 1845. Work then began at the south end with the lowest numbered houses on the east side and the Eversholt Street terrace, which had the highest numbers.

The first tenant was Donald Fraser, a surgeon and local politician who was living at No. 1 by March 1846, but only twenty-six of an eventual seventy-six houses had been built by 1851. Five years later thirty-four had found tenants and the square was complete by 1860. The duke tried to encourage builders and tenants by providing the site for a church and contributing to the cost. He was particularly insistent on a spire, to make this confidence-boosting symbol as visible as possible. St Matthew's was built at the north end of the west side in 1852–56, with John Johnson as architect. His Gothic vicarage next door was completed in 1871.

No architect's name has been mentioned in connection with the square itself, but it may be significant that William Hinton Campbell was the original tenant of No. 71, one of the first houses built. He was a pupil of Henry Goodridge of Bath and became an Associate of the RIBA in 1840. The hot-tempered artist Alexander Fussell, best known as an illustrator, lived at No. 2 in the 1850s.

The large, conventional houses proved popular and the square maintained a good reputation in the nineteenth century. Christina Rossetti gave it a testimonial in 1876: 'I like Oakley Square, with its freshness & greenness'. She was encouraging a friend who had to move out from Gordon Square as an economy measure. It was also given a good report by Charles Booth's assistant in 1898:

The garden lodge and east side of Oakley Square, c. 1905.

Large, well-built houses, the square keeping its character, with very few exceptions, as a good residential neighbourhood. At No. 4 the widow of a railway porter and at No. 20 a cabman are living, and No. 5 shows 'apartments' notice. But these exceptions. The garden of the square is still private.

Numbers 24–39 at the north end of the east side were destroyed during the Second World War, St Matthew's Church was wrecked and there was blast damage throughout the square. The rest of the east side was cleared in the 1960s as part of the site for the Ampthill Square Estate, a deeply depressing work by Eric Lyons. The church was demolished in 1977 and its walls now surround a more upmarket, but scarcely more inspiring, block of flats called St Matthew's Lodge. Opposite, at the northern point of the large public garden, a lodge managed to survive the bombing. Now the garden acts as a buffer between the original 1840s and 1850s houses and the busy road and council estate that face them.

The houses were among those destroyed by bombing.

This function is emphasised by the open railing on the west side of the garden and the thick hedge on the east.

Oakley Square

See Carlyle Square

Ogle Square

MARYLEBONE [WESTMINSTER]

The Ogles of Marylebone are complicated. The original Ogle Street was later Saville Street, but is now Hanson Street. Ogle Court was later Upper Ogle Street, but is now Ogle Street. Ogle Mews, a cul-de-sac off the east side of the present Ogle Street, no longer exists. Ogle Square was off the north side of Ogle Mews.

John Lockie explained it more clearly in his first edition of 1810 than in the 1813 revision: 'Ogle-Square, Upper Ogle-Street, Marybone, – a few small houses behind 10, three doors on the L. from 9 Upper Marybone-street'. He gave a cross reference from Ogle Court to Upper Ogle Street, and it was as Ogle Court that the present Ogle Street was named on the Horwood maps. The 1790s edition showed a small open space behind No. 10 Ogle Court, with no houses. The 1813 revision showed houses around the square, which was directly behind No. 10, as Lockie said, but had its entrance in Ogle Mews to the south.

There were four small houses in Ogle Square, valued at £8 per annum each when they were first rated in 1799. The occupants were a chair maker, turner and porter in 1841, a dressmaker, pewterer, cabinet maker and labourer in 1851, and bricklayers, a cabinet maker and a butler in 1861.

This was one of the slums of wealthy Marylebone and in the 1860s it became the focus for Roman Catholic missionary work. The St Charles Borromeo Church of 1862 is still on the west side of Ogle Street. In 1867 the east side, with much of Ogle Mews and all of Ogle Square, was demolished to make way for the St Charles elementary and grammar schools. They have gone in their turn and John Astor House now occupies most of the block.

Old Square

There were quadrangles of a collegiate kind at Lincoln's Inn from early in the sixteenth century, but they could not be called squares before that name came into fashion in the 1660s and there could not be an Old Square until there was a New.

New Square was built in the 1680s and 1690s, but its name did not become fixed until long afterwards. In 1708 Hatton wrote that apart from Searls court (our New Square) there were at Lincoln's Inn 'four other Courts which have no particular Names'. Even when Old Square did emerge as a name, which it had by the 1740s, there was great inconsistency in its use. At different times it was applied singly or collectively to all four of the courts mentioned by Hatton, only three of which still exist. It is best to describe those four courts as Old Buildings, to distinguish them from the later extensions, New Square to the south, Stone Buildings to the north and the new hall and library to the west.

In the eighteenth and nineteenth centuries Old Square was most often used to mean the two courts north and south of the chapel. The present practice of calling the southern of these Old Buildings and the northern Old Square did not become established until early in the twentieth century. By that time the Tudor chambers in the northern section had been rebuilt with the result that our Old Square – except for the chapel on the south side – is considerably less old than New Square. It was the rebuilding of the chambers between 1874 and 1886 that reduced the size of the irregular northern court and gave it a nearly square shape. The Elizabethan style was established in 1874 by Sir George Gilbert Scott's west side and followed faithfully by the architects of the north and east sides.

The eminent lawyers whose names are associated with Old Square nearly all had chambers in what is now regarded as Old Buildings. The present Old Square is too modern to have acquired such associations. With its four benches surrounding a flower bed and a young tree, it forms a pleasant enough open space, but the tall red chambers make it seem smaller than it is and only the heavily restored Jacobean chapel on the south side gives Old Square any architectural interest.

Old Square, Lincoln's Inn, from the north-west corner in 2013.

Old Square

In *Lost London: landmarks which have disappeared, pictured by J. Crowther c. 1879–87*, a book edited by Beresford Chancellor in 1926, there is a sketch of the Cheshire Cheese in Old Square, Surrey Street, Strand. The pub stood at the corner of Surrey Street and the now extinguished Howard Street, opposite the entrance to Strand Lane and the 'Old Roman Bath'. There was a slight widening of the road at this junction, but all the directories give the Cheshire Cheese as No. 10 Surrey Street, and this is the only reference I have seen to Old Square. If it was not a mistake, it can only have been an informal local name.

Old Street Square

See Bartholomew Square

Onslow Square

Henry Smith, a City merchant who died in 1628, established a charity, eventually of immense wealth, for the benefit of Barbary slaves and his own poor relations. The bulk of the charity's income came from some 100 acres of land in Westminster, Kensington and Chelsea. In the usual improvident eighteenth-century manner the trustees granted long leases at inadequate rents, but in 1807 the charity regained possession of the land, which soon became ripe for building development. In 1828 the trustees took the important step of appointing George Basevi, newly famous for Belgrave Square, as the surveyor of the London estate. He designed Pelham Crescent, Egerton Crescent and the associated roads, but the important land to the west remained open.

A small part of the site of Onslow Square was provided by the garden of Cowper House, a private lunatic asylum which stood on the south side of Brompton Road, where the west end of Melton Court is now, but most of the land came from Gibb's Nursery, the lease of which expired in 1843. In that

year a young man named Charles Freake was building St Jude's Church near the Royal Hospital, which was designed by George Basevi. This collaboration on a minor church now demolished and forgotten was probably the reason for Freake's success in bidding for the land made available by the removal of Gibb's Nursery, and was thus the foundation of a great career.

Basevi had been planning the development of the land for ten years or more in anticipation of the extinction of Thomas Gibb, and it was to this layout that Freake began his building operations in 1844. His agreement also bound him to use the elevations provided by the charity's surveyor. Freake started work on the first four houses in the square (Nos 1, 3, 5 and 7) in September 1845, and Basevi was killed in October, falling from scaffolding at Ely Cathedral. These houses were therefore begun according to Basevi's design, but probably altered during construction in line with Freake's own judgement and taste, which was a good deal less refined.

The next estate surveyor, Henry Clutton, took a far less active role than Basevi, and thereafter Freake was free to design and build without interference. Both sides benefitted: the charity's income rose to unprecedented heights and Freake ended his career as an immensely rich baronet, patron of the arts and friend of royalty. By the mid-1850s, when living at No. 79, he was describing himself as an architect.

Most of the roads on the Smith's charity estate honoured leading trustees. Onslow Square was carried over from Onslow Terrace in Brompton Road, a small development named after the 2nd Earl of Onslow, who died in 1827. Freake eventually extended Basevi's modest square to such an extent that the obscure earl is commemorated by something as large and grand as Eaton Square or Cadogan Place.

The first houses let so readily that Freake continued to take more and more land from the charity, building bigger houses and extending the square to a second garden and eventually to a third, although there the name was changed at an early stage to Onslow Gardens. Among many adjustments to the style of the houses, Freake abandoned the overall stucco favoured by Basevi and built the rest of the square in exposed grey brickwork with stucco trim. (See p.17.) Thirty-one houses were occupied by 1851, fifty-one by 1856 and the whole square was finished by 1865.

Landlords liked to include a church in any quality development, and one had been planned here from the start. Freake built and largely paid for St Paul's and became the patron of the living, an indication of his rapidly rising social status. He was also thought at one time to have been the architect, but that dubious honour is now given to James Edmeston. St Paul's was built in 1859–60 on a site given by the charity. It adjoined the back of Brompton Hospital and was not likely to be a popular site for houses.

The success of Onslow Square was with the middle classes more than the gentry and it also acquired a somewhat bohemian reputation, of a very respectable kind. The sculptor Baron Marocchetti, now best known for his 'Richard I' outside the Houses of Parliament, lived at No. 30 in the late 1840s and early 1850s, then at No. 34 until his death in 1868. At No. 34 he had a huge studio and foundry in the mews behind, and it was there that the amateur sculptor Sir Edwin Landseer cast his Trafalgar Square lions.

The square's convenience for the museums led to Sir Henry Cole living at No. 26 in 1856–57 and No. 17 from 1857 to 1863. Sir Edwin Lutyens was born

at No. 16 in 1869, the son of a painter. He lived in London squares for most of his life.

The great actress Helen Faucit lived at No. 31 from 1851, the year of her marriage to Theodore Martin, the biographer of the Prince Consort. Martin became a great favourite of Queen Victoria when the biography was well reviewed, and his wife was received at court after her retirement from the stage. They entertained widely at Onslow Square, which remained their London home for the rest of their lives. She died in 1898, he in 1909. Sir Theodore's final years were embittered by the noise from motor omnibuses passing his door. He wrote to *The Times* to complain about the nuisance in his ninetieth year. The house, on the busy north-east side of the square, was destroyed during the Second World War.

Thackeray lived at No. 36 from 1854 to 1862, when his house at Palace Green (now the Israeli Embassy) was ready. He was writing *The Newcomes* in 1854, so it is odd to find the Honourable Mrs Newcombe living at No. 25 in 1852. The proceeds of the book were spent on furniture, 'the old traps looking very decrepit in the new house'. According to his daughter, 'the result

The north-east corner of Onslow Square, *c.* 1850.

of my father's furnishings was a pleasant, bowery sort of home, with green curtains and carpets, looking out upon the elm-trees of Onslow Square'. A later writer was P.G. Wodehouse, who lived at No. 4 in the summer of 1922 and later made the square the home of one of Ukridge's many long-suffering girlfriends.

The historian H.A.L. Fisher (who was also in Lloyd George's cabinet as President of the Board of Education) was born here in 1865. His father was private secretary to the Prince of Wales until 1870, when the family moved to Sussex. Fisher begins his autobiography:

> I was born on March 21st 1865, at 3 Onslow Square, a little white slip of a house which somehow or other has continued to survive the transformations of seventy years, and still awakes as I pass it the sweet and affectionate memories of my Victorian childhood … From time to time we were warned that we should look carefully at two old gentlemen, Mr Froude and Mr Carlyle, as they strolled past the windows of No. 3, but their names meant little to us then …

Froude lived in Onslow Gardens. The Fishers' far from slip-like house, on the east side of the square, now has a bus stop outside. It is on one of the more direct routes from Kensington to Chelsea.

Onslow Square as Freake left it survives almost complete and in excellent condition. Malvern Court was built in the north-east corner in 1930–31. There were no other demolitions before the Second World War, although the charity was planning widespread rebuilding in 1939. During the war a number of houses at the north end of the east side were destroyed. They were replaced by flats, those next to Malvern Court in contemporary style, the ones facing the garden in a facsimile of the lost houses. Numbers 77–109, on the north side of the second garden, were altered after the war on conversion to flats, and many of the other houses have been treated in a similar way without the external disturbance. The square is now in excellent condition once again. The luxury of two private gardens allows for variety of treatment: the larger eastern garden has an open lawn with trees around the edge, the other offers more shade.

Orange Square

PIMLICO [WESTMINSTER]

'Orange Square' is a modern name, but as the place is old it may be as well to include it here. It is a square only in the same way as Leonard Square and others north of the City – an irregular opening where several roads meet. In this case it is Pimlico Road, Ebury Street and Bourne Street.

The name, taken from the Orange public house in Pimlico Road, was in common use long before it was adopted officially, but the place, as containing the only public conveniences in the district, was even better known to the natives as 'Karzy Square'.

For two centuries it had managed perfectly well as an anonymous junction so far as the local authorities were concerned. If the official naming had been delayed a little longer, Mozart Square would probably have been the choice, as his statue is now the most prominent feature of the paved space in the centre. The house a short way up Ebury Street where the young composer lodged during his English tour is marked by a blue plaque.

The Mozart statue in Orange Square in 2011.

The junction was the centre of a hamlet at the time of Rocque's map of the 1740s, although then only two roads met there. Rocque called them Strumbelo (Pimlico Road) and Five Fields Row (Ebury Street), which is where Mozart stayed. Farm buildings surrounded the junction itself. By the 1790s Bourne Street had appeared, as a single terrace, and most of the farm buildings had given way to modern houses in continuation of Ebury Street. A nursery on the south side was the only agricultural relic. A small building, probably a watch-house, had also appeared in the centre of the open space. Ebury Street was still Five Fields Row, but Pimlico Road was Queen Street east of the junction and Grosvenor Row to the west. This was part of the tentative, pre-Cubitt development of the Grosvenor estate in Pimlico.

Only on the north side does any of the late eighteenth-century development survive. The south, including the Orange pub, is Victorian. The central space, with trees and seats and Mozart, is probably a pleasanter spot to linger in than at any time in its urban career. An occasional serenade or divertimento piped from the base of the statue would make it even better.

Orme Square

Orme Square is named after its developer, Edward Orme, and appears as Orme's Square in some early references. He was an engraver and artist who made a fortune as the publisher of coloured prints and illustrated books like *British Field Sports* of 1807. He also published views of Russia, which may explain the names of two of his other developments, St Petersburgh Place and Moscow Road.

From 1809 Orme invested his profits in land ripe for building at Bayswater, and after 1817 retired from publishing to concentrate on its development. In 1818 he paid for the Bayswater Chapel, the forerunner of St Matthew's, to raise the tone of his estate. Orme Square was built between 1823 and 1826, when seven houses appeared in the ratebooks, all with tenants. Butler's 1824 map of Paddington showed only the houses on the north side, but it was complete on George Gutch's 1828 map. Most developers chose to live in one of their own houses and Edward Orme

Orme Square from Bayswater Road, *c.* 1905.

Numbers 1 and 2 Orme Square in 2006.

may have occupied No. 2 briefly but, an artist at heart, he preferred the atmosphere of Fitzroy Square, where he lived for nearly twenty years until his death in 1848.

In December 1825 an advertisement in the *Morning Post* announced the imminent opening of a new school: 'Under the Special Patronage of Her Royal Highness the Duchess of Kent: Kent House, No. 1 Orme-square, Bayswater, French boarding school for young ladies, conducted by Madame G. d'Ailhecourt, of Paris', who promised to pay 'most particular attention to the morals and manners of the Young Ladies' and assured parents that 'only the French language, in its utmost purity' would be spoken in the house. That enterprise was short-lived, but No. 1 later had a long history as a school for girls and later for boys. It was run by the Misses Margaret and Mary

Home in the 1840s and 1850s, by John Meiklejohn in the 1860s and by Robert Quick in the 1870s. Another important school was Herbert Wilkinson's at No. 11 (later 10 and 11), which lasted from the 1880s to the 1920s. Max Beerbohm was one of his pupils.

It is a very small square with only twelve houses, half of those facing the Bayswater Road rather than the garden, but it has punched well above its weight in the number of famous men and women who have lived there. The variety in the size of the houses made it available to both rich and comparatively poor.

It was as an economy measure that the legal writer John Austin moved to No. 5 in 1834, with his wife Sarah, best known as a translator, and their daughter, later Lady Duff Gordon. The Austins passed the house on to another writer, John Sterling, who lived there from 1835 to 1838, as described by Carlyle:

His house was in Orme Square, close by the corner of that little place (which has only three sides of houses) … A sufficiently commodious, by no means sumptuous, small mansion … His study-room in this house was perhaps mainly the drawing-room; looking out safe over the little dingy grassplot in front, and the quiet little row of houses opposite … On the right you had the continuous growl of the Uxbridge Road and its wheels, coming as lullaby not interruption. Leftward and rearward, after some little belt of houses, lay mere country …

The social scientist and sanitary reformer Edwin Chadwick is said to have lived at No. 7 from 1832 to 1839, presumably as a bachelor lodger with Daniel Connor (1754–1848) who was the ratepayer throughout that period. Chadwick married in 1839.

Number 1 was the first London home of Sir Rowland Hill, of the penny post, from 1839 to 1844. Lord Leighton had a studio at No. 2 from 1859 until 1866, when he moved to what is now Leighton House. He was visited in Orme Square by the Prince of Wales. Number 2 was the home of a very different artist, Bernard Partridge of *Punch*, in the 1920s.

Edward Dannreuther, the pianist, lived at No. 12 from the 1870s to 1893, and organised many notable performances of new music there. He was one of the foremost champions of Wagner, and the composer stayed with him during the 1877 Wagner festival. Dannreuther named his first four children Tristan, Sigmund, Wolfram and Isolde. The fifth, bathetically, was named Hubert, after Sir Hubert Parry. Nearly all of Parry's chamber music was premiered at Dannreuther's house.

Ernest Cassel (later Sir Ernest), the friend of the Prince of Wales, lived at No. 2 in the early 1880s, and Isambard Brunel, the son and biographer of Isambard Kingdom Brunel, died at No. 1 in 1902.

Because Bayswater was 'an airy suburb, half town, half country', as Carlyle could still describe it in 1835, Orme Square was built without the tight-packed formality of its contemporaries. It is more like the slightly later Lyndhurst Square at Peckham than any other. The houses are irregularly spaced and of individual design. Even the materials vary, with exposed brickwork towards the Bayswater Road, stucco on the east and west sides and stone on the north. The garden is too narrow to have much recreational value, but most of the houses have private gardens as well. The stone eagle on a column at the south end may, though it is not double-headed, be another allusion to Edward Orme's cherished imperial Russian connections, which he mentioned in his will.

Ovington Square

BROMPTON [KENSINGTON AND CHELSEA]

Ovington Square is part of the select group, also including the nearby Trevor Square and tiny Tibberton Square in Islington, that owe their narrow, rectangular shapes to their origin as the gardens of large houses. In the case of Ovington Square this was Grove House, where Sir John Macpherson, Governor General of Bengal in the brief interlude between Warren Hastings and Lord Cornwallis, died in 1821.

In 1823–24 it was the home of William Wilberforce, who called it Brompton Grove. He was succeeded by the journalist William Jerdan, who recorded that 'the drawing room had been built by Sir John Macpherson to entertain the Prince Regent' and that 'Mr Wilberforce, who had laid out several hundred pounds in putting the house into perfect order for his abode, though he hardly occupied it at all, requested the favour of me to let one of the cellars be appropriated to him till the seasonable weather in spring', when it would be safer to move his wines. Jerdan was amazed at the quality and variety of the wines possessed by the saintly and ascetic Wilberforce.

The house belonged to the Baroness Von Zandt of Ovington, Hampshire, the English widow of a Bavarian nobleman, who in 1844 made a development agreement with the architect William Wilmer Pocock. He was the son of William Fuller Pocock, the architect of Trevor Square, and was born in 1813 while Trevor Square was being built. W.W. Pocock and his brother-in-law Thomas Archbutt, a builder, set to work immediately, as they wished to get the square established before Kensington became subject to the London building regulations at the end of the year.

The north side of Ovington Square, *c.* 1904. The three houses on the right were destroyed during the Second World War.

Grove House was demolished to form the access street from Brompton Road, which was originally called Ovington Terrace but is now Ovington Gardens. The square opened out at the end behind the gardens of two houses that had stood next to Grove House until its demolition. The north side of Ovington Gardens, which also formed the short west side of the square, could not be built until those two houses were demolished in their turn in the 1860s.

After the first rush of building in 1844 the pace of development was slowed by the financial troubles of Thomas Archbutt. He withdrew, but Pocock was able to finish the square himself. Most of the houses on the two long sides were built in the 1840s, but the last was not let until 1852.

The square was an immediate and permanent success, the houses finding good tenants as soon as they were built. At first a few artists and actresses enlivened the middle-class mass, but the square became more stiff and exclusive later in the century when No. 18 was a fitting home for the killjoy politician Sir Wilfrid Lawson. He devoted most of his long years in Parliament to the attempted suppression of the drink trade, but in 1892 also found time to prevent the House of Commons adjourning for Derby Day, as it had always done until then.

The eastern end of the north side suffered serious bomb damage during the Second World War and Nos 22–26 were replaced by an inappropriate block of flats, all red brick and glass, built in 1957, when most architects had appallingly bad manners. It was designed by Walter Segal, who was wise to concentrate later on his self-build projects.

If the visitor stands with his back to these flats, Pocock's conventional Italianate stucco houses and the narrow private garden are pleasant enough. The little road leading to Walton Street, built by Pocock over a neighbouring estate in 1849–51, has some attractive smaller houses that are now numbered in the square. One has a fine oriel window.

Oxford Square

BAYSWATER [WESTMINSTER]

In the 1799 plan for the layout of Bayswater in co-operation with the Grand Junction Canal, the Oxford and Cambridge Squares area was to have been occupied by Buckingham Square, with two reservoirs in place of a garden. Later plans for the Bishop of London's estate showed a large polygon covering the area subsequently occupied by the squares and their attached crescents. A large Stanhope Square was the next idea, and even when the scheme for two squares emerged the southern one was originally to be called Southwick Square.

The final plans were not settled until 1838, when building began in Oxford Square. The first three houses appeared with tenants in an 1839 ratebook. The general style was laid down by George Gutch, surveyor to the estate, but individual clients could employ their own architects to plan the interiors. Henry Harrison, who also worked in Cambridge Square, designed No. 22.

Fourteen houses were listed in the 1840 rate and the square was all but fully occupied by 1841. The actor and writer Tyrone Power, the founder of a notable theatrical dynasty, was the first resident, listed at No. 1 from 1839. He was lost at sea in 1841, on his way home from an American tour, in the *President* steamboat disaster. The manuscript travel journal for 1840 of his son, William Power (in the Public Record Office of Northern Ireland), is dedicated to Mrs Tyrone Power, No. 1 Oxford Square, Hyde Park. She remained in the house until 1854. Such theatrical figures were not typical of the square, which for the most part was occupied by thoroughly respectable but rather dull and undistinguished tenants.

There were only two other real celebrities. Frederic Harrison, the leading English disciple of Comte and the author of many books, was born in Euston Square in 1831 but the family moved to No. 22 Oxford Square in the early 1840s. His father, a stockbroker, but the son of a builder, is said to have designed the house. Number 17 was the last home, in 1895–96, of George Du Maurier, the *Punch* cartoonist (most famous for *The Curate's Egg*) and the author of *Trilby* and other novels.

There was no significant bomb damage to Oxford Square in the Second World War, but the Ecclesiastical Commissioners had already marked it down for destruction in the 1930s, when they began a policy of rebuilding in Tyburnia as the original leases fell in. The whole of Oxford Square was demolished in the 1960s and the private garden is now overlooked by fourteen-storey tower blocks and 'town houses' with a strong flavour of Meccano.

Oxford Square

See Cavendish Square

The south side of Oxford Square, *c.* 1904.

Pack Horse Square

Pack Horse Square lay a few yards north and north-east of the Pack Horse public house, which still stands at the corner of Chiswick High Road and Acton Lane. A curving section of road led east from Acton Lane to the square proper, which had about a dozen houses on the four sides.

There was no trace of the square in the 1841 census, but the style of the houses that stood on the north side of the western arm proves that this section at least was a good deal older. It was named The Square on the 1848–50 skeleton Ordnance Survey map and appeared under the same name in the 1851 census. It then contained fifty houses, nearly all of them occupied by agricultural labourers, so the cottages in the narrow eastward extension later known as Essex Place were then clearly being counted as part of the square. It was Pack Horse Square in the 1861 to 1881 census returns. In 1871 most of the tenants were still working on farms, but that had changed ten years later when only a few gardeners represented dwindling agriculture and most of the residents were general dealers, hawkers or costermongers.

By 1891 the name had been abolished and in a reversal of fortune the square was counted as part of Essex Place, formerly its access lane from the east. Most of the cottages in the square proper were demolished to make way for the Chiswick Empire music hall, which was built between 1910 and 1912. The rest, including the oldest houses in the western arm, were swept away between 1935 and 1950 by slum clearance and the growth of the shopping centre. Essex Place still exists as a supermarket access road, but most of the site of the square is a carpark.

Palace Square

As its name suggests, Palace Square was planned in the heady 1850s, when developers supposed that any houses built within a few miles of the new Crystal Palace would quickly make their fortunes. Crowds of speculators rushed in, land prices in Norwood and district rose to unprecedented heights, the market was glutted, and many bankruptcies followed.

The first few houses in Palace Square were hastily built in the late 1850s but proved hard to let and

The east side of Palace Square, *c.* 1920, with the 1850s houses in the distance.

the development was completed gradually during the calmer recovery of the 1860s. In the first moment of excitement it was probably the intention to create a real square with a private garden, but during the more realistic completion of the estate two terraces of quite small houses filled the centre instead. The original houses on the periphery were much larger.

Of all this, very little survives today. This was partly the result of Second World War bombing, which destroyed most of the west side and two-thirds of the houses in the interior. The greater damage was done by Bromley Council in the 1960s and 1970s, when a redevelopment of the area involved the demolition of all but six of the original houses and the removal of the south, the west and most of the east side of the square. This leaves only a short, curving cul-de-sac to live up to the name of Palace Square. The surviving houses suggest that something of the quality of Grafton Square at Clapham might have been achieved if the original 1850s plan had been carried out.

Pancras Square

SOMERS TOWN [CAMDEN]

As the first project of the Metropolitan Association for Improving the Dwellings of the Industrious Classes, the first company set up on the 'Five Per Cent Philanthropy' principle, Pancras Square became the very model of a modern model dwelling and was visited by all the leading statesmen and social reformers of the day. The square was built in 1847–48 on a site just off Pancras Road, on the south side of a part of Platt Street that no longer exists. The architect was W.B. Moffat. In shape, if in nothing else, it resembled Alexander Square, with one long side, two very short and the fourth open to the road; but instead of a garden, Pancras Square had a paved forecourt, and five-storey tenements instead of elegant houses.

The Booth researcher who visited in 1898 called it St Pancras Square, 'rents from 5/6 to 9/6 (2 rooms & scullery 5/6 to 8/-, 3 rooms & scullery 7/6 to 9/6), dull but good, room for 105 families'. Like many pioneering works it was soon out of date, left behind by the technical improvements introduced in the

industrial dwellings built by the Peabody trustees and others, so it would probably not have survived even if it had come safely through the Second World War. In fact, it was entirely destroyed by a landmine on 17 April 1941. The Goldington Street Estate was built on the site, with tenements larger than the Victorians ever dreamt of.

Pancras Square had one celebrity, William Chiffney, the jockey and trainer of racehorses. He was born, naturally, at Newmarket, but being improvident like all his family he ended his days in these ugly tenements in 1862, having squandered the large sums he earned during a successful career.

Panton Square

SOHO [WESTMINSTER]

The main authority for the career of Colonel Thomas Panton is Theophilus Lucas's *Memoirs of the Lives, Intrigues, and Comical Adventures of the Most Famous Gamesters* (1714). According to Lucas:

> [Panton's] chief game was at Hazard, at which he got the most money; for in one night, at this play, he won as many thousand pounds as purchased him an estate of above 150l. per annum, insomuch that he built a whole street near Leicester-fields, which, after his own name, he called Panton-street. After this good fortune, he had such an aversion against all manner of games, that he would never handle dice nor cards again, but liv'd very handsomely on his winnings to his dying day.

Panton Street, which was built in 1671, still exists south of Coventry Street, but the colonel's other London development to its north, which he began in 1673, is long gone. It was Panton Yard, a name in use by 1681, four years before Panton's death. The work was carried out under the watchful eye of Christopher Wren, Surveyor General of the King's Works, as Charles II was anxious to raise the standard of building in Windmill Fields and Soho, and to make money from issuing licences.

Panton Yard was 'a very large place for stabling and coach-houses, there being one large yard within another'. The inner northern yard, which was later known as Queen's Head Court, continued to be a mews until it was destroyed during the construction of Shaftesbury Avenue. The larger southern yard, as Strype recorded in a passage written before 1720, 'is designed to be built into streets, taking up a large piece of ground, and according to probability will turn to better advantage than at present'. At this point it became known as Panton Square, although it was not included in William Stow's 1722 list.

The fashionable houses built a little before 1720 were eleven in the approach road from Coventry Street and seven in the miniature square at its north end, two each on the east and west sides and three on the north. These three houses were the largest and best. The one at the east end was rebuilt before the end of the eighteenth century.

The Duke of St Albans was among several aristocratic residents in 1720. The square was also popular with army officers and artists. The American painter Benjamin West, later president of the Royal Academy, lived there from 1768 to 1775, during his very successful early years in London. In 1813 Joseph Farington noted in his diary that 'West said that while He himself resided in Panton square, Coventry St, Wilson one day called upon Him & looking through the window pointed to a house in the square in which He, Wilson, had lodged before he went to Italy'. That was in the 1740s when Richard Wilson, later the founder of the English landscape school, was working as a portrait painter.

The status of the square may have tumbled in 1762, if a story told by the playwright John O'Keefe is to be believed:

Panton Square, c. 1840.

The Morocco Ambassador lived in Panton Square, near Coventry Street. One of his attendants happened to displease him: he had him brought up to the garret, and there sliced his head off. It was made no secret: he and his servants thought it was very proper, but the London people, who had somewhat of Christianity, were of another opinion. I saw a violent party gather before the house: they broke into it, demolished the furniture, threw everything they could lay their hands on out of the windows, and thrashed and beat the grand Moor and his retinue down the Haymarket.

O'Keefe is the only authority for this incident, which appeared in his *Recollections* (1826), dictated to his daughter when he was old and blind.

At first Panton Square was the name used for all the houses, but by the 1830s the approach road was called Arundel (or Arundell) Street, although the numbering of the houses in the street and square remained continuous. Colonel Panton's daughter had married Lord Arundell of Wardour, thus introducing two more names into the topography of Soho. In 1868 'Panton Square' was abolished (at the request of four residents) and for its last half-century the whole development was officially known as Arundel Street, although the old name continued to be used colloquially.

In the nineteenth century the square suffered a steep social decline. John Fielden, the radical MP and factory reformer, was living in Arundel Street in 1841 with solicitors and surveyors for company, but by the 1850s both square and street were dominated by hotels and boarding houses, many of them catering for French and Italian visitors. Mrs Gaskell lodged at No. 11 in 1849 ('our dusty noisy lodgings in Panton Square') and Stéphane Mallarmé lodged at No. 9 (on the east side of the square) during his visit to London in 1863.

The Lyons Corner House in Coventry Street, built in 1907–09, proved such a success that the company soon felt an urgent need to enlarge it. Property in Arundel Street and the square, west and north of the restaurant, was bought up and in 1913 a private Act of Parliament was obtained authorising the extinction of the right of way. The suspension of building during the First World War gave a short reprieve, but in 1921 the Corner House was extended over the site of the former Panton Square.

Papiet Square

See Nichols Square

Park Square

REGENT'S PARK [WESTMINSTER AND CAMDEN]

When John Nash began to lay out the Regent's Park in 1812 his plan called for a grand circus at its south-east corner, linking Portland Place to the park and bisected by the New Road. The southern half of this circus is the familiar Park Crescent, which was begun in that year. Unfortunately (or fortunately, according to taste) the builder was bankrupted in 1815, and before the crescent was completed in 1822 developments on the south side of the park had prompted a change of plan.

By that time Nash had a group of reliable builders keen to contract for his monumental terraces, but less likely to be interested in a crescent of smaller houses that would be more expensive to build and would turn their backs to the park. Instead Nash decided to extend the park to the Marylebone Road in the form of a square, with houses linked stylistically to Park Crescent, but in size and form more like those being built to the north. Park Square, with terraces on only two sides and open to the park and the crescent at north and south, had little claim to the title in any classical sense, but the 1820s was the decade of Eaton Square, Alexander Square, Brompton Square and others equally eccentric: 'square' was becoming a word of vague and elastic meaning.

Park Square was built between 1823 and 1825, the west side by William Nurse, who had already undertaken half of York Terrace, the east side by a newcomer, Jacob Smith. For him the houses were a minor consideration. Behind the central three he built the Diorama, a large auditorium for the display of panoramic paintings. Panoramas were familiar enough; here the novelty was that powerful machinery swung all the spectators round to view a fresh painting that had been preparing behind their backs while they admired the first. The architects and engineers who designed this marvel under Nash's supervision were his assistants Charles Morgan and Augustus

Charles Pugin. The Diorama was later converted into a Baptist church and has been turned to various uses since. Its shell is still standing behind the Prince's Trust.

Nash had the garden planted and laid out with great care, to enhance the beauty of the houses and the park. For Beresford Chancellor in 1907 the surroundings mitigated the contempt with which the architecture was generally regarded at that time:

> The houses are of that solid character, with pillar ornamentations between the windows, so characteristic of the period at which they were built; but the beauty of the garden and the proximity of the park ... gives them quite a green and suburban effect, which even the busy Marylebone Road is unable to greatly affect ... Between Park Crescent and the garden of Park Square there is a tunnel beneath the Marylebone Road, known as 'Nursery-maid's Walk,' on account of its being used by those guardians of the children resident in Park Crescent when passing thence to the more ample garden of Park Square. It is said that so tenacious were the residents of their rights in this subway, that when the railway that runs beneath was contemplated, gradients of 1 in 100 had to be resorted to in order that the line might pass below this tunnel.

In the 1940s and 1950s the garden was popular with the children of all the Regent's Park terraces. It was here that Anthony Powell saw the infant Jane Asher (later a radio Jean Templar) playing in the sandpit, and a youthful Joan Collins breasting dramatically through the bushes. In 1976 the garden, following the happy precedent of Gibson Square, acquired a Jubilee Line ventilation shaft in the form of a Regency summer house.

Considering the quality of the houses and the prominence of the position, Park Square has had surprisingly few famous residents. Sir Hudson Lowe, Napoleon's warder at St Helena, lived at No. 3 on the west side in the early 1830s. Lord Dunsany, the writer, was born in 1878 at No. 15, on the east side, and George Edwardes, one of the greatest of all theatrical impresarios, died at No. 11 on the west side in 1914. He began by assisting Richard D'Oyly Carte in the production of the Gilbert & Sullivan operas and then moved to the management of the Gaiety Theatre, where he was largely responsible for the creation of a new genre, the musical comedy.

This is one of the select band of politically divided squares. When built it was all in the parish of St Marylebone, but the boundaries were simplified in 1900 and now Park Square West and the garden are in Westminster and Park Square East in Camden.

Park Square East and the Diorama in 1827, the tower of Soane's Holy Trinity, Marylebone Road, rising behind.

Parliament Square

Until the end of the eighteenth century the Westminster slums wrapped round the abbey and St Margaret's, filling the space between Palace Yard and Storey's Gate with a maze of mean streets and alleys. This had long been regarded as an affront to the dignity of Parliament and a threat to its security. In 1734 James Ralph, after describing the slums, wrote:

> Surely such a place as this ought, at least, to be large and convenient, if not costly and magnificent; though, in my opinion, it ought to be the centre of our elegance and grandeur: and to do this effectually, all the buildings I have complained of, ought long since to have been levelled to the ground, and a space laid open from the Privy-garden to Westminster-hall, and from the west end of the abbey to Storey's-gate, on the other; this surrounded with stone buildings all in a taste, raised on a piazza or colonade, with suitable decorations; and the middle should be adorned with a group of statues, answerable to the extent of the circuit round it. It is easy to imagine what an effect such an improvement as this would have on the spectator, and how much more agreeable it would be to the honour and credit of the nation.

The government eventually took note. The slums north of St Margaret's, some attached to the church itself, were demolished, and a narrow rectangular garden (half the present size) was laid out there under powers given by Acts of Parliament of 1804 and 1806. Its width was exactly that of the church, from which it was separated only by a footpath. In January 1808 *Jackson's Oxford Journal* announced:

> The New Square in front of St Margaret's Church, Westminster, on the site of houses now pulled down, is to be called Parliament Square; it is inclosed with palisades; shrubberies are to be planted, and in the centre the Right Hon. the Speaker proposes to erect a statue of Mr Pitt. – The pedestal is to be an Atlas, with Mr Pitt on his shoulders.

The shrubberies were planted, but Pitt's statue failed to appear. An 1812 print showed the garden looking (but for the dramatic backdrop of the abbey) much like that of any fashionable London square. The 1814 plan illustrating the parliamentary commissioners' further recommendations showed the plantation as 'Garden Square' with an 'Occasional Carriage Way' between it and St Margaret's.

A rival proposal put forward by Edward Lapidge in 1809 had called for the rebuilding of the Houses of Parliament and the removal of St Margaret's to the south side of the abbey. Most of the space gained he wished to enclose within an enlarged abbey precinct, leaving room only for a small unnamed square at the south end of Parliament Street. In the centre there was to be a 'Naval Column'. This was not surprisingly rejected by the commissioners as being too visionary.

Lapidge revived his old plan in 1834, but even so he has never been suspected of setting fire to the Palace of Westminster. His ideas were still influential as late as 1845 when an official plan called for the demolition of St Margaret's and labelled the garden 'The Enclosure or Abbey Close'.

At about the same time that the square was being created, the streets north of the abbey were cleared and Samuel Pepys Cockerell's Westminster Guildhall or Sessions House was built on a small part of the site between 1804 and 1808. The rest remained vacant for years and was known jocularly as the 'Desert of Westminster'. The part to the west of the Guildhall was eventually filled in 1825–26 by Decimus Burton's Parliamentary Mews (later the Stationery Office) and by the Inwoods' Westminster Hospital of 1831–34. To the north of the Guildhall, surprisingly, the humble St Margaret's Church School was built, but the vacant space to the east developed into a secondary garden, almost as big as the one in the centre of the square.

That was the situation until the 1860s, when the Metropolitan Railway dug up the garden while constructing its line from St James's Park to Westminster Station, which ran diagonally across the centre of the square. Edward Middleton Barry was then engaged in completing his father's work on the Palace of Westminster and he was employed to redesign the garden. He dispensed with the shrubberies and any hint of a domestic square and treated the area

The Westminster Guildhall, Parliament Square, in 1827.

Parliament Square from the north-west in the 1920s.

formally as an additional forecourt to his father's building. The garden was divided symmetrically into two grassed enclosures with a broad footpath running between them from east to west. He encouraged the idea of using the garden as a site for statues by moving that of Canning from New Palace Yard to the green on the west side of the square, and the present cluster shows that Parliament was not slow to take the hint.

Like most of central London, Parliament Square emerged bruised and battered from the Second World War. There were already plans to enlarge the space by demolishing the last three houses in Great George Street, east of Little George Street. The approach of the Festival of Britain and the desire of the government to impress visitors with a shiny new London added urgency, and Grey Wornum's scheme was carried out between 1949 and 1951. This achieved a square garden double the size of the old one by pushing the secondary garden further west (the Canning statue with it) and making it narrower. The statues in the main garden were rearranged in avenues of trees on the north and west sides, with the rest given over to an impressively large lawn. The arrangement remains much the same, but with the passing years traffic has made the garden hard to reach and protesters have often made it a less desirable objective.

Parson's Square

SHOREDITCH [HACKNEY]

Parson's Square was a name used in its last few decades for the place that had been known for more than 100 years as Parson's Yard. The east side of Shoreditch High Street from St Leonard's churchyard to Jane Shore Alley was glebe land, but it belonged to the archdeacon of London, who was rector of Shoreditch, not to the vicar. When the glebe was sold in 1655 as part of confiscated church property a large number of small houses had already been built there.

Parson's Yard was the part of this land immediately south of the churchyard. It was mentioned by Hatton in 1708 and was shown as a square open space surrounded by houses on maps from the early eighteenth century to the middle of the nineteenth. In this poor area it was never much above the level of a slum.

In the late 1850s the square was rebuilt, with additional houses replacing the open space, and was given the new name of Calvert Street. It lasted only until the 1890s when the notorious slums to the east were replaced by the LCC's Arnold Circus, and Calvert Avenue was built over the site of Calvert Street as one of the approaches to the new estate.

Paternoster Square

CITY OF LONDON

The original Paternoster Square, which occupied only the north-western quarter of the present one, was the successor to Newgate Market. After the Great Fire the market dealt principally in meat, although Hatton in 1708 called it 'a large and very good Market, chiefly for Butchers Meat, Poultry, Fruit and Roots'. Hughson, who was disgusted by the rivers of blood running

Newgate Market, the forerunner of Paternoster Square, in 1860.

The site of the bombed Paternoster Square in the 1940s.

in all the neighbouring streets, described it in 1806: 'Newgate Market is commodious, and contained in a square, measuring 194 feet from east to west, and 148 feet from north to south, with a market house in the centre, under which are cellars.'

The opening of the new Smithfield in 1868 put Newgate Market out of business. It was sold by auction in 1869 for £20,000. The whole area was rebuilt and roofed over, and with the name of Paternoster Square it became an extension of the publishing and bookselling quarter of Paternoster Row. The interior, where the old market house had stood, was divided into four parts by glazed passages crossing it north to south and east to west. Where they met in the centre there was a slightly enlarged space open to the sky. Each of the four sections contained three shops. Other shops and a pub named the Red Cross occupied the periphery.

Number 26 was the birthplace in 1887 of the great Northcliffe publishing empire, and No. 2 was an early address of A.P. Watt, the first great literary agent. This publishers' Paternoster Square was entirely destroyed in the Second World War. The burning of the warehouses involved a terrible loss of book stock.

The second Paternoster Square, loved by Pevsner and other architectural modernists and hated by everybody else, was laid out between 1962 and 1967 and swept away in 1997, after one of the most important architectural debates of the century. Rival plans from the left and right wings of the profession came and went before the present very British compromise was adopted. Elizabeth Frink's 'Paternoster, Shepherd and Sheep' (set up in 1975) is the only survivor from the old square and for that reason, although innocent in itself, has unhappy associations for those who remember the desolate place in the 1980s.

The third and present square, built between 1997 and 2003 to a general plan by Sir William Whitfield, is the finest new public space in London. It began with the great advantages, so wasted by the planners of the 1960s version, of having St Paul's as a backdrop and another Wren building, the Chapter House, to grace its southern edge. Even luckier was the availability of Temple Bar for importation into the new square after 120 years of unhappy exile in Hertfordshire. But that was a piece of luck that might have been equally available to the owners of the 1960s square, who spurned it.

The Monument ventilation shaft, Paternoster Square, in 2007.

So now the southern side of Paternoster Square is a perfect gallery of Wren (or possible Wren), with the Chapter House and Temple Bar hung against the wall of St Paul's. As a mischievous extra exhibit a toy replica of the Monument has been erected in the square as a disguised ventilation shaft. Flushed with the success of their Temple Bar coup, the owners presumably asked the City fathers for the original, but were refused.

Patriot Square

BETHNAL GREEN [TOWER HAMLETS]

Patriot Square was built in the early 1790s on the estate of the Dickens family, London haberdashers who had been settled in Bethnal Green for nearly 200 years. In the eighteenth century patriotism often meant no more than opposition to government ('the last refuge of a scoundrel') so the name may perhaps reflect the Dickens' politics.

The earliest Sun insurance policy for the square is of 1792. In January of that year Robert Wissett of the East India House took No. 19 on the north side of 'a piece of ground whereon several houses are now building and intended to be called Patriot Square'. The sellers were Aaron Eele, a builder of Mile End New Town, and Daniel Bowyer, a carpenter of Whitechapel. The houses they produced were of two bays with three storeys plus semi-basement. The doors were round-headed, but not the windows.

The Horwood map of the 1790s showed thirty houses numbered as part of the square, but eight of those faced what is now Cambridge Heath Road and were usually called Patriot Place. The twenty-two in the square itself were in two terraces, north and south, facing each other across a wide road. There was no central garden. The high road was at the west end and the east end was open to the fields. These were among the best houses in what was then a pleasant suburb, and they attracted highly respectable tenants.

The amenities of Patriot Square suffered a serious blow in 1840 when an enterprising pawnbroker named John Kelday, noting the success of the big new private cemeteries on the outskirts of London, acquired the field at the east end of the square and opened it as the North-East London Cemetery. Even though the ground was not consecrated and Kelday himself sometimes acted as chaplain, he was soon overwhelmed with customers, his facilities being especially in demand during the great cholera epidemics of 1848–49 and 1853–54. Twenty thousand corpses were buried there, six deep, before the cemetery was closed by an Order in Council in October 1855. Over the western half of this pleasant spot, where no burials had taken place when the closure order was issued, extensions to the square and Peel Grove were built soon afterwards, the south side of the new section of the square being begun by 1861 and the north completed by 1864. It was at first sometimes considered part of Peel Grove rather than the square and was numbered there in the 1861 and 1871 census returns.

Kelday and his successors made repeated attempts to sell the used part of the cemetery east of Peel Grove as land for development. In 1883 there was a scheme to build industrial dwellings there, not removing the bodies but covering them with a platform of concrete. This was successfully opposed by the Bethnal Green Vestry and the Metropolitan Board of Works.

The square naturally went downhill, but in 1897 it was still 'quiet, respectable, working class'. The first breach in the 1790s houses occurred when the ones on the south side closest to Cambridge Heath Road were demolished to make a site for Bethnal Green Town Hall. It was built in 1909–10 to the designs of Percy Robinson and William Alban Jones.

The rest of the south side was destroyed when an extension was built in 1937–39. The town hall is now a hotel. The north side survived until the 1970s when it was replaced by the dull council block named James Docherty House. Patriot Square still exists as a name.

Paul Square

OLD STREET [HACKNEY]

Paul Square was off the east side of Paul Street, Finsbury, opposite Hill Street (now Bonhill Street). Horwood's 1790s map showed a terrace of four houses that may have been the tentative beginning of the south side of the square. The 1813 revision showed it fully built with about twenty small houses, and gave the name. The square was residential, occupied by carpenters, carmen, servants out of place and the like. It was short-lived, for in the 1860s all the houses were demolished to permit a major enlargement of the City Stone Yard in Worship Street. The area was heavily damaged during the Second World War. Offices and a private school are now on the site.

Paultons Square

CHELSEA [KENSINGTON AND CHELSEA]

Danvers House, built for the future regicide Sir John Danvers in 1623, stood where Danvers Street and Crosby Hall are now. The square occupies the site of its Italian garden north of the house, where 'Sir John was wont on fine mornings in the summer to brush his beaver hat on the hyssop and thyme, which did perfume it with its natural essence and would last a morning or longer', as John Aubrey records. The house was inherited by Lord Wharton, who married Sir John's granddaughter. Wharton's song 'Lillibullero' was almost as fatal to James II as Sir John's signature had been to his father Charles I.

Danvers House was hemmed in by the terraces of Danvers Street in the 1690s and demolished early in the eighteenth century. The garden, otherwise Dovehouse Close, became a nursery which was known as Shepherd's in 1822, when some remains of the Danvers House outbuildings were found there.

There was little further development on the estate until Danvers Street was extended in the early 1840s. It was only then that Paultons Square was laid out across the site of the Dovehouse Close nursery. The name came from Paultons near Romsey in Hampshire, a home of the Sloane Stanley family, the landowners. Two houses were built in 1841, nine by 1844, twenty by 1846, and the square was complete by 1851. One of the first residents was Alfred Allen, architect and surveyor, who lived at No. 54.

The houses are simple, of two bays and generally of three storeys plus basement, with a four-storey centrepiece on each side. The ground floors have rusticated stucco, with plain brickwork above. On the two long sides the ground-floor windows are round-headed, but not on the short south side, where the upper windows are ponderously decorated and the whole effect is heavier.

Like most of Chelsea, the square was not at all fashionable in its early days and the notable residents have all been from the arts or literature. Henry Fowler, the author of *The King's English* ('according to Fowler') and editor of *The Concise Oxford Dictionary* and *The Pocket Oxford Dictionary*, lived at No. 14 from 1899 to 1903. Lawrence Gowing, the painter, lived in Paultons Square briefly during the Second World War, before moving the short distance to Wellington Square. Kathleen Raine lived at No. 47, where she entertained many other writers and artists. Some lived in the basement flat, including the

sculptor Eduardo Paolozzi in the early 1950s and the translator Willa Muir (widow of Edwin) in the 1960s.

The brilliant historian Dorothy George, author of *London Life in the Eighteenth Century* and (like Joseph Grego of Granville Square) a leading expert on the English caricaturists, lived at No. 54, where she died at an advanced age in 1971. The only blue plaque is not on any of the old houses, but on the large block called Paultons House, on the eastern corner of King's Road, where the writer Jean Rhys lived in flat 22 from 1936 to 1938.

By the early twentieth century the square was dominated by boarding houses, with the odd dressmaker or French corset maker, and was so little regarded that just before the Second World War the LCC planned to run a tramline through it. Local opposition luckily prevented such a destructive intrusion. The houses were all shaken by blast during the war, but since then the physical and social improvement has been spectacular. The square features a narrow but well-planned private garden and one of the smallest houses in London: No. 56 is squeezed between Paultons House and No. 55, of which it was once a part.

The garden and east side of Paultons Square in 2007.

Pavilion Square

See Cadogan Square (2)

Peabody Square

The Blackfriars Road Peabody Square was built between 1870 and 1872 on the site of the Magdalen Hospital, an asylum for penitent prostitutes. It was the last, the largest and the grandest of the five designed for the trust by Henry Astley Darbishire. The odd shape of the land produced a double square.

The more formal of the two openings lies directly off Blackfriars Road, and from its south-west corner a second, more loosely organised, breaks away at forty-five degrees, reaching almost to Waterloo Road. From the beginning the central spaces were planned as gardens rather than courtyards. These, together with the smaller blocks, their elaborate entrances and the setting forward of the middle bays, create a faint illusion of a series of palaces ranged round a continental 'place'.

In 1899 the Booth survey reported, 'Large prison-like buildings, asphalt square in centre, fair open space planted with trees. Eagerley tenanted.' Today the immediately striking thing is the quantity of expensive cars parked in the two courtyards. Peabody housing, this close to the City at least, is clearly no longer occupied by the industrious working classes. Parts of the squares are still given over to trees and grass and you feel that they might have become two leafy private enclosures by now, were it not for the heavy demand for parking space.

This Peabody Square produced one man of genuine eminence. George Brown, Harold Wilson's rival for the Labour party leadership and later a famously tired and emotional foreign secretary, grew up here and was educated nearby at the West Square central school.

Peabody Square, Blackfriars Road, from the east in 1872.

Peabody Square

John Nelson Tarn called this set of industrial dwellings Peabody Square in his *Five Per Cent Philanthropy*, but Peabody Buildings was the usual name. It was completed in April 1870 after the Westminster Peabody Square and before Blackfriars. The architect, as usual, was Henry Astley Darbishire.

The site, smaller than the others, was between Cheyne Row and Lawrence Street, directly opposite Carlyle's house. It had only a narrow courtyard – hence the general use of 'Buildings' rather than 'Square' – and tenement blocks four storeys high. It was intact in 1973, but now only the north, east and west sides are standing, which means that the courtyard is larger, with trees.

Peabody Square

Because the first 'improved dwellings for the industrious classes' built with George Peabody's bounty were on a sharp-angled corner plot in Spitalfields, the Islington site became the first of the characteristic Peabody squares. It was opened in 1865, a year after Spitalfields.

The architect for both projects and for all the early Peabody buildings was Henry Astley Darbishire, who had become the leading expert in the field through his work at Columbia Square a few years earlier.

Peabody Square, Islington, was built on a site east of Essex Road and south of Greenman Street, very close to little Tibberton Square, to which it must yield the palm in all respects save two: it is perfectly preserved and perfectly square.

The four blocks – to which others were later added nearby – are of five storeys, the fifth being an attic for baths and washhouses. The baths were free 'for all who desire to use them'. The centre was originally just a large courtyard, but today it includes a small garden with trees, the rest being given over to car spaces.

Peabody Square

In its architecture, the 1866 Peabody Square at Shadwell is like the one built at Islington the year before, the only important differences being the extra storey, six instead of five, and the setting back of one bay instead of three at the end of each side. The four blocks are also placed rather differently in relation to each other to fit a rectangular site. (See pp.14–15) The land acquired was

Peabody Square, Islington, in 1866.

between Cable Street and the Highway, immediately south of Elm Row, which the LCC was characteristically to rename Elf Row. The square is as well preserved as its Islington brother, but in this poorer area seems more grim and forbidding. The courtyard has only a couple of trees and the cars are fewer and shabbier.

Peabody Square

WESTMINSTER

A Peabody Square at Westminster sounds odd today, but Westminster had its fair share of slums well into the twentieth century. This example of the standard Peabody range of tenement blocks was built in 1868, south of what was then Little Chapel Street but now Caxton Street, and east of Buckingham Row, now Buckingham Gate. It replaced one of the many sets of almshouses in this area.

The regular Peabody architect, Henry Astley Darbishire, was now entirely practised in the production of such housing, although he continued to experiment with technical improvements to sanitary arrangements and the provision of extra comforts for the tenants. The *Illustrated London News* noted with natural astonishment that 'some of the bed-rooms

have fireplaces'. There were three blocks on the north, east and west sides of the courtyard, the entrance being, rather oddly, from the narrow lane on the south side called Brewer's Green.

Buckingham Gate, so close to the palace, was a surprisingly poor area in the first half of the twentieth century and Peabody Square continued to provide a useful service. Between the wars the courtyard was given the luxury of a glass roof, which must have been shattered when the square suffered minor bomb damage. That was patched up but, tenements being increasingly out of place in post-war Westminster, Peabody Square was sold by the trust and demolished in the 1970s. Several generations of offices have risen and fallen on the site since then.

Peacock Square

NEWINGTON [SOUTHWARK]

Peacock Street was one of the oldest in Newington. It was shown, as Peacock Lane, turning off the southeast side of Newington Butts on Rocque's 1740s map. The irregular outline drawn by Rocque could have been intended to indicate what was later Peacock Square branching from it.

Peabody Square, Westminster, from the south, in 1869.

The square was shown without a name on Horwood's 1790s map, with between three and seven houses arranged around a narrow courtyard off the east side of Peacock Street. Immediately south of the square was a footpath leading to Frederick Place, later Hurlbutt Place. Lockie included the square in the 1813 edition of his *Topography*, but not in 1810.

The 1851 census listed seven houses numbered 9–15, plus an empty house with no number specified. The tenants were labourers, a milkman, a laundress and a schoolteacher. This was a poor part of a poor district and Peacock Street was already partially demolished when the Booth surveyor visited it in 1899.

The houses of the square survived until the 1950s and the name was used for the footpath until the 1970s. A large council estate was then built there, obliterating the old street pattern. Canterbury Place is roughly on the line of Peacock Street.

Peckham Rye Square

PECKHAM [SOUTHWARK]

'Peckham Rye Squ.' was boldly named on Greenwood's 1830 map near the narrow north-western point of the common. The words seem to refer to a feature – perhaps buildings on three sides of a courtyard – on the north corner of what is now Rye Passage, the footpath from Peckham Rye to Relf Road. There was no mention of the name in the 1830 ratebook. Dewhirst's 1842 parish survey showed Rye Cottage at this point and later maps nothing but conventional houses and shops. It may have been an unrealised scheme or a mere cartographer's blunder.

Pembridge Square

NOTTING HILL [KENSINGTON AND CHELSEA AND WESTMINSTER]

Beresford Chancellor confused Pembridge with Pembroke Square in his *History of the Squares of London*, but the names are the only point of similarity. Pembroke Square is simple and modest, Pembridge elaborate and grandiloquent. It is alone among the London squares in having been built with only detached houses, and nearly alone in having produced a handsome profit for everyone concerned. To complete the story of almost unprecedented success, thirty-two of the thirty-four houses are still standing, most of them in good condition.

The square must make a greater impression on absolute strangers – no doubt the status of many of the guests at the hotels – than on those who have been accustomed to seeing nearly identical houses all over the Holland Park district. Having made such a success with the design in Pembridge Square the builders continued to use it in their later developments.

They were Francis and William Radford, who began to take building leases on the Hall estate at Notting Hill in 1849 and over the next fifteen years built about 125 houses in the square and the surrounding roads. The younger brother Francis was the designer of the firm's spectacularly successful and infinitely repeatable houses, of which the type devised for the square was the last, nearly the largest, and the best.

The square was built between 1856 and 1864. The 1862 directory listed only Nos 1–3, an unnumbered Seerah House, and William and Francis Radford, builders. Numbers 1–3 are the biggest houses of all because they had to fill the awkward curving site between Pembridge Gardens and Pembridge Road, but the other thirty-one were originally identical. They are three bays wide and have three storeys plus basement and attic, with two-storey bay windows either side of the door. The attics are the most decorative and original feature, with the central of three dormers doubling as a highly elaborate chimney stack. The houses are stuccoed throughout, with the ground floor rusticated.

The square was too far west for the fashionable world and the houses too expensive for most professional men or artists, so the early tenants were nearly all merchants, a fair number of them Jewish. The most eminent resident was Field Marshall Sir John Fox Burgoyne, who died at No. 5 in 1871. The extraordinary element in his military career is that he directed sieges during the Peninsular War and in the Crimea, more than forty years apart. He was an illegitimate son of General John Burgoyne, the playwright, who surrendered at Saratoga in 1777, and the godson of Charles James Fox. His statue can be seen in Waterloo Place.

The east side of Pembridge Square, *c.* 1905.

The Palace Court Hotel, Nos 12–14 Pembridge Square, *c.* 1930; a photograph doctored to make the three detached houses appear like a single building.

The old parish boundary ran neatly behind the gardens of the east side, but the modern borough boundary runs down the centre of the road, placing those four houses in Westminster, while the rest of the square is in Kensington and Chelsea.

Pembridge Square escaped very lightly during the Second World War, with only one house on the south side suffering significant damage. That has been invisibly repaired. The only breach in the original design is made by Vincent House, a block of flats built in 1939 and now used as a residential hotel. It replaced the original Nos 4 and 5. The Commodore Hotel already occupied the corner house before the 1939 rebuilding.

There have been numerous private hotels in the square from early in the twentieth century, when they appeared in a rush. There are now also private schools. A few houses on the north side are in a deplorable condition and others have been altered in regrettable ways. The iron and glass canopies over some of the front steps are pleasant and useful ornaments, but they are not original features. The mass of stucco can be overpowering but it remains a very impressive square, with a large and beautifully maintained private garden.

Pembroke Square

In 1823 Lord Kensington, having finally got the troublesome Edwardes Square more or less finished, let some adjoining land to John Dowley, surveyor, and Robert Tuck, carpenter, as the site for another square. Pembroke was chosen as the name because Lord Kensington's family was from Trefgarne in that county.

The fact that the speculators were a surveyor and carpenter rather than an architect and builder indicates the quite lowly status of the intended development. Here there was to be only a narrow garden, not the huge paddock of Edwardes Square, and the houses were to be equally small. They were probably designed by Dowley, who was chief surveyor to the

The north side of Pembroke Square, *c.* 1905.

Westminster Commissioners of Sewers, but not otherwise known as an architect. The two partners began to build on a shoestring in the calm economic conditions of 1823, but got into difficulties during the financial crisis of 1825 and were bankrupted in 1826. They had completed the Pembroke Arms pub on the south-east corner (now the Hansom Cab) and a few houses, and had started work on most of the others on the south and north sides.

The houses left unfinished by Dowley and Tuck were completed in 1827–29 under the eye of the solicitor Thomas Longridge Hawks, one of the creditors. He also took responsibility for the west side, but had made little progress there when he died in 1829. His brother and executor George Hawks arranged for its continuation. In 1831 he sold the family's remaining interest to a local builder, William Collins of Edwardes Square, who had completed the main west side terrace by 1835. Here the houses have front gardens. In its north-west corner Pembroke Square almost meets Edwardes Square. The pleasant linking road features Nos 1 and 2 Pembroke Cottages, probably built by Collins about 1842 (No. 1 with a Sir William Rothenstein plaque) and the Scarsdale Arms of 1866–67.

William Weir described Pembroke Square in 1843 as 'plain enough in its exterior, and not unaptly characterised by the beer-shop on the corner'. It was distinctly bohemian, popular with minor artists and actors, but it did have its lions. Thomas Hofland, the landscape painter, lived at No. 6 in 1833–37. The poet Arthur O'Shaughnessy was born at No. 46 in 1844, the son of a minor artist. George Henry Lewes lived at No. 3 during the early years of his married life, between 1841 and 1843, which was eight years before the fateful meeting with Marian Evans. He and 'George Eliot' were later to live together in two other London squares. Number 19 was the last home of the architect Robert Lugar, who died there in 1855. He was noted for his villas and cottages, about which he published influential books.

Until modern gentrification the status of the square did not change much. In 1899 the Booth survey found: 'Three floors and basement, all alike. Houses well kept, servants. Many lodging houses, bills with "apartments". Grass plot in centre.'

The Pembroke Arms, at the corner of Pembroke Square and Earls Court Road, *c.* 1930. It is now the Hansom Cab. (Photograph courtesy of Maurice Friedman)

The garden was held by William Collins on lease from Lord Kensington and the tenants had access to it in the usual way. There was a lodge at the Earls Court Road end, presumably for a gardener. Late in the nineteenth century the lodge was let to various florists, and around 1897 was bought by a gardener named Charles Rassell, who also acquired the freehold of the whole central garden. The 1913 map showed it as a vacant plot with no trees or paths.

In 1923 Rassell applied to build two houses at the west end, but was refused permission. This was one of the warning signs that produced the London Squares Preservation Act of 1931. Rassell and the residents soon reached an agreement, and the enclosure is still divided between Rassell's Nursery at the east end, with a shop in Earls Court Road, and a private communal garden at the west end. The houses are in excellent condition and the square at its highest point of prosperity.

Percy Square

Percy Square, which was built between 1844 and 1850, was merely a short cul-de-sac of thirteen houses that filled the gap between Vernon Square and the backs of the houses on the west side of Holford Square and the north side of Percy Circus. The only square-like features it could boast were a main section that was wider than the entrance and two houses built across the east end, looking directly down the street. The houses were very like those of Vernon Square and Holford Square.

In 1906, for no obvious reason, as there was no clash of names, the LCC made Percy Square part of Vernon Square. Seven years later the whole of Percy Square was demolished to make way for the Vernon Square School, built between 1913 and 1916. It is now the Vernon Square Campus of the School of Oriental & African Studies.

Petticoat Square

The little Petticoat Square, off the south-western side of Petticoat Lane, was probably built in the 1720s, one of several that appeared in the eastern City and Whitechapel at that time. The Ogilby & Morgan map of 1676 and the Strype map published in 1720 showed Bate's Yard on the site, not Inkhorne Court as Harben says. 'Bates Yard very mean,' was Strype's only comment in 1720.

Petticoat Square was in William Maitland's list, published in 1756 but probably compiled in 1732. Rocque named it Petticoat Square in the 1740s. There were ten houses in 1751 (one occupied by Samuel Levy) and Horwood showed thirteen in the 1790s. In the middle of the nineteenth century the centre of the square, formerly an open space, was filled with twelve back-to-back cottages of the meanest kind, separated only by tiny yards.

It did not last long in that debased condition. Between 1877 and 1879 the Commissioners of City Sewers took advantage of the Artisans' & Labourers' Dwellings Act of 1875 to clear Petticoat Square and its neighbouring streets and alleys as dangerous slums. The 2 acres obtained also included the site of Ebenezer Square. The artisans' dwellings that replaced the 164 demolished houses in 1885 were given the name of Petticoat Square, although there was nothing square-like about them.

Perhaps the closely packed military square was in the mind of the architect, Colonel William Haywood of the London Rifle Brigade. The five large blocks, arranged in neat ranks, filled the whole space between Middlesex Street (the old Petticoat Lane) and the Metropolitan Railway cutting. They remained until replaced from 1965 by the City of London's Middlesex Street Estate, dreary flats in dark brick with concrete balconies and shops underneath. But even then the name would not die. The courtyard of this ugly block, decorated with a few seats and trees, is known even now as Petticoat Square, and the name is often applied to the flats, as making them sound less municipal.

Phoenix Square

Phoenix Square took its name from Phoenix House, on part of the garden of which it was built in 1841. The builder was William Seager, a man responsible for many much better houses in and around

The second Petticoat Square in 1885.

Blackheath. It was not in any sense a true square but a group of mean wooden cottages on either side of an alley branching north from the present Tranquil Passage. There were eight originally, but more were soon added.

The square was an instant slum, with poor water supply and little sanitation. There was a cholera death in 1849 and another in 1853. The *Daily News* reported on 8 November 1853 that a doctor 'found the condition of the houses in Phoenix-square, Dartmouth-passage, where the recent case of cholera has occurred, to be disgracefully bad, and inevitably endangering the lives of the tenants'.

The cottages were passed rapidly from landlord to landlord, each promising improvements but failing to carry them out, and the place became a scandalous blot on a prosperous and healthy suburb. The solution was found in the 1860s, not directly through slum clearance but as part of a major redevelopment of the triangle between Tranquil Vale and Montpelier Vale, with the building of Royal Parade. The much more respectable Brigade Street, named after its fire station, was built on the site of Phoenix Square in the 1870s.

Pitt's Square

SOUTHWARK

Between Green Bank and Stoney Lane, two turnings off the north side of Tooley Street, ran Pitt's Court, a winding alley so narrow and insignificant that it was not named on most maps. It was an honour that the elder Pitt would gladly have ceded to his son, and the younger to his father.

Rocque called it Farriers Yard in the 1740s, but it was anonymous on the Horwood maps of the 1790s and 1813. Pitt's Square was the name given by the skeleton Ordnance Survey map of 1848–49 to a tiny offshoot from its north side, but the census returns consistently failed to notice it or to distinguish it from Pitt's Court.

In the twentieth century Pitt's Court became wider and more distinct, but by then Pitt's Square had been extinguished. The large new offices on the eastern corner of Braidwood Street, the former Green Bank, now occupy the site of both court and square.

Plough Square

WHITECHAPEL [TOWER HAMLETS]

Plough Square was an occasional name for the lower end of Plough Street, Whitechapel, south of Buckle Street. Because there was no access south to Little Ayliff Street (now Goodman's Stile) this section of Plough Street formed a short cul-de-sac with three houses on each side. It was called Plough Square in the 1807 and later editions of *The Picture of London*, in some court cases in 1847, on the 1873 Ordnance Survey map and in the earlier LCC lists of streets, but most maps and directories treated it as part of Plough Street. In 1847 No. 6 Plough Square, and probably the other five houses too, were let out as lodgings by a man named George Sharpe, who also had a barber's shop in one of them.

The great changes that have taken place in the Aldgate area in modern times have left this southern 'square' section as the only part of Plough Street surviving. It is now the anonymous forecourt to one section of the huge Goodmans Fields housing development.

Plum Tree Square

ST GILES [CAMDEN]

Plum Tree Square is mysterious. It appeared as 'Plumtree Square, in Plumtree street, St Giles's' in William Stow's 1722 list of streets and as 'Plum Tree Square, Plum Tree street, St Giles' in the list of squares published by William Maitland in 1756, but compiled, he says, in 1732. Hatton had listed only Plum tree street in 1708, and in the 1740s Rocque showed Plumptre Street as a long cul-de-sac leading north from St Giles High Street nearly to Great Russell Street. It had a small offshoot named Plumptre Court, but nothing in street or court resembled a square.

Horwood's 1790s map showed the northern half of Rocque's Plumptre Street widened and extended to and beyond Great Russell Street under the new name of Charlotte Street. The southern half, which he named Plumbtree Street, was still very narrow at its junction with the High Street, but widened markedly at the halfway point, north of which the houses on the east side were set back from the original building line. That might possibly have justified giving the name of square to the wider section. The widening was more pronounced on the parish map of 1815 and Greenwood's map of 1827.

In 1829 Rowland Dobie wrote that 'Plumtree Street takes its name from Henry Plumtree, esquire, its builder, in 1686, or thereabout', the land having been leased to Plumtree by John Buggin in that year. Plumtree Street was close to the notorious St Giles Rookery, a criminal enclave swept away when New Oxford Street was driven through it in the 1840s. Dobie, however, said that 'this street and its continuation, Charlotte Street, is of a respectable description, especially the latter'. As part of the 1840 improvement scheme, Plumtree Street was widened by the demolition of all the houses on the west side.

The southern half of Bloomsbury Street, south of New Oxford Street, follows the line of the old Plumbtree Street, and perhaps of Plum Tree Square.

Polygon

See Clarendon Square

Pomeroy Square

See Carlton Square, New Cross

Pond Square

HIGHGATE [CAMDEN]

In 1898 Pond Square was described as 'a short row of old houses that have seen better days', an assessment that will seem strange to anybody familiar with this large and popular open space, seemingly surrounded with houses. But Pond Square is both accidental and illusory.

Most of the frame is provided by the backs of shops in Highgate High Street and West Hill and by the imposing buildings on the far side of South Grove. It is only on the short west side that genuine, long-standing Pond Square houses exist, and it was these, Nos 1–6, that were put down by the critical observer in 1898. They had certainly declined in the century or more since their building brought the square into being.

In the 1890s several of them were lodging houses and one was occupied by a boot repairer. The delightfully shady garden, so cool even on the hottest day, was another accident, for here until the 1860s was the malodorous pond that gave the square its name.

The Highgate Village ponds were supposed to be former gravel pits. The open area around them, known from the fifteenth century as Highgate Green, was originally much larger, but it was gradually reduced by encroachments and evolved into something close to the size and shape of Pond Square early in the eighteenth century. There was a house on the site of the present Nos 1–6 by 1739.

Numbers 1–5 Pond Square in 2011.

The pond in
Pond Square, c. 1860.

The two polluted ponds formed the only water supply for many of the villagers. They were joined to form a single pond in 1845, but in the 1850s the New River Company began to supply the village with piped water and the pond, no longer of practical value, was neglected. In the 1860s there were plans to build on the remains of the green, but instead the trustees drained the pond and planted the open space with a circular shrubbery crossed with paths, making it for the first time something like a square. There were further threats of building in the 1870s, but in 1885 Pond Square was taken over by the St Pancras Vestry and its future secured.

The south-facing Rock House, No. 6, the largest and most attractive of the Pond Square terrace, was built not long before 1777. It replaced the stable of the original house of 1739, which was on the site of Nos 2 and 3. Numbers 1, 4 and 5 were added at unknown dates before 1785 to create the continuous but very irregular terrace. As the owner of the original house from 1760 to 1785 was Richard Shillingfold, a carpenter, he probably built the terrace himself.

The other houses and flats now numbered in the square are either the hind parts of High Street shops adopting a domestic disguise to court the greater prestige of that address, or new buildings in the back gardens of the High Street. For much of the twentieth century there were only eleven properties in the square, but now there are twice as many.

If the original cottages suffered a social decline in their first century, they have more than made it up in their second. This is so much the case that recently the residents have been agitating to have the square gated and locked at night, a first step perhaps to creating an entirely private garden.

Poole's Square

SHOREDITCH [TOWER HAMLETS]

Poole's Square was a court off the south side of Quaker Street, like its close neighbour Quaker Square, in the account of which something about the history of the area can be found. Rocque's map of the 1740s had Dagger Court more or less on the site, but the various editions of the Horwood map showed nothing there.

Poole's Square was probably built in the 1820s and certainly existed by 1841. It had half a dozen cottages scattered around the court, which was bounded by Quaker Square on the west and a national school on the east. The names were casual and shifting: the 1848–50 skeleton map called Quaker Square Poole's Court and Poole's Square Poole's Place; the 1851 census called Quaker Square Pools Square and Poole's Square Pools Place. The inhabitants were poor – weavers, carpenters, chair makers, etc.

Poole's Square was demolished in 1936 and the LCC built Wheler House on the site of this and the adjoining slums.

Poplar Square

BAYSWATER [WESTMINSTER]

Poplar Place was the mews behind Upper Craven Place in Blackman or Lion Lane, now Queensway. It was built in the early 1820s by John Bark, a small-scale Bayswater developer, formerly a coal merchant. Poplar Square,

off the east side of Poplar Place, made its first appearance in the ratebooks in 1826, when the four cottages were owned by William Lawrence. It was promptly re-absorbed by Poplar Place for rating purposes, not to make a comeback until 1839, but the name was then used to describe the same four properties.

The cottages were arranged two and two on the north and south sides, with front gardens between. There was also a building on the east side, sometimes occupied as No. 5. Attached to the back wall of the southern block, to emphasise its poverty, was a ragged school. While Bayswater was growing strongly the cottages were occupied by carpenters and bricklayers, but later it was the haunt of coachmen and stablemen. When one of Charles Booth's assistants visited Poplar Square in 1899 he found 'four small one storied, two-roomed cottages, gardens in front'.

Poplar Square made its last appearance in the electoral register in 1912. That was when a temporary infants' school was opened there, in two dismounted horse trams. The 1914 map shows the site of the square and the ragged school as a vacant plot.

Poplar Place originally ran from Moscow Road to the Bayswater Road, but its south end was taken to enlarge the garden of a Bayswater Road house and the north end became part of the site of the Queen's Road or Bayswater underground station. The section that survived these amputations still exists obscurely and unexpectedly, but none of the old cottages are standing.

Porchester Square

WESTBOURNE GREEN [WESTMINSTER]

Porchester Square was built in the 1850s on part of the Bishop of London's land, just south of Westbourne Green, an old settlement. The developer was George Wyatt, one of the three architect sons of the sculptor, Matthew Cotes Wyatt. This branch of the great Wyatt family took a leading part in the building of Bayswater. George later designed similar houses in Leinster Square and Prince's Square.

John and William Scantlebury were the main builders engaged in Porchester Square, but the first was Thomas Wood. He was also the first occupant,

The front doors of the north side of Porchester Square, *c.* 1905. Across the road they confronted the more conventional houses of Gloucester Terrace. (Photograph courtesy of Maurice Friedman)

living at the little No. 32 in 1851, three years before any other houses were complete. Five had found tenants by 1854, Nos 1–20 and 32–46 were occupied in 1856 and the square was complete by 1858.

It is not a true square in its shape – a narrow rectangle – or its design. In south Kensington it would be called Porchester Gardens, as the road borders the garden on only three sides. This means that the houses on the north side turn their party faces to the garden, into which they open directly, but have their front doors in workaday elevations in the road to the north. That road has a split personality, the south side being Porchester Square and the north Gloucester Terrace. The houses on the south side of the square, across the road from the garden, are more attractive with restrained porches supporting a continuous balcony and large ground-floor windows.

One detached house, the Lodge, was included in the square for postal purposes, although not part of the development, being a surviving relic of the old Westbourne Green. It occupied the west side until replaced by Shepherd and Thomerson's Porchester Hall in the 1920s.

The square maintained a good reputation during the nineteenth century despite being on the northern edge of prosperous Bayswater, close to the area blighted by the railway. The only notable resident was Leslie Stephen, who lived with his mother at No. 19 in the years before his marriage to Thackeray's daughter Minny in 1867.

In the Edwardian postcards Porchester Square looks rather squalid. It was the beginning of a decline that accelerated until the Ecclesiastical Commissioners were glad to sell the houses to the LCC in 1955. The fact that the garden of the sleek square of today is open to the public and has a children's playground, gives a clue to this less prosperous past. The LCC and its successor the GLC made many alterations to the square and its environs from 1964, restoring the houses and converting them into flats. The Colonnades at the west end of the south side was designed by Farrell & Grimshaw and built in the 1970s. It replaced the pub on the corner, the first four houses, and Porchester Square Mews, which was entered through the archway that still survives. Above the arch are displayed the awards won by the scheme.

Portman Square

With new streets on the Harley estate approaching from the east and on the Grosvenor estate from the south, Henry William Portman's Marylebone fields were ripe for development when he inherited them in 1761. Perhaps he already had his plans matured, for he lost little time in laying out the ground.

The centrepiece of the scheme was the grand Portman Square, which was linked directly with its chief models and rivals, Cavendish Square and Grosvenor Square, by long, straight roads. It was reported to be 'now building' in January 1765, and the first houses were occupied, on the south side, in 1768. Abraham and Samuel Adams built all or most of the south, east and west sides as a speculation, completing them by 1773, and Samuel later built part of Manchester Square. There, except in the case of Manchester House, he probably relied on his own design skills, but in the larger and more prestigious Portman Square some clients brought in their own fashionable architects to finish the houses according to their tastes.

This was certainly true of the north side, which was the last to be built between 1772 and 1778. Here most of the plots were larger and all were more expensive, because they enjoyed an open outlook at the back and the much admired view of Hampstead and Highgate. John Johnson designed two of the houses and James Wyatt was responsible for seven, some as a private speculation. One of his clients was the dreadful Countess of Home, whose No. 20 he began in 1772. It is curious that the architect now most associated with Portman Square is Wyatt's great rival Robert Adam, who was only called in by the countess in 1775, after she had dismissed Wyatt, to complete Home House.

In 1783 the irregularities of the north side gave great offence to the anonymous editor and reviser of James Ralph's *Critical Review*:

> What pity it is, that the ground landlord did not confine his tenants to build according to an uniform plan! Or if symmetry, magnificence, and public order, be objects of no value, why does he not let out the area in the center to every one who has money to build a house, or a dog-kennel?

Portman had the original idea of getting extra profit from the sought-after north side by letting a large plot, almost as big as the square itself, off the north-west corner. The learned Elizabeth Montagu, queen of the bluestockings, took a ninety-nine-year lease of this land soon after her husband's death in 1775, and commissioned James Stuart to design a detached house for her in 1777.

The north side of Portman Square in 1813.

Montagu House, Portman Square, c. 1840.

'Athenian' Stuart was a slow worker and a steady tippler, so the house was not ready for occupation until 1781. The interior decoration was only completed in the 1790s, after Stuart's death. 'I had a letter lately from Mrs Montagu, who appears in delightful health and spirits, and proposes soon to be in town to take possession of her palace,' wrote her friend Elizabeth Carter in October 1781; and in January 1782 she was able to report that 'Mrs Montagu is in delightful health. I dined with her on Sunday in her palace, which is really beautiful, and in which she appears to be very happy …'

Mrs Montagu's assemblies at Portman Square were celebrated but far from comfortable, according to the reminiscences of Lady Louisa Stuart:

> As her company came in, a heterogeneous medley, so they went out, each individual feeling himself single, isolated, and (to borrow a French phrase) embarrassed with his own person; which might be partly owing to the awkward position of the furniture, the mal-arrangement of tables and chairs. Everything in that house, as if under a spell, was sure to form itself into a circle or semicircle.

After Mrs Montagu's death in 1800 the house was sometimes occupied by her heirs, including for a time Henry Goulburn, Peel's Chancellor of the Exchequer, who had married into the Montagu family, and was sometimes let to tenants, including the Turkish ambassador. The landowner, Lord Portman, obtained possession when the lease expired in 1874 and made it his own residence, changing the name to Portman House. He also made some heavy Victorian alterations and additions, which was some small consolation when the house was gutted by a firebomb in 1940 and demolished after the war.

The square had enough residents by 1777 to justify the laying out of the oval garden. In 1780 a private act was obtained for its management and the trustees set about planting and adornment. Although it had been built with no attempt at regularity, in 1807 Portman Square was described as second in beauty only to Grosvenor Square. One of its assets (incredible to the modern eye) was that 'north of it is Baker-street, perhaps the handsomest street in London'.

Inconvenient evidence of the success of the square is provided by the ever-changing numbering scheme. Under the original arrangement, which treated the corner houses as parts of the side streets, there were thirty-nine houses included, but as a Portman Square address became a social asset more and more residents attached themselves to it. At first they used 18a, 27a, etc. and when these were regularised in the final renumbering the thirty-nine houses were found to have risen to forty-seven. Although it was the main feature of Portman Square, Montagu House was numbered 1 Upper Berkeley Street until it became No. 22 in the square in 1858.

The most exciting event in the history of the square came as early as 29 April 1802, when Napoleon's agent Louis Otto illuminated his house on the south side in dramatic fashion to celebrate the signing of the preliminary articles of the peace treaty, and all London went to enjoy the show. Southey described the scene:

> Never before had I beheld such multitudes assembled. The middle of the street was completely filled with coaches, so immoveably locked together, that many persons who wished to cross passed under the horses' bellies without fear and without danger. The unfortunate persons within had no such means of escape ... We tried the first entrance to the square in vain; it was utterly impossible to get in, and finding this we crossed into the counter current, and were carried out by the stream. A second and a third entrance we tried with no better fortune; at the fourth, the only remaining avenue, we were more successful. To this, which is at the outskirts of the town, there was one way inaccessible by carriages, and it was not crowded by walkers, because the road was bad, there were no lamps, and the way was not known ... The inscription [of Otto's illumination] was Peace and Amity; it had been Peace and Concord, but a party of sailors in the morning, whose honest patriotism did not regard trifling differences of orthography, insisted upon it that they were not *conquered*, and that no Frenchman should say so.

An early print shows the inscription as the even more provocative 'Victory'.

The north side of Oxford Street was less popular than the south, as Trollope hinted in *The Small House*

The south-west corner of Portman Square, *c.* 1905.

at Allington in 1863, but Portland Square was nevertheless able to attract a galaxy of fashionable residents before and after that date. In 1898 Charles Booth's assistant wrote that 'Portman Square, as the residence of a Royal Duchess, is the most fashionable square north of Oxford Street, probably the only one which is still really fashionable'. The Duke and Duchess of Fife then lived at No. 15. The duchess, the Princess Royal, eldest daughter of Edward VII, died there in 1931.

Residents of personal rather than inherited distinction were rarer here than in the other large West End squares. Apart from the residents of Montagu House, the most eminent were Lord Grey, of the Reform Act, who occupied Home House from about 1814 to 1818, and the hostess Lady Ottoline Morrell who was born at No. 5 in 1873.

The death of the Princess Royal was the signal for the destruction of the square, which had remained fashionable until then. In the 1930s blocks of luxury

a restaurant, is the fourth survivor. It is really part of Portman Street, in which it was numbered until the 1850s. As in the other squares on the Portman estate, the garden remains private.

Powis Square

Powis Square and Colville Square were built together by George Frederick John Tippett on 17 acres of Portobello Farm land purchased in 1860. Tippett was then busy with Leinster Square and Prince's Square in Bayswater and soon transferred much the same plan to this new development. He is thought to have been his own architect for the Notting Hill scheme.

He did introduce one novelty in the shape of what was virtually a third square, called Colville Gardens, between Powis Square and Colville Square. It differed only in having a narrower strip of communal garden. Powis Square had the most generous, or least mean, of the three. All were of the type that would have been called 'Gardens' in South Kensington, with the houses on one side opening directly into the enclosure.

Powis Square was built slowly, Tippett undertaking some of the houses himself and letting plots to other builders. By 1871 the eastern terrace and the middle terrace (opening into the garden) were complete, but of the western terrace only two houses had been built. The short north and south sides, continuations of Talbot Road and Colville Terrace, were also finished and the garden was laid out and planted.

The remaining houses of the west terrace, completing the whole development, were built by 1875. The tall stucco houses, narrow and gaunt, with porches and canted bays, were much the same all over the estate, huge numbers of them packed in tightly.

The short first leases sold reasonably well, at the cost of admitting schools – including Walter Wren's Indian Civil Service coaching college – and the odd boarding house, but the area suffered an early and steep social decline. In 1885, weighed down with debt and with many empty houses on his hands, Tippett was bankrupted.

The Booth survey gave a graphic description of decay in 1899:

flats were built in the middle of the north side (on the site of her house among others), in the middle of the east, and at the east end of the south side.

In addition to Montagu House, a few on the south and west sides were badly damaged during the Second World War. Since then almost all the houses have been replaced by flats, shops and offices, and two hideous hotels: the Churchill, which fills the whole of the west side, and the Radisson Portman on the site of Montagu House.

Portman Square is now a depressing place to visit, with only four original houses remaining. Numbers 19–21 on the north side give some idea of the old scale and style. The great Home House, one of the finest in London, was saved when Samuel Courtauld acquired it in the 1920s and made it the Courtauld Institute of Art. The spy Anthony Blunt, director of the institute, lived in a flat at the top of the house. The Courtauld moved to Somerset House in 1989 and Home House became a club. Number 34, now

This and other squares in the district are built on the same plan. The houses on one side (in this case the east) back on to the square [garden] and have all their best rooms looking out on the square, to which they have direct access from a very small private court. The kitchens and sanitary offices look upon the street, into which the house's door opens. On the opposite side of the square the street door and the best rooms face the square, and the inhabitants have to cross the public road to reach the gardens. As a result of this arrangement the street between two squares is simply hideous. The houses have been re-drained and the pipes are carried up outside, so that each street door is flanked by a forest of pipes of all sizes, gradually diminishing in number as the roof is reached. The windows are dirty, and many of them glazed with ground glass. Some of the houses are fitted for two families and have small brass plates marked 'Flat No. 1' and 'Flat No. 2' and giving the name of the respective occupant.

The decline grew much steeper in the twentieth century, with most of the houses divided into flats or bedsits by the 1920s, some by the council and some by private landlords. There was not much serious bombing of the square during the Second World War, but general blast damage and poor maintenance added to the squalor. In the 1950s it became one of the centres of Rachmanism. The council began to restore some of the houses in the 1960s but the central terrace, opening into the garden, was rebuilt in plain brick in 1979.

Powis Square is now an ugly place, with a garden that is little more than a children's playground surrounded by untidy flats in various styles, some converted from the old houses and others new. Much the most attractive feature is the Tabernacle, which faces the garden on the north side. It was built as a Baptist chapel in 1887, designed by Habershon and Fawckner, but is now a community centre, well restored in the late 1990s.

The west side of Powis Square, c. 1905.

Prebend Square

Prebend Street commemorates the large estate that belonged to the Dean and Chapter of St Paul's Cathedral in the Middle Ages, this part of which passed into the hands of the Clothworkers' Company after the Dissolution.

When it was developed in the middle of the nineteenth century the Clothworkers chose the focal point, where the present Popham Road, Britannia Row, Bishop Street and Rector Street converge on Prebend Street, to establish their own institutions. In 1855 they built their almshouses, giving them the key position at the junction of all these roads with a well-planted garden in front of them. But the almshouses enjoyed this dignity for less than twenty years. In 1871 the Clothworkers obtained permission to sell one of their City charities, Lambe's Chapel in Wood Street Square (q.v.), on condition that they provided an equivalent. This they did by demolishing the front ranges of their almshouses (confining them to Bishop Road) to provide a suitably dramatic site for St James's Church, which was built between 1873 and 1875. It was designed by the company's own architect, Frederick William Porter, a pupil of Lewis Vulliamy.

The wide road junction in front of the new church, with its garden in the centre and a triangular frame of 1850s houses, soon became known as Prebend Square, and St James's Prebend Square was long the official name of the church. But as the houses were all numbered in their different roads, the name never became firmly attached to the junction and has long slipped out of use. Nearly all the framing houses were destroyed in the Second World War but the church, the almshouses and the leafy public garden still give something of the feeling of a square.

Prebend Square, *c.* 1910.

Prince's Square

Prince's Square was one of George Tippett's developments, built between 1856 and 1859 in conjunction with the neighbouring Leinster Square. In September 1857 *Building News* reported that Mr Chambers had just completed three first-class residences on the south side and had four more in a very advanced state, and on the north side Mr Edwards had erected two and had two others in active progress, while at the western end the Prince's Hotel was completed and occupied. These builders were perhaps Charles Chambers, who figured in the development of Notting Hill, and William Lloyd Edwards of Queen's Road, now Queensway. The Prince's Hotel, the first of many, was at No. 73.

The best features of the square are the bow-fronted houses on the west side and in the western extension, which are identical with those on the west side of Leinster Square. They were designed by George Wyatt. The houses facing the rather mean garden are dull and heavy and the road between the two squares, containing the entrances of the back-to-front houses, is ugly.

The new square proved popular enough at first but quickly lost favour. The original tenants tended not to renew their leases and after twenty years the weight of empty houses here and in his other squares forced George Tippett into bankruptcy.

In 1899 Charles Booth's researcher, revising the colour coding of the original poverty map, found that it looked 'dull and dirty, seven houses to let', and recommended that it should be relegated from a prosperous yellow to a merely respectable red. The sudden nature of its decline is shown by the fact that in 1902 almost every tenanted house was privately occupied, while in 1915, except for a YMCA at No. 28, a home for working girls at No. 47 and a Ladies' International Club at No. 74, it was entirely given over to boarding houses.

This is a most confusing square, with no central open space to focus it and the numbers running in all directions. The investigator is not helped by the London directory compilers who, in designating the various stretches as north, south, east and west, had got their compass in a twist. In 2011 there was a plan to convert the many small hotels in the square into one, two and three-bedroom flats. It has certainly become less seedy in recent years, and George Wyatt's bow fronts give it a pleasant air of seaside frivolity.

The west side of Prince's Square, Bayswater, *c.* 1905.

Prince's Square

Prince's Square, a turning off the east side of Wilson Street, developed gradually during the early nineteenth century from the mere alley shown by older maps. There were eight houses in 1817. The space it filled was between Horse Shoe Alley off Wilson Street, and Queen's Square off Finsbury Avenue. The name completed the set begun by Queen's Square and King Square, which was on the north side of Horse Shoe Alley.

Prince's Square can never have been salubrious. In 1841 the occupants included an ink manufacturer, a hat dyer, a Lucifer manufacturer, a hotpresser and a manufacturing chemist. The building of the Broad Street goods depot in the 1860s had the effect of shortening the square, and it was snuffed out entirely when the depot was extended on the west side of Finsbury Avenue in the 1890s.

Prince's Square

(now part of Gate Street)

This is perhaps the smallest of all the London squares or former squares. In 1810 John Lockie described it as 'Princes-Square, Princes-Street, Lincoln's-Inn-Fields, – a small recess on the S. side, nearly op. New Turnstile'. His Princes Street is now part of Gate Street.

Rowland Dobie wrote in 1829, 'We may remark, that as St Giles's parish contains the largest square [Lincoln's Inn Fields], so it also *may boast* of the smallest, which is situate near it, namely, Prince's Square, containing only one house!'

In 1907 Beresford Chancellor placed 'the tiny Princes Square … between Little Queen Street and Gate Street'. Maps show nothing resembling a square directly opposite New Turnstile, but a few yards to the west there was a small recess on the south side of Prince Street. Having narrowly escaped destruction in the great Aldwych improvement, it can still be found on the south side of

Gate Street, a few steps from Kingsway, serving as the forecourt to a betting shop. Kingsway follows in part the line of Chancellor's Little Queen Street, which it obliterated.

With such a minute place it is unsafe to conclude much from the evidence of maps, but the Strype map of St Giles, published in 1720, marked a tiny unnamed court south of Little Princes Street, Rocque in the 1740s did not, but in the 1790s Horwood showed it again south of what was by then Princes Street. Strype mentioned Little Princes Street, 'a Place of no great Account for Buildings or Inhabitants', but no courts turning from it except New Turnstile.

Prince's Square

(later Swedenborg Square)

John Prince, the self-styled 'Prince of Surveyors', has been credited with the creation of Prince's Square. He was Edward Harley's agent for the development of his Marylebone estate and a major builder there – of Princes Street, for example – and also worked for the Duke of Bedford in Covent Garden.

It was just to the east of the earlier Wellclose Square and, like its larger neighbour, was mainly occupied in the early years by merchants, sea captains and other mariners. It was described by John Noorthouck in 1773 as 'a neat place principally inhabited by the families of gentlemen that belong to the sea' – to the families, because the gentlemen themselves were absent more often than not. Parker's 1720 map, which showed 'Well Close' with its church, did not include Prince's Square and nor did the Strype map of Stepney or William Stow's 1722 list of streets.

The Swedish church in the centre was built in 1728–29. Prince's Square featured in Maitland's 1756 list, which was probably compiled in 1732, and the first mention of it in the Old Bailey proceedings was in January 1734. Rocque's 1740s map showed the church, with houses on the east, west and south sides of the square. The north side, where some of the houses were larger and more elaborate, was not built until the 1820s.

It was not a place likely to attract the famous. The only celebrity is the Scottish painter of miniature portraits, Anthony Stewart, who lived at No. 26 from 1807 to 1820, perhaps longer. He specialised in children and numbered Princess Charlotte, daughter of George IV, and the future Queen Victoria among his sitters. Emanuel Swedenborg was buried in the Swedish Protestant church, where he worshipped when in London, in 1772, but his remains – with the wrong skull – were removed to Sweden in a battleship in 1908. In 1938 the name was changed to Swedenborg Square.

The church closed in 1911, the timber trade that provided most of the congregation having moved to the Surrey Docks, and the building was demolished in 1921. The church had occupied most of the garden and its removal briefly gave the local children the advantage of a playground in the centre.

The square passed through the Second World War almost miraculously well, with houses damaged only at the south end of the west side. The unpretentious three-storey terraces, opening directly onto the pavement, were still in reasonable condition in the early 1960s, but the arrogant spirit of the age was against them. All were demolished to make way for the St George's Estate, built by the LCC and GLC between 1964 and 1970. At Wellclose Square the form survived the clearance, allowing for the faint possibility of a renaissance, but here every vestige of the square's existence was gleefully erased.

Prince's Square

See Cleaver Square and Cory Square

Printing House Square

CITY OF LONDON

Printing House Yard was the successor to the inner cloister of the Dominican friary known as Blackfriars. After the Dissolution a house was built on the north side of the cloisters. It was later called Hunsdon House after Henry Carey, Lord Hunsdon, a cousin of Queen Elizabeth.

The Swedish church in Prince's Square, Wapping, *c.* 1905.

In 1623, when let to the French ambassador, the house was the scene of a disaster. An over-large congregation at a Roman Catholic service in an upper room caused two storeys to collapse, killing as many as ninety-one men and women. It was probably while the house was in this ruinous condition, certainly between 1623 and 1628, that it was bought from the last Lord Hunsdon's daughter by the men who held the patent of King's Printer. Until then the King's Printing House had been in Aldersgate.

Hunsdon House was destroyed in the Fire of London, but rebuilt in the early 1670s. It appeared as 'The Kings Printinghouse' (at the end of Printing House Lane) on the Ogilby & Morgan map of 1676. Hatton, in 1708, described Printing House Lane as 'a passage to the Queens Printing house (which is a stately Building)'. The printing house on the north side of the yard and the printer's house on the west side were destroyed

Apart from the Printing House, which was No. 5, and the advertising office of *The Times* at No. 4, there were five houses. The square was partly residential, partly commercial and not monopolised by *The Times* until the 1870s. The great engraver, William Faithorne the elder, retired to a house in Printing House Yard in the 1680s and died there in 1691.

There was a coal merchant and a solicitor at No. 1, the big house on the south side, in the early nineteenth century; a carver and gilder at No. 3 from about 1815 until 1860; and in the 1830s and 1840s an artificial florist at No. 7. The printer's house, occupied by the Walter family, was on the west side. Number 1 was bought by John Walter of *The Times* in 1855, No. 3 in 1860 and No. 7 (by then rebuilt as part of a hotel facing south to Queen Victoria Street) in 1873. Most of the buildings around the square were demolished between 1868 and 1870 and the new *Times* office, with its main entrance in Queen Victoria Street, was opened in 1874.

Printing House Square was described by Max Schlesinger in 1853 as being in the middle of:

> … a labyrinth of the narrowest, the most wretched, ill-paved, and unsavoury streets of London … At length we turn to the left, into a narrow street, and reach a small square of the exact dimensions and appearance of a German back-yard. There are two trees quite lonely behind an iron railing, and a door with the words 'THE TIMES' on it.

Even after the offices were enlarged they remained obscure. Virginia Woolf used regularly lose her way when walking to Printing House Square with the manuscripts of her *TLS* reviews. 'I know a square wherein the wild *Times* grows' was William Titterton's only reference to it in his 1926 survey of the squares.

The true Printing House Square ceased to exist around 1960 when *The Times* began to rebuild its offices across the open space. The paper had obtained a statutory instrument for the stopping up of the square in 1955 and the new premises were completed in 1965. In 1962 Printing House Square was approved as the name for the new office's forecourt which was open to Queen Victoria Street. *The Times* moved out in 1974 and the building was used for a while by *The Observer*. The name was finally extinguished late

by fire again in 1738 but soon rebuilt. The connection of the building with the office of King's Printer was broken when Charles Eyre and William Strahan acquired the patent in 1769 and built a new and much larger printing house in New Street Square.

John Walter bought the old King's Printing House in 1784 for his Logographic Press, and began to print the *Daily Universal Register*, the forerunner of *The Times*, in 1785. The name Printing House Square came into use in the 1780s, probably because John Walter gave that as the address of the paper from the first issue on the first day of 1785. He thought, perhaps, that it sounded more dignified than 'yard'. It was the usual name by 1800, although Printing House Yard still turned up occasionally until 1810 or later. The Horwood maps of the 1790s and 1813 called it Printers Square (at the east end of Printing House Lane) but it was 'Printing House-Square' in Lockie's list of 1810.

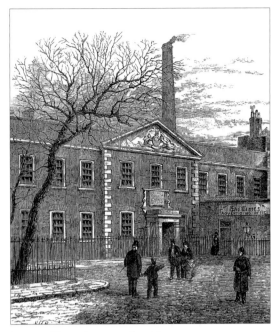

Printing House Square in the 1860s.

in the twentieth century when the Bank of New York Mellon Centre, No. 160 Queen Victoria Street, was built across the whole of the site with no open space. It was completed in 2003.

Providence Square

KINGSLAND [HACKNEY]

(later Sutton Place and Bonby Place)

Providence Square was probably of the front garden type, the long front gardens of the two sides collectively standing in for the more conventional communal garden. It was part of an early nineteenth-century development north of Kingsland Green, between the present Kingsland High Street and Boleyn Road.

Frederic Place, immediately to the south of the square, was built in 1826. A dense pattern of small streets and alleys had developed by then but most of the houses were soon destroyed by the railways. Providence Square survived, miraculously perhaps, when two of the lines of the North London Railway were dug a few yards to the north and south in 1850 and 1865. The first removed the north side of the square, reducing it to a mere terrace of eight cottages on the brink of the cutting.

Trapped in a tight triangle between the two railway lines and the backs of the High Street shops, it was never likely to be more than a slum, but as it offered so little scope for redevelopment it was not removed. About 1870 the eight survivors of the old square were rebuilt as a terrace of six, with two more facing Boleyn Road, and the former square was given the new name of Sutton Place. It did not produce much improvement, as the Booth survey found in 1897: 'Sutton Place also poor, drunken costers. The Lord Clyde Coffee House at the corner has been a noted brothel for years.' A second attempt was made by changing the name to Bonby Place in 1920.

It had been scheduled as a slum clearance area before the Second World War, during which all but the Lord Clyde was destroyed by bombing. The site, occupied since the 1960s by the rear parts of shops in Kingsland High Street, is immediately south of the Dalston Kingsland Station.

Prujean Square

CITY OF LONDON

The name of Prujean Square (or Court) came from Sir Francis Prujean, president of the College of Physicians, who lived in the parish of St Martin Ludgate, near the Old Bailey, from 1639 until his death in 1666. Various authorities say that he lived in the court, but his house was a large one, with twelve hearths in 1664, so it is more likely that his house was not rebuilt after the fire and provided the site for this new development. It was shown on the Ogilby & Morgan map of 1676 as 'Prigeons Court', and Hatton listed it in 1708 as 'Prugeon's Court, so named from the late Mr Prugeon the Owner'.

Prujean Court was a far better name for the place than the later Prujean Square. It was a rectangular yard, off the west side of Old Bailey and running parallel with it, north and south. Entry was by a narrow passage at the south end. There were no houses on the east side, which was occupied by the gardens of the Old Bailey houses. On the west side there were six, and perhaps another at the north end. Prujean Square was taking over as the name by the 1780s, although the old one continued to crop up long afterwards.

It was well tenanted at first, but entirely commercial by the early nineteenth century. Several of the Old Bailey houses with back entrances in the court were inns, which cannot have improved the amenities. Further drawbacks were the two nearest neighbours to the west, the Fleet Prison and the huge yard of the Belle Sauvage Inn, scene of bull and bear baiting and the place where a rhinoceros was exhibited in 1683.

In the eighteenth century hairdressers, bookbinders and shoemakers lived in Prujean Court, and later Prujean Square was popular with various trades connected with printing and book production. By the 1870s all the original houses had been rebuilt as a large printing works that occupied the whole of the west side until the area was destroyed during the Second World War. The site has been redeveloped several times since then.

Pump Square

SHOREDITCH [HACKNEY]

Pump Square appeared only in the 1851 census. It stood between Kingsland Road and Hackney Road, south of the present Cremer Street, on part of the White Bear Gardens, and not far from Harris Square. The tiny court of two or three houses, a turning off Orchard Place, was occupied in 1851 by a butcher and a 'horse hair manufacturer'. Like so much else in this poor district, Pump Square was swept away when the North London Railway built its line into Broad Street in the early 1860s. Workshops fill the streets that survive on either side of what is now the Overground viaduct.

Quaker Square

SHOREDITCH [TOWER HAMLETS]

Quaker Square, off the south side of Quaker Street, was known as New Square until 1909, and before it was New Square it was New Court. When it was new is hard to tell: probably in the 1650s or 1660s, when the banker and politician Sir William Wheler began to build on his estate here. That was also the time when a Quaker meeting was formed in Spitalfields.

The Ogilby & Morgan map of 1676, made when Quaker Street was still Westbury Street, showed an unnamed court in the correct position, with four or five houses. It was New Court by the 1740s and well into the nineteenth century, and New Square by the 1850s. Perhaps that change of name celebrated a rebuilding.

The 1873 map showed houses with long front gardens, some with trees. The gardens were mentioned in the Booth survey of 1898: 'New Square, quiet, 18 houses, well cared for little gardens in front, 2 storey houses, that at the east end had about eight cages hung out on wall'. As maps indicated no more than eight houses in New Square it is hard to see where the eighteen came in, unless those in the adjoining Poole's Square were being included. That is not unlikely in these interlocking and poorly demarcated courts: the 1848–50 skeleton map called Quaker Square Poole's Court and Poole's Square Poole's Place; the 1851 census called Quaker Square Pools Square and Poole's Square Pools Place. The LCC demolished most of the south side of Quaker Street and its offshoots in 1936 and built Wheler House on the site.

Queen Ann's Square

MARYLEBONE [WESTMINSTER]

Queen Ann's Square was a project of the 1770s that probably never got beyond the drawing board. John Noorthouck claimed in 1773 that 'Northward of Cavendish-square, towards Marybone, a new square is now compleating called Queen-Anne Square', and the 1772 map of London published with his history included a fully formed 'Queen Anns Square', larger than Cavendish Square, on the north side of Foley House. It even indicated buildings on the south side, though none on the other three. Such a scheme, unless with houses only to east and west, could hardly have won the approval of Lord Foley, who so prized his view to the north.

Only a year or two after Noorthouck described this fantasy square, James and Robert Adam were designing Portland Place, which was soon built on the site instead, its great width intended to placate Lord Foley. The Langham Hotel later replaced Foley House.

Henry Wheatley claimed that Bentinck Square was another name for this project, but then he said the same (correctly) about Manchester Square. Wilfred Whitten, the editor of Smith's *Book for a Rainy Day*, remarked in one of his discursive notes that it was 'intended to build a Queen Anne Square at the foot of Great Portland Street, but this project fell through'. That belief presumably arose from confusion between Great Portland Street and Portland Place.

Queen Anne's Square

See Manchester Square

Queen Square

BLOOMSBURY [CAMDEN]

Queen Square was planned as early as 1686 at the fag end of Nicholas Barbon's great campaign of expansion west of Gray's Inn. It was originally intended to be called Devonshire Square, after Devonshire Street (now Boswell Street) the approach from Red Lion Square in the south. The permanent name was loyally substituted during the reign of Queen Anne.

Hatton, writing in 1708, after describing Queen Square at Westminster, added that 'There is also another Square of this Name designed, at the N. end of Devonshire Street, near Red lion square'. The point was perhaps still undecided in 1725 or a little earlier, when Defoe referred to 'Ormond Street, and the great New Square at the West End of it'. It is curious that the queen commemorated in the garden is not Anne but Charlotte, consort of George III. Oliver Beckett, who lived at No. 26, erected her lead statue in 1775.

Most of the land, part of Lamb's Conduit Fields, belonged to Sir Nathaniel Curzon, who let a large part to Arthur Tooley for sixty-one years from 1705, 'wheron to erect houses'. Tooley's first work was the church. St George the Martyr was built by subscription as a chapel of ease to St Andrew Holborn in 1705–06, the cost being recouped by the sale of the pews. It was enlarged and beautified within by Nicholas Hawksmoor in 1717–20 as, appropriately, one of the 'Queen Anne' churches, and given its own parish in 1723. Defoe's account, published in 1725 but written

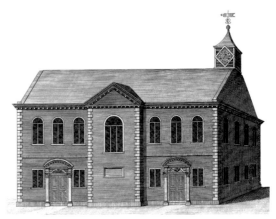

St George's, Queen Square, Bloomsbury, in the 1750s.

earlier, was, 'Here is also a very convenient Church, built by the contribution of the Gentry Inhabitants of these Buildings, tho' not yet made Parochial, being called St George's Chapel'. The present appearance of the church is largely the work of Samuel Teulon, who substantially altered it in 1867–68.

The houses were mostly built between 1710 and 1725, the west side before the east, by a number of speculating tradesmen and intending residents. Thomas Barlow, the carpenter who was later active in Hanover Square and Grosvenor Square and lived to be 'a very noted Master-Builder', was busy here between 1709 and 1714, when he received a lease of No. 6. The north side was 'left open for the sake of the beautiful landscape formed by the hills of Highgate and Hampstead, together with the adjacent fields', as Dodsley wrote in 1761.

Sir Nathaniel Curzon had the northern house on the west side, thus securing the best view but not hogging all of it like the Duke of Bedford in Bloomsbury Square. In 1773 Noorthouck wrote that 'though the distant beauties have occasioned the decoration of the area to be overlooked, a walk round it is as pleasant as any of the public gardens, none of which can boast so fine a prospect'. It was only the development of the Foundling Hospital estate in the 1790s that destroyed this amenity. In 1792 Edward Lind of Queen Square took legal action to restrain the governors, but lost his case. Even after this defeat the upper end of the square remained open to Guilford Street, from which it was protected by a garden until the late 1920s. In 1825 it was still possible to write that 'Queen Square, which, in point of fact,

The east side of Queen Square, Bloomsbury, *c.* 1905.

is a parallelogram, is neat-looking, and possesses some features of the rural', and even in 1907 it was, among the squares, 'one of the most retired in London'.

Although it was too remote to be in the forefront of fashion, Queen Square had its noble residents in its early days and remained a good address throughout the eighteenth century. Philip Norman quoted a lady who lived there until about 1820 as saying, 'When I came to the square I was the only lady who did not keep a carriage. Before I left I was the only one who did.'

The ratebooks show some famous names in Queen Square: Joseph Andrews at No. 9 in the 1750s, Jane Eyre at No. 28 from 1750 to 1752, and R. Acres (from the country, no doubt) at No. 2 in 1788–89. Real celebrities included Edmond Hoyle, the great expert on whist, who lived and taught his pupils here in the 1740s. This was probably at No. 14 on the west side, which was occupied earlier and later by members of the family. The ratebooks for the 1740s are missing.

The Burneys occupied No. 39, the southern house on the east side, from 1770 to 1774. In November 1770 Fanny Burney wrote: 'We have a charming house here.

It is situated at the upper end of the square, and has a delightful prospect of Hamstead and Hygate.' Her father, Dr Charles Burney, was then making his musical tour of France and Italy and did not see the new house until Christmas Eve. He was particularly pleased with it because a previous occupant was John Barber, Swift's friend and printer, who was Lord Mayor in 1732–33. Barber bought the house with the profits from successful speculation in South Sea stock and died there in 1741. York House, No. 37, is now on the site.

Until the arrival of the hospitals the most famous institution in the square was the school known as 'the Ladies' Eton', run by Jane Dennis at No. 31 from the 1740s and later extended into 29 and 30 by Judith Stevenson. The satirical poet Charles Churchill – a strange man to let loose in a girls' school – taught there in the 1750s, the future Mrs Thrale was an early pupil, and James Boswell's daughter, Veronica, was a boarder in 1788–89. There were then 220 pupils and the fees were over 100 guineas per annum. The girls sometimes made the short trip across the square to St George's in the school carriage so that they could learn to get in and out with dignity in their unwieldy skirts.

The gentry largely deserted the square after 1800, when it became popular with solicitors, architects, surgeons, clergymen, writers and artists, a few of them famous. The Christian Socialist Frederick Denison Maurice lived at No. 21 in the early 1850s, sharing the house with Sir Frederick Pollock, Lord Chief Baron of the Exchequer, and his huge family. Number 26 was the home of William Morris from 1865 to 1872 and remained the premises of his firm until 1881.

The poet William Allingham had lodgings at No. 1 in the mid-1850s and described its amenities in a letter:

> I have come to like my lodgings very much and they are admired by all my visitors; being both quiet and lively – for though there is no thoroughfare for carriages at the upper end of the Square, it has a great many foot passengers and is full of children, having a fine plane tree, several poplars and hawthorns, and a grass plot in front of my three windows. I can go into the garden when I like, and have the gardener to touch his gold-laced hat to me, under the shadow of Queen Anne, whose statue and title adorn the Square.

The mistake about the statue was a common one.

In 1891 Henry Wheatley noted that 'Queen Square has long ceased to be a fashionable place of residence, and several of the larger houses have been appropriated to commercial, educational or benevolent uses'. As Robert Louis Stevenson wrote in 1874: 'It seems to have been set apart for the humanities of life and the alleviation of all hard destinies. As you go round it, you read, upon every second door-plate, some offer of help to the afflicted.'

The charities were mainly hospitals. The first was Joseph Amesbury's Private Spinal Institution, which was at No. 31 in the late 1840s and early 1850s. The great National Hospital for paralysis and epilepsy began at No. 24 in 1860, the Alexandra Hospital for Children with Hip Diseases at No. 19 in 1867, and the Italian Hospital at Nos 40 and 41 in 1884. All of these expanded and were eventually rebuilt, the National in stages from 1881, the Alexandra and Italian in 1899. The London Homoeopathic Hospital expanded into the square from Great Ormond Street in 1909–11. The Alexandra moved away in 1920 and the Italian closed in 1990.

Queen Square suffered almost as much in the First World War – when a Zeppelin dropped a bomb in the garden, breaking most of the windows – as in the Second, when only the south-east corner was badly damaged.

The east and north sides are now nearly filled with hospital buildings of no beauty, but there is still much to enjoy: St George's and seven old houses on the west side and two houses and the former Italian Hospital on the south. The centre has from the first been arranged in an unusual way. The northern three-quarters is a garden, which had only a lawn while the famous view of Hampstead and Highgate lasted, but was planted afterwards to hide the infamous view of Guilford Street. The garden is still presided over by Queen Charlotte. In front of the church at the south end is a small paved space, once provided with a parish pump, and in the early twentieth century 'much used by the youth of the neighbourhood for cricket, roller skating and other recreations', but now a pleasantly shady area with seats.

Queen Square

The Aldersgate Queen Square was part of the complex of courts and alleys between Bartholomew Close and Aldersgate Street of which Cloth Fair still gives an idea. It was not shown on the Ogilby & Morgan map of 1676. The Strype map had a correction at this point to indicate something like a square, suggesting that it may have been built shortly before the map was published in 1720. William Stow included it in his 1722 list of streets as 'Queen's Square, in Bartholomew Close', and Maitland called it 'Queen Square, Little Bartholomew close' in his 1756 list, which was probably compiled in 1732. On Rocque's 1740s map it was 'Queen's S'.

There were eight or nine houses, approached from Aldersgate Street through an archway nearly opposite Jewin Street and along a narrow alley. The entrance from Bartholomew Close in the west was less restricted.

Though nothing more than a court, it was quite a good address in its early days and there were still a couple of private residents in 1841. It became entirely commercial soon afterwards. By 1915 nearly the whole of the square was occupied by a fancy leather goods manufacturer. The LCC abolished the name in 1939, calling the remaining buildings Nos 30–33 Bartholomew Close; new stationery would have been a sad waste, as they were destroyed in the Blitz a year or two later. Aldersgate Court and Mitre House are now on the site.

Queen Square

Queen's Row was the name for the houses on the west side of Hoxton Street, north of Turner's Square. Horwood's 1790s map showed an alley between two of the Queen's Row houses, apparently making no progress beyond their back gardens, but Cary's 1795 map named Queen Square behind Queen's Row.

The 1813 revision of Horwood indicated that the alley had been extended to Ivy Lane and that houses had been built on both sides of its east end, which was described as Queen's Row Walk. Queen or Queen's Square later became the usual name, with some justification because the nine houses, five on the north and four on the south side, had long front gardens which

gave a sense of space. But although the gardens gave this square-like feel to the east section, the lane was narrower there than in the westward extension leading to Ivy Lane, which was known separately as Queen's Place. At its extreme east end the lane grew even narrower as it entered a passage (the original alley of the 1790s) that passed through a shop into Hoxton Street.

The square lost its name late in the nineteenth century when the whole complex became known simply as Ivy Lane, but it retained its houses and its distinctive form until after the Second World War. A Hoxton Street supermarket is now on the site.

Queen Square

(now part of Queen Anne's Gate)

The site of Queen Square was an ancient inn called the White Hart, which was purchased in 1695 by Charles Shales, a goldsmith. He cleared the ground and between 1703 and 1705 built the twenty-four elaborate houses of the new square, plus a mews, containing a chapel.

Queen Square, Westminster (now Queen Anne's Gate), looking east in 1850.

He dignified his little estate with the statue of Queen Anne that still presides there. Hatton described it in 1708 as 'Queen Ann of Great Britain, erected in full proportion on a Pedestal at the E. end of Q. Square, Westminster'. The statue originally stood more prominently against the centre of the high wall that separated Queen Square from Park Street. This solid barrier was necessary because of the lower status of Park Street and the noise and disorder surrounding the Royal Cockpit at its east end. The cockpit already existed when Queen Square was built and survived until 1810. Shortly before 1814 the wall was replaced by a lower one with railings above and a gate in the centre, and the statue was then removed to its present position. The wall and railings were pulled down in 1873, the year before the two places were combined under the new name of Queen Anne's Gate.

Hatton described the development in 1708 as, 'Queen Square, a beautiful New (tho' small) Square, of very fine Buildings. On the N. side of the Broad Way, near Tuthil-street, Westminster.' In 1714 it was, 'A square called Queen's-square, well built, with noble hostells, and Her present Majesty's Statue at the End of it, which also opens into the Park by a curious Iron-gate. This Square hath a Chappel for the Conveniency of its Inhabitants.'

The first two residents were Lord Dartmouth, a fixture in all Queen Anne's governments, Whig or Tory, who was at the present No. 26 from 1704 to 1711, and William Paterson, one of the founders of the Bank of England and the promoter of the ill-fated Darien scheme of Scottish colonisation. He lived at the present No. 19 from 1704 to 1718. Dukes and earls quickly joined them and the square was an immediate success.

In 1728 the bishops of Carlisle, Norwich and Chichester were all living there. Shales sold the houses in 1713 to the future Duke of Chandos (Handel's patron) and he in 1720 to Sir Theodore Janssen of the South Sea Bubble. After the bubble burst in the same year, Parliament confiscated nearly all of Janssen's assets, which were disposed of by the South Sea Company trustees between 1723 and 1729. The Queen Square houses contributed £23,087 towards the compensation fund for the victims of the fraud.

Strype's account, published in 1720 but written earlier, called it 'a handsome open Square, with very good Houses, well inhabited, especially that Side that fronts St James's Park, having a delightful Prospect therein, with the Conveniency of Doors out of their Gardens into the same'.

The author of *Pietas Londiniensis* (1714) gives this account of 'The Chapel in Queen's Square by St James's Park', Westminster: 'This private Chapel was founded for the Use of the Tenants within Queen's Square by Mr Charles Shales, Proprietor, in 1706; it is very neat and fine, and beautified with a stately Gallery, Pulpit, and other Ornaments'. It was, however, only a room above the coach houses in Queen Square Mews. The date of its closure is not certain, but no chaplain is known after 1855.

The nobility soon moved on to newer squares in Mayfair, but Queen Square continued to attract very respectable tenants, some of moderate celebrity. The actress Peg Woffington died in 1760 at the present No. 28, the house of her protector, Colonel Julius Caesar. Admiral Sir Peter Parker, Nelson's friend and patron, lived in the same house from 1763 to 1793, and Sir John Hawkins, the historian of music and the first biographer of Dr Johnson, lived at the present No. 46 from 1777 to 1783.

The ornate and exquisitely decorative Queen Anne's Gate is the last place one would associate with the utilitarians, but it was the chosen residence of many members of the sect: rather like the taste of modernist architects for living in Georgian houses. Jeremy Bentham's father was the creator of Queen Square Place, an offshoot from the southern arm of Queen Square. Bentham himself lived at No. 2 Queen Square Place. He also had a lease of No. 1 Queen Square (now No. 40 Queen Anne's Gate) where he installed James Mill and his son John Stuart Mill from 1814 to 1831. The house was then taken over by Sir John Bowring, who had lived with Bentham as his secretary until then. Sir Edwin Chadwick succeeded to the role of resident secretary in 1831–32. John and Sarah Austin, more disciples of Bentham, lived at No. 1 Queen Square Place for a few years from 1819 or soon after; their daughter Lady Duff Gordon was born there in 1821. Queen Square Place was destroyed to make way for the monstrously utilitarian Queen Anne's Mansions, built from 1873 and demolished in 1971.

Sir James Pennethorne, the architect, Nash's assistant, lived at the present No. 42 in 1839–40. He was the first of many architects and civil engineers who lived or had offices there in the nineteenth and twentieth centuries. Sir Edwin Lutyens and Sir Aston Webb were side by side at Nos 17 and 19 in the 1920s. Other new features of that period were the offices of societies and companies and some hotels, but there were still a few private residents, like Lord Haldane at No. 28.

The narrower section of the square running south to the Broadway was always of lower status and became distinctly shabby in the nineteenth century. The Queen Square police court was at No. 19 (now 46) from 1793 to 1846, when the new Vincent Square

The north side of Queen Anne's Gate (formerly Queen Square, Westminster) in 2007.

office took over. Number 18 (now 44) was briefly a pub, the Hoop & Grapes, in the early 1840s, No. 20 (later 48) was occupied by a blacking manufacturer from the 1840s to the 1870s, and the chapel became a ragged school after it was closed in the 1850s.

Much has been demolished in that southern section, where the Orwellian Ministry of Justice now occupies the site of Bentham's house, but the vital eastern arm, the original square, has survived miraculously. Number 34 is an early nineteenth-century rebuilding and Nos 36–38 was built as the offices of an oil company in 1908–10 and later occupied by the National Trust. With those exceptions, the 1704 houses are still standing in peerless beauty, making this the finest street, if no longer the finest square, in London.

Queen's Head Square

LAMBETH

Queen's Head Square was at the western end of Upper Marsh. Its entrance was just east of Stangate Street and nearly opposite the Queen's Head (from which it was named) and Queen's Head Court.

The square, which was of three sides, the fourth being open to Upper Marsh, was shown without a name on Horwood's 1790s map. It cannot have been much older. Lockie gave its name and position in 1810.

By 1841 it had become known as Pembroke Place, perhaps because the Queen's Head pub had ceased to exist. In that year the inhabitants included labourers and a cook, but also a bookbinder and a bookseller. Slum clearance in this part of Lambeth began seriously in the 1890s. The 1893–94 Ordnance Survey showed the north side of the square demolished, and by 1914 it had been extinguished to make way for a long series of tenement blocks. The rear parts of the Ernst & Young offices in Lambeth Palace Road are now on the site.

Queen's Square

BATTERSEA

See St Philip Square

Queen's Square (Lime Street)

Strype's map, published in 1720 but earlier in date, showed a long winding Queen's College Passage running from Leadenhall Street to Lime Street with an opening labelled 'Square' near the Lime Street end, south of the East India House. Strype's account is the only authority:

> About the Middle of the Street [Lime Street] is a Place called Queens Square, or Queens Square Passage, as leading into Leadenhall Market, a well built Place, with a Free Stone Pavement; on the Ground, on which this Place is built, was a large House, the Habitation of a Merchant, and anciently supposed to belong to the Kings and Queens.

The Ogilby & Morgan map of 1676 showed a plain alley here without a name or any opening like a square. Rocque's map of the 1740s made the passage part of Paved Alley or Little Queen Street, with no substantial opening. Leadenhall Place is the nearest modern equivalent, but that is rather to the south of Strype's square; its site must lie beneath the heap of twisted metal to the north.

Queen's Square (Moorfields)

Queen's (or Queen) Square was off the north side of Moorfields, which is now represented by Eldon Street. Moorfields being the great holiday resort of Londoners, the roads around it were full of inns, and most of the courts branching from them began as the inn yards. Seventeenth and early eighteenth-century maps showed several off the north of Moorfields, but none resembling the later Queen's Square. Rocque's 1740s map had Maximus Court in the correct position and with something approaching the form of the future square.

As there was no queen between 1737 and 1761, and as the fashion for squares swept the City in the 1760s and 1770s, it is reasonable to conclude that Maximus Court was rebuilt as Queen's Square then, or soon after. Horwood's 1790s map showed it

Number 5 Queen's Square, Moorfields, *c.* 1922.

complete except for the end house, No. 5, which was included in the 1813 revision. That was the only one that survived long enough to be photographed. It was a double-fronted three-storey house of some pretentions, built in a standard late eighteenth-century style.

Queen's Square settled down to sixty or seventy years of obscure prosperity. The inconvenient entrance was under a shop at the corner of Eldon Street. A narrow passage led from it along the west side of the Eldon Arms, then turned ninety degrees west into the wider court containing the nine houses. The pub, the most prominent building, was the birthplace in 1842 of William Anderson, a surgeon and anatomist who taught in Japan and became the leading British expert on Japanese art. His *Pictorial Arts of Japan* (1886) is a classic and much of his superb collection is now in the British Museum.

The square was not affected by the upheavals to the south when Finsbury Circus was built over Moorfields in the 1820s, or by those to the east during the building of Broad Street Station in the early 1860s, but the construction of the goods station a few years later did mark the beginning of the end. It entailed moving the line of Finsbury Avenue to the west, chopping off half of Queen's Square in the process. The outlook of the five houses that remained was restricted to a tall brick wall.

In the 1890s the goods station was extended across Finsbury Avenue and the north side of the square was demolished, leaving only one house on the south side incorporated into a warehouse and the fine old merchant's house at the end, by then the premises of a chimney sweep. In 1938 the name was taken away, when the LCC decided to treat the stub that remained as a part of Finsbury Avenue. Even after the comprehensive rebuilding of this area in recent decades, there is still an indentation at One Finsbury Avenue, with sculpture, trees and seats – more of the attributes of a square than the old Queen's Square ever possessed.

Queen's Square

HIGHBURY [ISLINGTON]

Queen's Square, an oval at the east end of Queen's Road, later Queensland Road, was built in the 1840s. Victoria Place and Albert Place were turnings off Queen's Road, and Victoria Terrace was sometimes used as a separate name for the south side of the square, as Queen's Place was for the north.

There is no evidence that the interior of the oval was an open space for long, if at all, although the name suggests it was the intention. The main feature of the interior, the Marquis of Salisbury pub at the western point, was already standing in the mid-1850s. Mary Cosh reports that Queen's Road first appeared in the ratebooks in 1845 and Queen's Square in 1848. That was a time when the landowners of Highbury and Holloway were pursuing their plans in glorious isolation.

Queen's Road was built on a narrow field, which determined its form. Its owner evidently hoped that it would link with the quality Highbury Park development to the east, but Queen's Road was working class from the first and no connecting road was permitted. The moral barrier received powerful physical reinforcement in the 1870s when the railway line between Finsbury Park and Canonbury was built immediately to the east of the square.

Queen's Road was renamed Queensland Road in 1872, but Queen's Square retained its separate identity and soon acquired a very bad reputation. The Booth survey gave this account in 1897:

> The Queensland Road itself runs east out of Benwell Road, about the most vicious place in the subdivision … but there are some quite respectable people in it nevertheless. The west end has houses built in 1800 for a different class of tenant; on the north side are common lodging houses for women, on the south for men. Women troop home between 1 & 2 a.m. from the neighbouring streets and also from as far off as King's X … Instead of being an open square the oval at the east end is built over … Neighbourhood noted for thieves, prostitutes, rag pickers, and common labourers.

In the twentieth century the east end of the oval, with the eastern loop of road, was lopped off to make way for sidings and a carriage shed, turning Queen's Square into a pair of culs-de-sac, the south longer than the north. The square was made part of Queensland Road in 1940, and in the 1950s and 1960s the LCC cleared most of the area and scheduled it for industry rather than housing. One or two houses converted to industrial use survived precariously on the south side of the road.

The former square was surrounded by workshops and a single large building occupied the whole of the interior. Off the north side of the square the cul-de-sac formerly known as Emily Place was truncated by the Emirates Stadium, the bulk of which completely overshadowed Queensland Road in its last days. Road and square were replaced by massive ranges of flats in 2012–13.

Quinn Square

BETHNAL GREEN [TOWER HAMLETS]

The Bethnal Green Quinn (or Quinn's) Square was built by Thomas Quinn in 1882–83 on the site of the Russia Lane nursery and the nurseryman's house. It consisted of ten blocks of tenements, nine ranged around the perimeter and the last planted, rather meanly, in the middle of the courtyard. There were also Quinn model dwellings at Islington and a Quinn's Square in Waterloo Road.

In 1898 a police superintendent told Virginia Woolf's half-brother, George Duckworth (in his capacity as one of Charles Booth's investigators), that 'where the rules of Buildings are lax "there are no worse places to be found": he mentioned as an instance of the latter Quinn's Buildings in Russia Lane'. Despite this poor reputation, Quinn Square survived until the 1960s, when it was replaced by a later style of housing for the poor.

Quinn's Square

The Waterloo Road Quinn's Square was built at about the same time as the one in Bethnal Green and was similar in plan, this time with seven blocks around the edge and an eighth in the courtyard. It replaced a complex of tiny cottages in Ann's Place, Elizabeth Place and Wilson's Place, which were all extinguished.

The Bethnal Green tenements formed almost a perfect square. Here the angle at which Tower Street (now Morley Street) met Waterloo Road forced the northern blocks to splay, which is perhaps why this estate was known as Quinn's Buildings more often than Quinn's Square. It was a very poor area and the streets around had the sprinkling of thieves and prostitutes common near a railway terminus, but the Booth survey was able to report in 1899, 'Quinn's Buildings, 6-storey. Look poor, well kept inside.'

There was quite serious blast damage during the Second World War, but the blocks survived until the early 1970s. Lindsay Anderson shot some scenes of *O Lucky Man* there in 1972, while Quinn's Square was awaiting demolition. The London Ambulance Service headquarters was built on the site.

Ram Square

The original Ram Square was a short, triangular lane behind the houses on the east side of Red Lion Street, now Ram Street. It was named after the Ram Brewery, where many of the residents worked. The brewery, which closed in 2007, was on the other side of Red Lion Street. The main entrance to the square was very close to the High Street; the second, a mere alley, was 100 yards down Red Lion Street.

The John Corris map of 1787 showed nothing like the square, but two houses lying back from Ram Lane may later have been incorporated into its east side. This original square existed by 1835, when the particulars of Earl Spencer's sale included a 'freehold estate in Ram-square and Plough-lane, 8 brick-built cottages and gardens, on lease to Mr P. Blackmore'. It later had ten

or so cottages, plus some shops and a pub, the Duke of Cambridge, at No. 2. The 1841 census listed the predictable coopers and brewer's servant among the residents, but also a well digger and a rat catcher.

A stubby eastern offshoot existed by the late 1840s. In the 1860s it was extended into a long cul-de-sac, the north side built before the south, with fifty small terraced houses thrusting almost to North Street, now Fairfield Street. Its construction required the demolition of the terrace on the east side of the original square. The intricate entrance from Red Lion Street must have made the cul-de-sac secluded, perhaps threatening. It had no width of street or depth of garden to justify its being counted as part of the square, but it was not given a separate name. In 1899, the Booth survey described it as a paved cul-de-sac of two-storey houses with forecourts, the residents mainly poor.

The widening of Red Lion Street early in the twentieth century, to accommodate electric trams, swept away the remains of the original square and simplified the entrance to the cul-de-sac. Nearly three-quarters of it was demolished around 1935 to be replaced over the next two years by the Wandsworth Civic Centre, the stone-faced part of the present town hall at the corner of the High Street and Fairfield Street. The fourteen houses that survived at the west end were demolished in stages, Nos 2–14 in 1955–56 and the other side for a further town hall extension, built between 1973 and 1975, which finally extinguished Ram Square.

Ratcliff Square

Ratcliff Square was built very early in the eighteenth century. Unlike Wellclose Square and Prince's Square, the other early riverside experiments with the form, it was not of the classic shape, but a narrow rectangle with the short north side open to White Horse Lane.

By the time of Rocque's 1740s map the east and south sides were fully built, but only the southern two-thirds of the west side. Trees stood before the houses in the south-west corner. In the 1790s Horwood showed that the west side had been completed by a short terrace set forward from the old one, narrowing the entrance, but on the east side only the southern half of the original terrace was still standing. The blank space to the north was perhaps the result of the great Ratcliff fire of 1794: it had been filled by 1813. There was at least one pub in the square, the King's Arms, which existed in 1782. There was a change at the north end in the first years of the nineteenth century when the new Commercial Road took White Horse Lane as part of its route and extinguished it.

That the square was far from genteel was shown by an incident in 1837, when a jealous wife paid a mob of 200 to burn effigies, wave banners and shout libellous obscenities outside her rival's house. Any slight quality it may have retained was destroyed a year or two later when the Commercial Railway, soon to become the London & Blackwall Railway, built its viaduct south of the Commercial Road, cutting off the bottom of the square in the process and blighting the remaining part. The railway was opened in 1840 and arches at the bottom of the square were for sale in 1841.

The houses on the west side were soon demolished and the factories and warehouses that replaced them were built out across the open space, at the north end first, then down the length of the square. Though reduced to the width of a street, it continued to be called Ratcliff Square until the early 1920s, when the name was changed to Ratcliffe Cross Street.

It is now a dark, gloomy place occupied by garages and car workshops and almost a cul-de-sac, as it leads to a half arch in the railway viaduct that destroyed the square. The narrow stretch of Ratcliffe Cross Street to the south of the railway – the former Periwinkle Street – retained more of the old Ratcliff atmosphere until recently, but it has now been rebuilt on both sides.

Ravenscourt Square

RAVENSCOURT PARK
[HAMMERSMITH AND FULHAM]

Ravenscourt Square is a little like Addington Square in that its garden, now given over to tennis courts, merges into a large public park. The park is on the east side where there have never been any houses. From the south and west the square is menaced by one of those ever-expanding bodies, a hospital. But in spite of all this it is a quiet and confidently civilised little community. I found a pair of flip-flop sandals on the pavement outside one garden gate, the toes pointing left and right, waiting with serene confidence for the owner to emerge and slip them on. Nannies are no longer to be found in traditional abundance in Kensington Gardens, but in Ravenscourt Park they still flourish, and many of them seem to emerge from the square.

The houses are of three distinct periods. The west side existed as a lane long before the square was thought of. It had some importance as part of the route from the Roman road to the Chiswick High Road until the 1830s, when the building of the New Road (now the north–south section of Goldhawk Road) made it a backwater. The west side of this lane and its east side north of the square itself still feature some early nineteenth-century houses.

The south side of Ravenscourt Square, c. 1905.

Numbers 4a and 6a on the west side of Ravenscourt Square in 2008.

The square was formed in the 1850s by thrusting the north and south sides towards the perimeter wall of Ravenscourt Park house. Four houses, two detached and two semi-detached, were quickly built on the south side. Although the north side is slightly longer than the south, only a semi-detached pair was built there in the 1850s because an old house in the lane already occupied the corner plot. All of these 1850s additions survive. The rest of the houses are modern, either replacing some on the west side destroyed during the Second World War, or built over the gardens of the bigger houses.

The celebrity of Ravenscourt Square is the novelist 'Ouida' (Marie Louise de la Ramée), whose residence 'until 1874' at Bessborough House, No. 11 on the south side, is recorded by a blue plaque. The association of Harrison Ainsworth with the square seems due to a misunderstanding. Ouida's doctor, William Francis Ainsworth, who lived a few doors away at Ravenscourt Villa, was Harrison's cousin, and it was through his influence that Ouida's first stories were published in *Ainsworth's Magazine*.

Rectory Square

STEPNEY [TOWER HAMLETS]

Rectory Square was named after the former St Dunstan's Rectory, which still stands next to the long entrance from White Horse Lane. The square was built between 1861 and 1868, filling the gap south of Beaumont Square. It had three long, drab terraces of two-storey houses, with bays on the ground floor, paired doorways, heavy windows with rounded top corners on the first floor, and high parapets. The only good thing was the well-planted garden with the unusual shape of a blunted arrowhead, dictated by the elongated triangle of the square.

In 1898 the Booth survey reported '2 storey 6 roomed houses letting for £28 to £30, tenanted by small business men, small gardens'. Some cottages on the south side of the entrance lane, part of an earlier Stepney Green development, were demolished in the 1870s and replaced by the East London Synagogue. It was the first large one in the East End, built to the

Rectory Square, *c.* 1905.

designs of Davis and Emanuel in 1876–77. Like the cottages it replaced, the synagogue faced the more distant Stepney Green and had its less elaborate side turned to the square.

There was only minor bomb damage during the Second World War, but all the original houses were demolished between 1971 and 1975 and replaced by low-rise GLC houses and flats that are a good deal less drab than the Victorian terraces. The enclosed garden was converted into a raised lawn, well planted with trees. The two buildings of interest are the former synagogue, now flats called Temple Court, and the former rectory, a rambling Tudor house of 1843 that was subdivided in 1987 and renamed the Rosery.

Red Cross Square

CITY OF LONDON

The City's Red Cross Square was for the most part a narrow road running north from Nicholl Square and Maidenhead Court to Jewin Street. The feature that justified the name was a widening near the southern end. The Ogilby & Morgan map of 1676 and the Strype map of Cripplegate Ward (made before 1720) named it Red Cross Alley. Both showed the widened

south end, Strype making it more distinctly square.

A motive for its creation is suggested by its position immediately behind the large garden of Thanet House (later Shaftesbury House) in Aldersgate Street. This must have given the houses in the square, which at that stage were all on the east side facing the garden, a pleasantly open aspect. In the seventeenth century it was also very secluded, as the only entrance was in Jewin Street far to the north. By Strype's time several outlets had been made to Crowderswell Alley in the east. Strype describes Redcross Alley as 'very long, but somewhat narrow, with pretty good Houses; to many of which are Gardens, which occasions the Place to be the better inhabited'. The Red Cross Square name appeared on Rocque's 1740s map, by which time the Thanet House garden had been built over. Rocque showed trees in the square section, not in the centre but in front of the new houses on the west side.

Although this became in general a poor area of the City, Red Cross Square continued to be surprisingly well inhabited. Even in 1840 about half of the thirty or so houses were the private residences of reasonably substantial people. Most of them lived on the older east side. The west was more commercial, with a pub, the Red Lion, at No. 5. This was the last generation of wealthy City residents. Over the next thirty years many of the houses were rebuilt as offices and workshops, and in the process the narrow south-eastern entrance was widened to match the 'square' section. This robbed the name of its point and in 1870 it was changed to Hamsell Street. It was now entirely commercial and by the 1890s the rebuilding and widening had been continued north all the way to Jewin Street. The area was very heavily bombed during the Second World War, and cleared afterwards for the Barbican Estate. Mountjoy House is now on the site of the square section of Red Cross Square.

Red Cross Square

SOUTHWARK

One of the many narrow passages running between Borough High Street and Red Cross Street (now Redcross Way) was known as Red Cross Alley in the eighteenth century and Red Cross Court in the early part of the nineteenth. Its Borough High Street entrance was next to the Red Cross public house.

Before 1841 the southern side of the middle section of Red Cross Court was demolished and rebuilt some way south of its original line. This widened section became known as Red Cross Square, while the narrow entrances at either end (one in St George's parish, the other in St Saviour's) both retained the old name.

The square had twelve or thirteen of the new houses on the south side, about ten of the older cottages on the north. They were occupied by labourers, dress-makers, paviours, etc. Around 1890 the west end of Red Cross Court, in St Saviour's, was replaced by large blocks of model dwellings and the whole of the court and square was renamed Redcross Place. The blocks were opposite Octavia Hill's Red Cross Gardens. In 1914 the former square was demolished in its turn to make way for more tenements. Now streets and flats have all vanished from an area occupied entirely by Roman Catholic schools. The Borough High Street entrance to the extinguished Redcross Place was directly opposite the surviving Mermaid Court.

Red Cross Square

See Mark Lane Square

Red Lion Square

HOLBORN [CAMDEN]

Red Lion Square was built in 1684 and the following years by the notorious Nicholas Barbon. Its site was the open space called Red Lion Fields, which took its name from the Red Lion Inn, Holborn. Barbon's scheme, which may not originally have included a square, was a contentious one. Like their southern neighbours at Lincoln's Inn Fields in the previous generation, the lawyers of Gray's Inn regarded the open space as their especial amenity. The upshot was recorded by Narcissus Luttrell in 1684:

> Dr Barebone, the great builder, having sometime since bought the Red Lyon Fields, near Graies Inn walks, to build on, and having for that purpose employed several workmen to goe on with the same, the gentlemen of Graies Inn took notice of it, and thinking it an injury to them, went with a considerable body of one hundred persons; upon which the workmen assaulted the gentlemen, and flung bricks at them, and the gentlemen at them again; so a sharp engagement ensued, but the gentlemen routed them at the last …

The lawyers may have won this first battle, but nobody could stop Barbon for long. A compromise was reached, from which the idea of a square with a garden may first have emerged, and the work was soon resumed. It is unlikely to have proceeded quickly or smoothly to judge from the account given of Barbon's business methods in Roger North's autobiography:

> I once asked him why he dealt so much in building and to overrun his stock, and he not only forced to discontent everyone, but be perpetually harassed with suits. He said it was not worth his while to deal little; *that* a bricklayer could do. The gain he expected was out of great undertakings, which could rise lustily in the whole, and because this trade required a greater stock than he had, perhaps £30,000 or £40,000, he must compass his designs either by borrowed money or by credit with those he dealt with, either by fair means or foul.

Nevertheless, building must have progressed reasonably fast, as the 3rd Earl of Bridgewater was able to settle in Red Lion Square when his house in the City was destroyed by fire in 1687. By the 1690s it was a good address, but the tide of fashion was washing swiftly westwards in the early eighteenth century as bigger and better squares were built south and north of Oxford Street, and the high prosperity of the ones immediately to the west of the City did not last long.

In 1737 Red Lion Square tried to keep up with its younger rivals by obtaining a private Act of Parliament along the lines established by St James's Square in 1725, and quickly followed by nearly all the others. This enabled the inhabitants to form a garden committee and tax themselves 'to enclose, pave, watch, clean, and adorn' the square.

Like other squares in Holborn and Bloomsbury, it remained popular with the gentlemen of the law after the nobility had moved on. In 1756 Sir Matthew Lamb (grandfather of Lord Melbourne, the prime minister) who was evolving from a barrister into a politician and country gentleman, 'moved from Red Lion Square, an area inhabited by judges and senior counsel, to the more fashionable Sackville Street in Piccadilly', as his biographer Roger Turner explains. He lived at No. 3 on the west side of the square. The 1817 directory listed many solicitors.

In 1771 John Stewart described it after Hanover Square, of which he almost approved, and found the two very different:

Red Lion square, elegantly so called, doubtless, from some alehouse formerly at the corner, has a very different effect on the mind. It does not make us laugh; but it makes us cry. I am sure, I never go into it without thinking of my latter end. The rough sod that 'heaves in many a mouldering heap,' the dreary length of the sides, with the four watch-houses, like so many family vaults, at the corners, and the naked obelisk that springs from amidst the rank grass, like the sad monument of a disconsolate widow for the loss of her first husband, form, all together, a *memento mori*, more powerful to me than a death's head and cross marrow bones: and were but the parson's bull to be seen bellowing at the gate, the idea of a country church-yard in my mind would be compleat.

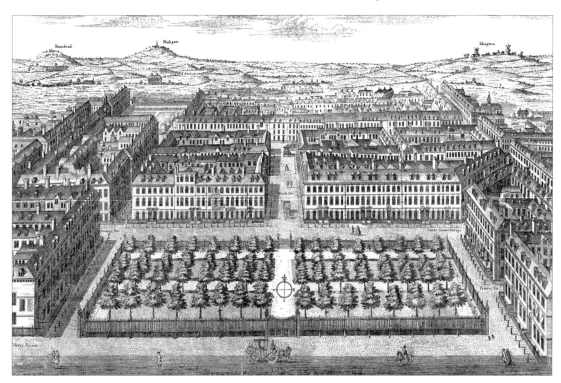

Red Lion Square, Holborn, from the south in 1731.

In 1843 William Weir found it 'the most disconsolate square in London … a bare and sterile desert … prosaic in the extreme'. It was then occupied mainly by solicitors plus a few architects.

The great philanthropist Jonas Hanway, who was to the eighteenth century what Lord Shaftesbury was to the nineteenth, was at No. 23 on the east side from 1768 until his death in 1786. He is now best remembered as the first man to brave ridicule by carrying an umbrella in the streets of London. In philanthropy his great success was the Hanway Act, which forced London parishes to send pauper children into the country instead of killing them in fever-ridden workhouses. His connection with the square seemed to set the tone for its future use, which has had much to do with charity, education, socialism and high-mindedness, just the things calculated to produce the effect the square had upon Weir.

The first free dispensary for poor children was opened at No. 7 in 1769 by William Armstrong, brother of the poet-physician, John. In the 1830s there was a philosophical club that met at a tavern in Red Lion Square. The young George Henry Lewes, later the historian of philosophy and the consort of

St John's, Red Lion Square, Holborn, c. 1905.

George Eliot, was a member. In 1841 Red Lion Square was home to the Mendicity Society, the National Apprenticeship Institution, the British & Foreign Mission, the Christian & Philanthropic Institute, the English Monthly Tract Society, the Indigent Blind Visiting Society, the London City Mission, the London Female Mission and the Apprenticeship & Agency Office. One is surprised not to find the Mothers'-Small-Clothes-Conversion-Society.

Frederick Denison Maurice founded the Working Men's College at No. 31, on the north side, in 1854 while he was living nearby in Queen Square. Rossetti, Burne-Jones and Ruskin taught at the college. The Pre-Raphaelite connection with the square had begun in 1851 when Rossetti occupied a studio at No. 17, the landlord insisting that the models should be kept 'under some gentlemanly restraint', as 'some artists sacrifice the dignity of art to the baseness of passion'. At Rossetti's suggestion Edward Burne-Jones and William Morris occupied the same rooms in 1856–58. Number 8 was the original workshop of Morris & Co. from 1861 to 1866.

Number 2 Red Lion Square, Holborn, on the west side, c. 1910.

The building of St John's Church, John Lough-borough Pearson's masterpiece, in 1874–78, can be seen as part of the same movement – an Anglo-Catholic mission to the Holborn slums. It replaced three of the five original houses at the short west end. The opening of the garden to the public from 1885, when it was laid out by the Metropolitan Gardens Association, was also intended to benefit the poor, especially the children. In 1907, this was Beresford Chancellor's summing-up:

> To-day Red Lion Square can hardly be said to preserve many, if any, of its original characteristics. Its houses, many of them rebuilt, are occupied almost wholly by professional and commercial undertakings ... The square has indeed undergone a change as radical and complete as that which is to be observed in the case of Soho and Golden Squares, with which it has much in common in its decline as it had in the period of its prosperity. Most of its houses are freehold, and a once well-known conveyancer was wont to say, when looking at the somewhat untidy state in which the Square was kept, that it was an example of the evils attendant on this sort of tenure.

Various authorities state that H.G. Wells taught at the University Tutorial College at No. 32 Red Lion Square (the former Cresswell sponge warehouse) from 1890 to 1893. In fact, the college did not move to the square until 1 September 1892 (as announced in the *Morning Post* of 20 July) so Wells only spent his last year as a tutor there. During his early days at the college its premises were in Holywell Street, which was destroyed in the creation of Aldwych. The eminent translator Willa Muir was a later tutor at the college.

The last of the advanced institutions established in the square was the Conway Hall, a temple of the agnostic religion. It was built in the north-east corner, for the South Place Ethical Society, in 1929 and named after its most famous minister, the American Moncure Conway.

It is fitting that a square created by the son of a revolutionary should have radical associations. The Red Lion Square disturbances of 1974, a violent clash between fascists and communists, with the police and innocent bystanders as the chief victims, set the

Cresswell's sponge warehouse on the north side of Red Lion Square, Holborn, in 1889.

pattern for much that has happened since. The most prominent monuments in the square are a bust of Bertrand Russell and a statue of the socialist politician Fenner Brockway, orating.

Red Lion Square suffered more severely during the Second World War than the other pioneers that promoted the growth of the West End in the seventeenth century. The short east and west sides were destroyed, as was more than half of the north side. The south side escaped much damage, but even there the houses at the extreme east end were wrecked. The most important single loss was St John's Church. Its disappearance was made the excuse for chopping off the west end of the square when Procter Street was created and Drake Street widened in 1961. The truncated square is now a sad and dreary place

The garden of Red Lion Square, Holborn, *c.* 1905.

surrounded by offices and flats, some of them painted in a hideous dirty pink. The only relief comes from the Conway Hall, designed by Alfred Waterhouse's assistant, Frederick Herbert Mansford, and the four surviving old houses, Nos 14–18, on the south side.

Red Lion Square

WANDSWORTH

The little Red Lion Square at Wandsworth was built in stages in the early nineteenth century. It had almost as many names as houses, for it was also known as Red Lion Court and Red Lion Yard and seems sometimes to have been considered merely a part of Dutch Yard.

Dutch Yard ran directly south from Wandsworth High Street for a short distance, then narrowed and swerved a little to the west before continuing south in front of a terrace of seven or eight small cottages known as Garden Place. These had detached front gardens opposite. In 1838 they belonged to George Cade senior, of the firm of George Cade & Son, carpenters and builders, who were listed in Wandsworth in the 1823–24 directory. At its south end Dutch Yard

swung east in front of a terrace of four cottages with front gardens. These four were later than the rest, not built until after 1838. They were usually considered as the genuine Red Lion Square, but sometimes Garden Place was also included.

Labourers and bricklayers were the typical tenants of both. In 1899 the Booth survey treated them all together: 'Dutch Yard, with court off it on west – two storey, some flush, some at south with front gardens.'

Most of the Red Lion Square cottages were swept away in the 1930s, creating for a time a much larger open space, but the southern terrace survived until the 1950s, when its houses were known as Nos 9–12 Garden Place. By 1964 they had been demolished and large warehouses covered the whole site. But the restored cachet of the name means that squares are not easily allowed to die, and when they do they are not always left to rest in peace. There is again a Red Lion Square more or less on the old site, but it is entirely modern. An estate agent described it when newly built as a 'lovely gated mews style complex, very secure'.

Red Lion Square

See Reliance Square

Redcliffe Square

Redcliffe Square was built on the Gunter estate at West Brompton between 1868 and 1876 by the firm of William Corbett and Alexander McClymont. The architects were almost certainly the brothers George and Henry Godwin, surveyors to the estate. They were the sons of George Godwin of Alexander Square.

The name is thought to be an allusion to George Godwin junior's restoration of the church of St Mary Redcliffe at Bristol. He had been designing houses on the Gunter estate since 1849, beginning in a fairly restrained Italianate style but growing more extravagant as the building line moved westward, especially after he was joined by his younger brother Henry.

By the late 1860s the style, verging towards the Gothic, had become too wild to be safely corralled within the formal discipline of a square. This was one of the last portions of the estate to be completed and it is noticeable that the houses in Redcliffe Square, although tall, are narrow and built on much more restricted sites than in many of the surrounding streets.

The houses in Redcliffe Gardens, Tregunter Road and, of course, the Boltons, are on large plots and have generous gardens. The back gardens of the houses in the square range from tiny to non-existent.

In form, Redcliffe Square is closest to Canonbury Square, with two gardens bisected by a busy road, but in this case the whole of the western garden is occupied by St Luke's. Corbett and McClymont had wanted a church from the beginning of their involvement with the estate, but it took some time to choose a site and longer to raise the money. For the first two years, from 1871 to 1873, the congregation met in a temporary iron church on the site later occupied by Nos 29–33. St Luke's, designed by the Godwins and named after St Luke's, Cheltenham, the first vicar's old parish, was built in 1872–73. It is a rare case of a large Gothic church made to seem quite restrained by the architecture of its surrounding houses.

William Corbett became the first patron of the living, but it proved a poisoned chalice, the exorbitant cost of the church contributing to the bankruptcy of Corbett and McClymont in 1878. By then, fortunately, the square had been completed and the bankruptcy had a much greater effect on their next venture, St Andrew's Square at Surbiton.

The east side of Redcliffe Square, *c.* 1905.

The houses in Redcliffe Square let well at first and the square was particularly popular with senior officers of the army and navy during the nineteenth century. The leading lion, Sir Henry Rider Haggard, must have felt at home in their company. He lived at No. 24 from 1888 to 1891.

The square shared the decline of the district in the early twentieth century, a period when a large number of its houses were occupied by women. That could often mean discreet boarding houses and sometimes discreet bawdy houses. The square escaped lightly during the Second World War, although St Luke's suffered some damage, but the comparative dereliction of the houses and poverty of the residents led the owner to give the garden to the council in 1949. It is now called a park. Since the 1950s the square has enjoyed a full measure of the rapid social recovery of West Brompton.

Reform Square

Reform Square was a tiny yard off the west side of Mount Street (now Swanfield Street) in the notorious rookery known as the Nichol, on the borders of Shoreditch and Bethnal Green. The name suggests a building date in the early 1830s, although the street pattern here was established twenty or thirty years earlier, when Nelson Street and Collingwood Street were created.

In 1848 Hector Gavin gave Reform Square a better than average report in his *Sanitary Ramblings*:

> This is one of the cleanest courts in the district; besides a dust-heap in a corner, there are two privies, which are nearly full; there is one water-pipe without a cock to the six houses. As the court, however, is paved, the run of water from the open pipe, when it comes on, is very useful in cleansing the drain in the court.

Things had deteriorated in 1861, when John Hollingshead explored the Nichol:

> The first court I go into with my guide is called 'Reform Square' – a bitter satire upon its aspect and condition. It is nearly opposite the Church of

St Philip, and is a square yard – not much larger than a full-sized dining-room. It is entered by a mountainous slope of muddy brick pathway, under an archway; and contains half-a-dozen houses, which look out upon two dust-heaps, a pool of rain and sewage, mixed with rotten vegetable refuse, and a battered, lop-sided public privy. The houses are like doll's houses, except that they are black and yellow. The windows are everywhere stuffed with paper – rags being in too much demand at the marine store-shop, or for the clothing of the human child-rats, who are digging into the dust-heaps, with muddy oyster-shells ... At the entrance to 'Reform Square' is a row of zigzag two-roomed houses, let for about four shillings a week; the street-doors of which open into the lower rooms, almost upon the wretched tenants' beds. The staircases leading to the upper apartments are little more than ladders in one corner, and there is no space for more than the usual furniture – a table, two chairs, and a bedstead. The flooring of the lower rooms in these houses is so high above the pavement in the street, that three stones are placed at each of the street-doors for the inhabitants to climb into their dwellings by. I say climb, for the lower stone is so lofty, and the whole three are so shallow on their flat surfaces, that it is with difficulty a full-sized man can stride up them. When you stand in the narrow doorway, and look down into the street, it is like looking down into a deep pit.

The inquest on a woman who died at No. 3 Reform Square in 1866 heard this from the doctor:

> The room in which she and another person lived contained 882 cubic feet of air; and the room underneath, in which seven persons lived, had a cubic space of 819 feet. Now, the minimum allowance consistent with health was set down as 800 cubic feet for each individual. The defective ventilation was a known cause of typhus fever, and the defective drainage, the accumulation of vegetable and other refuse, and the state of the closets, would produce typhoid fever ... Mr C.A. Christie, sanitary inspector, said that on the 17th of last month, while walking down Mount-street, he saw water flowing across

the pavement out of Reform-square, and he went up and made an inspection. He found the place in a very filthy state; and when he found out the landlord, he served him with notices, which were not yet fully complied with. His discovery of the state of the place was entirely casual; he had received no notification from the Board about it.

The landlord stated that:

There were two rooms in each house, and each room was let at 2*s*. 3*d*. per week rent. He held the property on lease, at £26 a-year ground-rent. He had been served with a notice from the parish authorities on the 26th of January, but it was dated on the 19th, and was left with a tenant. He had done some cleansing since. He had put the place into thorough repair, at a cost of £120, eighteen months ago. The people would not keep the place clean – that was the real matter.

Perhaps as a result of this bad publicity, the name seems to have been changed soon afterwards to Reform Court. It did not survive for long under that disguise, as the whole district of the Nichol was officially declared a slum and swept away by the London County Council in the 1890s to build the Boundary Street Estate.

Regency Square

KENNINGTON [LAMBETH]

Regency Square at Kennington was a much smaller and poorer neighbour of the surviving Cleaver Square, though not nearly so poor as the third in this group, White Hart Square.

The name suggests the early nineteenth century, but this was a development of the 1840s. Regency Place, which formed the north side of the square, had its origin in the days of the Prince Regent and passed on the name to its younger offshoot.

The first element of the square that emerged on the south side of Regency Place was the St James's National (Church of England) School, which had been built by 1843. The school, together with School House Villa for the master, occupied the whole of the centre, where

a garden might have been. St James's Church was in Kennington Park Road, immediately to the east.

The frame of houses around the school was still being built in 1851, when the residents of those completed were of very mixed occupations. The Booth survey of 1899 found mostly labourers. St James's Church was closed and demolished after the First World War, and before the Second the school and square had been replaced by the huge NAAFI HQ Warehouse. Now housing estates cover the whole area. The modern Cornwall Square is more or less on the site of Regency Square.

Regent Square

BLOOMSBURY [CAMDEN]

Regent Square was built in the 1820s and named, of course, in compliment to the Prince Regent. The land had belonged for nearly a century to a family of brick-makers named Harrison. Thomas Harrison began

St Peter's, Regent Square, in 1827.

tentative negotiations for joint development with the Foundling Hospital in 1802, and when they led nowhere he made plans on his own account in 1809–10. But the work going forward on the Foundling and Bedford estates generated a great demand for bricks and a glut of houses, two good reasons for delay.

The square was laid out by 1822, but the houses were not begun until six or seven years later and completed only in the late 1830s. An obscure architect named Henry Lent Keys lived at No. 6 from 1834 to 1852, but was probably too young in 1828 to have been entrusted with the design of the houses. No. other name has been suggested.

When the first residents arrived in 1829 they already had a choice of two churches to attend. As previous writers on the square have considered these as its only points of interest, it is sad to relate that both were demolished after Second World War bomb damage.

St Peter's Church (Chapel in its early years) was built on the east side between 1822 and 1825. The architects were the father and son team of William and Henry Inwood, who had achieved fame, or notoriety, a few years earlier with their building of St Pancras Church, Euston Square, in the most thoroughgoing Greek style ever seen in London. At Regent Square, with

much less money to spend, the style was more muted and conventional. The first incumbent of St Peter's was William Harness, who was at Harrow with Byron and was one of the closest of his early friends.

The National Scotch Church (now the Lumen United Reformed Church) was built for the immensely popular preacher Edward Irving between 1824 and 1827, as a miniature imitation of the west front of York Minster. It was the first work of William Tite, later Sir William, who is best known for the Royal Exchange. Beresford Chancellor said in 1907 that 'there are two towers to the church, which are 120 feet high, and from Hampstead are sometimes mistaken for those of Westminster Abbey'. These landmarks were seriously damaged during the war, and the church was rebuilt in a much less memorable style in 1965.

The bombing affected all parts of the square, but was most serious on the north and east sides. It was perhaps the proximity of ruined houses and bomb sites that made the garden the setting for excellent Guy Fawkes Night bonfires after the war. The north, east and west sides were cleared and rebuilt as council estates from the late 1950s, leaving only the terrace of seventeen on the south side to represent the original architecture. Numbers 9 and 10 were rebuilt in facsimile.

The west and part of the north side of Regent Square, *c.* 1905.

Regent Square has an unexpected musical association. Louis Spohr, in his day considered almost the equal of Beethoven, used to stay at No. 3 during his visits to London. It was the home of his friend, Edward Taylor, who translated the texts of his choral works into English. Number 2 was the home in 1848–49 of Sir Edward Creasy, whose *Fifteen Decisive Battles of the World* was once to be found in every library. The most notable twentieth-century residents were James Strachey and Vanessa Bell, who successively made a flat at No. 36 a northern outpost of 'Bloomsbury' for a few years after the First World War. William Hartnell, the original Doctor Who, was born at No. 24 in 1908.

Reginald Square

DEPTFORD [LEWISHAM]

Reginald Square was mostly built in the 1850s on a piece of land surprisingly left vacant or underused between the Broadway, the High Street, Church Street and Reginald Road. Leases of Nos 74 and 76 ran for ninety-nine years from 22 May 1855. The design allowed for an existing terrace of ten cottages tucked behind the Broadway to be incorporated as the south side.

It was one of those false squares of the later nineteenth century, with houses in the centre instead of a garden: in this case three terraces, two long ones facing east and west and a shorter one fronting Reginald Road, and thus not really part of the square. As the three sides were separately known as Reginald Street (west), Reginald Place (east) and Amelia Terrace (the slightly older cottages on the south side), the name Reginald Square was only used intermittently.

The Booth survey gave a good description in 1899:

Reginald Place. Broad street, 2-storey houses flush with pavement. Quiet working class. Paper hanger, people in regular work. Two families per house as a rule … At the end is Amelia Terrace. Row of old 2-storey cottages with flower gardens in front. On the front of centre house is a full-sized figure of a sailor holding a Union Jack … Reginald Street, 2-storey, six rooms. Exactly like Reginald Place.

The south side was nibbled away during the twentieth century as larger premises were built in Deptford Broadway, but otherwise Reginald Square remained much the same until destroyed at a stroke in June 1944 by one of the first wave of flying bombs. At least twenty-two people were killed. No attempt was made to recreate the old street pattern in the post-war rebuilding, but Reginald Square persists as the name for a very dull service road curving behind the High Street and Deptford Broadway.

Reliance Square

SHOREDITCH [HACKNEY]

Reliance Square was built between the 1790s, when Horwood's map showed the site vacant, and 1813, when the revised edition included 'Reliance Street' with twenty-three houses, perhaps not quite complete. There were fourteen in the east–west offshoot and nine (with room for a few more) in the main stem. John Lockie called it Reliance Square in 1813. In the 1841 and 1851 census returns it was inhabited by respectable working people, carpenters, shoemakers and the like.

The railway viaduct run into Broad Street in the 1860s destroyed the houses in the north–south section, leaving it as a mere access alley, and shaved a couple off the east–west offshoot. This made the square secluded, even claustrophobic, with only the narrow entrance from New Inn Yard. The viaduct overlooked that end and at the east were the backs of towering warehouses in Anning Street. The doors opened directly onto the paved court which sloped down from both sides to a central gutter. The three-storey houses had the peculiarity that there were no windows above the round-headed doors but three large, square windows to each house, ranged one above the other. Victorian maps called it Red Lion Square, but it reverted to the old name in the twentieth century.

The remaining part of the square was scheduled for slum clearance in the 1930s. If the LCC had not got round to demolishing it by 1940 it was saved the trouble, as this area was heavily bombed. Reliance Square is now just a stubby yard squashed against the railway viaduct that began its destruction. The east–west section has been entirely extinguished and the only notable feature is a gym located in the railway arches. The viaduct has been made part of the Overground system. New Inn Square and its offshoot Socrates Place formed a similar pattern on the west side of the viaduct.

Rochester Square

CAMDEN TOWN [CAMDEN]

Rochester Square is the poor elder brother of Camden Square, laid out in the 1830s before the Camden New Town development was undertaken seriously, but not built until after 1841. In 1835 the future 2nd Marquis Camden had married Harriet Murray, daughter of the Bishop of Rochester (of the family of the Duke of Atholl) and these connections gave names for the square and the nearby Murray Street.

Rochester Square was doomed from the first to be of a lower status than Camden Square, being smaller and having Richard Montgomery's nursery in the centre, where a garden should have been. The nursery was established there long before a house was built, Montgomery's address being No. 122 Camden Road Villas until the square took shape.

On the north and south sides most of the houses faced the nursery across a road, but on the west there was only a narrow lane in front of the houses, a rare and attractive feature seen also at Wilmington Square. In other respects the layout recalls Tyburnia, as the houses at the east end turn their backs to the nursery, with which their gardens would communicate directly were it only open. Their front doors are in Stratford Place where they are numbered.

Some houses were occupied by 1846, before any in Camden Square. The south side, Nos 1–14, was completed by 1851 (when John Shailer had taken over the nursery) and the north side, Nos 15–28, appeared in the 1852 directory. These houses were all semi-detached. The attractive terrace on the west side, Nos 29–36, was an afterthought of the late 1850s, built over part of the nursery.

Rochester Square has had one or two famous residents. R.D. Blackmore, the author of *Lorna Doone* and many less successful novels, lodged here in the early years of his marriage between 1853 and 1855. Despite his literary fame, the main business and

The north side of Rochester Square in 2007.

interest of his life was fruit farming at his Teddington market garden. Was he attracted here by the nursery garden in the centre? In the mid-1850s it was run by John Slipper, nurseryman and florist.

Sir Eugene Goosens, the composer, the son of a jobbing opera conductor, was born here in 1893

Rochester Square declined more rapidly than Camden Square and was full of boarding houses early in the twentieth century. In 1926 a little spiritualist temple, with a foundation stone laid by Sir Arthur Conan Doyle, was built behind the west terrace. The western end of the south side was badly damaged by the Rochester Place V1 late in the Second World War and although eight of the fourteen houses were still sound, the whole of the south side was replaced by three large blocks of council flats.

The state of the former nursery garden is the burning issue at Rochester Square. It is protected by the 1931 London Squares Preservation Act, but at present does more to damage than enhance the environment of the houses. As Camden's conservation area appraisal put it in 2011, 'The Square's vegetation has turned wild and the nursery is derelict. It is designated a private open space and is not accessible to the public. This is a major opportunity for landscape enhancement.' The task for the politicians is to make the garden either a private amenity for the residents or a public open space. This is a rare case where compulsory purchase would be a welcome solution.

Rose Square

OLD STREET [ISLINGTON]

Rose Alley was off the east side of Golden Lane, north of Play House Yard, now Fortune Street. It led to an open space that the 1813 Horwood map described as 'Thomas's Burying Ground' and the 1830s ratebooks as 'Brown's Burial Ground'. On the north side of Rose Alley, immediately north of the cemetery, were two offshoots called Rose Court and Rose Square.

Rose Square was a cul-de-sac of eleven houses by the 1870s. On the Horwood maps of the 1790s and 1813 only the east side was shown, built directly against the west side of Bear & Ragged Staff Court, which is now represented by Warwick Yard. The square was probably not completed until after 1830. This slum district was cleared in the late 1880s to build the tenements of the huge Peabody estate. Many of the blocks survive further east, but on the site of Rose Square Peabody Court has replaced them.

in a theatrical boarding house. It was perhaps No. 26, where several ballet ladies were lodging in 1891. His sister Marie, the harpist, was born in a similar establishment in Ampthill Square in 1894. It is a curious coincidence that one of Sir Eugene's professional appointments was as conductor of the Rochester Philharmonic Orchestra, New York.

Rose Square

The area between Bateman's Row and Hoxton Road (now part of Old Street) was a new development of the late eighteenth century. Its main feature was William Street, now Rivington Street. Off the north side of William Street were Rose Court and Pleasant Row, both quite short culs-de-sac. Around 1820 a link was established between their northern end, extending a little to the east, and north of the link a small court of eight houses was built and named Rose Square. The passage was no wider than an alley, but the front gardens of the cottages gave a sense of space.

Rose Square survived until the early 1860s, when it was one of the places demolished to make the site for the Shoreditch Vestry Offices in Old Street. They were built between 1863 and 1868 and are now the oldest part of Shoreditch Town Hall. Rose Court was later Rose Street and is now Rivington Place. Pleasant Row is no more.

Rosebery Square

The LCC built Rosebery Avenue between 1889 and 1893 across the site of numerous slum alleys so small that their names – Poole's Buildings, Bayne's Court, etc. – are hard to read on the map. Such improvement schemes always cleared a good deal more ground than was needed for the new road, creating an opportunity for speculative builders to bid for the leftovers.

A specialist in this work, James Hartnoll, acquired much of the awkward land on either side of the southern end of Rosebery Avenue – awkward because it was down in the Warner Street valley that the new road had bridged. Conventional houses were out of the question, but they were never what Hartnoll intended. Model dwellings, tall tenement blocks that would easily overtop the elevated road, were his speciality, so much so that he probably required no help from an architect to design the ones he planned here. The tenants he had in mind were of course the deserving poor, not the undeserving whose homes had been destroyed.

Rosebery Avenue, running between the east (right) and west blocks of Rosebery Square, *c.* 1905.

Rosebery Square Buildings was the original name for the ranges of flats that Hartnoll built east and west of the road in 1890–91. They are of five floors, though only four are apparent from Rosebery Avenue. From an early date the whole development became known as Rosebery Square, and in the 1990s, after modernisation, they were officially designated Rosebery Square East and West. But there is very little square-like about the overall design, except a slight setting back of the blocks from Rosebery Avenue. The 1914 map had it right when it put its 'Rosebery Square' in the courtyard behind the blocks on the west side. That is certainly a square of the Peabody type.

Most of Rosebery Square came through the Second World War unscathed, but the north wing of the west side was destroyed in 1940 and rebuilt in 1948 in a different style, with no windows on the flank wall.

Rothesay Square

See Woburn Square

Royal Mint Square

WHITECHAPEL [TOWER HAMLETS]

The dreadful slums between the Royal Mint and Dock Street, which included Cartwright Square, were demolished in the 1870s. They were replaced principally by model dwellings, blocks of tenements built by the Peabody Trust and other housing charities and private developers.

Royal Mint Square, built south of Royal Mint Street and east of Cartwright Street in 1884, was the most idiosyncratic result of this process. Its seven five-storey blocks achieved only an approximate square because the eastern side followed the curving line of a railway spur serving the London Docks. Royal Mint Square was not the work of Peabody or the other large industrial dwellings companies, but a commercial enterprise aimed at a slightly higher class and adorned with inappropriate architectural flourishes. Skilled workers from the Royal Mint were among the tenants.

The square was seriously damaged during the Second World War and demolished in the 1970s. John Nelson Tarn, writing in 1973, when it was still

standing, thought it 'a very poor example of private housing development'. Tower Hamlets Council built the Royal Mint Square Estate on an enlarged site between 1978 and 1982.

Russell Square

BLOOMSBURY [CAMDEN]

Russell Square has a prehistory, because the east side existed as a row of exclusive houses overlooking the garden of Bedford House and the open fields to the north long before any square was thought of. The northern houses of the original Southampton Row just reached the southern end of the future square, a large detached mansion known originally as Baltimore House was on the site later occupied by part of the Imperial Hotel, and the eight houses of Southampton Terrace on that of the Russell Hotel.

In his *Adelphi*, a spiritual autobiography, William Cowper recorded that in the early 1750s, 'I was at liberty to spend my leisure time, which was well nigh all my time, at my uncle's at Southampton Row'. Whether his uncle's house was one of those that later became part of the square is not certain, although the distinction has been claimed for No. 62, now part of the site of the Imperial Hotel.

Thomas Gray lodged in Southampton Row ('at Mr Jauncey's') from 1759 to 1761. In July 1759 he told a friend:

> I am now settled in my new territories commanding Bedford gardens, and all the fields as far as Highgate and Hampstead, with such a concourse of moving pictures as would astonish you; so *rus-in-urbe*-ish, that I believe I shall stay here, except little excursions and vagaries, for a year to come. What tho' I am separated from the fashionable world by broad St Giles, and many a dirty court and alley, yet here is air, and sunshine, and quiet, however, to comfort you: I shall confess that I am basking with heat all the summer, and I suppose shall be blowed down all the winter, besides being robbed every night; I trust, however, that the Museum, with all its manuscripts and rarities by the cart-load, will make ample amends for all the aforesaid inconveniences.

It was in 1759 that the Duke of Bedford made a private road extending Southampton Row northwards from the last houses to link with the New Road (now Euston Road at this point) which had just been laid out to the north. The private road became, in due course, the east side of Russell Square and Tavistock Square. It naturally encouraged the building line to creep northwards.

The big house of the private road was built in 1763 for the notorious 6th Baron Baltimore, who had to leave the country hurriedly in 1768 after being acquitted of abduction and rape on a technicality. In 1773 Noorthouck wrote that it was 'either built without a plan, or else has had very whimsical owners; for the door has been shifted to various parts of the house, being now carried into the stable-yard'.

Baltimore House was afterwards occupied by the Duke of Bolton and by Lord Chancellor Loughborough, introducing the law into the square at a very early date. As Loughborough was made Earl of Rosslyn as a consolation prize on being dropped from the cabinet in 1801, Rosslyn House was the last name of this mansion before it was overwhelmed by the square. It was converted into three houses as Nos 66, 67 and 71, and in that form survived until about 1910. Number 71 was the east wing, approached from Guilford Street and known as Bolton Gardens.

Broad St Giles and all the dirty courts and alleys mentioned by Gray as separating Bloomsbury from the fashionable world were the obstacles the Duke of Bedford had to overcome when he demolished Bedford House in 1800 and set about building on the fields behind it. That is perhaps why he and his surveyor James Gubbins chose to make Russell Square the largest in London after Lincoln's Inn Fields and to have the garden laid out by the great Humphry Repton. Sceptics were to be struck dumb with astonishment.

The development was placed in the safe hands of the builder-architect James Burton, who had recently shown his ability with Brunswick Square on the neighbouring Foundling Hospital estate. In 1800 Burton exhibited a design for the south side of Russell Square at the Royal Academy. The houses there were built in that year and the next, and after a short pause the west and north sides completed the frame of houses between 1807 and 1813.

In 1807 the author of *The Picture of London* declared that 'Russell and Tavistock-squares, when finished, will be capital additions to the metropolis'. In the 1825 edition the account of Russell Square mentioned that the 'extensive enclosure in the centre is a miniature landscape-garden; every possible feature, both of beauty and variety, having been introduced'. An indentation on the south side of the garden received Westmacott's statue of the Duke of Bedford, set up in 1809, facing that of Fox in Bloomsbury Square.

In 1829, Rowland Dobie introduced a panegyric upon the veteran James Burton into his history of St Giles and Bloomsbury:

The fields where robberies and murders had been committed, the scene of depravity and wickedness the most hideous for centuries, became, chiefly under his auspices, rapidly metamorphosed into splendid squares and spacious streets; receptacles of civil life and polished society. This pleasing transition, however, required firmness of nerve and energy of no common description, and these Mr Burton eminently possessed. If he accumulated a fortune by the vast improvement of these estates, he well deserved it … Let it be remembered that this vast speculation of Mr Burton's was begun and finished during a long disastrous war, most unfavourable to such an undertaking, yet he sternly persevered.

The square had its own watchman, a diminutive one, which proved an obstacle when Sir Thomas Lawrence tried to persuade Robert Peel to get him a better job in 1829. 'I have a petitioner – an honest watchman of our square for four years; with all certificates of good conduct; but alas! five feet *six*. It is not possible to have him included in the new Police!'

The example of Lord Loughborough, who was a resident even before the square was laid out, was quickly followed by other lawyers, who were the dominant group for much of the nineteenth century. Dobie noted this in 1829: 'It has, from its first formation, been a favourite residence of the highest legal characters; and here merchants and bankers have seated themselves and families, the air and situation uniting

The east side of Russell Square, Bloomsbury, *c.* 1905 showing the bow window of Baltimore House.

to render it a pleasant retreat from the cares of business.' As early as 1873 Sir Joseph Arnould wrote nostalgically that in the early years of the century Russell Square was 'in point of residence, the *ne plus ultra* of a successful barrister's ambition'. In 1893 W.J. Loftie called it 'Russell Square, once sacred to lawyers'.

Around 1812 Thomas Denman, later lord chief justice, moved from No. 5 Queen Square to No. 50 Russell Square, following the westward course of legal fashion. An even more eminent lawyer was Sir Samuel Romilly, who cut his own throat at No. 21 in 1818, one of the politicians who fell a victim to the suicide epidemic that followed the downfall of Napoleon.

Thomas Noon Talfourd, barrister, dramatist and judge, lived in the square from the 1830s to the 1850s and entertained a wide circle of friends, including Dickens and Thackeray, first at No. 56 and then at the larger No. 67, part of Baltimore House.

The invaluable diarist Henry Crabb Robinson, a retired barrister and the friend of many of the leading writers of his time, lived at No. 30 from 1839 until his death in 1867. He occupied an apartment there for most of that time, but took over the whole house from 1864. It was conveniently close to University College, of which he was a promoter and benefactor, and to University Hall in Gordon Square, which he helped to found.

The greatest of all the square's residents was Sir Thomas Lawrence, who lived from 1813 until his death in 1830 at No. 65, a house described as 'a museum containing the choicest specimens of painting, sculpture, architecture, and engraving'. The Soane Museum may give us an idea of the clutter. Like Soane, he was obliged to enlarge and alter his house, converting the attics into studios for his assistants and pupils. He wrote in 1821:

> These alterations in my house will be made by Mr R. Smirke. They will not be visible to my neighbours in the Square; and as I do not want the credit of 'extensive additions' to my house, I shall let the work proceed as quietly, but at the same time as rapidly, as possible. My workmen come in at the Mews behind my house.

His friendship with George IV and Sir Robert Peel did not allow him to enjoy his improved house in entire security. On one occasion, probably in June 1827, his windows were smashed by a Corn Law mob.

The most eminent of many architects were Philip Hardwick, who lived at No. 60 until his move to Cavendish Square in the 1850s, and George Edmund Street, who was at No. 51 from 1862 to 1870.

Miscellaneous celebrities have included George Edward Cokayne, author of *The Complete Peerage,* who was born at No. 64 in 1825; the theologian Frederick Denison Maurice who lived at No. 5 from 1856 to 1862; and Mrs Humphrey Ward, the best-selling novelist, who was at No. 61 from 1880 to 1891, when the family moved to a more fashionable West End address. The Pankhursts, Emmeline, Christabel and Sylvia, were at No. 8 from 1888 to 1893; Sir Julian Huxley was born at No. 61 in 1887; and the actor and writer George Grossmith lived at No. 55 from about 1904 to 1909. George Routledge died at No. 50 in 1888, and William Swan Sonnenchein, the founder of another notable publishing house, lived at No. 62 early in the twentieth century, moving to No. 58 when his old house was demolished to extend the Imperial Hotel around 1909. Number 24 was the Faber & Faber offices from the foundation of the firm as Faber & Gwyer in 1925, and the second home of T.S. Eliot during his long publishing career.

In 1898 the Booth survey found that the 'Russell Square district passed out of the hands of fashion to the Jews, who in turn are making way for Boarding houses … Across Russell Square leases falling in and houses being done up with terra cotta facings – not many what you'd call carriage people living here now.' Beresford Chancellor's history of the squares found a state of transition:

> Within recent years one side, the east, of the Square has become altered in a very striking way, for quite half that side has been absorbed in one of those vast hotels which appear to be springing up with the same frequency as new theatres, all over London. In this case, it is the sumptuous Hotel Russell; while next to No. 65, on the same side, several houses have been demolished to make way for the Imperial Hotel, now (1906) in course of erection. The Hotel Russell is constructed in terra-cotta, or brick which resembles it, and nearly all the houses on the north side and some in other parts of the Square have been refaced with the same material, which, perhaps artistically, carries out the scheme of the dominant building, but has not greatly conduced

The north side of Russell Square, Bloomsbury, partly modernised, *c.* 1905.

The Imperial Hotel, Russell Square, Bloomsbury, *c.* 1920.

to the preservation of the otherwise Georgian appearance of the houses, and inevitably suggests the idea that the surplus material, after the erection of the hotel, has been thus carefully utilised.

He also remarked on the obscurity of the square in his day, something that was soon to be changed by the hotels, the underground station, and the promotion (or degradation) of the east side into a main road as part of the Aldwych and Kingsway scheme.

The re-facing of the houses on the north and south sides with terracotta was an unfortunate policy of the Bedford estate in the 1890s, aimed vainly at halting the decline of the square by giving the houses a veneer of the latest fashion. The decline had not been rapid or disastrous, but gradually from the 1880s houses were divided into apartments or were taken over as the offices of a multitude of miscellaneous organisations. The process was accelerated by the building of the Hotel Russell in 1898 and the Imperial from 1906. The Imperial's stablemate, the Premier Hotel, replaced the old Baltimore House about 1910.

By the 1920s there were hardly any private residents left in the square, except in hotels and boarding houses.

The old buildings that remained were soon under threat from the University of London. Parts of the west and north side were demolished in 1939 and more would no doubt have followed but for the delay caused by the war.

From 1959 attempts were made by the university, aided by the damaging testimony of Nikolaus Pevsner, to revive the grandiose schemes of the 1930s and destroy the remains of Georgian Bloomsbury. The Bedford estate was also anxious to sweep away much of its legacy. Luckily, permission for most of these changes was refused as far as they affected Russell Square, and it retains buildings of interest on all four sides.

The grand Hotel Russell now has no competition on the east side, the Imperial and Premier hotels having been rebuilt in the 1960s in a style that was a disgrace even to that decade. The terracotta-trimmed original houses survive along most of the south side and part of the north. On the west side the unaltered original houses at the north and south ends are separated by the unconvincing pastiche flank of Stewart House, a university building of 1985. The garden, a park in the heart of the city, nothing can destroy.

Russell Square

The centre of the Gravel Pits district of Deptford, between Church Street and the Creek, was a notorious no-go area known as the City, built haphazardly in the second half of the eighteenth century and the early years of the nineteenth on land belonging to John Addey's charity.

The largely criminal and entirely poor population was left to govern itself. Hardly any attempt was made to collect rates in this dangerous area and map makers were no keener to penetrate it than other respectable men.

Russell Square was part of the tangle of alleys and courts that formed the City. It had thirteen houses in 1824, all classified as poor. The square was destroyed in 1835–36 during the building of the London & Greenwich Railway viaduct. James Wyld's 1832 plan of the proposed line of the railway named Russell Square just to the south of the viaduct, giving a grossly exaggerated idea of its size and importance.

Rust Square

When Addington Square was built early in the nineteenth century it was equipped with all the West End luxuries, including an extensive range of mews. By the 1870s there were few carriage folk left there and the coach houses and stables were largely redundant. Addington Mews was therefore rebuilt as Kitson Road and off the east side of it Rust Square was squeezed in. The name was approved in 1878. The style of the new road and square was the same, 'three storey houses, good working class', as the Booth survey said in 1899.

Although exactly of the shape, it was not a true square because the centre was filled by eight houses back to back, in north and south-facing terraces. There were seven houses each on the north, south and east sides and two more were hidden in an offshoot in the north-east corner. The west was formed by Kitson Road and numbered in it.

Rust Square, looking west towards Kitson Road in 2010.

The south side was quite badly damaged in the Second World War and the east side less seriously. They were demolished after 1976, with the eight houses in the centre, greatly to the benefit of those that remain on the north side and in Kitson Road. The new garden is not grassed but paved in a series of terraces stepping down towards the centre, and finely shaded by a grove of symmetrically planted trees, not quite a quincunx. Like that of its big brother Addington Square, the garden opens out to the south and east to link with Burgess Park.

the man who providentially blocked the intended northern outlet of Brompton Square. Elger made an agreement with the landowner in 1851 and began to build in 1853. Most of his houses are still standing.

Rutland Square

The revisers of Richard Horwood's map perhaps had an optimistic mole in John Nash's office, as their 1813 edition showed several streets and squares as achieved developments that never had existence except on the drawing board. Rutland Square was one of these.

The map placed it to the east of the Regent's Park and the Cumberland Basin, filling most of the space between Augustus Street and Hampstead Road, but although the map-makers provided the square with a solid frame of houses, none of this was ever built. The site remained vacant until the 1830s when Stanhope Street, Harrington Street, Granby Street and Rutland Street were built there. The old plans had evidently been carefully filed, as Granby Street and Rutland Street were the names given by the Horwood map to the roads that continued the north and south sides of the fantasy square, and they occupied the same positions in the real development. But instead of a garden, Harrington Street filled the space between them. Granby Street is now Granby Terrace, and Rutland Street (the ghost of a ghostly square) is now Mackworth Street.

St Agatha's Square

Union Court, a small cul-de-sac off the north side of Willow Street, just east of Willow Court and a stone's throw from Tabernacle Square, was replaced by the Willow Street United Methodist Free Church in the middle of the nineteenth century. In 1872 everything on the north side of Willow Street east of the church was demolished as part of the clearances for Great Eastern Street.

In the redevelopment of the land that remained vacant after the new road was completed, St Agatha's Square was built immediately to the east of the church by the

Rutland Square

Rutland Square was an occasional alternative name for Rutland Gate, or perhaps only for its southern section. It was used, for example, on the map published in 1850 by Day & Son, to show the estate of the commissioners for the 1851 exhibition. The northern section of Rutland Gate was built in the late 1830s and early 1840s, but the southern extension was a separate development by John Elger,

Improved Industrial Dwellings Company. It consisted of two buildings with bay windows on the Willow Street building line, and between them four buildings set back behind a courtyard, after the style of Pancras Square.

These fancifully designed model dwellings were presumably resorted to because the taller tenement blocks that filled the rest of the surplus land would have robbed the church of all its light. Even on this more humane scale the square provided forty-eight dwellings. It was called St Agatha's Buildings by the Booth survey of 1898, which found it thoroughly respectable. The name was taken from the new parish church of St Agatha, Finsbury Market.

St Agatha's Square survived until about 1970, but with the northern expansion of the City model dwellings were as little in request there as United Methodist Free churches. The Hoxton Urban Lodge Hotel now stands on the site of both.

St Agnes Square

OLD STREET [HACKNEY]

St Agnes Square, Tabernacle Walk, appeared only in the 1851 census. Its two houses, occupied by a cabinet maker and a cheesemonger, were listed between St Agnes Place and Tabernacle Walk. Tabernacle Walk is the present Tabernacle Street, and St Agnes Terrace was its northern section, between Cowper Street and Old Street. St Agnes Square was perhaps a passing name for a small court off the east side of Tabernacle Walk, nearly opposite Cowper Street. It was shown on the 1872 map, but had been built over by the 1890s.

St Andrew's Square

SURBITON [KINGSTON-UPON-THAMES]

St Andrew's Square takes its name from Sir Arthur Blomfield's church in Maple Road, which was built in 1871. The square, just 50 yards to the south, was begun in 1876. It forms a group with Westcroft Square at Hammersmith and Nightingale Square at Balham, as defiant suburban attempts at the classical form in a period when the square had been largely abandoned in the centre.

A design for houses on the south side of St Andrew's Square by Richard Lano Pearce, published in 1893. The semi-detached houses are Nos 32 and 33, but the house on the right is not No. 31, as built. The floor plan is of No. 33.

terraces before giving up the struggle. They came here fresh from a not much more successful development at Redcliffe Square in Brompton, overreached themselves like so many other Victorian builders, and were bankrupted in 1878 with debts of nearly £1.5 million.

The short west side and the west end of the south side were eventually completed in the late nineteenth and early twentieth centuries with a curious medley of houses, bungalows and flats. The east side is formed by Maple Road, which existed before the square.

The large and attractive garden was private until 1972, when Kingston Council rather surprisingly acquired it by compulsory purchase and opened it to the public. It has now been restored to something like its original form.

St Catherine's Square

See St Katherine's Square

St Charles Square

NORTH KENSINGTON
[KENSINGTON AND CHELSEA]

This was a late entry into the roll of London squares, in which it is one of the largest and one of the least satisfactory examples. In the mid-1860s the site was a field between Portobello Farm and Notting Barn, in a landscape entirely rural except for the isolated Notting Hill Station (now Ladbroke Grove) to the south. It took the builders some time to catch up with the Metropolitan Railway, which had opened the station in 1864.

St Charles Square was created as a frame for the St Charles College, a Roman Catholic rival to the public schools, which occupied the whole of the centre in lieu of a garden. The college, which was founded in 1863, had outgrown its original premises in Paddington, and a new school was built here in the open fields in 1873–74. By 1874 the professor of music at the new college was living at Chilterne House, which was probably No. 52 on the north side of the square. Many houses were occupied by 1876 and all had been built by 1882, although thirteen were still standing empty.

The Booth survey gave this description in 1899:

The other two were completed much as planned, but here in Surbiton William Corbett and Alexander McClymont, the builders, only managed to fill one and a half of the three sides with their tall, florid

... 3 and 3½ storey, well to do, servant keeping. The north side backs upon poor Rackham Street. Rents £50 plus rates and taxes. Business men. The open space in the centre is the playground of St Charles Catholic College, all nations taught, is a boarding school. The houses opposite the school hard to let, have been turned into flats. Note in window of one house: '5 and 8 rooms, self contained, £45 and £50 inclusive'.

In 1907 Beresford Chancellor wrote that 'St Charles's Square contains nothing of interest beyond the college, which practically absorbs it'.

One interesting resident he overlooked was Alfred Domett, a minor poet who was the hero of his friend Browning's 'What's become of Waring since he gave us all the slip?' The answer was that he had gone to New Zealand, where he spent thirty years and was briefly prime minister. He came home in 1871, bought No. 32 St Charles Square (now demolished) in March 1876 and died there in 1887.

Another celebrity was the artist Montague Dawson, who lived at No. 2A in the 1920s and 1930s. Later in life his paintings of ships and seascapes made him the world's most commercially successful living artist after Picasso.

There were about seventy large houses, but even so they only surrounded two and a half sides of the enclosure. At first they had an open outlook, as the only buildings in the centre were the college and the Carmelite convent built on the north edge in 1877–78, the rest being playing fields and gardens. But in the twentieth century the Roman Catholic buildings multiplied and now the only open space is the convent garden in the north-west corner, which cannot be seen from any of the houses. They look out onto various undistinguished schools and the former college chapel, now a parish church. The college itself, the only notable building, was demolished after Second World War bomb damage. All the houses on the north side were also destroyed in the war.

The Training College (formerly the St Charles College), St Charles Square, in 1907 or a little earlier.

St George's Square

The 1790s edition of Horwood's map showed St George's Square just built, with four houses each on the north, south and east sides, and the west side open to an unfinished street then called George's Row, but in 1813 known as George's Mall. John Lockie defined the square's position in 1813 as 'Saint George's Mall, St George's Fields, middle of the east side'.

The square had a very short life. It was destroyed in the 1820s when a new road was constructed leading almost due north from the main entrance of Bethlem Hospital, nearly parallel with George's Mall on its east (the square) side, to link it with Westminster Bridge Road. Bethlehem Hospital is now the Imperial War Museum. This new layout also did not last long, for in the 1830s St George's Road, which used to swing left to join Lambeth Road directly in front of the hospital, was extended north-westwards along its present line to meet Westminster Bridge Road. In the process the new road of the 1820s and George's Mall were both extinguished, with the result that St George's Road now runs across the site of the fleeting St George's Square.

St George's Square

Although Thomas Cubitt is rightly regarded as the founder of modern Pimlico, a good many of its original houses were built after his death in 1855. This was particularly the case with St George's Square, of which only seventeen houses (of 123) were listed in the 1856 directory.

The square was an afterthought, for when Cubitt laid out the ground in 1839 it was as Gresford Street and Pulford Street. Mean streets they would have been, with only the width of the present garden to form their other sides, but the square that was substituted by 1842 is also mean. It is not just that none of the houses have back gardens, some of them barely have a yard. In fact, it is a shabby-genteel square, all front and display with no back or substance. The saving graces are the great length of the garden, almost the equal of Eaton Square, the triangular extra green

north of Lupus Street, and the opening to the river at the south. St Saviour's Church at the north end of the garden (built in 1864 to designs by the Grosvenor estate surveyor Thomas Cundy) adds variety.

The oldest houses are those of the early 1850s at the north end, around the triangular green. The northern ends of the two long sides were barely begun at the time of Cubitt's death and the southern halves were built very slowly. Most of the terrace south of Chichester Street on the west side remained only half-built until the 1870s, and some at the south end of the east side was not even begun in 1869.

The slow development and the lack of Cubitt's controlling hand meant that there was no consistency in the style of the houses. This is particularly noticeable on the east side where between Nos 77 and 79 and again between Nos 105 and 107 the houses change from the normal flat-fronted style to sections with bay windows through four storeys. The eight houses with bay windows from No. 107 to No. 121 were the last to be built.

The square's famous residents have been from the arts and sciences. Thackeray's daughter Annie, Lady Ritchie, herself a novelist and biographer, lived at No. 109 from 1901 to 1912. The square's other leading writers had Irish birth and commercial success in common, but not much else. Bram Stoker, the author of *Dracula*, lived at No. 26 in his later years, dying there in 1912. Writing was just a sideline for him, the serious business of his life being to manage the Lyceum Theatre for his friend Sir Henry Irving. Bill Naughton, creator of Alfie and chronicler of northern working-class life, lived rather incongruously at No. 64 from the 1940s to the 1960s, when deeply involved in radio, television and film work.

The valuable scholar William John Thoms, the founder of *Notes and Queries* and the inventor of the word 'folklore', lived and died at No. 40, and Sir Joseph Barnby, the composer, died at No. 9 in 1896.

The most bizarre celebrity was Walter Wingfield, who died at No. 33 (where there is a plaque) in 1912. He is usually regarded as the inventor of lawn tennis, although his chosen name for the new sport – 'sphairistike' – was hardly calculated to promote it. Francis Crick, Nobel prizewinning scientist, lived in a flat at No. 56, which also has a plaque, from 1945 to 1947.

St George's Square, Pimlico, the south end of the west side, *c.* 1905.

Numbers 72 and 74 on the west side were destroyed during the Second World War and have been replaced by flats that are good in themselves but do not blend well with their stucco neighbours. The most elaborate terrace in the square, between Lupus Street and Chichester Street, built with pilasters in 1854, was demolished in the early 1960s for the sake of Pimlico School. This was a case of mindless destruction, as the frontage to the square was not used for buildings, but left a blank wall guarding a drop to a games area. The school was an experimental design by the GLC and proved an environmental disaster, under repair as often as not. But for these blemishes, the square is in good preservation, of growing popularity, and with its fine garden still private.

St George's Square

SOUTHWARK

St George's Square in the Borough was known as Three Ton or Three Tuns Court in less sophisticated and more truthful days. It was entered beneath an archway on the north side of White Street, now the western end of Long Lane, and there was an exit at the north end into Angel Alley, just a few yards from the Borough Gaol. Between the two entrance passages the court was slightly wider and here there were eleven cottages.

In the 1740s Rocque showed Blue Boar Alley, with a very different shape, at this point. Horwood's map of the 1790s had Three Ton Court. In Lockie's 1813 edition it was Three Tuns Court, White Street, Borough, at No. 18, fourth east of St George's Church. The change to St George's Square in the 1850s may have marked some alteration to the cottages, for Three Tun Court was unoccupied in the 1851 census, and when it reappeared under its new name there was no longer any access at the south end. By that time the alley to the north was considered part of Collier's Rents.

The new square did not last long after its elevation. In the 1880s a warehouse was built in what was by then Long Lane, obliterating everything on the west and south sides of Collier's Rents, including the square. The flats known as Brenley House are now on the site.

St George's Square

It might seem that the developer who imposed this name was telling a barefaced lie. For the many other so-called squares it is easy to find some element in the form or design that might conceivably justify the name, but St George's Square at Upton Park is a mere road, and not a good one.

The explanation is that the development was begun in the 1860s but not completed until much later. The late 1860s houses, the only ones with the slightest pretension to architectural display, are Nos 36–50 at the east end of the south side. When they were built there was an intention to form a square between them and St George's Road to the north. The roads

that would have framed it were shown, laid out all alone in the fields, on the 1867 map. The only houses then built were a few on the north side of what is now St George's Road.

The failure of Upton Park to grow into the prosperous suburb hoped for evidently prevented the plan from being completed. In 1889, all hopes of a real square having been long abandoned, the north and west sides were made part of St George's Road and St George's Avenue. Small houses were built over the intended garden, on the south side of St George's Road and the north side of the road that continues to be called St George's Square.

St George's Square

See Chalcot Square and George Square

Numbers 36–50 on the south side of St George's Square, Upton, in 2010.

St James's Gardens

See St James's Square, Notting Hill

St James's Square

NOTTING HILL [KENSINGTON AND CHELSEA]

(now St James's Gardens)

I once visited an elegant house in Islington that had stained glass in the rear windows, an aberration I could not understand until I discovered that the view was over a rough council estate. This was the experience of the early residents of the Notting Hill St James's Square, which was the last outpost of the middle classes before the notorious Pottery Lane slums began. The houses of the north side were much harder to let than the rest because they had that unwelcome outlook and only a short garden as a sanitary zone.

The square was designed without any outlets to the north. Sirdar Road, the central north–south axis of the Pottery Lane district, was meant to lead straight to St James's Church in the centre of the square, but had been brusquely blocked. In 1899 the Booth survey reported: 'Sirdar Road, end is a cul-de-sac, black [semi-criminal]. There is no through communication with St James Square, as shown on map, "though they have long wished to make one".' Nothing could have been further from the wishes of the residents of the square, who must have felt that their precarious respectability was under constant siege from the denizens of Pottery Lane.

The site of St James's Square was on the northern edge of the Norland estate, the development plan for which had been laid down in the 1830s before the Pottery Lane scandal broke. Royal Crescent and Norland Square were built without any disturbance from the trouble in the north, but it was very different when the builders reached St James's Square. By then the state of the potteries and piggeries had been thoroughly exposed by the newspapers.

Faced with a hard sell, the Victorian developer's first thought was often a church, and St James's, planted grandly in the centre of the square, was the first element here. It was built in 1844–45 to the designs of Lewis Vulliamy, whose clockmaker father had once owned the estate. Like his church in St Peter's Square, Bethnal Green, it is a pleasing example of his fantasy Gothic, more Walpole than Pugin.

The north side of St James's Square, Notting Hill (now St James's Gardens), *c.* 1905.

The west side of St James's Gardens (formerly St James's Square, Notting Hill) in 2007.

For several years the church stood all alone. The first houses built were Nos 1–8, after which there was steady progress until 1851, but all of it on the south side, at the short west and east ends, and at the west end of the north side, furthest from Pottery Lane. These attractive three-storey terraces were designed by John Barnett. If only the square had been completed to this pattern! But there was a pause of a decade – a decade of architectural disintegration – before builders could be found to take on the unpromising north side plots that remained. The tall and ugly houses that begin at No. 26 spoil what could have been a near-perfect square.

The new name of St James's Gardens was imposed by the LCC in 1939, to avoid confusion with its venerable West End namesake. St James's Square looks dowdy in the old postcards, but St James's Gardens is attractive in the gleaming brick and stucco. It is more prosperous than at any time in its career and the houses more carefully looked after. In the 1990s sitcom *As Time Goes By*, the home of the heroine, a successful businesswoman, was played by No. 21.

St James's Square

ST JAMES'S [WESTMINSTER]

A 300-page history of St James's Square was published 120 years ago and a great deal has happened since then. Several new buildings are under construction even as I write. In a general survey of this kind a comprehensive account of this aristocrat among London squares will not be expected.

Representatives of most of the noble families of England (and many of Scotland and Ireland) have lived there during its three and a half centuries of unbroken fashion and prosperity. Elsewhere a Lord Chancellor or a Chancellor of the Exchequer would rank as a major celebrity, but here few but prime ministers stand out.

Henry Jermyn, Earl of St Albans, the creator of St James's Square and in a large measure of the West End, was the servant and near contemporary of Charles I. At the Restoration he was almost an elder statesman. His interest in Pall Mall Field, the site of the square, came through the Queen Mother, Henrietta Maria, to whom he had been attached in various capacities since 1628. The field, part of her jointure, was leased to him in 1661. In the next year he persuaded Charles II to extend his lease, and in 1665 he was granted the freehold.

The king's first object was the rewarding of meritorious service, but he was also personally interested in the success of the scheme, 'his Majesty intending those Places near unto his Majestie's Pallaces of White-Hall and St James's should be Built for the conveniency of the Nobility and Gentry who were to attend upon his Majestie's Person, and in Parliament; and for the better Ornament of the Place'. The clamour for 'lodgings' at Whitehall was a constant source of annoyance to the king and an obstacle to the improvement of the palace. A third motive was the provision of suitable houses for the royal mistresses, his own and his brother's.

The new town was unpopular with Lord Clarendon, the Chancellor, who did not like to see royal estates given away; with Lord Southampton, the Treasurer, who was engaged in a rival development at Bloomsbury; and with the Lord Mayor and aldermen, who wished to keep the palaces of the free-spending nobility within the City walls.

Jermyn had begun to lay out the ground for building by 1663, but found clients unwilling to build the very large houses envisaged without the security of freehold. The plague and the fire further delayed Jermyn's plans but soon proved invaluable by accelerating the flight from the City. The first house was at the south-east corner and its original entrance was probably from Pall Mall; it was occupied by Jermyn himself in 1667. The south side was defined by that time, but the houses there faced Pall Mall and had only back entrances, if any, in the square. Apart from Jermyn's own, the great houses on the east, north and west sides were not begun until about 1670; then they came with a rush, and the square was complete by 1676.

The original houses, of which none survive, followed the style set by Jermyn and achieved a fair degree of uniformity, even though their widths varied from 120ft to only 27ft. There were four exceptionally wide houses, two on the east side, one on the north (a second and better house for Jermyn himself) and one on the west. But the uniformity did not last for long: the residents had bought the freeholds and were nearly all rich and wilful. The houses were rebuilt one by one to suit the tastes of new owners, usually by the best architects of the

St James's Square, St James's, from the south-east corner, in 1812.

The east side of St James's Square, St James's, *c.* 1904.

day, many in the eighteenth century, some in the nineteenth and one even in the twentieth century. The few original houses that escaped the ravages of fashion and ostentation were eventually condemned as old-fashioned or decayed and replaced by clubs or offices.

The ground in the centre of the square was not included in the grants to Jermyn and remained Crown property. No attempt was made to imitate the garden laid out in Soho Square about 1680. The centre of St James's Square remained an unadorned open space surrounded by posts and a low railing, useful as a site for firework displays. In the centre of each side there was an ungated opening and from these entrances well-worn pedestrian tracks soon defined the routes from King Street to Charles Street and from York Street to Pall Mall.

In this state, it was favourably noticed by Edward Hatton in 1708: 'St James's square, a very pleasant, large and beautiful Square … all very fine spacious Building (except that side towards Pall Mall) mostly inhabited by the Prime Quality'. But then as now, an unguarded open space soon became a rubbish tip. To improve it there had been plans for a statue of William III in 1697 and 1724, and of George I

in 1721. These came to nothing at the time, but in 1726 the residents, most of them peers or members of the lower house, obtained a private act empowering them to form a committee and levy a rate for the adornment and protection of the garden and the roads. This became the model for the private acts obtained by nearly all the other early squares. The changes the committee made in 1727 left a wide roadway round the garden, but introduced a circular pond with a fountain into the centre. The garden was enclosed by an ornamental railing, forming an irregular octagon, with a lamp at each corner (see p.9).

The lighting and watching did not protect the residents and their visitors from the assaults of high-waymen, as Mrs Harris (the wife of James '*Hermes*' Harris) reported to her son in 1773:

A most audacious fellow robbed Sir Francis Holburne and his sisters in their coach, in St James's Square, coming from the opera. He was on horseback, and held a pistol close to the breast of one of the Miss Holburnes for a considerable time. She had left her purse at home, which he would not believe. He has since robbed a coach in Park Lane.

St James's Square was the only one in London that met with the qualified approval of John Stewart in 1771:

> Though far from perfect in that stile, and altogether uncompleted on one side, [it] still strikes the mind (I judge from my own feelings) with something of more ease and propriety than any square in London. You are not confined in your space; your eye takes in the whole compass at one glance, and the water in the middle seems placed there for ornament and use.

His approval did not extend to Norfolk House, now so much lamented: 'Would any foreigner, beholding an insipid length of wall broken into regular rows of windows … ever figure from thence the residence of the first duke of England? "All the blood of all the Howards" can never ennoble Norfolk house.' John Noorthouck added in 1773 that 'in such mansions we expect something beyond roominess and convenience, the meer requisites of a packer or a sugar baker'.

The style praised by John Stewart in 1771 was already becoming old-fashioned, and by 1825 it was despised. A critic wrote then that St James's Square:

> … was long, and in a great measure continues to be, more celebrated for its distinguished residents than for the beauty of its buildings. Latterly, however, its inner area, which used to form an unsightly object, having been much enlarged, and laid out and planted with walks, shrubs, etc., its general appearance has been much improved. A large circular sheet of water occupies the centre; from the midst of which rises a pedestal, surmounted by a statue, in a stiff and artificial style, of William III.

This statue, first proposed during the lifetime of the king, was more than a century in contemplation, as it was not erected until 1808. The stagnant pond was removed as a health hazard in the 1840s. The changes to the garden praised by the anonymous critic in 1825 had been carried out by John Nash in 1817.

The residents were indeed distinguished. Many ambassadors lived in the square in its early days, but the most exalted foreign visitor preceded them all: Cosimo de Medici, who was to succeed in the next year as Cosimo III, Grand Duke of Tuscany, lived at Jermyn's house in the south-east corner in 1669, during his European tour. Our own royal family also

Numbers 11–13 on the north side of St James's Square, St James's, *c.* 1904.

The Junior Carlton Club on the south side of St James's Square, St James's, in 1874.

patronised the square. Frederick, Prince of Wales, moved to Norfolk House in 1738, after his quarrel with George II, and remained until his move to Leicester House in 1743. George III was born in 1739 in a detached building behind Norfolk House.

A number of leading ministers of the Crown were residents in the seventeenth century and early in the eighteenth, and since Sir Robert Walpole gave the office something like its modern form, there have been eight prime ministers. Sir Robert himself was the first. From 1732 until 1735 (when he moved to No. 10 Downing Street) he rented Lord Ashburnham's house, the predecessor of No. 32. Spencer Compton, Lord Wilmington, Walpole's nominal successor as prime minister in 1742–43, lived at what might be called No. 22 (the northern section of the Army & Navy Club site) from 1720 to 1743. Lord Chatham, the elder Pitt, lived at No. 10 from 1759 until 1762. He had also occupied an unidentified house in the square (possibly the same or No. 33) in 1743–46.

Three prime ministers-in-waiting who lived in the square were Lord Grenville at No. 20 from 1789 to 1792, Lord Liverpool at No. 6 from 1803 to 1806 – the house belonged to his father-in-law, the Earl-Bishop of Bristol – and Lord Grey at No. 15 in 1819.

Lord Derby had a much longer association with the square, being at No. 10 from 1837 to 1854, and then at No. 33 until his death in 1869. Number 33 remained Derby House until his grandson moved to Stratford Place (see Aldborough Square).

The last St James's Square prime minister was Gladstone, who lived at No. 10 in 1890; the house has a joint plaque in honour of Chatham, Derby and Gladstone. The great Foreign Secretary Lord Castlereagh, a more distinguished man than some of these prime ministers, lived at No. 18 from 1806 until his death in 1822. In 1820 the hated Castlereagh had the mortification of living next door to the mob's idol Queen Caroline, who had been lent No. 17 during her trial in the House of Lords.

The square has fewer literary associations. Its two great writers were also statesmen. The Marquess of Halifax ('the Trimmer') lived at Halifax House, the site later taken by Nos 17 and 18, between 1673 and his death in 1695. Lord Chesterfield was born at No. 32 in 1694 and lived at No. 18 from 1727 to 1733.

The London Library, which moved to No. 14, the smallest house, in 1845, and rebuilt it in 1896, has given any number of great writers an association with the square. It was not the first important library there. The 2nd Earl of Oxford, whose tracts formed *The Harleian Miscellany* and whose manuscripts are in the British Library, lived at No. 3 in 1716 and probably for a few years before, and the wonderful collection of the 3rd Duke of Roxburgh, one of the most determined of bibliophiles, had been dispersed from his house at No. 13 some thirty years before the London Library was established next door.

The London Library proved the most durable of the institutions that invaded the square from the 1830s and had come almost to monopolise it by the end of the nineteenth century. Private clubs were the most important, the square being quite as much a part of clubland as Pall Mall or St James's Street. The Oxford & Cambridge Club was the first, at No. 18 from 1831. By the 1890s a third of the houses were clubs, or had been rebuilt as part of them, and half of the south side was occupied by the back of the Junior Carlton Club in Pall Mall.

Number 1 became the London & Westminster Bank from 1844 and No. 3 the offices of the Tithe Commission from 1854. The War Office had branches at Nos 19 and 21 (the Intelligence Department) and by 1900 an insurance company occupied No. 15. This left few houses in private hands, but those few,

in the north-east corner and on the north side, were still occupied by the rich and titled, who continued to adapt them to their changing needs. One of the first private swimming baths in London was installed at No. 11 in the 1860s.

The aristocracy lingered at Nos 4, 5, 6 and 11 until the Second World War. Number 4, now the Naval & Military Club, has a blue plaque honouring Nancy, Lady Astor, who lived there from 1912 to 1942.

The two world wars brought great changes to the square, physical and moral. In 1918 the 'Washington Inn', a club for American officers, was built over part of the garden by the YMCA of America. It was still open in 1920, delaying long-planned alterations to the garden, which were carried out in 1922–23. Norfolk House, the last of the huge palaces that once existed on three sides of the square, was demolished in 1938.

During the Second World War the railings were removed from the garden as part of the scrap metal drive and the lawn was dug up for allotments. 'It is curious to see cabbages growing round the empty plinth of King William's equestrian statue in St James's Square,' James Lees-Milne wrote in September 1943. There was serious bomb damage on the west, south and east sides of the square. Number

The Washington Inn American Officers' Club, in the garden of St James's Square, St James's, *c.* 1919.

4, the Astors' house, which escaped the bombing, became the London headquarters of the Free French forces from 1943 to 1945.

In the barbarous decades after the war the old houses that had survived came under threat and some were lost. In 1957 the Royal Institute of International Affairs even wanted to demolish Nos 9 and 10 (the home of three prime ministers) but permission was refused.

Since then there has been a steady revival. Clubs have returned and so have a few private residents. In March 2008 a flat in St James's Square sold for what was reported to be the record price for any British home. The garden is now semi-private, being maintained by a garden committee at no public expense, but generously opened for the benefit of office workers and passers-by during weekday business hours.

The houses that survive are fully protected and give examples of the work of some distinguished men. The best are three early 1770s works of Robert Adam: Nos 20 and 33, which he designed, and No. 11 which he remodelled. Number 15 is by James Stuart, 1764–66; Nos 9 and 10 by Benjamin Timbrell, 1735–36; No. 4 by Edward Shepherd, 1726–28; No. 5 by Matthew Brettingham, 1748–49 and No. 13 probably also by him, 1735–36. The star of the nineteenth-century houses is No. 32, designed by S.P. and C.R. Cockerell for the Bishop of London in 1819–21. But even when a house had been the work of an eminent architect, later generations could not resist calling in lesser men to tinker: if St James's Square is a gallery of architecture, it is one where the retouchers and restorers have been rampant.

St John's Square

CLERKENWELL [ISLINGTON]

The Priory of St John at Clerkenwell, the English headquarters of the Knights Hospitallers, was founded about 1144. Its inner precinct extended from the eastern end of Clerkenwell Green (now Aylesbury Street) in the north to the surviving gatehouse in St John's Lane in the south. After the priory was suppressed in 1541 the precinct came to be known as St John's Court and eventually St John's Square, a name first recorded in 1712.

It was far from square in shape, more like an irregular cross, with odd protrusions in all directions. The greater part of the priory church was blown up by Protector Somerset to provide building materials for Somerset House, but the choir was patched up in the reign of Queen Mary and again in the eighteenth century, and became St John's Church. The prior's lodgings, to the north and east of it, became the premises of the Master of the Revels under Queen Elizabeth, and in the seventeenth century were converted into a large mansion known as Aylesbury House.

From the early seventeenth to the early eighteenth century St John's Court was a fashionable residential area, with a series of large houses, most of them on the west side. In 1708 Hatton described it as 'St John's Priory, a spacious and pleasant Place, more like a square than a street (especially that end next to Clerkenwell)'. Many aristocrats and courtiers lived there, in semi-retirement from the bustle of the City and court. One of the last was Bishop Gilbert Burnet, the Whig historian, who died in 1715. His funeral procession was stoned by a Tory mob on its way to St James's Church. By that time the name was changing to St John's Square and the mansions were being divided into tenements or replaced by smaller houses.

As a place of residence St John's Square was mostly favoured after 1715 by merchants and the Nonconformist clergy, but there were a couple of aberrations. John Wilkes, the extraordinary politician, writer, pornographer and rogue, was born there in 1725, the son of a distiller. The distillery was next to St John's Church. John Camden Hotten, the extraordinary publisher, writer, pornographer and rogue, was born at No. 45 (a number also significant in the career of Wilkes) in 1832. He was the son of a builder. Were they both named in honour of the square?

By the beginning of the nineteenth century Clerkenwell had been overwhelmed by the City. The rich merchants were moving to the West End or to new suburbs, and their place was taken by printers, watchmakers, jewellers and metal workers. The square was well on the way to becoming a slum by the time the wide new Clerkenwell Road was smashed through the centre in the 1870s, dividing it into two parts. Most of the old houses that

St John's Gate and the south-eastern corner of St John's Square in 1829.

St John's Gate and the south-western corner of St John's Square, *c.* 1905.

survived this destruction were replaced by offices and workshops later in the century, and more were destroyed in the Second World War.

Nevertheless, St John's Square remains a place of extraordinary interest, as it is topped and tailed by two of London's most important medieval relics. The gatehouse and St John's Church were acquired by the revived order of St John in 1874 and 1931. The church is the main feature of the northern half of the square, but the visible buildings give little hint of antiquity, being Lord Mottistone's rebuilding of the 1950s. The interior retains some medieval fabric, and the crypt is a remarkable twelfth-century survival. The northern half of the square also has a late eighteenth-century terrace, but it is only a façade, everything behind having been rebuilt as offices in the 1980s.

The part of the square south of Clerkenwell Road has Victorian tenements and warehouses on the east side and modern, glassy offices on the west. It is entirely redeemed, however, by the St John's Gate of 1504. This has been frequently and heavily restored during its post-Dissolution career as printing office, tavern and headquarters of the Order of St John – until about 1770 the opening was 'encumbered with a billiard room which filled all the upper part from the spring of the arch' – but it is still one of the most valuable monastic relics in London.

St John's Square

See Smith Square

St John's Wood Square

The Greenwood maps of 1827 and 1830 gave the name of St John's Wood Square to a gap in the houses on the south side of St John's Wood Terrace, close to the High Street, but showed only one or two houses facing the open space.

The *Standard* reported on 26 September 1827 that, 'On Friday last, as Captain Lawson, of the 15th Hussars, late of No. 2 St John's-wood-square, was driving down the Park-road in his chaise', the horse bolted and Mrs Lawson and the children were injured.

Numbers 1, 2, 4 and 5 first appeared in the ratebooks in 1825 and No. 3 was included in 1826. As at Orme Square, which it would have resembled if completed, the houses on either side of the entrance were perhaps numbered as part of the square. Five houses were as far as it proceeded. The 1828 ratebook transferred them to St John's Wood Terrace and listed Nos 3, 4 and 5 as empty properties.

The 1834 survey of St Marylebone, like all later maps, showed a continuous run of houses on the south side of St John's Wood Terrace, the unmatching Nos 7 and 8 having filled the gap where the abortive square had been. The Charles Lane mews behind had replaced the intended garden, of which the kink at the south-west end of the lane is perhaps a relic.

The square was a very short-lived and unsuccessful experiment in an area where development had only begun about 1820. The failure was significant, as St John's Wood, with its villas, was at the forefront of a new style of suburban development that largely superseded formal geometrical arrangements.

St Katherine's Square

St Katherine's (or Catherine's) Square, close to the Thames east of the Tower of London, was part of a large irregular opening called St Katherine's Court until the middle of the eighteenth century. By the 1790s, in line with the prevailing fashion, the more compact western half had been formalised as St Katherine's Square, leaving the eastern end as the Court.

The square, with about a dozen houses, some of them Elizabethan, was at the centre of a dense network of alleys – including one named Cats Hole – between the Tower and St Katherine's Church. This was a royal peculiar, an enclave free from the jurisdiction of the City and its guilds, and consequently home to a teeming population of foreigners, fugitives and entrepreneurs.

The City was naturally delighted to throw its weight behind a scheme to drown the whole inconvenient suburb like a litter of unwanted kittens. The St Katherine's Dock Act was passed in 1825 and within three years the church, the square and the court had all been replaced by a busy system of basins and locks. The dock, which was not large enough to be permanently successful, closed in 1968 and is now a marina.

St Leonard's Square

KENTISH TOWN [CAMDEN]

This late 1850s development was sometimes known in its early years as St Leonard's Place. That would have been a more appropriate name, as it is a broad, stubby cul-de-sac, not by any conventional definition a square. But it is possible to see what led to the present name winning the contest, as there are some elements in the design that were clearly inspired by the architecture of squares.

The first two houses of the north and south terraces are advanced beyond the building line of the rest, which gives a sense of increasing space even though the fences of the front gardens are all on the same line. At the east end a formal composition of five houses, the middle one set slightly forward, appears to make a decent stab at a third side to the square. It is partly illusion, as only the middle three houses are really facing west; the two flankers are the advanced end houses of the north and south terraces. To the south of the square there is even a mews, though it is unlikely that any carriage folk ever lived here.

There was bomb damage at the east end of St Leonard's Square, especially in the north-east corner, but it has all happily been made good. The trim, uniform, three-storey terraces are attractive, especially in the sunshine, and the exotic trees in some of the front gardens help to maintain the illusion of a square.

The north side of St Leonard's Square in 2011.

St Margaret's Square

When the Corporation of London planned the development of the Bridge House Farm estate at Ladywell and Brockley in the 1880s its surveyor envisaged various opulent architectural flourishes. These gradually fell away under economic pressure as the social character of the area declined towards the end of the century, and St Margaret's Square was the only fancy feature that survived.

It was merely a setting back of ten houses in Adelaide Avenue, with a green in front of them. The single houses on the short east and west sides used to have their front doors facing the garden, but the one to the west was destroyed during the Second World War (with the house at the western end of the terrace) and the house on the east side has been largely or wholly rebuilt and is now entered from Adelaide Avenue.

The garden was originally a private amenity for the residents of the twelve houses, but as they were divided into flats the green began to be neglected and the LCC took over its upkeep. In 1952 St Margaret's Square was offered to Lewisham Council on a twenty-one year lease at £1 per annum, if Lewisham would

lay it out and maintain it as a public open space under the terms of the London Squares Preservation Act. The lease was granted in 1954 and Lewisham still looks after the shady sunken garden.

St Mark's Square

By the middle of the nineteenth century the projectors of ambitious middle-class housing schemes had grown so accustomed to the idea of a square as the centrepiece that they sometimes included a ghost square from mere force of habit. The area of broad avenues and sweeping crescents that grew up around St Mark's Church at Dalston in the 1860s had its inevitable St Mark's Square, even though it never achieved more than the most spectral existence.

The name was half-heartedly applied to the houses that framed the church on the north, west and south sides, but they formed a more natural part of Sandringham Road, St Mark's Road (now Rise) and Colvestone Crescent, in which the LCC officially incorporated them in stages until the name was finally laid to rest in 1914. The tall Gothic terraces of the 'square' still surround the Gothic church.

Number 30 Adelaide Road, which formed the west side of St Margaret's Square, seen from the garden in 1909.

St Mark's Square

Like St Mary's Square at Paddington, which it resembled in other ways, this is not a square at all but two short stretches of road to the west and north of St Mark's Church, which itself faces Prince Albert Road and the zoo. The Regent's Canal encloses the churchyard to the west.

St Mark's was built in 1851–52, the architect being Thomas Little. The semi-detached houses on the west side are contemporary with the church, the terrace on the north side a little later. They might just as well have been included in Princess Road and in Regents Park Road, the numbering of which is confusingly interrupted by the square. But the houses are attractive and well preserved and provide a dignified setting for the church.

The square was popular and did not rapidly sink into boarding houses and institutions like so many in north London, but the area did decline towards the end of the nineteenth century. In 1898 the Charles Booth surveyor was told by the police inspector who acted as his guide that the houses were 'not now inhabited by so good a class as formerly; does not think that any of them keep a carriage'.

St Mark's was gutted in 1940 and some of the houses were damaged by blast, but all have been finely restored. Now they look bright and prosperous, as though refreshed by the invigorating air of the canal.

St Mary's Gardens

See St Mary's Square, Kennington

St Mary's Square

This is a tiny two-sided relic of what was once a substantial village square, the enlarged meeting place of several roads, west of St Mary's Church at the southern end of Ealing.

The gradual widening of St Mary's Road, Church Lane and South Ealing Road has obscured its original form, but Westfield House, at the corner of St Mary's Road and Church Lane, was formerly the main, almost the sole, feature on the north side of the square. Trees stood in front of this fine house, where the traffic now roars.

The modern name did not become attached to the square until the 1880s, when its decline was well advanced. It was Church Square in 1881 and 1861

The north side of St Mark's Square, Regent's Park, c. 1905.

The east side of St Mary's Square, Ealing, in 2013.

and before that 'near the Old Church' or 'opposite the Old Church' or merely 'Ealing' were the usual addresses for this part of the village. In the 1861 census Westfield House was one of the six listed in Church Square. It was occupied by a lunatic with a staff of four servants, one of them a 'lunatic's attendant'. The parish clerk and tax collector also lived in the square. Later in the century there were ten or a dozen houses, some of them very small.

The green shrank throughout the nineteenth century and the square reached more or less its present size in 1894, when the number of houses fell to six during the widening of South Ealing Road. By then the square was largely commercial, No. 5 in the corner being occupied by a cow keeper. The council continued to chip away at the green, but no more houses were lost.

There are now two cottages and a larger house on the south side, and on the east three cottages and the Old Fire Station – of 1888 – which is no bigger than its neighbours. Some of the cottages are perhaps of the late eighteenth or early nineteenth century. The path before them is lavishly decorated with flowers and shrubs in pots after the manner of Bonnington Square. The triangular green is enclosed by a low post and rail fence and completely shaded by its single tree.

St Mary's Square

KENNINGTON [LAMBETH]

(now St Mary's Gardens)

St Mary's Gardens, which was known as St Mary's Square until 1936, was part of the same development as Walcot Square, its neighbour to the north, and shares many of its characteristics. The name comes from St Mary Lambeth, the parish in which it stands and which administered this charity estate. (See Walcot Square for more about the development and the residents.)

The north side of St Mary's Gardens, formerly St Mary's Square, Kennington, in 2009.

St Mary's Gardens is, like Walcot Square, attractive and quiet, with a well-kept if rather dull private triangle of grass and trees in the middle – for these are triangles rather than true squares. On two sides St Mary's Gardens is also like Walcot Square in being lined by neat terraces of small houses, very early Victorian in date (before 1841), but late Georgian in spirit. The difference is on the south-west side where the taller houses were built a good deal later, in the 1860s, in a style that is uncompromisingly Victorian. This was because the land to the south did not belong to the Walcot charity estate and the development here had to await the convenience of the neighbouring landowner.

St Mary's Square

PADDINGTON [WESTMINSTER]

This was only ever a two-sided square, with Harrow Road to the south and St Mary's churchyard to the east. There was one large house and a terrace of ten on the west side and a terrace of seven on the north.

The roads had been laid out by the 1820s as part of the Park Place development, but the houses in the square did not appear immediately. The west side, known at first as Park Place Terrace, was built in 1841–42. The north side, which was added in 1843–45, was originally called Stanley Place and had

The west side of St Mary's Square, Paddington, *c.* 1910.

Stanley Mews behind. It may be of significance that James Banting, architect and surveyor, was the first occupant of No. 5 Stanley Place from 1845.

The St Mary's Square name did not come into use until the early 1860s. By then part of the garden had been annexed as the site for the Paddington Vestry Hall, built in 1853; but even when the building was enlarged after becoming the town hall in 1900 a third of the garden was left open, and with the churchyard and Paddington Green adjoining to the east the residents suffered no lack of air or outlook. The square settled down to tranquil prosperity.

Its troubles began in the Second World War when the north terrace was badly damaged and eventually replaced by flats. In 1965, with the abolition of the Borough of Paddington, the town hall became redundant and was demolished. At the same time the construction of Westway entailed the loss of the west terrace. St Mary's Square is now a sad squashed remnant, with no houses remaining, blocks of flats to the north, and the truncated western arm pointing accusingly towards the motorway.

St Matthias Square

See Goldsmith Square

St Pancras Square

See Pancras Square

St Peter's Square

BETHNAL GREEN [TOWER HAMLETS]

St Peter's Church at Bethnal Green was built in 1840–41. It was designed in the Norman style by the versatile Lewis Vulliamy, who could readily turn out churches in various forms of fanciful and free and easy Gothic, before it became too scholarly and stereotyped. The vicarage behind the church was also by Vulliamy, but has been enlarged, and the National Schools, now a factory, were built soon afterwards. Then there was a pause before a broken frame of houses ended the isolation of the church in the early 1850s.

What developed was a peculiar square of only two sides, the north and south, both of them ending abruptly at the backs of houses in the older Elizabeth Street (now Mansford Street) to the east. On the west side was St Peter's Street, its pitiful remnant now St Peter's Avenue, and the centre, where a garden might have been, was occupied by the church and vicarage.

The whole of the north side was given over to the church school, which left only the south side for houses. There were ten of them in two terraces of five, facing the flank of the church and the garden of the vicarage, and in a short extension to the east there were three more behind the vicarage garden, facing south. All were demolished in the 1960s, together with the houses in St Peter's Street. In 1938 the LCC decided to call the southern side St Peter's Close, a name that might have been more appropriate to the north side, with its width and its purely ecclesiastical buildings, but that continues to be known as St Peter's Square.

St Peter's Square

St Peter's Square was the main element of an ambitious venture in town planning that was more urban than suburban, taking its lead from the mid-eighteenth-century Hammersmith Terrace on the riverfront.

The new estate was built between Hammersmith Terrace and King Street, on land belonging to George Scott of Ravenscourt Park. Its first feature was St Peter's Church in Black Lion Lane, which was designed for the New Church Commissioners by a local man, Edward Lapidge, and built between 1827 and 1829.

The extraordinary houses of the square followed over the next decade. They were built in terraces of three, but each terrace was made to resemble a palace, or at worst an immense semi-detached pair, the door of the middle house being cunningly hidden

The former National Schools, St Peter's Square, Bethnal Green, in 2009.

The west side of St Peter's Square, Hammersmith, *c.* 1905.

in a loggia. The stucco fronts are adorned with eagles, pineapples, recumbent dogs.

As the church and square were clearly meant to complement one another, Edward Lapidge must be a candidate for the vacant honour of having designed the houses. Another possible architect is the landscape gardener, John Claudius Loudon. As early as 1839 Thomas Faulkner claimed in his *History and Antiquities of Hammersmith* that Loudon had laid out and planted the garden of the square, and he sometimes dabbled in architecture in conjunction with his landscaping.

Among the early residents were two notable journalists. Thomas Payne, the printer and publisher of the *Morning Post*, lived in the square in the 1830s and 1840s, and John Doran, the historian and editor of *Notes and Queries*, was there in the years around 1840. There was a decline later in the century, with industry and a few lodging houses infiltrating from the 1880s. Robert Pate, the would-be assassin of Queen Victoria, who was living at No. 12 in 1881, gave the square little to boast about.

In 1899 the Booth survey found the square occupied by Hammersmith tradesmen, and thought that the underused garden might be advantageously opened to the public. That happened not long afterwards.

In 1913 the LCC contributed £4,000 to the £7,500 required by Hammersmith Council to purchase the garden and compensate the builders who had already begun to destroy it. The council laid it out in 1914 at a cost of £834 and opened it in the following year. *The Greek Runner* by Sir William Richmond, which graces the centre of this lovely, tranquil garden, was presented by his family and placed there in 1926.

St Peter's Square was artistic and bohemian – perhaps another way of saying cheap – from the 1920s to the 1950s. Robert Graves and Laura Riding lived at No. 35a, a second-floor flat, from 1927 until her suicide attempt in 1929 – by leaping from a window – broke up their strange ménage. Graves also had a barge or houseboat moored close to the south end of the square. John Piper, the artist, lived in a flat at No. 29 from 1929 until 1934, when his first wife left him for a neighbour. Alec Guinness was one of a number of actors who settled in Hammersmith after the war. He lived at No. 7 from 1946 to 1955, when he moved to the country.

The present perfection of the square is partly an illusion. Its original unity of design was breached late in the nineteenth century when meaner streets were built to the south. The two western houses of the south side were demolished for the sake of Eyot Gardens and the southernmost and largest on the west side, deprived of its extensive grounds, became a dye works and later had a laundry built over its remaining garden.

The other big house of the square was at the west end of the north side, with its entrance in the access road from King Street. It was demolished with the adjoining house to provide part of the site for the Commodore Theatre, which was built in 1929. This huge combined cinema and variety theatre, later a bingo hall, filled the whole space between King Street and the square, where it had its back entrance. It was a serious disruption to the scale and atmosphere until it was demolished in 1982. In the rebuilding the opportunity was happily taken to place houses on the frontage to the square, designed to harmonise with their neighbours.

The renewed respect for squares in the twenty-first century has led to the demolition of the last house in North Eyot Gardens and the reinstatement in handsome external facsimile of the two lost houses on the south side.

St Philip Square

BATTERSEA [WANDSWORTH]

St Philip Square is the centrepiece of the Park Town estate at Battersea, which the developer, Philip Flower, tried to promote as a southern extension of Cubitt's Belgravia and Pimlico. It was designed by James Knowles, an architect who had the ill luck, or bad judgement, to be associated with several ambitious town planning schemes that ended in disappointment.

Numbers 27 and 29 on the west side of St Peter's Square, Hammersmith, seen from the garden in 2008.

St Philip's Church, St Philip Square, *c.* 1910.

Here, the hopes of the projectors were dashed when Battersea was cut to ribbons by the railway companies. The wealthy tenants they hoped to attract never penetrated beyond the tangle of tracks and bridges.

An impressive church was an essential element in housing developments of this kind. A square was becoming less common by the 1860s, so Knowles combined the two economically by placing St Philip's in the middle of the square instead of a garden. The houses were built before the church in the late 1860s, so the first tenants had a brief taste of an open outlook. Indeed, until a church was included the intended name was Queen's Square.

Its east side formed part of a long and unbroken three-storey terrace in Phillip (now St Philip) Road. At that stage Thackeray Road, the eastward continuation of the south side of the square, had not been thought of; when it was, houses in Phillip Road had to be demolished to make room for it. But although the St Philip Road terrace is continuous it is not uniform, the houses facing the square being twice the width of the rest and disfigured with porches.

The other sides of the square were treated more formally, with three-storey terraces featuring a single four-storey bay-windowed house at each end. The shorter north and south sides have the widest houses, but they are built almost flush with the road, with an oppressive effect. On the west side the houses have semi-basements and attics with tall dormers and are set well back from Queenstown Road behind dramatically wide and long flights of steps. It must have been an impressive group, but four of the ten houses were destroyed in the Second World War.

St Philip's Church was built in 1870. The modest vicarage, tucked away behind it, forms a pleasant contrast to its neighbours. A square with a church in the middle is rarely a success, unless the central enclosure is large enough to also include a garden. St Philip Square, like Bonnington Square, benefitted from the Second World War when it received a garden courtesy of the Luftwaffe. But here the bombsite that became a public garden is on the far side of the busy Queenstown Road and remains a dull patch of grass and shrubs, whereas the Bonnington garden is in the centre of the square and has been central to its remarkable improvement.

St Stephen's Square

Samuel Teulon's St Stephen's Church was completed in 1850, but was already shown on the 1848–49 skeleton Ordnance Survey map, by which time the square in which it stood had taken the name in anticipation. A frame of thirty or so small houses was begun soon after the church.

In 1851 the only resident was a bricklayer, probably placed in one house to keep an eye on the twenty-five being built. Maps from Horwood's of the 1790s onwards had shown a few buildings on the site, arranged round a smaller, anonymous open space with a square shape.

As the only entrance was the narrow one from Kent Street, now Tabard Street, it should have been a quiet spot; pious, too, as it was dominated by St Stephen's, with the church in the centre instead of a garden, the hall and infants' school in the south-west corner and the vicarage in the south-east. But the district was very poor and the square was infiltrated by industry from an early date. Peace was unlikely to have been maintained beyond Sunday, if then.

All the houses except the vicarage were demolished in the 1930s with a view to the redevelopment of the district as the Tabard Estate, but little had

The former vicarage of St Stephen's, St Stephen's Square, Southwark, from Hankey Place in 2013.

been done, and nothing in the square, when the war put a stop to building. The church and the vicarage were damaged by bombing, but repaired. The respite for St Stephen's proved only a short one, for it was closed in 1961 and demolished in 1965. The former vicarage, now at the corner of Hankey Place and Manciple Street, is thus the only relic of the square. A new rectory for St George the Martyr, the mother parish, was built on the site of the church.

St Stephen's Square

(now part of St Stephen's Gardens)

St Stephen's Square was built in 1861, at the fag end of the great Paddington housing boom that had begun at Connaught Place by Marble Arch more than fifty years earlier. By 1860 the land available was too far from the West End and too close to the great railway yards for any great success to be likely.

So many houses were on the market that new developments had to be very striking to gain attention, and the St Stephen's Square houses were entirely standard. The owners found them hard to let, attracted few people of rank or note, and were soon glad to allow the Governesses' Home to occupy No. 9. By the 1890s a military academy and a boarding house had also been admitted. During the First World War there was a Jewish working girls' club and three houses were occupied by a dressmaker and her sweated labour.

The square's only celebrity was the great scholar Sir Frederic Madden, keeper of manuscripts at the British Library, who died at No. 25 St Stephen's Square (now No. 60 St Stephen's Gardens) in 1873.

The modern St Stephen's Gardens combines two originally separate elements, the old St Stephen's Square with its garden to the west and the old St Stephen's Road to the east. This means that the numbering of the former square has changed completely. There was at one time a further complication, because the old Burlington Road, which balanced St Stephen's Road at the west end of the square, was also incorporated in the new St Stephen's

The north side of St Stephen's Square, Westbourne Green, *c.* 1904.

Gardens in 1938, but the LCC obliterated the old Burlington Road section soon after the war as part of the site of a housing estate. The square was lucky to escape the same fate, as it had become very down-at-heel in the twentieth century; that is how the attractive garden comes to be public. The legal protection enjoyed by the garden probably deterred potential developers from molesting the houses, which are now in better condition than at any time since the nineteenth century.

St Thomas's Square

HACKNEY

St Thomas's Square was laid out in 1771–72 on land belonging to St Thomas's Hospital. It has an unusual shape, a rectangle squeezed at the Mare Street end.

Now the public garden is the only point of interest, but even in its prime the square had just one side, the east, of any importance. The eight houses there (the only ones shown on Faden's 1785 map, and Cary's of 1795) were large and well-built, with substantial private gardens. On the north side there was a much meaner terrace of nine houses with only front gardens, their back doors opening directly into Burford Lane. On the west was Mare Street, unconnected with the square. The south was occupied by the side of the Hackney Congregational Chapel (opened in 1772) together with the minister's house and a large detached villa.

St Thomas's Square has a bizarre connection with children's books. Talbot Baines Reed, the son of Sir Charles Reed, MP for Hackney and chairman of the London School Board, was born in 1852 at the big house on the south side. T.B. Reed was the author of countless popular public school stories, the most famous being *The Fifth Form at St Dominic's* (1887). Number 2 on the east side was the home in the early years of the nineteenth century of the Hennell family. Caroline Hennell, later Mrs Bray, was the author of improving works for children with titles like *Our Duty to Animals* (1871). Her brother and sister, Charles and Mary, were also writers, and all the family were friends of Marian Evans (George Eliot), whose religious thought they influenced.

The Congregational church, once distinguished, suffered a humiliating decline into a Presbyterian chapel, a cinema (the Empress, later the Essoldo) and eventually a bingo hall, before being put out of its misery in 1996. Although it had been remodelled in 1933 with a new front to Mare Street, the building was essentially the church until the end.

The square sustained quite serious bomb damage during the Second World War but could have been saved. Instead the eighteenth-century houses were compulsorily purchased and demolished by the council in the 1950s, leaving just a late Victorian pair in the south-east corner. The only really old thing remaining in St Thomas's Square is the '1772' date stone reset in the new building that replaced the former chapel at the corner of Mare Street. Just to the south is the archway that used to lead to the Congregational schools.

Numbers 7 and 8 St Thomas's Square in 2015.

Salisbury Square

The 1633 edition of Stow's *Survey of London* described Salisbury Court:

> ... a place so called, for that it belonged to the Bishop of Salisbury, and was their Inne, or London house, at such time as they were summoned to come to the Parliament, or came for other businesse. It hath of late time been the dwelling, first of Sir Richard Sackville, and after of Sir Thomas Sackville, Baron of Buckhurst, Lord Treasurer, who very greatly enlarged it with stately buildings.

Lord Treasurer Buckhurst, the poet, was later 1st Earl of Dorset. As John Aubrey recorded, ''Twas this lord that gott Salisbury house *cum appurtenantiis* juxta St Bride's, in exchange for a piece of land, neer Cricklade in Wilts, I thinke called Marston, but the title was not good, nor did the value answer his promise.' The former bishop's palace was called Salisbury House, alias Sackville Place, alias Dorset House in 1611.

In 1629 the 4th Earl, through poverty or thrift, chose to let the house, as a gossiping letter of Sir George Gresley announced:

> My Lord of Dorset is become a great husband; for he hath let his house in Salisbury Court unto the queen for the Ambassador Leiger of France, which is daily expected to come over, to lie in, and giveth for it £350 by the year, and for the rest of his stables and outhouses towards the water side, he hath let for £1000 fine and £100 by the year rent, unto the master of the revels, to make a playhouse for the children of the revels.

The playhouse that opened in 1630, the last one founded before the Civil Wars, was not a new building but a converted barn. Plays were performed there with varying success until the closure of the theatres in 1642, and after that there were clandestine revivals. The last was in 1649, when the actors were arrested on stage and taken to Whitehall in their

costumes. The sequel was violent: 'divers Souldiers by force & Armes entered ye said Playhouse, Cutt down ye Seates, broke down ye Stage and utterly defaced ye whole buildinges'. They were not totally destroyed, however, and the theatre was patched up at the Restoration.

In the 1640s, after the ruin of the Royalist cause that he had half-heartedly supported, the 4th Earl returned to Dorset House, which he is said never to have left after the execution of Charles I in 1649. He died there in 1652 and Cromwell followed royal precedent by using the house to lodge the Swedish ambassador, Christer Bonde, who came to seek his alliance in 1655.

The economical earl had allowed houses to be built in the courtyard of the great mansion. In his diary, which he kept in the third person, Bulstrode Whitelocke recorded how in 1633, 'his wife not contented with her living in the Countrey, especially in her husbands often absence, was desirous to have a house in London, he was willing to satisfy her, & tooke a convenient house in Salisbury Court'. While they lived there Whitelocke was deputed to supervise the music for a masque the Inns of Court decided to produce for the delight of the king and queen:

> [He] chose the Masters & others for the musicke the best he could meet with in London, of all Nations, and had 4 of the Queens Chappell the more to please her Majesty, he caused them all to meet in practise att his house in Salisbury Court, where he might be with them, & had sometimes 40 lutes, besides other instruments & voyces, in consort together.

So perhaps Samuel Pepys, the most famous son of Salisbury Court, who was born there on 23 February in that year (in the modern Court not the Square) acquired his love of music in the cradle. For his love of the stage the Salisbury Court Theatre, opened three years before his birth, may claim the credit.

Dorset House and the old theatre were destroyed in the Great Fire of London, and the courtyard or square was rebuilt with three-storey houses all around it, those on the west and south sides with front gardens. Most were of three bays but a few had five. The centre was cobbled, with no garden.

Between the square and the river the sumptuous Dorset Garden Theatre was opened in 1671 and Salisbury Court (sometimes called Dorset Court) became a favourite place of residence for actors, including Betterton, and dramatists, notably Dryden and Shadwell. A less likely resident was John Locke.

In the seventeenth century 'Salisbury Court' meant not only the square but the approach to it from Fleet Street (which now has the exclusive use of the name) and also the street running south to the river, later Dorset Street and now Dorset Rise. The modern usage with regard to Salisbury Square and Salisbury Court was only established in the middle of the eighteenth century. In 1708 Hatton listed 'Salisbury Court, a considerable street between Fleet street N. and the Thames S. in the middle whereof is a small pleasant square'. In 1722 William Stow gave 'Salisbury-court' and 'Salisbury-square' separate entries.

Because of this changing use of the name it cannot be assumed that all those known as residents of Salisbury Court before 1750 lived in the square. Those with Salisbury Court addresses after 1750 probably did not. The most eminent eighteenth-century resident was Samuel Richardson. He had his London home and printing business in Salisbury Court from 1739 or earlier, and published his novels there. In 1754 he took a house at No. 11 Salisbury Square, set back in the north-west corner, where he died in 1761. The printing works he moved to Blue Ball Court, off the east side of the square.

A theatrical quarter was naturally well supplied with pubs. Salisbury Court had the Red Balls in 1679, the Two Black Posts in 1680 and the Blue Ball or Ball & Star in the 1690s. Because of their history as part of a larger entity, the eighteen or nineteen houses in Salisbury Square were not numbered as a unit until after the First World War, being treated instead as continuations of the various access streets. In 1841 and 1905 the only pub then surviving in the square, the Barlow Mow, was No. 135.

In 1817 David Hughson gave this account: 'Salisbury-Square, is now adorned by a very neat pillar in the centre, from which arises a superb gas lamp, illuminating the circumference in a beautiful manner. Here is the Church Missionary Society, and the office or warehouse of the Bible and Homily Society.'

The east and part of the north side of Salisbury Square in 1927, with the tower of St Bride's, Fleet Street, behind. The pub was the Barley Mow at No. 9.

In 1841 there was an MP living in the square – the honourable member for Stoke-upon-Trent – but the rest of the houses were occupied by solicitors and surgeons, or were being used as hotels or business premises. In the first half of the twentieth century it was largely occupied by newspaper and publishers' offices.

Salisbury Square passed through the Second World War with little damage, but most of the old buildings had gone by then. Since the war the west and south sides have been taken over by large office blocks and the heavily restored No. 1 on the north side is the only reminder of the domestic past. A road still passes down the east side, but the rest of the square is semi-pedestrianised. In the centre is a small paved area with flower beds and seats, surrounding an obelisk. This is not the pillar mentioned by Hughson in 1817 but the peripatetic memorial to the radical Lord Mayor Robert Waithman, who died in 1833. It spent more than a century opposite his shop in Farringdon Street, twenty years in Bartholomew Close and has been in Salisbury Square since 1972.

The garden of Salisbury Square from the south in 2007, showing the Waithman memorial and No. 1.

Sandy Square

'Sandy Sq.' was the name given by Wallis's 1801 map of London and Westminster to the southern section of Sandys (or Sandy's) Street, Bishopsgate, where it met Catherine Wheel Alley. Wallis showed this junction as a much wider space than other contemporary map makers – although the 1873 Ordnance Survey made it quite wide – and he was not supported by them or topographers in calling it a square. It must either have been a local and temporary name, or a mere mistake.

This part of Sandy's Street was later known as Windsor Street. It was demolished in the 1890s, when the new northern section of Middlesex Street was created. Sandy's Row, a little to the north-east, keeps the name alive. There may be some connection with Catherine Wheel Square (q.v.).

Scrub Square

Scrub Square does not appear on the map of Christ Church, Southwark, in Strype's 1720 revision of Stow, a map that may be earlier than that date. It was shown as quite a large, loose open space on Rocque's map of 1746, but during the remainder of the eighteenth century it shrank away to a small court.

Rocque indicated five or six houses or groups of houses scattered around the west, north and east sides of some garden ground, with the south side defined by one of the many drainage ditches on this stretch of reclaimed river bank. He called it Scrubs Square, suggesting that the name was that of an owner or developer. Horwood's 1790s map showed a much smaller Scrub Square off the west side of Bennett Street (now Rennie Street) with just nine houses, six on the north and three on the south side. The 1813 revision indicated a deteriorating situation, with one house on each side demolished. These riverside streets were becoming more industrialised, with houses increasingly giving way to wharves, warehouses and factories, and Scrub Square had been extinguished before 1840.

By the 1860s most of the area in the angle of Upper Ground and Bennett Street was occupied by the large works of Shand, Mason, & Co., hydraulic engineers of No. 75 Upper Ground, a firm noted for their fire engines, but part remained open as the factory yard. Industry having deserted the Southwark waterfront, the site is now covered by the shops of Milroy Walk and the flats above.

Searle Square

See New Square, Lincoln's Inn

Shaft's Square

Lockie gave this direction in 1810: 'Shafts or Shaftsbury-Square or Court, York-Street, Westminster, – between Horse-shoe-alley and Smith's Rents'. He left out 'Court' in the 1813 revision, probably more for conciseness than accuracy.

The square was built in the second half of the eighteenth century. Rocque's 1740s map showed Horse-shoe Stable Yard and Smith's Rents, but nothing between, and the ratebooks lumped together Smith's Rents and the offshoot that became the square under the name of Smith's Court, not disentangling the two elements until the 1840s.

The stuttering attempt at an aristocratic name did not last long. By the 1841 census the square had subsided into the appropriately humdrum Smith's Place. It was a court with six houses on the east and north sides in the 1790s and in 1813, to which two more had been added on the west side by 1869. The entrance was from George Street (now Vandon Street) in the south, and the square ran up behind Horseshoe Alley for a third of its length.

In the 1860s it just survived the construction of the Metropolitan Railway, which shaved past the southern end, but in the 1890s Smith's Place and Smith's Rents were demolished and replaced by several large buildings. These newcomers lasted barely forty years before giving way in their turn, with the east side of Horseshoe Alley, to the even larger Vandon Court. York Street is now Petty France, and Horseshoe Alley is Vandon Passage. The southern section of Vandon Court, lying back from the north-east angle of Vandon Street, is now on the site of Shaft's Square. Its courtyard was the entrance to the square and also gave access to Smith's Rents to the east.

Shard's Square

PECKHAM [SOUTHWARK]

Shard's Square was part of Peckham New Town which replaced the market gardens south of the Surrey Canal in the 1820s and 1830s. The square existed by 1841, when the houses were occupied by labourers and bricklayers, plus the odd clerk or excise officer. The name came from the Shard family, who lived at the nearby Manor House of Peckham in the eighteenth and early nineteenth centuries.

The Booth survey gave a poor report in 1899: 'Shard Square, cul-de-sac, four room cottages, fronts. Has a bad name, "low labouring class", drunken. South side worse than north.' It was not a true square, but a road with about twenty cottages on each side and only the front gardens to give it the broadness that suggested the name. It may not have been entirely a cul-de-sac,

either. The main and only official entrance was in Peckham Park Road, but the south end was separated from the better Edwin's Row only by a wall or fence, which local ingenuity must surely have found a way to circumvent.

Large blocks of council flats were built on the site of the houses around 1930, and Shard's Square was reduced to its present humble form, as a stubby cul-de-sac off Peckham Park Road.

Sharp Square

See Granville Square

Shepherd's Square

MAYFAIR [WESTMINSTER]

(now part of Shepherd Market)

Shepherd Market, the original Mayfair shopping centre, has had much the same form since Edward Shepherd laid it out in the 1730s, even though most of the houses and shops were rebuilt in the nineteenth century. The naming of the various parts has been less stable.

The former Shepherd's Square, Market Street, Shepherd Market, in the 1920s.

Shepherd's Square was the late eighteenth and early nineteenth-century name for the court immediately south of the main Curzon Street entrance, opposite Queen Street. South of the archway through Nos 42–43 Curzon Street the court opens out in two stages, a feature unchanged since Rocque's map of the 1740s. Horwood and Lockie both used the Shepherd's Square name, but by 1841 Shepherd's Court had replaced it, and later it was regarded as part of Market Street, the lane crossing at its south end. Now it is numbered in Shepherd Market.

Sherry Square

GREENWICH

Sherry Square, Sherry Court and Sherry Place were tiny offshoots from Thames Street, built before 1838. They were entered via alleys or archways between or under the houses on the north side, east of Horseferry Road, now Horseferry Place. Around 1870 there was a major reorganisation of this complex, involving the consolidation of the surviving parts under the name of Sherry Court. Then or soon afterwards there was also some demolition and rather less rebuilding.

The Sherry Square houses were among those rebuilt, and they even had their amenities improved when the brewery that had been hard up against their east side was replaced by a hay and straw yard. In 1899 the Booth survey commented on Sherry Court, 'Four houses, two rooms and scullery. Have been rebuilt recently … Further west is another court with one house.'

The LCC made almost everything between Thames Street and the river a slum clearance area in the 1930s and replaced the cottages with the blocks of flats that still dominate what is left of Thames Street. Page House is on the site of the Sherrys.

Sidney Square

WHITECHAPEL [TOWER HAMLETS]

Sidney Square and Ford Square, which have always been bracketed together, are sisters certainly but not twins. The development of this part of Stepney

The garden of Sidney Square, looking north, in 2007.

proceeded from west to east, which meant that Ford Square was built (as Bedford Square) in the early 1820s and Sidney Square in the late 1820s and early 1830s. They were rectangular rather than square in shape, but the rectangles were not unduly elongated. The houses all had private back gardens of a decent size, but at the front they opened directly onto the pavement.

The early residents were clerks, master mariners, customs officials, plus the odd labourer. In 1898 Charles Booth's researcher, coming from Ford Square, found Sidney Square 'equally uncared for. Better class of inhabitants on east side than west, some servants kept on the east side.'

The LCC, anxious to preserve open spaces in the crowded East End, bought the Ford and Sidney Square gardens in 1903 and opened them to the

Sion Square

A large riding school known as Jones's Equestrian Amphitheatre was built in Union Street, Whitechapel, south-east of St Mary's Church, before 1786. The site had been a mulberry garden. The building was circular – it was a pioneer circus – with extensions to east and west. All the leading trick-riders and acrobats of the period performed there during its brief career, when not engaged at Astley's more celebrated establishment.

In 1790 it was acquired for use as the Sion (or Zion) Methodist Chapel, one of those attached to Lady Huntingdon's Connexion. Around it there had quickly grown up a neighbourhood of small streets that included Sion Square.

The building remained a stronghold of Calvinistic Methodism until it was acquired by the German Catholic Mission in 1862 and used as its church until 1873. Then, during a service, 'several pieces of plastering fell from the dome-shaped roof. Mr Dalton advised the congregation, about a hundred in number, to leave the building as quietly as possible, but they had scarcely got outside when the whole of the roof fell in with a terrible crash.' The chapel was rebuilt in more conventional style as St Boniface in 1875, and supplied with bells by the almost adjoining Whitechapel Bell Foundry.

In 1841, when there were twenty-three houses, carman was the most common occupation in Sion Square, but there were also gun makers, farriers and a pianoforte maker among a wide miscellany of trades. The Booth survey of 1895 found three-storey houses, 'a few, but very few, flower pots on window sills'. What was left of the square, a tiny opening with a garden at the north-east corner of the chapel, had been made part of Union Row by then, but the old name persisted.

St Boniface was not the only German church to suffer from enemy action during the Second World War, but surely the only one hit in the First World War as well, during a Zeppelin raid. That damage was easily repaired, but the destruction in 1940 was total. Many of the surviving houses in the southern part of

public in the following year. The Sidney Square garden is maintained in a rather dull municipal style like a very small park.

The south side of the square had been demolished before the Second World War and now consists of undistinguished flats. The original houses on the other three sides were all damaged in the bombing. The north side was entirely rebuilt in the 1990s as flats in a mock Georgian style. The east and west sides are largely original but with a good deal of patched brickwork and some rebuilding in pastiche.

The lion of Sidney Square, its lion comique, was the music hall star Charles Coborn, who was born at No. 25 in 1852. He is remembered as the singer of 'Two Lovely Black Eyes' and 'The Man Who Broke the Bank at Monte Carlo'. His real name was Colin Whitton McCallum.

the square and in Mulberry Street were also flattened and no attempt was made to recreate the complicated street pattern in rebuilding what had become a purely commercial district. The square ceased to exist, but the church was rebuilt at the corner of Adler Street and the new Mulberry Street in 1959–60. The present St Boniface has, appropriately, the most extraordinary belfry in London.

Sir William Warren's Square

From his yards at Wapping and Rotherhithe, the great naval contractor Sir William Warren had very nearly a monopoly in the supply of timber to the royal dockyards for much of the Restoration period. He obtained the position in part by bribing Samuel Pepys and no doubt other less recklessly indiscreet naval officials.

Because of the marshy nature of much of the ground at Wapping, only lightweight (and combustible) timber buildings could be supported. Warren's house and yard there were burnt down in 1673 and 1682, and after the second fire he moved entirely to Rotherhithe. The land at Wapping was part of the estate of Bridewell Hospital. After the fires the governors of the charity invested heavily in piling, which made it possible to rebuild the destroyed houses in brick. Sir William Warren's Square presumably took over the site of his house and yard.

In his *New View of London* of 1708 Edward Hatton included a supplement of streets that were 'either omitted upon my first View or were erected and added since, during the time this Book was in the Press'. In this section appears 'Warren's (Sir William) his Square near King Edward Stairs, Wapping', but Hatton unfortunately does not say whether it was new or overlooked. The Strype map published in 1720 showed the square with trees around the south, east and west sides. It remained little changed during the eighteenth century. In the 1790s there were five houses on the east side and seven on the west, which extended south to Wapping High Street. The north side was counted as part of Cinnamon Street.

In 1837 the Charity Commissioners found the estate in a deplorable condition, largely because of Wapping's loss of trade to the London Docks. 'Many of the houses situate in Sir William Warren's Square are unoccupied and, with very few exceptions, the small streets, and indeed some parts of the main street, present an appearance by no means superior to the worst part of St Giles's.'

As tenants could no longer be found for the houses, the west side of the square was soon rebuilt as warehouses and the east side was similarly treated in the 1860s. By then the south side was occupied only by the Golden Anchor public house, which had its main entrance in the High Street. The former square soon degenerated into a mere passage between two towering warehouses, which until the 1960s had raised walkways crossing from one to the other as at Shad Thames. Only the eastern warehouse is still standing and that has been converted into flats called Prusons Island. The line of four trees running north from Wapping High Street, between Clave Street and Hilliard's Court, marks the site of Sir William Warren's Square.

The site of Sir William Warren's square from the south, in 2013.

Sloane Square

Beresford Chancellor omitted Sloane Square from his *History of the Squares of London* on the grounds that it was 'too much in the nature of a public square to be included in this work'. On that basis he ought also to have excluded Leicester Square, which was equally commercial in 1907, but that he rightly dealt with at length because its historic use was very different. The same is true of Sloane Square, although its days as a residential centre were a good deal shorter and less glamorous.

The square was laid out in the 1770s as part of Henry Holland's Hans Town development on the Cadogan estate, and most of the fifty-one houses were occupied by 1780. The best, on the north and south sides, were in formal terraces with the end houses set forward. None survive, but some idea of the style can be seen in the few original houses still standing in Sloane Street.

Repton planned the garden for Lord Cadogan around 1806, but from the first it was compromised by the roads crossing it, particularly the diagonal King's Road. Horwood's 1790s map had a rare advertisement in the square, a hand indicating No. 34 at the east corner of Lower Sloane Street, and the mysterious words, 'Green Temperated Air'.

In its early days it was popular with horticulturalists and artists, being on the rural edge of town. Charles Varlo, the agricultural theorist, lived there in 1784, and John Fraser's American Nursery at 'King's Road, Sloane Square' was established about 1789. He died there in 1811. The Scottish engraver Francis Legat was living in the square by 1790, and the artists Thomas Burgess and his father William died there in 1807 and 1812.

The increasing importance of the King's Road prevented Sloane Square from remaining residential. Although most of the good houses survived on the south side and at the east end of the north until the close of the nineteenth century, and the smaller ones on the west side until the 1930s, the square was almost entirely commercial, with only five private residents, by 1852. William Weir was scathing in 1843: 'Sloane Square, as bare and intersected with crossings

Sloane Square from the north-west corner in 1896.

The south-west corner of Sloane Square, *c.* 1905, showing the Star & Garter. In 1907 P.G. Wodehouse called it 'the last outpost of respectable, inartistic London'.

The Bibesco Hut, the YMCA's Chelsea soldiers' canteen, *c.* 1919. It stood in the south-east corner of the Sloane Square garden, outside the Royal Court. The hut was the gift of Asquith's son-in-law, Prince Bibesco.

as Kennington Common, as tiny in its proportions as Red Lion Square and combining with a rare excess of common-place all that is uninteresting in both'.

The houses at the west end of the north side were demolished when the Metropolitan & District Railway tunnel was dug across the square in the late 1860s; Sloane Square Station was opened in 1868. The remaining houses on the north, east and south sides were demolished early in the twentieth century, as part of the Cadogan estate's policy of sweeping away the original Hans Town buildings.

Sloane Square is now dominated by the Royal Court Theatre of 1888 and by large twentieth-century shops, most notably Peter Jones of 1935–37, which replaced the last original houses on the west side. The garden, finally freed from the King's Road, is now a pleasant oasis from the encircling traffic, paved not grassed but with abundant trees and seats and sculptured entertainment. It could have been very different, as there were serious plans in the early 1960s to build shops in the centre.

Smith Square

WESTMINSTER

Thomas Archer's baroque St John's, the most remarkable of the 'Fifty' new churches, was built on a marshy field between 1713 and 1728. Smith Square is the descendent of the yard of the new church, which was at first almost without connection to the surrounding streets; the present ample access is mostly modern.

The name comes from the landowners, who provided the site for St John's. In 1708 Hatton mentioned Smith Street (now Great Smith Street), 'so called from Sir James Smith the Ground Landlord, who has here a fine House'. The two names, Smith's Square and St John's Church Yard, existed side by side for a century and a half until they were both ousted by Smith Square; this despite the fact that the name 'Smith's Square' with the date '1726' had been there all along on the wall of No. 5. Lediard's 1739 map showed it as Smiths Square, with only two access roads, North Street and Church Street. In 1868 an attempt was made to change the name to St John's Square, but the Metropolitan Board of Works refused permission.

Apart from the two short terraces on the north side built in 1726 or thereabouts there were hardly any houses in the square until early in the nineteenth century, and it was only then that it began to achieve its present neat shape. In the eighteenth century the churchyard was much larger and extremely irregular, bounded to east and west by the back gardens of Mill Bank and Tufton Street, and to the south by those of Vine Street (the present Romney Street), which used to continue east to Mill Bank. In the north-west corner there was a large extension of the churchyard where John Street, now Gayfere Street, was slowly built in the second half of the eighteenth century, and not completed until the nineteenth. Church Street, now Dean Stanley Street, was a very short stub until it was extended towards the church late in the eighteenth century.

The problem with Smith Square was the south end, where the only exits were the narrow Little Tufton Street, some way south of the present Dean Trench Street, and the very narrow Church Passage in the south-west corner. When houses were built on the south side in the nineteenth century they were pierced by two archways leading to mews. These were eventually taken over by the carriers, Carter Paterson, because so few people here kept carriages. At the south-east corner there was an offshoot called Scott's Rents that surprised the Booth investigator in 1899: 'a picturesque corner; quaint, tiled cottages; very small; astonished to hear a piano in No. 8, but no information obtainable as to occupants. Rabbit hutches; hens. A queer corner to find within a quarter of a mile of the Houses of Parliament.' North of Little Tufton Street was the tall St John's Residential Chambers, a cheap lodging house that had 'helped to bring down the square'.

Beresford Chancellor wrote in 1907 that:

Smith Square today is a scene of desolation except for a few remaining Georgian houses with picturesque over-doorways and iron railings, for the whole of the south and west sides has been demolished, and where the houses stood are heaps of brick rubbish awaiting a final levelling, and probably the erection of the inevitable flats. On the east side are modern erections, a warehouse, and some apparently artisan dwellings.

St John's, Smith Square, from Dean Bradley Street, *c.* 1910.

The north side of Smith Square in 1926.

The result was not as bad as Chancellor anticipated. The old access roads and alleys on the west and south sides were abolished and the new Dean Trench Street and Dean Bradley Street gave the square its present regularity. The cheap lodging houses were swept away and the new buildings were some fine houses on the west side and offices of the 1920s elsewhere. Compton Mackenzie remembered Smith Square as 'emerging from slumdom' when he moved to (Lord) North Street in 1912.

Since then Smith Square has had some notable political residents. Mulberry House, No. 36, which was designed by Lutyens and built in 1911 for Reginald McKenna, was later occupied by Sir Edward Grey (Lord Grey of Falloden) and Henry Mond, Lord Melchett. Sir Oswald Mosley lived at No. 8 in the 1920s and 1930s, and Rab Butler at No. 3 from 1938. A plaque on the Lord North Street wall of No. 5 records the residence there of the journalist W.T. Stead from 1904 to 1912.

Smith Square suffered considerable bomb damage in the Second World War. St John's was burnt out and restored as a concert hall in the 1960s. Numbers 1 and 2 on the north side were destroyed, but have been replaced by houses in pastiche, much taller than the originals, and Nos 36 and 37, the distinguished houses on the west side, were badly damaged and restored to other uses. Most of the large offices in the square have been rebuilt since the war. The shrinking of the churchyard made St John's in the centre overpowering, but the removal of the offices of the political parties has had the happy effect of reducing the oppressive security.

Smith's Square

GREENWICH

Smith's Square was the last name for a place known in the 1850s as Three Tuns Square. The site was vacant on the 1838 map of Greenwich, and the 1841 census did not include it under either name. In 1851 only two houses were occupied, by a chaff cutter and hostler. It grew into a T-shaped court of ten or a dozen houses behind the Three Tuns in London Street, now the northern end of Greenwich High Road.

The square was off the south side of Smith's Buildings, a narrow extension of the inn yard that led eventually to Straightsmouth via Carr's Court. The area was cleared in the 1870s for the building of the railway line between Greenwich and Maze Hill stations that opened in 1878. The street pattern was severely disrupted: the Three Tuns just survived, but all the courts and alleys behind were swept away. The footbridge over the railway from Straightsmouth to Greenwich High Road passes more or less over the site of Smith's Square.

Soho Square

SOHO [WESTMINSTER]

Soho Square, which was licensed in 1676 and built from 1677, was known at first as Frith Square, after Richard Frith, the originator and chief builder, and then as King Square.

Controversy over whether this name referred to Charles II or the herald and statistician Gregory King has raged for centuries. In his autobiographical notes King claimed to have been involved in the planning of the square, but there is no independent confirmation of this. Modern opinion favours the case for King Charles, whose statue, now sadly battered, presides over the garden as an appropriate patron for Soho.

A fourth name was also current in 1693 when Colsoni, in his *Guide de Londres*, one of the earliest town guides, entreated his tourists to '*Souvenez vous sur tout d'aller voir la belle place de Soho, qui s'appelle aussi Kings Square & Monmouths Square, à cause qu'il y a dans le quarré la Statue de Charles Second, & le grande Maison de deffunt My Lord Monmouth, on appelle tout ce quartier là Soho*'. ('Above all be sure to visit Soho Square, which is also called King's Square and Monmouth's Square, as it contains the statue of Charles II and the great house of the late Lord Monmouth; the whole district is known as Soho.') It was just 'Soho' on Edward Hatton's map of 1707, and 'Kings (or Soho) square' in his text of 1708. As late as 1739 it was described as 'the stately quadrate denominated King's-square, but vulgarly Soho-square'. Vulgarity won the day, as usual.

The first house leases were granted in 1679, fourteen houses were occupied in 1683, twenty-three in 1685 and a full complement of forty-one in 1691. By that time Frith and most of the men involved with him in the development were bankrupt.

Soho Square was of the great house type, where all or most of one side is occupied by a single mansion, often the proprietor's. Nearly always the great house was set on the north, to enjoy the views to Hampstead and Highgate, but here the close proximity of Tyburn Road, with all its unpleasant associations, led the Duke of Monmouth to choose the south side.

Frith began work on the house at the beginning of 1682. The duke was one of the early residents of the square, in occupation of part of the unfinished Monmouth House by 1683 or early in 1684, but he left England in that year and only returned for his fatal rebellion. After his execution the empty and

Monmouth House on the south side of Soho Square in 1727.

Soho Square from the south in 1731.

unfinished house was left to decay for more than twenty years, while the duchess and various creditors argued over its fate.

The house was certainly unlucky: even when a buyer, Sir James Bateman, the Lord Mayor, was found in 1717, he died before the alterations he had ordered were finished. The work was completed in 1719 by his son, later the 1st Lord Bateman. These very extensive and dramatic changes have long been attributed to Thomas Archer on stylistic grounds, although there is no documentary evidence of his involvement. Monmouth House was occupied by the Batemans until the 1750s and by the French and Russian ambassadors in the 1760s. By then fashion had migrated west and the house had become so hard to let that it was demolished in 1773.

It might have been expected that the misfortunes of Monmouth House, blighting the south side, would have damaged the prospects of Soho Square, but it nevertheless managed to attract very fashionable residents in its early years and to maintain a reasonably good reputation for most of the eighteenth century. The most celebrated of the early settlers were the Whig leader Lord Wharton at No. 22 from 1683 to 1686, and Admiral Sir Cloudesley Shovell at No. 31 from 1705 until his death in 1707. The historian Gilbert Burnet, Bishop of Salisbury, lived at No. 26 for at least part of the period from 1703 to 1709.

In addition to the regular residents there were those like John Evelyn who took a house for the season. In November 1689 he noted, 'I went to London with my family to Winter at Sohò in the greate Square'. In addition to the French and Russians at Monmouth House, the Venetian, Spanish and Neapolitan ambassadors lived in the square at various times in the eighteenth century. The Soho Academy, the best private school in London, was at No. 1 from 1717 to 1725/26 and at No. 8 until 1805.

It is an indication of the continuing popularity of the square that many of the houses were rebuilt in the middle of the eighteenth century as the original leases expired. The big houses were mainly on the south side, flanking Monmouth House, and on the east. The most important there were No. 20 at the north end and Carlisle House, where St Patrick's Church and its presbytery are now. It was built for

Charles Howard, later 1st Earl of Carlisle. He was living there by 1685 and it remained the family's town house until 1753. It became the most celebrated pleasure resort in London between 1760 and 1772, when occupied by the opera singer and adventuress Teresa Cornelys, who attracted the whole town to her subscription assemblies, masquerades, balls and musical entertainments.

The Bach-Abel concerts were given there in 1765–68 and 1774, after which they moved to the Hanover Square Rooms. In 1764 the wife of James (*Hermes*) Harris told her son, 'If his Lordship has an inclination for a good concert, he may have one and twenty, at Mrs Cornely's, for five guineas; seven of Bach's, seven of Cocchi's, and seven of Abel's. We approve the place so much that both your father and I have subscribed.' In 1771 she reported sadly:

> The Harmonic is over, and, what is worse, they threaten hard to indict Mrs Cornelly's as a house of ill-fame, and say that forty beds are made and unmade every day, which is hard, for a friend of ours says it is never more than *twenty*; but (joking apart) if they choose to demolish Mrs Cornelly all elegance and spectacle will end in this town, for she never yet had her equal in those things, and I believe got but little, as all she undertakes is clever to a degree.

In 1773 the historian John Noorthouck was less indulgent than Mrs Harris. To him Carlisle House was where 'the nobility of this kingdom long protected Mrs Cornelys in entertaining their masquerade and gaming assemblies, in violation of the laws, and to the destruction of all sober principles'. Mrs Cornelys always lived on the edge, threatened by the theatre owners for her illegal opera performances and by the magistrates for those scandalous private rooms, but it was her creditors who brought her down in 1772. Carlisle House was used for other entertainments after her bankruptcy, but was demolished in 1791. One part of its function was continued at No. 21, on the north corner of Sutton Row, where Hooper's Hotel, known as the White House, was a notorious fashionable brothel during the last quarter of the eighteenth century.

From the time of Mrs Cornelys the square became more mixed, with a fair number of writers, artists and scientists among the country gentlemen, the bankers, and a dwindling number of aristocrats. Alderman William Beckford lived at No. 22 from 1751 to 1770, and his son William, the author of *Vathek*, was born there in 1759. Other literary figures were the dramatist George Colman, at No. 26 from 1776 to 1787; Richard Payne Knight, the antiquary, at No. 3 from 1808 to 1824; and Thomas Barnes, the editor of *The Times*, at No. 25 from 1836 (when he left Nelson Square) until his death in 1841. The John Cleland who lived at No. 32 from 1770 to 1772 was probably the author of *Fanny Hill*, enjoying a rare moment of prosperity. The soldier, novelist, playwright and eminent theatre architect Samuel Beazley lived in great style at No. 29 from 1826 until his death in 1851.

The square was still fashionable enough to be a good location for portrait painters. Allan Ramsay lived at No. 31 from 1761 until 1767. The house became almost a factory for the mass production of his royal portraits by a team of assistants. The most famous of the many nineteenth-century artists was Henry William Pickersgill, who lived at No. 18 from 1822 or earlier until the early 1850s. He later moved to Blandford Square, where he died in 1875.

The great scientist of Soho Square was Sir Joseph Banks, who used No. 32 as his home and research institute from 1777 to 1820. It became a centre of intellectual life in London and a great meeting place for European botanists. Sir Joseph's botanical collections were moved to the British Museum at Montague House in 1827–28. His house became the premises of the Linnean Society from 1822 until 1857. Second to Banks in fame was the surgeon and anatomist Sir Charles Bell, who lived at No. 34 from 1811 to 1831.

The commercialisation of the square in the nineteenth century was begun in grand style by Trotter's Soho Bazaar. John Trotter, who made a suspicious fortune as Storekeeper General during the Napoleonic Wars, had rebuilt Nos 4–6 in 1801–04 as warehouses. They were no longer needed after 1815 and were converted into 'the most celebrated Bazaar in the Metropolis, and the first of this kind, opened by Mr Trotter in 1815', as David Hughson recorded in 1817. This cross between a craft fair and a franchise department store survived until 1889.

The west side of Soho Square in 1813.

There were some twenty-five businesses by 1838, with manufacturers of pianos and harps striking the dominant note. Publishers and billiard table makers were later prominent, but much the biggest firm in the square was that of Crosse & Blackwell, 'Italian warehousemen', who came to monopolise the north-east corner. By the 1850s there were very few private residents.

Hospitals and other charities found homes in the square in the nineteenth century, together with two churches. St Patrick's on the east side was founded in 1791 in the assembly rooms built by Mrs Cornely's behind Carlisle House. The church later acquired the pair of 1790s houses that replaced Carlisle House. The present church, extending into the square over the site of one of them, was built in 1891–93. The second house was retained as the presbytery. Sir Aston Webb's French Protestant church on the north side was also built in 1891–93.

The square was invaded by film companies in the twentieth century. The GPO Film Unit at No. 21 was the most worthy, and Twentieth Century Fox at the massive Twentieth Century House in the south-west corner the most obtrusive.

The majority of the square's old houses were replaced by shops and offices, but the few that remained sheltered the last celebrities. The composer Benjamin Frankel, perhaps attracted by the film companies, lived at No. 17, and Rupert Hart-Davis had his flat and publishing house at No. 36.

The garden was laid out as early as 1680, when the leases began to stipulate an annual contribution to its upkeep, and it became the model copied sooner or later by all the West End squares. Cibber's statue of Charles II, which was introduced at an early date if not immediately, was far more impressive than the mutilated remains. It stood on a tall pedestal in a basin of water and was guarded by allegorical figures representing the Thames, Severn, Tyne and Humber. When the square ceased to be residential, attempts were made to open the garden in the 1870s and 1890s, but the Duke of Portland objected and the public had to wait until the twentieth century.

Soho Square is now a curious medley of architectural styles, most of them bad, but the battered remains of a few seventeenth-century and rather

The south-west corner of Soho Square, c. 1910.

more eighteenth-century houses survive to hint at the more seemly original appearance. Number 10 was built as two houses about 1680 and combined from 1696. Numbers 14, 15, 17 and 36 are probably of the late 1670s, but all altered to a greater or lesser extent. Numbers 2 and 38 were rebuilt in 1735, and No. 1 Greek Street between 1744 and 1754. It is the most distinguished house in the square, though not numbered in it. Number 26 was rebuilt between 1758 and 1761, No. 37 in 1766 (but now much altered), Nos 12 and 13 in 1768–69, and St Patrick's Presbytery (No. 21a) in 1791–93. Number 21, originally of the 1670s, was greatly altered or entirely rebuilt for Crosse & Blackwell between 1838 and 1840. Even the Hospital for Women retains the exterior outline of the two houses from which it was cobbled together. The nineteenth-century decline led to these survivors being converted to other uses rather than replaced by luxury flats, as happened in some of the more fashionable squares.

Somerset Square

STRAND [WESTMINSTER]

Somerset Square was a name sometimes used for the great quadrangle of Somerset House, as for example on the 1790 map of the parish of St Mary le Strand by William Simpkins.

South Audley Square

See Audley Square

South Square

GRAY'S INN, HOLBORN [CAMDEN]

Holborn Court, the most southerly of the quadrangles at Gray's Inn, was sometimes known as Holborn Square in the early nineteenth century, but had its name changed officially to South Square in 1829. This did not accompany any physical change; that had happened in the eighteenth century (see p.210), when the Elizabethan chambers were rebuilt gradually over several decades, after the society appointed Thomas and John Gorham as surveyors 'of the new buildings in Holborn Court'. They designed Nos 2 and 3, which were built in 1738. Number 4, designed in matching style by Henry Keene, was built in 1750, and No. 1 (the sole survivor) is dated 1759.

South Square was less regular than Gray's Inn Square, as it had the hall and chapel on the north side, the library on the east, and entrances to north and south. Although the chambers had numbers up to 14, the creation of offices and a common room and the enlargement of the library meant that eventually only ten sets remained in use.

There were always a few private residents among the mass of lawyers occupying the chambers, and also the odd artist, engraver, civil engineer or architect. The most eminent of the architects was George Frederick Bodley; he and his partner Thomas Garner had offices at No. 14 in the 1870s and 1880s before moving to the quieter Gray's Inn Square.

South Square was badly damaged during the Second World War, with only the south-west corner escaping entirely. Number 1 shows the style of the destroyed chambers. The rest were rebuilt by Sir Edward Maufe in the 1940s and 1950s. He also designed the new library on the east side and partly restored, partly rebuilt the damaged chapel and hall on the north side. The result is pleasant but entirely modern, like the quadrangle of a superior new university.

The east side of South Square in the 1920s.

Left and right of the entrance to Gray's Inn Square are two works by Raymond Erith, the common room and buttery. The bronze statue of Sir Francis Bacon at the east end of the garden is by F.W. Pomeroy, best known for his *Justice* with her shining sword at the Old Bailey.

Southwark Square

SOUTHWARK

Southwark Square, genuinely square and almost classical in design, was built as part of the Southwark Bridge and Bridge Street development between 1814 and 1819. It was largely residential with only the odd solicitor or house agent introducing a hint of trade, but its prosperity did not last long.

In 1841 the tenants were mainly clerks and there were servants in most of the houses, but it had become distinctly more working class ten years later. The north side and part of the west were lopped off by the creation of Southwark Street in 1862 and much of the south side a few years later by the South Eastern Railway viaduct carrying the line into Cannon Street. In 1872 the only houses standing were five or six on the west side. By 1894 they too had been swept away, the name was abolished, and an open yard occupied the site.

It is now the car park south of Southwark Street, with its entrance adjoining Lambert House.

Southwick Square

See Oxford Square

Spital Square

SPITALFIELDS [TOWER HAMLETS]

The ancestor of Spital Square was Spital Yard, which had been the cemetery of the St Mary Spital priory that stood here until the Dissolution. In the centre was the pulpit cross where the Spital sermons were preached at Easter. It was quite a small open space, no bigger than the garden of Staple Inn, and of a nearly square shape.

The Central Foundation School, Spital Square, *c.* 1910.

The Ogilby & Morgan map of 1676 showed few buildings abutting directly on it, and those looking more like stables than houses. On the west side was the garden of Spital House, a mansion belonging to the St John family, earls of Bolingbroke, and later to the Tillards.

It is curious that by the time Spital Square is first heard of the space was losing any approach to squareness. That was in 1716, when it was called 'the New Court or Square within the Spittle Gate'. By the 1740s it had become a mere crossroads, with arms running north, south, east and west. In fact it was the first instance in London – to be followed by so many others – where the name of 'square' was applied to a place with none of the distinctive attributes. The change was the result of the houses built here from the last years of the seventeenth century being arranged across the open space rather than around it. The western arm, which was the first, was built over the Spital House garden, leaving the mansion (perhaps rebuilt at that time) as the chief feature of its south side.

The square was begun while the St Johns were still the owners, perhaps as early as 1697, and the western arm was fully formed by 1711, but most of the houses were built after they sold the estate to Isaac Tillard in 1716. The northern and eastern arms were created in the 1720s and all the houses completed by 1739, mostly by William Goswell, a prominent local builder. The southern arm, which remained a cul-de-sac, was formed across part of the Spital House garden in the early 1740s. It had only one house, the large No. 33 on the west side, built between 1770 and 1773. The houses of the square were of high quality, up to the best West End standard of the period. They were intended for the wealthy Spitalfields silk manufacturers and merchants, who were their main occupants for the first century or more. Their privacy and quiet were protected by bollards at the three entrances, preventing through traffic, and by the services of a watchman.

There were a few celebrities. The Spital Square Academy at No. 3 was a well-respected school for much of the eighteenth century, run in succession by Samuel Watkins, John Canton and William Canton. John Canton was a noted scientist, a friend of Benjamin Franklin and one of the pioneers of electrical research. Parents might have been alarmed if they had learned the details of some of the experiments with lightning that he conducted at the school. Thomas Stothard, the painter and illustrator, served his apprenticeship from 1770 to 1777 in the house of a Spital Square silk weaver. John Wallen, an architect much employed in the City for warehouses and other commercial buildings, lived at No. 11 from the 1830s to the 1850s and had been in practice at No. 5 with his partner George Ferry as early as 1811.

The dignified seclusion of the square broke up late in the nineteenth century. The German synagogue was built in the 1880s on the site of Nos 10 and 11, at the crossroads, and the Central Foundation School for Girls replaced Spital House and No. 33 in 1890. The bollards maintaining the privacy of the square were removed in 1917 to ease traffic congestion at Spitalfields Market, and in the 1920s most of the houses were demolished for the extension of the market and the widening of the access from Bishopsgate.

Now No. 37, probably rebuilt about 1740 and occupied appropriately by the Society for the Protection of Ancient Buildings, is the only surviving house. A Victorian warehouse and part of the former school adjoin No. 37, but elsewhere a 1980s pastiche of an eighteenth-century house in the northern arm is the only relief from modern glass and steel.

The Square

BRENTFORD

See Ferry Square

The Square

CARSHALTON [SUTTON]

The small recess off the south side of the High Street that formed the original Square was ancient. It had a seventeenth or early eighteenth-century terrace on the east side and on the west a detached house that may have been of Tudor origin. The south side was formed by the gates of Carshalton Place and the north was open to the High Street.

The Orangery, The Square, Carshalton, in 2013.

The name, although probably applied casually and unofficially long before, did not come into regular use until late in the nineteenth century. The earliest example I have seen is Tatton Winter's painting, which the artist captioned 'The Square Carshalton 1884'. The local directory first used the name, as a subdivision of the High Street, in 1891 and did not give The Square a substantive entry until 1907. The census first included it in 1901. In the 1891 and earlier returns the cottages that later formed The Square were listed as part of the High Street.

The history of The Square hinges at 1900, when the Urban District Council made it the centre of the town's municipal life. The council acquired offices in a purely rural little yard, where its neighbours in 1901 were servants, a carpenter, a plumber and a bootmaker. The fire brigade had found temporary premises in The Square in 1899.

These moves coincided with the break-up of the Carshalton Place estate, which was about to be developed by the Carshalton Park Estate Company. The garden of the big house had occupied the land behind the square, blocking its growth, but now it was possible to extend it south as a mere suburban road. The eight semi-detached villas built on the west side of this extension over the next few years included three for the curates of All Saints' Church. The suburban respectability of the new section of The Square soon spread to the north end, which was widened, paved and adopted by the council in 1907–08. The old houses were swept away and the council built itself fine new offices and a new fire station in 1908, next to the slightly older All Saints' parish rooms. There was also a bank at the corner of the High Street. The east side of the extension was offered for sale as building land in 1907, but the typical suburban terrace that occupies it was built only in 1928.

Recently two detached houses have been built on the site of the parish rooms, and the former council offices, which were later used as the public library, have been converted into a children's nursery. The only reminders of the old square are two Carshalton Place outbuildings that formerly stood inside its gates: the luxurious Georgian stables, now converted into offices and called the Orangery, and Ivy Cottage, the much humbler coachman's house attached.

The Square

HAMPSTEAD

See Hampstead Square

The Square

HESTON [HOUNSLOW]

This was, like The Square at Carshalton, an occasional local name for a group of old houses set back from the main road. In this case the houses were of the eighteenth century or earlier and they occupied the east and south sides of a paved yard off Heston Road, opposite the Old George inn.

The form of the square and the style of the buildings suggested that it might have begun as a farmyard, but in the nineteenth century the large house on the south side became the grocery and post office run by the Paines family, and one of the cottages on the east side a bootmaker's shop. In 1891, the only time the census returns described the houses as 'The Square', a third was occupied by a farm labourer.

In the early 1920s the short section of Heston Road immediately to the north-west was widened and the post office was rebuilt as part of a new terrace of shops. That effectively destroyed The Square, but the east side, with the boot shop, survived rather longer. It was demolished before 1955, in preparation for the widening of the south-eastern end of Heston Road. The curious angle between the shops and houses opposite the Old George is a relic of the square.

The Square

RICHMOND [RICHMOND UPON THAMES]

The Square at Richmond is of the same nature as Battersea Square, an irregular opening at the meeting place of five roads, of the kind to be found in towns and villages all over the world, and long pre-dating the invention of the square as a sophisticated element in urban planning. The 1770 Richmond map labelled the spot 'late town pond'. It had acquired the name

The south side of The Square, Richmond, in 2011.

of The Square by 1813, when it appeared several times in the parish registers. They did not include addresses before that year.

The Square was entirely commercial from an early date. In 1855, in addition to numerous shops and several schools, it included the Rose & Crown public house and the office of the Richmond Omnibus Conveyance Company. The south side still features some of the original modest cottages converted into shops. The north side is dominated by two former public buildings: a mechanics' institute of 1843 that was later expanded as a swimming pool and baths and acquired a dome early in the twentieth century, and an 1870 fire station with a clock tower.

The Square

TURNHAM GREEN

See Pack Horse Square

The central portion of Lancaster Gate, formerly The Square, Upper Hyde Park Gardens, c. 1920.

The Square

UPPER HYDE PARK GARDENS,
BAYSWATER [WESTMINSTER]

The Square was the name given to the central portion of Upper Hyde Park Gardens, now Lancaster Gate, when its houses were begun in 1858–59. Most of the open space in the centre was occupied by Christ Church, which had been built in 1854–55. The southern third was a small, square, formal garden.

In 1861 East India merchants, barristers and fashionable doctors were the tenants of the eight occupied houses. Six more were being built or were in the hands of caretakers. The full circuit of about thirty houses, which Bridget Cherry attributes to John Johnson, was completed in 1865. The Square

had then become Lancaster Gate, although the great terraces to the south continued to be known as Upper Hyde Park Gardens for a little longer. By 1869 the whole complex had adopted the new name.

The houses of the former square all survive, but only the tower and spire of Christ Church. The rest has been replaced by Spire House, a nightmare concrete parody of Gothic built in 1983.

The Square

WOODFORD GREEN
[REDBRIDGE AND WALTHAM FOREST]

Small open spaces of this kind were common in loosely planned villages, built when land was less valuable than it is today. In Woodford Green itself, there are openings as big or bigger in Savill Row and Mill Lane, to the south and west of the Square. Although it must have existed from the early nineteenth century, The Square was not so called, officially at least, until the 1870s. In 1882 it was occupied by a carpenter and joiner, a grocer, a shoemaker, a corn dealer, a tailor and by the George & Dragon Temperance Hotel.

It was originally three-sided, the south being formed by Mill Lane, and is now effectively reduced to two, as the four houses of the west side (in Waltham Forest) have been replaced by modern council flats set back behind a lawn. There are four houses of interest, the early nineteenth-century brick pair, Nos 1 and 3, on the east side, and the weather-boarded pair, Nos 12 and 14, probably not much older, on the north. There is also an early Victorian shop on the south-east corner, numbered in Mill Lane. All these are in Redbridge. The open space, just a wide section of road, is now largely devoted to parking.

The Square, Woodford Green, from the south, in 2013.

Stanhope Square

See Cambridge Square, Hyde Park
Square and Oxford Square

Stanton Square

SYDENHAM [LEWISHAM]

Stanton Square was built in the 1870s on a small field next to the original gas holders of the Crystal Palace District Gas Company at Bell Green. The seemingly eccentric decision to build a square on a spot where fashion or smartness could never be hoped for was dictated by the shape of the field. It had a narrow entrance from Bell Green Lane giving access to an almost square plot of land tucked behind the Bell public house and its neighbouring shops in the curving section of Southend Lane. As a result, the working people who lived here – many of them labourers from the gasworks – enjoyed one of the most classically planned squares in London. There was a single entrance at the south-west corner, unbroken

ranges of uniform houses on all four sides, and a well-planted garden in the centre. What is more, it was nearly square, the east and west sides being only a little longer than the others and the south side set at a slight angle for the convenience of the approach road.

Fifty small and plain two-storey and two-bay houses were squeezed into the square and its approach. Most were in terraces, but at the three corners away from the entrance a semi-detached pair was fitted in, set back from the terraces. All the houses had tiny front and back gardens in addition to the use of the communal garden in the centre. At an early stage the square lost its unwelcome neighbours, the gas holders, as the company concentrated production at its larger site north of Southend Lane, but the works there were not much further away and they got larger and noisier and more polluting as the decades passed.

Stanton Square came through the Second World War, during which gasworks were an obvious target, with hardly any damage. The houses were still in quite good condition in the 1970s, when Lewisham Council decided to demolish them all and establish

Stanton Square and environs, *c.* 1925.

the Stanton Square Industrial Estate there. A new road called Stanton Way was cut through the site, but industry is now almost as much forgotten as the square.

Stepney Square

This stubby extension of Stepney High Street north of what is now Ben Jonson Road developed gradually into a square during the eighteenth century. Newcourt's map showed no opening there in 1658. It could possibly have been the 'Dunstan's Square, in Whitechapel' that William Stow included in his 1722 list, being close to St Dunstan's but far from Whitechapel. In the 1740s Rocque showed only what appeared to be a single large house on the west side of an unnamed open space. From later evidence of maps and photographs we know that this was two houses, one facing east onto the square, the other facing south. They survived in industrial use until 1943, when they were known collectively as the Manor House.

By the 1790s three houses had been built on the east side of what was by then called Stepney Old Square. This was because Stepney New Square was being built just to the north. When that became Trafalgar Square in 1809 – it is now Trafalgar Gardens – the 'Old' was gradually dropped.

Three houses on the east side and one or two on the west was as much as Stepney Square achieved. The south was the entrance, open to Ben Jonson Road and the High Street, and nothing was ever built at the north end. The houses remained residential until the 1880s, when they began to be converted into factories and workshops. By 1914 the only remaining house on the east side was a Catholic school, the other two having been replaced by a cinema. All were destroyed during the Second World War and Stepney Green School was extended over the site in the early 1960s, extinguishing the square.

Stepney New Square

See Trafalgar Square

Stewarts Square

The 1841 census included Stewarts Buildings, Alley and Square, Devons Lane, but in 1851 and later, only Stewarts Buildings appeared, listed in Back Alley, the footpath from Mile End to Bow. In 1841, 'The Square', with numbers from 1 to 20, was the chief feature of Stewart's Buildings. In 1861 Stewarts Buildings had three sets of numbers, 1–4, 1–7 and 1–20, the alley and square having been absorbed.

The complex was built between 1800 and 1813 off the north side of Back Alley, close to its junction with Bromley High Street. The name evidently came from the proprietor: a Robert Stewart, 'independent', lived in Stewart's Buildings (not the Square) in 1841.

Immediately to the west of Stewarts Square were the Drapers' Almshouses of 1706, of which the central block miraculously survives south of Rainhill Way. The square was about half the size of the almshouses, but equally formal in its layout, with a well-planted rectangular garden and terraces on the long east and west sides. On the old maps it appears a pleasant backwater, but the Booth survey gave a dismal report in 1897: 'On the West side where the High Street joins the Devons Road, Back Alley & Stewarts Buildings, both should be black [vicious, semi-criminal], notorious brothels, & have been so for years. Here it was that Barrett who stole the silver ingots from the London & North Western Railway hid.'

Despite its reputation, Stewart's Buildings survived for a surprisingly long time. It was replaced in 1932 by the St Agnes Roman Catholic Primary School, which also cut off Back Lane from Bromley High Street.

Sun Square

Sun Square was included by Lockie in his 1810 list of streets and located more precisely in the 1813 edition as being in 'Sun Street – at 18, 1st on the left from 149 Bishopsgate-without'. It was squeezed into the very narrow strip of land between Sun Street and Dunnings Alley in the first decade of the nineteenth century. Harben, who placed it on the wrong side of Sun Street in his *Dictionary of London*, found no earlier reference than 1810.

In 1841 the three houses listed were occupied by respectable sounding ironmongers, plus a clerk and a cane dealer, but by 1851 there were seven houses shared by twenty-four families. Most of the inhabitants then and later were very poor and not very honest.

The square was demolished in the early 1870s, when extensive clearances were made west of Bishopsgate in preparation for the building of Liverpool Street Station.

Surrey Square

Surrey Square was a short-lived court of five or six houses between China Square and the Methodist chapel in Lambeth Road, now rebuilt as the Lambeth Methodist Mission. The ground was part of the garden of Surrey Villa, the large house at the corner of Kennington Road and Lambeth Road. When that became derelict in the 1880s its outbuildings were converted into, or replaced by, the houses of the square. They must have been of a reasonable standard, as the tenants in 1891 included a mining engineer and a shipping foreman, alongside a carpenter and a bricklayer. The improvised square was snuffed out when the Lambeth Vestry built its public baths on the site of Surrey Villa and some neighbouring houses in the late 1890s. The baths were destroyed in the Second World War and tall flats are now on the site.

Surrey Square

Surrey Villas, just off the south-east side of Nunhead Green, was perhaps intended to complement Linden Grove to the south, a spacious road lined with large detached houses. The area failed to develop into the quality middle-class suburb hoped for, and few houses appeared in Surrey Villas.

Around 1860 eight cottages, without gardens or even back yards, but arranged around a small communal garden or court, were built on the south side of Surrey Villas, at the Nunhead Green end. The site may originally have been set aside for mews or a livery stable. They were known at first as Surrey Cottages, a name later transferred to a road opposite, but were Surrey Square by 1870.

The ratebook for that year, when the cottages had the modest rateable value of £7–10, indicated that the owner was named Ellis. In 1871 the tenants were labourers, a carman and (this being close to Nunhead Cemetery) a grave digger and a stone mason's assistant. The building of this actual or potential slum was a first indication of the abandonment of high ambitions for Surrey Villas, which was given the more modest name of Banstead Street in the 1880s.

Surrey Square lasted for little more than thirty years and was in decline throughout. In 1881 only three of the cottages were occupied and in 1891 only No. 2, by a clothes mangler. The 1894 map showed the square extinguished and small terraced houses on the site.

Surrey Square

In so unpromising a location, Surrey Square comes as a pleasant surprise. It was built on land belonging to the Driver family. 'Drivers Seed Shop' was shown on a 1795 map at the corner of the present Old Kent Road and East Street, and Surrey Place was the terrace in Old Kent Road to the south of it.

Michael Searles, the talented surveyor to the neighbouring Rolls estate, began Surrey Square with his usual high hopes in 1793–94, by designing the north terrace, a grand palace front of twenty-nine houses. If the rest of the very large square, which was bigger than Lincoln's Inn Fields, had been completed in the same style it would have been one of the finest in London, but there the project stalled. Before the death of Searles in 1813 three detached villas (long vanished) were built on the short east and west sides. The big house that filled the whole of the east side was occupied by the owner, William Driver. By 1830 semi-detached houses had been built along the south side, which had acquired the separate name of Surrey Grove, and the garden had been laid out and planted.

Number 46 Surrey Square, Old Kent Road, in 2011.

Thus Surrey Square remained, like a sleeping beauty, while slums crowded round the palace on all sides, until it was rudely awoken in 1864 by the laying of the foundation stone of All Saints' Church in the garden, directly opposite the cobwebbed north terrace. The building of the church in 1865 opened the way for disintegration.

Aldbridge Street was laid out to the south, across the centre of the garden, which thus ceased to exist,

the three villas were demolished and Surrey Grove lost all connection with the square. The Surrey Arms (now No. 5 and closed) was rebuilt in florid style in the approach from the Old Kent Road, and mean terraces filled the remainder of the garden on either side of the church. In 1884 the west end of the north terrace was pulled down to build the Surrey Square School, leaving the eighteen Searles houses that survive today as the only fragment of a broken dream.

There was a good deal of bomb damage to the square during the Second World War, luckily not affecting the Searles terrace too severely. The church and much of the south side were destroyed. All Saints' was rebuilt in 1959; it is now the Church of the Lord. The rest was cleared and replaced partly by a council estate, partly by Surrey Square Park, thus restoring a fragment of the old garden.

The square's most famous son is Samuel Palmer, the artist, who was born at the present No. 42 (where there is a plaque) in 1805 and remained until 1818, when his mother died. Although the family then moved north of the river, Palmer remained a south Londoner at heart, with Dulwich and the country beyond as his rural ideal. Number 1 was the birthplace in 1808 of a very distinguished civil engineer, William Lindley. He is hardly known in his own country because nearly all his work was done abroad and especially in Hamburg, a city he largely rebuilt between 1840 and 1860. The demolished No. 31 was the home in the 1880s of the architect and professional (perhaps fantasist) Scot, Charles Niven McIntyre North.

The scene in Surrey Square today illustrates the survival of Disraeli's two nations. From the elegant houses of the raised north terrace families of well-behaved children are packed into expensive cars and whisked away to their private schools, while from the council estate on the south side gangs of dangerous-looking youths slouch towards the Old Kent Road. It is a thoroughly traditional English arrangement, far removed from the alien concept of the gated estate. Here the rich and poor live face to face in intimate incomprehension.

Sussex Square

Sussex Square would not look out of place in Surbiton or Woking, but here in the heart of grandiloquent Bayswater it is surreal to turn a corner and step suddenly into this displaced fragment of suburbia. The mature beauty of the garden only adds to the sense of confusion. Is it a fragment of the Green Belt?

The east side of Sussex Square, *c.* 1904.

As with several of the Bayswater squares, there was indecision about the name. In 1834 Bathurst Square was thought of, in honour of Lord Bathurst, one of the best but least remembered ministers in the Liverpool cabinet, who died in that year. The delay in getting the development started was fatal to his chances, except for the consolation prize of the little Bathurst Street. By the time the houses were built he was forgotten and the Whiggish Duke of Sussex was honoured instead.

Sussex Square was begun in the early 1840s, No. 1 being the only house included in the 1841 ratebook. All but the west end of the north side was shown on Lucas's 1842 Paddington map, but only six houses were listed as occupied in the 1843 directory and seventeen in the 1845 rate. The full complement of thirty was completed in 1848. Nothing of that period survives.

From the 1930s, as the original leases fell in, the short-sighted Ecclesiastical Commissioners engaged in piecemeal rebuilding on their Bayswater estate. Sussex Square was the most thoroughgoing expression of this policy, and how deplorable the results are! Every original house was replaced in the late 1950s and early 1960s by bland terraces, or by blocks of flats scarcely better than the municipal standard of the period.

This is one of the few genuinely square squares of London, something that enabled the designer to indulge in a circular garden. It had houses only on the north, east and west sides, as the south was occupied by the very dull rear elevation of Hyde Park Gardens. Now the north side is also excluded from the numbering of the square, the Clifton Place name having been extended west to annex it. The original houses were big, three bays wide and alternating between four and five storeys plus basement, the taller houses being set forward.

The leading residents were the usual Bayswater mix of baronets, politicians and generals. In 1898 the Booth survey noted 'Jews coming in'. Few peers were attracted north of the park, but there was an exception in 1924 when the future 8th Earl Spencer, father of Diana, Princess of Wales, was born at No. 24. That was the year in which his distant relation Winston Churchill left the old No. 2, where he had lived since 1920. The present No. 3 has a Churchill plaque recording the association.

Sutherland Square

As originally built in the 1840s and 1850s, Sutherland Square was the egg with two yolks, a single entity with two tiny gardens, each with its own frame of houses. This very rare distinction, this suburban presumption indeed, was soon put a stop to by the London, Chatham & Dover Railway, which smashed its viaduct through the eastern garden in 1861. As a result, the pretty houses of its east side, which alone survived the outrage, have ever since had a gloomy and restricted brick outlook, though it has been softened by some trees and shrubs planted next to the viaduct. They were known separately as Sutherland Square East until unity was restored in 1868.

The western garden and its houses were not directly affected by the railway and have even benefitted from the barrier that the viaduct has placed between the square and the raucous Walworth Road. The schools built for St Paul's Lorrimore Square on a part of the cleared site not required for the railway were destroyed during the Second World War. Their '1871' date stone has been reset in the terrace now on the site.

The square had been begun between 1841 and 1845 in an area of precarious countryside, dotted with tea gardens and other delights, long a favourite haunt

The east side of the western section of Sutherland Square in 2013.

of Cockneys on the razzle. They continued to be troublesome even after the square was begun. One at least of the gardens must have been laid out by 1846, for in June of that year (in a case designed to show that nothing changes) three lads were convicted of stealing the iron heads from the railings and selling them to the local scrap metal dealer – marine store dealer then – for fourpence:

> I was playing with these boys in the field on the 28th May. Jones took up a stone and happened to hit one of the knobs of the rails, and it came off – then he, Hobden, and all of them threw at them, and knocked nine more of the knobs off. Jones picked them up and said 'Let us go and sell them.'

The iron belonged to Henry Groom and was 'fixed to a certain garden of his'. A newspaper report added, 'The property consisted of the ornamental tops of the iron railings placed round Sutherland-square, Walworth-road, and which the boys were enabled to break off from their being cast-iron; and the quantity removed has much disfigured the appearance of the railings'. The magistrate drew a very modern moral about working parents and children running wild.

The Booth survey painted an interesting picture of Sutherland Square in 1899:

> Talleymen, very few servants. Berstein the sarsparilla seller lives in corner house, 'sells himself all over London, and owns a tidy list of house property.' Next to him is a retired provision merchant who keeps a carriage, but the majority of inhabitants don't keep servants. Tie factory employing 50 girls on south side.

Henry Berenstein, 'herbalist', lived at No. 34, his neighbour with the carriage at the detached No. 35. The tie factory was in Sutherland Place, now Macleod Street.

Maimed as it is, Sutherland Square still comes as a pleasant surprise. I was searching for Lorrimore Square – which barely repays the trouble of finding – when I stumbled upon its close neighbour quite by chance. The garden, which Southwark Council bought for the princely sum of £75 and

opened in 1922, is a charming miniature. From here the regrettable council flats that replaced some bombed houses on the north side are almost hidden. Fortunately they lie in the less conspicuous section of the square that linked the surviving with the lost garden.

Swedenborg Square

See Prince's Square, Ratcliff Highway

Sweet Apple Square

SHOREDITCH [TOWER HAMLETS]

Sweet Apple Square was known alternatively as Sweetapple Court, a more appropriate name as it was merely a long, narrow cul-de-sac leading north through an archway from the junction of the present Austin Street and Virginia Road. The name is supposed to come from Joseph Sweetapple, who lived nearby in 1770. It is not as uncommon as one might suppose: there was an earlier Sweetapple Court in Bishopsgate, named after an alderman.

The square had been built by 1775. Hector Gavin described it in 1848, under the name of Sweet-Apple Court, as part of his sanitary ramblings amid the Bethnal Green slums:

> The gutter in the centre of this court was very filthy; garbage was strewn about, the privies were quite full and dilapidated. Each house has water supplied to it, but by a cock let through the wall; and as the house is parcelled out, whenever the person who inhabits the first floor is from home, and the door therefore locked, no one can procure water. This may happen when the water is on, and a great difficulty in obtaining it may thence arise. From the dripping of the water-pipe the place had become damp, and on opening the door, a horrid odour of nastiness, like putrid paste, was found to pervade the room.

But somehow Sweet Apple Square survived the clearances that replaced most of the old Bethnal Green slums with new ones. There were sixteen houses at first, but they were reduced to eight when the west side was demolished to accommodate the Mildmay Mission Hospital when it was moved here in 1890. The east side houses must have been rebuilt then or earlier if the Charles Booth investigator was any judge of architecture, for he described them in 1898 (again under the name of Sweet Apple Court) as '8 houses, 2 storeys, cement pavement, houses new, rather poor and some rough'.

The southern half of the surviving side was destroyed during the Second World War and the whole area to the east of the hospital was soon covered by the flats known as Wingfield House. The line of the square still persists as the footpath off the north side of Virginia Road, nearly opposite Hocker Street.

Sydney Square

PECKHAM [SOUTHWARK]

Sydney Square was a range of tenements of the model dwellings kind built on the south side of Latona Road around 1880. It was close to the much larger and older Leyton Square and just south of the Surrey Canal.

The land had been used for market gardening until development began in the 1870s. The Booth survey of 1899 found 'several blocks of buildings let in sets of from 2 to 4 rooms; quiet'.

The quiet was shattered on 8 June 1944 by a flying bomb that exploded in Unwin Road just to the south, causing widespread destruction. The surviving blocks were cleared and redeveloped around 1960, but little has changed except that the tenements are now of the flimsier post-war variety.

Tabernacle Square

OLD STREET [HACKNEY]

The name came from Whitefield's Tabernacle, the hastily built and temporary first church of his branch of the Methodists after his breach with Wesley. It was built in 1741 on the west side of Windmill Hill, now Tabernacle Street. The square did not emerge until about fifty years later.

'Emerge' is the correct word, as it was only the casual open space left when three roads met awkwardly as they approached the south side of Old Street. Horwood's 1790s map shows it just beginning to take anonymous shape. He still marked most of it as rough open ground, although the name was in use by 1794. The 1813 revision of Horwood gave it the wrong name, from a very easy confusion with the similar Leonard Square just to the south. John Lockie had got it right in 1810: 'Tabernacle-Square, Old-Street-Road, – the N. end of Paul-st. from Finsbury-square'.

The twenty or more original houses (a number that dwindled over the decades) were mostly commercial from the first, but the odd surgeon continued to live there throughout the nineteenth century. The creation of Great Eastern Street in the 1870s opened up the north side, but apart from that the shape of the square has not changed much in over 200 years. The buildings have changed a good deal and are now mostly Victorian.

The name was abolished late in the nineteenth century, but proved hard to eradicate. It is still very much a distinct place, dignified since 1880 by a granite column and drinking fountain erected by the Shoreditch Vestry.

Tabernacle Square from the south-west in 2007.

Talbot Square

This was the last and least of the squares of Tyburnia. Its site was the Lower Reservoir of the Grand Junction Waterworks Company, which was filled in during the 1840s. The stucco houses are of the standard first-rate Bayswater type, five storeys plus basement, with balustraded porches and balconies.

Number 1 was occupied in 1855, but most of the twenty-six houses were built in 1858. It is a three-sided square, open at the south end to the wide Sussex Gardens. In the early development of Bayswater the area north of Sussex Gardens was of lower standing than that to the south because of the canal. The superior houses of Talbot Square and Norfolk Square (begun a year or two earlier on the site of the South Reservoir) drove the tide of fashion a little further north.

Talbot Square was solidly middle class until the First World War, after which houses began to be divided into flats. A large notice at the entrance declared, 'No barrel organs, street criers, or itinerant musicians are allowed in this square'.

The most notable house was No. 10, which had a double Churchill connection. His brother Jack lived there from 1910 to 1913, followed by his cousin Shane Leslie, the Irish nationalist and miscellaneous writer, who remained until 1918.

During the Second World War there was serious damage to the north-west corner and less serious to the rest of the north side. A large hotel replaced these houses and the building is now the University of London's Lilian Penson hall of residence. It is of the same height and colour as the rest of the square, but not otherwise a good match.

The narrow, rectangular garden was private until 1996. Westminster Council improved it in 2008–09, with new railings, gates, and an arch at the south entrance. A curious feature of the square was its numbering, with the odds of the west side and the evens of the east meeting in the middle of the short north side, but this has been lost in the rebuilding.

The west side of Talbot Square, *c.* 1904.

Tavistock Square

Like Russell Square, Tavistock Square has a prehistory. The east side was an extension of Southampton Row and was built before the rest, rather as a completion of James Burton's Foundling Hospital development than as part of the great Bedford plan. The square's most famous building, Burton's own Tavistock House, faced north to enjoy a view of Highgate and Hampstead and only became part of the square when the road in front of it failed to develop into a direct link with Burton Crescent.

Even before Tavistock House and the east side of the square were built there was a similar detached villa just north of Tavistock Place, but facing Southampton Row, of which it was originally a part.

It was later No. 37 Tavistock Place and the home of Francis Baily, President of the Royal Astronomical Society. The villa was replaced by the Tavistock Square Settlement (Mary Ward House) in the 1890s.

The east side of the square was built by James Burton, probably to his own design, between 1800 and 1806, and in 1807 the author of *The Picture of London* wrote that 'Russell and Tavistock-squares, when finished, will be capital additions to the metropolis'. 'When finished' was the rub, for in the difficult economic conditions of the war Burton and the Bedford estate found they had overstocked the market for such large houses. The completion of Tavistock Square had to wait until the boom of the early 1820s, when the new star, Thomas Cubitt, built the south side in 1821–22 and the north and west sides in 1824–27. The clients for the houses on the west side brought in Lewis Vulliamy to improve Cubitt's design.

Tavistock House, Tavistock Square, *c.* 1900. The five central bays were the original villa, the wing on the right the Dickens house.

The southern end of the west side of Tavistock Square, *c.* 1905.

Tavistock Square from the south-east corner, *c.* 1905.

Like the other expensive parts of Bloomsbury, Tavistock Square suffered in the 1820s and later from the competition of Cubitt's more fashionable developments in Belgravia. As a result there were as many doctors as gentlemen among the early tenants, a prefiguring of the square's future, and a good many Jewish names. The Booth surveyor noted in 1898 that there 'used to be many Jews here, but they are leaving – going to Hampstead'.

The famous residents were mostly at Tavistock House. Burton was followed by James Perry, editor of *The Morning Chronicle*, who was a friend of Sir Thomas Lawrence of Russell Square. After Tavistock House was enlarged and divided into three, the part closest to the square (which retained the name) was the home of Charles Dickens from 1851 to 1860. A theatre erected in the garden was used by his famous private company.

Georgina Weldon, the indefatigable litigant, ran her strange orphanage at Tavistock House from 1869, and having drawn Charles Gounod into her toils, kept him a virtual prisoner there from 1871 to 1874, when his wife came from France to rescue him.

Celebrities in the houses of the square itself have included the great singer John Braham, who was at No. 3 from 1816 to 1821; Virginia and Leonard Woolf at No. 52 from 1924 to 1939, with the Hogarth Press in the basement; and Anthony Powell in a flat at No. 33 from 1929 to 1932.

Tavistock Square was one of the best on the Bedford estate, all four sides being the work of good architects and builders, and of good dates. Like most of the others it suffered a sad decline in the twentieth century. The three parts of Tavistock House were the first casualties. They were demolished in 1901 and after a long delay replaced by what Lutyens intended as the headquarters of the British Theosophical Society, but which was eventually finished for the British Medical Association.

The east side of the square was demolished in 1938 for an extension to the BMA, begun in that year, and for offices and flats to the south of it. The remaining houses were all damaged in the Second World War. The south side, with the Hogarth Press, was replaced by an enlarged Tavistock Hotel, the north by blocks of flats. That left just Vulliamy's west side, which would

no doubt have been demolished by the University of London but for the controversy over the wanton destruction in Woburn Square. Instead it has been restored as offices and a hall of residence.

The popular public garden is full of memorials, the most notable being Fredda Brilliant's Gandhi statue, erected in the centre in 1968. Most of the London squares saw the last of the bombs in 1945, but here there was the sad epilogue of the bus bomb of 7 July 2005, which killed thirteen passengers and passers-by.

Tedworth Square

CHELSEA [KENSINGTON AND CHELSEA]

Tedworth Square and the contemporary Cadogan Square were the last two in London of real quality. Tedworth Square was built on the site of a nursery in the late 1870s and early 1880s. It was in two quite different styles representing those two decades, although the modern rebuilding of the north side has confused the picture. That was laid out first as part of the present Redesdale Road, before there was any thought of a square. It continued to be numbered as part of the road and in the directories was tossed back and forth between road and square.

The surviving parts of Redesdale Road and the west side of the square display all the porches and pillars, the balustrades, pediments and architraves of Paddington or South Kensington, and the north side was originally the same. Two of the houses on the west side were included in the 1880 directory, No. 37 occupied by the builder, Henry John Wright. The south side was begun in that year with Nos 25–31, with 21 and 23 added in 1881. The south side and east side (built in the mid-1880s) feature the horrible, glaring red brick that looks almost like terracotta. For some reason this style rather than that of the demolished houses, was the inspiration for the new flats of the north side when it was rebuilt in the late 1970s, so from being half-and-half, Tedworth Square is now one-quarter South Kensington and three-quarters Pont Street.

It was never so fashionable as Cadogan Square: barrister and solicitor were the most common occupations in the early years. Beresford Chancellor wrote in

1907 that 'it has no history, and beyond being a square, no particular interest', but Tedworth Square has not been without celebrities. A notable resident at No. 19 from 1920 until her death in 1936 was the Marchioness of Dufferin and Ava, perhaps the most widely travelled diplomatic wife of the nineteenth century, as the marquis was Governor of Canada, Viceroy of India, and ambassador to Russia, Turkey, Italy and France. She published lively accounts of her experiences. Sir Edward Thornton, who succeeded Lord Dufferin in his Russian and Turkish embassies, lived at No. 5 after his retirement, and died there in 1906.

Lillie Langtry lived at No. 15 from 1900 to 1904 – she was 'Emily de Bathe, actress', in 1901 – and Mrs Patrick Campbell, a much more serious actress, was at No. 15 from 1919 to 1921, moving from the more expensive Kensington Square. After Tedworth Square, her next London home was in a mews – 'this horse's house', as she called it.

The most famous men associated with the square were visitors rather than householders. Mark Twain rented No. 23 in 1896–97, a residence commemorated by a plaque, and Edward Elgar borrowed No. 3, the home of his friend Basil Nevinson, in 1899.

Tedworth Square was smarter in the early twentieth century than in the nineteenth, but like nearly all of London became shabby after the Second World War. The low point in its history came in the 1970s, when the council permitted the demolition of the dilapidated houses of the north side. Since their rebuilding as luxury flats the square has participated in the irresistible rise of Chelsea.

Theberton Square

See Gibson Square

Thessaly Square

BATTERSEA [WANDSWORTH]

Like Cheriton Square at Balham, this was not a true square at all but a crescent off New Road (which later became Thessaly Road) with houses on the inner and outer sides. It was built on the south-western perimeter of the Nine Elms railway yards in the late 1880s, unpromisingly on the site of a chemical works, but it was found to be quite salubrious by the Booth survey in 1899.

The south side of Tedworth Square, *c.* 1905.

Not surprisingly, given its position in the middle of the great tangle of Battersea locomotive works and marshalling yards, it was damaged during the Second World War, but the death blow was the decision in the 1960s to move the Covent Garden market to Nine Elms. The square was demolished to enlarge the market and its site is now usually buried beneath a mountain of pallets.

Thorburn Square

BERMONDSEY [SOUTHWARK]

The plans for Thorburn Square and its satellite streets were put forward in 1868 by the Bermondsey-born architect, Alfred Porter. He was perhaps also responsible for St Anne's Church, which was built in 1869–72 on land formerly used for market gardening. It occupied the whole centre of the square. The church has usually been attributed to an otherwise unknown 'J. Porter'.

St Anne's, Thorburn Square, in 1909 or a little earlier.

The 1871 map showed it standing all alone in a field, with roads converging on it north, south, east and west. The surrounding houses were added during the 1870s.

A fascinating feature copied from Belgrave Square was the placing of detached houses with large gardens at the corners. Thorburn Square even improved on its model by giving them plots of the same size, although the likeness to Belgrave Square was restored when the north-eastern house's garden was cut up by the building of the Monnow Road School. These houses had individual names like Thorburn Villa and West Villa, and the one at the north-western corner was St Anne's Vicarage. They were tall and distinctly Gothic, with gables. In a poor district, between Grange Road and the Old Kent Road, this was an island of relative prosperity, with a few houses still employing servants to the end of the nineteenth century.

The square suffered minor blast damage during the Second World War but the houses were in good condition when they were demolished in the 1960s. Their replacements are three-storey flats with balconies that respect the shape and scale of the square and do not overwhelm the restored St Anne's, but there are, alas, no villas at the corners.

The slightly earlier and well-preserved Longley Street to the north was part of the same development, but the houses in the square were larger and in a different style. From Longley Street the new square is approached dramatically via an arch that gives a glimpse of the church.

Thornhill Square

BARNSBURY [ISLINGTON]

The large and ambitious Thornhill Square, which with Thornhill Crescent has the shape of an elongated egg, was built between 1847 and 1852 on the estate of George Thornhill, MP for Huntingdonshire. His surveyor was Joseph Kay of the Foundling Hospital. Kay died in December 1847, but no doubt had time to formally approve the plans for the first houses, which set the style for the rest.

The architect of Mecklenburgh Square could not have approved them wholeheartedly. The houses verge towards the Italianate and individually are

The public library in Thornhill Square, Barnsbury, *c.* 1908. (Photograph courtesy of Maurice Friedman)

The south-eastern curve of Thornhill Square, Barnsbury, *c.* 1910.

rather heavy and over-decorated, but seen across the wide garden and in the mass – and there are nearly 100 of them – they are effective. They benefit further from the sloping site and the gentle curve, which brings the mature trees into all perspectives.

The large enclosure of the square proper became a private garden for the residents. The interior of Thornhill Crescent was reserved for St Andrew's Church, which was built in 1852–54, the architects being Francis Newman and John Johnson. It comes as a shock in the centre of this classical piece of town planning to find it an example of thorough-going Gothic of which Joseph Kay would not have approved at all. St Mary-in-the-Castle at Hastings was his idea of a church.

The square was very respectable but did not attract famous residents. One minor celebrity was John George Edgar, who died at No. 30 in 1864, aged only 36. In his short life he managed to write a great many popular stories for boys, mostly set in the Middle Ages. *Cressy and Poitiers*, his most famous work, was serialised during his lifetime but not published in book form until 1865. It was once to be found in every second-hand bookshop.

The square was declining by the end of the century, with a few boarding houses springing up. The Booth survey of 1897 urged the vestry to open the garden 'as a playground for the Gifford Street district', but it still belonged to the Thornhill family. The new Islington Council which replaced the vestry in 1900, did begin to make the square more public when it demolished two houses as the site for a public library, built at the corner of Bridgeman Road in 1905–07. It is a very interesting example of the work of Beresford Pite, who also designed the impressive insurance offices (now the Royal College of General Practitioners) in Euston Square. The church and the library, with a pub and shops nearby, make this the centre of what is almost a village community.

The square escaped very lightly during the Second World War and the few houses seriously damaged have been well restored. The garden, which had run out of control, was handed over to the council in 1946, and is now the glory of one of the least altered and most impressive squares in London.

Thornhill Square

Thornhill Square was built in 1862, according to a date stone noted by the Booth surveyor in 1899. It was not a true square, but it was quite a complicated development. There were twelve houses in the broad north–south section branching off Westmacott Street (formerly Wellington Street), seven on the west side and five on the east. A terrace of fifteen more filled the south side of an alley that crossed the bottom of this main stem and at the east end of the alley there were four houses on the north side: thirty-one in all, on a very small plot of land. The report in 1899 was 'two storey houses, dirty children playing about'.

The LCC changed the name to Westmacott Gardens in 1938, in deference to the slightly older and considerably bigger and better Thornhill Square in Islington. Westmacott Gardens came through the Second World War unscathed, but in the 1950s Camberwell Council embarked on a massive rebuilding programme that swept away this and many other roads and courts, changing the street pattern dramatically. The site is now occupied by Draycott Close, which has a central garden in humble imitation of a square.

Thorold Square

Thorold Square was built, probably in the early 1790s, as part of the halting development of 'the New Road to Bethnal Green'. The land belonged to the Tyssen family of Hackney, who began to let their estate to potential developers in the 1760s.

The area had been largely given over to market gardens until the road was improved from the 1740s. It was 'just a country extension of Spitalfields', as an old man later recalled, and the gardens were not entirely replaced by houses until well into the nineteenth century. The houses were the work of a poor class of builders and attracted a poor class of tenants: the classic recipe for a slum.

When the appalling state of Bethnal Green became a public scandal, Hector Gavin gave this description in 1848:

This is a very filthy but open square of twenty-two dilapidated houses; the gutters are full of foetid fluid; the clay-soil is covered, in many parts, by water, and the whole surface is muddy. Around the square are collections of garbage, and heaps of dust and ashes; the privies are full and offensive. It is stated that the dustman never comes to remove the refuse though repeatedly applied to. The houses are four-roomed, and are let to two families; for the ground-floor 3s. a week is the rent, for the floor above, 3s. 6d. The water is supplied to this court from a sunk tank communicating with the main. A pump in the centre of the square raises the water when wanted.

Things had not improved when *The Illustrated London News* sent a reporter in 1863:

The visitor who, after having threaded the labyrinth of Friars-mount, remembers that it is principally to Thorold-square that attention has been called, will wonder in what that place can be worse than the neighbourhood he has just left. The truth is, that it is in nothing worse – nay, is many degrees better, since it is approached from the main road; but that such a den should for so long have been suffered to open from a broad public thoroughfare is in itself a pretty good evidence of what must be the condition of the old places which are hidden in almost unexplorable corners. Thorold-square is a repetition of these, but on a large, lighter, and airier scale. It is true that it is muddy, that its houses are ruinous, and that the rotten, ruined, wooden pump, stuck full of nails, which adorns its filthy area is a pretty good representative of the usual water supply. It is equally true that on entering it from the main street the visitor will feel a sickly feeling creep over him, and would, if he were previously hungry, discover within himself a sudden loathing for food and a desire for strong drink. But Thorold-square is by no means an unfavourable specimen of Bethnal-green, although the parish authorities are making much of it, as though for its condition alone they had been liable to censure.

This public exposure eventually alarmed the landlords and some of the worst slums were cleared, including Thorold Square. It was demolished in 1872 and replaced by Thorold Street. Damaging associations of this kind helped to end – temporarily – the long run of fashion that the name of 'square' had enjoyed since the middle of the seventeenth century. Few of any quality were built after the 1860s.

Three Crown Square

Three Crown Court, later Three Crown Square, was presumably named after an inn that it displaced. 'Three Crown Court, in the Borough' featured in Edward Hatton's 1708 and William Stow's 1722 lists of streets. It was on the Strype map published in 1720 (but probably earlier) and Rocque's of the 1740s, as '3 Crown Court'. Rocque showed Foul Lane to the north and Dirty Lane and Whores Nest nearby, but in spite of its neighbours it was rather smart.

The sixteen tall early eighteenth-century houses were rather in the style of Dr Johnson's in Gough Square, though by the 1820s many had been converted to shops. The centre of the court was paved not grassed, but shaded by a few trees. In 1793 or soon afterwards it was dignified by a statue of Charles II, removed from the front of the old Southwark town hall, and this may have been the inspiration for promoting the court to a square. Greenwood's 1827 map still described it as 'Court' but the 1830 edition as 'Square'.

Edward Walford gave this account in 1878:

On the occasion of the rebuilding of the hall in 1793, the statue of the king, instead of being replaced in its original situation, was sold, and set up in a neighbouring court called Three Crown Court, upon a pedestal of brickwork, the inside of which, strange to say, was made to serve as a watch-box for a 'Charley' … After remaining for some time in Three Crowns Court, the poor unfortunate monarch, we believe, found a resting place in the shady nook of a garden in the New Kent Road.

Deprived of royal protection and that of the watchman, Three Crown Square soon fell on evil days.

By 1840 nearly all the houses were occupied by hop and seed merchants, although two solicitors and the Southwark Savings Bank clung on for much of the nineteenth century, and Mrs Ann Drewett, sextoness, was at No. 5 in 1843.

It was increasingly hemmed in by the growth of the Borough Market, so that in 1899 the Booth survey found 'only one house lived in at the north west end, potato salesman. Full of porters carrying sacks, and small carts. There is a passage through to the Borough Market at the north west end.'

Three Crown Square was effectively snuffed out when the market expanded east in 1932, but it remained an address within the market until 2009. Work on the new Thameslink Railway viaduct then required the demolition of that part of the building.

Three Falcon Square

See Falcon Square, Southwark

Three Tun Square

CITY OF LONDON

Three Tun Square, off the east side of Redcross Street, was an occasional name for what was more often and more appropriately called Three Tun Court, although Strype in 1720 had a different name altogether: 'Three Faulcon Court, very good, and well built, with a Free stone Pavement'. It was Three Tun Court on Rocque's 1740s map and on most others until the nineteenth century.

The Three Tuns pub was at No. 53 Redcross Street, at the corner of the square and later at the corner of Paper Street. Much of Redcross Street was demolished when the Metropolitan Railway was constructed in the early 1860s. Three Tun Court just escaped, but it was a reprieve only. In 1890 it was demolished and replaced by Paper Street, a collection of offices where unsuccessful businesses went to die. That was destroyed during the Second World War and the Barbican Centre is now on the site.

Three Tuns Square

See Smith's Square, Greenwich

Thurloe Square

SOUTH KENSINGTON
[KENSINGTON AND CHELSEA]

After the completion of Alexander Square in the early 1830s, the new owner Henry Alexander expected to wait a decade before he could initiate development on the

The east side of Thurloe Square, c. 1905.

rest of his South Kensington estate. The lease of John Harrison and William Bristow's nursery, which occupied the land, was not due to expire until 1842. In fact, his opportunity came almost immediately when Harrison and Bristow were bankrupted in 1832, but the depression that had brought them down affected the building trade to an even greater extent. Alexander took no immediate steps, probably on the advice of his surveyor, George Basevi, who was busy designing houses on the adjoining Smith's Charity estate (see Onslow Square) and would naturally be nervous of glutting the market.

The preparatory work for 'a new square ... intended to be called Thurloe Square' was carried out in 1840, the houses were built between 1840 and 1846 by various firms and all were let by 1849. The architect was Basevi, who was killed in October 1845, just before the square was completed. The style is an interesting transitional one, midway between the Basevi of Belgrave Square

The west side of Thurloe Square in 2006.

and the Freake of Onslow Square. The name chosen for the new development, which included Thurloe Place and Thurloe Street, commemorated a distant connection between the Alexander family and John Thurloe, Cromwell's Secretary of State.

In 1866 the Metropolitan Railway Company made a compulsory purchase of all the houses (Nos 1–11) on the south side of Thurloe Square and Nos 45–56 on the west side. They were needed for the building of South Kensington Station and the track running east towards Sloane Square. Only Nos 52–56 on the west side and 1–5 on the south were demolished, but Nos 6–11 were blighted by the truncation of their gardens and the digging of a deep cutting within a few feet of their back rooms.

The scars were hidden behind ornamental walls for twenty years but then, proving, if proof were needed, that the Victorians were as insensitive as any 1950s brutalist, the awkward sites were filled with buildings in the most shocking red brick. On the south side this was the set of wedge-shaped artists' studios numbered 5 Thurloe Square, built in 1885–87. On the west side it was No. 52, a house built in 1888–89 in gaudy Queen Anne style. It is lower than its neighbours, but fills the eye. Since this early mishap the square has gone on serenely from strength to strength and is now one of the best in London.

The first tenants were the usual mix for this type of housing in Kensington, the odd knight or baronet, senior army and navy officers, doctors, barristers, clergymen and wealthy widows, but the Rajah of Coorg added a little exotic excitement when he occupied No. 56 (one of the few houses now demolished) in the mid-1850s. He was in England to sue the East India Company.

There have been other moderately famous residents at all periods. Number 37 was the last home, in 1863–64, of Thomas Potter Cooke, who was a powder monkey at the Battle of Cape St Vincent in 1797 and went on to be the most popular actor of nautical roles on the Victorian stage. He was also the first, or one of the first, interpreters of Frankenstein's monster. Sir Henry Cole lived at No. 33, the first house on the east side, from 1873 to 1877. Its front door directly faces the Victoria & Albert Museum, of which he was the first director.

The square's most distinguished writer was Emily Morse Symonds, who enjoyed success as novelist, biographer and playwright, always under the pen name of George Paston. She lived for many years, from the 1890s, at No. 7. Neville Conder, the architect, partner of Sir Hugh Casson, lived at No. 49 in his later years. The Ismaili Centre, built just round the corner in Thurloe Place between 1978 and 1983, is one of his best works.

Thurlow Square

BETHNAL GREEN [TOWER HAMLETS]

Thurlow Square was a short cul-de-sac off the north side of Thurlow Place. It was opposite Chester Place, now Bessy Street, of which it might just as well have been considered a continuation. Thurlow Square had only four houses, all on the west side. At the northern end they almost touched the southern houses of Burnham Square.

There was no sign of Thurlow Square on the 1790s Horwood map, but it appeared as Thurlow Place in the 1813 revision, when the more substantial Thurlow Place to the south had hardly been started. Lockie included Thurlow Place, Bethnal Green, in his 1810 list of streets. Lord Thurlow's death in 1806 may have been the occasion for the naming. Thurlow Square appeared in the 1851 census returns, but not in 1841 or 1861, so the name was a short-lived affectation. In 1851 the tenants were labourers and a tailor. Like Burnham Square, the place was swept away in the 1930s and replaced by Bethnal Green Council's Burnham Estate.

Tibberton Square

ISLINGTON

Tibberton Square was built by Thomas Wontner over the garden of his own house in Greenman's Lane (now Greenman Street) between 1823 and 1828; a third of the houses were still seeking tenants in 1830. Wontner was married at Worcester, his wife's birthplace, in 1770, and named his square after the village of Tibberton, which is now nearly a suburb of that city.

He was a hatter, with a factory in Greenman's Lane employing forty to fifty hands. An 1832 London directory lists 'T. Wontner jun. and J. Wontner, Skinners and Furriers, 17 Tibberton sq., Islington', so the smells from the factory probably added little to the amenities of the square. The founder died in 1831 and the business had been inherited by his two sons, Thomas and Joseph. The family continued to live in the square beyond the middle of the century but their handsome double-fronted house, with Venetian windows on the ground and first floors, has not survived.

Adjoining his own house, Wontner had built on the west side of the square and at the west end of the north side seven large houses, three of them with extensive gardens. All have been demolished. The rest of the north side and the whole of the south consisted of the two terraces that now make up the square. The first tenants were mostly given the courtesy of an 'Esq.' by the directories and included John Arthur Cahusac, FSA, but the square became distinctly working class after the factory and the big houses at the west end had been replaced by public baths and washhouses in 1894–95. Even so, they were much above the level of the tenement blocks of Peabody Square to the west and the smaller and meaner houses, including those in Adelaide Square, to the east.

By great good fortune Tibberton Square escaped significant bomb damage in the Second World War. If there had been any it is likely, in this area of large

The north side of Tibberton Square in 2007.

council estates, that it would have been demolished. Instead it has prospered, is attractive, and the flats into which the houses were divided in the 1970s are much in demand. In its modest way it is reminiscent of Trevor Square at Knightsbridge, being narrow and sloping, of a similar date, size and architectural style, and built in a back garden. In the nineteenth century their social pretensions would not have been so widely different.

Tobin Square

NOTTING HILL [KENSINGTON AND CHELSEA]

Little Tobin Square was at the heart of Notting Hill's Pottery Lane slum, one of the worst in London and far and away the worst of the West End. It was also stubborn and long-lasting, persisting through nearly the whole of the nineteenth century and to a lesser degree beyond, despite immense remedial efforts.

Its history had two distinct stages, before and after the 1870s. The first ended when the brickmaking and the pottery industry petered out, and the thousands of pigs – four-legged pigs – that infested the district were expelled by the sanitary authorities. Gradually, during the 1870s and 1880s, many hovels were demolished, sewers were laid, and the street pattern became less amorphous. But this only ushered in a second phase characterised by dreadful overcrowding, poverty, prostitution and a ferocious workhouse.

Tobin Square was built at this point of transition, at the south end of Tobin Street, now Avondale Park Road. It was, literally and metaphorically, next to the workhouse, which even had a postern at the end of the court. There were nine two-storey houses, two each on the south and west sides, and five on the north, which was extended to the workhouse gate. Although it was still almost new, Tobin Square was found to be 'very poor and rough' in 1899.

Tobin Square was demolished as part of the general rebuilding of the area by housing charities and Kensington Council between the wars. The houses now on the site, Nos 1–5 Avondale Park Road, have a courtyard entrance that almost pays homage to the departed square. Just behind, replacing the workhouse, are the million-pound houses of Avondale Park Gardens, a square built by the council in 1920.

Tolmers Square

REGENT'S PARK [CAMDEN]

Tolmers Square was built by William Sawyer between 1861 and 1864 on the site of a New River Company reservoir and waterworks. It was squeezed in between older streets that were poor and becoming squalid. The St Pancras Congregational Church that filled the whole of the cramped centre instead of a garden was built in 1863, with John Tarring as its architect, but that is no reason to hold him responsible for the houses. Tarring's innumerable Gothic churches and chapels led to his being called the Gilbert Scott of the Dissenters. It was he who induced the nonconformists to relax their prejudice against spires, a sad moment for architecture.

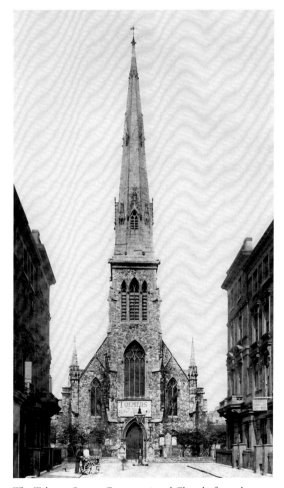

The Tolmers Square Congregational Church, from the east, *c*. 1905.

Sawyer obviously hoped to create a middle-class enclave at the heart of this poor area, but his effort was an instant failure. Nearly all the houses were occupied by several families as early as 1871. The police inspector who assisted the Booth surveyor in 1898 knew the square well: "'A family on each floor,' said Wait. "Several prostitutes live here.'"

Beresford Chancellor described it in 1907 as 'a small enclosure formed by two semi-circles of exceedingly dreary-looking houses'. It grew poorer in the twentieth century, with waves of immigrants filling the flats. After the First World War the church, with its spire removed, was converted into a cheap cinema. It closed in 1972 and was demolished in the following year.

From the 1950s to the 1970s the square was the focus of a highly political battle between residents, squatters, property companies and the local authorities over redevelopment proposals. Architecturally, it would have been hard to find anything less defensible than these unloved Victorian houses, but the aim of the residents' association was always to achieve a redevelopment in which housing for local people predominated over offices and luxury flats.

The new Tolmers Square, built between 1975 and 1982, was a happy compromise. This pedestrian haven from the horrors of the Euston Road underpass is one of the most successful of the modern interpretations of the square. The design and planting of the garden is attractive, the houses, with their archways and round-headed windows, are inventive, and the restaurant and popular pub make the square lively without being raucous. Even the children racing around on their bikes seem picturesque rather than threatening.

Torrington Square

Torrington Square was named after George Byng, Viscount Torrington, father-in-law of the 6th Duke of Bedford. The houses, which were built between 1821 and 1827, at the start of the second phase of development on the Bedford estate, were the work of James Sim, who went on to build the similar Woburn Square. It is not known what architect, if any, he employed.

Torrington Square was very long and narrow, which made the garden seem little more than a strip of greenery. The houses, of two bays and four storeys plus basement, were all on the long east and west sides. They were smaller than those built by Burton and Cubitt in the estate's major squares and proved easier to sell as the social status of Bloomsbury declined. Although it was only a fraction of the size of Russell Square, Torrington Square contained the same number of houses.

Rowland Dobie gave this description in 1829:

Torrington Square is also on the Duke of Bedford's estate, and is lately in a state of completion. It contains seventy houses of a moderate size, and is so pleasantly situate on an elevated healthy spot, as to have been filled with occupants, as fast as it progressed in building. Its form is rectangular, or what is called, improperly, a long square; and it has proved a very successful speculation to its very industrious and worthy builder, Mr Sims.

Torrington Square was not fashionable, its characteristic residents being doctors, clergymen, solicitors and actors. The celebrities were from the arts rather than society and politics. Torrington Square had more than its neighbour Woburn Square only because it was nearly twice as large. The actress Anne Maria Tree lived at No. 3 as early as February 1823, and Charles Kean, the actor, had the same house from 1853 to 1855. George Scharf, a topographical artist to whom every London historian owes a debt of gratitude, lived at No. 1 from 1848 to 1856, and the philosopher Herbert Spencer at No. 18 from 1860 to 1862. Christina Rossetti was at No. 30, one of the few surviving houses, from 1876, when she left Euston Square, until her death in 1894. The biographer and critic Hugh Kingsmill Lunn, who wrote under the name of Hugh Kingsmill, was born at No. 46 in 1889.

Lodging houses existed from the earliest days, became common from the 1850s, and by the end of the century almost monopolised the square. It was marked down for destruction from the 1920s, when the University of London began buying houses there and in the neighbouring streets and squares as a site

Torrington Square, looking south-east from Torrington Place, *c.* 1905.

for its planned expansion. Work was delayed by the slump, but demolition got underway in the late 1930s, when the whole of the west side and the southern end of the east were cleared. Birkbeck College was begun on the west side and the School of Oriental & African Studies on the east before the war brought all building to an end.

Some of the remaining houses on the east side were destroyed in the Blitz. Immediately after the war, Birkbeck was completed and the Students' Union was built on the remainder of the west side of the square, which had by then become an empty name. The extension to the School of Oriental & African Studies cut across the south end in the early 1970s and now only six of the seventy-one houses survive, in a forlorn terrace at the north end of the east side. There is no longer even a garden, just a few trees scattered around a paved area, part of which is the roof of the students' union swimming pool.

Tottenham Square

KINGSLAND [HACKNEY]

Tottenham Road was laid out in the 1820s as part of the grand design for the De Beauvoir estate, which was intended to be splendid and achieved solid respectability in parts, notably at De Beauvoir Square. The north-east corner, close to the Dalston crossroads, was never smart and often rough.

Tottenham Square, a short cul-de-sac off the north side, began as the access – more garden than road – to two detached houses built in the gap between Tottenham Road and the Balls Pond Road. They lay back to the west of the cul-de-sac, but did not enjoy their seclusion for long; the 1831 Hackney parish map showed the first two of what would soon become a terrace of much meaner houses built directly onto the east side.

By 1860 the detached houses had been demolished and the square had achieved a regular shape, with six houses on each side and one at the north end. The number was soon reduced by the establishment of a Gospel Mission Hall on the west side and a fancy cabinet maker's works at 'Tottenham House', and the character was further established by a beerhouse at the corner of Tottenham Road.

In 1897 the Booth survey found that 'Tottenham Square … has a rough common lodging house in it, beds 6d per night and 2/6 per week'. The rest of the west side was lost to the expanding Tottenham Road Board School (now De Beauvoir Primary), and although five houses on the east side and the one on the north survived until the 1960s, and the name a little longer, the square has now been entirely extinguished.

Trafalgar Square

(later Buller Square)

This was not a true square but a broad cul-de-sac with houses on the north, south and east sides. St Leonard's Square at Kentish Town is similar in its layout, though not in its houses. At Trafalgar Square the terraces, built in 1842, were stylish in a heavy, late Georgian manner, with the doors and all the windows enclosed within tall, round-headed recesses, three to each house. They were of two storeys and semi-basement. The surviving side of the adjoining Nelson Square (now part of Furley Road) has similar houses, evidently the work of the same builder.

Rows of trees on both sides of Trafalgar Square were some compensation for the lack of a garden. It was quiet, respectable and almost entirely residential, with a mission room in connection with the nearby St Andrew's Church as the only intrusion. The most notable resident was the boxer, Tom Belcher, younger brother of the champion, Jim. He died at No. 19 in 1854.

Peckham's Trafalgar Square lost its name in 1937, when the LCC gave the monopoly to the one below Nelson's Column. Peckham's rival became Buller Square, but it did not long survive the change of name. The short east side was badly damaged during

the war. The houses on the north and south sides were demolished in the late 1960s and early 1970s, and not a trace of the square remains today.

The site is occupied by a community centre, a patch of grass, and a floodlit area for basketball and other games. The south end of Peckham Park Road has been renamed Buller Close.

Trafalgar Square

(now Trafalgar Gardens)

Stepney's Trafalgar Square was built in the 1790s, a decade or more before the great battle, and was known at first as Stepney Square or Stepney New Square. The 'new' was to distinguish it from the Old Square, a tiny northward continuation of the High Street that was later the undisputed Stepney Square. In 1809 the name of the newcomer was patriotically changed to Trafalgar Square, and thus it remained until 1938, when the LCC was busy eradicating duplications. It then became Trafalgar Gardens.

The square was quite large, with thirty-seven houses shared between the north, south and east sides, facing a circular garden. On the west side was the old-established White Horse Lane, which was never counted as part of the square, and in which there were no houses at this point when the square was built. The north side was the first to be completed, followed by the east. The south side, where the houses were less regular and slightly larger, came last, early in the nineteenth century. On all three sides the houses opened directly onto the pavement, with no front garden or area. The north and east sides featured terraces of modest three-storey, two-bay houses.

The only notable resident was John Carvell Williams, Congregationalist, MP, editor of the *Liberator*, and leading advocate of disestablishmentarianism. He was born there in 1821.

The south side was the first to be destroyed, when the School Board for London demolished all the houses in the 1880s to make room for its Trafalgar Square School. This removed the wealthiest residents and was no doubt the occasion for the garden, by then

The east side of Trafalgar Gardens (formerly Trafalgar Square, Stepney) in 2007. Taller Flats now stand here.

square not circular, to be offered to the vestry, which opened it to the public in 1885. The Booth survey reported in 1898 that the square was 'now tenanted by poor Jews and labourers'.

In this heavily bombed area, the terraces on the north and east sides survived the Second World War almost miraculously, but what enemy action could not achieve was well within the compass of Stepney Council, which demolished them in 1948–49 and built blocks of flats in their place.

The buildings framing the square changed again as part of a major reconstruction of the Stepney Green area that began in 2010. Private flats now wrap around the north and east sides of the square and the school on the south side has been rebuilt. The garden is still largely a paved games court and playground, with trees only on the perimeter. The pleasant, irregular houses facing it on the west side of White Horse Lane were built in the 1830s, but the three-storey houses in this group are not unlike the destroyed terraces in the square.

Trafalgar Square

WESTMINSTER

Trafalgar Square and Parliament Square are the only two in London created deliberately, in the continental manner, with a view to public magnificence. Abroad such ceremonial squares were generally the work of kings anxious to state their ambitions or record their triumphs, so it is appropriate that Trafalgar Square owed a good deal to George IV, our last grandiloquent sovereign, and his architect John Nash.

The Mews, home to the king's falcons from the time of Edward I and to his horses from the sixteenth century or earlier, was a heterogeneous collection of buildings, altered and added to as the need arose. Architecture was not considered necessary until 1732, when the north range of the large Mews was rebuilt by William Kent. His very grand stables lasted until the early 1830s and the chaotic tangle of old houses and barns around them until 1825, by which time the new Royal Mews at Buckingham Palace had made them redundant.

Such a pivotal site, the hinge in the route from Westminster to London, was seized upon by projectors from an early date as the natural spot for a great public open space. Defoe mentioned it in 1725, not as his own idea but as something long under consideration:

> From this place [the statue of Charles I] due North, are the King's Stables, called the Meuse, where the King's Horses, especially his Coach-Horses, are kept, and the Coaches of State are set up; it is a very large Place, and takes up a great deal of Ground, more than is made Use of: It contains Two large Squares, besides an Out-let East, where is the Managerie for teaching young Gentlemen to Ride the great Saddle; in the middle of the first Court is a Smith or Farryer's House and Shop, a Pump and Horse-Pond, and I see little else remarkable, but old scatter'd Buildings; and, indeed, this Place standing where a noble Square of good Buildings might be erected, I do not wonder that they talk of pulling it down, contracting the Stables into less Room, and building a Square of good Houses there, which would, indeed, be a very great Improvement, and I doubt not will be done.

When Kent's scheme was carried out a few years later, those hoping for a 'noble Square of good Buildings' were disappointed. Two large open spaces were indeed retained north and south of Kent's Crown Stables, but they were private courtyards, one for the King's Mews where the west half of Trafalgar Square now stands, and the other for the smaller Queen's Mews on the site now occupied by the rear parts of the National Gallery.

The frequent reprinting of Defoe's *Tour* kept this ideal before the public. James Ralph mentioned it in 1734, wishing 'that a view was opened from hence to St Martin's Church', and in 1766 it was revived in John Gwynn's *London and Westminster Improved, to which is prefixed a Discourse on Public Magnificence*. In Gwynn's plan the great open space intended to replace the northern half of the Mews was named King's-square. It was not the last proposal for

the site. In 1815 Sir Frederick Trench, a 'Gentleman who fancies Himself a Man of Taste', put forward a scheme for a Napoleonic War memorial in the form of a huge pyramid.

The first decisive move was made by John Nash in the 1820s. He had been recommending a square here since 1812, but the opportunity did not arrive until after the death of George III. The decision was then taken to build a new royal mews at Buckingham House, which Nash was soon to transform into Buckingham Palace for George IV. All the southern parts of the old mews were to be demolished, leaving Kent's great range standing more or less on the site now occupied by the front part of the National Gallery and creating an inchoate open space corresponding to the western half of the present Trafalgar Square.

It was in 1822, with the square still largely hypothetical, that Nash's nominal masters, the Commissioners for Woods, Forests & Land Revenues, let the west side to the Royal College of Physicians and the Union Club, and Robert Smirke designed for them the block that later became Canada House. This was already standing when the miscellaneous mews buildings were cleared in 1825. To the east of the new open space was a clutter of old shops, houses and inns south of St Martin's.

The space revealed by the 1825 clearance was so disappointing that Nash was asked to prepare a plan for its extension, and his Pall Mall East & West Strand improvement scheme was published in 1826. It included a proposal to replace Kent's stables with a new national gallery. The *Quarterly Review* commented on the plans in that year:

> It is now probable that a splendid building, designed for the use of the National Gallery of Paintings and Sculpture, will be erected on the north side of the new square at Charing Cross, to supplant the Mews, and to extend from Pall Mall East to St Martin's church … The removal of all the houses on the west side of St Martin's-lane, as far as the church, including the Golden Cross Inn, and the whole of the contiguous buildings, will form a noble square facing Whitehall, and will rescue the noble palace of the Percys … from the Strand.

St Martin-in-the-Fields from the Royal Mews, part of the site of Trafalgar Square, Westminster, in 1810.

Sadly, the rescued Northumberland House was sacrificed for the sake of Northumberland Avenue in 1874.

The demolition of the small houses around St Martin's was proceeding in 1828, but the main range of the mews still survived and a penny-pinching Commons committee was urging the king 'that the present building of the Royal Mews at Charing-cross, the upper floor of which, being lighted by sky-lights, can, at a very small expense, be made available for a National Gallery, or other public purposes, may be preserved'. The building was retained for a time and used for the National Repository, a display of 'useful mechanical arts and manufactures', as James Elmes called it, forming a feeble foretaste of the Great Exhibition of 1851.

In September 1830 it was reported that the public records stored in Westminster Hall were to be removed to 'the building lately the King's Mews at Charing-cross' as part of the preparations for the coronation of William IV. Kent's masterpiece was becoming a general dump.

Just two months later the embryo square ('the open space before the National Repository') became the scene of the first of its many riots, the building materials lying about in heaps providing perfect ammunition for the mob. At a subsequent trial:

Thomas Tull, Secretary to the National Repository, stated that he witnessed the outrageous conduct of the mob towards the police from a window; large stones flew in all directions, and one lady was severely injured by a stone hitting her; there was a cry of 'Down with the new Police,' which appeared to be a kind of watchword for riot.

It was in that year of 1830 that much of the necessary demolition in St Martin's Lane, the Strand and the surrounding streets was completed, including the sweeping away of the ancient Golden Cross Inn. This proved – as what does not? – a great boon for the lawyers, with special courts sitting to resolve disputed levels of compensation.

The next point to be decided was the name of the new square. In the first flush of enthusiasm at the start of the new reign, King William IV Square was suggested, and it was called King William Square on James Wyld's plan of the improvements published in 1832. The architect George Ledwell Taylor, who knew the king through their shared naval interests, claimed the credit for persuading him to accept Trafalgar Square instead. Taylor designed the large block on the east side, built as chambers in 1830, that soon became Morley's Hotel and was later the South

The King's Mews as the National Repository in 1829, seen across the emerging Trafalgar Square, Westminster.

African High Commission. It was replaced by South Africa House in 1930–33.

If George IV had lived a little longer John Nash would probably have left his mark on the buildings of Trafalgar Square. But the death of his unpopular patron ended Nash's career and Suffolk Place, the United Service Club in Pall Mall (now the Institute of Directors), the St Martin's parochial building and the Lowther Arcade block in the Strand are the nearest examples of his work.

Northumberland House, Trafalgar Square, Westminster, c. 1870.

There was no competition for the National Gallery, only private lobbying for the plans of various eminent men. The succession of a Whig government gave the advantage to William Wilkins, who was known to Whigs and Radicals as the architect of University College. He had already worked on a scheme to convert Kent's mews into a national gallery. His plans for a new building were submitted in 1831, Parliament voted the funds in 1833, and the gallery was built between 1834 and 1838. The Royal Academy occupied the eastern half for the first thirty years.

Wilkins was obliged to use the portico of the demolished Carlton House, donated to the project by George IV. This has always caused architects to scorn the gallery, which amateurs have liked. The buildings around the square were generally disparaged in their early days. In 1843 William Weir wrote that 'it is odds but Charles I, indignant at being surrounded by such a crockery-shop, claps spurs to his horse and rides off'. In 1852 the German visitor Max Schlesinger wrote, 'Politeness induces us to say as little as possible of Trafalgar-square'.

With the frame of buildings completed, attention turned to the centre of the square and the nature of the monuments to be placed there. The first question was whether it should be a paved and entirely open space

The statue of Charles I and the Union Club, Trafalgar Square, Westminster, in 1827.

fit for great public assemblies and national events, or a railed garden planted like those of other squares. With the riot of 1830 so fresh in their minds, many nervous people favoured the idea of a private enclosure from which the mob could be excluded, and when a paved square was decided upon the large basins were introduced to limit the space available for rioting.

The newly formed Nelson memorial committee was granted a site in 1839 and staged an open competition for the monument, won by William Railton's column. In 1840 Charles Barry was asked to lay out the square and a select committee of the Commons heard criticisms and suggestions from all the leading architects. The work on the square and the building of Nelson's column proceeded side by side and Baily's statue took its place at the top just six months before the square was opened in May 1844. There were no fountains in the basins and no lions on the plinths, but the square was nearly finished.

Trafalgar Square was at its peak for less than a decade, between the completion of Landseer's lions in 1867 and the demolition of Northumberland House in 1874. With dignified ranges of the 1820s and 1830s on the three dominant sides, the monuments in the centre

new and fresh, and fine buildings, St Martin's and Northumberland House, in the north-east and south-east corners, the square could justly be acclaimed as a great national achievement, a worthy centre of empire. But the shameful destruction of Northumberland House, followed in the next decade by the worst of the Trafalgar Square riots and, soon after, the arrival of the motor car, were setbacks only feebly offset by the building of Admiralty Arch in 1908–11. That project removed a third of the houses in the south-west corner which, as a pre-existing element – the south side of Cockspur Street – had always been a minor and largely unnoticed part of the square. The houses there were popular with architects and engineers.

The main events of the interwar years were the acquisition and alteration of the Union Club for the Canadian High Commission; the rebuilding of Morley's Hotel as Sir Herbert Baker's South Africa House; and Lutyens' redesign of the centre of the square and replacement of Barry's fountains, a job not completed until the 1940s. This meant that the busts of the First World War admirals, Jellicoe and Beatty, associated with the new fountains, were unveiled in the aftermath of the Second World War.

The north side of Trafalgar Square, Westminster, in 1829, showing the King's Mews, St Martin-in-the-Fields and the Royal College of Surgeons.

Trafalgar Square, Westminster, in the 1920s, showing the demolition of the former Morley's Hotel.

Trafalgar Square, Westminster, from the west, c. 1840.

Political conflicts continued to rage in the square as always, but the most important battles of the late twentieth century were fought for its architectural integrity. There were threats in the north-west and south-east corners from the proposed new wing of the National Gallery and a replacement for the decaying Grand Hotel. The 'monstrous carbuncle' speech by the Prince of Wales certainly saw off the first and produced the popular Sainsbury Wing. The speech also helped to smooth the path for Grand Buildings, which positively improved the unsatisfactory south side of the square.

Since the 1920s the traffic problem had been getting out of hand. The open space designed for the enjoyment of the public became ever more dangerous to approach and increasingly noisy and polluted when reached.

The twenty-first century began its trusteeship of Trafalgar Square in fine style by finding a partial solution to the problem. Sir Norman Foster's redesign of 2002–03, with the closing of the north side to traffic and the building of the great stairs, has revitalised the centre of the square and rehabilitated the National Gallery, though at the cost of making Charles I's unfortunate south side more hideous than ever.

Trafalgar Square

See Chelsea Square

Tredegar Square

One of the architectural showpieces of London hides modestly here in the Mile End Road. It was built on the land of Sir Charles Morgan, who became the 1st Baron Tredegar in 1859. Morgan Square was an alternative name in the early years, but the family had lived at Tredegar Park in Monmouthshire long before they took it as their title.

The most perfect squares often emerge from the midst of economic disaster. Sir Charles entrusted the development of his Mile End estate to Daniel Austin, a brickmaker and builder who began the development in 1822 and soon settled at No. 14 Cottage Grove, now Rhonda Grove. Austin failed in 1827, and two Tredegar Square builders followed him into the bankruptcy courts in 1830, William Miller in January and Edward Bumford in November.

Austin had been a sugar refiner and coal merchant before burning his hands with bricks. Bumford, who in 1812 pursued the safe trade of an engraver in Islington, moved into speculative building in that year and between then and 1830 was responsible for the development of a large area between Whitechapel Road and Bethnal Green Road. By 1828 he was describing himself as a surveyor. William Miller and his partner Richard Leavitt were among the builders who took plots from Bumford on these estates. They were involved in a fraudulent bankruptcy in 1813, when Bumford was one of the principal creditors. Their attempt to step up from these modest East End streets to the grandeur of Tredegar Square ended in predictable ruin.

Daniel Austin may have intended to build two roads similar to Cottage Grove rather than a square. Before his bankruptcy in 1827 two pairs of houses had been built in the south-west approach to the future square (then only a stub of road) that were identical to Austin's houses on the east side of Cottage Grove, where most of them survive. Cavendish Terrace, which now occupies the entrance to the square, is a stylish continuation of the west side terrace in pastiche, replacing Austin's pairs which were destroyed during the Second World War.

Whatever Austin's intentions may have been, Miller and Bumford evidently decided immediately on a square in the very grandest West End style, and completed it, with Miller as the principal builder, between 1827 and 1830. Credit for the design has been tentatively awarded to William King, an obscure architect who lived at No. 18 Cottage Grove, only a few doors from Daniel Austin. Another candidate must be Austin himself, as he emerged from his bankruptcy to co-design Trinity Church, which closed the vista at the north end of Cottage Grove. A third possibility is Edward Bumford, who styled himself 'surveyor'.

Whoever designed the square does not deserve his obscurity, as the stuccoed north side is a fine piece of work. It was evidently inspired by Nash and would not disgrace Regent's Park. The other three sides have excellent but much plainer brick terraces of a standard 1820s type, similar to those on the New River estate at Clerkenwell.

The north side of Tredegar Square, *c.* 1910.

Those involved in the development were local men who, in spite of their serial failure, must be supposed to have known the market. The later history of the square proves that there was a demand for houses of this quality from the commercial and administrative elite of the East End. Those whose work obliged them to live 'east of Aldgate' occupied the square throughout the nineteenth century: large shopkeepers, managers, senior clerks, solicitors, architects and surveyors, doctors and dentists, clergymen and proprietors of schools. It continued to be very respectable until late in the nineteenth century when, like Trevor Square a little earlier, it was suddenly colonised by a host of travelling drapers.

The most celebrated resident was Stella Richman, the television producer and restaurateur (once the wife of Alec Clunes) who was born at No. 7 in 1922. Her father was a Jewish leather merchant.

The Mile End Vestry hoped to buy the garden in 1898, to avert the possibility of its being built over when the leases of the houses expired in 1902. Lord Tredegar declined to sell, but the land remained a private garden, increasingly neglected, until it was converted into a children's playground in the late 1930s under the King George's Fields scheme. Now it is happily a garden again, a public one, planted with a formality to match the houses.

Trevor Square

KNIGHTSBRIDGE [WESTMINSTER]

Trevor Square was built on the site of Powis House, a late seventeenth-century mansion on the Kensington Road that had a number of distinguished tenants in its career of 120 years. It belonged to the Trevors of Brynkinalt in Denbighshire, who decided to demolish it and build the present square and satellite streets in 1810, after the founding of the barracks opposite had spoilt its outlook and amenities. The square they built had to struggle with the same blighting influence during its first century.

Powis House was demolished in 1811 or shortly afterwards, when Charles Street (now Trevor Street) was laid out across the site of the house and Trevor Square in its garden. This garden origin dictated the narrow

rectangle and gave it a family resemblance to the contemporary Tibberton Square at Islington, though in its newfound eminence Trevor Square would probably not wish to acknowledge its poor relation.

The architect employed to plan the new estate by Lord Dungannon, the Trevor of the day, was William Fuller Pocock. He not only laid out the streets but designed some of the houses, establishing the pattern followed by the various builders involved, and took many of the building leases himself. Work began in 1818 on the east and south sides and the last houses on the west were completed in 1827.

With the barracks to the north, and Harriette Wilson to set the tone from the start, Trevor Square had a dubious reputation, with boarding houses and similar establishments becoming more frequent throughout the nineteenth century, until the Booth survey in 1899 said it was 'all lodging houses; poorer class than Hill Street and Charles Street'. The other notable trend was the colonisation of the square by travelling salesmen. In 1882 nine of the houses, a quarter of the total, were occupied by 'travelling drapers'.

The most exciting year in the history of the square was 1886. Number 3, which had been the Westminster Board of Works Free Public Library since 1858, was then enlarged and extended back across its garden. (It closed in 1907.) The Japanese Village, which inspired *The Mikado*, had an entrance at the north-east corner of the square that must have brought exotic guests to the lodging houses in 1886. It was also then that the Dilke scandal revealed No. 9 as a house of ill-repute.

Trevor Square has some literary associations. The courtesan and writer Harriette Wilson occupied No. 16 from 1828 to 1830, and the chronically poor playwright and actor Thomas Dibdin died at No. 22 on the south side in 1841. That he could afford a house there indicates the low status of the square at that time. Since its gentrification Ben Travers, the playwright, has lived at No. 10 and Max Reinhardt, the publisher, and owner of the Bodley Head and other imprints, at No. 16. He liked to boast of the Harriette Wilson connection.

The square had sunk to such a level when Lord Trevor sold it shortly before the First World War that the new owner planned to demolish the whole estate. An architectural competition was held to determine a fresh layout, but nothing was ever done and the south side, which had always been the most working class, was sold to Harrods in 1913. It was demolished in that year to make way for the Harrods depository and a garage, and in 1918 its continuations east and west, formerly called Arthur Street, were made part of the square. The depository was not completed until the early 1920s.

There was serious damage to the central houses on the east side of the square during the Second World War and the south-east corner was shaken by the V1 that fell near the south end of Lancelot Place. These scars have been healed and now narrow neo-Georgian houses have been built in front of the garage entrance on the south side and have inherited the numbers of two of the demolished houses. Should the depository ever be removed, more numbers will be available.

The small size of the houses, which was a serious objection during the Victorian age, has become a positive advantage since the war. With Georgian architecture firmly back in favour and the convenient proximity of Harrods, if not of its depository, Trevor Square has gone from strength to strength and is now one of the most attractive in London.

Trinity Church Square

SOUTHWARK

(formerly Trinity Square)

Trinity Square, which was renamed Trinity Church Square in 1939 to distinguish it from its godfather by the Tower, is the centrepiece of a 20-acre estate in Southwark belonging to the Corporation of Trinity House. The land was given in 1661 for the support of sick and aged seamen and their families, by Christopher Merrick, after whom the neighbouring Merrick Square was later named.

The intention of the corporation to build on their estate, previously used mainly for market gardening, was probably signalled by their appointment of the experienced architect Daniel Asher Alexander as surveyor in 1807. He was best known for warehouses and prisons – his Dartmoor Prison was begun in 1806 – but he had also designed country houses and was busy with the porticoes and wings of the Queen's House at Greenwich in 1807.

The general layout of the estate and the positioning of Trinity Square were probably his work, and it

The west side of Trevor Square, *c.* 1904.

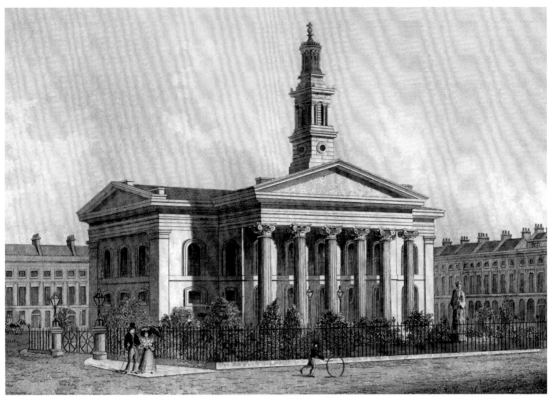

Holy Trinity, Trinity Square (now Trinity Church Square), Southwark, in 1830.

was stipulated in building agreements that the plans of all intended houses should be submitted to the surveyor for approval. It was common practice for the estate surveyor to provide elevations for the most important part of a new development, to set the tone, and it may have been the case here. But Daniel Alexander was succeeded in 1822 by his pupil Richard Suter, later the architect of Merrick Square, so any designs supplied for Trinity Square could have been by either man or the two in collaboration.

Work began in 1814 with the creation of Trinity Street, originally called Great Suffolk Street East, the central part of which forms the north side of the square and is now numbered as part of it. Few houses appeared in the new street until the early 1820s, when the present Nos 60–62 Trinity Church Square were built. As they balance the identical Nos 51–53, forming the two ends of a symmetrical composition marking the north side of the square, they were evidently designed after it was laid out.

If not part of the estate plan from the beginning, the square must have been decided on by 1820, when authority for Holy Trinity Church was included in an Act of Parliament. The church, occupying the southern two-thirds of the potential garden ground, was built in 1823–24. The architect was Francis Bedford, who had just completed St Luke's at West Norwood for the Commissioners for New Churches. He used much the same design here, on a less dramatic site.

The builder of the houses surrounding the church was William Chadwick, who made an agreement with the corporation in 1824 and was given a lease of the remaining part of the interior to form a garden for his tenants. It was presumably Chadwick who acquired and got the Coade workshop to repair the medieval statue that adorns the garden. It is called *King Alfred* and is thought to have come from Westminster Hall, which Sir John Soane altered in 1822–25, when adding his law courts. The statue was in place by 1830. (There is an alternative theory that it came from the garden of Carlton House, which was demolished in the 1820s.)

The west side of the square was built first in 1825–26, and the east side was begun in 1826. Chadwick did not fall victim, like so many others, to the banking crisis of those years, but his operations were obviously held up by the financial pressures, and the south side was not completed until 1832. Despite the delay, he was able to achieve creditable consistency; too much in fact, as the uniformity of the long terraces is oppressive. It would have been better to break them up with pediments or pilasters, with balconies or verandas. Whittuck's 1830 view indicates that the slightly advanced central five houses of the west, and presumably also the east side, were originally further emphasised by a balustraded parapet, and that must certainly have helped.

The square was a success in its early years, with a very respectable population of merchants, solicitors, surgeons and architects, mostly obscure, but with one or two of some interest. Francis Pouget, who is best known for the Queen's Hotel at Upper Norwood, lived at No. 52 from 1828 to 1856, promoting himself from surveyor in the 1840s to architect and surveyor in the 1850s. John Belcher, who designed many City offices and shops, lived at No. 60 from 1849 to 1852. It was one of the childhood homes of his son, Sir John, later president of the RIBA.

Literature was also represented. Thomas Tegg, the publisher, one of the pioneers of cheap editions of the classics, lived at No. 11 from 1848 to 1852. John Oxenford, the playwright and translator of Goethe, who was born in Camberwell and remained loyal to south London, died at No. 28 in 1877. He was the author of more than 100 plays in a career of forty years. His farce *A Day Well Spent* (1836) was the remote original (via a German version) of Thornton Wilder's *The Matchmaker*, of *Hello Dolly!* and of Tom Stoppard's *On the Razzle*.

By the 1850s boarding houses had infiltrated the square and it fell out of favour with the professional classes. In 1899 the Booth survey found 'three storey houses with basements, forecourts, some private, but mostly lodgings. Many Guy's students here and hereabouts.' In 1907 Beresford Chancellor gave a slightly revised report: 'Once inhabited by well-to-do City people, its houses have now become largely lodgings once affected by students of Guy's

The garden of Trinity Church Square, looking east, in 2007.

Hospital and others – the "others" now being in the majority, as the medical student has sought other fields.'

The square suffered during the Second World War, with Nos 49–51 on the north side nearly destroyed, serious damage to the church and all the other houses shaken. The three demolished houses were quickly rebuilt in an excellent facsimile. Most of the others were divided into flats, some running across several of the original house widths, but the exteriors are perfectly preserved.

Trinity Square

(now Trinity Gardens)

Trinity Gardens, which was known as Trinity Square until 1937, when the one by the Tower was given exclusive rights, is a little gem in the middle of Brixton. It was built in 1850–51 behind the Trinity Asylum almshouses in Acre Lane, which had been established in 1822. To the north were other almshouses built in the 1830s and later taken over and enlarged by the City of London, so the new square was very favourably located.

The land belonged to Thomas Bailey Illidge, son of John Illidge of Bethel House, Brixton. The father had died in 1846, which was perhaps the occasion for the development. The builders were John and Charles Ellis who, according to custom, were bankrupted in 1855. John lived at No. 17 and Charles at No. 22, the present 46 and 51. The architects may have been Willshire and Parris who in 1849–50 produced for Thomas Illidge and his brother John a number of house plans and elevations that are preserved at the London Metropolitan Archives. Among them is a layout dated 1850 for an unnamed square just to the south, intended to be built where Horsford Road and Torrens Road eventually appeared instead.

Trinity Gardens is small and less than thirty houses ever opened directly onto the garden, but the total numbered as part of it has varied considerably. The west side was originally part of Trinity Road, all of which is now included in Trinity Gardens, as is a small north-eastern offshoot formerly called Trinity Grove. The terraces facing the garden were built to a simple plan, with the advancing of the end and centre houses as the main feature. Those on the north and east sides are of two storeys plus basement and attic, with rusticated stucco and round-headed windows to the ground floor, and the advanced houses with porches. The demolished south side was almost certainly the same. The houses on the west side, part of the long Trinity Road terrace, are of two storeys only and of plain brick, but the eight opposite the garden have the same pattern of the two end and

Holy Trinity was closed in 1960 and was further damaged by fire in 1973, soon after being chosen for conversion to a rehearsal and recording hall by the London Philharmonic and London Symphony orchestras. They went ahead with a rebuilding more than a conversion project and the church was reopened as the Henry Wood Hall in 1975. The small garden in front, mainly grassed, with the statue in the centre and mature trees around the edge, is private – a necessary precaution, perhaps, for the protection of the statue and the hall. The square is well looked after by an active residents' association.

The east side of Trinity Gardens (formerly Trinity Square, Brixton) in 2008.

the two central houses advanced, proving that they were carefully planned as one side of a square.

A general and a lieutenant of the Royal Navy were among the early residents of Trinity Square and it remained a respectable address throughout the nineteenth century, with trades appearing only in the smaller houses in the former Trinity Road, south of the garden.

The square declined with the rest of Brixton in the twentieth century, but passed through the Second World War almost unscathed. The houses on the south side were sacrificed afterwards for a very dull block of council flats called Daisy Dormer Court, but the others are intact. Like Cleaver Square it has a pub, the Trinity Arms, in the north-west corner. This one still occupies the original two houses, although the front has been altered in line with changing tastes in pub architecture. The landlord had the use of the garden as an allotment until Lambeth Council acquired it for an open space in 1931. It is now paved, not grassed, and features young trees and uncomfortable-looking seats, but at least there are railings once more. Gentrification has restored the houses to pristine perfection.

Trinity Square

CITY OF LONDON [AND TOWER HAMLETS]

Samuel Wyatt was appointed surveyor to Trinity House in 1792 and was immediately instructed to design a new headquarters for the corporation at the north end of Tower Hill. It was Wyatt's most prominent public building, the climax of his career, so as soon as the new hall was completed in 1796 he obtained permission to lay out a large oval garden in front of it as a suitable setting for the jewel.

The northern section of Tower Hill was ripe for conversion into a square, as it already had a frame of good houses on the east and west sides and the Tower of London defined most of the south. In 1708 Hatton had mentioned the 'many good new Buildings mostly inhabited by Gentry and Merchants'.

The garden was an immediate success, described enthusiastically in 1805: 'The area before the Trinity House, formerly the awful scene of public executions and of midnight plunder, is now very handsomely railed in, and encloses a very beautiful shrubbery.

Trinity House, Trinity Square, City, in 1829.

Numbers 37 and 36 on the east side of Trinity Square, City, *c.* 1860.

So that Tower Hill is formed into an airy and beautiful square.' The new name was not accepted immediately, but it was in occasional use by 1804 and was given by John Lockie in the 1810 edition of his *Topography of London*.

The long, splayed terrace on the west side was tenanted by ship agents, ship brokers and others in nautical occupations, plus merchants of all kinds, although wine merchants came to predominate late in the nineteenth century. The east side had a number of fine private houses, especially at the north end, where some of them survive. The largest (long demolished) was No. 37, the official residence of the Secretary to the Customs.

There were three pubs in the square, the Coopers' Arms at No. 25, the Old George at No. 31 and the Tower Shades at No. 36, but only the Old George survived into the twentieth century. Institutions included the Brewers' Company Grammar School at No. 9 from the 1850s, and the offices of the Thames Conservancy at No. 41 from the 1860s.

Events of the 1880s seriously affected the square. Between 1882 and 1884 the Metropolitan Railway's inner circle, now the Circle Line, was completed with a tunnel dug across the south side of the garden. At the same time the present Byward Street was constructed and the garden slightly reduced and flattened to continue the new east–west road at the same width.

A great change came over Trinity Square at the beginning of the twentieth century, when all the old buildings west of Trinity House were demolished to make way for the offices of the Port of London Authority, successor to the Thames Conservancy. Sir Edwin Cooper's immense building took a full decade in preparation and construction from 1912 to 1922. The small part of the west side not required for it was filled with offices during the same period. There was heavy bomb damage in the Second World War, with Trinity House gutted and even the great PLA building shaken.

Trinity Square is one of the few in London divided between two local authorities, Trinity House and the PLA building being in the City, the garden and the east side in Tower Hamlets. It still retains many attractions, although the constant roar of traffic is

The garden of Trinity Square, City, in the early 1890s by William Luker, Jr.

The First World War merchant seamen's memorial, Trinity Square, City, in 2008.

Trinity Square, City, *c.* 1925.

certainly not one of them. The former PLA building, now 10 Trinity Square, is the dominating presence, but for those who find it too assertive Trinity House next door provides an immediate corrective and reproof. It was restored and extended in the 1950s by Sir Albert Richardson. In the north-eastern corner the two surviving houses are a reminder of the style and scale of the square created by Wyatt in 1797.

The garden, which has been extended to the east and lost its original oval shape, has many points of interest. Pride of place goes to the impressive stretch of Roman and medieval City wall exposed in the eastern extension. Within the original garden the chief feature is Lutyens' noble memorial to the merchant seamen killed in the First World War. Such perfection scarcely needs the backdrop of the Tower of London. The 1939–45 memorial does not attempt to compete with Lutyens but sinks its head in justified modesty. The Falklands memorial is better, and does take full advantage of the Tower. The 1939–45 memorial nearly covers the site of the scaffold, where so many men and women suffered on Tower Hill.

Trinity Square

KENSAL TOWN [KENSINGTON AND CHELSEA]

Kensal New Town, a working-class suburb squeezed between the Grand Junction Canal, the Great Western Railway and the Western Gas Works, was begun in the 1830s and greatly expanded in the 1840s. That was when the land between East Row and Middle Row was filled with a network of cottages approached via alleys. The ones closest to East Row were known in the 1850s as Trinity Cottages and Trinity Square, but later they were all called Trinity Cottages.

The area was largely cleared in the 1880s to make way for a school, a church institute and a bus garage, but the Booth description of the other side of East Row in 1899 gives a good idea of what the Trinity Square area was like: 'a small village of one storied red tiled hovels which stretch back from the main road, probably the habitations of labourers when Kensal New Town was a brickfield or a market garden'.

St Mary's School and the former bus garage still occupy the site of the square.

Truman Square

BERMONDSEY [SOUTHWARK]

Truman Square, otherwise known as Truman Place, was the northernmost of three courts off the west side of Prospect Street – the prospect being over the marshy ground that became Southwark Park. The Booth survey of 1899 found that one of the other courts, Arica Place, was built in 1845.

Truman Square, which took its name from the owner, George Frederick Truman, was probably of a slightly later date. It certainly existed by 1860 but perhaps not in 1857. The Booth survey, which called it Truman's Place, noted that the people were poor and the houses of two storeys, arranged on the north and west sides only.

The 1914 map showed five in the square, plus four in Prospect Street that looked like part of the same development. There was a small open space in the centre that might at a pinch have justified the name of 'square'. Truman Square still existed in 1934, but had gone before the Second World War.

Prospect Place is now a service road on Southwark Council's Kirby Estate, with a prospect only of washing hanging from the walkways of ugly blocks of flats.

Turner Square

HOXTON [HACKNEY]

Turner Square, later known as Turner's Square, was the central stem of a network of alleys between Hoxton Street and Pitfield Street, in an area now occupied by the Arden Estate. There was nothing about it to justify the name of 'square' except a slightly wider section towards the east end. It was otherwise long and narrow and the forty-odd cottages did not even have front gardens to give a sense of space.

It was shown incomplete and nearly surrounded by fields on Horwood's 1790s map, and Cary's 1795 map indicated only the north and south sides, not the west. It had reached its final form by the time of the 1813 revision of Horwood.

It was never much better than a slum. There was a brewery in the square in the 1830s and 1840s, and in 1898 the Booth surveyor described it as '2 or 3 storey,

poor, cement paved'. Turner Square survived the Second World War, but was reduced to a short stub at the east end in the 1950s. The stub was extinguished in the 1960s, when more shops and flats were built on the site.

Turner Square

WHITECHAPEL [TOWER HAMLETS]

The East End Turner Square was a terrace of seven houses set back from the south side of Whitechapel Road between the present New Road and Ivy Court. There was nothing resembling it on the Strype map, published in 1720 but probably surveyed earlier. It was shown distinctly on Rocque's 1740s map, with a grove of trees in front sheltering it from the road. Horwood numbered it 213–219 Whitechapel Road in the 1790s and Lockie placed it at No. 219, '4 doors W. of Cannon-st. road', in 1813. In his first edition of 1810 he had described it as 'about seven houses that stand back from the line of the pavement'. It had already disappeared by 1827, either because the houses had been rebuilt or because shopfronts had extended them forward to the Whitechapel Road building line. The shops now on the site are late Victorian.

Turner's Square

CITY OF LONDON

The tiny Turner's Square, which was probably not built until the 1830s, was a late addition to the collection of mean squares in the Houndsditch and Aldgate area. Only seven houses were listed in 1841 but each sheltered several families of labourers, porters and tailors. In 1852 there were six, each valued at £4 per annum.

Access was difficult, as the square was approached via a long alley on the south side of Gravel Lane and then through an archway on the south side of Amelia Place. There was no way out to Aldgate High Street.

The square's existence was as brief as it was obscure. It was demolished during the building of Aldgate Station, just to the south, which was opened in 1876. The site is now occupied by St Botolph Street and the open space to the north of it between the St Botolph Building and Beaufort House.

Ulster Square

This was one of several anticipations of John Nash's plans for Regent's Park, included in great detail on the Horwood map of 1813 but never carried out. It was shown with a large number of houses but only a small, tapering garden, west of Clarence Market, now Clarence Gardens. Chester Terrace and Chester Mews were built instead.

Unicorn Square

Unicorn Yard on the north side of Tooley Street was obviously named after an inn, although in the nineteenth century the pub at the corner was the Admiral Hood. The yard was named by Hatton in 1708 and it had the same general shape in all maps from 1720 until the 1860s: an alley opening at the north end into a square court that extended east and had a narrow outlet in Vine Yard.

Rocque showed a small building in the court in the 1740s, but by the 1790s it was entirely open. Horwood called the place Union Yard, but that was clearly an error. Unicorn Yard was the name for both alley and court well into the nineteenth century, but by 1841 the court was separately known as Unicorn Square. The Unicorn Yard Baptist Chapel existed south of the square for seventy years or more without disturbing it, but when the chapel was turned into a Roman Catholic school about 1870 the square was soon extinguished, first to make a playground and then to provide the site for a new school.

Unicorn Yard is now Unicorn Passage, and the Unicorn Theatre has taken the place of chapel, school and square.

Union Square

Union Square, Minories, was included by Maitland in his 1756 list but is not found elsewhere. It was probably his name for New Square, Vine Street.

Union Square

Union Square was the first name for Cranmer Court, which still forms a small open space off Clapham High Street, just north-east of the railway bridge, with the Royal Oak pub at the corner. It was built between 1827 and 1838, when the workhouse stood directly opposite on the south-east side of the High Street.

In 1841, when it was still called Union Square, the tenants of the four or five houses included a labourer, a painter, a grocer and a butcher. By 1851, the new and more appropriate name of Cranmer Court had been adopted. The corner was shaved off when the London, Chatham & Dover Railway built the bridge across the High Street in 1862 and opened its Clapham Station (now Clapham High Street) just to the north.

All the buildings in and around Cranmer Court were destroyed or badly damaged by two flying bombs that fell close by towards the end of the Second World War, but they have been reinstated.

Union Square

Union Square demonstrates better than any other the triumphant renaissance of the garden square in the twenty-first century. The developer responsible for the two squares north of the canal at Islington was Henry Rydon. Unluckily for its future, Union Square was half on the Clothworkers' and half on the Packington estate.

The houses were built in 1851–52, slightly later than those in the neighbouring Arlington Square. Union Square was mentioned in the 1851 census enumerator's description of his district, but no houses were included among the schedules. The style of the two squares is very similar, although the builders to whom Rydon sublet the plots were not the same. Two of the wide streets of the Clothworkers' estate (St Paul Street and Linton Street) cut across the short north and south sides of Union Square, and both have side turnings immediately opposite the garden.

The east side of Union Square, Islington, in 2007.

This meant that it was only the terraces on the long east and west sides (twelve on the west, thirteen on the east) that were thoroughly part of the square, although a few at the corners of Union Street and Bevan Street were numbered in it or enjoyed a distant view of the garden.

The square has only become prosperous and fashionable in modern times. It was built with clerks, shopkeepers, and skilled craftsmen in mind and they, with the odd doctor or schoolteacher, were the early residents. It declined later in the nineteenth century as the houses were subdivided, and was shabby even before the Second World War, in which some minor damage was done.

Islington Council bought the Packington estate compulsorily in 1963, to protect the tenants (as said) from their landlords, but soon announced plans to rebuild the whole area, moving the tenants to council flats around the borough. A planning battle ensued

with those who wished to see the old houses rehabilitated. Richard Crossman, the housing minister, visited the area. He thought that it 'wouldn't become as good as Canonbury but it could become a second-class Canonbury', but he weakly caved in to his undersecretary, Bob Mellish, who told him, 'We want to pull the whole bloody thing down and we are determined to develop the area for council building'. The new Packington Square Estate was built in the late 1960s, the demolitions for it including the west side of Union Square in 1966. The garden, which had been owned by the council since 1946, was protected by the 1931 Act, but it was soon overshadowed by the high flank wall of the estate.

The brutalists won that battle, but within twenty-five years the Packington estate was falling apart. In 2010 the revived prestige of the garden square had changed even local council sentiment to such an extent that when the crumbling estate was demolished to general joy, a facsimile of the lost side of Union Square was built as the eastern boundary of the new development. Strangest of all, the building firm employed was Rydon. But Islington Council would still not admit to a mistake. Visiting the square to celebrate the completion of the second phase of the project in 2012, the mayor claimed that the Packington estate had served the people well for fully forty years and that only 'slum Victorian housing' had been demolished to make way for it; this while gazing across the garden at the immaculate surviving houses, 'slums' that now change hands for well over £1 million.

Union Square

PENTONVILLE [ISLINGTON]

Building began on the Pentonville estate in the 1770s but proceeded slowly. Union Square was on its mean northern fringe, the last part to be dealt with, so the event commemorated by the square's name was perhaps the parliamentary union of England and Ireland in 1800. It was certainly built at about that time. Cary's 1795 map showed no development north of Chapel Street, but the square was named on James Tyrer's 1805 Clerkenwell map.

The houses lay back behind front gardens of which the privies took up the greater part. Drinking water came from a pump in the centre of the court. In 1841 the tenants were mainly labourers, porters and shoemakers, but there was also the odd jeweller or watchmaker. The Booth survey of 1897 included it among 'rough courts out of Chapel Street'. 'Union Square has 15 2-storied cottages … A roughish set of costers and fish curers, no trouble to the police.'

It was off the north side of Chapel Street, running back towards another court named Mount Sion. Union Square probably communicated with Mount Sion either officially or via a hole in the wall, as it gave access to the south side of Mantell Street, formerly Sermon Lane but now included in Tolpuddle Street. The little square must have been demolished sometime between 1912, when it appeared in the LCC list of streets, and 1914, when the Ordnance Survey showed the site cleared and vacant.

Union Square

See Dickens Square

Upper Square

ISLEWORTH [HOUNSLOW]

The Upper Square at Isleworth is not to be considered as part of the formal tradition that began with Covent Garden in the 1630s. As a widened opening at the junction of several roads it is older than that, but it was not called a square until the West End made the name fashionable.

The west side of Upper Square, Isleworth, in 2011.

It was very much the junior partner to the present Lower Square, which was known emphatically as 'The Square' until early in the twentieth century. The Upper Square had mainly smaller houses, which by 1850 had nearly all become shops. The most important building was the Swan, at the corner of Swan Street.

The square was given a little more civic importance late in the nineteenth century with a drinking fountain and cattle trough on the little green and a bank on the most prominent corner. Today the chief interest lies in the much-altered eighteenth-century houses, now shops and restaurants, on the west side.

Upton Square

See Gibson Square

Vauxhall Square

VAUXHALL [LAMBETH]

Horwood's 1790s map showed twenty-eight houses with private gardens of a reasonable size in Vauxhall Square, but no communal garden in the centre, although the space was quite big enough to accommodate one. The only access was a narrow passage between the houses of Vauxhall Row to the west. Just north of the square was a much less common feature, two confronted crescents (almost forming an oval) called Glasshouse Street. This is the clue to the history.

All of these houses were built on the site of the huge Vauxhall glassworks. It was set up by the 2nd Duke of Buckingham in 1670 and closed about 1780, although the buildings were still shown on a possibly outdated map of 1795.

Vauxhall Square and Glasshouse Street were clearly built with some pretentions to smartness and they must have been pleasant enough in the early days. But Vauxhall never shook off its long industrial heritage and the square soon embarked on a downward path that grew steeper as the nineteenth century advanced. The first serious blow came in 1848, when the London & South Western Railway was extended from Nine Elms to Waterloo, the viaduct slicing off the western end of the square.

Vauxhall Row was widened in stages from the late 1860s to conform with the new Albert Embankment to the north, in which it was later incorporated. The railway viaduct was widened bit by bit as more tracks were added, eating further into the square. By 1871 only twenty houses were standing and a pottery had been established in the north-east corner.

In 1890 or soon afterwards the square was acquired as part of the site of the huge Guinness Trust Buildings, tenements that were themselves demolished in 1975. They were replaced by the unexpected park known as Spring Gardens, which is now almost verging into a wood.

Vernon Square

The tiny Vernon Square was built in the early 1840s on an outlying corner of the New River Company's estate. It never had more than three sides, the fourth being taken by Bagnigge Wells Road, or King's Cross Road as we call it. Even a third side is doubtful, as the houses to the west of the garden were numbered in Penton Place.

Most of the east side was occupied by the Vernon Baptist Chapel, which left very little space for houses. The LCC added a few in 1906 when it incorporated with Vernon Square the even smaller offshoot known as Percy Square. But what the LCC gave with one hand it took with the other. In 1913 both the north side of Vernon Square and the Percy Square addition were demolished to make way for the Vernon Square School, built between 1913 and 1916. It is now the Vernon Square Campus of the School of Oriental & African Studies.

The Vernon Baptist Chapel was built for the Reverend Owen Clarke, secretary of the British & Foreign Temperance Society, in 1843–44. The architect may have been his builder, William Smith, or possibly James Harrison of the nearby Holford Square. Clarke also had the two flanking houses built, completing the east side of the square. The one to the north was replaced by the church hall in 1933 and the one to the south (which was bombed in 1941) by the manse, so now there are no houses in the square. Only the chapel survives, as the King's Cross Baptist Church.

Beresford Chancellor wrote in 1907 that 'Vernon Square has been lopped away, to increase the adjoining road, and is no more a square'. It was certainly never much of a square, but even today it retains the most important element, a garden, with four trees and a few seats and bushes, forming a welcome oasis in the Kings Cross Road.

Victoria Park Square

Bethnal Green would be of no more concern to this book than Camberwell Green or Newington Green, had the government not changed the name of the road facing the east side to Victoria Park Square in 1868. This was in belated response to the opening of Victoria Park, the grand approach road of which begins 100 yards away.

It is only a one-sided square, the roads to north, south and west being too long and important to be included, although the eighteenth-century houses at the north end, which turn their backs to Old Ford Road, might have made half of a north side and Paradise Row part of an east.

Bethnal Green stood in for the garden, but at the time of the renaming it was being seriously reduced in size by the erection, on the northern half, of the Bethnal Green Branch of the South Kensington Museum. This was the old Brompton Boilers, the long-lasting temporary home of the Victoria & Albert Museum, re-erected at Bethnal Green between 1868 and 1872. There, it was first used to exhibit the Wallace Collection while Hertford House was being enlarged. It is still an outstation of the V&A, now as the Museum of Childhood.

The east side of Vernon Square, *c.* 1905.

It was not the only intrusion on the green: at the south end is Soane's St John's Church of 1826–28. The open section between the two intruders is known as Museum Gardens, having been acquired by the government with the site of the museum in 1868.

Number 17 Victoria Park Square in 2013.

Bethnal Green itself was ancient, immemorial, and detached houses were built on its eastern edge from at least as early as the sixteenth century. Late in the seventeenth century a continuous terrace began to replace the large Tudor houses. East Side was the only name applied to the whole of it before 1868, but the northern end was known separately as Grove Place.

Today Victoria Park Square contains a miscellany of buildings ranging in date from the seventeenth century to the end of the twentieth. The most important are the 1680s pair numbered 17 and 18, the most prominent Our Lady of the Assumption, a Roman Catholic church of 1911–12 at the north end.

Much of the south end, including the vicarage on the west side, was destroyed in the Second World War, and two houses were lost at the north corner of Sugar Loaf Walk, but otherwise the square escaped with only blast damage. The south end is now made hideous by flats on part of the vicarage site and by a police station and fire station that are equally ugly in their very different styles. The police station is on the site of the Royal Engineers' volunteer barracks.

The barracks, Victoria Park Square, c. 1905.

Victoria Square

Victoria Square was the creation of the architect and developer Sir Matthew Wyatt, one of the extended family that produced twenty or more architects in the eighteenth and nineteenth centuries.

Wheatley said, not quite accurately, that it 'was built circ. 1836, or rather scooped out of the back gardens of Arabella Row and Ranelagh Street'. Before the square was created there was a yard or court on the site with two or three houses, and it was from the extinction of these that the space was obtained, more than from the gardens of the surrounding streets. The houses in Arabella Row (now Lower Grosvenor Place) and Ranelagh Street (now Beeston Place) retained some of their gardens. The lease under which the old houses were held only expired in 1836 and Wyatt and his associate John Howell did not obtain a new one from the Marquess of Westminster until 1837.

The estate surveyor Thomas Cundy had a street in mind but Wyatt persuaded him to accept a more prestigious square. His plan was submitted to Cundy in 1838 and the houses were built in 1839–40. A statue of Queen Victoria was already in the centre in Thomas Campbell's day, as it is mentioned by his first biographer. The Thomas Tuckey who lived at No. 1 in 1841 was perhaps the builder. Between 1841 and 1851 he moved to No. 3 and evolved from a builder into a gentleman.

Victoria Square has been mainly occupied by courtiers and minor politicians, the least minor being the rebarbative John Arthur Roebuck, who lived at No. 12 in the 1840s. The most notable resident was the brilliant but far from courtly Admiral Thomas Cochrane, 10th Earl of Dundonald, one of the liberators of Chile, Peru and Brazil, who was the first tenant of No. 2.

A few writers intruded among the courtiers. The most prominent could scarcely have been more different. Thomas Campbell lived at No. 8 from 1841 to 1843, towards the end of his long decline, when his fame as a poet was fading and he had sunk into an inefficient journalist and publishers' hack. He died at Boulogne the year after leaving the square.

Ian Fleming bought No. 16 in 1952, soon after his marriage to the divorced Lady Rothermere, and moved in at the start of 1953. It was his London home until his death in 1964. He told a friend that he had 'bought a beautiful Regency house in Victoria Square – between the Queen and the Goring Hotel. Whatever Anne says it is the same size as the flat, only vertical instead of horizontal. An expensive shift of position!' The house was not Georgian, but built at the start of Victoria's long reign, and the Flemings moved there at the start of Queen Elizabeth's longer reign. The move coincided with the publication of *Casino Royale*, the first of Fleming's Bond novels, so the years in Victoria Square were the most prosperous of his life, but not the

The garden of Victoria Square from the east in 2007.

happiest. His part of the vertical house was at the top, to which he retreated to escape from his wife's endless parties. The connection between Campbell and Fleming – not a startling coincidence in their profession – is that drink certainly shortened the life of both.

Other writers who have lived in the square are Henry Chorley, the music critic, at No. 15 in the early 1850s; Margaret Oliphant at No. 14 in 1880; and Leonard Woolf at No. 24 from 1943. When his short lease expired he bought another of ninety-nine years from the Grosvenor estate, to ensure he would always have a London home, even if he lived to be 150.

The Booth survey gave Victoria Square a reasonably good report in 1899:

Three and four storey houses with basements, all occupiers said to be 'independent, except a doctor', but on east side there are two or three houses that take lodgers. But the square has always had a good class of occupants. The Earl of Mount Edgecumbe is at No. 5.

In 1907 Beresford Chancellor called it 'a tiny cul-de-sac at the north end of Ebury Street', a curious mistake, as for such a small square it has the generous allowance of three entrances.

The diminutive size and the Nash-inspired architecture have always made it one of London's prettiest squares. The only drawback was the lack of a garden, which at one time threatened to make it an ugly car park. That objection has been overcome by the creation of a small paved private garden with trees, flower beds and seats, so the Queen's neighbours now enjoy every comfort.

Victory Square

CAMBERWELL [SOUTHWARK]

Victory Square was built in the mid-1880s, mainly on the site of a pair of houses with long gardens. In form it was not unlike Ludgate Square in the City, a narrow curving lane describing one quarter of a poorly drawn circle, but Victory Square was entirely residential.

The main entrance was in New Church Road. From there it swung jerkily round to emerge in an access lane at the side of a mineral water factory. Twenty-five houses were squeezed onto a small plot of ground. They were mostly in dull, bay-windowed terraces opening directly onto the pavement, but one group of five, probably built a little later, had front gardens.

The date of the square is of no help in deciding after which victory it was named, as the much older houses on the New Church Road frontage were called Victory Terrace or Victory Place.

The square survived until the late 1970s, but since the 1940s its fate had been sealed as part of the land required for the ever-growing Burgess Park, which now covers the site.

Victualling Office Square

It is hard to see how this came to be considered a square. From the first half of the eighteenth century the buildings, never more than six, occupied only the north and east sides, the rest being open to Little Tower Hill. The earliest maps did have some faint suggestions that there may once have been west and south sides.

The main building on the north was the Black Horse pub at the corner of Queen Street, which had a shop or two adjoining it. The east side was entirely taken up by the St Botolph Aldgate charity school and the house of the St Botolph beadle. The school stood next to the main entrance of the Royal Mint, on the site once occupied by the entrance to the Victualling Office. The square was destroyed, together with Queen Street, when the Mansell Street extension was driven through the site in 1907.

Vincent Square

Dr William Vincent's creation of Vincent Square in 1810 had two disposing causes, one long-standing, the other immediate. The first is illustrated by a report in the *Morning Post* of 9 July 1804 under the heading 'Westminster Club versus Westminster College':

Queen Elizabeth granted by charter to the Dean and Canons of Westminster, a piece of ground in the neighbourhood of Tothill-fields. The inhabitants of Westminster have for a number of years enjoyed the right of commonage on the piece of ground alluded to, and have long been in the habits of playing there at cricket. The Westminster Scholars insist that they have an exclusive right of playing at cricket on the ground, and the inhabitants on the other hand, contend they have an equal right. We understand that the Masters on Tuesday gave the Scholars a half holiday. About half-past five o'clock, while the Westminster Club were playing a match, the Scholars belonging to the College arrived and waited for one of their Ushers to head them, against the members of the Club … about six o'clock a person belonging to the College arrived on horseback, and made a grand charge on the innocent amusers wickets.

The gentlemanly conduct of the King's Scholars prevented this exciting scene from degenerating into a free-for-all, but the potential for serious town and gown riots was obviously there.

Nor was it the only sort of violence to be feared on the ground. Robberies were common, as were boxing matches, and in 1806 the *Morning Chronicle* recorded that 'at a bear-baiting on Monday in Tothill-fields, one of the bears having broke loose, fastened upon a person named Shawe, whom he tore very much with his paws'.

Victualling Office Square (on the left) and the Royal Mint in 1829.

Watching a match from the north side of the Westminster School playing field, Vincent Square, *c.* 1905.

The school authorities may also have been worried about the morals of the scholars, to judge from this *Morning Post* report of 1 September 1808, 'On Tuesday evening three young women ran, not incommoded with cloathes or modesty, three times round a given space in Tothill Fields, for a Holland shift and half-a-guinea, during which they afforded abundance of sport to a numerous company of curious spectators.'

The immediate occasion of the development was Vauxhall Bridge ('the Regent's Bridge') which was planned from 1808 and built between 1811 and 1816. A *Morning Post* report of 24 May 1811 on the progress of the bridge noted that, 'Various roads and streets are now cutting out, and Tothill-fields will shortly be graced with noble squares, stately buildings, with warehouses, etc., and the banks of the Thames very considerably improved.' The new Vauxhall Bridge Road, which cut across part of their land and made it accessible, was too good a commercial opportunity for the Dean and Chapter to pass up.

Dr Vincent, who had been headmaster of Westminster School from 1788 to 1801 and dean since 1803, was in the perfect position to shape the development in a way that would benefit his beloved school. By making an open space as large as Lincoln's Inn Fields the central feature of the estate he preserved

and improved the playing field and secured to the scholars the exclusive right to its use. In the process he created one of the very few squares with a private enclosure in the centre that is not accessible to the residents. The great size of the playing field disguises, on the ground, the fact that it is not square in shape, the west side following the line of the older Rochester Row and the south being splayed to conform with Vauxhall Bridge Road.

Two builders involved in the development were Alexander Copland and Henry Rowles (see Cadogan Square [1]) the nephew of Henry Holland. Copland was an architect in addition to being the first building contractor on an industrial scale. Work proceeded quite quickly and Dr Vincent had the satisfaction of seeing the square well advanced before his death in 1815.

The Horwood map of 1813 described the centre as 'Play Ground for the Westminster Scholars'. Houses, mostly semi-detached, were shown as built or being built on the north and west sides. One pair only appeared at the north end of the east side and not even a road was set out on the south. The 1815 sewer map showed eight houses on the west side, twelve on the north and two on the east.

In 1817 David Hughson gave a better account of progress:

We may add, that a part of this district, nearly as bad as the worst part of St Giles's, is now formed into a neat square, and one of the most spacious in London: each side consists of elegantly-constructed houses, somewhat in the cottage style. The area still serves as a play-ground to the Westminster scholars, and the square itself derives its name from their late venerable preceptor, Dr Vincent.

This original 'cottage style' survives in two pairs, Nos 3 and 4 on the east side and Nos 84 and 85 on the north. The detached No. 86 (which all the early maps showed as a pair) is of the same period. Hughson exaggerated the extent of the early development: Greenwood's 1827 map, like Horwood's, showed the east side almost entirely unbuilt. Greenwood did include the south side, naming it Douglas Street. The north and east sides he called 'Vincent Square' (as on Horwood's map) and the west side he left nameless.

A numbering system was already established by 1816, when lodgings at No. 28 were advertised. This and other notices stressed the convenience for the Houses of Parliament, but there is little sign that the hint was taken in the early days, while the ugly slums of Westminster lay between the square and Whitehall. It was only in the twentieth century that prominent politicians like Richard Crossman, Duncan Sandys and Harold Wilson settled in the square.

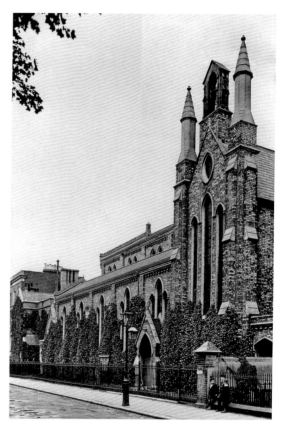

St Mary's, on the east side of Vincent Square, in 1907 or a little earlier.

The earliest celebrity was John Payne Collier, the literary scholar and forger, who lived there around 1816 (the year of his marriage) while working for *The Times* as a parliamentary reporter. Otherwise the square attracted clergymen, schoolmasters, solicitors and architects.

The circuit of houses was never completed because, from an early period as institutions found the square a convenient place to build. Edward Blore's St Mary's Church was first in 1836–37, and with its schools and vicarage it soon occupied a good deal of the east side. The Westminster Police Court on the west side, designed by Charles Reeves, was praised when it was built in 1847 as a great improvement on its predecessor in Queen Square, now Queen Anne's Gate. 'The cells for prisoners are constructed on the most approved principle,' said *The Illustrated London News*, 'combining with security a thorough ventilation and warming.' By the early twenty-first century the cells looked like a serious disincentive to crime.

Numbers 3 and 4 Vincent Square, on the east side, in 2013.

The Westminster Technical Institute on the north side of Vincent Square, *c.* 1910.

A few years after the court was opened the Coldstream Guards' Hospital was built next door. It was the first of a number of hospitals and nursing homes that dominated the west and south sides by the early twentieth century. On the north side most of the original pairs of houses were replaced by the Westminster Technical Institute and the Royal Horticultural Society's hall at the turn of the nineteenth and twentieth centuries.

A good many of the institutions have now gone. St Mary's was closed in 1923 and replaced by Vincent House in 1932. The hospitals have been demolished or converted into flats. The police court and the rear parts of the police station have given way to a lavish range of private apartments, complete with topiary, a garden god and eclectic decorative flourishes.

The architectural frame is now extremely miscellaneous, with more misses than hits, but the wide expanse of playing field provides ample compensation. The Westminster scholars, now boys and girls, are still to be seen trudging up field in their sports gear through the Westminster back streets, but now that the school has bought the Horticultural Society's new hall they will perhaps find life easier.

Walcot Square

KENNINGTON [LAMBETH]

Edmund Walcot left 17 acres to the poor of Lambeth and Southwark in 1667, and the half of the Walcot Estate assigned to St Mary Lambeth in 1713 is today the main source of income for the Lambeth Endowed Charities. Walcot Place was the old name for the fine eighteenth-century houses that still survive so plentifully in Kennington Road, between Brook Drive and Chester Way. The fields to the east remained as market garden ground until the 1830s, but the gap left in the Walcot Place terraces seems to indicate that a building development was long in contemplation. When it was finally carried out the main element was called Walcot Square. The name is not accurate, as the enclosure is a triangle, as is southern offshoot St Mary's Gardens, formerly St Mary's Square.

Walcot Square was built between 1837 and 1839, so this is perhaps London's earliest Victorian example of the form, but the three builders involved were still clinging precariously to the wreckage of the Georgian style. Their houses were small and plain, and they became plainer as the development proceeded, with the round-headed windows and fanlights of the south side giving way to simple lintels to the north and west.

In its early days the Walcot estate was popular with artists and journalists, including the editors of two leading newspapers. Thomas Barnes of *The Times* lived in Walcot Square and Lackland Mackintosh of *The Morning Post* in St Mary's Square. Another St Mary's Square journalist was Edward Barrow, the uncle of Charles Dickens; and in *Bleak House* Dickens gave Walcot Square a distinguished legal resident, for it was there that Mr Guppy intended to set up his practice after qualifying as an attorney.

There was much bomb damage in Walcot Square, with a number of houses destroyed on the south side, but the gap has been made good with inoffensive replicas. At the eastern end there was a small parade of shops. One surviving oddity is a blind-ended extension to the square in the north-west corner that features a tiny single-storey detached house with a semi-basement – almost a bungalow.

In 1899 Charles Booth's researcher had found the estate in decline, with 'mess in street'. Today Walcot Square is very tidy and more prosperous than at any time in its history.

Warburton Square

HACKNEY

Warburton Square existed for seventy years between the south-eastern point of London Fields and the toe of Victoria Park. It was one of the sorry apologies for a square that appeared in the second half of the nineteenth century, when the real thing was going out of fashion. Like Cheriton Square at Balham it was planned with houses in the centre, where a garden should have been.

Cheriton Square still exists, but Warburton Square and the nearby Duncan Square featured poor-quality houses that have not survived. Warburton Square was built in the 1860s and demolished in 1935 as part of a slum clearance programme that swept away most of the neighbouring streets. The large block of council flats called Warburton House is on the site.

The north side of Walcot Square in 1967, with the Imperial War Museum in the background. (Photograph by M.D. Trace, courtesy of Lambeth Archives)

Warren's Square

See Sir William Warren's Square

Warwick Square

Warwick Square is exceptional in the City of London in that it clung to its original name of Warwick Court for 140 years while dozens of others, far less deserving of it, were being promoted to the fashionable name of square. It had some of the attributes of a fine square – shape, quality of houses, uniformity of design – but

no central garden. Instead there was a wide expanse of roadway, with a lamp in the middle.

Warwick Court took its name from Warwick Lane, from the west side of which it branched. It was first recorded, fully formed, on the Ogilby & Morgan map of 1676. As Warwick Lane was destroyed in the Fire of London, Warwick Court must have been built or rebuilt between 1666 and 1676, a date that agrees well with its formal design and the original architectural style. The canons' houses in Amen Court just to the south were built in 1671–73.

The curious features of Warwick Court were the extensions at the south-west and north-west corners, rather like those at Barnsbury Square, except that

Warwick Square, City, from Warwick Lane, in 2007.

there the houses in the extensions are larger, and here they were smaller than those in the main part. There were fourteen houses in the square itself, plus eight distributed between the two extensions. The major houses were of three storeys plus attic and basement and were three bays wide on the short west side, two bays on the north and south sides.

Warwick Court was popular with doctors in the seventeenth and eighteenth centuries, being so close to the College of Physicians. Lawyers also lived there. Lord Truro, the son of an attorney who rose to be Lord Chancellor, was born in Warwick Court in 1782.

It was beginning to be known as Warwick Square by 1813. On the Horwood map it was called Warwick Court, but John Lockie, in the second edition of his *Topography of London*, published in the same year, listed it as Warwick Square with a cross reference from Warwick Court. In 1810 he had given the cross reference but neglected to write the substantive entry. It was a common case, no doubt, of an extended struggle between fashion and tradition.

In the nineteenth century it was very much a part of the Paternoster Row quarter of the City, full of printers, booksellers, newsagents, engravers, stereotypers, bookbinders, publishers (especially of newspapers) and one of the first advertising agencies.

Nearly the whole of the north side was demolished in the 1860s and replaced by an extension to the huge brass foundry of Tylor & Sons, which extended to Newgate Street. The firm had taken over the old College of Physicians in Warwick Lane in 1829 and later expanded south. In the rest of the square the original red brick Restoration houses survived for a little longer, except for one rebuilt in discordant stucco on the south side and another on the west.

Nearly every building in Warwick Square was damaged during the Second World War and those at the south-east corner were totally destroyed. Now the north and west sides are occupied by the rear of the 1960s extension to the Old Bailey and the south side by a 1960s office block, but now the square does at last have a garden, albeit a miniature one, where two trees make a brave show in summer. There are flower beds and benches, and in the south-west corner a view of Ewan Christian's minor canons' houses in Amen Court.

Warwick Square

KENSINGTON [KENSINGTON AND CHELSEA]

(now part of Warwick Gardens)

Warwick Square was the original name for the wide northern end of Warwick Gardens, a development begun in 1822. The contractors were Joseph and Thomas Brindley, shipbuilders who dabbled in house building, and the architect was William Cutbush, surveyor to Lord Kensington, the landowner.

Things proceeded slowly for three or four years, the developers paying tradesmen and architects by assigning leases to them, but in 1826 the great financial crisis that ruined Sir Walter Scott bankrupted the Brindleys. Work came almost to a halt for several years while legal arguments raged, but a criminal case in May 1827, when a man was transported for stealing tools from a carpenter working on an unfinished house, shows that something was still being done to complete the existing carcases.

A compromise was reached between Lord Kensington and the other Brindley creditors (who included John Nash) in 1829. The unfinished houses were completed and sold, but no new ones were begun for nearly twenty years, faith in the original scheme having been fatally undermined. When a new builder was persuaded to try his luck in the late 1840s it was only at the price of abandoning the square and continuing the development south in the form of a street called Warwick Gardens East and West. Warwick Square was retained as the name for the wide north end until the 1870s.

After it had lost its original identity, the square had two celebrated residents. In 1881 Holman Hunt was living at No. 2 Warwick Gardens, the large house at the north-west corner. It has been demolished, but was a mirror image of the surviving No. 1. At No. 11, the first of the houses that began the tapering of the square into a road, there is a blue plaque to G.K. Chesterton, who spent much of his childhood and youth there.

The garden that was planned for the square was never provided, but the wide expanse of road was given some definition in 1934, when the Queen

The east side of the northern section of Warwick Gardens (formerly Warwick Square, Kensington), *c.* 1905.

Victoria memorial column from Kensington High Street was moved to the centre. Now, with its satellite cattle trough and flower beds, it gives the space something of the feeling of a square that it so signally failed to achieve in the 1820s. The surviving houses of that date, Nos 1–9 (odd) on the east side, show how grand a square it might have been if the trade cycle had been kinder.

Warwick Square

PIMLICO [WESTMINSTER]

According to Anthony Trollope's fine discrimination, in the 1860s Warwick Street, cutting across diagonally between Eccleston Square and Warwick Square, marked the boundary of fashionable London. Eccleston Square was an honorary part of Belgravia, but everything south and east of it was beyond the pale. This probably had something to do with the protracted building history of Warwick Square, which was not even complete when Trollope was writing *The Small House at Allington*.

Thomas Cubitt obtained a lease of the marshy Pimlico land from the Marquess of Westminster in 1825, but he then spent a decade in raising and levelling the ground to make it suitable for building. The planning and naming of the streets and squares was a gradual process, subject to change as building progressed. It appears from this report on the opening of Belgrave Road and Eccleston Street published in the *Era* of 1 January 1843, that Marlborough Square was the original name. 'Mr Cubitt has also opened a commodious road from Vauxhall-bridge through Lincoln-place, Besborough-place, Marlborough-square, Eccleston-square, Eaton-square, and Belgrave-square, to Albert-gate at Knightsbridge.' St George's Square cannot have been meant, as it was named in the same article.

Pimlico was a slightly anticlimactic end to the triumphant career of Thomas Cubitt. It was a great technical achievement, and his prudence prevented it from being a disaster, but it did not repeat the financial success of his earlier developments. During Cubitt's lifetime Warwick Square was one of the more disappointing parts of Pimlico, with less than

The north-west side of Warwick Square, Pimlico, c. 1905.

half the houses finished and the rest left for his heirs to deal with. Cubitt himself built only Nos 1–5 on the north side and 64–66 on the south, and those few house occupied him throughout the 1840s, for want of tenants, not manpower or resources. Numbers 6–11 were added by another builder between 1851 and Cubitt's death in 1855. There he left the square which his executors, mainly leasing plots to other builders, could not get finished until 1869.

The houses on the short Belgrave Road side of the square were not considered part of it by Cubitt, although the numbering has always included them. They were built before most of the houses on the north and south sides. The west side is mainly occupied by St Gabriel's Church, built in 1851–53 to the designs of the estate surveyor, Thomas Cundy, on land reluctantly surrendered by Cubitt.

South and south-east of the church are the oddities of the square. Number 33 is a studio house built in 1860–61, and as defiantly out of keeping with its surroundings as any piece of modern brutalism. It was built for the fashionable Scottish portrait painter James Swinton, so some fine ladies were obliged to cross the Warwick Road boundary to visit his studio.

The architect was George Morgan. Opposite this oddity is the large private garden of the last house on the south side of the square, which was built for Cubitt's daughter in 1865. This is an anomaly of a more traditional kind, a throwback to the proprietor's house of some of the earlier West End squares.

The lists of occupants confirms Trollope's verdict on the square. Viscount Torrington, who lived at No. 4 in the early days, was a rare aristocratic tenant. He was a relation of the Duke of Bedford and probably known to Cubitt since his Bloomsbury days. Such was the cachet that his residence in the new square was thought to confer that he was able to negotiate a reduced rent. But although Warwick Square did not scale the social heights it did maintain a reasonable reputation throughout the nineteenth century, being particularly popular with admirals. A rare celebrity was George Earle Buckle, the editor of *The Times*, who lived at No. 64 during the later years of his editorship, which lasted from 1884 to 1912.

Even more than Eccleston Square, Warwick Square declined in the first half of the twentieth century, when most of the houses were broken up into flats, but having got through the Second World War with very little damage, and retaining a private garden, it recovered more quickly than most of Pimlico. Among those who have lived there since the war are the great London novelist William Sansom in the 1940s and Churchill's son-in-law Duncan Sandys, who spent his last years in a flat at No. 12.

Warwick Square

SOUTHWARK

A late eighteenth-century yard just north-east of St George's Circus was variously known as Ebdin, Ebden, or Ebdon Court from the 1790s to the 1860s. It was off the west side of Pearl Row, which became Warwick Street in the 1850s. In the next decade Ebdin Court was renamed Warwick Square to match, although it was not square in shape and had only two or three houses.

In 1905 the LCC decided that there were too many places called Warwick Street and Square and changed both of these to Milcote Street. In that guise the houses of the former square survived the Second World War but were swept away in comprehensive redevelopment in the 1950s. Only the southern end of Milcote Street survives. The site of the square is the yard north of Milcote House.

Waterhouse Square

HOLBORN [CAMDEN]

It is doubtful whether Waterhouse Square should be included in this list, as it is merely the modern name for the great courtyard of the Prudential Assurance Offices in Holborn. The building was begun in 1876, but the courtyard was the last part to be built, between 1895 and 1901. Alfred Waterhouse was the architect. The square was named in his honour after

Waterhouse Square from the south-west in 2009.

the Prudential had given up the building, which was converted into sets of offices between 1990 and 1993.

Here is one Gothic square that does work, because Waterhouse was not thinking of a square at all, but of the courtyard of a mighty castle or palace. It is all done in bright red brick and terracotta. The Prudential war memorial stands in the corner and the centrepiece is an imaginative domed light-well for the basements, that incorporates lamps for the square and seats for loiterers. It all looks especially fine when the rain glitters on the patterned pavement.

Waterloo Square

CAMBERWELL [SOUTHWARK]

The original Waterloo Square was a tiny court off the west side of George Street (later Lomond Grove) and part of a dense network of small streets, generally called 'Place' or 'Row', that extended to Camberwell Road. The square was built in the 1840s; its name did not come directly from the battle but from Waterloo Street, which ran east from George Street.

In the late 1880s half of this district was demolished to make way for a huge range of tenements to which the name Waterloo Square was transferred, perhaps because that was the best-sounding place among those supplanted. It was certainly not the largest, as it consisted only of four cottages facing each other two and two across front gardens that represented the square. They were approached from the south end of George Street via an archway and a long alley.

The big new Waterloo Square had a narrow courtyard running down the centre. There were seven blocks on the west side of the court and six on the east, where a few small terraced houses had survived at the north end. When the Charles Booth poverty map was being revised in 1899 these model dwellings were described as 'less well looked after [than the blocks further north in George Street] but said to be the more expensive', and the tenants were in reasonably comfortable circumstances.

There was serious damage to the south end during the Second World War and blast damage to all the other blocks. They were demolished in the 1960s and replaced by council housing set to a different pattern. The flats between Lomond Grove and Bullace Row are on the site of the extinguished square.

Waterman Square

PENGE [BROMLEY]

Waterman Square is the modern name for the former Watermen's Company almshouses built in 1840–41, so this is a dubious case like Waterhouse Square. The Free Watermen & Lightermen's Almshouses, to give them their full name, were designed by George Porter in a full-blooded Tudor style with grand twin clock towers flanking the chapel and gateway. Some of the eccentricities have been attributed to Porter's celebrated pupil Samuel Teulon, but he left to set up his own practice in 1838.

The company found the almshouses hard to repair and maintain after serious bomb damage in 1941, and they were closed in 1973 when the company moved its pensioners to Watermen's Close, Hastings. The old houses were occupied by council tenants at first, but as they passed into private ownership from the 1980s the estate was smartened up and given its smart new name. It is now – faint praise perhaps – the glory of Penge.

Waterman Square from the south-west in 2013.

Watt's Square

See Chamber Square

Webb's Square

Webb's (or Webb) Square, which lay off the east side of Shoreditch High Street, was built about 1718 on land that had formerly belonged to the priory of St Mary Spital. By the late seventeenth century this portion of the priory estate had passed into the hands of John Hudson of Bovington, Hertfordshire, after whom the square was nearly named. In a mortgage deed of 11 November 1718 some land to the south was described as 'two parcels of ground … abutting north on the square intended to be railed in 12 feet from the demised premises and to be called Hudson's Square'. In the event, the godfather was John Webb, who held a lease of part of the property in 1718. The 'Strype' map of 1720 showed 'Webbs Square' surrounded with the rail, and in Rocque's map of 1746 with trees. The open space, more court than garden, was square in shape but the houses were mostly on the extended north and south sides. In John Stow's 1722 list it appeared as 'Web's Square, in Shoreditch'. There is an 1806 plan in the Crace Collection showing the internal arrangement of several of the houses in some detail.

The square's only celebrity was John Joseph Griffin, who was born there in 1802. He had a successful career in Glasgow and London as a publisher, chemist and manufacturer of chemical apparatus. He was the author of the often reprinted *Chemical Recreations* (1823).

Webb's Square was demolished about 1839 to make way for the old Shoreditch Station, the terminus of the Eastern Counties Railway, which was opened in 1840 and renamed Bishopsgate Station in 1847. Shoreditch High Street Station is now more or less on the site.

Wellclose Square

Wellclose Square was sometimes known as Marine Square 'from the number of sea-officers who live there', as John Noorthouck explained in 1773. It was created by the notoriously ruthless and unscrupulous developer Nicholas Barbon in 1682–83. The diagonal alleys at the corners were a trademark, seen also at his Red Lion Square. Defoe, in an account published in 1725, remembered it in its earliest days and incidentally explained the name:

> Well Close, now called Marine Square, was so remote from Houses, that it used to be a very dangerous Place to go over after it was dark, and many People have been robbed and abused in passing it; a Well standing in the middle, just where the Danish Church is now built, there the Mischief was generally done.

The Danish church in the centre was built in 1694. The sculptor Caius Cibber, himself born a Danish subject in Schleswig-Holstein, designed it without charging a fee and was buried there in 1700.

The square was built slowly, in a variety of styles and materials – number 26 was small and weather-boarded – but Parker's 1720 map showed 'Well Close' with a full frame of terraces round the church.

The houses were mostly three bays wide, but varied in height from two to four storeys. The larger ones were inhabited by substantial sea captains, merchants and officials during the eighteenth century. It was from this group that the square's chief celebrity sprang. Thomas Day, author of *Sandford and Merton*, a children's classic in the days before *Alice*, was born at No. 36 on the south side in 1748. He was the son of the deputy collector outwards of customs in the port of London. *Sandford and Merton*, written in the 1780s under the influence of Rousseau, is now largely forgotten, but Day is still remembered for his extraordinary attempt to educate two foundling girls on the principles set out in *Émile*, with the idea of making one of them his wife. The experiment was a predictable failure.

The Swedish mystic Emanuel Swedenborg, who worshipped at the Swedish church in the adjoining Prince's Square and was buried there, is said to have lodged in Wellclose Square during some of his frequent visits to London.

Being so far off the beaten track, the square changed little during two and a half centuries. Houses were rebuilt from time to time but generally it was cheaper to adapt the old ones to new uses. When the painters James Northcote and Joseph Farington toured the East End in 1811, 'in walking through Wellclose square and that neighbourhood [Northcote] said it appeared to Him like a Country town, and excited in his mind a melancholy feeling such as He always had in those places'.

The south-west corner was the first to be broken up, with a large cooperage at No. 27, Joel Emanuel's Almshouses (opened in 1840 and later known as the Jews' Almshouses) at No. 29, and the Sessions House for the Tower Liberty at No. 33. There was also a factory at No. 48 on the east side before the end of the eighteenth century.

The Danish church was given a brief new lease of life as the Mariners' Church in 1845, and a painting made to commemorate the occasion shows a very spruce square with a luxuriantly planted garden. This must have been largely propaganda, as the area was becoming very poor and the square was in serious decline. In 1840 half the houses were in commercial use and by the 1850s there were only three or four private residents. The church was demolished in 1869

St Paul's School, Wellclose Square, *c.* 1910.

The Danish Church, Wellclose Square, in the 1750s.

and the St Paul's Schools (attached to St Paul's Church for Seamen in Dock Street) were built on the site and opened in 1870. In 1900 the square was full of Jewish and maritime charities and missions.

In spite of – or perhaps because of – all this poverty and decay, many of the original houses survived. Some were shaken during the Second World War but few were seriously damaged. As late as the 1960s it would have been possible to restore the square if the will had existed. Instead, the houses were all demolished as slums, only the school in the centre being spared, but very little was done with the site. Barbon's alleys are still in use in the two western corners, Grace's Alley having the unique Wilton's Music Hall on its north side, but much of the square is surrounded by wasteland.

Wellington Square

BLOOMSBURY [CAMDEN]

Wellington Square lay due north of Mecklenburgh Square and south-east of Regent Square. It was attached to the east end of the twin burial grounds belonging to St George's Bloomsbury and St George the Martyr, Queen Square. 'Near the Foundling' was how one early resident described it.

The land belonged to Thomas Harrison, a brick-maker, who had prepared the way for the development of his estate with a private act obtained in 1810. (See Regent Square.) The name sufficiently indicates the date. It was an early tribute to the Iron Duke, built indeed before he was raised to that rank, as it was begun in 1811. Sir Arthur Wellesley was created Viscount Wellington in 1809 and duke in 1814.

The 1813 Horwood map indicated seventeen tiny houses and a tiny garden in the centre. The houses on the south side were back to back with those in Prospect Terrace and on the west side they were built against the burial ground wall, with no front or back gardens, so it was not a tribute of which Wellington would have felt proud, had he ever stumbled across it.

Small though they were, the eighteen houses sheltered more than sixty families in 1851, plus numerous lodgers. Most of the tenants were labourers, bricklayers, house painters, etc., but one was 'Attendant

in Library in British Museum'. The square was demolished and Prospect Terrace Board School built on the site in 1890. For a short time the approach road from Sidmouth Street was called Wellington Place, but soon even the ghost was banished when it was made part of Prospect Terrace. That and the school have now gone with the whole of the old street pattern and the new building of the Westminster Kingsway College occupies the site, with entrances in Gray's Inn Road and Sidmouth Street.

Wellington Square

CHELSEA [KENSINGTON AND CHELSEA]

Most Wellington place names were given during the great man's days of military glory between 1809 and 1815, but Wellington Square at Chelsea commemorates his declining years as a deaf elder statesman in the 1840s.

The site of the square was occupied by Downing's floor cloth factory until 1836 or a little earlier. When houses were built on the King's Road frontage at that time a gap was left for 'Johnson's Square', but it went no further than the name. Howard Colvin says that Francis Edwards, best known as an industrial architect, 'completed' Wellington Square for Thomas Goding between 1840 and 1847. Goding was the proprietor of the Lion Brewery and Edwards had designed several brewery buildings for him, including the famous one on the South Bank.

'Completed' is a more unlikely word to use of Wellington Square than of any other in London, for besides being one of the most attractive, it is unusually regular and uniform. Most squares (like most films) are messy collaborations; there are few that express so completely as Wellington Square the pure conception of a single mind. One other is Gibson Square, also designed by Edwards. Perhaps Goding, as financial backer or mortgagee, stepped in to rescue the abortive Johnson's Square scheme and brought in his favourite architect to carry it through. The principal builder was Robert Cox.

Like nearly all the Chelsea squares, this one rose only gradually to its present popularity. The houses were built between 1847 and 1852 and the first half dozen were occupied early in 1849. Two sold in October were let at £120 per annum and held for a term of eighty years. Twenty-five of the thirty-five houses had been disposed of by 1851 and there were solid tenants, including the architect Thomas Tyerman at No. 7, but also several boarding houses. In 1856 the residents included a solicitor, a builder and a professor of pianoforte. Wellington Square had an equivocal reputation in the late nineteenth century, when men who could not rise to a St John's Wood villa were apt to keep their mistresses in the discreet seclusion of a Chelsea square.

Wellington Square, Chelsea, from the north, *c.* 1905 (above) and *c.* 1920.

The Booth survey of 1899 reported 'many prostitutes here'. In 1902 it was almost entirely given up to apartments and boarding houses, except for the St Mary's Home for Women and Children at No. 15.

Wellington Square's ascent to its present eminence began modestly with the bohemian invasion of the King's Road early in the twentieth century. Artists and writers settled here, including Sir Lawrence Gowing, the painter and art historian, who lived at No. 25 in the 1940s after leaving Paultons Square. One might say that Mrs Miniver lived at No. 16. That was the home during the 1930s, when the Miniver stories were being written, of Mrs Joyce Maxstone Graham, who wrote them under the name of Jan Struther. It was widely assumed that Mrs Miniver, the perfect wife, was a self-portrait, but 'Jan Struther' spent the war in America, being fêted in Hollywood during the making of the famous film, and afterwards divorced her husband, who had been a prisoner of war.

Wellington Square is now delightful. Particularly attractive are the two hidden extensions at the south end, forming extremely quiet and secluded sub-squares in the corners. The garden is too narrow to be a social amenity and there are no seats, but the trees are well-grown and a fountain plays in the central pond.

Wellington Square

See Chelsea Square

Wesson Square

See Mansion House Square, Camberwell

West Square

SOUTHWARK

West Square, one of the finest in south London, has nothing whatever to do with the points of the compass. It was built on land belonging to Jane West and her son, Temple. She was the widow of Colonel Temple West who had died in 1784, leaving her a life interest in his Lambeth estate. In 1791 the mother and son granted a building lease to Thomas Kendall and James Hedger.

The principal in the transaction was Hedger, who was popularly known as 'the King of St George's Fields'. He had made money as the proprietor of the Dog & Duck public house and medicinal spa in Lambeth Road, just to the west, and invested it in leasehold property. The major part was the 70 acres belonging to the Bridge House, the division of the City Corporation that looked after London Bridge and the other river crossings. Hedger built many houses in St George's Fields, on Bridge House land and on plots leased from minor landowners, but as his right to develop the Bridge House land was doubtful he spent as little as possible on the houses there and they were all swept away soon after his lease expired in 1810.

With West Square Hedger was on firmer ground, legally if not physically – for St George's Fields were marshy – and the houses he built there are the unique surviving examples of his work. The Wests no doubt insisted on better quality in a development that was, for them, a long-term investment.

The square was built quite quickly, the north and east sides first. Horwood's 1790s map showed it almost complete, with only the four corners to be tidied up, and with an octagonal central garden laid out formally in a somewhat bizarre fashion. There were eventually minor outlets at three of the corners and at the south-west a large private garden for No. 20. The two major access roads were in the middle of the north and south sides. The southern approach was known originally as South Street, the northern somewhat confusingly as West Street. That is now treated as part of the square and South Street is Austral Street. It was there that James Hedger built a detached house for himself, with a garden running behind that of No. 20. Hedger's house was replaced in 1875–76 by Charlotte Sharman's orphanage, now the All Saints annexe of the Imperial War Museum.

There were some fifty houses in the square, plus the City Arms on the eastern corner of West Street. Another house ceased to be private in 1796, became in effect a ship, when the Admiralty acquired No. 36 as the first station on its shutter (and later semaphore) telegraph line to Deal and Sheerness. This system made it possible to send orders or receive news rapidly from the ports. Hughson recorded in 1817 that 'a single signal has been communicated, in a clear day, from the Admiralty to Deal in two minutes and a half'. A signalling tower was built on the roof, destroying the pediment intended to mark the two central houses of the east side. Here ratings spent their days peering through telescopes, north-west to the Admiralty and south-east to the next station at Telegraph Hill, New Cross. An officer commanded the little crew. The telegraph was in use until 1822 and the house continued to be occupied by a naval officer at least until the 1850s.

Robert and Henry Barker, panorama painters and showmen, were the square's first celebrities. Robert, the inventor of panoramas and the proprietor of the Panorama in Leicester Square, was at No. 14 from 1799 until his death in 1806; his son, assistant and successor Henry moved to No. 13 on his marriage in 1802 and remained until 1824. The panoramas were painted in a wooden rotunda erected for the purpose in the garden of No. 14.

Thomas Richard Williams, the pioneer photographer, famous for his stereo views, lived and worked at No. 35 from 1851 to 1859. At No. 19 there is a Royal Society of Chemistry plaque to John Alexander Reina Newlands ('born and raised here') as the inventor of the Periodic Law. This is an act of reparation, as during his lifetime the chemical establishment was very reluctant to accept Newlands' claim to priority in this discovery. He was born in 1837, the son of a Presbyterian minister.

Charlie Chaplin claimed to have lived in a large house in West Square, sometimes identified as No. 39, in the early 1890s, but that part of his life is badly documented.

West Square was a good address until the 1870s, but then it began to decline with the introduction of orphanages, lodging houses, factories and workshops, and a Board school built just off the north-west corner in 1884. In 1899 the Booth survey found 'the east side keeps a few servants, but rest rather poor. Messy square, great deal of loose paper.'

In 1907 there was a proposal to build houses over the central garden, a threat only averted when the LCC and Southwark Council bought it for £3,500.

The north-east corner of West Square in 2007.

The City Arms, No. 56 on the north side of West Square, *c.* 1930. (Photograph courtesy of Maurice Friedman.)

It was laid out for public use by the Metropolitan Public Gardens Association and opened in 1910.

The western half of the north side of the square was demolished before the Second World War, to provide a playground for the school, now named after Charlotte Sharman. During the war the school was badly damaged and most of the houses in the square were shaken by blast. The worst affected were at the east end of the north side, and there the houses and the City Arms were demolished and replaced in the late 1940s with a terrace in simplified pastiche.

After the war there was a plan to demolish the old houses and add the garden to the Geraldine Mary Harmsworth Park – a fad of the time that damaged or destroyed several squares – but the danger was happily averted. The prefabs built in the garden were removed, the damaged houses repaired, and the square was gradually raised to its present fine condition.

Westbourne Square

WESTBOURNE GREEN [WESTMINSTER]

Westbourne Square, which was a rough triangle, was built in 1858–59 by the Ramsays, a family heavily but unsuccessfully involved in the development of Notting Hill. It lay midway between the northern arc of the Grand Junction Canal and the southern arc of the Harrow Road, and these two curves dictated that the land between should be developed largely in crescents. The central section of Bourne Terrace (a modern crescent shaped by the same imperative) follows the line of the now north side of the square.

Allan A. Ramsay was listed as the owner of the twenty-nine houses when they first appeared in the ratebooks in 1859. In March, Henry Malcolm Ramsay of Highgate, surveyor, advertised them in the *Morning Post*:

… good modern family residences to be let in this fashionable locality, having elegant elevations, substantially built, tastefully decorated, and finished with every requisite. The houses contain 8 bedrooms, bath-room, closets, spacious and lofty drawing-rooms, enclosed hall, dining, breakfast-rooms, and library, excellent kitchen, housekeeper's-room, butler's pantry, scullery, and larder, with all other domestic conveniences. Rents very moderate, being from £95 to £150 per annum.

Ramsay was experienced in the marketing of such properties, having built similar ones in Ladbroke Grove and Elgin Crescent. Despite his assertion, this was never a very fashionable locality, the residents of the square not rising above the odd major general, and over the decades it slipped a notch or two from its respectable beginnings. In 1898 it was described as 'much less good than formerly. One or two have manservants, but others let apartments.'

The unusual shape gave Westbourne Square some interest, but the houses were not attractive. One must regret the loss of No. 16, however, as it might have borne a blue plaque to George Butterworth, the immensely promising composer killed on the Somme in 1916. He was born there in 1885.

Number 27 was one of the childhood homes of Aldous Huxley, whose father Leonard had moved there in 1909. The sofa would have made a good exhibit for a Huxley museum, as it was there that Aldous discovered sex, with the aid of an au pair girl he picked up in the street in 1913 and brought back to the temporarily empty house: a sofa being an eccentric choice with those eight bedrooms lying idle. There is a description of the house in *Antic Hay* (1923) that makes a stark contrast with Mr Ramsay's in 1859:

Gumbril senior occupied a tall, narrow-shouldered and rachitic house in a little obscure square not far from Paddington. There were five floors, and a basement with beetles, and nearly a hundred stairs, which shook when anyone ran too rudely down them. It was a prematurely old and decaying house in a decaying quarter. The square in which it stood was steadily coming down in the world. The houses which a few years ago had all been occupied by respectable families, were now split up into squalid little maisonnettes [*sic*], and from the neighbouring slums, which along with most other unpleasant things the old bourgeois families had been able to ignore, invading bands of children came to sport

Westbourne Square from the north-west corner, *c.* 1905.

on the once sacred pavements. Mr Gumbril was almost the last survivor of the old inhabitants. He liked his house, and he liked his square. Social decadence had not affected the fourteen plane trees which adorned its little garden, and the gambols of the dirty children did not disturb the starlings who came, evening by evening in summer-time, to roost in their branches.

The district surveyor's plan of the effects of the V1 rocket that plunged into the square in 1944 shows four houses totally destroyed, seven damaged beyond repair and the remaining eighteen so badly damaged that it was doubtful whether they could be saved. In the event the whole area was cleared for comprehensive redevelopment. This was a mercy, perhaps, as the future of the square would have been bleak in the shadow of Westway.

Westcroft Square

HAMMERSMITH

[HAMMERSMITH AND FULHAM]

The land on which Westcroft Square was later formed had its potential for building development damaged in 1868, when the London & South Western Railway ran its Kensington and Richmond Line through the middle of the fields. The area was broken up into awkward plots with limited access from the main roads. As the largest of them, south of the tracks, had a nearly square shape this very late attempt to make a success of a classical square was resorted to in 1878. The near neighbourhood of St Peter's Square to the south and Ravenscourt Square to the north perhaps suggested the idea. The field name was carried over to the square.

The north side of Westcroft Square in 2008.

It was built by Thomas Hussey of Kensington High Street, who had his brickfields nearby at Stamford Brook. For some of his more important projects, like Albert Hall Mansions, Hussey employed Norman Shaw as his architect, but not here at Hammersmith.

In 1899 the Booth survey found the square dingy, the houses ugly and the garden ill-kept: 'Houses cheap and large, £60 a year, but not approved by the public. Many don't keep a servant.' Now it strikes one as a decent Victorian square, notable only for its unusually late date. The uniform houses are tall, with bay windows rising through three storeys and linked round-headed porches. There are a few mildly Gothic touches, but designing for a square seems to have restrained the architect from going far in that direction. The style does well enough in the open spaces of a square, but would not merit a second glance in a street.

The exciting moment in the history of Westcroft Square came in 1927, when the garden was threatened with building development just four years before the London Squares Preservation Act gave all such enclosures protection. Fortunately the residents were able to buy the garden and hand it over to the council. It is small but well maintained. A council gardener was there when I paid my visit, resting on one of the benches.

White Hart Square

KENNINGTON [LAMBETH]

White Hart Square was the close neighbour of Cleaver Square, almost communicating with it in its south-eastern corner, but even the fragile respectability of Cleaver Square would have been very anxious to maintain that 'almost', as White Hart Square was certainly a slum. There are about sixty houses in Cleaver Square; in White Hart Square, only a third of the size, there were forty.

White Hart Square was built before 1831, when it appeared fully formed on a map under the name of Prince's Buildings, evidently borrowed from Prince's Square, the old name for Cleaver Square. White Hart Square, a name adopted in the 1850s, came from

White Hart Street to the north, which used to extend from Kennington Lane to Kennington Park Road but is now truncated. The street was named from a pub in Kennington Lane.

There was a Sunday school on the north side of the square and the 1871 map showed the curious feature of five separate strips of garden, three with trees, in the centre of the widest section. They were perhaps allotments, or possibly the remains of a communal garden. In 1899 the square, which had never been good, was found to be going downhill: 'Two storey, poor and very poor, labourers and carmen, messy'. The cottages were demolished between the wars and replaced by tenements.

White Lion Square

CITY OF LONDON

Old Bethlem, the forerunner of Liverpool Street, is shown on seventeenth and eighteenth-century maps with an offshoot to the north, where the southern entrance to Liverpool Street Station now stands. On the 1676 map it was named Bethlem Court, but later it was often counted as part of Old Bethlem. It was square in shape, but the interior, where a garden might have been, was full of houses.

Early in the nineteenth century the inconvenience of one name covering a complex of streets led to a change, and by 1813 the northern offshoot was becoming known as White Lion Square. There was a White Lion alehouse in Bethlem Court in 1795, when John White was the landlord.

Old Bethlem was widened, straightened and smartened up in the late 1820s as part of the Finsbury Circus development, and renamed Liverpool Street after the prime minister. Not long afterwards some of the little streets to the north, including White Lion Square, were replaced by a broad cul-de-sac known as Liverpool Street Buildings. In 1841 there was a White Lion, perhaps relocated, at No. 44 Liverpool Street, close to Liverpool Street Buildings.

The extinction of the square in the 1830s only anticipated its fate, as it would otherwise have been one of the many victims of Liverpool Street Station, which was opened in 1874.

White's Square

White's (or White) Square was a fair-sized rectangle at the south-west end of the long, narrow Nelson's Row. That was the only substantial entrance to the square but there was later a pedestrian postern into Crescent Road, under an arch. The terraces on the two short sides extended beyond the open space, which meant that the number of houses was about the same on all four.

The name of Nelson's Row suggests its date. White's Square was begun by 1808 when Edward Morden, a carpenter, insured four unfinished houses there, but was not completed until the 1860s. In 1894 there were at least fifty houses, plus the St James's Infant School on the south-west side, but the LCC kept confusing the issue by renumbering parts of the square in Nelson's Row.

The Booth survey found it poor but slightly improved in 1899, 'White Square, 2½ storey, unpaved, quiet, many costers, children rather dirty, once notorious den of iniquity and rowdyism, but much better, though still occasional drunken rows.'

White's Square was rebuilt by the LCC in the 1930s as three quite elegant four-storey blocks of flats, with the garden reduced to a wide road, but the name persists.

Whitechapel Square

'Whitechapel Square, at Whitechapel' appeared in William Stow's 1722 list of London streets, but is not otherwise heard of. He cannot have meant Sion Square, which was not built until later. It might just possibly have been his name for Montague Square.

Whitmore Square

Whitmore Square was originally called Windmill Square. It was a feature on the south side of Canal Road and thus a by-product of the Regent's Canal, this part of which was dug between 1816 and 1820. It was shown fully formed but without a name on the 1827 Greenwood map, and called Windmill Square in the 1830 revision. In 1827 the windmill was marked north of the square between Canal Road and the canal, but in 1830 it was placed at the south-east corner of the square, adjacent to Mill Road.

Canal Road is now Orsman Road and Mill Road (which existed before the canal) is Mill Row. The Whitmore Square name, which soon displaced Windmill Square, came from Whitmore House,

White's Square from Nelson's Row in 2008.

an exclusive private lunatic asylum just north of the canal. It had been the home of Sir George Whitmore, Lord Mayor in 1631.

The square's life was short, as in 1863 it was cleared to provide a site for St Andrew, Canal Street. The church was badly damaged during the Second World War and demolished when the parish was combined with St Anne's, Hoxton. Large blocks of council flats have replaced it. Harland Square was an offshoot of Whitmore Square.

William Square

BERMONDSEY [SOUTHWARK]

William (or Williams) Square was one of the pest-holes of Jacob's Island, where Bill Sykes met his timely end. William is probably right, as Edward, John and Jacob were street names nearby.

London Street, now Wolseley Street, was on the south bank of one of the tidal ditches that made the rookery an island. Until the ditch was filled in the 1850s the hovels on the north bank opposite London Street were in Water Lane, which was connected with the island's main road, Jacob Street, by Farthing Alley. The three-sided William Square was at the corner of Farthing Alley and Water Lane, open to the former on the east.

Many of the houses on the island were ancient, overhanging the ditches like a nightmare parody of Venice. William Square was a late addition, just emerging at the beginning of the nineteenth century. The block west of Farthing Alley was the only part of Jacob's Island where the slums were not cleared and replaced by warehouses soon after the exposure in *Oliver Twist*, but William Square was rebuilt as a simple terrace facing Farthing Lane late in the nineteenth century.

Wolseley Street is still a social boundary, but whereas it used to be between crime and squalor on the north and comparative respectability to the south, it is now between council flats on the south and expensive private developments and warehouse conversions to the north. The site of William Square is the gravelled area with trees and seats between Farthing Alley and the Ship Aground pub.

Wilmington Square

CLERKENWELL [ISLINGTON]

The part of the Northampton estate on which Wilmington Square and the surrounding streets were built was Spa Fields, the scene of the notorious political meetings and riots of 1816–18. The radicals were only moved on when the progress of the building work left them no ground to stand on.

Wilmington Square was planned in 1817 and built from 1818. The name came from the Earl of Wilmington, an ineffective prime minister in 1742–43, who was a son of the 3rd Earl of Northampton and left his considerable fortune to his nephew, the 5th Earl.

The west side of Wilmington Square in 2007.

The overall management of the estate was in the hands of the agent, Edward Boodle, and the surveyors, Samuel Pepys Cockerell until 1827 and thereafter his son, Charles Robert. The builder who contracted for the square and its satellite streets was John Wilson, who was also apt to describe himself as an architect. To him the design of the houses is probably due, although S.P. Cockerell or his son (who assisted his father in his old age) must have approved the plans.

Progress was slow because of Wilson's financial problems. Numbers 15–21 on the east side were built in 1818–21, most of the other houses gradually during the 1820s, but Nos 38 and 39 on the west side only in 1840–41.

The square was originally intended to be bigger and squarer, reaching further north, as Greenwood's over-eager 1827 map showed it doing, but Wilson was allowed to squeeze in more houses on the south side of Margaret Street instead. This parsimonious truncation, although preventing it from achieving the classic form, has in the long run worked wonderfully well in favour of Wilmington Square. It has made it much more quiet and secluded and given it an attractive and unusual feature in the narrow lane on the north side between the houses and the garden.

The garden was originally private but became neglected as many houses were converted to commercial use, notably the local trade of artificial flower making, and the district descended into a slum. In the 1880s there was some idea of building a church in the centre, but instead the garden was made public and somewhat municipal in 1895–96. The Booth surveyor believed in 1898 that this had 'improved the square if anything (i.e. the character of the inhabitants) certainly has not driven respectable people away'.

There is said to have been a private theatre in Wilmington Square in its very early days, where the celebrated actress Louisa Nisbett made her debut in 1822 or earlier. There is another theatrical association in Edward Laman (or Leman) Blanchard, who lived in the square in the 1850s. He wrote the popular Drury Lane pantomimes from 1852 to 1888.

There were few other notable figures in Wilmington Square until late twentieth-century gentrification brought a change of fortune. A number of houses were reconverted to single occupation at that time, and Lord Mandelson was one of those who colonised the newly fashionable square.

Wilmot Square

BETHNAL GREEN [TOWER HAMLETS]

Wilmot Square was named after David Wilmot, who began to acquire leasehold and freehold land adjoining the Bethnal Green New Road in 1766. He and his tenants built hundreds of houses in the next few decades, including Wilmot Square, which was begun in 1777.

Cary's map of 1795 also showed a larger green to the north of the square, with Wilmot's Folly to the east and houses on its west side called Wilmot's Grove. The Folly was David Wilmot's own house, which had a bowling green adjoining. On the Horwood map of the 1790s Wilmot Square consisted of sixteen houses, with the south side open to Bethnal Green Road. There was a burglary at No. 15, close to the main road, in 1797. The square became increasingly commercial during the nineteenth century, but there were still private residents in the 1860s and the well-planted little garden survived until the end.

Wilmot Square was destroyed in 1878 when the new Mansford Street was built to provide a better link between Hackney Road and Bethnal Green Road, and incidentally clear some of the notorious Bethnal Green slums. One of the blocks of model dwellings built in Mansford Street was named Wilmot House.

The only famous son of Wilmot Square was Andrew Garran, who was born there in 1825. He became editor of the *Sydney Morning Herald* and an influential figure in the New South Wales legislature. His real name was Gamman, but given the comic resonance of 'gammon' for the Victorians it is understandable that a politician chose to modify it.

Wilton Square

ISLINGTON

A small fragment of the Clothworkers' Company estate was marooned on the north-east side of the New North Road when it was built soon after 1812. The shape of this piece of ground necessarily produced one of the oddest squares in London, for it is not square or rectangular or triangular, but a compromise between the three.

There was an abortive development scheme in the late 1840s, before Arlington Square or Union Square on the same estate had been built, but the lessee had overextended himself and backed out. As a result, Wilton Square was the last of the three to be built. Edward Rowland and Thomas Evans, fresh from Arlington Square, began work in 1851 or perhaps a little earlier, as they were granted leases by the Clothworkers' Company for newly built houses in Wilton Square in

The garden of Wilton Square, looking north-west, in 2007.

1851 and 1852. The square did not appear in the 1851 census. Rowland and Evans produced plain but attractive terraces of two-storey houses with deep areas and steps up to the pedimented doors.

It was once a very devout square. The Bethel Welsh Methodist Chapel was built on the south side in 1853 and the Salem Scotch Baptist Chapel, which occupied the whole of what is now the central garden, was begun in the same year. The Bethel Chapel was rebuilt in 1884, but closed soon after the Second World War. It was used as a hostel from 1955 and rebuilt in its present undisguised form in 1986.

The congregation of the Salem Chapel was riven, in the usual manner of Victorian Baptists, by feuds and schisms. In 1897 it was reported that the square had 'a dilapidated Salem Chapel in its midst; is private property and let to whatever sect cares to

Winchester Square

The old courtyard of the bishop's palace was named Winchester Yard in Strype's 1720 edition of Stow and on Rocque's 1740s map, where it had the same form as on the Strype map of twenty-five or more years earlier. Strype described it as 'Winchester Yard, a long square Place pretty well built, hath three out lets, one into Stony street, another into St Mary Overies Dock and the third into another Part of Stony street'. It was shown without a name on the 1790s Horwood map, with just a wall or fence on the south side, a terrace of houses at the southern end of the east side, two detached houses on part of the north side and warehouses occupying the rest of the periphery.

Goods stored in hop warehouses in 'Winchester Square' were insured with the Sun in 1802, but the name was then only an occasional variant. In the 1813 edition of Horwood more warehouses were shown on the south side and the open space was again called Winchester Yard. That was still its name in 1872, when it was nearly surrounded by large hop warehouses. It is not very different today, although some of the warehouses have been rebuilt as offices and others converted into them, but between 1901 and 1912 the Winchester Square name became firmly established.

rent it'. It closed in 1913, was used by the Church of England for a time, then by the YMCA, but was demolished in the 1960s.

The square had begun to decline almost as soon as it was finished. By 1897 it had 'gone down in character' and was 'very untidy', and things grew worse in the twentieth century with the problems of the chapels, serious bomb damage, and most unsympathetic replacement of the lost houses.

The 1960s and 1970s were, uncharacteristically, the salvation of Wilton Square. The demolition of Salem gave it a garden for the first time and the closure of Wilton Villas to vehicles made it effectively a cul-de-sac. The square is now quiet and the tall trees in the small, irregular garden make it pleasantly shady. If the 1950s council houses and the 1980s hostel were replaced by buildings in a sympathetic style it would be a gem.

Winchester Square from the north-east corner in 2010.

Windmill Square

See Whitmore Square

Windsor Square

Windsor Square was the name given in Leverington's *Descriptive Street Routes* (published in 1859) to the crescent at the south end of Windsor Terrace, where it meets the City Road. Leverington's route was 'on by shops to City-road, at St Luke's Workhouse; then by Windsor-square, into Wharf-road …' Contemporary maps and directories were unanimous in treating the open space as part of Windsor Terrace, which was built in the first five years of the nineteenth century, so this may be the mysterious Leverington's personal contribution to London topography. The LCC sought to protect the garden in 1905 under the usual name of Windsor Terrace. There is still a green there, with trees and seats – a welcome relief from the City Road – but it is now surrounded by dull municipal flats.

Winter's Square

The tiny Winter's Square was surprisingly complicated. The site of the square section was shown as an open yard on the 1813 Horwood map, with a terrace of four cottages in an alley to the west which seem later to have been numbered as part of the square. In the 1790s edition of Horwood the four cottages looked newly built and the square section (which had no houses on either map) was less distinct.

In 1822 the Hon. Douglas Kinnaird, the banker (Byron's friend), let a timber building and some land to Frederick Farrand, carpenter and builder. This was later the cooperage, No. 206 Long Lane, adjoining the site of the square to the east. In 1824 John Terry of Long Lane, builder, let a house and ground in Winters Court to Frederick Farrand. Greenwood's map of 1830 (but not the 1827 edition) showed houses in the formerly open yard and named them Winter's Square, and in a lease of 1860 the place was described as Winters Square formerly Winters Court. From all

The green at Windsor Terrace (formerly perhaps Windsor Square) from the south in 2013.

this it appears that the main part of the square was built in the 1820s, probably by John Terry.

Maps indicated only about five houses in the main section, but in 1887 there was mention of a No. 9, which suggests that the western offshoot had by then been incorporated, probably as Nos 1–4. In 1899 the Booth Survey only found four houses: 'Winter Square (south side of Long Lane) four 2 storey houses, facing north'. These were almost certainly four surviving in the main section, the western offshoot having by then been cleared to create a yard for George Elliott & Co., the printers' engineers of Nos 186 and 188 Long Lane.

The last terrace survived until the 1930s, when the building of the Elim Estate destroyed it.

Woburn Square

BLOOMSBURY [CAMDEN]

Woburn Square was the last to be begun of the seven on the Duke of Bedford's Bloomsbury estate. In his history of Bloomsbury and St Giles published in 1829, Rowland Dobie noted the importance of the New Road (Marylebone Road, Euston Road, City Road) in the development of the area. Since it

was laid out in 1756 all the Bedford fields had been 'covered with houses, except a new square parallel with Torrington Square, which is now in progress, intended to be called Rothesay Square'. Although Rothesay Square may have been the name favoured by rumour, Woburn Square was in use at least as early, and more officially.

To squeeze in another square was a late change of mind. The 1820 plan for the layout of the ground from Russell Square to the New Road had proposed an 'Upper Montague Street' at this point.

The builder of both Torrington Square and Woburn Square was James Sim, who was already at work on Woburn Square in 1828, when Thomas Cubitt contracted to lay out the garden. The houses were largely finished and occupied by 1834. If Sim employed an architect, his name is not recorded. He built comparatively small and simple houses in these second-rate squares and found them easier to dispose of than Cubitt did his larger three-bay houses in Gordon Square.

Woburn Square was long and narrow, but as it was not quite so long as Torrington Square the garden did not seem so mean. The outstanding feature was Christ Church, which was built in the centre of the

The east side of Woburn Square from Gordon Square, c. 1905, showing Christ Church.

east side between 1831 and 1833. The architect was Lewis Vulliamy, who designed jolly Gothic churches for a number of London squares.

Woburn Square was dull but respectable in its early years, not rising higher than the odd MP, nor sinking lower than an architect. One architect of interest was William Hosking of No. 23, who spent more time writing and lecturing than designing buildings.

He was a professor at King's College in the 1840s. The square had few other notable residents. Clement Scott, the dominant Victorian theatre critic, died at No. 15 in 1904, the year in which Richard Addinsell, the composer of film music, was born at No. 31. They were neighbours for a few months.

In 1907 Beresford Chancellor wrote that of Woburn Square 'there is little to be said, for, like

The east side of Woburn Square in 2006.

a happy country, it has no history'. Its happiness ended not long afterwards when it began to be acquainted with the University of London. Its fate was sealed in the 1920s when the university began to buy property north of the British Museum. Various plans involving the replacement of Woburn and Torrington Squares with university buildings came and went during the 1930s, but were not carried out because of the war.

It was only a reprieve. Part of the west side was demolished in the 1950s to make way for the Courtauld Institute, and in the early 1970s the square was truncated when the library of the School of Oriental & African Studies was built across the south end. Half of the east side, including Christ Church, was demolished at the same time. The church was included in the clearance despite widespread protests, on the pretext of its being a dangerous structure: its site has remained vacant.

Now just fourteen houses survive, nine on the east side, five on the west. The only comfort is that the controversy surrounding these demolitions helped to save other threatened squares in the next decade.

Wood Street Square

CITY OF LONDON

Within the Barbican Estate, by the modern Monkwell Square and south-west of St Giles's Church, a section of the City wall and part of its corner bastion are preserved. In the eleventh century a hermitage was built against the south side of the wall there, which came to be known as St James-in-the-Wall. In 1543 it was bought by William Lambe, 'Citizen and Clothworker', and was thereafter called Lambe's Chapel. He is thought to have lived in a house attached to its west end.

Lambe left the property to the Clothworkers' Company, of which he was master in 1569–70. An open space known as Lamb's Court or Chapel Court had developed to the south, and there the company built a second house. One of the two became the residence of the Clerk of the Chapel. In 1825 the company removed Heath's Almshouses to Monkwell Street, at the corner of Lamb's Court, the originals at Islington having become ruinous.

The interior of Lambe's Chapel, Wood Street Square, in 1825 or a little earlier. The print on the right shows the exterior.

At the same time they rebuilt the clerk's house and the chapel, which became the chapel of the almshouses.

Before 1871 the name of the open space was changed from Chapel Court to Wood Street Square. It was probably a gradual rather than an instantaneous change, as local conservatism was always antagonistic to new names, and before the days of the LCC there was no imperious authority to enforce them. If the change was intended to make the place more fashionable, it came too late. Private residents had long been deserting the area, which was becoming almost entirely commercial. In 1871 the Clothworkers, surrendering to this trend, leased the almshouses at the corner of the square to Thomas Loveridge, who demolished them and built warehouses on the site. The almshouses were removed to Essex Road.

In 1872 the Clothworkers obtained a private act enabling them to sell the chapel, building St James's Islington (see Prebend Square) as an equivalent. As they explained in the preamble:

> … by reason of the changes which have taken place in the city of London, there is no longer a resident population in the neighbourhood of Lambe's Chapel capable of receiving the benefits contemplated by the said William Lambe … and the expense of keeping up the said chapel and paying a chaplain to perform divine service therein is in fact uselessly incurred.

When the chapel was demolished, part of the medieval crypt was rebuilt adjoining Clothworkers' Hall in Dunster Court, south of Fenchurch Street, where it can still be seen. The private act obliged the Clothworkers to erect within two years 'substantial buildings of the value of two thousand five hundred pounds at the least' on the site of the chapel and in 'the vacant space, square, or court formerly known as Lambe's Court, but now known or distinguished as Wood Street Square, Monkwell Street'.

In this area in the 1870s they inevitably built warehouses and offices, in the process narrowing the old square to the width of a street. The name remained in use for the west end of Hart Street until the Second World War, when the whole area was flattened – except for those resilient City walls.

Worship Square

SHOREDITCH [HACKNEY]

At the junction of Worship Street, Clifton Street and Holywell Row, north-east of Finsbury Square, there is still a rectangular open space with a traffic island and parking spaces for many motorbikes. For much of the nineteenth century this was known as Worship Square. The area was developed in the second half of the eighteenth century.

In the 1790s Clifton Street did not exist and the houses that later constituted Worship Square were considered part of Holywell Row. One of them, the Bald Faced Stag, was described as in Holywell Row in 1787, when Samuel Gregory was the landlord. By 1801, when William Dickinson was landlord, the name 'Worship Square' had been adopted. The pub was at No. 2. Most of the other houses were in industrial or commercial use, in a wide variety of trades. James Collier, the coffee roaster at No. 10 in the 1840s, must have made the district pleasant for the passer-by, if not the resident.

The style of the original houses can be judged from the ones that survive in Holywell Row, just to the north. The Worship Square name was abolished in 1872 when the opening was made part of Clifton Street. There were only a dozen houses. Those on the east side had front gardens that were lost when they were replaced by a printing works in the 1890s. The open space is therefore larger and squarer now than when it bore the name of square.

Clifton Street in 2013, showing the former Worship Square from the north.

York Square

York Square was presumably named in honour of the Duke of York – the 'Grand Old Duke' – who was popular in proportion to the unpopularity of his elder brother, George IV. There was a Duke of York pub in Salmon Lane just to the north by 1826.

The square, which was part of the St Paul's School estate, was built in the mid-1820s for the Mercers' Company under the supervision of its surveyor, George Smith. It was usual for the landowner's architect to lay down the general principles of a development and perhaps provide a sample design or two, but to leave the details of the houses to the individual builders. For such simple two-storey terraces as these it is unlikely that they needed to call on the services of any other architects. One of the firms engaged in the building was the partnership of George Watkins the younger and William Robert Fry. Their houses were empty and in various degrees of forwardness in February 1826, when a young man was transported for seven years for stealing 20lb of lead, value 6s, from the roof of one of them.

The houses were mainly occupied by seafarers, or those engaged on the river as lightermen, boat builders and the like. In 1898 the garden was said to be 'fairly kept by the residents', but nevertheless it was offered to the LCC for £3,000 in 1903, together with that of Arbour Square, another Mercers' Company development. The LCC pleaded poverty and the Mercers agreed to lease the two gardens for twenty-one years at a nominal rent. They were tidied up and opened to the public in 1904. The council noted hopefully that the lease was likely to be renewed, as having the gardens well looked after benefitted the Mercers' Company.

There was no bomb damage, so this is an almost perfectly preserved miniature square, only a step from Limehouse Station and the squalid Commercial Road. There are pubs at two of the corners, the Queen's Head in the original premises, the Old Ship in an early twentieth-century building that is, remarkably, less tall than the modest terrace to which it is attached. The Queen's Head was so named by 1836, when Simon Williams was the landlord. In more recent times it is celebrated as the pub where the Queen Mother pulled a pint in 1987.

Just off the south-east corner there is an equally remarkable survival in Flamborough Walk, an irregular terrace of four stucco houses started before the square. They used to face the Commercial Road behind long front gardens, but early in their history they were separated from it by the curving railway viaduct. This diminished them in one sense, but has probably been the main reason for their preservation.

York Square

See Munster Square

The garden and west side of York Square in 2011.

ABOUT THE AUTHOR

JOHN COULTER was born in Croydon in 1951 and educated at the John Ruskin Grammar School there, and at the University of Sussex. He worked for many years in the Lewisham Archives and Local History Centre, retiring as Local Studies Librarian in 2011. He has written twelve books about that borough, including histories of Lewisham (1994) and Sydenham and Forest Hill (1999).

About Norwood, where he lives, John has written four books, including a history, *Norwood Past*, published in 1996. He was also the editor of *London of One Hundred Years Ago* (1999), a portrait of the city between 1887 and 1914 in contemporary words and pictures.

John Coulter is a book collector and has written for the journal of the John Meade Falkner Society (of which he is a member) an account of the creation and dispersal of Falkner's remarkable library.

Since 2006 John Coulter has been working on a survey of the London squares. This began with the idea of a centenary revision of Edwin Beresford Chancellor's *The History of the Squares of London* (1907), but grew into a separate work when it became clear how many squares Chancellor had overlooked and how much had changed in those he did include. In the last decade John Coulter has visited every square at least once, taking notes and thousands of photographs, some already of historic interest.

SELECT BIBLIOGRAPHY

The bibliography is restricted to standard works constantly used and to histories of individual squares. It does not include the many historical and topographical accounts of London, or the biographies, autobiographies, letters and diaries of the residents of London squares from which the odd fact or assertion has been taken.

Adcock, St John, *Wonderful London* (3 vols, 1926–27. Vol. 2 includes 'Among the Squares and Circuses' by William Richard Titterton).

Booth, Charles (ed.), *Life and Labour of the People in London* (1st ed., 3 vols, 1889–91; 4th ed., 17 vols 1902–03; with poverty maps). [And the police notebooks at the Charles Booth Online Archive]

Bradley, H. Gilbert, *Dorset Square in the Parish of St Marylebone: A Short History* (1984).

Chancellor, E. Beresford, *The History of the Squares of London, Topographical & Historical* (1907).

Colvin, Howard, *A Biographical Dictionary of British Architects 1600–1840* (4th ed. 2008).

Cosh, Mary, *The Squares of Islington* (two parts, 1990–93).

Cunningham, George H., *London: Being a Comprehensive Survey of the History, Tradition & Historical Associations of Buildings & Monuments Arranged under Streets in Alphabetical Order* (1927).

Dasent, Arthur L., *The History of St James's Square and the Foundation of the West End of London* (1895).

Dictionary of National Biography.

Dobie, Rowland, *The History of the United Parishes of St Giles in the Fields and St George Bloomsbury* (1829).

Dodsley, Robert and James (pubs), *London and Its Environs Described* (6 vols, 1761)

Elmes, James, *A Topographical Dictionary of London and its Environs* (1831). [This is, in general, a slavish copy of Lockie's first edition of 1810, but it has some original entries for later streets and buildings.]

Gavin, Hector, *Sanitary Ramblings: Being Sketches and Illustrations of Bethnal Green* (1848).

Hamilton, Godfrey Heathcote, *Queen Square, Its Neighbourhood and Its Institutions* (1926).

Handover, P.M., *The History from 1276 to 1956 of the Site in Blackfriars Consisting of Printing House Square …* (1956).

Harben, Henry A., *A Dictionary of London* (1918).

Hatton, Edward, *A New View of London* (2 vols, 1708).

Hobhouse, Hermione, *Thomas Cubitt, Master Builder* (2nd ed. 1995).

Hood, Jean, *Trafalgar Square: A Visual History of London's Landmark through Time* (2005).

Hughson, David [David Pugh], *London* (6 vols, 1805–09).

Hughson, David [David Pugh], *Walks through London* (two volumes, 1817).

Johnson, B.H., *Berkeley Square to Bond Street: The Early History of the Neighbourhood* (1952).

Kings, Eric, *Thomas Ross of Kilravock House* (2006. Chapter 6, on Grafton Square).

Knight, Charles, *London* (six volumes, 1841–44. Vol. 6 includes 'The Squares of London' by William Weir).

Leigh, Samuel, *New Picture of London* (1818 & 1834 editions).

Lockie, John, *Topography of London* (1st ed. 1810, 2nd ed. 1813).

Longstaffe-Gowan, Todd, *The London Square: Gardens in the Midst of Town* (2012).

Maitland, William, *History of London* (1756).

Noorthouck, John, *A New History of London* (1773)

Paul, Anthony, *A History of Manchester Square* (1971).

Pevsner, Nikolaus, et al., *London: the Buildings of England* (six volumes, 1983–2005).

Phillips, Hugh, *Mid-Georgian London* (1964).

Powell, Gary, *Square London: A Social History of the Iconic London Square* (2012).

[Ralph, James], *A Critical Review of the Publick Buildings [etc.] in and about London and Westminster* (1734; and the revised 1783 edition, by an anonymous editor).

Rhind, Neil, *Blackheath Village and Environs 1790–1990* (Volume 1: 'The Village and Blackheath Vale'. 2nd ed. 1993).

[Stewart, John], *Critical Observations on the Buildings and Improvements of London* (1771).

Stow, William, *Remarks on London* (1722).

Stroud, Dorothy, *George Dance, Architect* (1971).

Stroud, Dorothy, *Henry Holland, his Life and Architecture* (1966).

Stroud, Dorothy, *The South Kensington Estate of Henry Smith's Charity* (1975).

Stroud, Dorothy, *The Thurloe Estate, South Kensington* (1959).

Strype, John, *A Survey of the Cities of London and Westminster* (1720; a revision and continuation of John Stow's survey).

Summerson, Sir John, *Georgian London* (1945, revised edition 1988).

Summerson, Sir John, *The Life and Work of John Nash, Architect* (1980).

Survey of London (from 1900, in progress).

Tarn, John Nelson, *Five Per Cent Philanthropy: An Account of Housing in Urban Areas between 1840 and 1914* (1973).

Thomson, Gladys Scott, *Life in a Noble Household 1641–1700* (1937).

Thomson, Gladys Scott, *The Russells in Bloomsbury 1669–1771* (1940).

Thornbury, Walter, and Edward Walford, *Old and New London: A Narrative of its History, its People, and its Places* (6 vols, 1873–78).

Titterton, William Richard, see Adcock.

Victoria County History (from 1900, in progress).

Walford, Edward, *Greater London: A Narrative of its History, its People, and its Places* (2 vols, 1882–83).

Wates, Nick, *The Battle for Tolmers Square* (1976).

Weir, William, see Knight.

Wheatley, Henry B., *London Past and Present* (3 vols, 1891).

SQUARES BY BOROUGH

(If no district is named, it is the same as the borough or city)

Brent (1)

Kilburn Square, Kilburn

Bromley (5)

Heath Square, Penge
Kelsey Square, Beckenham
Market Square
Palace Square, Upper Norwood
Waterman Square, Penge

Camden (50)

Ampthill Square, Somers Town
Argyle Square, St Pancras
Augustus Square, Regent's Park
Baldwin's Square, Holborn
Bedford Square, Bloomsbury
Belsize Square, Belsize Park
Bloomsbury Square, Bloomsbury
Brunswick Square, Bloomsbury
Camden Square, Camden Town
Carmarthen Square, Bloomsbury
Chalcot Square, Primrose Hill
Clarendon Square, Somers Town
Cummings Square, Regent's Park
Euston Square, Bloomsbury
Fitzroy Square, Fitzrovia
Gordon Square, Bloomsbury
Gray's Inn Square, Holborn
Hampstead Square, Hampstead
Hampstead Square, South Hampstead
Harrington Square, Somers Town
Holsworthy Square, Holborn
Lincoln's Inn Fields, Holborn [part]
Mecklenburgh Square, Bloomsbury
The Mount Square, Hampstead

Munster Square, Regent's Park
New End Square, Hampstead
New Square, Lincoln's Inn, Holborn
Oakley Square, Somers Town
Old Square, Lincoln's Inn, Holborn
Pancras Square, Somers Town
Park Square, Regent's Park [part]
Plum Tree Square, St Giles
Pond Square, Highgate
Prince's Square, Holborn
Queen Square, Bloomsbury
Red Lion Square, Holborn
Regent Square, Bloomsbury
Rochester Square, Camden Town
Rosebery Square, Holborn
Russell Square, Bloomsbury
Rutland Square, Regent's Park
St Leonard's Square, Kentish Town
St Mark's Square, Regent's Park
South Square, Gray's Inn, Holborn
Tavistock Square, Bloomsbury
Tolmers Square, Regent's Park
Torrington Square, Bloomsbury
Ulster Square, Regent's Park
Waterhouse Square, Holborn
Wellington Square, Bloomsbury
Woburn Square, Bloomsbury

City of London (70)

America Square
Angel Square
Austin Friars Square
Bell Savage Square
Bell Square (Blomfield Street)
Bell Square (St Martins-le-Grand)
Billiter Square
Bowling Square

Bridgewater Square
Bury Square
Car Square
Catherine Wheel Square
Charterhouse Square [part]
Chatham Square
Chequer Square
College Square
Cook Square
Cook's Square
Crosby Square
Crosley's Square
Cross Key Square
Devonshire Square
Ebenezer Square
Falcon Square
Gough Square
Gould Square
Green Arbour Square
Gun Square
Haberdashers' Square
Hanover Square
Haydon Square
Honesty Square
Honeysuckle Square
Jeffrey's Square
King's Square
Lime Street Square
Little College Square
Little Haydon Square
London Bridge Square
Ludgate Square
Mansion House Square
Mark Lane Square
May Square
Mitre Square
Monument Square
Moor Square
New Square
New Street Square (1)
New Street Square (2)
New Street Square (3)
Nicholl Square
Nixon's Square
Paternoster Square
Petticoat Square

Prince's Square
Printing House Square
Prujean Square
Queen Square
Queen's Square (Lime Street)
Queen's Square (Moorfields)
Red Cross Square
Salisbury Square
Sandy Square
Sun Square
Three Tun Square
Trinity Square [part]
Turner's Square
Union Square
Warwick Square
White Lion Square
Wood Street Square

Ealing (1)

St Mary's Square

Greenwich (8)

Beresford Square, Woolwich
Carey Square, Woolwich
Catherine Square, Woolwich
Lyons Square, Woolwich
Mortgramit Square, Woolwich
Mount Nod Square
Sherry Square
Smith's Square

Hackney (50)

Albion Square, Dalston
Basing Square, Hoxton
Bath Square, Old Street
Belmont Square, Shoreditch
Brunswick Square, Haggerston
Charles Square, Hoxton
Christopher Square, Shoreditch
Clapton Square
Colebrook Square, Hoxton
Crosby Square, Shoreditch
De Beauvoir Square, De Beauvoir Town

Duncan Square

Fassett Square, Dalston

Gainsborough Square

George Square, Hoxton

Goldsmith Square, Stoke Newington

Goldsmiths' Square, Haggerston

Hammond Square, Hoxton

Hare Square, Hoxton

Harland Square, Hoxton

Harriet Square, Shoreditch

Harris Square, Shoreditch

Hoxton Square, Hoxton

Jerusalem Square

King's Head Square, Shoreditch

Leonard Square, Old Street

Little Louisa Square, Hoxton

Louisa Square, Hoxton

Marian Square, Haggerston

New Inn Square, Shoreditch

Nichols Square, Haggerston

Parson's Square, Shoreditch

Paul Square, Old Street

Providence Square, Kingsland

Pump Square, Shoreditch

Queen Square, Hoxton

Reliance Square, Shoreditch

Rose Square, Shoreditch

St Agatha's Square, Old Street

St Agnes Square, Old Street

St Mark's Square, Dalston

St Thomas's Square

Tabernacle Square, Old Street

Tottenham Square, Kingsland

Turner Square, Hoxton

Warburton Square

Webb's Square, Shoreditch

Whitmore Square, Hoxton

Windsor Square, City Road

Worship Square, Shoreditch

Hammersmith and Fulham (5)

Goldrings Square, Walham Green

Imperial Square, Walham Green

Ravenscourt Square, Ravenscourt Park

St Peter's Square, Hammersmith

Westcroft Square, Hammersmith

Hounslow (7)

Chiswick Square, Chiswick

Ferry Square, Brentford

Golden Square, Brentford

Lower Square, Isleworth

Pack Horse Square, Turnham Green

The Square, Heston

Upper Square, Isleworth

Islington (50.5)

Adelaide Square

Albert Square, Barnsbury

Alwyne Square, Canonbury

Arlington Square

Arundel Square, Barnsbury

Banner Square, Old Street

Barnsbury Square, Barnsbury

Bartholomew Square, Old Street

Beckford Square, Old Street

Bell Square, City Road

Bull's Head Square, Clerkenwell

Canonbury Square, Canonbury

Charterhouse Square, Clerkenwell [part]

Chequer Square, Old Street

Cherry Tree Square, Old Street

Claremont Square, Clerkenwell

Cloudesley Square, Barnsbury

Cobden Square

Coldbath Square, Clerkenwell

Compton Square, Canonbury

Eagle Square, Clerkenwell

Edward Square

Elder Square

Finsbury Square, Old Street

Gibson Square

Gloucester Square, City Road

Granville Square, Clerkenwell

Holford Square, Clerkenwell

King Square, Clerkenwell

Lamb Square, Clerkenwell

Lloyd Square, Clerkenwell

Lonsdale Square, Barnsbury

Milner Square
Myddelton Square, Clerkenwell
New Square, Clerkenwell
New Street Square, Old Street
Norfolk Square
Northampton Square, Clerkenwell
Peabody Square
Percy Square, Clerkenwell
Prebend Square
Queen's Square, Highbury
Rose Square, Old Street
St John's Square, Clerkenwell
Thornhill Square, Barnsbury
Tibberton Square
Union Square
Union Square, Pentonville
Vernon Square, Clerkenwell
Wilmington Square, Clerkenwell
Wilton Square

Kensington and Chelsea (40.5)

Albert Square, Kensington
Alexander Square, Brompton
Beaufort Square, Notting Hill
Brompton Square, Brompton
Cadogan Square, Knightsbridge (1)
Cadogan Square, Knightsbridge (2)
Camera Square, Chelsea
Campden Hill Square, Holland Park
Carlyle Square, Chelsea
Chelsea Square, Chelsea
Colville Square, Notting Hill
Colville Square North, Notting Hill
Earl's Court Square, Earl's Court
Edwardes Square, Kensington
Gillray Square, Chelsea
Hereford Square, South Kensington
Kensington Square, Kensington
Ladbroke Square, Notting Hill
Lansdowne Square, Notting Hill
Lowndes Square, Knightsbridge [part]
Markham Square, Chelsea
Marlborough Square, Chelsea
Nevern Square, Earls Court
Norland Square, Notting Hill

Onslow Square, South Kensington
Ovington Square, Brompton
Paultons Square, Chelsea
Peabody Square, Chelsea
Pembridge Square, Notting Hill
Pembroke Square, Kensington
Powis Square, Notting Hill
Redcliffe Square, West Brompton
St Charles Square, North Kensington
St James's Square, Notting Hill
Sloane Square, Chelsea
Tedworth Square, Chelsea
Thurloe Square, South Kensington
Tobin Square, Notting Hill
Trinity Square, Kensal Town
Warwick Square, Kensington
Wellington Square, Chelsea

Kingston-upon-Thames (1)

St Andrew's Square, Surbiton

Lambeth (30)

Acre Square, Clapham
Albert Square, Kennington
Bedford Square, Clapham
Bonnington Square, Vauxhall
Bown Square
Carfax Square, Clapham
Carlisle Square
Chester Square, Kennington
China Square
Cleaver Square, Kennington
Cory Square, Bankside
Factory Square, Streatham
Grafton Square, Clapham
Greyhound Square, Streatham
Hanover Square, Kennington
Histed's Square, Streatham
Knight's Hill Square, West Norwood
Lambeth Square
Leavis Square, Vauxhall
Melbourne Square, Stockwell
Queen's Head Square
Regency Square, Kennington

St Mary's Square, Kennington
Surrey Square
Trinity Square, Brixton
Union Square, Clapham
Vauxhall Square, Vauxhall
Walcot Square, Kennington
White Hart Square, Kennington
White's Square, Clapham

Lewisham (16)

Avenue Square
Black Horse Square, Deptford
Broomfield Square, Deptford
Brunswick Square, Deptford
Collins Square, Blackheath
Copperas Square, Deptford
Dacre Square, Lee
Davis's Square, Deptford
Elliott's Square, Deptford
Finsbury Square, Deptford
Midway Square, Deptford
Phoenix Square, Blackheath
Reginald Square, Deptford
Russell Square, Deptford
St Margaret's Square, Brockley
Stanton Square, Sydenham

Merton (1)

Belvedere Square, Wimbledon

Newham (7)

Albert Square, Stratford
Channelsea Square, Stratford
Chant Square, Stratford
Davey Square, North Woolwich
Hudson's Square, Stratford
Maryland Square, Stratford
St George's Square, Upton

Redbridge (0.5)

The Square, Woodford Green [part]

Richmond upon Thames (2)

Golden Square, Richmond
The Square, Richmond

Southwark (72)

Addington Square, Camberwell
Alpha Square, Walworth
Avondale Square, Old Kent Road
Azenby Square, Peckham
Bear Garden Square, Bankside
Belgrave Square, Peckham
Bermondsey Square, Bermondsey
Bloomsbury Square, Newington
Brook's Square
Brunswick Square, Camberwell
Buckenham Square, Newington
Camden Square, Peckham
Canterbury Square
Carlton Square, New Cross
Castle Square, Peckham
Charlotte Square
Chatteris Square, Newington
Choumert Square, Peckham
Clifton Square, Peckham
Cottage Square, Newington
Crown Square, Camberwell
Crown Square, Newington
Dickens Square
Ellis Square, Newington
Falcon Square
Fells Square, Bermondsey
Goodwin Square
Grosvenor Square, Camberwell
Hamilton Square
Hargreave Square, Bermondsey
Leyton Square, Peckham
Lock Square, Walworth
Lorrimore Square, Walworth
Lyndhurst Square, Peckham
Mansion House Square, Camberwell
Merrick Square
Mint Square
Molesworth Square, Bermondsey
Nelson Square

Nelson Square, Peckham
New Square, Bermondsey
Peabody Square, Blackfriars Road
Peacock Square, Newington
Peckham Rye Square, Peckham
Pitt's Square
Quinn's Square, Waterloo
Red Cross Square
Rust Square, Camberwell
St George's Square
St George's Square, Newington
St Stephen's Square
Scrub Square, Bankside
Shard's Square, Peckham
Southwark Square
Surrey Square, Nunhead
Surrey Square, Old Kent Road
Sutherland Square, Walworth
Sydney Square, Peckham
Thorburn Square, Bermondsey
Thornhill Square, Camberwell
Three Crowns Square
Trafalgar Square, Peckham
Trinity Church Square
Truman Square, Bermondsey
Unicorn Square
Victory Square, Camberwell
Warwick Square
Waterloo Square, Camberwell
West Square
William Square, Bermondsey
Winchester Square
Winter's Square, Bermondsey

Sutton (1)

The Square, Carshalton

Tower Hamlets (71.5)

Albert Square, Ratcliffe
Arbour Square, Stepney
Beaumont Square, Stepney
Bell Square, Spitalfields
Ben Jonson Square, Mile End
Burnham Square, Bethnal Green

Busby Square, Bethnal Green
Carlton Square, Mile End
Caroline Square, Bromley-by-Bow
Cartwright Square, Whitechapel
Castle Square, Bethnal Green
Chamber Square, Wapping
Charles Square, Wapping
Claremont Square, Shadwell
Columbia Square, Bethnal Green
Coopers Square, Ratcliffe
Cornwall Square, Bethnal Green
Cottage Square, Stepney
Cowper's Square, Whitechapel
Cox's Square, Spitalfields
Crossland Square, Bethnal Green
Dalston Square, Stepney
Dunstan's Square, Whitechapel
Elger Square, Whitechapel
Ford Square, Whitechapel
Goulston Square, Whitechapel
Great Eastern Square, Whitechapel
Gun Square, Limehouse
Hooper's Square, Whitechapel
Ion Square, Bethnal Green
Jeffery's Square, Whitechapel
John's Square, Whitechapel
King Square, Shoreditch
Love Lane Square, Ratcliffe
Montague Square, Spitalfields
Mount Square, Bethnal Green
New Alley Square, Limehouse
New Square, Limehouse
New Square, Whitechapel
North Square, Bethnal Green
Patriot Square, Bethnal Green
Peabody Square, Shadwell
Plough Square, Whitechapel
Poole's Square, Shoreditch
Prince's Square, Wapping
Quaker Square, Shoreditch
Quinn Square, Bethnal Green
Ratcliff Square, Ratcliffe
Rectory Square, Stepney
Reform Square, Bethnal Green
Royal Mint Square, Whitechapel
St Katherine's Square, Wapping

St Peter's Square, Bethnal Green
Sidney Square, Whitechapel
Sion Square, Whitechapel
Sir William Warren's Square, Wapping
Spital Square, Spitalfields
Stepney Square, Stepney
Stewarts Square, Bromley-by-Bow
Sweet Apple Square, Shoreditch
Thorold Square, Bethnal Green
Thurlow Square, Bethnal Green
Trafalgar Square, Stepney
Tredegar Square, Mile End
Trinity Square, City [part]
Turner Square, Whitechapel
Victoria Park Square, Bethnal Green
Victualling Office Square, Whitechapel
Wellclose Square, Wapping
Whitechapel Square, Whitechapel
Wilmot Square, Bethnal Green
York Square, Limehouse

Waltham Forest (1.5)

Jeffrys Square, Walthamstow
The Square, Woodford Green [part]

Wandsworth (9)

Battersea Square, Battersea
Brassey Square, Battersea
Cheriton Square, Balham
Nightingale Square, Balham
North Square
Ram Square
Red Lion Square
St Philip Square, Battersea
Thessaly Square, Battersea

Westminster (76.5)

Albermarle Square, Mayfair
Aldborough Square, Marylebone
Alma Square, St John's Wood
Arlington Square, Mayfair
Artillery Square
Audley Square, Mayfair

Bearbone Square, Soho
Belgrave Square, Belgravia
Berkeley Square, Mayfair
Blandford Square, Marylebone
Bryanston Square, Marylebone
Cambridge Square, Bayswater
Cavendish Square, Marylebone
Chester Square, Belgravia
Cleveland Square, Bayswater
Cleveland Square, St James's
Connaught Square, Bayswater
Covent Garden, Strand
Cressey Square, Bayswater
Cumberland Square, St John's Wood
Dorset Square
Dorset Square, Marylebone
Eaton Square, Belgravia
Ebury Square, Pimlico
Eccleston Square, Pimlico
Fulmers Square
Gloucester Square, Bayswater
Golden Square, Soho
Grosvenor Square, Mayfair
Hanover Square, Mayfair
Harewood Square, Marylebone
Hyde Park Square, Bayswater
Kensington Gardens Square, Bayswater
Kildare Square, Bayswater
Leicester Square, Soho
Leinster Square, Bayswater
Lincoln's Inn Fields, Holborn [part]
Lowndes Square, Knightsbridge [part]
Manchester Square, Marylebone
Marlborough Square
Montagu Square, Marylebone
Montpelier Square, Knightsbridge
New Square
Norfolk Square, Bayswater
Ogle Square, Marylebone
Old Square, Strand
Orange Square, Pimlico
Orme Square, Bayswater
Oxford Square, Bayswater
Panton Square, Soho
Park Square, Regent's Park [part]
Parliament Square

Peabody Square
Poplar Square, Bayswater
Porchester Square, Westbourne Green
Portman Square, Marylebone
Prince's Square, Bayswater
Queen Ann's Square, Marylebone
Queen Square
Rutland Square, Knightsbridge
St George's Square, Pimlico
St James's Square, St James's
St John's Wood Square, St John's Wood
St Mary's Square, Paddington
St Stephen's Square, Westbourne Green
Shaft's Square

Shepherd's Square, Mayfair
Smith Square
Soho Square, Soho
Somerset Square, Strand
The Square, Upper Hyde Park Gardens, Bayswater
Sussex Square, Bayswater
Talbot Square, Bayswater
Trafalgar Square
Trevor Square, Knightsbridge
Victoria Square, Belgravia
Vincent Square
Warwick Square, Pimlico
Westbourne Square, Westbourne Green

SQUARES BY DISTRICT

Balham

Cheriton Square
Nightingale Square

Bankside

Bear Garden Square
Cory Square
Scrub Square

Barnsbury

Albert Square
Arundel Square
Barnsbury Square
Cloudesley Square
Lonsdale Square
Thornhill Square

Battersea

Battersea Square
Brassey Square
St Philip Square
Thessaly Square

Bayswater

Cambridge Square
Cleveland Square
Connaught Square
Cressey Square
Gloucester Square
Hyde Park Square
Kensington Gardens Square
Kildare Square
Leinster Square
Norfolk Square
Orme Square
Oxford Square
Poplar Square
Prince's Square
The Square, Upper Hyde Park
  Gardens
Sussex Square
Talbot Square

Beckenham

Kelsey Square

Belgravia

Belgrave Square
Chester Square
Eaton Square
Victoria Square

Belsize Park

Belsize Square

Bermondsey

Bermondsey Square
Fells Square
Hargreave Square
Molesworth Square
New Square
Thorburn Square
Truman Square
William Square
Winter's Square

Bethnal Green

Burnham Square
Busby Square
Castle Square
Columbia Square
Cornwall Square
Crossland Square
Ion Square
Mount Square
North Square
Patriot Square
Quinn Square
Reform Square
St Peter's Square
Thorold Square
Thurlow Square
Victoria Park Square
Wilmot Square

Blackfriars Road

Peabody Square

Blackheath

Collins Square
Phoenix Square

Bloomsbury

Bedford Square
Bloomsbury Square
Brunswick Square
Carmarthen Square
Euston Square
Gordon Square
Mecklenburgh Square

Queen Square
Regent Square
Russell Square
Tavistock Square
Torrington Square
Wellington Square
Woburn Square

Brentford

Ferry Square
Golden Square

Brixton

Trinity Square

Brockley

St Margaret's Square

Bromley

Market Square

Bromley-by-Bow

Caroline Square
Stewarts Square

Brompton

Alexander Square
Brompton Square
Ovington Square

Camberwell

Addington Square
Brunswick Square
Crown Square
Grosvenor Square
Mansion House Square
Rust Square
Thornhill Square
Victory Square

Waterloo Square

Camden Town

Camden Square
Rochester Square

Canonbury

Alwyne Square
Canonbury Square
Compton Square

Carshalton

The Square

Chelsea

Camera Square
Carlyle Square
Chelsea Square
Gillray Square
Markham Square
Marlborough Square
Paultons Square
Peabody Square
Sloane Square
Tedworth Square
Wellington Square

Chiswick

Chiswick Square

City of London

America Square
Angel Square
Austin Friars Square
Bell Savage Square
Bell Square (Blomfield Street)
Bell Square
    (St Martins-le-Grand)
Billiter Square
Bowling Square

Bridgewater Square
Bury Square
Car Square
Catherine Wheel Square
Chatham Square
Chequer Square
College Square
Cook Square
Cook's Square
Crosby Square
Crosley's Square
Cross Key Square
Devonshire Square
Ebenezer Square
Falcon Square
Gough Square
Gould Square
Green Arbour Square
Gun Square
Haberdashers' Square
Hanover Square
Haydon Square
Honesty Square
Honeysuckle Square
Jeffrey's Square
King's Square
Lime Street Square
Little College Square
Little Haydon Square
London Bridge Square
Ludgate Square
Mansion House Square
Mark Lane Square
May Square
Mitre Square
Monument Square
Moor Square
New Square
New Street Square (1)
New Street Square (2)
New Street Square (3)
Nicholl Square
Nixon's Square
Paternoster Square
Petticoat Square
Prince's Square

Printing House Square
Prujean Square
Queen Square
Queen's Square (Lime Street)
Queen's Square (Moorfields)
Red Cross Square
Salisbury Square
Sandy Square
Sun Square
Three Tun Square
Trinity Square
Turner's Square
Union Square
Warwick Square
White Lion Square
Wood Street Square

City Road

Bell Square
Gloucester Square
Windsor Square

Clapham

Acre Square
Bedford Square
Carfax Square
Grafton Square
Union Square
White's Square

Clerkenwell

Bull's Head Square
Charterhouse Square
Claremont Square
Coldbath Square
Eagle Square
Granville Square
Holford Square
King Square
Lamb Square
Lloyd Square
Myddelton Square
New Square

Northampton Square
Percy Square
St John's Square
Vernon Square
Wilmington Square

Dalston

Albion Square
Fassett Square
St Mark's Square

De Beauvoir Town

De Beauvoir Square

Deptford

Black Horse Square
Broomfield Square
Brunswick Square
Copperas Square
Davis's Square
Elliott's Square
Finsbury Square
Midway Square
Reginald Square
Russell Square

Ealing

St Mary's Square

Earl's Court

Earl's Court Square
Nevern Square

Fitzrovia

Fitzroy Square

Greenwich

Mount Nod Square
Sherry Square

Smith's Square

Hackney

Clapton Square
Duncan Square
Gainsborough Square
Jerusalem Square
St Thomas's Square
Warburton Square

Haggerston

Brunswick Square
Goldsmiths' Square
Marian Square
Nichols Square

Hammersmith

St Peter's Square
Westcroft Square

Hampstead

Hampstead Square
The Mount Square
New End Square

Heston

The Square

Highbury

Queen's Square

Highgate

Pond Square

Holborn

Baldwin's Square
Gray's Inn Square
Holsworthy Square

Lincoln's Inn Fields
New Square, Lincoln's Inn
Old Square, Lincoln's Inn
Prince's Square
Red Lion Square
Rosebery Square
South Square, Gray's Inn
Waterhouse Square

Holland Park

Campden Hill Square

Hoxton

Basing Square
Charles Square
Colebrook Square
George Square
Hammond Square
Hare Square
Harland Square
Hoxton Square
Little Louisa Square
Louisa Square
Queen Square
Turner Square
Whitmore Square

Isleworth

Lower Square
Upper Square

Islington

Adelaide Square
Arlington Square
Cobden Square
Edward Square
Elder Square
Gibson Square
Milner Square
Norfolk Square
Peabody Square
Prebend Square

Tibberton Square
Union Square
Wilton Square

Kennington

Albert Square
Chester Square
Cleaver Square
Hanover Square
Regency Square
St Mary's Square
Walcot Square
White Hart Square

Kensal Town

Trinity Square

Kensington

Albert Square
Edwardes Square
Kensington Square
Pembroke Square
Warwick Square

Kentish Town

St Leonard's Square

Kilburn

Kilburn Square

Kingsland

Providence Square
Tottenham Square

Knightsbridge

Cadogan Square (1)
Cadogan Square (2)
Lowndes Square
Montpelier Square

Rutland Square
Trevor Square

Lambeth

Bown Square
Carlisle Square
China Square
Lambeth Square
Queen's Head Square
Surrey Square

Lee

Dacre Square

Lewisham

Avenue Square

Limehouse

Gun Square
New Alley Square
New Square
York Square

Marylebone

Aldborough Square
Blandford Square
Bryanston Square
Cavendish Square
Dorset Square
Harewood Square
Manchester Square
Montagu Square
Ogle Square
Portman Square
Queen Ann's Square

Mayfair

Albermarle Square
Arlington Square
Audley Square

Berkeley Square
Grosvenor Square
Hanover Square
Shepherd's Square

Mile End

Ben Jonson Square
Carlton Square
Tredegar Square

New Cross

Carlton Square

Newington

Bloomsbury Square
Buckenham Square
Chatteris Square
Cottage Square
Crown Square
Ellis Square
Peacock Square
St George's Square

North Kensington

St Charles Square

North Woolwich

Davey Square

Notting Hill

Beaufort Square
Colville Square
Colville Square North
Ladbroke Square
Lansdowne Square
Norland Square
Pembridge Square
Powis Square
St James's Square
Tobin Square

Nunhead

Surrey Square

Old Kent Road

Avondale Square
Surrey Square

Old Street

Banner Square
Bartholomew Square
Bath Square
Beckford Square
Chequer Square
Cherry Tree Square
Finsbury Square
Leonard Square
New Street Square
Paul Square
Rose Square
St Agatha's Square
St Agnes Square
Tabernacle Square

Paddington

St Mary's Square

Peckham

Azenby Square
Belgrave Square
Camden Square
Castle Square
Choumert Square
Clifton Square
Leyton Square
Lyndhurst Square
Nelson Square
Peckham Rye Square
Shard's Square
Sydney Square
Trafalgar Square

Penge

Heath Square
Waterman Square

Pentonville

Union Square

Pimlico

Ebury Square
Eccleston Square
Orange Square
St George's Square
Warwick Square

Primrose Hill

Chalcot Square

Ratcliffe

Albert Square
Coopers Square
Love Lane Square
Ratcliff Square

Ravenscourt Park

Ravenscourt Square

Regent's Park

Augustus Square
Cummings Square
Munster Square
Park Square
Rutland Square
St Mark's Square
Tolmers Square
Ulster Square

Richmond

Golden Square

The Square

St Giles

Plum Tree Square

St James's

Cleveland Square
St James's Square

St John's Wood

Alma Square
Cumberland Square
St John's Wood Square

St Pancras

Argyle Square

Shadwell

Claremont Square
Peabody Square

Shoreditch

Belmont Square
Christopher Square
Crosby Square
Harriet Square
Harris Square
King's Head Square
King Square
New Inn Square
Parson's Square
Poole's Square
Pump Square
Quaker Square
Reliance Square
Rose Square
Sweet Apple Square
Webb's Square
Worship Square

Soho

Bearbone Square
Golden Square
Leicester Square
Panton Square
Soho Square

Somers Town

Ampthill Square
Clarendon Square
Harrington Square
Oakley Square
Pancras Square

South Hampstead

Hampstead Square

South Kensington

Hereford Square
Onslow Square
Thurloe Square

Southwark

Brook's Square
Canterbury Square
Charlotte Square
Dickens Square
Falcon Square
Goodwin Square
Hamilton Square
Merrick Square
Mint Square
Nelson Square
Pitt's Square
Red Cross Square
St George's Square
St Stephen's Square
Southwark Square
Three Crowns Square
Trinity Church Square
Unicorn Square

Warwick Square
West Square
Winchester Square

Spitalfields

Bell Square
Cox's Square
Montague Square
Spital Square

Stepney

Arbour Square
Beaumont Square
Cottage Square
Dalston Square
Rectory Square
Stepney Square
Trafalgar Square

Stockwell

Melbourne Square

Stoke Newington

Goldsmith Square

Strand

Covent Garden
Old Square
Somerset Square

Stratford

Albert Square
Channelsea Square
Chant Square
Hudson's Square
Maryland Square

Streatham

Factory Square

Greyhound Square
Histed's Square

Surbiton

St Andrew's Square

Sydenham

Stanton Square

Turnham Green

Pack Horse Square

Upper Norwood

Palace Square

Upton

St George's Square

Vauxhall

Bonnington Square
Leavis Square
Vauxhall Square

Walham Green

Goldrings Square
Imperial Square

Walthamstow

Jeffrys Square

Walworth

Alpha Square
Lock Square
Lorrimore Square
Sutherland Square

Wandsworth

North Square
Ram Square
Red Lion Square

Wapping

Chamber Square
Charles Square
Prince's Square
St Katherine's Square
Sir William Warren's Square
Wellclose Square

Waterloo

Quinn's Square

West Brompton

Redcliffe Square

West Norwood

Knight's Hill Square

Westbourne Green

Porchester Square
St Stephen's Square
Westbourne Square

Westminster

Artillery Square
Dorset Square
Fulmers Square
Marlborough Square
New Square
Parliament Square
Peabody Square
Queen Square
Shaft's Square
Smith Square
Trafalgar Square

Vincent Square

Whitechapel

Cartwright Square
Cowper's Square
Dunstan's Square
Elger Square
Ford Square
Goulston Square
Great Eastern Square
Hooper's Square
Jeffery's Square
John's Square
New Square
Plough Square
Royal Mint Square
Sidney Square
Sion Square
Turner Square
Victualling Office Square
Whitechapel Square

Wimbledon

Belvedere Square

Woodford Green

The Square

Woolwich

Beresford Square
Carey Square
Catherine Square
Lyons Square
Mortgramit Square

SELECT INDEX

This is essentially an index to the owners, developers, architects, builders and residents of the squares, usually listed under the most familiar form of their names. 'Marquis' and 'marquess' have been regularised as 'marquess'. Railway stations, embassies, and a few major buildings and events are also included.

Banks, Mrs G. Linnaeus (Isabella Varley) 181

Banks, Sir Joseph, baronet 450

Banner, Henry 44

Banner, John 44

Banner, Peter 44

Banting, James 427

Barber, Anthony, Baron Barber 299

Barber, John 375

Barbican Estate 75, 101, 222, 236, 288, 300

Barbon, Nicholas 50, 159, 160, 245, 313, 386, 521, 523

Baring, Sir Francis, 1st baronet 161

Bark, John 360

Barker, Robert & Henry 259, 526

Barlow, Frederick Pratt 24

Barlow, Thomas 214, 223, 374

Barmby, Sir Joseph 409

Barnard, J. & E. 317

Barnes, Thomas 307, 450, 514

Barnes, William Pemberton 102

Barnett, John 412

Barrallier, Francis Louis 189

Barratt, Thomas 303

Barrow, Edward 514

Barry, Sir Charles 134, 135, 267, 488

Barry, Edward Middleton 151, 342

Basevi, George 28, 55, 329

Bateman, Sir James 449

Bateman, William, 1st Viscount Bateman 449

Bates, Henry 179, 212, 233

Bathurst, Henry, 3rd Earl Bathurst 463

Bavarian Embassy 197

Baxter, George 324, 325

Baxter, Richard 71, 115

Baynard, Edward 136

Baynes, Walter 136

Beatles 30, 297

Beatty, David, 1st Earl Beatty 488

Beaumont, Sir George Howland, 7th baronet 217

Beaumont, John Thomas Barber 50

Beaumont, William 50

Beazley, Samuel 450

Beck, Thomas 292

Beckford, William (senior) 51, 450

Beckford, William (junior) 282, 450

Bedford, Francis 493

Bedford, Francis Russell, 4th earl of 148

Bedford, Francis Russell, 7th duke of 326

Bedford, Francis Russell, 9th duke of 151, 168

Bedford, Gertrude Russell, duchess of 51

Bedford, John Russell, 4th duke of 51, 400

Bedford, John Russell, 6th duke of 71, 74, 150, 176, 200, 400, 537

Bedford, Wriothesley Russell, 3rd duke of 71

Bedford New Town 32, 229, 326

Beecham, Sir Thomas, 2nd baronet 152

Beerbohm, Sir Henry Maximilian 333

Belcher, John & Sir John 494

Belcher, Tom 482

Bell, Charles 277, 278

Bell, Clive 202

Bell, Sir Charles 450

Bell, Vanessa 100, 202

Beloe, William 63

Benedict, Sir Julius 282

Benhill Road 84

Bennett, Arnold 91, 137, 209

Bennett, Jill 120, 123

Benson, Edward Frederic 80

Bentham, Jeremy 378

Bentinck, Lord George 110

Berenstein, Henry 464

Beresford, William, Viscount 61

Berkeley of Stratton, Christian, Lady 62

Berkeley of Stratton, John, 3rd baron 63

Berkeley of Stratton, William, 4th baron 63

Berkeley House, Piccadilly 62

Berlioz, Hector 227

Bernard, Jeffrey 221

Berry, Daniel 229

Bessborough, Edward Ponsonby, 8th earl of (Viscount Duncannon) 109

Betterton, Thomas 436

Betty, William Henry 33

Bibesco, Prince Antoine 444

Bingley, Robert Benson, 1st baron 109

Birkenhead, Frederick Edwin, 1st earl of 172

Bishop & Sirkett 248

Bishop, Thomas 93

Bishops of London 142, 153

Blackburn, James 269

Blackmore, Philip 382

Blackmore, Richard Doddridge 396

Blackstone, Sir William 266

Blanchard, Edward Laman 96, 533

Blanchard, William (actor) 95

Blanchard, William (landowner) 252

Blewitt, Jonas 68

Blewitt, Samuel 236

Blomfield, Sir Arthur 167, 297, 406

Blood, Sir Bindon 91

Blore, Edward 282, 512

Blore, John 79, 232

Blow, Detmar 217

Blunt, Anthony Frederick 365

Blunt, Sir John 241-42

Bodley, George Frederick 209, 452

Campbell, William
  Hinton 326
Campbell-Bannerman,
  Sir Henry 57
Canadian High
  Commission 217
Canning, Charles John,
  1st Earl Canning 216
Canning, George 65, 344
Cannon Street Station 453
Canonbury Tower &
  Road 99
Canterbury,
  Archbishops of 290
Canterbury, Dean &
  Chapter of 162
Canton, John &
  William 454
Cantwell, Robert 323
Carlisle, Charles
  Howard, 1st earl of 449
Carlyle, Thomas 103,
  128, 173, 331, 333-34
Caroline of Ansbach,
  Queen 245
Caroline of Brunswick,
  Queen 84, 179, 225,
  417
Caron, Leslie Claire
  Margaret 299
Carpenter, Richard 271,
  272
Carpenter, Richard
  Cromwell 271, 304, 305
Carpenter, Thomas 271
Carter, Elizabeth 363
Cassel, Sir Ernest 334
Casson, Sir Hugh 123,
  477
Casson, John & Lewis
  105

Castlereagh, Robert
  Stewart, Viscount,
  2nd Marquess of
  Londonderry 133, 417
Catherwood, Frederick
  113
Catling, W. T. 37
Cato Street Conspiracy
  216
Caulfield, Patrick 60
Cavalier, Pierre 68
Cavendish, Henry 52
Cawdor, John Campbell,
  1st baron 225
Chadwick, Sir Edwin
  334, 378
Chadwick, William
  493-94
Chamberlain, Joseph 99
Chamberlain, Neville 168
Chambers, Charles 368
Chandos, James
  Brydges, 1st duke of
  108, 197, 257, 378
Changeur, Louis Léon 173
Channon, Sir Henry 57
Chantrey, Sir Francis 227
Chaplin, Charlie
  (Sir Charles) 526
Charles I 70, 148, 257,
  264, 347, 413, 435,
  487, 489
Charles II 113, 133, 256,
  338, 414, 447, 451, 474
Charles, Prince of Wales
  489
Charlesworth, Maria
  Louisa 46
Charlesworth, Tim 279
Charlotte, Queen 289,
  374, 376

Charterhouse 115, 313
Chatham, William Pitt,
  1st earl of 118, 196,
  357, 417
Chelmsford, Frederic
  John Napier Thesiger,
  1st viscount 168
Chelmsford, Frederic
  Thesiger, 1st baron 168
Chelsea Park Gardens 96
Cherry, Bridget 303, 455
Chesterfield, Philip
  Stanhope, 2nd earl of 71
Chesterfield, Philip
  Dormer Stanhope,
  4th earl of 71, 216, 417
Chesterfield House,
  South Audley Street 39
Chesterton, Gilbert
  Keith 96, 174, 516
Chifney, William 338
Chinnery, George 203
Chorley, Henry 509
Choumert, George 125
Christian, Ewan 73,
  221, 516
Christopher, Henry 171
Churchill, Charles 375
Churchill, John Strange
  Spencer 466
Churchill, Sir Winston
  Spencer 97, 172, 463
Cibber, Caius Gabriel
  451, 521
Cibber, Colley 66
Clairmont, Claire 307
Clancy, Michael 135
Clapham (High Street)
  Station 502
Clare, John Fitzgibbon,
  2nd earl of 276

Clarendon, Edward
  Hyde, 1st earl of 70
Clarendon, George
  Herbert Hyde Villiers,
  6th earl of 120
Clark, Kenneth
  McKenzie, Baron
  Clark 217
Clarke, Owen 506
Clarke, Samuel 227
Claxton, Robert 191
Cleaver, Mary 131, 222
Cleland, John 450
Cleveland, Barbara
  Palmer, duchess of 133
Cleverdon, Douglas 46
Clive, Robert, Baron
  Clive 65
Clothworkers' Company
  37, 367, 502, 534
Clough, Arthur Hugh 202
Clutton, Henry 151,
  320, 329
Coates, Robert 297
Cobden, Richard 135
Cocchi, Gioacchino 449
Cochrane, William 242
Cock, Edward 63
Cockerell, Charles
  Robert 419, 533
Cockerell, Samuel Pepys
  81, 142, 288, 324-25,
  342, 419, 533
Cohen, Morris 25
Cokayne, George
  Edward 402
Cole, Sir Henry 330, 477
Coleridge, Mary 240
Collier, James 540
Collier, John Payne 80,
  178, 512

Fielden, John 340

Fielder, John 119

Fielding, Henry 10

Fiennes, Celia 77

Fife, Princess Alexandra, duchess of 364

Fife, Alexander William George Duff, 1st duke of 364

Finch, Francis Oliver 36

Fire of London 153, 179, 271, 284, 299, 344, 414, 435

Fisher, Herbert Albert Laurens 331

Fisher, Jasper 159

Fitzroy, Robert 323

Flanders, William 35

Flaxman, John 177

Fleay, Frederick Gard 42

Fleming, Ian Lancaster & Ann 508

Flitcroft, Henry 66, 72

Flower, Philip 430

Foley, Thomas Foley, 1st baron 373

Forbes-Robertson, Sir Johnston 46, 53

Fonblanque, Albany 142

Ford, Henry 35

Ford, James 35

Forster, Edward Morgan 82

Forster, John 268

Forster, William Edward 172

Foster, Norman Robert, Baron Foster 489

Foundling Hospital 18, 81, 82, 288, 374, 394, 400, 467, 471

Fourdrinier & Hunt 277, 278

Fowler, Charles 150, 200

Fowler, Henry Watson 348

Fox, Charles James 73, 74, 352, 400

Francis, Edward 165, 166

Frankau, Pamela 172

Frankel, Benjamin 451

Fraser, Lady Antonia 97

Fraser, Donald 326

Fraser, Hugh 97

Fraser, John 443

Freake, Sir Charles James, 1st baronet 167, 329

Frederick, Prince of Wales 257, 417

French Embassy 370, 449

Frink, Elizabeth 345

Frith, Richard 22, 245, 256

Frost, David 105

Froude, James Anthony 331

Fry, William Robert 541

Fulmer, Samuel 190

Furniss, Harry 111

Fussell, Alexander 326

Galsworthy, John 298

Gandhi, Mohandas Karamchand 469

Gardelle, Théodore 258

Gardiner, Samuel Rawson 202

Garland, Robert 171

Garner, Thomas 452

Garnett, David 202

Garran, Andrew 534

Gaskell, Thomas 285

Garrard, Stephen 97

Gaskell, Elizabeth Cleghorn 340

Gelding Close 196

George I 214-15, 257, 258, 415

George II 197, 245, 257

George III 52, 64, 146, 257, 417, 484

George IV 131, 144, 280, 393, 483, 484, 487, 541

George, Mary Dorothy 348

George, Sir Ernest 23, 90, 179

Gielgud, Val 166

Gilliatt, Penelope 120, 123

Gillray James (senior & junior) 192-93, 208

Gladstone, William Ewart 61, 417

Glascock, William Nugent 29

Glenbervie, Sylvester Douglas, Baron 225

Glenn, John 23

Goddard, Henry 229

Goding, Thomas 523

Godolphin, Sydney, 1st Earl of Godolphin 133

Godwin, George (the elder & the younger) 28, 391

Godwin, Henry 28, 391

Godwin, Mary Jane 130

Godwin, William 85, 130

Goldring, Robert 198

Goldsmith, Oliver 211

Gomme, Sir Laurence 163

Gondomar, Diego Sarmiento de Acuña, conde de 77

Gonella, Nat 173

Goodall, Frederick 94

Goodridge, Henry 326

Goosens, Sir Eugene & Marie 396-97

Gordon Riots 8, 72

Gorham, Thomas & John 452

Goswell, William 454

Gotobed, John 146

Gough, Alexander Dick 37, 159, 293

Gough, Sir Richard 202

Goulburn, Henry 363

Gould, Elizabeth & James 204

Goulston, Sir William 204

Gounod, Charles 469

Gover, Richard 43

Gowing, Sir Lawrence Burnet 348, 525

Grace, William Gilbert 90

Grafton, Augustus Henry Fitzroy, 3rd duke of 216

Grafton, Henry Fitzroy, 5th duke of 205

Graham, George 300

Graham, Joyce Maxstone 525

Grand Junction Canal 91, 320, 335, 466, 527

Grand Surrey Canal 20, 69, 262, 439, 465

Grant, Albert, Baron Grant 258

Grant, Duncan 100

Grant, John 271

Graves, Robert von Ranke 429

Graves, Walter 308, 309

Gray, Thomas 399

Green, John Richard & Alice Stopford 246

Grego, Joseph 208

Grenville, William Wyndham, Baron Grenville 417

Gresley, Sir George, 1st baronet 435

Grey, Charles, 2nd Earl Grey 65, 364, 417

Grey, Edward, 1st Viscount Grey of Fallodon 172, 447

Gribble, William 252

Griffin, John Joseph 521

Grimshaw, Sir Nicholas 361

Groom, Henry 464

Grossmith, George 70, 163, 402

Grossmith, Weedon 53

Grosvenor, Henrietta, baroness 215

Grosvenor, Sir Richard, 4th baronet 214

Grosvenor, Sir Robert, 6th baronet 63

Grosvenor Park 212

Grub Street 219, 222, 235

Gubbins, James 400

Guinness, Sir Alec 429

Gutch, George 92, 336

Gunter, Robert & John 63

Gurney, Edmund 299

Gutch, George 239

Gwyn, Eleanor 266

Gwynn, John 484

Habershon, William Gilbee 366

Hackshaw, Robert 236

Haggard, Sir Henry Rider 392

Hailsham, Douglas McGarel Hogg, 1st viscount 133

Hailsham, Quintin McGarel Hogg, 2nd viscount 133

Hakewill, Henry 167

Haldane, Richard Burdon, Viscount Haldane 379

Haldimand, George & William 54, 55

Halifax, George Savile, 1st marquess of 266, 417

Hall, Christopher Newman 221

Hall, Edwin Thomas 84, 90, 120

Hamilton, Emma, Lady 118, 216

Hamilton, Sir William 216

Hamilton-Fairlie, Gordon 98

Hammack, Henry Lawrence 102

Hammett, Sir Benjamin 31

Hanbury, Bridget 196

Hanover Square Rooms 226-27

Hansard, Thomas Curson 118

Hansard, William 307

Hanson, Joshua 96-7

Hanway, Jonas 388

Harben, Henry Andrade 143, 271, 317, 460

Harbin, Robert 95

Harcourt, Simon, 1st Viscount Harcourt 109

Hardinge, Agnes 315

Hardwick, Philip 57, 109, 402

Hardwick, Thomas 249

Hardwicke, Philip Yorke, 1st earl of 216

Harewood, Henry Lascelles, 3rd earl of 227

Harman, Sir George 121

Harmsworth, Cecil, 1st Baron Harmsworth 203

Harness, William 394

Harrington, Caroline, countess of 216

Harrington, William Stanhope, 2nd earl of (Lord Petersham) 216

Harris, Elizabeth 227, 415, 449

Harris, Susan 75

Harrison, Charles 92

Harrison, Frederic 178, 336

Harrison, George Henry de Strabolgie Neville Plantaganet 244

Harrison, Henry 92, 336

Harrison, James 234, 506

Harrison, John 476

Harrison, Thomas 393-94, 523

Harrison & Beal 321

Harrowby, Dudley Ryder, 1st earl of 216

Hart-Davis, Sir Rupert 451

Hartnell, William 395

Hartnoll, James 398

Haszlang, Josef von 197

Hatherley, William Page Wood, 1st baron 179-81

Hawkins, Sir John 378

Hawks, Thomas Longridge & George 354

Hawksmoor, Nicholas 77, 374

Hawtrey, Sir Charles 163

Haydn, Joseph 227

Haymerle Road 57

Haywood, William 356

Headlam, Walter 321

Hedger, James 525

Helps, Sir Arthur 122

Hennell, Charles & Mary 433

Henrietta Maria, Queen 414

Henslowe, Philip 49

Herbert, Sidney, 1st Baron Herbert of Lea 55

Herbert, William (bibliographer) 204

Herbert, William (antiquary) 314